musicHound CONTENTS

Artie Shaw recently made the rather astute comment that swing is a verb, not an adjective. In other words, one shouldn't label "swing music" as such, because any great piece of music—a Bach fugue, a bluegrass hoedown, or a Duke Ellington suite—swings in its own fashion. Shaw's broader conception of swing is especially relevant in the late 20th century, when America is smitten once again with the music of its past.

Today's "neo-swing" resurgence, although styled in '40s gangster chic, actually comprises a patchwork of influences that covers nearly every chapter of classic American music. Because swing history is American history, we do ourselves a great disservice if we limit our definition only to the genre's golden age, from 1935 to 1945.

Thankfully, the folks at MusicHound had the foresight to side with Mr. Shaw, chronicling all manner of American swingers, from Cab Calloway to Bob Wills to Bill Haley, from the old-school pioneers to the zoot-suit rioteers.

As a member of Royal Crown Revue, I've had the pleasure of watching this so-called movement develop from a tiny clique of bands and dancers into an international phenomenon. In an age of blurred morality and political disillusionment, people have gravitated toward its ideals with an unexpected ferocity.

Naysayers complain that the popular new sound is a watered-down attempt to cash in on nostalgic times, a pale comparison to the technical artistry of yesteryear. In their cynicism, however, these critics have failed to understand the original intent of the movement, which spent years below the radar screen as an alternative youth culture. With little formal schooling (but lots of enthusiasm) most of neo-swing's proponents found their way to the music primarily through a love of roots styles like punk, ska, rockabilly, and jump blues. They never claimed to be heirs to the masters.

Having performed this music for every conceivable kind of crowd (we once played with Kiss and Neil Diamond in the same week), I'm convinced modern, rock-bred audiences are fully capable of "getting it." Neo-swing works in a rock environment because it has the same youthful rebelliousness. It reinjects a wilder element into big-band music that nostalgic memories may have sterilized over time. Remember: in their day, America's classic artists were as provocative and controversial as Elvis Presley, Marilyn Manson, or any number of other "dangerous" rock innovators. They crossed color lines, challenged musical standards, and, initially, were condemned for "corrupting" the youths who packed ballrooms by the thousands. They expressed the same sort of revolutionary zeal that would play out in every major musical movement of this century, from bebop jazz to punk to rap.

So, are we merely having a fling with our past before moving on to an unknown future? Can a backward look be meaningful in setting a standard for how to live in the modern world? From my swingin' experience, the answer is an overwhelming "yes."

We seem once again to appreciate playing real instruments, singing real melodies, and that most congenial means of breaking ground with the opposite sex—partner dancing. Americans are starting to understand their musical heritage is not an antiquated piece of history to be appreciated only by grandparents. Nor is it an abstract museum piece accessible only to an intellectual elite. Old or new, classic American music swings, while forging a meaningful link to our past.

If you don't believe me, check out a swing show sometime. You'll likely find kids in Megadeth T-shirts there with their parents—all of them dancing. Now that's perspective.

Daniel Glass drums for Royal Crown Revue, which dubs itelf the "Johnny Appleseed of the neo-swing movement." In reaction to the predominant Los Angeles hair-metal bands of the '80s, the septet retreated into history, dressing up in 1940s-style costumes and playing Louis Prima/Louis Jordan–style music around 1989. They first gained recognition in hipster L.A. swing clubs, then via touring throughout the world (and on the Vans Warped Tour). The Revue's latest album, The Contender, *came out in 1998. Glass has written several articles on big-band history for* Modern Drummer *magazine.*

musicHound FOREWORD

by steve perry

Ask a kid in my neighborhood about the history of American popular music and you'll get something like this: "OK, like, there was this thing at the beginning called the big bang, I think. That was in 1968 or something. Then there was disco. Then MTV started and Kurt died. Now we bust rhymes and play Nintendo, dude."

This was pretty much me as a young man. I dropped out of school in the early '80s, and for no good reason started hanging out at this delicatessen/coffee house in Eugene, Oregon, called Lenny's Nosh Bar. Lenny's was open until 4:00 A.M., so all the late-night party action always ended up there.

The owner, Lenny Nathan, could be an ornery old codger, but he was nothing if not a savvy businessman. He sculpted an atmosphere of coolness that carefully appealed to smug bohemians of every conceit: punks, mods, beats, greasers, and hippies. He had such great and diverse taste in jukebox singles that I never heard anyone bitch.

Now, a lot of this music Lenny couldn't stand. He was in his mid-60s and had been a trumpet player as a young man. So he always had somebody like Bunny Berigan, Satchmo, or Harry James somewhere in the box for the slow hours during the day.

I was there most of the day because Lenny's had a pinball machine that was easy to beat up on. I would play for hours winning free games while Lenny made matzoh balls. Tunes like Glenn Miller's "Moonlight Serenade" or Harry James's "I Can't Get Started" would float through those pastrami-scented afternoons.

Understand, I was a die-hard punk rocker at the time. I lived for bands like the Damned, the Stooges, and the New York Dolls. But, slowly, saxophones began to melt my heart and stir my chain-smoking little soul. I became the soft-hearted cream puff who slow dances with the sad new-wave girl and tries to cheer her up. In other words, my friends thought I was beginning to show signs of becoming very unpunk and totally uncool.

I couldn't help it. I guess when I heard a four-string jazz banjo, or Count Basie, I recognized another part of myself besides the cynical nihilist, a part I hadn't been in touch with since I was a little kid. I felt joy.

Lenny started taking a liking to me. He began to open up about his own tender years. When he was 13, he had worked at his uncle's bar in Albany, New York, serving trays of drinks to Al Capone and his cronies during their frequent back-room poker games. He would always add one extra to every tab—for himself. Later, he joined the Merchant Marines, lost his virginity in a whorehouse, and smoked pot (still legal then) like it was tobacco.

What can I say, I'm a big fan of these kind of hard-boiled stories from swingin' antiquity. And Lenny had a million of 'em. His stories conjured a black-and-white underworld of leggy spider women and small-time hustlers. He made retro culture appealing. He inspired me to find a 78-rpm record player and start a collection of hand-painted ties and double-breasted suits. Soon I was frequenting estate sales and acquiring old vinyl by exotic-sounding groups like the Chocolate Dandies (because I liked the name). My interests included big band, R&B, race records, bebop, rockabilly, western swing, and early shufflin' Jamaican ska. I bought any permutation of that jumpin', swaggerin' feel.

I enjoy records that have what we call a pocket—a groove that's good for dancing or for an instrument to solo. If you could roll it down a hill it would go like an egg, not a baseball. I like this feeling so much I started a band. Its mission was to satisfy the diametric poles of my personality by hybridizing the kinds of music I loved the most, punk rock and swing. In Duke Ellington's "Ko Ko," whenever I heard those sweeping, blustery chords that sound like the wind, my eyes watered.

If only I'd had *MusicHound Swing*. I could have found out a lot more, a lot quicker. Essentially, this volume is like Ralph Nader does swing. In exhaustively researched, erudite entries, the critics have taken the time to figure out which of an artist's recordings is a Rolls-Royce and which is a lemon. What's also really cool is that contemporary swing bands are in here, cross referenced to where we stole our ideas. (Personally I'm just thrilled to be listed on the same page as Charlie Christian—although we're actually more of a rock band, and not even worthy to shine Charlie's shoes. Oh well.)

Lenny's Nosh Bar no longer exists. A nearby hospital bought up the street, evicted all the funky tenants, and tore that mother down. In its place is a parking garage. Up here we call it "getting Californicated."

But this year I've seen swing music, which had been a cultural footnote for 40 years, rise from the dead like bright flowers atop a garbage heap of hipster cynicism. So I can't help but be optimistic about the fate of that soulless, plastic, functional little street. Someday, maybe, seekers, romantics, fools, and artists will count for something more than an inspiration for some new ad campaign you see on the back of a bus. In the meantime, I'll remain proudly out of touch, while I try to understand what holds true value for me. With a little help from *MusicHound Swing*, old records, and guys like Lenny.

Steve Perry is lead singer for the Cherry Poppin' Daddies, the Eugene, Oregon, rock-and-swing septet that began in 1989 as a scruffy punk band living in a bassist's tiny garage. After experimenting with many different styles, including ska, grunge, and lounge, the Daddies settled on an upbeat Louis Jordan jump-blues style in the mid-1990s. In 1998, the band's song "Zoot Suit Riot" earned tons of MTV coverage and radio airplay and became a huge hit, pushing the same-titled album to platinum status. Perry lives in Oregon.

musicHound INTRODUCTION

by steve knopper

In the middle of the slow shuffle "Milkcow Blues Boogie," the famous story goes, Elvis Presley abruptly stopped his band. "Hold it, fellas," he declared in 1954. "That don't move me. Let's get real, real gone for a change." Guitarist Scotty Moore and bassist Bill Black stepped up the tempo, and rock 'n' roll began.

It's one of the cuddliest legends in popular music, but it wasn't original. Benny Goodman had done the same thing, two decades earlier, at a Hollywood ballroom called the Palomar. His big band had been playing superslow dance music in the style of the day's syrupy sweet bandleaders, Guy Lombardo and Kay Kyser. But nobody danced, and Goodman's band was in distress.

Finally, drummer Gene Krupa approached Goodman with a suggestion: "If we're gonna die," he said, "let's die playing our own thing." So, that night in 1935, Goodman broke out hot Fletcher Henderson arrangements like "King Porter Stomp," the crowd went nuts, and the swing era officially began.

"Whatever its virtues, rock 'n' roll doesn't swing," critic Francis Davis recently wrote in the *Atlantic Monthly.* But he's wrong. Swing rocks. Rock swings. The famous Krupa solo in Goodman's "Sing, Sing, Sing" has the same manic hysteria as Keith Moon's drums on the Who's "I Can't Explain." Though historians consider swing a jazz movement, and rock a pop movement, both styles are links on the same musical chain.

So today, what's surprising is not that Big Bad Voodoo Daddy plays the Super Bowl halftime show or that swing songs like the Brian Setzer Orchestra's "Jump, Jive, an' Wail" and the Squirrel Nut Zippers' "Hell" appear among videos by Mariah Carey and Beck on MTV. It's how long "swing" has been shorthand for "square."

After World War II, the swing bands foundered, done in by the financial strain of dragging dozens of musicians around the country and by the advent of bebop jazz and, later, rock. The big bands were pushed into one endless nostalgia circuit, no longer relevant to a generation raised on the guitar heroics of rock 'n' roll. That didn't change until the 1990s, more than six decades after Goodman's Palomar shows. Subtly, slowly, the style graduated once again from underground phenomenon to mainstream culture. The hipster dance movie *Swingers* became a cult hit; Brian Setzer built an extremely large band; other neo-swing groups like Royal Crown Revue and the Cherry Poppin' Daddies gained airplay on alternative rock stations; and the "Khakis Swing" Gap ad froze dancers in mid-air. Swing was back.

"Kids come up—my son's 11—'Guess what, Mr. Setzer? I play trombone in my school band, I'm going to start a swing band!'" Setzer recently told *Down Beat.* "It's probably been 50 years since that kid has been cool, you know?"

MusicHound Swing is the first album-buying guide to link the swing era, roughly 1935 to 1942, with the jump bands of today. Of course, we've included their common forebears—sadly unheralded (at the time) African American bandleaders such as Count Basie, Fletcher Henderson, and Jay McShann; New Orleans jazz inventors like Jelly Roll Morton and Sidney Bechet; jive-talking R&B shouters like Louis Jordan, Louis Prima, and Cab Calloway; and the transcendent Louis Armstrong and Duke Ellington.

For spice, and because today's jitterbuggers hear this stuff in clubs, we've also included a smattering of rockabilly, jump blues, and boogie-woogie. And we haven't ignored western swing, which isn't as unrelated as some people think. The Dorsey Brothers, Krupa, and trombonist Jack Teagarden backed hillbilly minstrel man Emmett Miller on his mysterious late-'20s recordings; New Orleans pre-swinger Joe "King" Oliver covered country yodeler Jimmie Rodgers's "Everybody Does It in Hawaii"; and '30s western-swing hero Bob Wills sounds more like Goodman than either bandleader's fans usually admit.

In suggesting which CDs to buy and which to avoid, *MusicHound Swing* encourages jazz, rock, and jump-blues fans to make these connections.

What's swing? The most devoted Goodman fan couldn't define it in 1935, and it's still a "know it when you hear it" situation. Some say it was merely a better word for "jazz," which once referred not to a hot Count Basie night in Harlem but to ballroom dwellers like "King of Jazz" Paul Whiteman. (For historical purposes, we've included Whiteman, Guy Lombardo, Kay Kyser, and the like, too.) Most critics agree it has a strong rhythmic pulse, complex waves of horns, and plenty of solos by pianists, guitarists, banjoists, singers, or drummers.

There are countless historical reasons why swing and rock shouldn't be segregated into distinct "jazz" and "pop" camps. Presley and his contemporaries sped up squawking R&B music and sold it to teenagers in the '50s. Before that, R&B shouters like Big Joe Turner, Louis Jordan, Louis Prima, and Cab Calloway were scaled-down outgrowths of horn-heavy big bands like the Duke Ellington, Count Basie, and Fletcher Henderson orchestras. And those bands, directly or indirectly, come from New Orleans, home of Sidney Bechet, Jelly Roll Morton, Louis Armstrong, and the "second-line" marching rhythm that runs through it all.

Here's a sad parallel: both styles became popular only after white practitioners learned to excel at African American music. Presley became the King of Rock 'n' Roll by covering "race records" such as Arthur "Big Boy" Crudup's classic jump blues "That's All Right (Mama)." Goodman became the King of Swing after hiring Fletcher Henderson—a black bandleader who's hugely influential today but never once landed above #8 on the pop charts—to speed his arrangements into swing.

But the main reason for linking swing and rock is simple. People can dance—the lindy hop, the jitterbug, even the fox-trot—to both. Maybe in 1955 Harry James lived in Squaresville and Bill Haley came from Cool. Today, James's "Perdido" and Haley's "Shake, Rattle, & Roll" sound great back-to-back on the dance floor. Not to mention Carl Perkins's "Blue Suede Shoes" and Count Basie's "Moten Swing."

So it is that Elvis Presley appears in a swing book. Frank Sinatra might have disapproved. But Cab Calloway, we think, would have responded with an "oodlee-odlyee-odlyee-oodlee-doo."

Nothing against music lovers who meticulously archive old Benny Goodman and Fletcher Henderson recordings for home-stereo use—MusicHound critics are occasionally known to do that themselves. But for years, the best way to experience swing music has been on the dance floor, whether it's couples twirling smoothly in elegant ballrooms or sweaty men in zoot suits tossing women so high their hoop skirts fly up Marilyn Monroe–style. Thanks to Richard M. Stephenson's *The Complete Book of Ballroom Dancing* (Doubleday, 1992), the U.S. Swing Dance Server Web site, and Elizabeth Gilbert's superb December 1998 *GQ* profile of Harlem legend Frankie Manning for help with the following dance information:

Fox-Trot: After vaudeville actor Harry Fox invented this dance in 1914, it became a huge craze, dominating classes and clubs all over New York City. As part of his act, Fox did trotting steps to ragtime music—and worked his "Fox's Trot" act to the roof of the prestigious New York Theatre. Though Fox once declared bankruptcy and died a minor Hollywood actor in 1959, his namesake dance, an adaptable mixture of slow and fast steps, lives in ballrooms everywhere. The fox-trot begat the Peabody, the lindy and the hustle, among many others.

Jitterbug: Though it's a standard upbeat ballroom dance today, the word "jitterbug" was a loaded racial term in the '30s. Blacks used it to describe white swing lovers who tried unsuccessfully (and with humorous jerky movements) to imitate the lindy hop. In terms of steps, it's similar to the lindy—and East Coast swing, for that matter—but usually not as acrobatic or jumpy. Sometimes jitterbug and lindy hop are used interchangeably.

Lindy Hop: Named for Charles Lindbergh's 1927 flight to Paris, this two-step-and-fancy-breakaway dance initially became famous at Harlem's Savoy Ballroom. The sexy, often-acrobatic dance was a cultural force in the black community, performed to the music of Fletcher Henderson, Count Basie, and other African American big bands. Following swing's loose path from Henderson to Benny Goodman, the lindy spread to white dancers, becoming hugely popular during the mid-'30s swing era. Eclipsed by its successor, the jitterbug, the lindy died down for years—until young swing revivalists tracked down Frankie Manning and other originators for lessons in the early '90s. *GQ* magazine recently called it "powerful, lusty, quicker than whiplash."

Cha-Cha: A more structured version of the mambo, this "one, two, cha-cha-cha" Latin dance became a craze of its own in the late '50s. Its name comes from a Haitian percussion instrument, and it took hold when a Cuban orchestra, America, performed sort of a slow mambo for dancers in 1953. Unlike the short-lived mambo, the cha-cha never really went away. According to *The Complete Book of Ballroom Dancing,* it's the most popular Latin dance in the U.S.—perhaps because it's so easy to pick up and doesn't rely on fancy acrobatics.

Mambo: Though the name has Haitian origins, the mambo began with a 1943 Perez Prado performance in Cuba—then spread to the U.S. via Prado, Rosemary Clooney, and Nat King Cole as a bona fide "craze." As acrobatic as the lindy hop, the jerky, fast-and-slow dance grew out of the more conservative rumba and led to the more enduring cha-cha. Despite now-quaint singles such as Clooney's "Mambo Italiano" and Cole's "Papa Loves Mambo," the craze burned itself out fairly quickly. But some advanced dancers still pull it off.

Tango: Born in Buenos Aires, Argentina, the tango took off in Spain, absorbed black and Creole influences from the "New

World," and became hugely popular in the mid-1800s. In 1914, not long after European dance teachers banned the romantic, costumed "dance with a stop" for being seductive and immoral, it caught on in the U.S. and endures as a ballroom mainstay. Though it has no direct connection to swing dancing, the tango's popularity around 1930 helped create interest for couples exhibition dancing in general—thus setting up the swing era. It has inspired several movies, most recently 1998's *Tango.*

West Coast Swing: This adaptation of the lindy hop was originally called "western swing"—because it happened on the West Coast—but the name changed to avoid confusion with country-western dancing. In the 1930s, a dancer named Dean Collins learned the Savoy Ballroom–style lindy and moved to Hollywood to make it in the movies. Known as the "Father of West Coast Swing," Collins choreographed the swing scenes in many dance movies from the '30s to the '60s. A syncopated dance where the man usually stands in one place while the woman jumps and twirls all around, it emphasizes improvisation. Because the dance, unlike, say, the waltz, is in constant flux, West Coast swingers distance themselves from ballroom dancers.

Country-Western Swing: Just as the great western-swing fiddler Bob Wills took inspiration from late-'20s and early-'30s big-band music, so did his fans derive their two-step and couple dances from lindy hoppers and jitterbuggers. The dancing continued in this vein until the late '70s, when it started taking cues from the slow-slow, quick-quick steps of West Coast swingers. So dancers were prepared in 1981, when John Travolta's *Urban Cowboy* movie spread it everywhere. It devolved for a while into the "Achy Breaky Dance," a simple line dance encouraged by hunky singer Billy Ray Cyrus.

East Coast Swing: Basically another name for the lindy hop, East Coast swing has been so-called since the '40s, when dancers distinguished themselves from their West Coast swinging counterparts. The term is frequently used by major dance studios.

Hustle: Disco-swing fusion? That's probably not how most people remember Van McCoy and the Soul City Symphony's corny 1975 hit "The Hustle," but in retrospect most dance teachers view the craze as a variation on the six-count lindy hop. It's actually a challenge dance, especially with complex variations like the Latin hustle and the three-count hustle. In some ways, although it's more couples-oriented, the neo-swing movement is another way of luring disco dancers back to the clubs they deserted two decades ago.

So how do you use *MusicHound Swing*? Here's what you'll find in the entries, and what we intend to accomplish with each point:

• An introductory paragraph, which will give you not only biographical information but also a sense of the artist's or group's sound and its stature in the swing—and overall music—pantheon.

• **what to buy:** The album or albums that we feel are essential purchases for consuming this act. It may be a greatest hits set, or it may be a particular album that captures the essence of the artist in question. In any event, this is where you should start—and don't think it wasn't hard to make these choices when perusing the catalogs of swing giants like Benny Goodman, Duke Ellington, and Count Basie. Note that for acts with a limited catalog, **what's available** may take the place of **what to buy** and the other sections.

• **what to buy next:** In other words, once you're hooked, these will be the most rewarding next purchases.

• **what to avoid:** This category could include albums the world would be better off without, or it may designate work that newcomers to the particular artist are better off saving for later. Checking the bone ratings—and of course the writer's comments—usually makes it clear whether we're saying "avoid this forever, and cover your ears if anybody plays it in your vicinity," or merely indicating that it's "for completists."

• **the rest:** Everything else that's available for this act, rated with the Hound's trusty bone scale (see below for more on this). Note that for some artists with sizable catalogs, we've condensed this section down to **best of the rest.**

• **worth searching for:** An out-of-print gem. A bootleg. A guest appearance on another artist's album or a film soundtrack. Something that may require some looking but will reward you for the effort.

• ⏪: The crucial influences on this act's music.

• ⏩: The acts that have been influenced by this artist or group. Used only where applicable; it's a little early for George Gee & His Make-Believe Ballroom Orchestra or Red & the Red Hots to have influenced anybody.

We should also remind you that *MusicHound Swing* is a *buyer's* guide. Therefore, for the most part we only discuss CDs that are currently in print and available in the United States.

Now, you ask, what's with those bones? (Down, boy! Sheesh. . . .) It's not hard to figure out—🦴🦴🦴🦴🦴 is nirvana (not Nirvana), a **woof!** is dog food. Keep in mind that the bone ratings don't pertain just to the act's own catalog, but to its worth in the whole music realm. Therefore a lesser act's **what to buy** choice might rate no more than 🦴🦴🦴; some even rate 🦴🦴½, a not-so-subtle sign that you might want to think twice about that act. Note that for recent releases that were not available to be reviewed before press time, "N/A" will appear instead of a bone rating.

As with any opinions, all of what you're about to read is subjective and personal. MusicHound has a bit of junkyard dog in it, too; it likes to start fights. We hope it does, too. Ultimately, we think the Hound will point you in the right direction, and if you buy the 🦴🦴🦴🦴🦴 and 🦴🦴🦴🦴 choices, you'll have an album collection to howl about. But if you've got a bone to pick, the Hound wants to hear about it—and promises not to bite (but maybe bark a little bit). If you think we're wagging our tails in the wrong direction or lifting our leg at something that doesn't deserve it, let us know. If you think an act has been capriciously excluded—or charitably included—tell us. Your comments and suggestions will serve the greater MusicHound audience and future projects, so don't be shy.

Editor

Steve Knopper has been swinging most of his life, from the time he fell off a swing, onto his stomach, at age six. He grew up imitating Ringo Starr while banging on chairs in his bedroom; much later, he traced the Beatles' lineage to skiffle jazz, R&B, rockabilly, jump blues, and the big bands, especially Gene Krupa and Count Basie. Today he hears swing in everything, from Louis Prima's "Just a Gigolo" to Buddy Greco's "The Lady Is a Tramp" to Public Enemy's "Fight the Power." Armed with this logic, he edited *MusicHound Lounge: The Essential Album Guide to Martini Music and Easy Listening.* Knopper is a Chicago-based freelance writer whose stories have run in *Rolling Stone, George, Musician, Newsday, Chicago,* the *Chicago Tribune, Request, Billboard, Yahoo! Internet Life,* and many other publications. He also writes a regular column, "Blues," for the Knight-Ridder Newspapers wire service and has contributed hundreds of entries for *MusicHound Country, MusicHound Blues, MusicHound Rock,* and *MusicHound R&B.* His daily column, "Net Buzz," is humorous at least 25 percent of the time and can be found at www.dailynetbuzz.com.

Series Editor

Gary Graff is an award-winning music journalist and series editor of the MusicHound album guides. A native of Pittsburgh, Pennsylvania, his work is published regularly by Reuters, *Guitar World, ICE,* the *San Francisco Chronicle,* the *Cleveland Plain Dealer,* the *Pittsburgh Post-Gazette,* Michigan's *Oakland Press,* SW Radio Networks, *Country Song Roundup,* and other publications. A regular contributor to the Web site Mr. Showbiz/Wall of Sound, his weekly "Rock 'n' Roll Insider" report airs on Detroit rock station WRIF-FM (101.1). He also appears on public TV station WTVS's *Backstage Pass* program and is a founding board member of the Music Critics Organization and co-producer of the annual Detroit Music Awards. He lives in the Detroit suburbs with his wife, daughter, and two stepsons.

Managing Editor

Jeff Hermann, a swinger in spirit if not on the dance floor, is an editor at Visible Ink Press where he enjoys the respect of his co-workers except when they refer to him as "monkey boy." Hermann resides in a quaint apartment in a Detroit suburb, but the love of his life lives in New York, New York.

Associate Managing Editors

Dean Dauphinais is an obsessive-compulsive senior editor at Visible Ink Press and the managing editor of several MusicHound titles. While he can count the number of times he's been swing dancing on one hand (actually, on no hands), he routinely taps his foot to music that swings and lists Joe Jackson's *Jumpin' Jive* among his favorite albums of all time. A devotee of Diana Krall and Frank Sinatra (R.I.P.), Dauphinais lives in suburban Detroit with his wife, Kathy, and two sons, Sam and Josh.

Judy Galens is a senior editor with Visible Ink Press and managing editor of several MusicHound titles. She swings, but only on playgrounds. Galens lives in domestic bliss (most of the time) with her husband and their new baby, Graham, in a suburb of Detroit.

Copy Editors

Barbara Cohen is a copyediting and indexing whiz, and has had a hand in a number of Visible Ink titles. She also lectures and writes on indexing and the training of indexers.

Christina Fouco is a contributor to *MusicHound Swing!*

Pamela Shelton is a freelance writer and copy editor living in Connecticut. She used to write a bluegrass column for *Country in the City News*.

Publisher
Martin Connors

MusicHound Staff
Michelle Banks, Christa Brelin, Jim Craddock, Justin Karr, Diane Maniaci, Brad Morgan, Carol Schwartz, Devra Sladics, Christine Tomassini

Proofreading
Kathy Dauphinais

Art Direction
Tracey Rowens, Michelle DiMercurio, Cindy Baldwin

Contributing Photographers
Jack and Linda Vartoogian grew up in late-1950s Detroit and heard, but did not get to see, some of the best performers in music. To compensate, they have devoted themselves to photographing musicians (and dancers) from across the country and around the world. While their New York City home virtually guarantees that, eventually, most acts come to them, they continue to seek opportunities to discover new talent and new venues—the farther from home the better. Their images appear regularly in the *New York Times, Time, Newsweek, Living Blues, JazzTimes*, and many other periodicals, as well as in numerous books, including their own *Afropop!* (Chartwell Books, 1995) and *The Living World of Dance* (Smithmark, 1997), and *MusicHound Blues, MusicHound R&B, MusicHound Lounge, MusicHound Folk, MusicHound Jazz* and *MusicHound Rock*. The forthcoming *MusicHound World* features nearly 200 Vartoogian photographs.

Ken Settle is a Detroit-area photographer who has specialized in music photography for over 17 years. His photos have been published worldwide in magazines such as *Rolling Stone, People, Guitar Player, Playboy, Audio*, Japan's *Player*, France's *Guitarist*, and Australia's *Who Weekly*, as well as major newspapers like the *Atlanta Journal Constitution* and the *Arizona Republic*. The Hard Rock Cafe recently acquired 67 of his exhibition prints for their international collection, and several of his images were exhibited in *People* magazine's traveling exhibition, "Through the Years with *People*." His work also appears in *MusicHound Rock, MusicHound Country, MusicHound Blues, MusicHound R&B, MusicHound Lounge, MusicHound Folk*, and *MusicHound Jazz*. Ken dedicates his photo contributions to the memory of his beloved cats, Angie and Squeaky.

Graphic Services
Randy Bassett, Pam Reed, Barbara Yarrow

Permissions
Edna Hedblad

Production
Mary Beth Trimper, Dorothy Maki, Deborah Milliken, Evi Seoud, Wendy Blurton, Rita Wimberley

Technology Wizard
Jeffrey Muhr

Typesetting Virtuoso
Marco Di Vita of the Graphix Group

Marketing & Promotion
Marilou Carlin, Kim Marich, Lauri Taylor, Betsy Rovegno, Nancy Hammond

MusicHound Development
Julia Furtaw

Contributors
Susan K. Berlowitz has worked for the past several years as a photojournalist for a monthly jazz publication and as a radio DJ and producer. She operates a freelance publicity business in New York City and is a member of the jazz faculty at Merkin Hall.

Stephen L. Betts is a Nashville-based columnist for *Country Song Roundup* magazine and researcher for the TNN shows *Today's Country* and *This Week in Country Music*. He is a contributor to *MusicHound Country* and *MusicHound Folk*.

Will Bickart, a contributor to *MusicHound Jazz*, is a clinical psychologist living in San Francisco. He has been listening to jazz for over 20 years and his knowledge of the idiom is extensive.

Dan Bindert has contributed to *MusicHound Jazz* and is music editor and jazz columnist at *City Newspaper* in Rochester, New York, and a regular contributor to the Canadian magazine the *Jazz Report*. His work has also appeared in *Blues Connection, Urban Network*, and *Frederick Douglass Voice*. Bindert is a radio announcer at Rochester NPR-affiliate WXXI, where he has been hosting *Blues Spectrum* and various jazz programs since 1989.

John Bitter, photojournalist and *MusicHound Jazz* contributor, is a retired procedures analyst whose hobby since his early teens has been jazz record collecting, sparked by working six years as a full-time jazz buyer in a Lakewood, Ohio, record shop. He is a contributing editor for *Mississippi Rag*, a traditional jazz publication.

Steve Braun is a Washington-based national correspondent for the *Los Angeles Times* and a contributor to *Blues Access* magazine. He does not own a zoot suit with a reet pleat, or call strangers "Gate."

Keith Brickhouse is a jazz journalist/independent radio producer who lives and works in New York City. The *MusicHound Jazz* contributor has produced the nationally syndicated Public Radio programs "Highlights of Montreux Live" (a 13-part series) and "A Postcard from Bern," a two-hour special as part of the *Jazz Traveler* series.

Stuart Broomer writes regularly on music for *Cadence, Coda,* and *Toronto Life.* He contributed the "Monster Solo" sidebars to *MusicHound Jazz.*

G. Brown has written about popular music for the *Denver Post* for the last 21 years (even longer than he spent in high school). The *MusicHound Lounge* contributor is also the popular host of several specialty programs on Denver-area radio stations and has served as a kids' show host on local television (Uncle G!).

Ken Burke is a singer-songwriter whose column, "The Continuing Saga of Dr. Iguana," has been running in discerning small press publications since 1985. A contributor to several MusicHound guides, Burke is proud to announce that sales of his CD, *Arizona Songs*, are rapidly approaching double digits.

Salvatore Caputo is a freelance writer who lives in Phoenix, which is as far from Tuxedo Junction as he cares to be. A college-age swing band plays Friday nights at his local YMCA as he works out to shed the effects of a not-so-swinging lifestyle. His wife and three kids thank him for getting in the mood.

Jay Dedrick is entertainment editor at the *Daily Camera* newspaper in Boulder, Colorado, where the spirit of Glenn Miller swings to this day.

Chris Dickinson has written for *MusicHound Country,* the *St. Louis Post-Dispatch, Journal of Country Music, New Country,* the *Chicago Tribune,* and *Request.*

Josh Freedom du Lac, who once thought the only swing in the world that mattered was Will Clark's, is co-editor of *MusicHound R&B.* When he's not falling off of his mountain bike or obsessing over a bottle of California Cabernet, he writes about music and all sorts of other stuff for the *Sacramento Bee.*

Daniel Durchholz is co-editor of *MusicHound Rock* and a freelance writer and editor for numerous print and Web publications. He lives in St. Louis with his wife and four kids. Most of his swinging is done from chandeliers.

Geoff Edgers, a staff writer for the *News & Observer* in Raleigh, North Carolina, has contributed to *Spin, Details,* the *New York Times Sunday Magazine, Salon,* and the *Boston Phoenix.* He is author of *The Midnight Hour: Bright Ideas for After Dark,* a children's book.

George Foley is a nationally known ragtime pianist who cut his first album while still in his teens. He performs regularly in the Cleveland area and elsewhere in North America. George's work can also be found in *MusicHound Jazz.*

Jon Hartley Fox is an award-winning writer and record producer who lives in Sacramento, California. He is a 20-year veteran of the bluegrass wars and a contributor to *MusicHound Country* and *MusicHound Folk.*

Christina Fuoco is the music reporter for the *Observer & Eccentric Newspapers* chain based in Livonia, Michigan. She lives in Berkley, Michigan, with her cat, Spedliann.

Lawrence Gabriel is a Detroit-based writer, poet, and musician who is also editor of Detroit's *Metro Times.* He has contributed to *MusicHound Rock, MusicHound Folk, MusicHound Jazz,* and *MusicHound R&B.*

Andrew Gilbert, *MusicHound Jazz* contributor, is a Bay Area–based writer who contributes regularly to the *San Diego Union-Tribune, Contra Costa Times, East Bay Express,* and *Salon.* His writing on jazz has also appeared in the Los Angeles *Reader,* the Los Angeles *View,* the San Jose *Metro,* the Santa Cruz *County Sentinel, Musician,* and *Jazziz.*

Gary Pig Gold, a veteran of *MusicHound Rock, MusicHound Country, MusicHound Folk, MusicHound R&B,* and even *MusicHound Lounge,* has been publishing his own rag, *The Pig Paper,* since A.D. 1975. He also scribbles for various online 'zines, runs his own band and record label out of Frank Sinatra's hometown, still cherishes his father's old Columbia 78 of Benny Goodman's "Boy Meets Horn," and honestly believes Chet Baker to be a better vocalist than he is a trumpeter.

Alex Gordon is associate editor of *Basketball Digest,* co-author of the book *College: The Best Five Years of Your Life* (Hysteria Press), a contributor to *MusicHound Lounge,* and former managing editor of the late, lamented *Internet Underground* magazine.

Gary Graff is MusicHound's series editor and co-editor of *MusicHound Rock* and *MusicHound Country.*

Ben Greenman is an author and critic living in Brooklyn. His work has appeared in *Rolling Stone, Wired,* the *Village Voice, TimeOut New York, Yahoo! Internet Life,* the *Miami New Times,* the *Chicago Reader, MusicHound Lounge,* and many other publications.

Larry Grogan has been writing about music, both aboveground and underground, for 15 years. In his 'zines *Incognito, Evil Eye,* and *Gone,* as well as in several New Jersey newspapers and *MusicHound Jazz,* he has annotated his love for everything from Monk to Piazzolla to Mose Allison and Hamza El Din. He is 35 and lives in South River, New Jersey.

Ed Hazell is a freelance jazz writer who contributes regularly to the *Boston Phoenix.* He is the author of *Berklee: The First 50 Years,* an authorized history of the Berklee College of Music, and a contributor to *Jazz: From Its Origins to the Present* (Prentice Hall). His articles have also appeared in the *Boston Globe, MusicHound Jazz,* and *Coda, Cadence,* and *Planet Jazz* magazines.

Steve Holtje is co-editor of *MusicHound Jazz* and is classical, jazz/blues, and world/soundtracks/new age editor of CDnow. He also freelances for the *Wire, Jazziz,* the *Big Takeover,* and various other publications, including most of the MusicHound volumes. Though he lives primarily in Lansdale, Pennsylvania, he returns to Brooklyn every weekend to maintain his reputation as a feared softball player.

Chris Hovan, a freelance musician and full-time teacher, writes about music for the *Crusader News, Jazz and Blues Report,* and the *Cleveland Free Times.* He has been a radio DJ, jazz buyer for a Cleveland-area record store, Northeast Ohio Jazz Society trustee, and producer/writer of WCPN Cleveland's jazz educational program *Milestones.* Chris has also contributed to *MusicHound Jazz.*

B.J. Huchtemann, *MusicHound Blues* and *MusicHound Jazz* contributor, is a staff music reviewer and interviewer for the *Reader* in Omaha, Nebraska. She also writes for *Blues Access,* plus advertising and promotional copy for radio, television, and print media.

Jack Jackson, who has written for the *Miami Herald* and Denver's *Westword,* struts regularly with barbecue. He lives in a thatch-roof house in Denmark.

Dan Keener, *MusicHound Jazz* contributor, is a 23-year-old from Denver, Colorado. He has a real-life job that is about as removed from writing about swing as you can get—he teaches lawyers how to use computers.

Chris Kelsey is a saxophonist who has studied the instrument with Lee Konitz and jazz history with Max Roach. He has written about music for *Jazz Now, Jazziz,* and *Cadence.*

George W. Krieger, a.k.a. "The Rock 'n' Roll Dentist," is a general dentist in Elizabeth, Colorado, and has written articles for *Goldmine, Colorado Heritage,* the *Pueblo Chieftain,* the *Roundup of Denver Westerners, MusicHound Lounge, MusicHound Rock,* and the *Journal of the Colorado Dental Association.*

Mark Ladenson, *MusicHound Jazz* contributor, has written for *Coda, JazzTimes,* and the *IAJRC* (International Association of Jazz Record Collectors) *Journal.* His reviews appear regularly in *Marge Hofacre's Jazz News* and his photographs appear regularly in *Cadence.*

Nancy Ann Lee is a Cleveland-based music journalist who confesses that she danced to swing music in grade school when it was called the "jitterbug." Lee has interviewed and photographed some of the world's greatest jazz musicians, and her articles and reviews have appeared online and in various print publications, sometimes accompanied by her photos. She is co-editor of *MusicHound Jazz.*

Jim Lester, *MusicHound Jazz* contributor, is a retired psychologist, moonlighting musician, and author of *Too Marvelous for Words: The Life and Genius of Art Tatum* (Oxford University Press, 1994).

Garaud MacTaggart is a *MusicHound Jazz* contributor and a Buffalo, New York–based freelance writer with 20 years of experience in music retailing (management/buyer). His work has appeared in newspapers such as the *Buffalo News,* the *Royal Oak* (Michigan) *Tribune,* Detroit's *Metro Times,* the *Orlando Weekly,* the *Columbus Guardian,* and Chicago's *In These Times.*

Tali Madden is a contributing writer for *Blues Access* magazine and a freelance music journalist who has written for *MusicHound Blues.* A former NPR-affiliate jazz and blues broadcaster/programmer, he is based in Portland, Oregon.

Brian Mansfield is the co-editor of *MusicHound Country* and *MusicHound Folk.* He currently serves as Nashville correspondent for *USA Today* and Nashville editor for CountryNow.com. He couldn't dance if his wife depended on it.

Lynne Margolis, a contributor to *MusicHound Rock, MusicHound R&B, MusicHound Folk,* and *MusicHound Lounge,* lives in the lovely city of Pittsburgh—where there's not only no more smoke, there's no more steel. The former pop music critic for the *Pittsburgh Tribune-Review,* she's now cranking out the Trib's TV and radio coverage—with a decidedly musical slant.

Sandy Masuo has written about a bewildering variety of music for a wide range of publications, including the *Boston Phoenix,* the *Los Angeles Times, Musician, Rolling Stone, RayGun, Music-*

Hound Lounge, and several online publications, including *Allstar, MTV Online,* and *Launch.* She is the associate editor at *Request* magazine and lives in Los Angeles with her anti-social cat, Spot.

Ronnie McDowell is a *MusicHound Country* contributor and the nationwide telemarketing sales director for *New Country* magazine. Ronnie is no kin to the singer of the same name (though it helps him get good dinner reservations).

Ajay Mehrotra is a graduate student in American history at the University of Chicago. A frustrated musician, he is now freelancing and working on his dissertation.

Chris Meloche is a composer, broadcaster, and music writer (for *MusicHound Jazz,* among other publications). Based in London, Ontario, his music has been featured around the world. His radio program *Wired for Sound* can be heard locally on CHRW-FM as well as internationally via RealAudio on the Internet.

David Menconi is the music critic for the *News & Observer* in Raleigh, North Carolina. He has also written for *Billboard, Spin, No Depression, Blues Access, Request,* and *MusicHound Rock, MusicHound Lounge, MusicHound Country, MusicHound Blues, MusicHound Folk,* and *MusicHound R&B.*

David Okamoto is the music editor for the *Dallas Morning News* and a contributing editor to *ICE* magazine. In between writing for *MusicHound Lounge, MusicHound Folk, MusicHound Country, MusicHound Jazz,* and *MusicHound Rock,* he helped produce a compilation of Martin Mull's music for Razor & Tie Records. Really.

Alan Paul is an associate editor at *Guitar World* and editor of *Guitar World* Online (www.guitarworld.com). His articles have run in *People, Entertainment Weekly,* the *New Yorker, MusicHound Blues, MusicHound Rock,* and many other publications. He likes piña coladas and making love at midnight.

Matt Pensinger has written for the *Colorado Springs Gazette* and Digital City Denver (a site on America Online), as well as *Blues Access, No Depression,* and *MusicHound Blues.*

Randy Pitts is a contributor to *MusicHound Country, MusicHound Rock,* and *MusicHound Folk* who has labored in the vineyards of traditional music in various circumstances for nearly 20 years, most recently as artistic director of the Freight and Salvage in Berkeley, California, where he worked from 1989 until 1996.

Bryan Powell is a Lawrenceville, Georgia, journalist who performs in the Atlanta area with the band Rough Draft. He contributes to *Blues Access* and has written for *MusicHound Blues, MusicHound Folk, MusicHound Lounge, MusicHound Rock,* and the Atlanta-based *Creative Loafing.*

Bret Primack has been writing about jazz musicians since 1977. A former East Coast editor of *Down Beat* and director of Jazz Central Station, his articles and interviews have appeared in publications such as *Down Beat, JazzTimes, Swing Journal, MusicHound Jazz,* and *People* magazine. Co-founder of the Jazz Theater Workshop and author of *The Ben Hecht Show,* Primack has also written liner notes for artists such as McCoy Tyner, Ella Fitzgerald, Clark Terry, and Arturo Sandoval.

Jim Prohaska, *MusicHound Jazz* contributor, is a resident of Lakewood, Ohio, and an avid collector and enthusiast of vintage jazz and blues of the 1920s and 1930s, owning well over 20,000 jazz and blues 78 rpm records and 10,000 LPs. Prohaska has donated and/or loaned material from his collection to the Rock and Roll Hall of Fame and Museum, the Western Reserve Historical Society, and the Cuyahoga Community College (Tri-C) JazzFest, and he buys and sells vintage recordings worldwide.

Doug Pullen is the music and media writer for the *Flint* (Michigan) *Journal* and Booth Newspapers. He is a regular contributor to the MusicHound series.

Carl Quintanilla, a Mel Tormé fanatic and *MusicHound Lounge* and *MusicHound Rock* contributor, is a staff reporter for the *Wall Street Journal.*

Judy R. Rabinovitz, *MusicHound Country* contributor, is an aspiring singer/songwriter and freelance music writer based in Nashville. She is currently on staff at *New Country* magazine.

John K. Richmond has produced jazz history programs for radio, has written about jazz for two major daily newspapers, the *Cleveland Press* and the *Plain Dealer,* and frequently conducts lectures and film programs on jazz. A contributor to *MusicHound Jazz,* Richmond serves as executive director of the Northeast Ohio Jazz Society (a jazz support organization), is a jazz history instructor at Cleveland State University, and is a working jazz musician.

Leland Rucker is editor of *MusicHound Blues* and contributor to all the MusicHound volumes. He is managing editor of *Blues Access,* a quarterly journal of blues music, and co-author of *The Toy Book: A Celebration of Slinky and G.I. Joe, Tinkertoys, Hula Hoops, Barbie Dolls, Snoot-Flutes, Coonskin Caps, Slot Cars, Frisbees, Yo-Yos, Betsy Wetsy and Much Much More* (Alfred Knopf, 1992). He lives in Boulder, Colorado.

Joel Selvin has covered pop music for the *San Francisco Chronicle* since 1970 and is the author of several books on the subject (in addition to his entries for *MusicHound Rock* and *MusicHound Country*). He co-produced Dick Dale's *Tribal Thunder* album.

Jim Sheeler is a *MusicHound Lounge* contributor and a staff writer for the *Boulder Planet* in Colorado, where he makes most excellent mix tapes.

Craig Shelburne lives in Nashville and has written for the *Nashville Scene, Gospel Voice, Music City News, MusicHound Country,* and *New Country.*

David Simons is a New England–based writer/editor who has contributed to *Musician, New Country, Guitar, Country Songwriter,* and other publications, in addition to *MusicHound Country, MusicHound Folk,* and *MusicHound Rock.*

John Sinclair is a poet, performer (with his Blues Scholars), music journalist (for *MusicHound Blues,* among other publications), radio host (WWOZ-FM), and record producer (Big Chief Productions) based in New Orleans. His recordings include *Full Moon Night; Full Circle* (with Wayne Kramer); *If I Could Be with You* (with Ed Moss & the Society Jazz Orchestra; and *thelonius: a book of monk—volume one.*

Mario Tarradell is the country music critic for the *Dallas Morning News.* His work has also appeared in *Replay* and *New Country* magazines, and in *MusicHound Country.*

Tom Terrell is a *MusicHound Rock* contributor and a freelance music journalist based in New York who claims to know everything about pop music since 1955—and remembers it all despite a longtime backstage association with George Clinton

ject (in addition to his entries for *MusicHound Rock* and *MusicHound Country*). He co-produced Dick Dale's *Tribal Thunder* album.

Jim Sheeler is a *MusicHound Lounge* contributor and a staff writer for the *Boulder Planet* in Colorado, where he makes most excellent mix tapes.

Craig Shelburne lives in Nashville and has written for the *Nashville Scene, Gospel Voice, Music City News, MusicHound Country,* and *New Country.*

David Simons is a New England–based writer/editor who has contributed to *Musician, New Country, Guitar, Country Songwriter,* and other publications, in addition to *MusicHound Country, MusicHound Folk,* and *MusicHound Rock.*

John Sinclair is a poet, performer (with his Blues Scholars), music journalist (for *MusicHound Blues,* among other publications), radio host (WWOZ-FM), and record producer (Big Chief Productions) based in New Orleans. His recordings include *Full Moon Night; Full Circle* (with Wayne Kramer); *If I Could Be with You* (with Ed Moss & the Society Jazz Orchestra; and *thelonius: a book of monk—volume one.*

Mario Tarradell is the country music critic for the *Dallas Morning News.* His work has also appeared in *Replay* and *New Country* magazines, and in *MusicHound Country.*

Tom Terrell is a *MusicHound Rock* contributor and a freelance music journalist based in New York who claims to know everything about pop music since 1955—and remembers it all despite a longtime backstage association with George Clinton

Without contributors, generous with their time, expertise, and writing talents, neither *MusicHound Swing* nor any of the rest of the MusicHound series would have amounted to anything. Thanks to them for delivering consistent work after another round of my begging, threatening, and pleading e-mails. And to my wife, Melissa, who had to endure Bing Crosby and Guy Lombardo for yet another holiday season.

Ken Burke isn't this book's official "assistant editor," but judging from the number of "Thanks, Ken" e-mails I've sent, he may as well be. With his tireless churning of clean and colorful copy, suggestions for new entries, unmatched rockabilly expertise, well-timed humor, and one incredible brush–with–Jerry Lee Lewis story, he helped make *MusicHound Swing* a much smoother process than I expected it to be. Special thanks, also, to his assistant, the esteemed Nez Nurkley.

I started writing MusicHound entries simply to make some extra cash while researching my favorite rock 'n' roll bands. After *MusicHound Rock* editor Gary Graff rejected my initial attempts to bail out, he submerged me even further, and by the time I was offered the editorship of *MusicHound Lounge,* I was hooked. Since then, I've befriended Gary and several terrific Visible Ink Press people, including Martin Connors, Dean Dauphinais, Jeffrey Hermann (who never once complained about my constant demands for archive material), Marilou Carlin, and Judy Galens. Fellow single-book editors Leland Rucker, Josh Freedom du Lac, and Dan Durchholz provided excellent advice (or patiently listened to me whine), as usual, during this project. *MusicHound Jazz* co-editor Nancy Ann Lee shared her knowledge of the swing era and helped polish the artist list.

During the final editing weeks, I pushed some of my regular writing assignments to the deadline limits. For putting up with this, I thank Ben Greenman, Scott Alexander, Rob Bernstein, and Barry Golson of *Yahoo! Internet Life*; Stephen Williams at *Newsday*; Pat Kampert, Mo Ryan, and Heather Lajewski at the *Chicago Tribune*; John Price of the Knight-Ridder/Tribune news service; Lucinda Hahn at *Chicago*; Amy Weivoda, Susan Hamre, and Sandy Masuo of *Request*; and many others.

Thanks to these musicians, publicists, and swing experts for biographical material and crucial CDs: Robert Crowe of rockabilly.net; Howard at Swing-out Chicago; Brad Altman, promoter at Chicago's Liquid; Julie Mertz of Big City Swing; Doug Engle at Delmark; Doug Bell with Bellevue Cadillac; Steve Kaplan at Collectables; J.R. Rich at Blue Note; Eddie Dattel at Memphis Archives; Ali O. at Cleopatra; Yvonne Garrett, publicist for the Cherry Poppin' Daddies; Monica Seide, Royal Crown Revue's Warner Bros. publicist; Doug Myren at Mouthpiece; Bill Elliot at Wayland; Michael Rothschild at Landslide; Sujata Murthy and Brenda Hansen at Capitol; Tom Muzquiz at Rhino; Cary E. Mansfield at Varese Sarabande; Kerry Murphy at Rounder; Kelly Watson at Deep South Records; Anders Janes and Ray Gelato; Marc Pucci Media; Aimee at Dionysus; J. Kregg Barentine at Ghost Note; members of Jet Set Six, Hot Rod Lincoln, and George Gee's band; Diamond Cut Productions; Mark Lipsius at Alligator; Michael Andrew at Colossal; George H. Buck Jr. at Solo Art; Jo Motta and Greg Geller at Warner Archives; Bernard Brightman at Jazz Classics Catalog; Lazy S.O.B Recordings; Red Young Productions; Melissa Adams at Yeprock Records; and Fantasy Records. Special thanks are due to Ellen Taintor, John Cain, and Dave Bartlett of Rounder Records for helping supply *MusicHound Swing* with its swingin' CD.

We've used these valuable sources: various articles in the *Chicago Tribune*; liner notes from Columbia's *Swing Time!* and GRP/ Decca's *An Anthology of Big Band Swing 1940–1955*; George T. Simon's *The Big Bands* (Schirmer, 1967/1981); *Swing! The New Retro Renaissance* (Re/Search, 1998); Ross Firestone's *Swing, Swing, Swing: The Life and Times of Benny Goodman* (Norton, 1993); Joel Whitburn's *Pop Memories, 1890–1954* (Record Research, 1986); and Michael Moss's *Swing Time* magazine. Several *MusicHound Lounge* sources were also helpful: Roy Hemming and David Hajdu's *Discovering Great Singers of Classic Pop* (Newmarket Press, 1992); Peter Gammond's *The Oxford Companion to Popular Music* (Oxford University Press, 1991); the CDnow (www.cdnow.com) and CD Universe (www.cduniverse.com) Internet sites; and Brad Bigelow at the Space Age Pop Music Standards homepage (home.earthlink.net/~spaceagepop/index.htm).

musicHound
SWING!

A

Howard Alden

Born October 17, 1958, in Newport Beach, CA.

While many of his '80s contemporaries were playing hipper jazz like bebop and cool, guitarist Howard Alden went back farther, to the records of Charlie Christian and Duke Ellington. After playing banjo in California pizza restaurants before he was 18 years old, Alden sought the sources, learning swing music directly by playing with Woody Herman, Dizzy Gillespie, Benny Carter, and Red Norvo, among many others. Swing-era veteran George Van Eps himself introduced Alden to the seven-string guitar, and he found the extra low string aided him in playing piano-based tunes by Ellington and Thelonious Monk. The house guitarist for the influential Concord Jazz label, Alden has recorded some two dozen albums since he started out in the '80s.

what to buy: Alden's use of the seven-string guitar for *Your Story—The Music of Bill Evans* (Concord Jazz, 1994, prod. Carl E. Jefferson), an exercise in swing, allows him a wider sonic range, all the better to play music by the great pianist Evans. Ken Peplowski, the superb clarinet player, gets co-billing on the marvelous *Live at Centre Concord: Encore!* (Concord Jazz, 1995, prod. Carl E. Jefferson), which peaks when Peplowski pulls out his tenor saxophone for two tunes.

what to buy next: On *Misterioso* (Concord Jazz, 1991, prod. Carl E. Jefferson), Alden revisits Bud Freeman's forgotten gem "Song of the Dove" and does an exemplary job with two Monk pieces, the title track and "We See," a pair of Ellington-style numbers, some Broadway show chestnuts, a Jelly Roll Morton classic (the delightful "The Pearls"), and one of Alden's own compositions. The variety of settings found on *Take Your Pick* (Concord Jazz, 1997, prod. Allen Farnham, John Burk) include a welcome reminder of how well Alden plays when paired with a really good horn player in a quintet.

the rest:

(With the Howard Alden/Dan Barrett Quartet) *Swing Street* (Concord Jazz, 1988)
The Howard Alden Trio (Concord Jazz, 1989)
(With the Howard Alden/Dan Barrett Quartet) *ABQ Salutes Buck Clayton* (Concord Jazz, 1989)
(With Jack Lesberg) *No Amps Allowed* (Chiaroscuro, 1989)
Snowy Morning Blues (Concord Jazz, 1990)
(With George Van Eps) *13 Strings* (Concord Jazz, 1991)
(With George Van Eps) *Hand Crafted Swing* (Concord Jazz, 1992)
A Good Likeness (Concord Jazz, 1993)
(With George Van Eps) *Seven & Seven* (Concord Jazz, 1993)
(With Ken Peplowski) *Concord Duo Series, Vol. 3* (Concord Jazz, 1993)
(With Frank Vignola and Jimmy Bruno) *Concord Jazz Guitar Collective* (Concord Jazz, 1995)
(With George Van Eps) *Keepin' Time* (Concord Jazz, 1996)

worth searching for: The two-CD set *Fujitsu-Concord 25th Jazz Festival Silver Anniversary Set* (Concord Jazz, 1996, prod. Carl E. Jefferson) includes six tunes from the Howard Alden Trio along with seven from Gene Harris and another seven from Marian McPartland.

influences:

◀◀ Charlie Christian, Barney Kessel, Bucky Pizzarelli

▶▶ Ron Affif

Garaud MacTaggart

Alien Fashion Show

Formed 1996, in Los Angeles, CA.

Eldon Daetweiler, vocals, trumpet; Jeff Daetweiler, drums, vocals; Todd Thurman, guitar, vocals; Jeffrey Alan, electric and acoustic upright bass, vocals; Kenji Saito, keyboard, vocals.

After doing their separate things in various Los Angeles bands, Daetweiler brothers Jeff and Eldon joined forces in 1996, merging their own experience and the big-band influences their musician parents imparted on them from a young age. Sultry is the word most often used to describe Alien Fashion Show's sound; the band's version of the Police's "Roxanne" is as sexy as the original, with a bluer mood. Its "Detroit Swing City" take on Kiss's "Detroit Rock City" impressed rock's clown princes themselves when the band performed it at Gene Simmons's birthday party. (They also play Anne Rice's Halloween ball each year, and toured with neo-swing king Brian Setzer.) The band claims it owes as much to surf music and rockabilly as big band and lounge, but you'll have to listen closely to pick out those influences.

what's available: *Alien Fashion Show* (Surfdog/Hollywood, 1998, prod. Jim Wirt, Dave Kaplan) is fresh yet fully cognizant of where it came from—the swinging days of the first supper-club acts. In addition to the aforementioned covers, Alien Fashion Show does the jazziest "White Wedding/Rebel Yell" medley since Billy Idol dyed his hair platinum and hooked a dog collar around his neck. (Maybe if he tried this version, he'd resuscitate his career.) One troubling point, though: Many of these songs depend on female lead vocals, yet singer Rachelle Berry is relegated to background vocal status under the "additional musicians" category. If she's not in the band, why use her out front on so much of the disc?

influences:

Frank Sinatra, the Dorsey Brothers, Louis Prima, Count Basie, Kiss, Tony Bennett, Brian Setzer

Lynne Margolis

Henry "Red" Allen

Born Henry James Allen Jr., January 7, 1908, in Algiers, LA. Died April 17, 1967, in New York, NY.

An early jazz trendsetter and transitional figure between New Orleans jazz and the swing era, Henry "Red" Allen was one of the last great trumpeters to emerge from the Crescent City after Louis Armstrong. A fixture in the influential big bands of Luis Russell, Fletcher Henderson, and the Mills Blue Rhythm Band, Allen went solo in 1940 and helped set the standards for the early swing era. Early in his career, he played in the New Orleans brass band led by his father, Henry Allen Sr., and other parade bands, as well as the famous bands of George Lewis and King Oliver. From 1928–29, Allen played in the St. Louis–based Fate Marable's Mississippi riverboat bands; Victor Records scouts discovered him while searching for a trumpeter to rival Armstrong's popularity on OKeh, a competing label. Later, after playing with Russell, Henderson, and the Mills band, he recorded New Orleans–style music with early jazz trendsetters, such as pianist Jelly Roll Morton and clarinetist Sidney Bechet. Gaining visibility during the 1940s and 1950s as a prominent figure in mainstream jazz, Allen further adapted his Dixieland-based style to perform with early swing masters such as saxophonist Coleman Hawkins, clarinetists Buster Bailey and Pee Wee Russell, trombonist J.C. Higginbotham, and other luminaries. During the 1950s–1960s, Allen held lengthy club engagements and toured Europe several times, remaining active until his death.

what's available: His only in-print domestic recording, *World on a String* (RCA/Bluebird, 1957/1991, prod. Fred Reynolds) features Allen in an exuberant octet romp, backed by a perky rhythm crew, including Cozy Cole (drums). Influential soloists Coleman Hawkins (tenor sax), J.C. Higginbotham (trombone), and Buster Bailey (clarinet). While toe-tapping classic New Orleans numbers such as "St. James Infirmary," "Sweet Lorraine," "Ain't She Sweet," and eight more tracks may not be danceable, they best represent Allen's late-career talents in a small ensemble session.

worth searching for: The European import *Volume 6, 1929–1933* (Jazz Chronological Classics, 1994) is the first of a five-disc series. Capturing Allen in his early 20s, the 23-tune compilation finds him fronting the Luis Russell Orchestra and co-leading a group with tenorman Coleman Hawkins. Another import disc, *Collection, Vol. 6: 1941–1946* (Storyville, 1997) documents Allen performing a mix of originals and early standards, including Allen originals such as "Siesta at the Fiesta," "Red Jump," and "Get the Mop."

influences:

Louis Armstrong, King Oliver

Clark Terry, Rex Stewart, Harry "Sweets" Edison, Roy Eldridge, Freddie Hubbard

Nancy Ann Lee

Albert Ammons

Born September 23, 1907, in Chicago, IL. Died December 2, 1949, in Chicago, IL.

Albert Ammons learned the art of the rolling bass line, so essential to the boogie-woogie piano style, in his hometown of Chicago—where he drove a cab to support himself in the '20s.

Red Allen **(Archive Photos)**

Technically the most gifted of his peers, such as fellow boogie-piano heroes Meade "Lux" Lewis and Pete Johnson, Ammons leaned closer to jazz than blues, although he was heavily influenced by the young blues prodigy Hersal Wallace and the dirty house-rent style of Jimmy Yancey. He played with just about everybody: R&B pioneers Joe Turner and Louis Jordan, country-bluesmen Big Bill Broonzy and Lonnie Johnson, bandleader Harry James, and jazz groups like the Port of Harlem Jazzmen and his own Rhythm Kings. With Lewis and Johnson, he played keyboards at John Hammond's important 1938 concert "Spirituals to Swing" at Carnegie Hall. Boogie-woogie became a craze after that, generating several chart hits and influencing many of the era's popular big bands. Gene Ammons, his son, was one of the most important post-war tenor sax players and recorded for Mercury with the senior Ammons in 1947. Albert joined the Lionel Hampton band in 1949, mere months before he died.

what to buy: *1936–1939* ♪♪♪♪ (Jazz Chronological Classics, 1993, prod. various), a good overall introduction, begins with four cuts from 1936 featuring Ammons and His Rhythm Kings. Everything else is from 1939, including two pieces with Harry James, the Boogie Woogie Trio, and the Port of Harlem Jazzmen. But the heart of the album is the 10 solo tunes, including a romping "Boogie Woogie Stomp" and a finely nuanced "Backwater Blues." The first recording sessions for Alfred Lion's new Blue Note label, *The First Day* ♪♪♪♪ (Blue Note, 1939/1992 prod. Alfred Lion, reissue prod. Michael Cuscuna) was a treasure trove of excellent piano playing. The CD is split between solo Ammons material, duets with Meade "Lux" Lewis, and some fine Lewis solo tunes.

what to buy next: *Master of Boogie* ♪♪♪ (Milan, 1992), mostly live 1938 and 1939 recordings from Le Hot Club de France, has Ammons playing solo, dueting with Meade "Lux" Lewis, accompanying Big Bill Broonzy, and collaborating on a three-piano date with Lewis and Pete Johnson.

the rest:

1939–1946 ♪♪♪ (Jazz Chronological Classics, 1997)
Boogie Woogie Man ♪♪♪ (Topaz Jazz, 1997)
Alternate Takes/Radio Performances ♪♪♪ (Document, 1998)
Boogie Woogie Stomp ♪♪♪ (Delmark, 1998)

The Andrews Sisters **(Archive Photos)**

worth searching for: Mosaic, the mail-order company for audiophiles, put out a box set on vinyl, *The Complete Blue Note Albert Ammons and Meade Lux Lewis* ₰₰₰₰ (Blue Note/Mosaic, 1944, prod. Alfred Lion, Michael Cuscuna, Charlie Lourie), including eight otherwise unavailable songs. A limited edition of 5,000, it's now out of print.

influences:

◀◀ Hersal Wallace, Jimmy Yancey, Pine Top Smith

▶▶ Judy Carmichael

Garaud MacTaggart

The Andrews Sisters

Formed 1930s, in New York City, NY.

Laverne Andrews (born July 6, 1915, in Minneapolis, MN), vocals; Maxine Andrews (born January 3, 1918, in Minneapolis, MN), vocals; Patti Andrews (born February 16, 1920, in Minneapolis, MN), vocals.

With their close harmonies and all-American looks, the Andrews Sisters were so popular in the 1940s their sound came to define World War II popular music—and swing, in particular. Shortly after starting their careers with a small orchestra in New York, they made it big with their first hit, "Bei Mir Bist du Schoen," in 1937 and achieved virtual immortality with "Boogie Woogie Bugle Boy" in 1941. For the next decade, they toured the country and appeared —playing themselves—with actors such as Bing Crosby, in films like 1947's *The Road to Rio*. Their most famous tune with Bing, "Mele Kalikimaka," can still be heard on radios around Christmastime. Although some listeners are bound to dismiss the Andrews Sisters as 1940s malt-shop Muzak, a closer listen shows their harmonies are surprisingly complex. And no one can deny the girls have a gift for swing; a cover of "Bei Mir Bist du Schoen" appears in the film *Swing Kids*. While a little Andrews Sisters can go a long way, the group shows wartime nostalgia can be endearing.

what to buy: *50th Anniversary Collection, Vols. 1 & 2* ₰₰₰₰▽ (MCA, 1987) is the best retrospective of the Andrews Sisters' career, complete with standards that made them famous, as well as some rarer renditions of "Tuxedo Junction" and "Sing,

Sing, Sing." *Their All-Time Greatest Hits* (Decca/MCA, 1994), a comprehensive two-disc set, is a good buy for devoted fans.

what to buy next: *The Andrews Sisters* (ASV, 1992) features annoyingly short recordings, but offers a good overview.

best of the rest:

Andrews Sisters Greatest Hits: The 60th Anniversary Collection (MCA, 1998)

worth searching for: *Rum & Coca-Cola* (Golden Stars, 1996) is a collection of the Andrews Sisters' best-known work. It contains probably the purest swing of any Andrews Sisters compilation—including versions of "Boogie Woogie Bugle Boy" and the wonderfully titled "Beat Me Daddy, Eight to the Bar."

influences:

Ella Fitzgerald, Bing Crosby

Lambert, Hendricks & Ross, Manhattan Transfer, Mel Tormé and the Mel-Tones

Carl Quintanilla

Ray Anthony

Born Raymond Antonini, January 20, 1922, in Bentleyville, PA.

Ray Anthony is one of the most vital living links to the big-band era. A young trumpet player in the Al Donahue, Glenn Miller, and Jimmy Dorsey orchestras, Anthony formed his own band after World War II and kept it alive and flourishing well into rock 'n' roll's heyday. Besides blowing a cool Harry James–inspired trumpet, when his band's regular singers, the Skyliners and Tommy Mercer, went on break, Anthony sang with warmth and humor. Recording for Capitol, Anthony's orchestra scored its first hits in 1950 with "Sentimental Me," "Count Every Star," and "Harbor Lights," but really hit it big when "The Bunny Hop" inspired a national dance craze. Anthony himself achieved a bit of pop-culture immortality when he co-wrote the hit theme for Jack Webb's classic TV cop show *Dragnet* in 1953. Anthony's band played both reed-oriented Glenn Miller–era standards and picked up on the brassier new pop sounds of the burgeoning rock 'n' roll scene. His popularity spread to Hollywood, where he wrote a paean to the reigning movie goddess Marilyn Monroe and appeared in such films as 1955's *Daddy Long Legs* (with Fred Astaire) and 1956's *The Girl Can't Help It* (with Jayne Mansfield). This won the handsome Anthony even more fans, including his soon-to-be-wife, B-movie Monroe-wannabe Mamie Van Doren (completing the triumverate of Big Blondes from the Fabulous '50s). Anthony appeared in 15 films and even got a chance to portray his old boss Jimmy Dorsey in the 1959 Red Nichols biopic *The Five Pennies*. Anthony's orchestra had a few more hits in the late '50s with "Skokiaan" and Henry Mancini's "Peter Gunn Theme," but was unable to keep a large orchestra going into the '60s. He continued recording with a sextet until his departure from Capitol (where he recorded nearly 100 albums) in 1968. These days, besides re-releasing his classic masters on his new record label and cutting fresh tracks, the never-idle Anthony vigilantly promotes the resurgence of big-band sounds on the radio.

what to buy: Make every effort to track down the recently deleted *Ray Anthony: Capitol Collector's Series* (Gold Rush, 1991/1996, compilation prod. Bob Furmanek, Ron Furmanek), a 22-track disc with his hits "(The Theme from) Dragnet," "Theme from Peter Gunn," "The Bunny Hop," and much more. Barring that, the more concise *The Best of Ray Anthony* (Aero Space, 1995, reissue prod. Ray Anthony) is a fine introduction to Anthony's vast catalog.

what to buy next: Short on hit power but long on first-rate music, *Swing Back to the '40s* (Aero Space Records, 1991, reissue prod. Ray Anthony) and *Young Man with a Horn, 1952–54* (Hindsight, 1988/1993, compilation prod. Thomas Gramuglia) contain the swinging cream of Anthony's crop.

what to avoid: Anthony has the pedigree, but lacks inspiration on *I Remember Glenn Miller* (Aero Space Records, 1953/1993, reissue prod. Ray Anthony), a by-the-numbers tribute LP. Also, though the budget-priced *Ray Anthony/Nelson Riddle: Back-to-Back Hits* (Cema Special Products, 1997, prod. various) contains the original hits, you could get a more satisfying full disc by either bandleader for the same dough. Finally, there's just no excuse for *Macarena Dance Party* (Aero Space Records, 1996, prod. Ray Anthony).

the rest:

Jam Session at the Tower (Aero Space Records, 1953/1990)
Sweet & Swingin' 1943–53 (Circle, 1953/1991)
1988 & All That Jazz (Aero Space Records, 1990)
Dancing in the Dark (Aero Space Record, 1990/1997)
Hooked on Big Bands (Aero Space Records, 1990/1995)
Dance Party (Aero Space Records, 1990/1995)
In the Miller Mood (Aero Space Records, 1992)
Dancing & Dreaming (Pair, 1992)
In the Miller Mood, Vol. 2 (Aero Space Records, 1993)
Dream Dancing 2 (Aero Space Records, 1994)
Touch Dancing (Aero Space Records, 1995)
Swing's the Thing (Aero Space Records, 1995)
Dancing Alone Together/Dream Dancing Around the World (Aero Space Records, 1995)
Dream Dancing Christmas (Aero Space Records, 1995)
Tenderly (Aero Space Records, 1995)
Boogie Blues & Ballads (Aero Space Records, 1997)
Dream Dancing in Hawaii (Aero Space Records, 1997)
Trip through 50 Years of Music (Aero Space Records, 1997)

Dirty Trumpet for a Swinging Party (Aero Space Records, 1997)
Dream Girl/Moments Together (EMI, 1997)
Dream Dancing in a Latin Mood (Aero Space, 1998)
1953 Chesterfield Shows (Magic, 1998)

worth searching for: The import *Ray Anthony Capitol Collection* (Capitol, 1998, prod. Ray Anthony) is as solid a compilation as anything stateside. Also, Anthony aficionados who own a VCR will probably dig *Club Anthony* (Aero Space Video, 1995, prod. Ray Anthony), a nice video showcase featuring Red Norvo, Vikki Carr, and an all-star big band.

influences:

◀◀ Glenn Miller, Harry James, Billy May

▶▶ Al Hirt, Mamie Van Doren, Doc Severinsen

Ken Burke

Harold Arlen

Born Hyman Arluck, February 15, 1905, in Buffalo, NY. Died April 23, 1986, in New York City, NY.

Cole Porter and Irving Berlin became more famous, but Harold Arlen had more natural swing in him than any of his songwriting contemporaries. The man famous for some of this century's most familiar standards—"Over the Rainbow," "Stormy Weather," "That Old Black Magic," "Ac-cent-tchu-ate the Positive," and "Get Happy"—began his career as a ragtime singer. Later, he was an arranger for Fletcher Henderson's influential swing outfits. Where songs by Porter, Berlin, and the Gershwins transformed into swing in the hands of performing talents like Frank Sinatra and Count Basie, Arlen frequently wrote them with big bands in mind. As a young man, Arlen learned how to perform from his father, a cantor at a Buffalo synagogue. Though his parents encouraged him to get a respectable job as a music teacher, Arlen instead wrote music, with lyricists such as Ted Koehler. Arlen and lyricist E.Y. Harburg earned an Oscar for *The Wizard of Oz,* which launched Judy Garland's acting and singing career as well as "Over the Rainbow," the dreamiest song of the 1930s. His flops were sensational—though he co-wrote excellent scores for *St. Louis Woman* and *House of Flowers* with Johnny Mercer and author Truman Capote, respectively, both shows took box-office dives. But his successes were even better—his music helped *Jamaica* become a Broadway smash late in the 1950s, and he earned Oscar nominations through the mid-1950s.

what to buy: You won't find many albums with Arlen performing his own songs, but maybe you'd settle for Frank Sinatra, Ella Fitzgerald, or Louis Prima. Though Frank Sinatra was more exhaustive with Sammy Cahn's catalog, he and bandleader Nelson Riddle put Arlen's "I Gotta Right to Sing the Blues" and "Don't Like Goodbyes" (with lyrics, from the musical *House of Flowers,* by author Truman Capote) through their naturally swinging paces on *The Capitol Years* (Capitol, 1990, prod. Ron Furmanek). Fitzgerald recorded several volumes of Arlen's work, including "Let's Fall in Love" and "Over the Rainbow," of course, in the early 1960s—the best CD reissue is *Harold Arlen Songbook* (Verve, 1961/1990, prod. Norman Granz). And there's no better example of the chemistry between one-time lovers Louis Prima and Keely Smith than on Arlen's "That Old Black Magic," in which Prima practically goes into excited convulsions during the opening verses; it's on *Louis Prima: Capitol Collector's Series* (Capitol, 1991, prod. Voyle Gilmore).

what to buy next: The familiar big-band beat is obvious on "I Love a New Yorker," the first song on *The Music of Harold Arlen* (Harbinger, 1998), although it's mostly performed in the early-century style of Broadway musicals. *Rosemary Clooney Sings the Music of Harold Arlen* (Concord Jazz, 1983, prod. Carl E. Jefferson) is more straightforward but less shimmering than Fitzgerald's work.

what to avoid: Much more corny is pianist Andre Previn's *Come Rain or Come Shine: The Harold Arlen Songbook* (Philips Classics), a pop-classical tribute album featuring soprano singer Sylvia McNair.

best of the rest:

(Dick Hyman) *Harold Arlen Songs: Blues in the Night* (Musicmasters, 1990)

worth searching for: *Harold Sings Arlen (With Friend)* (Vox Cum Laude, 1966) is difficult to find, but it's nice to hear Arlen's own voice (and, oh yes, it includes collaborations with Duke Ellington and Barbra Streisand).

influences:

◀◀ Cole Porter, Irving Berlin, Hoagy Carmichael, Scott Joplin, Art Tatum

▶▶ Ella Fitzgerald, Johnny Mercer, Barbra Streisand, Louis Prima, Frank Sinatra

Steve Knopper

Louis Armstrong

Born August 4, 1901, in New Orleans, LA. Died July 6, 1971, in New York, NY.

Despite his groundbreaking career and his serious reputation as one of the giants of 20th-century music, Armstrong had a warm, exuberant sense of humor. As a result, for every "What a Wonderful World"—the moving R&B hit that took on new life after its inclusion in the film *Good Morning, Vietnam*—he pulled off a comedic vamp like the playful Dixieland-in-a-stripjoint "Heebie Jeebies." Or he transformed the Kurt Weill showtune "Mack the Knife" into a humor anthem simply by shouting, exuberantly, "Take it, Satch!" before a trumpet solo. (Neither Bobby Darin nor Frank Sinatra ever wrenched as much fun out of it.) Armstrong's gruff, personable voice had immeasurable soul, of course, but his trademark bulging eyes and gigantic smile gave his music a vaudevillian, crowd-pleasing charm. From the mid-'30s to the mid-'40s, he transcended the swing era, fronting a big band and maintaining respect as a pioneer from both white and black bandleaders. Like many early jazzmen, he focused on pop standards, like those written by Hoagy Carmichael and other major American songwriters. Born and raised in New Orleans as the jazz age was taking off, Armstrong was the first improviser to blend disparate riffs and accents into extended solos that hung together as unified musical statements. This was obvious during his early days with the King Oliver and Clarence Williams groups, but his recordings with his own bands—Hot Five and Hot Seven—are some of the most important works of any music. These were just studio bands, but their musical treatments took New Orleans jazz out of the collective improvisation mode into that of the featured solo improviser. Pieces such as "Potato Head Blues," "Hotter Than That," and "Cornet Chop Suey" set standards for improvisation and composition. Armstrong's unequaled technical mastery so overshadowed his contemporaries that he was held as a model for all to follow.

what to buy: Armstrong's early recordings are historic, and many of them are included on the four-CD set *Portrait of the Artist As a Young Man, 1923–1934* (Columbia/Legacy, 1994, compilation prod. Nedra Olds-Neal). This is an essential Armstrong collection, with recordings from his Oliver and Williams days in addition to seminal collaborations with Bessie Smith ("St. Louis Blues"), Lonnie Johnson, Jimmie Rogers (yes, the country-western guy), and others. The Hot Five/Seven stuff is here, along with some of his early big-band work. *The Complete Studio Recordings of Louis Armstrong and the All Stars* (Mosaic, 1993, compilation prod. Michael Cuscuna) completes the picture with a six-CD set of Armstrong recordings spanning 1950–58. This is a great collection showing the band in top form with the likes of Earl Hines, Jack Teagarden, and Gene Krupa on board. Many of the standards ("Muskrat Ramble," "Struttin' with Some Barbecue," "Body and Soul," "Lazy River") are here, captured fresh without the burden of an audience to entertain. "Baby, Your Slip Is Showing" provides a taste of how Armstrong could still capture the old feeling. Both sets include excellent booklet essays and photos.

what to buy next: *Hot Fives and Hot Sevens—Vol. 2* (CBS, 1926/Columbia, 1988, prod. various) shows Armstrong's first flush of maturity and defining of the art of jazz.

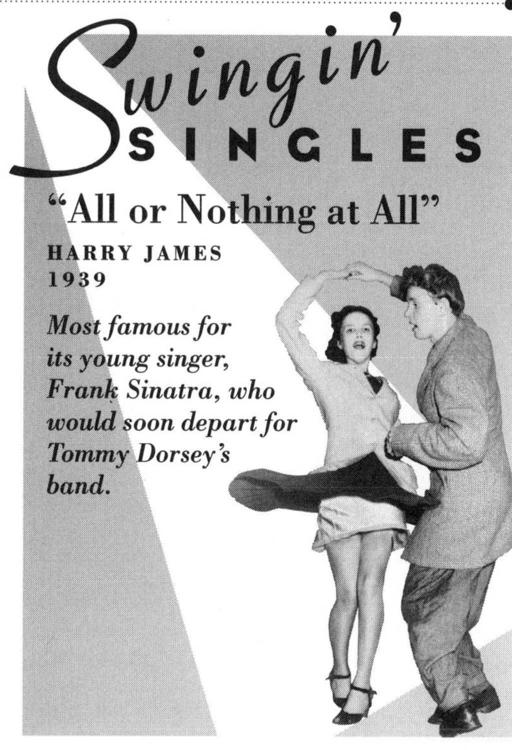

what to avoid: *What a Wonderful World* **woof!** (Decca, 1970, prod. Bob Thiele) contains little of what made Armstrong great, pandering to the rock generation with electric bass and guitar on covers that include "Give Peace a Chance" and "Everybody's Talking."

best of the rest:

Louis Armstrong and Earl Hines (CBS, 1927/Columbia Jazz Masterpieces, 1989)
Disney Songs the Satchmo Way (Disneyland, 1968/Walt Disney Records, 1996)
The Essential Louis Armstrong (Vanguard, 1987)
Stardust (CBS, 1988)
Laughin' Louie (RCA, 1989)
The Sullivan Years (TVT, 1990)
Mack the Knife (Pablo, 1990)
Rhythm Saved the World (Decca, 1991)
In Concert with Europe 1 (RTE, 1992)
Blueberry Hill (Milan, 1992)
The California Concerts (MCA, 1992)
Sings the Blues (BMG, 1993)
Young Louis Armstrong (1930–1933) (BMG, 1993)
Louis Armstrong and His Friends (Pasadena Civic Auditorium, 1951) (GNP, 1993)

Louis Armstrong **(Archive Photos)**

Happy Birthday Louis (Omega, 1994)
Swing that Music (Drive, 1994)
Pocketful of Dreams, Vol. III (Decca, 1995)
Satchmo at Symphony Hall (MCA, 1996)
Greatest Hits (RCA Victor, 1996)
This Is Jazz #1: Louis Armstrong (Sony, 1996)
Now You Has Jazz (Rhino, 1997)
Revue Collection (One Way, 1997)
This Is Jazz #23: Louis Armstrong Sings (Sony, 1997)
What a Wonderful Christmas (Hip-O/MCA, 1997)
Complete RCA Victor Recordings (RCA Victor, 1997)
American Icon (Hip-O/MCA, 1998)
Best of Louis Armstrong (Vanguard, 1998)
More Greatest Hits (RCA Victor, 1998)
Priceless Jazz: More Louis Armstrong (GRP, 1998)

worth searching for: *Ella Fitzgerald and Louis Armstrong* (Verve, 1957, prod. Norman Granz) offers a double treat with two of the world's greatest classic jazz singers swinging together. A great cast of Oscar Peterson, Herb Ellis, Ray Brown, and Buddy Rich back them up.

influences:

◀◀ Joe "King" Oliver, Buddy Bolden, Kid Rena

▶▶ Bix Beiderbecke, Dizzy Gillespie, Wynton Marsalis, Louis Prima

Lawrence Gabriel and Steve Knopper

Asleep at the Wheel

Formed 1970, in Paw Paw, WV.

Ray Benson, guitar, vocals; Lucky Oceans, pedal steel; Leroy Preston, drums, guitar, vocals; and a cast of nearly thousands.

The brainchild and passion of its towering frontman and sole surviving founding member, Ray Benson, Asleep at the Wheel began as an attempt to keep the spirit of traditional country and western music, particularly western swing, alive. Benson moved the band to Austin, Texas, during the early 1970s and weathered myriad personnel changes while keeping his artistic vision intact. Musically the group pays tribute to and updates Texas swing, blues, rock, and even pop—along with jazz, Cajun, blues, rock, and hardcore country. Its various lineups have included double fiddle, accordion, pedal steel, sax, guitar, mandolin, keyboards, and harmonica, with each new face bringing something fresh to the mix. Recognition has come slowly to this eclectic, elastic band of Texas transplants. But it has come. Among the group's recent accolades are two Grammys for its loving Bob Wills tribute album.

what to buy: The box set *Still Swingin'* (Liberty, 1994, prod. various) has a wide range of material, from previously unreleased obscurities to remakes of AATW staples with high-profile guests like Garth Brooks and Dolly Parton. This exhaustive collection contains 51 tracks, including Wheel spokes like "Take Me Back to Tulsa," "Route 66," "The Letter That Johnny Walker Read," and some of its best lesser-known stuff, like the torchy "Ruler of My Heart" (featuring former AATW vocalist Chris O'Connell).

what to buy next: *Asleep at the Wheel: Tribute to the Music of Bob Wills and the Texas Playboys* (Liberty, 1993, prod. Ray Benson, Allen Reynolds) is the most ambitious album this little swing band from Texas ever attempted. Wills is the band's sturdiest musical root, so with surviving Playboys Johnny Gimble and Eldon Shamblin in tow, the Wheels and guests (country stars Lyle Lovett, Chet Atkins, Vince Gill, George Strait, and Garth Brooks) eloquently and faithfully recreate Wills's signatures, including "Red Wine" and "Corine, Corina." The album won two Grammys and spawned a line-dance remix album, *Tribute to the Music of Bob Wills and the Texas Playboys—Dance Versions* (Liberty, 1994, prod. Ray Benson, Allen Reynolds).

what to avoid: Benson has spent most of the 1990s looking back on the band's career, with hits albums, live albums, and a box set. A misguided attempt to combine all of those formats, *Greatest Hits (Live & Kickin')* (Arista, 1992, prod. Ray Benson), doesn't do the band's live show, or its legacy, any justice.

the rest:

Asleep at the Wheel (MCA, 1985)
10 (Epic, 1987)
Western Standard Time (Epic, 1988)
Keepin' Me Up Nights (Arista, 1990)
The Swingin' Best of (Epic, 1992)
The Wheel Keeps on Rollin' (Capitol, 1995)
Back to the Future Now: Live at Arizona Charlie's, Las Vegas (Sony, 1997)
Merry Texas Christmas Y'All (High Street/Windham Hill, 1997)

worth searching for: The Wheel's earliest, edgier efforts are long out of print. *Collision Course* (Capitol, 1978, prod. Ray Benson) captures the band in all its stylistic diversity, with two fiddlers, velvet-voiced singer Chris O'Connell, and pedal steel guitarist extraordinaire Lucky Oceans.

influences:

◀◀ Bob Wills, Phil Harris, Count Basie, Merle Haggard

▶▶ Lyle Lovett and His Large Band, Marty Stuart, Mark O'Connor, Alison Krauss

Doug Pullen

Fred Astaire

Born Franz Austerlitz, May 10, 1899, in Omaha, NE. Died June 22, 1987, in Los Angeles, CA.

Hard as it is to picture Fred Astaire doing anything but lifting the gossamer Ginger Rogers through the air, the truth is the "song" side of his "song-and-dance man" title is well worthy of rediscovery through his few CDs in release. And his swing chops can be just as impressive as his ability to croon a hokey ballad. Astaire began his professional career at age five, starring in vaudeville with his sister, Adele. They performed in marginal shows on Broadway until composer George Gershwin wrote *Lady Be Good* for them in 1924, a show that skyrocketed Astaire's career. He appeared in the original versions of Gershwin's *Funny Face* and Cole Porter's *The Gay Divorcee*. And, of course, Hollywood eventually nabbed him. (One Tinseltown legend has it that casting directors, after his first screen test, wrote: "Can't act. Slightly bald. Also dances.") The Astaire music that has been collected is largely his film and stage soundtracks. Historians sometimes overlook his treatments of Gershwin's "Fascinating Rhythm" or Porter's "Night and Day"—both extremely skillful in their delivery. He manages a confident vocal presence even when surrounded by musicians of a much higher caliber. Moreover, there's something about that quaint, Midwestern accent that cloaks a very real sophistication in jazz singing. Astaire may never be noted among the great vocalists of his time, but he proves repeatedly he's more than a footnote.

what to buy: *Stepping Out* (Verve, 1994, prod. Norman Granz) features some of Astaire's best swing—from the early 1950s when his career was rebounding from a rare slump. It also features a catchy tune normally associated with Sinatra: "The Continental." *The Irving Berlin Songbook* (Verve, 1986), a must-have for Astaire fans, offers all of Berlin's classics—from "Puttin' on the Ritz" to "I'm Putting All My Eggs in One Basket"—and features a dream trio with Oscar Peterson on piano and Ray Brown on bass. *Fred Astaire at MGM* (Rhino, 1997, prod. George Feltenstein, Bradley Flanagan), a two-disc set, has tons of rare and previously unreleased performances, including a good mix of familiar and obscure tunes. *Let's Sing and Dance with Fred Astaire* (Promo Sound, 1997) is a good original mix of Astaire tunes, from, among other sources, *Top Hat* and *Swing Time*—two films for which Astaire is arguably most famous.

what to buy next: *Top Hat: Hits from Hollywood* (Columbia, 1994, compilation prod. Didier C. Deutsch) offers traditional Astaire tunes, but sounds better than many other albums that have repackaged the dancer-singer's career.

what to avoid: *Crazy Feet* (ASV, 1986) is an unremarkable collection of Astaire tunes—and short ones, at that. It's nothing you can't get from a more creative compilation.

best of the rest:
Puttin' on the Ritz (Golden Stars, 1996)

worth searching for: The outstanding but hard-to-find collection *The Astaire Story* (Verve, 1988) has Astaire alongside Brown and Peterson, singing Gershwin and Porter tunes. Besides the fine digital remastering job, it has Astaire's personal liner notes. The import *The Incomparable Fred Astaire: Love of My Life* (Halcyon, 1994, prod. John Wadley) is a respectable collection highlighting Astaire's flair for ballads. Finally, *Nice Work: Fred Astaire Sings Gershwin* (Conifer, 1989) contains renditions of Fred singing with his sister, Adele, on some truly unknown Gershwin songs.

influences:
◀◀ Bill "Bojangles" Robinson
▶▶ Bing Crosby, Mel Tormé, Gene Kelly, Bobby Short

Carl Quintanilla

The Atomic Fireballs

Formed 1996, in Detroit, MI.

John Bunkley, vocals; James Bostek, trumpet; Duke Kingins, guitar; Geoff Kinde, drums; Randy "Ginger" Sly, trombone; Shawn Scaggs, upright bass; Eric Schabo, tenor saxophone.

Like so many nuevo swingsters, John Bunkley came from another musical realm—in this case, ska, through the Detroit band Ganster Fun. But Bunkley also had a substantial jazz background, and as Ganster Fun ended, he and trumpeter James Bostek hatched plans for a group that would take the '40s jump of Louis Jordan and fortify it with more contemporary influences—although the band that resulted, the Atomic Fireballs, hardly strays from standard swing conventions. Through heavy touring, the nattily attired group won a strong Midwest following and appeared on several modern rock bills, including the Vans Warped Tour, while fans scooped up more than 8,000 copies of its independent release *Birth of the Swerve*. That made the Fireballs the subject of a bidding war won by Atlantic Records, whose chairman, Ahmet Ertegun, was enamored by the group's sound and found a kindred spirit in Bunkley.

what's available: *Torch This Place* (Atlantic, 1999, prod. Bruce Fairbairn) is a hot soundfield that – thanks to rock producer Fairbairn's generous hand on the volume control – captures the energy of the group's live performances and the lively interchange between Duke Kingins's guitar, Randy Sly's piano, and the three-part horn charts. Bunkley's charged, throaty vocals give these 12 tunes (five drawn from *Birth of the Swerve*) an aura of dusty authenticity. And tracks such as "Spanish Fly," "Caviar & Chillins," "Mata Hari," and "Man With the Hex" will give any Brian Setzer or Cherry Poppin' Daddy a run for his money.

worth searching for: *Birth of the Swerve* (Orbital, 1998, prod. Charlie Baby, dB, and the Atomic Fireballs), still available in Detroit, spotlights the recording birth of what promises to be a major new entry on the contemporary swing scene.

influences:

Louis Jordan, Cab Calloway, the Specials, Wilson Pickett, Joe Tex

Gary Graff

B

Mildred Bailey

Born Mildred Rinker, February 27, 1907, in Tekoa, WA. Died December 12, 1951.

Long before Sonny and Cher, even before Steve Lawrence and Eydie Gorme, there was Mr. and Mrs. Swing. Singer Mildred Bailey and vibraphonist Red Norvo joined forces personally (they were married for 12 years) and professionally for most of the 1930s. Prior to that, Bailey had been a regular singer with Paul Whiteman's ensemble though she recorded with a small galaxy of pre-bop jazz musicians, including Coleman Hawkins, the Dorsey Brothers, Benny Goodman, and Gene Krupa. After her stint as Mrs. Swing (she and Norvo eventually divorced) she continued to play live in the New York area, was featured regularly on Benny Goodman's radio show *Camel Caravan,* and even hosted her own radio program from 1944 to 1945. The amply proportioned Bailey had a sweet, lilting voice that she adeptly applied to stylized swing, moodier bluesy songs, and pop standards. Roughly a contemporary of both Billie Holiday and Ella Fitzgerald, she shared a similar diva-esque vocal presence though she wasn't quite as sultry as the former or as jazzy as the latter. Over the years she recorded several versions of her signature song, "Rockin' Chair" (penned for her by Hoagy Carmichael), but the first was with a Whiteman side group. During the late '40s, Bailey's health began to fail and after many hospitalizations for diabetes and cardiovascular ailments, she suffered heart failure and died in 1951.

what to buy: *In Love* ♪♪♪♪ (Simitar, 1998, compilation prod. Peter Kline), recorded later in Bailey's career (1946–47), benefits from better recording quality and refinements in her singing style. The tunes, as the title suggests, revolve around the ups and downs of romance, but they don't swing too vigorously. The warm arrangements flatter Bailey's vibrant, expressive vocals, which convey the wry humor of "Don't Worry About Strangers" as convincingly as the earnest yearning of "All of Me." *The Rockin' Chair Lady (1931–1950)* ♪♪♪♪ (Uni/Decca/GRP, 1994, reissue prod. Orrin Keepnews), a nicely assembled package with lots of detailed liner notes, compiles recordings made with various backing ensembles from seven sessions for Decca Records. The sound is great all around, and Bailey's vocals are sharp—a bit more quavery and stylized than Judy Garland on the early tracks but slyly evocative during the later sessions ('40s and '50s). There's even a touch of proto-scat singing in "When It's Sleepy Time Down South."

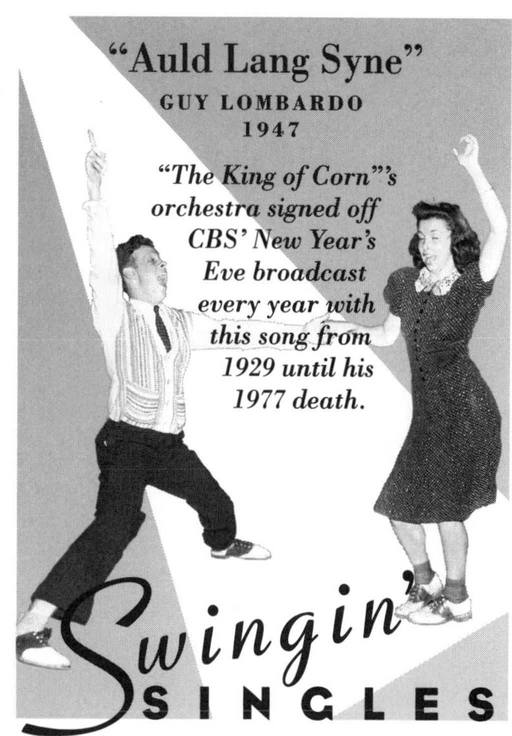
"Auld Lang Syne"
GUY LOMBARDO
1947
"The King of Corn"'s orchestra signed off CBS' New Year's Eve broadcast every year with this song from 1929 until his 1977 death.
Swingin' SINGLES

what to buy next: *American Legends: Mildred Bailey* ♪♪♪♪ (Laserlight/Delta/Telarc International, 1996, prod. Rod McKuen), though skimpy on liner notes (which cite two different birth dates for the singer, misspell "Whitehead," and feature lots of plugs for the U.S. Postal Service), is rich on sound. Backed by various ensembles (including Red Norvo and His Orchestra, Eddie Sauter and His Orchestra, and the Ellis Larkin Trio), the mood swings from sweetly melancholy love songs to lively jazz numbers. *Volume One* ♪♪♪ (The Old Masters/World's Records, 1995, prod. George Morrow) and *Volume Two* ♪♪♪ (The Old Masters/World's Records, 1995, prod. George Morrow) conveniently compile 43 recordings, most from the early '30s. The rhythms are livelier than Bailey's later, more pop-influenced recordings, though the sound quality was a bit on the tinny side.

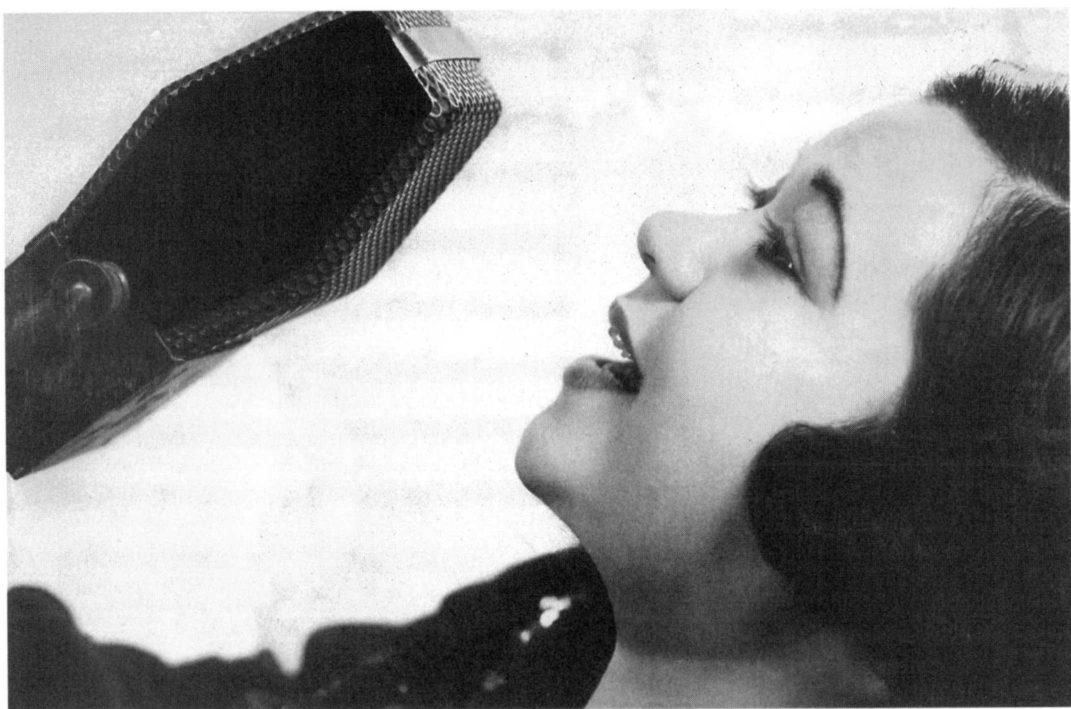

Mildred Bailey **(Archive Photos)**

worth searching for: *That Rockin' Chair Lady* ♪♪♪ (Pearl/Topaz Jazz/Koch, 1994), though virtually identical in title to GRP's compilation of Bailey's Decca recordings, is comprised of almost entirely different material. There are a number of mysterious compilations of Bailey's work on obscure import labels. Some, handled by domestic distributors, are fairly easy to find—though difficult to find out about.

influences:

◀◀ Bessie Smith, Ma Rainey

▶▶ Ella Fitzgerald, Peggy Lee, Kay Starr

see also: *Red Norvo*

Sandy Masuo

Pearl Bailey

Born March 29, 1918, in Newport News, VA. Died August 17, 1990, in Philadelphia, PA.

A legendary cabaret performer, Tony Award–winning actress, best-selling author, movie star, and the U.S. Goodwill Ambassador to the United Nations under three presidents, Bailey brought a touch of droll humor and class to everything she did. Her supple alto vocals embraced both the blues and Broadway pop, and her trademark comic asides created the persona of a performer willing to tell it like it is. Bailey began singing and dancing in her father's Pentecostal revivals at age three. After picking up a few steps from her brother (dancer Bill Bailey), she was good enough at age 15 to sing and dance for Noble Sissle's Band. She also sang with bands fronted by Edgar Hayes, Cootie Williams, and Count Basie before making her 1944 solo debut at the Village Vanguard, where Greenwich Village bohemians and the cream of cafe society alike dug her off-the-cuff remarks almost as much as her singing. Bailey replaced Sister Rosetta Tharpe in Cab Calloway's band until she was cast in the Broadway production of *St. Louis Woman,* for which she won a Donaldson Award. Soon she was alternating starring theater roles such as *Arms and the Girl* and *House of Flowers* with scene-stealing film appearances in *Variety Girl* and *Porgy & Bess.* Recording prolifically for several different record labels, Bailey didn't have many hit singles; songs such as "Tired" (which prefigured rap), "It Takes Two to Tango," and "Baby It's Cold Outside" became associated with her sexy, slurred delivery. Her reputation as a risque sophisticate also caused her *For Adults Only* LP to be banned from radio play—which, of course, only helped it sell more copies. Bailey's career peaked in 1967 with her Tony Award–winning performance in the all-black cast version of *Hello, Dolly!* In 1970, President Nixon named her America's "Ambassador of Love" and she became a special delegate to the U.N. under the Ford, Carter, and Bush administrations. She continued to host her own TV show, wrote the first of many books about her life and times, and played all the top nightspots until ill health forced her to slow down. President Reagan awarded her the Medal of Freedom in 1988.

what to buy: Several of Bailey's greatest early performances (c. 1945–50), including "St. Louis Blues," "Baby It's Cold Outside," and "Saturday Night Fish Fry" are on *16 Most Requested Songs* (Columbia/Legacy, 1991, compilation prod. Michael Brooks). It's an essential introduction to the talents and style of this sassy, one-of-a-kind personality.

what to buy next: Bailey's Tony Award–winning performance is preserved on *Hello, Dolly!* (RCA, 1967/1991, prod. George R. Marek, Andy Wiswell); its superior cast includes Clifton Davis, Cab Calloway, Joe Williams, and Mabel King in supporting roles.

the rest:

Won't You Come Home, Pearl Bailey (Compose, 1995)
It's a Great Feeling (Sony Music Special, 1995)
Some of the Best (Laserlight, 1996)
More of the Best (Laserlight, 1996)

worth searching for: Bailey's best moments from her many so-called "adults-only" LPs for Roulette are on *Best of Pearl Bailey—The Roulette Years* (Roulette, 1991, prod. various). Her provocative charm still resonates through "It Takes Two to Tango" and many others. Also, you can witness a prime example of the famous "Pearl Bailey attitude" on the home video version of *Sentimental Journey* (Tapeworm Video, 1993), one of her many network TV specials.

influences:

◄ Ethel Waters, Billie Holiday, Sister Rosetta Tharpe

► Abbe Lane, Freda Payne, Sylvia

Ken Burke

Charlie Barnet

Born October 26, 1913, in New York, NY. Died September 4, 1991.

A hugely popular bandleader of the swing era, saxophonist Charlie Barnet was almost as influential for his recordings as he was for breaking racial barriers in music. He led the first white band to play the Apollo Theater at a time when his color-blind hiring practices (Lena Horne, Roy Eldridge, and Benny Carter were among the important names who were in his bands) prevented him from playing many venues in racist America during the '30s and '40s. Barnet could afford to be a liberal dilettante (he was born into a wealthy family), but, as a big fan of the Fletcher Henderson and Duke Ellington bands, he also became a solid musician. His outfits of the early 1930s were like the white society bands of Paul Whiteman with a jazzier edge; by the mid-1930s, they had a more swinging jazz flavor. Around that time, he cut records with fellow bandleader Red Norvo that included clarinetist Artie Shaw and pianist Teddy Wilson backing up Barnet's Coleman Hawkins–inspired tenor playing. In 1939, "Cherokee," the Ray Noble barnburner, became Barnet's theme and one of the most frequently played of all jazz standards. Thanks to that hit song, Barnet's peak lasted well into the mid-'40s. In his autobiography *Music Is My Mistress*, Ellington remarked: "He constantly bolstered my ego by playing a book almost full of our compositions." Barnet was so enamored of Ellington he would sometimes hire Duke's band for his own private parties. Even after Barnet gave up his big band, he went out with an occasional sextet/septet or, in the case of his 1958 studio dates, worked with an amazing big band. But he spent most of his time in comfortable retirement.

what to buy: *An Introduction to Charlie Barnet: His Best Recordings, 1935–1944* (Best of Jazz, 1996) is a well-conceived overview of Barnet's most popular and important recordings for the Bluebird and Decca record labels. The set's minor weakness is the under representation of Barnet's hottest band of the mid-1940s.

what to buy next: For the mid-1940s material, get *Drop Me Off in Harlem* (Decca Jazz, 1992), which contains Barnet's biggest hit from the post-Bluebird years, "Skyliner." Barnet's band of the early- to mid-1940s included a fair number of swing and early bebop musicians (such as trumpet king Roy Eldridge and guitarist Barney Kessel) playing together in harmony.

the rest:

Clap Hands, Here Comes Charlie (Bluebird, 1987)
Cherokee (Bluebird, 1992)
Charlie Barnet and His Orchestra: 1941 (Circle, 1992)
Charlie Barnet and His Orchestra: 1942 (Circle, 1992)
Cherokee (Evidence, 1993)
More (Evidence, 1995)
Swell & Super (Drive, 1996)
Capitol Big Band Sessions (Blue Note, 1998)

worth searching for: In the days of vinyl, Bluebird had an awesome six-volume set of "twofers," *Complete Charlie Barnet, Vols. 1–6* (Bluebird, 1942, prod. various)—which, if it were in print today, would go to the top of the list.

influences:

⏪ Coleman Hawkins, Johnny Hodges, Duke Ellington

⏩ Pete Christlieb

Garaud MacTaggart

Dan Barrett

Born December 14, 1955, in Pasadena, CA.

A contemporary swing musician known for his gorgeous trombone sound, Dan Barrett began performing at age 15. Because he started so early, he had the opportunity to play with many of his big-band heroes, such as Tommy Dorsey, Barney Bigard, Jack Teagarden, Benny Goodman's last big band, and, at Carnegie Hall, the Woody Herman Orchestra. Barrett learned trombone and trumpet in junior high school, heard his first live jazz from the South Frisco Jazz Band and, by age 15, was subbing in the band. Barrett spent most of the late 1970s and early 1980s on the West Coast working with prominent jazz musicians and playing various festivals. In 1983, he joined fellow swing-obsessed jazzman Howard Alden, a guitarist, in New York City—where he wound up playing lead trombone in Goodman's band in 1985 and 1986. By the mid-1990s, Barrett was one of the busiest jazz musicians in the U.S. and international festival scene. He appears on numerous recordings, and on movie soundtracks for *The Cotton Club, Brighton Beach Memoirs,* and Woody Allen's *Bullets Over Broadway,* where he is seen briefly on camera.

what to buy: A laid-back duo album, *Two Sleepy People* ♪♪♪♪ (Arbors, 1996, prod. Rachel Domber, Mat Domber) teams two world-class players, Barrett and pianist John Sheridan, both tune-sleuths who explore fairly obscure melodies. They play 10 gems from the American popular songbook, such as "Remember Me" and "Oh, You Crazy Moon." A trombone buff's delight, *Jubilesta!* ♪♪♪♪ (Arbors, 1992, prod. Rachel Domber, Mat Domber) pays tribute to saxophonist Chu Berry ("Blue Chu"), trumpeter Roy Eldridge ("Little Jazz"), bandleader Duke Ellington ("Jubilesta"), and a wide range of trombone stylists. On the warmly rendered studio session *The A-B-Q Salutes Buck Clayton* ♪♪♪♪ (Concord Jazz, 1989, prod. Howard Alden, Dan Barrett), Barrett and Alden send their solid little band through a relaxed set of originals by swing-era arranger Buck Clayton.

what to buy next: *Swing Street* ♪♪♪½ (Concord, 1987, prod. Howard Alden, Dan Barrett) finds the Alden-Barrett Quintet making easy work of swing classics with their comfortable but solid approach to tunes such as "Cottontail," "Stompin' at the Savoy," and "Lullaby in Rhythm." Guitarist Alden has effortless technique—a marvelous sense of rhythmic concept, somewhere between swing and modern jazz. Barrett is a licensed swinger with an endless bag of dynamic trombone sounds. *Strictly Instrumental* ♪♪♪½ (Concord, 1987, prod. Carl Jefferson) features the Dan Barrett Octet, especially the leader's trombone and Howard Alden's guitar, but probably underutilizes front-line players Ken Peplowski and Warren Vaché Jr.

the rest:

Reunion with Al ♪♪♪ (Arbors, 1992)
(With George Masso) *Let's Be Buddies* ♪♪♪ (Arbors, 1994)
Dan Barrett and Tom Baker in Australia ♪♪♪ (Arbors, 1997)
Moon Song ♪♪♪ (Arbors, 1998)

worth searching for: Excellent examples of Barrett's arranging skills can be found on *Bobby Short with the Alden-Barrett Quintet: Swing That Music* ♪♪♪♪ (Telarc, 1993, prod. John Snyder), which was nominated for a Grammy Award.

influences:

⏪ Al Jenkins, Lou McGarity, Jack Teagarden

⏩ Howard Alden

John T. Bitter

Dave Bartholomew

Born December 24, 1920, in Edgard, LA.

You've probably never heard Dave Bartholomew's voice or trumpet, yet he is one of the most instrumental men in the creation of 1950s R&B from the shards of swing, blues, and jazz. And Bartholomew is a titan of New Orleans music, the guy behind the scenes in the success of Fats Domino and the creation of the irresistibly danceable sounds that have emanated from the Crescent City since the 1950s. For years, Bartholomew led a driving big band that played in the roadhouses around New Orleans, and while a few records document the crack unit he led, Bartholomew's heyday—the mid- to late 1940s—passed almost without recordings. But the craftsmanship he learned in those days molded the stream of swinging hits Domino released throughout the 1950s. Bartholomew played with a string of bands after leaving high school, but gained renown during a sting with Fats Pichon's band on a Mississippi riverboat, the S.S. Capitol, in the late 1930s. Drafted, Bartholomew returned from the Army to start up a band with legendary musicians like saxist Red Tyler, bassman Frank Fields, and drummer Earl Palmer. Playing behind everyone from blues crooner Roy Brown to local piano king Archibald, Bartholomew quickly became the town's musical kingmaker. From the late 1940s through the early 1960s, Bartholomew authored or produced scores of hits—all designed to get people out of their seats.

what to buy: *The Genius of Dave Bartholomew* ♪♪♪♪♪ (EMI, 1992, prod. Bruce Harris) contains 50 reasons to hail this man as an American original. They are all written or helmed by Bartholomew, a three-decade run that stretches from Tommy

Ridgley's tinny 1949 "Shrewesbury Blues" to Earl King's funky 1962 version of "Trick Bag." There are only four cuts here by Bartholomew himself, but to find more there's *In the Alley* ♪♪♪♪ (Charly, 1991, prod. Syd Nathan), a set of 20 stomping cuts for the Federal label from the late '40s and early '50s that include a raw version of what Chuck Berry later recorded as "My Dingaling."

what to buy next: *Crescent City Soul: The Sound of New Orleans (1947–1974)* ♪♪♪♪♪ (EMI, 1996, prod. Bruce Harris) purports to be a four-CD survey of the history of Crescent City classics, but Bartholomew's scent is all over this puppy. The highlight is Bartholomew's version of "Good Jax Boogie," a beer jingle so infectious that it has become a New Orleans standard long after the beer company went belly-up.

the rest:
New Orleans Big Beat ♪♪♪ (Landslide, 1998)

influences:

◀◀ Fats Pichon, Louis Armstrong

▶▶ Fats Domino, Smiley Lewis, the Neville Brothers, Dr. John, Allen Toussaint, Earl King

Steve Braun

Count Basie

Born William Basie, August 21, 1904, in Red Bank, NJ. Died April 26, 1984, in Hollywood, CA.

If music alone (as opposed to, say, race) had been the criteria for crowning jazz royalty, William Basie would have been the King of Swing, not merely a Count. Basie's riff-based big band was the epitome of swing. The band's streamlined "All American Rhythm Section" had its rhythm firmly locked in, providing a perfect springboard on which the band's jazz giants could launch their developing solo skills. In the early 1920s Basie became a professional New York pianist, learning at the feet of stride masters such as James P. Johnson and Fats Waller. In 1927 he made a western tour with the Gonzel White vaudeville company. When the company became stranded in Kansas City, Basie joined Walter Page's Blue Devils, then Bennie Moten's Kansas City Orchestra, introducing his already modified New York stride to the hard-riffing Kansas City jazz. This electrifying combination was the foundation on which Count Basie built his new band of 1935, which he formed from remnants of the Moten orchestra. In 1936 Basie and his band gave New York its first extended taste of hard-swinging Kansas City jazz. The band's influence was unquestionable. So too was the influence of Basie drummer Jo Jones, tenor saxophonist Lester Young, and trumpeters Buck Clayton and Harry Edison. Jones and Young, in particular, laid the groundwork for the boppers waiting just over the horizon.

The rising cost of touring a big band, coupled with diminishing revenue, led Basie to disband at the end of 1949. After that he led an influential small group—with a rhythm section that swung harder than ever. Then, bucking economic trends, Basie organized another big band in 1952 and led it for the remainder of his life (it would still be performing into the late 1990s under the direction of Grover Mitchell). While Basie's 1930s–40s band, now referred to as the "Old Testament" band, based much of its repertoire on head arrangements developed in rehearsal and on gigs, this "New Testament" band relied heavily on its arrangers, although it still boasted great soloists. Two 1955 hit recordings, the instrumental "April in Paris" and "Everyday I Have the Blues," featuring band vocalist Joe Williams, assured success for the new band. Basie continued recording for various labels, including Norman Granz's influential jazz label Verve, through the early '70s.

what to buy: *The Complete Decca Recordings* ♪♪♪♪♪ (GRP–Decca Jazz, 1992, compilation prod. Orrin Keepnews) magnificently documents the Basie band's first New York recordings, from 1937–39. The transfers are first class, and the annotation thorough, but most importantly, the band's tremendous sense of swing and soloists Lester Young, Buck Clayton, Benny Morton, Jimmy Rushing, among others, constantly show their bristling creativity. *The Essential Count Basie, Vol. I* ♪♪♪♪♪ (Columbia/OKeh, 1988, prod. Bob Altshuler, Mike Berniker), *The Essential Count Basie, Vol. II* ♪♪♪♪♪ (Columbia/OKeh, 1988, prod. Bob Altshuler, Mike Berniker), and *The Essential Count Basie, Vol. III* ♪♪♪♪♪ (Columbia/OKeh, 1988, prod. Bob Altshuler, Mike Berniker) contain many moments equal to those on the Decca reissue, but are a little less consistent, and not as well produced. These three CDs still include a lot from Lester Young and the other stars of the Decca sides, although by 1941, which hits mid-way through Volume III, there were quite a few defections, including Young, who is replaced by Coleman Hawkins on two tunes. The 10-CD set *The Complete Roulette Studio Recordings of Count Basie & His Orchestra* ♪♪♪♪♪ (Roulette/Mosaic, 1993, prod. Teddy Reig, reissue prod. Michael Cuscuna) and the eight-CD set *The Complete Roulette Live Recordings of Count Basie & His Orchestra* ♪♪♪♪♪ (Roulette/Mosaic, 1991, prod. Teddy Reig, reissue prod. Michael Cuscuna) include a few alternate takes on the studio sessions, keeping these CDs listenable.

what to buy next: *April in Paris* ♪♪♪♪♪ (Verve, 1956, prod. Norman Granz) includes 1955–56 Basie classics such as the hit title tune (a Wild Bill Davis arrangement), Freddie Green's fine "Corner Pocket," and Frank Foster's "Shiny Stockings." Also from 1955, *Count Basie Swings, Joe Williams Sings* ♪♪♪♪♪

Count Basie **(Archive Photos)**

(Verve, 1955/1993, prod. Norman Granz) is arguably the finest vocalist-and-big-band album ever. Everything clicks. Williams is at his peak; the band cooks, playing fine charts mostly by Frank Foster, and the soloists shine, especially Foster and section-mate Frank Wess on tenor sax. The album includes the classic "Everyday I Have the Blues," the equally fine "The Comeback," and the nearly as good "Roll 'Em, Pete." *Basie* (Roulette, 1957/1994, prod. Teddy Reig), which retains the famous atomic bomb album cover, includes arranger Neal Hefti's best charts: "The Kid from Red Bank" (with kicking Basie stride-piano), "Whirly-Bird" (with drummer Sonny Payne's rim shots adding punch to the work of the trumpet section), and the slow and sexy "Lil' Darlin'," (which quickly attained "jazz standard" status). *Sing Along with Basie* (Roulette, 1959/1991, prod. Teddy Reig) was a change of pace from Basie's usual big-band fare, featuring the star vocalese group, Lambert, Hendricks & Ross, singing many of the band parts and vocally recreating previously improvised instrumental solos. Unlike many later vocalese groups, whose strident singing too often reflects Broadway roots, LH&R had cut their teeth in jazz clubs of the era, and their work swung like mad.

what to avoid: Basie albums with Sammy Davis Jr. (Verve, 1964), the Alan Copeland Singers (ABC, 1966), Jackie Wilson (Brunswick, 1968), and Bing Crosby (Daybreak, 1972) just don't work. Other flops include bland attempts at the music from *Half a Sixpence* (Dot, 1967) and Walt Disney's *The Happiest Millionaire* (Coliseum, 1967), lame musicals to begin with, and *Basie Meets Bond* (United Artists, 1966) and *Basie on the Beatles* (Happy Tiger, 1970). Professional musicianship is up to par and good solo moments do occur but they are few and far between.

best of the rest:

Basie in London (Verve, 1957/1988)
Count Basie at Newport (Verve, 1957/1989)
Count Basie & the Kansas City Seven (Impulse!, 1962/1996)
First Time (Columbia, 1987)
88 Basie Street (Pablo, 1987)
The Golden Years, Vol. I–III and V (EPM, 1988–93) (Air checks and broadcast transcriptions)
Beaver Junction (VJC, 1991) (Air checks and broadcast transcriptions)
Corner Pocket (Laserlight, 1992)
Shoutin' Blues (RCA Victor/Bluebird, 1993)
Count Basie & the Stars of Birdland (Jazz, 1996)
Live at the Sands (Reprise/Warner Bros., 1998)

worth searching for: As exciting as the Basie Band's first Decca studio recordings were, broadcast recordings from the same period kick even more. The earliest, from a February 1937, Pittsburgh date, are on *The Count at the Chatterbox* (Jazz Archive, 1974). The LP *Featuring Wardell Gray* (Ozone, 1951) spotlights tenorist Gray in live sessions by Basie's big band of 1948, and the kicking small group of 1951. Although the music is top-notch, it's a poorly produced LP. A fantastic, full-fidelity LP performance by Basie's Band, including trumpeter Roy Eldridge and tenor saxophonist Eddie "Lockjaw" Davis, was recorded at the 1966 Newport Jazz Festival and issued on one side of *Basie, Lambert, Hendricks, Ross* (Europa/Giganti Jazz). It's top notch, with Lockjaw's sax work and the trumpet section tearing up "St. Louis Blues." The LH&R side isn't bad, but you'll never go back to it after you hear Basie. Basie's "New Testament" band's best period is thoroughly documented on two limited-edition sets available by mail-order only from Mosaic (phone: 203-327-7111 or FAX: 201-323-3526).

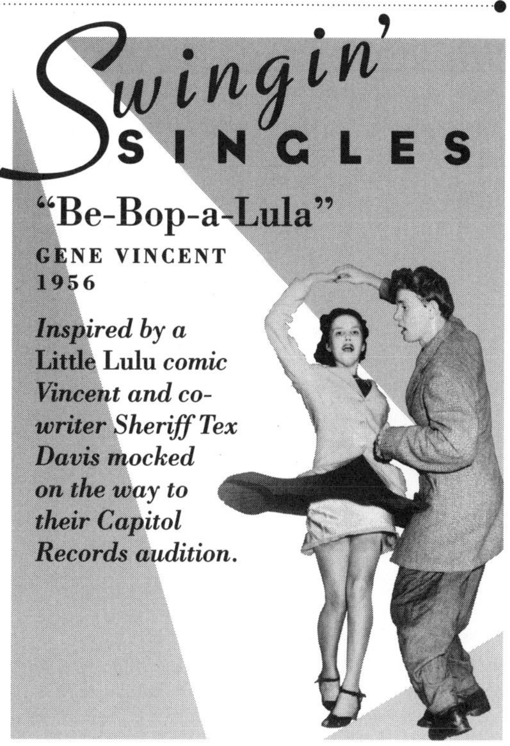
Swingin' Singles
"Be-Bop-a-Lula"
GENE VINCENT
1956
Inspired by a Little Lulu comic Vincent and co-writer Sheriff Tex Davis mocked on the way to their Capitol Records audition.

influences:

◀◀ Fats Waller, James P. Johnson, Bennie Moten

▶▶ Harry James, Benny Goodman, Glenn Miller, Charlie Parker

John K. Richmond

Beat Positive

See: Jet Set Six

The Beau Hunks

Formed 1991, in Amsterdam, Holland.

Menno Daams, trumpet; Jos Driessen, trumpet; Jilt Jansma, trombone; Robert Veen, alto and soprano sax, clarinet; Ronald Jansen Heijtmajer, alto sax, baritone sax, clarinet; Leo van Oostrom, tenor sax, clarinet, bass clarinet; Ilona De Groot, violin; Tineke de Jong, violin, viola; Eelco Beinema, cello; Jan Robijns, piano; Ton Van Bergeijk, banjo, guitar; Louis Debij, percussion; Peter Stove, tuba; Gert-Jan Blom, bass.

While most of us giggled at Bugs Bunny, a bunch of guys from Holland were watching more than the wabbit. While we giggled at the Little Rascals, a number of Dutch musicians were taking notes. Literally. With painstaking precision, Amsterdam's Beau Hunks have re-created the sounds of some of America's best-known, yet unrecognized, composers. The 14-piece band—which can expand to 30 pieces or shrink to a sextet—began with the works of Leroy Shield, who scored Little Rascals and Laurel and Hardy films. (More recently, they took on the symphonic jazz works of Ferde Grofe, who wrote songs for the swing-era bandleader Paul Whiteman.) To re-create Shield's music, the Beau Hunks worked from Library of Congress films, meticulously cataloguing and transcribing notes from each frame to compile a database of more than 2,000 sound cues. To re-create the true feel of the music, the takes were recorded with the band huddled around one pair of overhead microphones. The results—two CDs and more than 100 tracks of Shields's works—are staggering both in quantity and quality. While the original music of underrated '40s bandleader and inventor Raymond Scott has been recently rediscovered and released (on Columbia's *Reckless Nights and Turkish Twilights* and other compilations), the Beau Hunks continue to dig, unearthing even more of the unearthly sounds of Scott, whose music is known to anyone familiar with Warner Bros. cartoons or the more recent sloppy animated heroes Ren and Stimpy. There's something strange about hearing the music clearly and cleanly on CD without either the scratchy, warbling soundtracks that usually accompanied "Our Gang" shorts, or without the familiar cartoon characters that accompanied Scott's music. Somehow, because of the new technology—or perhaps despite it—the Beau Hunks stay true to the tunes, bringing the background to the forefront.

what to buy: Beginning with "Good Old Days," the opening theme of *The Beau Hunks Play the Original Little Rascals Music* (Koch Screen, 1994, prod. Gert-Jan Blom), it's difficult not to imagine the pictures that accompanied this music in the classic 1930s Hal Roach comedies. Thanks to the extensive liner notes, the pictures are provided, detailing the uses of each song in each film. Contrary to most jazz albums, the Beau Hunks play the cues in mostly less than a minute, but the 50 tracks segue together surprisingly well. *On to the Show: The Beau Hunks Play More Little Rascals Music* (Koch Screen, 1995, prod. Gert-Jan Blom, Piet Schreuders) begins with the trademark roar of the MGM lion, with the sound quality perfectly reflecting the era, boasting that it is "newly recorded in authentic Lo-Fi." There's even CD art by Shield fan R. Crumb.

what to buy next: On *The Beau Hunks Sextette Manhattan Minuet* (Koch Screen, 1996, prod. Gert-Jan Blom), from the raggedy trumpets to the frenetic clarinets, the sextet captures the sounds of Scott so precisely it's difficult not to join in with mouth-made sound effects and cartoon noises. The CD includes accolades (though not appearances) from Elvis Costello and Irwin Chusid, and even provides an excerpt from a bad review of the band in *Rhythm* magazine titled "You Can Keep Raymond Scott." *The Beau Hunks Sextette Celebration on the Planet Mars: A Tribute to Raymond Scott* (Koch Screen, 1995, prod. Gert-Jan Blom) has the distinction of including the Scott tune with the longest name, "Dedicatory Piece to the Crew and Passengers of the First Experimental Rocket Express to the Moon." Though that's exactly what the tune sounds like, there's still plenty left to the imagination. Liner notes are, as usual, detailed and wonderful. Noticing the song "Ectoplasm" is one of Scott's more somber tunes, a Beau Hunk called it "music to bury your mother-in-law by."

the rest:

The Modern American Music of Ferde Grofe (Basta, 1998)

worth searching for: Collectors may want the tidy double CD combining *Original Little Rascals* and *On to the Show*, although novice Beau Hunks (and Little Rascals) fans are advised to stick to the individual albums.

influences:

◀◀ Raymond Scott, Leroy Shield, the Little Rascals, Carl Stalling, Danny Elfman

▶▶ Don Byron

Jim Sheeler

Sidney Bechet

Born May 14, 1897, in New Orleans, LA. Died May 14, 1959, in Paris, France.

While Sidney Bechet never really received the public acclaim he deserved during his lifetime, or even since in the United States, his status among musicians and jazz connoisseurs as a true jazz giant (and, along with fellow New Orleans bandleader King Oliver, an early pioneer of the swing movement) has never been in question. Bechet learned to play clarinet as a child growing up in New Orleans, falling under the influence of early jazz notables such as Lorenzo Tio and Big Eye Nelson. In 1917

Sidney Bechet **(Archive Photos)**

he made his way to that cauldron of early jazz, Chicago, and played in the bands of such pioneers as Freddie Keppard, King Oliver, and Lawrence Duhe. Bechet's genius was already apparent, and became even more so when he went to Europe as a member of Will Marion Cook's Orchestra and took up his primary instrument, the soprano saxophone. The soprano was always a signature of Bechet's, and its powerful tone allowed Bechet to dominate early jazz ensembles as only trumpets had before. Bechet made his recording debut in 1923 with the Clarence Williams Blue Five, and joined an early incarnation of the Duke Ellington Orchestra in 1924, where he had a profound influence on young saxophonist Johnny Hodges. In 1925, Bechet recorded again with Williams in a group called the Red Onion Jazz Babies, and for the first time matched wits with a young Louis Armstrong. As early jazz progressed in the 1920s, so did Bechet's prominence, and he became the first jazz soloist on record in 1925. His virtuosity and presence as a soloist was unmatched by any other reed player at the time, and really only Armstrong on trumpet can be considered his equal. During the late 1920s, Bechet was back in Europe, wandering and playing and even spending some time in jail. After returning to the States in the 1930s, Bechet was veiled in obscurity, as more popularly pleasing ensembles led by the likes of Ellington and Armstrong were garnering all the attention. But in the late 1930s, due to a Dixieland revival, Bechet was again being hailed by critics as a luminary, and he began making some classic recordings (for Hughes Panassie) on Bluebird, and also on the fledgling Blue Note label. During the late 1930s and early 1940s, Bechet met once again with Armstrong on record, and also with Jelly Roll Morton, Earl Hines, and Eddie Condon. When Bechet returned to France, this time for good, he was surrounded by an adoring French audience. His celebrity status there would last until his death from cancer.

what to buy: The single-CD compilation *Really the Blues* ♪♪♪♪♪ (Living Era, 1993, prod. Vic Bellerby) includes highlights from one of Bechet's most prolific and important periods. Of particular interest are "2.19 Blues" with Armstrong and "Blues in Thirds" with Hines. *Volume 2: 1923–1932* ♪♪♪♪♪ (Masters of Jazz, 1992, prod. Alain Thomas, Fabrice Zammarchi) is classic early Bechet, including his first recordings with Clarence Williams and the Red Onion Jazz Babies sides from 1925. *Best* *of Sidney Bechet on Blue Note* ♪♪♪♪♪ (Blue Note, 1953, prod. Alfred Lion/1994, reissue prod. Michael Cuscuna) includes his now-famous readings of "Blue Horizon" and "Summertime."

what to buy next: The exciting live recording *Jazz at Storyville* ♪♪♪♪ (Black Lion, 1953/1992, prod. Alan Bates) was made during one of Bechet's visits to the U.S. later in his life. Most of *In Paris, Vol. 1* ♪♪♪½ (Vogue, 1953/1995) features Bechet as a soloist for two ballet scores, "La Colline du Delta" and "La Nuit Est une Sorciére." The settings are not typical for the Dixieland master, and he almost sounds out of place at times, but the combination works for the most part.

what to avoid: The title of *Sidney Bechet and Art Tatum* ♪½ (Bechet, 1940/Collectables, 1995) is quite misleading, for the two giants Bechet and Tatum never appear together on this CD of questionable sound quality. The Bechet sides are from a rather unsuccessful endeavor at early Latin jazz titled *Haitian Moods.*

best of the rest:
Summertime ♪♪♪ (Musical Memories, 1940/1992)
New Orleans Jazz ♪♪♪½ (Columbia, 1949/1989)
Spirits of New Orleans ♪♪½ (Vogue, 1949/1993)
The Complete Blue Note Recordings ♪♪♪♪½ (Blue Note, 1953/Mosaic)
(With Muggsy Spanier) *Double Dixie* ♪♪½ (Drive Archive, 1957/1994)
Live in New York, 1950–1951 ♪♪ (Storyville, 1989)
Master Takes: The Victor Sessions (1932–1943) ♪♪♪♪ (Bluebird, 1990)
Olympia Concert, October 19, 1955 ♪♪½ (Vogue, 1990)
1923–1936 ♪♪♪ (Classics, 1991)
1937–1938 ♪♪♪ (Classics, 1991)
1938–1940 ♪♪♪½ (Classics, 1991)
1940 ♪♪♪½ (Classics, 1991)
1940–41 ♪♪♪ (Classics, 1991)
Volume 1: 1923 ♪♪♪½ (Masters of Jazz, 1992)
Sidney Bechet in New York, 1937–1940 ♪♪♪½ (JSP, 1992)
Volume 3: 1931–1937 ♪♪♪½ (Masters of Jazz, 1994)
Volume 6: 1939 ♪♪♪♪ (Masters of Jazz, 1995)
Volume 7: 1940 ♪♪♪½ (Masters of Jazz, 1995)
En Concert avec Europe 1: 1957–1958 ♪♪♪ (RTE, 1995)
Volume 8: 1940 ♪♪♪♪ (Masters of Jazz, 1996)
Runnin' Wild ♪♪♪♪ (Blue Note, 1998)

worth searching for: RCA thoughtfully reissued all the Bechet sides they had on three groups of two CDs: *The Complete, Vol. 1 & 2* ♪♪♪♪½ (RCA, 1932–41/1994, prod. Jean-Paul Guiter), *The Complete, Vol. 3 & 4* ♪♪♪♪½ (RCA, 1941/1994, prod. Jean-Paul Guiter), and *The Complete, Vol. 5 & 6* ♪♪♪♪½ (RCA, 1943/1994, prod. Jean-Paul Guiter). However, they are already out of print.

influences:

◄◄ Lorenzo Tio Jr., Big Eye Nelson, Lawrence Duhe

►► Johnny Hodges, Bob Wilber, Steve Lacy

Dan Keener

Bix Beiderbecke

Born Leon Bix Beiderbecke, March 10, 1903, in Davenport, IA. Died August 6, 1931, in New York, NY.

One of the true legends of jazz, Bix Beiderbecke's stunning trumpet tone, unique phrasing, and impeccable rhythmic sense made him the idol of other early jazz musicians as well as the collegiate crowd of the "Roaring Twenties." Listening today to his solos in the hitmaking big bands of Paul Whiteman, Jean Goldkette, Frankie Trumbauer, and others, Beiderbecke's velvet sound remains as attractive as it was when first recorded during the 1920s and 1930s. Beiderbecke showed an early precociousness for music. By age seven he was a prodigy on piano, yet had never taken a lesson. When his older brother returned from World War I with some Original Dixieland Jazz Band records, Beiderbecke became infatuated with the music and borrowed a neighbor's cornet. Thus, he learned how to play jazz entirely on his own, developing a style and approach that were absolutely unique. He started playing professionally while still in high school. Beiderbecke's parents, trying to discourage his musical career, sent him away to school at Lake Forest Academy in the Chicago area, where he promptly spent most of his time absorbing the exploding jazz scene. Music ultimately won out over schooling, and Beiderbecke joined a band called the Wolverines, with whom he made his first recordings in February of 1924. The Wolverines, quite often unjustly maligned by some critics, were an enthusiastic and inspired young group whose music seems perfect for Beiderbecke's inspired horn. The acoustic recordings the Wolverines made for Gennett records showcase a self-assured and remarkably creative young cornetist. Beiderbecke then joined Frankie Trumbauer's band in St. Louis in September of 1925. When Trumbauer disbanded in mid-1926, he and Beiderbecke joined the Jean Goldkette Orchestra, whose recordings and radio broadcasts brought Beiderbecke national recognition. During the summer of 1927, Beiderbecke started to record both under his own name and with Frankie Trumbauer for OKeh records. These sessions yielded some of his finest solo work, and are high-level marks of jazz improvisation. Beiderbecke then joined Paul Whiteman and His Orchestra in October 1927. Sadly, Beiderbecke's acute alcoholism quickly brought about a decline in his career, and ultimately killed him.

what to buy: Although a definitive CD has yet to be compiled, *Bix Beiderbecke 1924–1930* ♪♪♪♪♪ (Jazz Classics in Digital Stereo, 1995, prod. Robert Parker) is a good introduction. The Wolverines titles can be found on *Bix Beiderbecke and the Wolverines* ♪♪♪♪♪ (Timeless, 1993, prod. Chris Barber, Wim Wigt) and *The Complete New Orleans Rhythm Kings, Vol. 2 (1923)/The Complete Wolverines (1924)* ♪♪♪♪♪ (King Jazz, 1923–24/1992, prod. Alessandro Protti, Roberto Capasso, Gi-

Bix Beiderbecke **(Archive Photos)**

anni Tollara). The Timeless compilation includes two Sioux City Six titles, two Bix and His Rhythm Jugglers titles, and two Wolverines titles (featuring Jimmy McPartland) made after Beiderbecke left. The King Jazz CD contains only the Wolverines titles, but also has the last six titles (plus alternates) recorded for Gennett by the New Orleans Rhythm Kings (who were influential not only to Beiderbecke, but to a whole generation of young, white Chicago musicians). Any doubts about the prowess of the Wolverines as a jazz unit can be quickly laid to rest by listening to "Fidgety Feet." Beiderbecke's solos on two tunes, "Oh Baby" and "I Need Some Pettin'," quickly prove his young genius. *Bix Beiderbecke, Vol. 1: Singin' the Blues (1927)* (Columbia, 1990, prod. Michael Brooks) and *Bix Beiderbecke, Vol. 2: At the Jazz Band Ball (1927–28)* (Columbia, 1991, prod. Michael Brooks) provide recordings from Beiderbecke's zenith. The rightly touted "Singin' the Blues" (some say one of the finest early jazz records made), "Riverboat Shuffle," and "I'm Coming Virginia" (dig the breathtaking "blue" note Beiderbecke takes in the 32nd bar of his solo) are a few examples of his best.

what to buy next: *Bix Lives* (Bluebird, 1991, prod. Steve Backer) and the two-CD *The Indispensable Bix Beiderbecke 1924–1930* (RCA, 1924–1930/1995, prod. various) feature Beiderbecke in the Goldkette and Whiteman bands. All Beiderbecke's critical recordings with these RCA Victor bands are covered here. Full, well-arranged scores present Beiderbecke and other fine soloists in wonderful period tune settings.

best of the rest:

Bix Beiderbecke 1924–27 (Classics, 1994)
Bix Beiderbecke 1927–30 (Classics, 1994)
Masters of Jazz Series: The Complete Bix Beiderbecke (Media 7, 1997)

influences:

◀◀ Louis Armstrong, Dominick "Nick" LaRocca, Emmet Hardy, New Orleans Rhythm Kings

▶▶ Louis Armstrong, Rex Stewart, Lester Young, Jimmy McPartland, Red Nichols, Andy Secrest, Roland "Bunny" Berrigan

Jim Prohaska

Bellevue Cadillac

Formed 1992, in MA.

Doug "The Professor" Bell, guitar; "Gentleman Joe" Cooper, lead vocals; Pete "The Cat" Wood, bass; Tim "Miles" Long, piano, Hammond organ, B3 electric vibes; Russell "Holly" Wood, percussion; Bob "The Breeze" Hoffelder, trombone; Russell "Hot Sauce" Hill, trumpet; Jeff "Be-Bop" Giacomelli, tenor sax; Bruce "Mr. Memphis" Cummings, baritone sax.

If you were to enter an audio laboratory somewhere and mix elements of Louis Jordan, Glenn Miller, Cab Calloway, T-Bone Walker, Freddie King, Little Milton, and everyone who ever recorded for the Stax-Volt soul record label, the result might come out like Bellevue Cadillac. The band's horns wail fat and brassy, the guitar work is some of the finest in any field, and the songs update the old rhythms and rhyme schemes with contemporary humor. The sound is not strictly swing, but the Cadillac is much beloved among the zoot-suit and contemporary bobbysoxer crowds. Unlike many swing bands with weak vocalists (or singing bandleaders who shouldn't), Bellevue Cadillac has a genuine talent in "Gentleman Joe" Cooper, whose bluesy, gospel delivery brings the band's eclectism together quite convincingly. Initially, Bellevue Cadillac's zany, tell-it-like-it-is founder, Doug Bell, had played guitar in several rock and blues bands before becoming a real-estate developer. Battles with the tax man, bankruptcy, and cancer made him realize he had labored too long without a creative outlet. Without even knowing (or caring) what was on the contemporary charts, he began to write songs from a big-band and jump-blues perspective, and sought out band members (all of whom are with him today). The energetic Bell writes most of the songs and co-arranges with sax player Jeff Giacomelli, and he insists on a very high level of musicianship. The first neo-swing band in the New England area, the band has shared bills with acts as diverse as Ray Charles and the Royal Crown Revue, yet appearing with big-name acts can only take a band so far. Recently, *Swing This, Baby!*, a compilation disc featuring "Black & White," a song from the Cadillac's first album, has scaled the *Billboard* charts, and talks with major labels have begun.

what's available: The debut, *Black & White* (Ardeon, 1996, prod. Rob Fraboni), is less a true swing album than a satisfying resurrection of the '60s Stax-Volt sound. Tunes such as "Black & White," "Body and Soul," and "Short Fuse" feature a fat Memphis Horns approach, Steve Cropper–style guitar licks, some churchy Hammond organ, and Cooper's evocative gospel/soul vocals. "Shoulda Coulda Woulda," "Cruisin'," and "Lay Your Money Down" work the jump-blues side of the big-band street, but for the most part, this is a good soul album. The band's second outing, *Prozac Nation* (Hep Cat, 1998, prod. Rob Fraboni), is weighted more heavily with sassy swinging jumpers. On "Prozac Nation," "Pull the Plug," and "Hey, Who Knew," the group twits its youngish audience with satiric observations on psychotherapy, euthanasia, and jive-talk while musically evoking dancefloor rhythms of a bygone era. Of special note for purists, "Call of the Wild" sports effective Gene Krupa–style drumming and wild brass.

influences:

◀◀ Cab Calloway, Blood, Sweat & Tears, Stax-Volt, Louis Jordan, Little Milton, T-Bone Walker, Roomful of Blues

Ken Burke

Tex Beneke

Born Gordon Beneke, February 12, 1914, in Fort Worth, TX.

It has become too easy to dismiss Tex Beneke as "the guy who took over the orchestra when Glenn Miller died," especially when he helped make Miller's sound popular in the first place. During the early to mid-'30s, Beneke had played sax in Ben Young's band before signing with Miller's struggling outfit. A talented soloist, Beneke could blow cool jazz, hot swing, or romantic mood music. In addition to his soaring tenor sax work (best heard on Miller's beloved "In the Mood"), Beneke's pleasant baritone gave voice to such great Miller hits as "Chattanooga Choo Choo," "Don't Sit Under the Apple Tree," and "I Got a Gal in Kalamazoo." After the Miller band broke up, Beneke worked briefly with the Modernaires and Horace Heidt before joining the Navy. Late in 1946, Beneke entered into an agreement with Miller's estate and began touring and recording as "The Glenn Miller Band with Tex Beneke." Post-war audiences went wild for the reconstituted group, which scored a string of Top 10 records. However, the band's manager and producer (working for the estate) insisted Beneke keep the sounds as faithful to Miller's pre-war work as possible, with no experiments. By 1950, the frustrated Beneke broke with Miller's estate and formed his own band. He still played the great hits of Glenn Miller—after all, they were his, too—but he also laid down fresh sounds and followed his own musical instincts. Big-band music was pretty much dead by then, but Beneke worked constantly, appearing on TV's *Cavalcade of Big Bands,* and touring the world with various aggregations well into the '80s.

what to buy: All 16 of Beneke's great RCA hits with Glenn Miller's orchestra are on *The Best of Tex Beneke* (Collectors' Choice, 1998, prod. various), which includes such jumping jive as "Hey! Ba-Ba-Re-Bop," "A Gal In Calico," and the silly "The Woodchuck Song." You can dig this superior 20-song collection, listed in the Collectors' Choice mail-order catalog, as both an extension of the great Miller sound and for Beneke's own mastery of the genre.

what to buy next: Those wishing to hear Beneke on a wider selection of standards and swing workouts should get *Palladium Patrol* (Aero Space, 1990), a 21-song compilation.

what to avoid: Played as one continuous loop, *Tex Beneke* (Canby, 1996) may prove a bit irritating to those preferring separation between tracks and songs.

the rest:

Jukebox Saturday Night (Vintage Jazz Classics, 1992)
Dancer's Delight (Magic, 1997)
Live in Hi-Flat at the Hollywood Palladium (Jazz Hour, 1997)

worth searching for: The import *Tex Beneke & the Glenn Miller Orchestra* (Halcyon, 1998) is yet another strong collection of post-war sides, many of which aren't on the Collectors' Choice set.

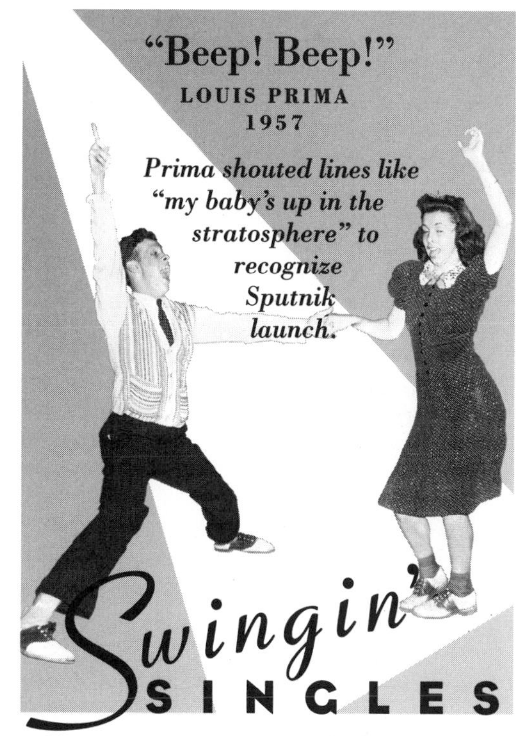

influences:

◄◄ Ben Young

►► Ray Anthony, Ralph Flanagan

see also: *Glenn Miller*

Ken Burke

Tony Bennett

Born Anthony Dominick Benedetto, August 3, 1926, in New York, NY.

There is no stronger candidate for the "Greatest Interpreter of American Song" award during the past half-century than Bennett. Frank Sinatra and Bing Crosby singled him out as the best singer in the business, and who's to argue? His impeccable tone, which has only grown deeper and stronger over the years, and swinging phrasing are the archetypal traits that traditional vocalists have aspired to for the past four decades. His greatest commercial success came in the early 1960s, but triumphant returns in the mid-1980s and early 1990s cemented his stature as a musical icon. By 1994's *MTV Unplugged* appearance, even the cynical grunge-loving crowd had championed the optimistic smoothie as an ironic hero. Growing up in Queens, Bennett spent his teens as a singing waiter. After a stint in the military during World War II, he studied singing at the American Theatre Wing School. Bob Hope and Pearl Bailey discovered him and dished out advice, and Bennett signed with Columbia Records and earned his first hit, "Boulevard of Broken Dreams," in 1950. Through 1964 he notched two dozen Top 40 hits, including "Because of You," "Cold, Cold Heart," "Rags to Riches," "Stranger in Paradise," and his signature number, "I Left My Heart in San Francisco." His emphasis shifted from singles to albums in the mid-1960s, but he continued to draw on material from what he called the "Great American Songbook," filled with George and Ira Gershwin, Irving Berlin, and Johnny Mercer. He also nurtured strong ties to swing and jazz, working with Count Basie, Dizzy Gillespie, and Duke Ellington. He recorded infrequently in the 1970s and 1980s—partly because he resisted pressure from Columbia to record more mainstream pop—and instead concentrated on touring and his other talent, painting. The first high-profile beneficiary of the lounge revival in the early 1990s, Bennett found new popularity—showing up on late-night talk shows and *The Simpsons,* starring on and releasing an album from *MTV Unplugged,* touring, and recording several well-executed tribute albums to Sinatra, Fred Astaire, Billie Holiday, and others. His voice today has a smokier edge than the impossibly smooth tone of his younger days, but it also has grown richer.

what to buy: If you can afford it, by all means go for *Forty Years: The Artistry of Tony Bennett* (Columbia, 1991, prod. Didier Deutsch), a chronologically arranged 87-song anthology and one of the best box sets of the box-set era. The four-disc collection, which covers his big-band beginnings and the start of his recent comeback, was re-released in 1997 in an unabridged but smaller, more affordable package. The Grammy-winning *MTV Unplugged* (Columbia, 1994, prod. David Kahne) took the momentum built by the box set and launched a full-fledged revival; Bennett gives a confident, commanding performance of career highlights—plus, Elvis Costello and k.d. lang make cameos. *The Art of Excellence* (Columbia, 1986/1997, prod. Ettore Stratta, Danny Bennett) marked Bennett's return to Columbia and significant sales. It mixes standards with great new finds like "How Do You Keep the Music Playing."

what to buy next: *I Left My Heart in San Francisco* (Columbia, 1962/1997 prod. Ernest Altschuler) is Bennett's first great studio album, containing "Smile," "The Best Is Yet to Come," and the unforgettable title track, which won two Grammys. *At Carnegie Hall: The Complete Concert* (Columbia, 1962/1997, prod. Ernest Altschuler, Robin McBride) is an expanded version of the original live album.

what to avoid: *Tony Sings the Great Hits of Today* (Columbia, 1969, prod. Wally Gold) is the type of corporate collection that Bennett loathed and that led to his retreat from the business. "MacArthur Park," "My Cherie Amour," and three Beatles tunes represent one ill-fitting choice after another.

best of the rest:
The Beat of My Heart (Columbia, 1957/1997)
In Person! With the Count Basie Orchestra (Columbia, 1959/1994)
Tony Sings for Two (Columbia, 1960/1996)
I Wanna Be Around (Columbia, 1963/1995)
Who Can I Turn To? (Columbia, 1964/1995)
If I Ruled the World: Songs for the Jet Set (Columbia, 1965/1997)
The Movie Song Album (Columbia, 1966/1988)
Snowfall: The Christmas Album (Columbia, 1968/1997)
Something (Columbia, 1970/1995)
All-Time Hall of Fame Hits (Columbia, 1970/1987)
The Very Thought of You (Columbia, 1971/1995)
All-Time Greatest Hits (Columbia, 1972/1987)
Rodgers and Hart Songbook (DRG, 1973/WMO, 1997)
Jazz (Columbia, 1987)
Bennett/Berlin (Columbia, 1987)
Astoria: Portrait of the Artist (Columbia, 1989/1997)
Perfectly Frank (Columbia, 1992)
Steppin' Out (Columbia, 1993)
Here's to the Ladies (Columbia, 1995)
On Holiday (Columbia, 1997)
The Playground (Columbia, 1998)

worth searching for: Never released commercially, *Selections from the Box Set 40 Years: The Artistry of Tony Bennett* (Columbia, 1991, prod. various) is just what the title indicates: a sampler of 12 tracks from the exceptional anthology. Also, the out-of-print *Tony's Greatest Hits, Vol. III* (Columbia, 1965, prod. various) is a snapshot of his peak impact era, anchored by "I Left My Heart in San Francisco," "I Wanna Be Around," and "When Joanna Loved Me."

influences:
◀◀ Art Tatum, Mildred Bailey, Frank Sinatra, Mel Tormé
▶▶ Sammy Davis Jr., Barbra Streisand, Jack Jones, k.d. lang, Elvis Costello, Harry Connick Jr.

Jay Dedrick

Bunny Berigan

Born Roland Bernard Berigan, November 2, 1908, in Hilbert, WI. Died June 2, 1942, in New York, NY.

Bunny Berigan's fiery trumpet tone and unmistakable growl provides excitement for even the casual jazz listener. No ordinary big-band sideman or leader, Berigan's sheer force and in-

Tony Bennett (© Jack Vartoogian)

ventive attack could spark any variety of musical settings. His musical career began at age eight on violin. By age 13, he had started to play trumpet, and by the next year, he played well enough to join some local bands. Soon, he quit school and became a professional musician. His travels ultimately took him to New York City, where he joined Hal Kemp's Orchestra and made his first recordings in 1930. After quitting Kemp, Berigan freelanced extensively around New York, spending brief periods with the bands of Paul Whiteman, Fred Rich, Ben Selvin, Bennie Krueger, and others. He was continually in recording studios because of his quick reading skills and improvisational expertise. Berigan was a regular fixture on 52nd Street, and his presence on many small-group swing records of this period are gems of 1930s jazz. After a short stint with Benny Goodman's Orchestra in 1935 and Tommy Dorsey's Orchestra in 1937, Berigan formed his own big band and recorded for RCA Victor from mid-1937 until the band went bankrupt in 1940. Bunny Berigan was a stellar trumpet player and a workaholic. Unfortunately, he was not a good businessman, and was also a heavy drinker. These factors ultimately brought on his death at age 33.

what to buy: Some of Berigan's best recordings from the early to mid-1930s can be found on *Portrait of Bunny Berigan* (ASV Living Era, 1992) and *Swingin' High* (Topaz, 1993). Berigan is featured with the Dorsey Brothers, Glenn Miller ("Solo Hop" is a Berigan tour de force), and others. *Bunny Berigan and His Boys: 1935–36* (Jazz Chronological Classics, 1993, prod. Gilles Petard), *Bunny Berigan: 1936–37* (Jazz Chronological Classics, 1993, prod. Gilles Petard), *Bunny Berigan: 1937* (Jazz Chronological Classics, 1994, prod. Gilles Petard), *Bunny Berigan: 1937–38* (Jazz Chronological Classics, 1994, prod. Gilles Petard), and *Bunny Berigan: 1938* (Jazz Chronological Classics, 1995, prod. Gilles Petard) cover possibly the best period of Berigan's career. The Bunny Berigan and His Boys period was Berigan's 52nd Street group before forming his big band. Unfortunately, the 1936–37 Classics reissue copies the old Epic LP, which chopped out Chick Bullock's vocals, also axing some beautiful Berigan solo work. To make up for it, the CD includes four tasty Frank Froeba and His Swing Band titles from Columbia (1936). On the other volumes, Berigan's classic "I Can't Get Started," "Black Bottom," and "Prisoner's Song" are primary examples of what made Berigan popular.

what to buy next: *Bunny Berigan: Pied Piper* (Bluebird, 1995, prod. Steve Backer) offers a nice cross-section of Berigan's Victor recordings. Berigan's entire output on radio transcription recordings have been released on the two-CD set *Bunny Berigan and the Rhythm Makers* (Jazz Classics, 1996). Although many titles are pop tunes, Berigan's solos add quite a bit of spark to these performances. "Shanghai Shuffle," "Sing You Sinners," and other titles make this acquisition most worthwhile.

best of the rest:

The Complete Bunny Berigan, Volume III (Bluebird, 1993)
Bunny Berigan: 1938–1942 (Jazz Chronological Classics, 1996)

worth searching for: Berigan was always at his best in a small group setting. The 1935 and 1936 recordings with Red McKenzie's group, the *Mound City Blues Blowers* (Timeless, 1994, prod. Chris Barber, Wim Wigt) feature Berigan extensively. Titles such as "What's the Reason," "Indiana," and "I'm Gonna Sit Right Down and Write Myself a Letter," should leave the listener in awe as Berigan rips through his solos, teases with muted accompaniment, then pounces once again. *Harlem Lullaby* (Hep, 1992, prod. Alastair Robertson, John R.T. Davies) or *Best of the Big Bands: Dorsey Brothers* (Columbia, 1992, prod. Michael Brooks) have his awe-inspiring solos on "She's Funny That Way," "Shim Sham Shimmy," and "She Reminds Me of You" (which might well be one of Berigan's best-ever offerings).

influences:

◀ Louis Armstrong, Bix Beiderbecke, Bob Mayhew

▶ Pee Wee Irwin, Roy Eldridge, Johnny Best, Billy Butterfield, Charlie Spivak

Jim Prohaska

Elmer Bernstein

Born April 4, 1922, in New York City, NY.

A Hollywood legend, Elmer Bernstein was one of the first movie composers to rely heavily on jazz idioms for his scores, thereby influencing the master of the swinging soundtrack, Henry Mancini, and every other composer who came of age in the '50s and early '60s. He studied music at Juilliard and worked for a brief time as a pianist. During World War II he worked as an arranger for Glenn Miller's Army Air Force Band as well as Armed Forces Radio. He eventually migrated to Hollywood, where he continues to work steadily as a film composer, having written music for more than 100 films, and earned 13 Oscar nominations. He also contributed the "Peter Gunn"–like title song for the '50s crime show *Staccato*. Bernstein's swaggering, jazz-tinged scores for films like *The Man with the Golden Arm* and *The Sweet Smell of Success* played an integral role in setting a mood of moral dissipation and urban grit for those seminal films.

what to buy: One of the best, and most familiar, of Bernstein's original soundtracks is *The Return of the Magnificent Seven* (MGM, 1966/Rykodisc, 1998), which set out to create an enduring heroic anthem and succeeded. After hearing it again even once, you'll march around the house singing the western "dum, DUM, dum, dum" theme all day.

what to buy next: *The Great Escape* (MGM, 1963/Rykodisc, 1998), music from the 1963 Steve McQueen adventure, has some of the *Magnificent Seven* power but isn't quite as distinctive.

what to avoid: *Elmer Bernstein with RPO Pops* (Denon, 1993), a collaboration with the Royal Philharmonic Orchestra on famous film music, including "The Magnificent Seven" and "Ghostbusters" applies overblown arrangements to familiar pop tunes.

worth searching for: Though almost of all of Bernstein's original albums, including his soundtracks, are out of print, he shows up repeatedly on volumes of Capitol's excellent *Ultra-Lounge* series. You can find the theme to *Stacatto* as well as "Thinking of Batty" on *Ultra-Lounge, Vol. 7: Crime Scene* (Capitol, 1996, compilation prod. Brad Benedict).

influences:

Glenn Miller, Benny Goodman

Henry Mancini, John Barry, Lalo Schifrin

Marc Weingarten and Steve Knopper

Big Bad Voodoo Daddy

Formed 1992, in Los Angeles, CA.

Scotty Morris, vocals, guitar; Josh Levy, piano; Andy Rowley, saxophone; Karl Hunter, saxophone; Glenn Marhevka, trumpet; Jeff Harris, trombone; Dirk Shumaker, bass; Kurt Sodergren, drums.

It's an absolute rarity: a low-budget independent film gets a huge buzz, finds a cult audience, and along the way catapults its featured musical act to significant national attention. As capable and catchy as its jumping jive may be—and it really took off in 1998, when the single "You & Me & the Bottle Makes 3 Tonight (Baby)" became a swing-revival smash and MTV buzz clip—Big Bad Voodoo Daddy owes its fame to Doug Liman's hip 1996 art-house favorite *Swingers*. In that film, the octet's then-mushrooming weekly appearance at Hollywood's famed Derby nightclub was played up for sharply effective cinematic energy. The band had been toiling away at its own brand of Cab Calloway/Louis Jordan swing and city-blues since 1992, releasing a pair of now-out-of-print homemade albums that earned it a well-regarded reputation among the hep-set of L.A.'s burgeoning lounge revival. After *Swingers* struck gold (and its accompanying soundtrack started selling in moderate numbers), BBVD's local gigs were soon teeming with cool cats and hot chicks decked out in the snazziest vintage clothing. The band took a year to capitalize on this notoriety, but it finally followed its Dixie-laden colleagues, the Squirrel Nut Zippers, along with the Cherry Poppin' Daddies and the Brian Setzer Orchestra, into the modern-rock camp. The band's visibility (along with that of the neo-swing movement) surged during halftime of the 1999 Super Bowl, when BBVD performed on a bill with pop megastar Gloria Estefan.

what to buy: *Swingers* (Hollywood, 1996, prod. various) has classics by old standbys such as Dean Martin, Tony Bennett, George Jones, and Bobby Darin, and cheeky tunes by fresh upstarts such as Love Jones and Joey Altruda. BBVD's three cuts—the Brian Setzer-ish "Go Daddy-O," a splendid cover of the Disney samba classic "I Wan'na Be Like You," and the group's signature number, "You & Me & the Bottle Makes 3 Tonight (Baby)"—are knockouts that give you a strong sense of what future releases hold.

what to buy next: Digging this '90s version of Cab Calloway? Then keep swinging to *Big Bad Voodoo Daddy* (Coolsville/EMI/Capitol, 1998, prod. various), the band's major-label debut. If your jump-blues brain is still a fairly clean slate, it will likely be a revelation—a blast of high-spirited fun amid a world of whiny noise and aimless thunder. If you've heard Calloway, Louis Jordan, and the best of the big bands, however, you'll probably find it all a bit sterile. As with Squirrel Nut Zippers, there's a spark and vitality that's lacking, despite the band's proficiency. And BBVD hasn't made an attempt to suffuse the exuberance of a bygone era with a dose of cutting '90s irony. (To think of what could have been done with Cab's "Minnie the Moocher"! It's rotely covered here.) Instead, BBVD merely mimics what it can never match.

worth searching for: BBVD's earlier home-grown works—*Big Bad Voodoo Daddy* (Hep Cat, 1993, prod. Big Bad Voodoo Daddy) and *Whatchu' Want for Christmas?* (Hep Cat, 1995, prod. Big Bad Voodoo Daddy)—are both fine, if not expertly produced, efforts.

influences:

Cab Calloway, Louis Jordan, Louis Prima, Bill Haley

Squirrel Nut Zippers, the Wonderful World of Joey, the Slackers, Big Sandy and His Fly-Rite Boys

Ben Wener

Big Dave & the Ultrasonics

Formed 1990, in Ann Arbor, MI.

"Big Dave" Steele, vocals, guitar; Dave Morris, harmonica; Dale Jennings, bass (1998–present); Pieter Struyk, drums (1993–present); Ben Wilson, keyboards (1992–present).

A solid rhythm section keeps this modern blues, swing, and boogie-woogie band's grooves going. They play mostly original material, obviously written to showcase each player's skills.

Leader Dave Steele's seasoned bass voice is superb and his sturdy guitar-playing is muscular but non-intrusive. Plus, his original songs have been performed and recorded by other groups, including the Roger Montgomery Blues Band. In addition to widely touring, this cohesive combo has opened for blues artists such as Albert King, Koko Taylor, John Mayall, and Buddy Guy, and appeared at numerous festivals. The Ultrasonics made their debut *Love & Money* and 1996 follow-up, *No Sweat*, for Schoolkids Records.

what to buy: The band's third album, *Big Dave & the Ultrasonics* (Burnside, 1998, prod. Ron Levy), showcases steady drummer Pieter Struyk and the boogie-woogie piano skills of Ben Wilson.

what to buy next: At last word, the Ann Arbor, Michigan–based Schoolkids Records had filed for bankruptcy, but you can probably still get copies of Big Dave & the Ultrasonic's first album, *Love & Money* (Schoolkids Records, 1993, prod. Big Dave & the Ultrasonics), in select stores and online sites. Performing mostly original material featuring Steele's vocals and rationed guitar accompaniment, and Morris's energetic blues-harp, the band shows its potential as an all-around blues/swing band.

what to avoid: Recommended for completists, *No Sweat: Live* (Schoolkids Records, 1996, prod. Big Dave & the Ultrasonics), kicks off with a rousing version of Louis Prima's "Jump, Jive, an' Wail," but doesn't quite sustain that energy. In spite of some fine solos from Steele, Morris, and Wilson (especially on the Hammond B-3), this CD doesn't quite compare with their studio-recorded efforts.

influences:

Louis Jordan, Louis Prima, Ray Charles, Muddy Waters, Mitch Woods

Nancy Ann Lee

Big Joe & the Dynaflows /Big Joe Maher

Born July 13, 1953, in Washington, DC.

As leader of Big Joe & the Dynaflows, which he formed in 1987, Big Joe Maher has developed into a thoroughly entertaining performer and tasteful singer. He has gone a long way toward mastering the nuances of swing and jump R&B vocals, style, and persona. Growing up in the suburbs of Washington, D.C., Maher fell under the spell of his father's swinging blues and R&B records. After years of working in and around the metro D.C. area as a drummer and vocalist, he began recording in 1988, first for the local independent label Powerhouse, for which he released *Good Rockin Daddy*. Blues guitarist Anson Funderburgh introduced Maher to Hammond Scott of Black Top Records, leading to the 1994 release *Layin' in the Alley*. He also has done session work on drums for blues artists such as Bob Margolin and, more recently, Saffire—the Uppity Blues Women singer-pianist Ann Rabson.

what to buy: *I'm Still Swingin'* (Severn, 1998, prod. Big Joe Maher, David Earl) benefits from a clever choice of material and capable support from guitarist Alex Schultz, formerly of Rod Piazza & the Mighty Flyers, among others.

what to buy next: *Layin' in The Alley* (Black Top, 1994, prod. Hammond Scott, Nauman S. Scott) is a convincing set of jump R&B and swing with a fun attitude.

the rest:

Good Rockin Daddy (Powerhouse, 1989)
(With Jeff Sarli) *Mojo* (Wildchild/Mapleshade, 1994)

influences:

Smiley Lewis, B.B. King, Louis Jordan, Percy Mayfield, Little Milton, Bobby Charles, Roscoe Gordon

Bryan Powell

Big Sandy & His Fly-Rite Boys

Formed as Big Sandy & the Fly-Rite Trio, 1988, in Orange County, CA. Became Big Sandy & His Fly-Rite Boys in February 1993.

Big Sandy (born Robert Williams), vocals, acoustic guitar; Wally Hersom, upright bass; Will Brokenbourgh, drums (1988–89); Bobby Trimble, drums (1989–present); T.K. Smith, guitar (1988–93); Ashley Kingman, guitar (1993–present); Lee Jeffriess, steel guitar (1991–present).

Exactly why hefty frontman Robert Williams transformed himself into Big Sandy isn't clear. Maybe it's because Robert Williams & His Fly-Rite Boys doesn't ring right. Whatever the name, this ensemble shuffled its way into the "alternative country" movement during 1994, with a melting pot sound that tapped into the traditions of rockabilly, western swing, and hillbilly music. Hailing from the West Coast environment that spawned legends Merle Haggard and Buck Owens, Big Sandy & His Fly-Rite Boys concentrate on the "western" half of country & western. Dressed in duds your grandfather might have worn back in his heyday—complete with colorful scarf ties—this quintet brings the past to the present with unabashed authenticity and verve. Both live and on record, Big Sandy & His Fly-Rite Boys revel in a no-frills musical philosophy that clashes with every over produced note of Nashville's mainstream country repertoire. The group has opened shows for acts as diverse as country upstarts the Mavericks, psycho-trashbilly kingpin Reverend Horton Heat, and mopey alternative rocker Morrissey.

what to buy: *Swingin' West* (HighTone, 1995, prod. Dave Alvin) offers a swinging, more streamlined approach than the band's versatile debut. Whether it be the sly pleasures of "My

Sinful Days Are Over" and "Blackberry Wine" or the blues-tinged wonder of "Let Me in There, Baby" and "If I Wrote a Song (about Our Love Affair)," this effort cuts to the heart of Big Sandy & His Fly-Rite Boys.

what to buy next: On his first album without the Fly-Rite Boys, *Dedicated to You* ♪♪♪½ (HighTone, 1998, prod. Robert Williams, Larry Sloven, Bruce Bromberg), Big Sandy sheds most of the western-swing and rockabilly and aims straight for soft, crooning R&B ballads. He's a terrific singer, especially on the opening "Lonely Guy," although he occasionally brings to mind an over-the-top Elvis Presley.

what to avoid: Without Big Sandy to provide the charisma and focal point, the Fly-Rite Boys' rudderless *Big Sandy Presents the Fly-Rite Boys* ♪♪½ (HighTone, 1998, prod. the Fly-Rite Boys) is an interesting take on western swing, but it lacks the punch of great rock 'n' roll instrumental music.

the rest:
Jumpin' from 6 to 6 ♪♪♪½ (HighTone, 1994)
Feelin' Kind of Lucky ♪♪♪ (HighTone, 1997)

worth searching for: Big Sandy & the Fly-Rite Trio recorded one album that was released in the United States, *Fly Right* ♪♪♪ (Dionysis, 1990, prod. Robert Williams). Another album as the Fly-Rite Trio, *On the Go* ♪♪♪ (No Hit Records, 1991, prod. Robert Williams), was released only in England.

influences:
◀◀ Tex Williams, Bob Wills, Hank Williams, Asleep at the Wheel
▶▶ Derailers, Dale Watson, Cowboys & Indians

Mario Tarradell and Steve Knopper

Eubie Blake

Born February 7, 1883, in Baltimore, MD. Died February 12, 1983, in New York, NY.

Ragtime pianist Eubie Blake exerted an influence on early jazz players with his energetic style. By 1915, he had teamed up with Noble Sissle in vaudeville and songwriting. Their 1921 hit show *Shuffle Along* introduced jazz dancing to New York and included the perennial favorite "I'm Just Wild about Harry," which Harry Truman used as his campaign song years later. Benny Goodman used Blake's 1930 gem, "Memories of You," throughout his career to great effect. From the 1940s through 1960s, Blake was in semi-retirement, though he practiced every day. The 1969 double-LP, *The 86 Years of Eubie Blake*, now out of print, jump-started a second career that lasted almost until Blake's death at age 100, plus five days.

what to buy: *Tricky Fingers* ♪♪♪♪ (Quicksilver, 1994) and *Piano Jazz with Eubie Blake* ♪♪♪♪ (The Jazz Alliance, 1993) capture Blake in good form. The latter (from Marian McPartland's NPR radio show) gives the best sense of his warmth and humor.

what to buy next: Blake's piano rolls of blues, spirituals, and rags are among the most exciting of the 1920s. His combination of syncopation, the blues, and a kind of earthy sophistication highlight the few available Blake rolls on *The Greatest Ragtime of the Century* ♪♪♪♪♪ (Biograph, 1987, prod. Arnold S. Caplin) and *Memories of You* ♪♪♪♪ (Biograph, 1990, prod. Arnold S. Caplin).

worth searching for: There have been several LPs released that feature Blake, even a few from the 1950s. But, without a doubt, the one most ripe for CD reissue is *The 86 Years of Eubie Blake* ♪♪♪♪ (Columbia, 1969, prod. John Hammond). Blake's close friends Bolcom and Morris showcase an overview of his beautiful compositions on *Wild about Eubie* ♪♪♪♪½ (Columbia, 1977, prod. Sam Parkins) including Blake on three solos and a duo.

influences:
◀◀ Jesse Pickett, Will Turk, Kitchen Tom
▶▶ James P. Johnson, Willie "The Lion" Smith, Terry Waldo, Mike Lipskin

George Foley

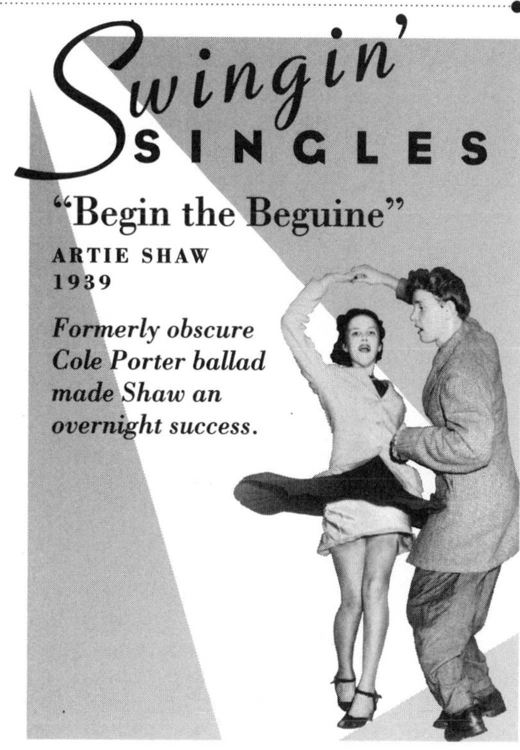
Swingin' SINGLES
"Begin the Beguine"
ARTIE SHAW
1939
Formerly obscure Cole Porter ballad made Shaw an overnight success.

Eubie Blake **(© Jack Vartoogian)**

The Blasters

Formed 1979, in Los Angeles, CA. Disbanded 1986. Re-formed 1996.

Phil Alvin, vocals, guitar (1979–85, 1996–present); Dave Alvin, guitar (1979–85); John Bazz, bass (1979–85, 1996–present); Bill Bateman, drums (1979–85); Gene Taylor, piano (1979–85); James Intveld, guitar (1996–present); Jerry Angel, drums (1996–present).

The Blasters were at the forefront of the late '70s/early '80s rockabilly revival that expanded into a renaissance of what the band accurately tagged "American Music." But that and $3.50 will get them a Frappuccino at Starbucks. One of the tragically underrated and now almost forgotten bands, the Blasters combined the energy of the burgeoning Los Angeles punk scene with a solid base in rock 'n' roll history and a taste for R&B and country. Theirs was a shared sensibility that drew on, but didn't ape, Jerry Lee Lewis, Big Joe Turner, and many other heroes. There's a complicated mix of ingredients and influences happening in the Blasters' music, but you'd be a fool if you didn't say it swung. After several critical triumphs, but almost no commercial success, the group split, with Dave Alvin going on to pursue a successful solo career. Phil Alvin released a couple of solo albums as well, but mainly concentrated on graduate school where he studied advanced mathematics. Eventually he re-formed the band, but without brother Dave's vision, it just didn't work.

what's available: Thanks to a much-needed rerelease on CD, it's no longer necessary to fork over the $100 or more it once cost to own a copy of the Blasters' independent debut *American Music* (Rollin' Rock, 1980/HighTone, 1997, prod. the Blasters). The album finds the band at its raw, raucous beginnings, and features songs such as "Marie Marie," "Barn Burning," and "American Music," that would later be found on the group's major-label releases. There are also six bonus tracks not found on the pricey vinyl version. Altogether, it's a jumpin' little record I'd ask my jockey to play.

worth searching for: The United Nations, or some other global authority, should look into the internationally criminal fact that none of the other Blasters albums besides *American Music* are currently in print. Only a couple were ever offered on CD, which a separate committee should investigate. Meanwhile the man (or woman) in the street can search the used CD bins for *The*

Blasters Collection ꝏꝏ (Slash/Warner Bros., 1990, prod. the Blasters, Jeff Eyrich), a definitive overview of the group's output. Their major-label debut, *The Blasters*, is their best single effort thanks to versions of "Marie Marie," "American Music," and "So Long Baby Goodbye." *At Home* ꝏ (Private, 1997, prod. John Porter) features the latter-day lineup and is for Phil Alvin completists—you know who you are—only.

influences:

◀◀ Big Joe Turner, Jerry Lee Lewis, Elvis Presley

▶▶ Big Sandy and His Fly-Rite Boys, the Rev. Horton Heat, the Flat Duo Jets, BR5-49

Daniel Durchholz

Blue Plate Special

Formed 1996, in Chico, CA.

Kevin Wright, guitar, pedal steel (1996–97); Charles Mohnike, guitar, drums (1996–97); Todd Clark, bass; James Vlahos, trombone (1996–97); Fred Stuart, vocals; Randall Keith, guitar (1998–present); Ken Charlson, piano; Adam Bankhead, drums (1998); Mike Newman, tenor sax (1998–present); Nathan Dreyfus, alto and baritone saxes (1998–present); Anthony Marchesi, vocals (1998).

Though it started more or less as a western-style swing band, Blue Plate Special fell apart, re-formed, dropped the pedal steel, and became a classic swing band in the jazz/R&B/big-band mode. The band wears its classic swing influences with fondness and skill—heavy on such touches as piano, horns, and smooth-moves vocals, Blue Plate Special would be just as comfy in a smoky, dimly lit jazz club as it would be in a bright, raucous dance hall. The boys certainly owe more to traditional swing than they do any neo–Louis Jordan, funk-punk, updated, overinflated incarnations inhabiting today's swing scene. And they certainly shouldn't be relegated to diners, regardless of their name (taken, of course, from the Jordan song "Boogie Woogie Blue Plate," which the band released as its first recording, a blue-vinyl 45 backed with Amos Milburn's "Don't Do It"). Blue Plate Special doesn't try to clutter its sound with modern or "alternative" influences, preferring to sound new by truly rebirthing the old for audiences who might not yet have heard the real thing. Though James Vlahos left to write for *National Geographic* magazine, he still writes charts for the band and his influence is heard throughout the band's disc, *A Night Out with . . . Blue Plate Special*. That album is loaded with originals written with a sense of history, shaken and stirred with some classic touches (like "Tango of Sorrow," with rhythm so vivid it inspires desires for a little cheek-to-cheek dance-floor action).

what's available: *A Night Out with . . . Blue Plate Special* ꝏꝏ (Slimstyle, 1998, prod. Jacquire King, Blue Plate Special) is anything but slung hash or you-know-what on a shingle. It's a deliciously jazzy disc full of bebop and blues flavorings more likely to cause finger-popping than Lindy hopping. "A Message for Paul Drake" conjures the *Perry Mason* theme; "The Hornet" is just a good old kick-ass instrumental. "Evening" is a standout, but "Work That Skirt" is swing in the true big-band sense.

influences:

◀◀ Louis Jordan, Count Basie, Wynonie Harris, Ike Turner & His Kings of Rhythm, Woody Herman, Benny Goodman, Artie Shaw, Bob Wills, Billy Jack Wills, Bill Haley, John Coltrane, Miles Davis, Amos Milburn.

Lynne Margolis

Blues Jumpers

Formed 1992, in New York City, NY.

Eldridge Taylor, lead vocals; Joe Geary, drums; Joe D'Astolfo, bass; Mike Girao, guitar (1992–93, 1997–present); Billy Rouse, guitar (1993–95); Nick Palumbo, guitar (1995–97); Jim Jedeikin, tenor sax; Matt Hong, alto sax.

One of the most popular East Coast swing bands, the Blues Jumpers have been garnering rave reviews practically from the start, regularly packing dance clubs with 1940s-garbed fans. The Bronx-based band members are former rockers (Lucky 7) and jazz musicians (Barrelhouse 6) who have also recorded with jazz bands led by swing stalwarts Illinois Jacquet and Lionel Hampton; as the Jumpers, they play songs by such neo-swing heroes as Louis Jordan and Cab Calloway. While still playing with the Lucky 7, Joe Geary and Joe D'Astolfo started this intended all-instrumentals band on the side. Nick Palumbo apprenticed with the band before breaking off to form his own East Coast unit, Nick Palumbo & the Flipped Fedoras.

what's available: The Blues Jumpers' sublime debut recording *Wheels Start Turning* ꝏꝏ (Ridge Recordings, 1997, prod. Joe D'Astolfo, Joe Geary) is a highly polished project that rivals the finesse of longer-established West Coast bands. Musicianship is flawless and first rate, and the unit satisfies the listener with its saucy mix of jump-blues classics and two ballads. Highlights include "Chartreuse," a jump-blues tune with lyrics that will make you chuckle; the catchy, chugging locomotive "High Ballin' Daddy"; the classic Roy Milton boogie "Baby I'm Gone"; and drummer Gene Krupa's rocking "Ball of Fire," which gives front-line horns a classy workout.

worth searching for: Although a seasonal album, *Swingin' Holiday* ꝏꝏ (National Music Distributors, 1998, prod. the Blues Jumpers) is a CD you'll enjoy year-round, especially Taylor's dramatic vocals on "You're a Mean One, Mister Grinch." If you can't find this CD in local stores, phone/fax National Music Distributors at 718-409-1172.

influences:

◀◀ Louis Jordan, Big Joe Turner, Cab Calloway, Wynonnie Harris, Royal Crown Revue, Big Bad Voodoo Daddy, Lavay Smith & Her Red Hot Skillet Lickers

Nancy Ann Lee

Tiny Bradshaw

Born Myron Bradshaw, September 23, 1905, in Youngstown, OH. Died January, 1959, in Cincinnati, OH.

Tiny Bradshaw's prevailing legacy may be as the author of such tunes as "The Train Kept A-Rollin'," which he cut in 1951 and passed down to Johnny Burnette, the Yardbirds, Aerosmith, and beyond. Big Joe Williams, Barney Kessel, Benny Goodman, Twisted Sister, Doc Severinsen, and Django Reinhardt have recorded his songs. Bradshaw began his career in the early 1930s, forming his own swing orchestra in 1933, and signing to Decca Records soon after. He served as a major in World War II, leading a 20-piece Armed Forces orchestra that toured abroad. Bradshaw's popularity increased in the late 1940s amid a rising tide of demand for jump R&B. He left the Savoy label, signing with King Records, and between 1949 and 1952 had hits with "Gravy Train," "Well Oh Well," and the instrumental "Soft." Bradshaw's popularity diminished with the advent of rock 'n' roll. Heart problems ended his career in 1958 and he died of a heart attack a year later.

what's available: Remarkably, given his sphere of influence as a songwriter, only one Bradshaw collection is in print in the U.S. *Great Composer—He Wrote and Played Them All* ♩♩♩♩ (King, 1994) offers 16 cuts from his King days. It features superb material; however, it does not include many of his finest moments on King.

worth searching for: *Breaking Up the House* ♩♩♩♩♪ (Charly, 1985) features several of Bradshaw's most glorious King sessions not found on *Great Composer*, including the title track, "T-99," "Walkin' the Chalk Line," and "Bradshaw Boogie."

influences:

◀◀ Cab Calloway, Wynonie Harris, Louis Jordan, Big Joe Turner

▶▶ Asleep at the Wheel, Johnny Burnette, Billy Wright, Little Richard, Tom Principato

Bryan Powell

Ruby Braff

Born Reuben Braff, March 16, 1927, in Boston, MA.

One of the few jazz musicians today performing solely on cornet, Ruby Braff is a remarkable classic-jazz stylist—fans and critics alike have said he's the most artistic cornetist to emerge since Louis Armstrong. Whether he's playing relaxed, mid-tempo swing, ballads, or up-tempo New Orleans–style tunes, Braff harbors a distinctive flowing, fat-toned, warm sound. Braff built his reputation in Boston during the 1940s before moving to New York in 1953. Although Braff's work, soloing in various bands and recording with trombonist/bandleader Vic Dickensen, was highly respected and critically acclaimed, jazz fans expected trumpeters to adhere to the Dizzy Gillespie style of playing. Thus, as a classic-styled player Braff had a difficult time finding work in clubs during the later 1950s. By the 1960s, Braff was working more regularly as a soloist, touring the U.S. and Europe with bands led by others. In 1973, he formed one of his few regular working groups, a short-lived quartet with guitarist George Barnes that fashioned its small-group traditional jazz after Louis Armstrong's Hot Five and other similar hot-and-sweet swing units. Following their final quarrel, the leaders broke up the band and Braff returned to performing as a small-group soloist and leading his own groups into the 1990s. In recent years, Braff has recorded as leader with elder swing stylists such as pianists Dick Hyman and Ellis Larkins, and younger players such as tenor saxophonist Scott Hamilton and guitarist Howard Alden.

what to buy: By the time Braff and Hamilton joined together for their 1991 recording, *Ruby Braff and His New England Songhounds, Vol. 1* ♩♩♩♩♩ (Concord, 1991, prod. Carl E. Jefferson), they had made a couple of successful albums together for the Concord label. Their liveliest remakes cover classics such as "I'm Crazy 'Bout My Baby (And My Baby's Crazy 'Bout Me)," "This Can't Be Love," and "Down in Honky Tonk Town." Recorded during the same studio session, *Ruby Braff and His New England Songhounds, Vol. 2* ♩♩♩♩♩ (Concord, 1992, prod. Carl E. Jefferson) features more of the same with 12 sterling performances from all on both catchy swingers and lush ballads. *A First* ♩♩♩♩♪ (Concord, 1985, prod. Carl E. Jefferson) was among the first of many sessions Braff has recorded with tenor saxophonist Scott Hamilton. These two musicians have a like-minded, easy-going approach to swing, and their talents for interpreting time-honored swing classics is impeccable. Top tracks for dance fans (though too short for real workouts) are "Romance in the Dark," "Dinah," "Shine," and the finale, a bursting jam on Count Basie's "Bugle Blues." *A Sailboat in the Moonlight* ♩♩♩♩♪ (Concord, 1986, prod. Carl E. Jefferson) is an eight-tune set that swings with abandon on intelligently improvised swing-jazz classics such as "'Deed I Do," "Jeepers Creepers," and "Lover Come Back to Me." The speedball pace of "Lover Come Back to Me" is a dancer's challenge.

what to buy next: *Being with You* ♩♩♩♩♪ (Arbors, 1997, prod. Arbors Records) finds cornetist Braff reminiscing on Louis Armstrong tunes with an all-star swing "little big band." Braff performs with his usual verve, contributes arrangements, and even sings on the Cole Porter ballad "Little One." Included are songs Satchmo helped make into classics, such as "Twelfth Street Rag," "Royal Garden Blues," and "Keepin' Out of Mischief Now." In his characteristic warm and intimate style, Braff is spotlighted on *You Can Depend on Me* (Arbors, 1998, prod. Arbors Records), a light-swinging, eight-tune session with a robust, toe-tapping interpretation of the Earl Hines title tune, perky versions of "That Big Butter & Egg Man" and "S'posin'," an up-tempo take on the Gershwin classic "The Man I Love," and agreeable renditions of "Little Old Lady," "Time on My Hands," and "Just You, Just Me." *The Ruby Braff/George Barnes Quartet Plays Gershwin* (Concord, 1975, prod. Carl E. Jefferson) contains 10 palatable swing versions of Gershwin classics such as "I Got Rhythm," "But Not for Me," "Somebody Loves Me," "Love Walked In," "Embraceable You."

what to avoid: Wait until you're totally enthralled with Braff's expert cornet renderings to pick up *Me, Myself, and I* (Concord, 1989, prod. Carl E. Jefferson) and *Bravura Eloquence* (Concord, 1990, prod. Carl E. Jefferson), gorgeous trio albums (13 and 14 tracks, respectively) with guitarist Howard Alden and bassist Jack Lesberg. The lush, lazy tunes performed on both CDs are best for his devoted jazz fans.

best of the rest:
Hustlin' and Bustlin' (Black Lion, 1955/1992)
Hear Me Talkin' (Black Lion, 1967/1992)
Cornet Chop Suey (Concord, 1991)
Controlled Nonchalance (Volume 1) (Arbors, 1994)
Live at the Regattabar (Arbors, 1994)

influences:
◀◀ Bunny Berigan, Bix Beiderbecke, Jimmy McPartland, Bobby Hackett, Buck Clayton
▶▶ Warren Vache, Jim Cullum

Nancy Ann Lee

Jackie Brenston

Born August 15, 1930, in Clarksdake, MS. Died December 15, 1979, in Memphis, TN.

"The Big Noise from Winnetka"
BOB CROSBY
1938
Bassist-songwriter Bob Haggart's whistling inspired by tray-spinning waiter at New York's Hotel President.
Swingin' SINGLES

Jackie Brenston's minor fame rests on a whim of fate. One of a rotating crew of hornmen who fronted Ike Turner's raw Mississippi Delta jump-blues combo, the Kings of Rhythm, Brenston had the good fortune to be taking lead as a vocalist when Turner blasted off on "Rocket 88," a chart-topping 1951 R&B hit that some longhairs believe is the first true rock 'n' roll recording. Made for Elvis Presley discoverer Sam Phillips, the record was leased to Chicago's Chess brothers and credited to Brenston, a mistake old Ike no doubt still rues to this day. Starry eyed, Brenston split from Turner's band but despite gigs with jazz pianist Phineas

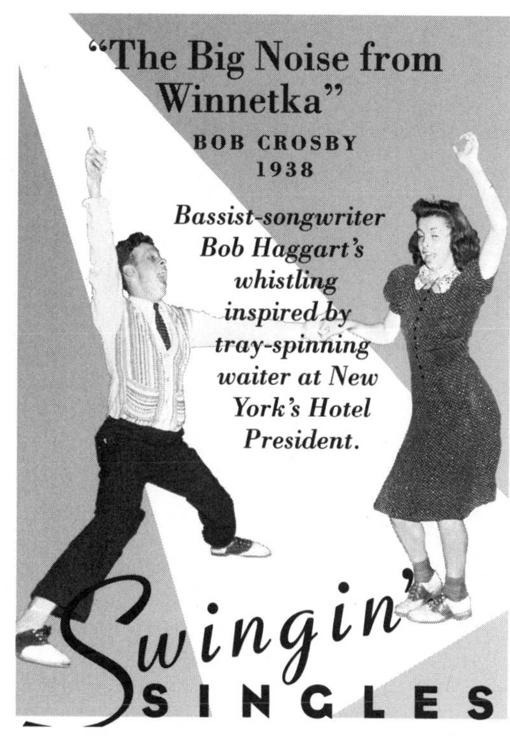

Newborn Jr. and guitar slinger Lowell Fulson, he went nowhere without Ike. Slinking back in the mid-'50s, Brenston drank heavily and left for good in 1962, just as Tina Turner's career took off.

what to buy: "Rocket 88" shows up on a variety of collections, but the true aficionado will ante up the big bucks for *Sun Records: The Blues Years 1950–58* (Charly, 1996, prod. Sam Phillips), a monstrous eight-disc, 202-track set that overwhelms the listener with everything from jazzy urban-piano R&B to backwoods gutbucket stompers.

what to buy next: Brenston rejoined Ike for sessions waxed for Syd Nathan's Federal label in 1956 and 1957, blowing baritone and singing on four tracks on *Kings of Rhythm* (Charly, 1991, prod. Syd Nathan).

influences:
◀◀ Ike Turner

Steve Braun

Teresa Brewer

Born Theresa Breuer, May 7, 1931, in Toledo, OH.

What in heaven's name is Teresa Brewer doing in a book on swing? Well, though Brewer initially made her mark as a cute

Teresa Brewer **(Archive Photos)**

girl singer with a string of nostalgia-oriented hits, as an adult, over half of her recorded catalog contains forays into jazz and swing. Critics may carp that Brewer's voice is too chipper and one-dimensional for these genres, but her legions of loyal fans say otherwise. During the late '40s and mid-'50s, Brewer was America's singing sweetheart. A teenager blessed with good looks, a perky disposition, and a sassy-but-sweet vocal style, she charmed adults and amazed her peers. Her run of hits not only established her as a powerhouse entertainer, but set the stage for the boom in teen-oriented music that would come later in that decade. In 1949, Brewer signed with London Records and recorded her classic "Music! Music! Music!," which sold more than a million copies despite a pressing-plant strike. She quickly followed with "Choo'n Gum," "Molasses," and "Longing for You," and, beginning in 1951, a string of hits for Coral Records (including her infamous tribute to Mickey Mantle, "I Love Mickey"). She also dabbled in country sounds with "A Tear Fell" and "Bo Weevil Song," and R&B with cover versions of Ivory Joe Hunter's "Empty Arms" and Sam Cooke's "You Send Me." Despite her willingness to expand her style, Brewer's youthful image was so successful her label refused to let her grow up. For every hit adult ballad she recorded, such as Joan Weber's "Let Me Go, Lover!" and Johnny Ace's "Pledging My Love," Coral saddled her with juvenalia like "The Hula Hoop Song" or "Pickle Up a Doodle." By 1961, she had left the label, and with producer-husband Bob Thiele, set out to record more serious grown-up sounds. Throughout the '60s, she mined the country and jazz markets, though her cute-as-a-button, perfect-pitch vocal technique never changed. Brewer semi-retired in the late '60s, cutting occasional singles, but Thiele brought her back in a big way the following decade, teaming her with jazz greats Count Basie, Dizzy Gillespie, Wynton Marsalis, and many others for a string of jazz and big-band LPs. Her '80s highlight, an LP recorded in London with Chas and Dave, Peter Frampton, and Albert Lee, featured Brewer's inspired rock remake of her first hit, "Music! Music! Music!" These days, despite the death of her husband (her most ardent and powerful supporter), Brewer remains ever youthful and cheery, and still performs before capacity crowds worldwide.

what to buy: The best of Brewer's hits from her early years at London and Coral Records are on *Music! Music! Music! The Best of Teresa Brewer* (Varese Vintage, 1995, compilation prod. Cary E. Mansfield, Marty Wesker). Eschewing the sticky kid stuff, this disc effectively showcases her versatility on material from perky sass ("Silver Dollar," "Ricochet"), to torch-song sophistication ("Till I Waltz Again with You," "A Tear Fell") and music-hall nostalgia ("Music! Music! Music!," "The Banjo's Back in Town"). Whether she sings like a broken-hearted chanteuse or a little girl sucking her thumb, Brewer is utterly convincing and occasionally compelling.

what to buy next: Brewer's later years as an unfailingly chipper pop and jazz singer are captured on *16 Most Requested Songs* (Legacy, 1991, compilation prod. Michael Brooks), which includes material recorded with Albert Lee and Peter Frampton.

what to avoid: The cobbling of classic tunes of the '40s into endless medleys makes *I Dig Big Band Singers* **woof!** (Signature, 1983/CBS Special Products, 1989, prod. Bob Thiele) a particularly tedious experience.

the rest:

Midnight Cafe (A Few More for the Road) (Sony Special Music, 1982/1995)
Best of Teresa Brewer (MCA Jazz, 1989)
American Music Box—Vol. 2: The Songs of Harry Warren (Red Baron, 1993)
Teenage Dance Party (Bear Family, 1994)
Good News: The World's Greatest Jazz Band of Yank Lawson & Bob Haggart (Sony Special Music Products, 1995)
Good Ship Lollipop (Sony Special Products, 1995)
It Don't Mean a Thing If It Ain't Got that Swing (Sony, 1995)

worth searching for: Brewer's tribute to Louis Armstrong, *Teresa Brewer & Friends: Memories of Louis Armstrong* (Red Baron, 1991, prod. Bob Thiele), features guest stars Wynton Marsalis, Freddy Hubbard, and Dizzy Gillespie on a rather fun compilation of tunes associated with the great Satchmo. Also, Brewer sounds fine on the variety of big-band and jazz standards assembled on *Softly I Swing* (Red Baron, 1992, prod, Bob Thiele), which has top tenor sax work by David Murray.

influences:

◀◀ Jo Stafford, Kay Starr, Joan Weber

▶▶ Connie Francis, Brenda Lee, Donna Fargo, Lorrie Morgan

Ken Burke

The Brigadiers

See: Horace Heidt

Clarence "Gatemouth" Brown

Born April 18, 1924, in Vinton, LA.

Clarence "Gatemouth" Brown is one of the foremost architects of modern blues guitar, second only to T-Bone Walker in terms of influential Texans. But with Gate, that's just the start of the story. A multi-instrumentalist (violin, harmonica, piano, mandolin, viola, and drums, as well as guitar), Brown embraces a host of musical categories, throwing Cajun, country, bluegrass, and jazz into his blues-dominated arsenal. It's a shame his 1997 album, *Gate Swings*, a jumping salute to the music Brown heard growing up in Texas, wasn't timed right for a chance to hit the charts with the Brian Setzer Orchestra, the Cherry Poppin' Daddies, and the others. Gate's versatility sometimes works against him—even his best albums often include one misguided venture—but it also informs everything he does with a wide-ranging sense of possibility. And he remains a damn fine blues guitarist.

what to buy: Brown returned to a big-band format more than 40 years after he first heard this stuff on *Gate Swings* (Verve, 1997, prod. John Snyder, Jim Bateman), with smashing, jazzy results. Though some modern swing fans lump "jump blues" and "swing jazz" into the same danceable category, this album really shows how the two come together. Among the highlights are superb, horn-rich covers of Duke Ellington's "Take the 'A' Train," Count Basie's "One O'Clock Jump," and Louis Jordan's "Caldonia." For a more thorough Gate collection, *The Original Peacock Recordings* (Rounder, 1990, prod. Scott Billington, Clarence Brown) has his 1950s work and is the best indication of how and why his playing was so influential on several generations of Texan guitarists. *Pressure Cooker* (Alligator, 1987, prod. Bruce Iglauer) reissues 1973 French sessions, in which Brown is backed by jazz greats including Jay McShann, Arnett Cobb, and Milt Buckner. The result is a predictably swinging set.

what to buy next: Brown stuck to horn-driven blues on his comeback album, *Alright Again!* (Rounder, 1982, prod. Scott Billington, Jim Bateman), which won a Grammy and quickly reestablished him as an American original and a musical force. Most of his many subsequent albums have been quite strong, but *Standing My Ground* (Alligator, 1989) stands out.

what to avoid: On *Long Way Home* (Verve, 1996), Brown is mostly just hindered by guest stars ranging from Eric Clapton, who lays down a few generic solos, to John Loudermilk, who sings a wretched version of his own "Tobacco Road." The album does, however, include several excellent and unexpected acoustic tracks. *Gate's on the Heat* (Verve, 1975) found him saddled with a lame, stiff band.

the rest:

One More Mile (Rounder, 1983)
Real Life (Rounder, 1987)
Texas Swing (Rounder, 1987)
Just Got Lucky (Evidence, 1993)
Man (Verve, 1995)
San Antonio Ballbuster (Drive Archive, 1995)

worth searching for: Brown has been around so long and created so many kinds of music, he winds up on several various-artist CD compilations. An excellent jump-blues archive, *Blues Masters, Vol. 5: Jump Blues Classics* (Rhino, 1992, prod. James Austin) stacks Brown's "Rock My Blues Away" with Big Joe Turner's "Shake, Rattle, and Roll," Louis Prima's "Jump, Jive, an' Wail," Roy Brown's "Rockin' at Midnight," and many other terrific R&B hits.

influences:

T-Bone Walker, Louis Jordan

Johnny Copeland, Johnny Winter, Albert Collins, Roy Clark

Alan Paul

Junior Brown

Born June 12, 1952, in Cottonwood, AZ.

There's something delightfully off-center about western-swing revivalist Junior Brown, and it's not just the angle of his cowboy hat. Maybe it's his instrument of choice, a self-invented combination six-string and steel guitar that he calls a "guit-steel." Maybe it's songs with such titles as "My Wife Thinks You're Dead," "Venom Wearin' Denim," and "What's Left Just Won't Go Right." Or maybe it's his unflappable allegiance to a brave vision that melds the hardcore honky tonk of Ernest Tubb with the string-bending, mind-blowing fury of Jimi Hendrix, with everything from Ray Price to Don Ho thrown in. Such a hip hybrid immediately made him a hero in his home base of Austin, Texas, but most of America—whose exposure to Brown has come chiefly from goofy CMT videos for "My Wife Thinks You're Dead" and truckstop songsmith Red Simpson's "Highway Patrol"—still thinks of him as a poker-faced novelty act. Listen carefully and you'll realize that beneath the tailored two-piece suits and the clever wordplay is a soft-spoken preservationist for the roots of country music and a hard-nosed champion for the brave struggles of working-class America who just happens to have a great sense of humor.

what to buy: "My Wife Thinks You're Dead" and "Highway Patrol" are the hilarious CMT hits that drew listeners to *Guit with It* (Curb, 1993, prod. Junior Brown), but the hidden treats are the pun-filled "Still Life with Rose," in which the singer tells an ex-flame she can't hold a candle to a painting of his new love ("Still life with Rose is better/Than life with you could ever be"), and the 11-minute instrumental "Guit-Steel Blues."

what to buy next: On *Semi Crazy* (MCG/Curb, 1996, prod. Junior Brown), Brown seamlessly works his stunning fretwork into his songs without turning them into jams, and showcases his narrative flair with his ode to blue-collar pride, "Joe the Singing Janitor," and "Parole Board," a hope-deprived prisoner's suicide lament that would even bring tears to Merle Haggard's eyes. However, the out-of-place, disc-capping medley of surf classics like "Pipeline" and "Walk Don't Run" is a conceptual wipeout.

Junior Brown **(© Jack Vartoogian)**

what to avoid: *Junior High* (MCG/Curb, 1995, prod. Junior Brown) is a five-song EP boasting barely discernible remakes of "Highway Patrol" and "My Wife Thinks You're Dead," designed chiefly to give radio the illusion that the label was working songs from a "new" album instead of the two-year-old *Guit with It*. It also fooled Grammy voters, who nominated it for Country Album of the Year, and consumers, who bought it without knowing that its much-superior predecessor existed.

the rest:

12 Shades of Brown (Curb, 1993)
Long Walk Back (Curb, 1998)

worth searching for: Brown and Red Simpson duet on "Nitro Express" from *Rig Rock Deluxe* (Upstart, 1996, prod. various), a collection of truck driving anthems sung by the likes of Don Walser, Buck Owens, Kelly Willis, and others.

influences:

Ernest Tubb, Jimi Hendrix, Red Simpson, Buck Owens

Cornell Hurd Band, BR5-49

David Okamoto

Les Brown

Born Lester Raymond Brown, March 14, 1912, in Reinerton, PA.

Best known as the house band on *The Dean Martin Show* and countless Bob Hope TV specials, Les Brown and His Band of Renown was arguably the most versatile orchestra of the big-band era. Brown's outfit could blow sweet and reedy like Isham Jones or Sammy Kaye, update the classics like Freddy Martin and Frankie Carle, and wail hot and brassy à la Glenn Miller or Stan Kenton. And you could always dance to it. A clarinetist, Brown led his first band at Duke University (the Duke Blue Devils), and worked as a professional arranger for orchestras led by Ruby Newman, Isham Jones, Jimmy Dorsey, Larry Clinton, and Red Nichols before going out on his own. Immediately, his sense of organization and professionalism won him the respect of bookers and top vocalists alike, and he scored some fair-sized hits with "'Tis Autumn," "Bizet Has His Day," and "Mexican Hat Dance." The turning point in Brown's career came when he hired Doris Day away from Bob Crosby's band. Their collaboration on such hits as "Sentimental Journey," "You Won't Be Satisfied Until You Break My Heart," and "My Dreams Are Getting Better All the Time" made them both household names. After Day's departure, Brown's orchestra continued to thrive with records like "I've Got My Love to Keep Me Warm" and their jumpin' theme "Leap Year." Never lacking for fine warblers, at one time or another Brown's orchestra employed Miriam Shaw, Betty Bonney, Ray Kellog, Lucy Polk, and novelty singer-saxophonist Butch Stone. During the '50s, while competing bands were retiring or being forced out of the business by rock 'n' roll, Brown's orchestra was busier than ever and won *Down Beat* magazine's Best Dance Band Poll five years in a row. They even hit the charts a few times, scoring a hit with an Ames Brothers remake of "Sentimental Journey." By 1962, Brown had tired of the road and settled his orchestra into a staff job at NBC, recording occasionally. His band's work behind Dean Martin, the Golddiggers, and Bob Hope was the best of any prime-time orchestra, and led in no small part to a big-band resurgence in the late '70s. These days, the retired Brown has handed the baton to his son, Les Brown Jr.

what to buy: The best-known numbers by Brown and His Band of Renown are on *Les Brown: Best of the Big Bands* (Legacy, 1990, compilation prod. Michael Brooks), including "Leap Frog," "Sentimental Journey," and "My Dreams Are Getting Better All the Time."

what to buy next: Brown's best singers (including Doris Day) are on *Best of the Big Bands: His Great Vocalists* (Legacy, 1995, prod. Didier C. Deutsch), which parades romance aplenty in "I Guess I'll Have to Dream the Rest," "I Got It Bad and That Ain't Good," and the flirty "Rock Me to Sleep." Equally fine is *The Essence of Les Brown* (Legacy, 1994, compilation prod. Michael Brooks), which contains some similar tracks, plus the good-humored jive of "Joltin' Joe DiMaggio." For Brown's Coral Records sound in the '50s, *The Les Brown Songbook* (Varese Vintage, 1998. compilation prod. Cary E. Mansfield, Marty Wesker) is a 16-track collection featuring singers Teresa Brewer, the Ames Brothers, Herb Jeffries, and the Modernaires. Brown remakes some of his most famous tunes for Columbia ("Leap Frog," "Sentimental Journey," and "New Mexican Hat Dance") but the arrangements are fresh and distinctly different.

what to avoid: The song selection is good but the sound is thin on the budget-rack curio *Giants of the Big Band Era* (Pilz, 1994), for completists only.

the rest:

The Uncollected Les Brown & His Orchestra 1944–46 (Hindsight, 1977/1994)
The Uncollected Les Brown & His Orchestra, Vol. 2 (Hindsight, 1978/1994)
Digital Swing (Fantasy, 1986)
22 Original Big Band Recordings (Hindsight, 1987/1992)
Jazz Collector Edition (Laserlight, 1992)
1944–1946 (Circle, 1992)
Greatest Hits (Curb, 1993)
Les Brown and His Band of Renown (Hindsight, 1994)
Live at Elitch Gardens 1959 (Status, 1994)
Live at Elitch Gardens 1959, Part 2 (Status, 1994)
Sentimental Journey (Columbia Special Products, 1994)
Anything Goes (USA, 1994)
America Swings—The Great Les Brown (Hindsight, 1995)
Band of Renown (Classic, 1995)
Lullaby in Rhythm (Drive Archive, 1995)
Sentimental Journey (MCA Special Products, 1995)
Live from Jantzen Beach (Jazz Band, 1998)

worth searching for: Featured vocalists Margaret Whiting, Johnny Mercer, and Jimmy Wakely bring extra zest to *The Les Brown Show from Hollywood 1953* (Magic, 1994, prod. various). Also, Brown fans consider the hard-to-find import *At the Hollywood Palladium* (Starline, 1995) one of the orchestra leader's many career highlights.

influences:

◀ Isham Jones, Jimmy Dorsey, Red Nichols, Glenn Miller

▶ Si Zentner, Randy Brooks, Les Brown Jr.

Ken Burke

Roy Brown

Born September 10, 1925, in New Orleans, LA. Died May 25, 1981, in San Fernando, CA.

Roy Brown's wild jump-blues and boogie records of the late 1940s and early 1950s were a spirited prelude to the joyous cacophony known as rock 'n' roll. His gospel-drenched cries and shouts predated Little Richard and Clyde McPhatter, and by extension, the soul sounds of the 1960s. Brown's first recordings for Gold Star Records reflected his early love for the smoother sounds of Bing Crosby and Billy Eckstine, but starting in 1947 he gave full vent to his wilder, more salacious influences, and indulged in fast, fast, fast tempos. A talented songwriter as well as musician, Brown wrote the classic "Good Rocking Tonight" and offered it to his friend and idol Wynonie Harris (who didn't record his higher-charting version until after Brown's rendition began to get airplay). Another friend, the great Cecil Gant, loved the song and made Brown sing it over the phone to Deluxe Records president Jules Braun, who signed the singer immediately. Between 1947 and 1952, Brown scored an impressive string of hits with wailing blues and jump tunes such as "Hard Luck Blues," "Boogie at Midnight," and "Rockin' at Midnight." After King Records bought out his contract in 1952, sales of his remarkable music declined dramatically; a later switch to Imperial Records led to the Top 40 pop hit "Let the Four Winds Blow," but a limp version of "Party Doll" stalled his momentum. He continued recording and touring throughout the '60s, supplementing his income by selling encyclopedias.

what to buy: Jump blues run rampant on *Good Rocking Tonight: The Best of Roy Brown* ♪♪♪♪♪ (Rhino, 1994, compilation prod. James Austin), an 18-track compilation of his biggest hits and most influential sides for Deluxe, King, and Imperial. Though the Rhino compilation offers much more, *Greatest Hits* ♪♪♪♪ (King Blues, 1997, prod. Henry Glover) is a nice budget starter set, with "Good Rockin' Tonight," "Hard Luck Blues," and "Rockin' at Midnight."

what to buy next: Brown's toughest tracks from his 1953–59 stint at King are on *Mighty Mighty Man* ♪♪♪♪ (Ace, 1993, prod. Henry Glover), a 23-track compilation with real-gone gassers "Ain't Rockin' No More," "Gal from Kokomo," and "Shake 'Em Up."

what to avoid: Brown never gave a bad performance in his life, but the sound quality on *Good Rockin' Tonight* ♪♪ (Pilz, 1993), which contains nine undocumented live and studio tracks, is atrocious.

the rest:

(With Wynonie Harris) *Battle of the Blues* ♪♪♪♪ (King, 1986)
The Battle of the Blues, Vol. 2 ♪♪♪♪ (King, 1989)
Battle of the Blues, Vol. 4 ♪♪♪♪ (King, 1989)
Greatest Hits ♪♪♪ (Classic, 1995)
Good Rockin' Brown's Back in Town ♪♪ (Aim, 1998)

worth searching for: The out-of-print *The Complete Imperial Recordings of Roy Brown* ♪♪♪♪ (Capitol Blues Collection, 1995, prod. Dave Bartholomew, compilation prod. Pete Welding) is a worthwhile 20-track collection including Brown's last chart record, "Let the Four Winds Blow," in addition to such later gems as "Hip Shakin' Mama," "Slow Down Little Eva," and "We're Goin' Rockin' Tonight," plus seven previously unreleased cuts. The import *Blues Deluxe* ♪♪♪♪ (Charly, 1993) has 24 tracks from Brown's big years at Deluxe and King, with some additional material from his mid-1970s stay at Gusto Records.

influences:

◀◀ Louis Jordan, Wynonie Harris, Bing Crosby, Billy Eckstine, Cecil Gant

▶▶ Bobby Bland, Hank Ballard, Clyde McPhatter, Fats Domino, Jackie Wilson

Ken Burke

Ruth Brown

Born Ruth Alston Weston, January 30, 1928, in Portsmouth, VA.

Though she is a versatile purveyor of jump blues, jazz, and pop music, Ruth Brown's most resonant legacy is her string of hits for Atlantic Records, which not only helped establish that label but also R&B's crossover appeal in the early rock era. Brown's first hits ("So Long," "Teardrops from My Eyes," "I'll Wait for You") were torchy jazz à la Billie Holiday and Dinah Washington, but as rock 'n' roll dawned, she developed her own rough style. Tunes such as "(Mama) He Treats Your Daughter Mean," "Wild Wild Young Men," "Mambo Baby," and "As Long As I'm Moving" were squealing, rocking paeans to youthful expectations, sexuality, and intimate groove. Brown mixed her bawdy rocking with sensual, romantic songs such as "Oh What a Dream" (written for her by Chuck Willis), "Love Has Joined Us Together" (with Clyde McPhatter), and "It's Love Baby." Her biggest hits were 1957's "Lucky Lips," a mainstream pop record that seems beneath her today, and the 1958 teen romper "This Little Girl's Gone Rockin'" (written by Bobby Darin), which eventually inspired a popular video on the Disney Channel. From the beginning of her career, Brown played to as many jazz audiences as R&B, and she attracted fans from all genres, including an impressed Frankie "Mr. Rhythm" Laine, who graciously dubbed her "Miss Rhythm." By the end of the 1950s, Brown's string of hits had played out, and she felt lost in the shuffle on Atlantic's crowded roster of stars. Signing with Phillips/Mercury, she recorded two solid LPs and had a minor hit single with her version of Faye Adams's "Shake a Hand" in 1962. Brown's career tailspinned badly after that. Though she cut well-regarded LPs for the DCC and Capitol Jazz labels, sales were slow and live gigs were not plentiful. To keep her family fed and clothed, Brown joined the Head Start program and trained to be a beautician while working as a maid, nurse's aide, cashier, and babysitter. During the mid-1970s, comedian Redd Foxx helped revive Brown's career by bringing her to Los Angeles and casting her in bit parts on his hit sitcom *Sanford & Son.* Brown also had recurring roles on the ill-fated sitcoms *Hello Larry* and *Checking In,* but her experiences in live theater would ultimately prove more rewarding. Roles in *Amen Corner* and *StaggerLee* won her critical praise and led to her Tony Award–winning role in 1989's *Black & Blue.* Yet, modern audiences probably know Brown best as Motormouth Mabel in John Waters's 1988 film *Hairspray,* or as the host of NPR's *Blues Stage.* Brown signed with Fantasy Records in 1988 and recorded four well-regarded discs featuring fresh interpretations of jazz and blues standards as well as occasional rip-it-up R&B. Her decade-old legal battle with Atlantic over unpaid royalties was finally resolved in her favor, and her old label helped set up the Rhythm & Blues Foundation as part of the settlement. Brown was elected to the Rock 'n' Roll Hall of Fame in 1991. These days, Ruth Brown still records and plays live dates whenever time and health permits (often with protégé Bonnie Raitt), and 1996 saw the release of her autobiography *Miss Rhythm.*

what to buy: The great string of records which resulted in Atlantic Records being nicknamed "The House That Ruth Built"

Ruth Brown (© Ken Settle)

are on the excellent *Rockin' in Rhythm: The Best of Ruth Brown* (Rhino, 1996, prod. Ahmet Ertegun, Jerry Wexler, Herb Abramson, Jerry Leiber, Mike Stoller, reissue prod. James Austin, Peter Grendysa), a 23-track compilation featuring her biggest hits from the 1950s as well as previously unreleased live versions of "(Mama) He Treats Your Daughter Mean" and "Oh What a Dream" from 1959. The excellent booklet will whet your appetite for Brown's revealing biography and the music is essential. Or skip right to *Miss Rhythm: Greatest Hits and More* (Atlantic, 1989, prod. Ahmet Ertegun, reissue prod. Bob Porter), a 40-song, two-CD set that not only includes all her Atlantic hits but also several pleasing LP tracks and four fine previously unreleased songs.

what to buy next: For a smart introduction to Brown's resurrection as a purveyor of soulful jazz, check out *Blues on Broadway* (Fantasy, 1989, prod. Ralph Jungheim), which earned her a Grammy Award for Best Jazz Female Vocal Performance, and mixes torch songs with such ribald sass as "If I Can't Sell It, I'll Keep Sittin' on It" and "Tain't Nobody's Biz-ness If I Do." Also, Brown proves she's lost none of her vocal chops or dramatic verve on *R+B = Ruth Brown* (Bullseye Blues/Rounder, 1997, prod. Scott Billington), a potent grab-bag of blues, R&B, and jazz featuring highly entertaining guest spots by Johnny Adams, Clarence "Gatemouth" Brown, and Bonnie Raitt.

what to avoid: *Fine Brown Frame* (EMI/Capitol, 1993, prod. Sonny Lester, reissue prod. Michael Cuscuna) is not so much a bad LP as it is a disappointing one. Brown is in fine voice, but the Thad Jones/Mel Lewis Orchestra distracts from her performance with its brassy jazz.

the rest:

Black Is Brown and Brown Is Beautiful (DCC Records, 1981)
Takin Care of Business (Mr. R&B/Stockholm, 1984/1991)
Have a Good Time (Fantasy, 1988)
Black and Blue—Original Cast Recording (DRG, 1989)
Fine and Mellow (Fantasy 1991)
The Songs of My Life (Fantasy, 1993)
Live in London (Jazz House Records, 1995)
You Don't Know Me/Touch Me in the Morning (Indigo, 1997)

worth searching for: Completists should be aware Brown makes guest appearances on several LPs by other artists. These include Charles Brown's *All My Life* (Bullseye Blues/Rounder, 1990, prod. Ron Levy); B.B. King's *Blues Summit* (MCA, 1993) and *How Blue Can You Get: Classic Live 1964–1996* (MCA, 1996); Manhattan Transfer's *Tonin'* (Atlantic, 1995); Benny Carter's *Songbook* (MusicMasters, 1995) and *Songbook Volume II* (MusicMasters, 1997); and Bonnie Raitt's *Road Tested* (Capitol/EMI, 1995).

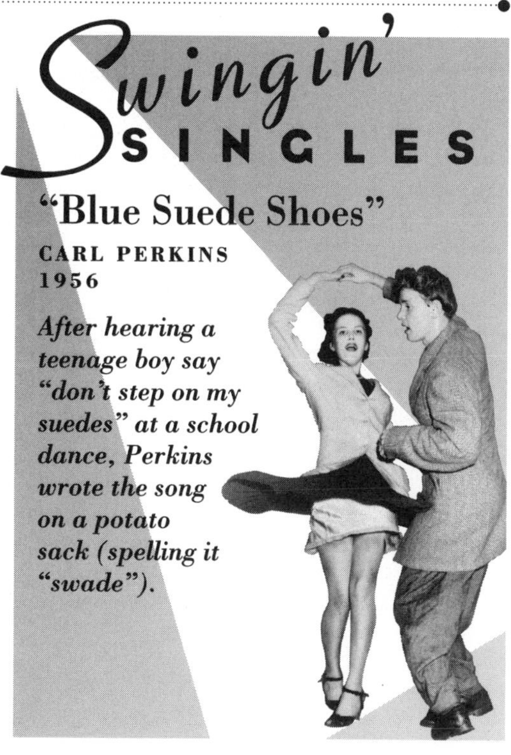
Swingin' SINGLES
"Blue Suede Shoes"
CARL PERKINS
1956
After hearing a teenage boy say "don't step on my suedes" at a school dance, Perkins wrote the song on a potato sack (spelling it "swade").

influences:

Bessie Smith, Billie Holiday, Dinah Washington, Sarah Vaughan

Irma Thomas, Little Richard, Koko Taylor, Bonnie Raitt

Ken Burke

Dave Brubeck

Born December 6, 1920, in Concord, CA.

History will recognize Dave Brubeck primarily as an innovator who redefined the jazz boundaries of counterpoint, harmony, and—most significantly—musical time. The Dave Brubeck Quartet transcended the 4/4, 2/4, and occasional 3/4 rhythms that had characterized the genre, creating masterworks in time signatures such as 9/8 ("Blue Rondo à la Turk") and 5/4 ("Take Five") that, while not uncommon now, were groundbreaking innovations in their day. However, it was as a pioneer of swinging, small-combo California jazz that Brubeck rose to fame in the early- to mid-1950s. Brubeck was a principal architect of the modern jazz combo, augmenting the piano trio with saxophone as a featured solo instrument. Along the way, the quartet crossed over from the traditional jazz audience to the then-untapped college market and to mainstream popularity, as evidenced by his appearance on the cover of *Time* magazine in 1954. The quartet demonstrated a relentless capacity for swing. Alto saxophonist Paul Desmond, who died in 1977, created a definitive alto sax tone, which he described as a "dry martini" sound. The "classic" edition of the quartet (including, beginning in 1958, Brubeck, Desmond, bassist Eugene Wright, and drummer Joe Morello) disbanded in 1967 after touring the world for the better part of a decade. During that time, they recorded and performed with Louis Armstrong, Carmen McRae, Charles Mingus, Jimmy Rushing, and others. After the quartet disbanded, Brubeck turned a portion of his energies to composing, creating religious and secular works for orchestra and chorus. He continued to perform and record in a jazz quartet setting, however, often with baritone saxophonist Gerry Mulligan. A 1970s version of the group, first dubbed Two Generations of Brubeck and later the New Dave Brubeck Quartet, featured Brubeck's sons, Darius, Chris, and Danny, on electric keyboards, bass (and bass trombone), and drums, respectively. Brubeck continues to perform in the U.S. and abroad and create vital recordings.

what to buy: Brubeck's definite recording is *Time Out* (Columbia/Legacy, 1959/1997, prod. Teo Macero), a landmark exploration of unorthodox time signatures that includes "Blue Rondo à la Turk" and Desmond's classic, "Take Five." The "blues suite" follow-up, *Time Further Out* (Columbia/Legacy, 1961/1996, prod. Teo Macero) is an essential companion piece. However, if swing is your thing, you'll want to begin with Brubeck's earlier efforts. *The Dave Brubeck Quartet featuring Paul Desmond* (Fantasy, 1986) repackages almost all of the material from *Jazz at Oberlin* (Fantasy, 1953/1987) and *Jazz at the College of the Pacific* (Fantasy, 1954/1987). It's a superb, 65-minute look at the early years with Desmond and includes a scintillating version of "Perdido." *Dave Brubeck/Paul Desmond* (Fantasy, 1982) offers 76 minutes of the quartet's early work (1952–54). *Interchanges '54* (Columbia, 1954–55/1991) compiles all of *Brubeck Time* (Columbia, 1954) and the out-of-print *Jazz: Red Hot and Cool* (Columbia, 1955).

what to buy next: *The Great Concerts* (Columbia, 1988, prod. Teo Macero, Cal Lampley) collects 74 minutes of cuts from live shows in Amsterdam and at Carnegie Hall in New York (both 1963) and Copenhagen (1958). Included is a vigorous 12-minute romp through "Blue Rondo" from the Carnegie Hall set. Brubeck's career is gloriously recapped on *Time Signatures: A Career Retrospective* (Columbia/Legacy, 1992, compilation prod. Dave Brubeck, Russell Gloyd, Amy Herot), a four-disc box set including 59 cuts in chronological order recorded between 1946 to 1991. Also included is a 76-page book, printed on heavy stock, detailing Brubeck's life and career and detailing the recordings included in the set. The previously unissued *Buried Treasures* (Columbia/Legacy, 1998) captures the classic quartet in an outstanding live performance in Mexico City in 1967. *We're All Together Again for the First Time* (Atlantic/Rhino, 1973, prod. Dave Brubeck, Siegfried Loch) is a live set recorded on a fall 1972 European tour, featuring both Desmond and Mulligan. Look out for 16 riveting minutes of "Take Five"; as with all of Brubeck's best live material, it's pure improvisation that remains true to the song's structure and character. Brubeck's 1990s releases on Telarc are consistently gorgeous. The gentle *Night Shift: Live at the Blue Note* (Telarc, 1995, prod. Russell Gloyd, John Snyder) showcases Brubeck's gift for blues piano.

what to avoid: There are a plethora of Brubeck anthologies on the shelves, such as the two-CD *Jazz Collection* (Columbia/Legacy, 1995, prod. Dave Brubeck) and *I Like Jazz: The Essence of Dave Brubeck* (Columbia/Legacy, 1991, digital prod. Michael Berniker). Choose carefully to avoid redundancy—clearly, you don't need them all.

best of the rest:

The Dave Brubeck Trio: 24 Classic Original Recordings (Fantasy, 1950–51/1982)
Stardust (Fantasy, 1951–54/1983)
Jazz Goes to College (Columbia, 1954/1989)
Brubeck Time (Columbia/Legacy, 1955/1998)
Brubeck Plays Brubeck (Columbia/Legacy, 1956/1998)
Dave Brubeck Octet (Fantasy, 1956/1991)
Dave Digs Disney (Columbia, 1957/1994)
Dave Brubeck Plays and Plays and Plays (Fantasy, 1957/1992)
Jazz Impressions of Eurasia (Columbia, 1958/1992)
Brubeck à la Mode (Fantasy, 1960/1990)
Near Myth/Brubeck Smith (Fantasy, 1961/1995)
Jazz Impressions of New York (Columbia, 1964/1990)
Bravo! Brubeck! (Columbia/Legacy, 1967/1998)
Last Set at Newport (Rhino/Atlantic, 1972)
All the Things We Are (Rhino/Atlantic, 1976)
Back Home (Concord, 1979)
Tritonis (Concord, 1980)
Concord on a Summer Night (Concord, 1982)
Music from "West Side Story" (Columbia, 1987)
Moscow Night (Concord, 1988)
The Dave Brubeck Quartet with the Montreal International Jazz Festival Orchestra: New Wine (MusicMasters, 1990)
Quiet As the Moon (MusicMasters, 1991)
Once When I Was Very Young (MusicMasters, 1992)
Trio Brubeck (MusicMasters, 1993)
Just You, Just Me (Telarc, 1994)
Late Night Brubeck: Live from the Blue Note (Telarc, 1994)

Dave Brubeck Trio & Gerry Mulligan: Live at the Berlin Philharmonie (Columbia/Legacy, 1995)
A Dave Brubeck Christmas (Telarc, 1996)
In Their Own Sweet Way (Telarc, 1997)
So What's New (Telarc, 1998)

worth searching for: *Marian McPartland's Piano Jazz with Guest Dave Brubeck* (The Jazz Alliance, 1993, prod. Dick Phipps) was taken from a National Public Radio program. It's an entertaining hour-long set that features Brubeck performing solo and in duets with McPartland. Approximately half of the recording is conversation and interview. Contact Jazz Alliance at P.O. Box 515, Concord, CA 94522. The aforementioned 1963 Carnegie Hall show, complete in one package, is available in the two-CD Japanese import, *Brubeck Quartet at Carnegie Hall* (Columbia, 1997), but be prepared to pay more than $45.

influences:

◀◀ Art Tatum, Cleo Brown, Fats Waller, Billy Kyle, Darius Milhaud, Duke Ellington, Erroll Garner

▶▶ Bill Evans, Vince Guaraldi, Ramsey Lewis, Jeff Lorber Fusion, Keith Jarrett, Keith Emerson, Cecil Taylor, Danny Zeitlan

Bryan Powell

Lord Buckley

Born Richard Myrle Buckley, April 5, 1905, in Tuolumne, CA. Died November 12, 1960, in New York, NY.

Lord Buckley, comedian and founder of the Church of the Living Swing, was an American original. He made his comedy routines swing with hep talk the way free-form musicians worked over jazz. Taking the stage in a pith helmet, waxed moustache, tuxedo, and looking every inch the British dignitary, Buckley jacked up his monologues with erudite King's English, hip slang, gangster argot, black dialects, and sub references galore. He called his technique "Hipsemantic," and used it to pack his routines with historical lessons on tolerance, prejudice, and the kinks of humankind. Jesus of Nazareth became "The Nazz," Albert Einstein "The Hip Eine," and years before the Stones sang "Sympathy for the Devil," Buckley played despot's advocate with "The Bad Rapping of the Marquis de Sade." Less a yuk-a-minute comic than a nightclub spell-weaver and social commentator, Buckley was every bit as revolutionary in style as Lenny Bruce, though nowhere near as successful.

Buckley got his start working burlesque houses during the '20s, and according to legend, he was Al Capone's favorite funnyman. The gang boss even set him up with his own club for a time. It was there he began to reinterpret such classics as "The Gettysburg Address" and "Marc Antony's Funeral Oration" with the syntax of black jazzmen. Working under the name Dick Buckley, he veered in and out of vaudeville and burlesque throughout the '40s, fine-tuning his character, and polishing his routines. He didn't officially become Lord Buckley until 1950, and once he took on the identity he never abandoned it—not even for a second. He referred to his home as the "Crackerbox Palace" (which George Harrison turned into a hit song), called his wife "Lady Elizabeth" and knighted his friends with such bizarre titles as "Prince Owlhead," "Princess Water Lily," and "Baron Clyde." Like Andy Kaufman's later absorption into his characters, it was all just a shuck, an extended piece of performance art which fed the comedy and garnered much-needed publicity. It nearly worked, too. Buckley had a feature role in the 1952 Ginger Rogers flick *We're Not Married*, appeared on network TV, and recorded several comedy singles that received airplay on late night jazz stations. Yet his career never really caught fire. His drinking earned him a bad rep with bookers, and an early drug bust resulted in the revocation of his cabaret card, so he couldn't work in New York. As a result, he remained something of a West Coast cult-hero, a fringe oddity best appreciated by those in the know. Under tragic circumstances, Buckley died just as Lenny Bruce and Mort Sahl were making smart, hip comedy fashionable and profitable.

what's available: Recorded just months before his death, *Bad Rapping of the Marquis de Sade* (World Pacific, 1996, reissue prod. Michael Cuscuna) contains selections ("The Chastity Belt," "H-Bomb") from Buckley's 1960 concert at the Golden Nugget, and two studio monologues ("Maharajah," "Scrooge") accompanied by bongos. The latter are especially fine, with the artist giving poignant and focused dramatic performances in several convincing dialects.

worth searching for: Buckley's first peak as a monologist came with *His Royal Hipness* (Discovery, 1992, prod, Jim Dickson), a collection of his groundbreaking routines ("The Nazz," "Jonah and the Whale," "Gettysburg Address") recorded during the early '50s. Some online services are still offering this out-of-print item.

influences:

◀◀ Harry "The Hipster" Gibson, Slim Gaillard, Babs Gonzales

▶▶ Lenny Bruce, Mort Sahl, Cheech and Chong, Andy Kaufman, Robin Williams, George Harrison

Ken Burke

Milt Buckner

Born July 10, 1915, in St. Louis, MO. Died July 27, 1977, in Chicago, IL.

Pioneering jazz organist Milt Buckner began as a pianist and arranger in the swing era. He arranged for McKinney's Cotton Pickers in 1934, but it was during a long and fruitful run with Lionel Hampton's orchestra in the 1940s (he reunited with Hamp a few times in later years) that Buckner really started to attract attention. Many successors, including jazzman George Shearing, used his unique "locked hands" piano technique. While associated with Hampton, Buckner penned the classic "Hamp's Boogie Woogie," among others. By the early 1950s Buckner was playing organ and fronting a small group of his own. The jumping R&B and blues of this era, including Buckner's minor hit "Trapped," has survived much better than the ballads. He continued to occasionally perform and record on piano (and vibes), but it was on the organ, both as a sideman with frequent partner Illinois Jacquet and on his own, that his exuberant personality was expressed most fully. His ability to create a swelling, pulsating flow of sound was perhaps put to its best use on the European recordings he made in the early 1970s with Clarence "Gatemouth" Brown and others. Often, Buckner could be heard on recordings grunting, singing, and shouting encouragement to himself as he played. Buckner, younger brother of the Jimmie Lunceford band's swing/hot sax star Teddy Buckner, played happy, good-time music that had more to do with lifting the spirits of the listeners than with technical virtuosity, though his skills were considerable.

what to buy: There's nothing in print under Buckner's name. A good sampling of his work with Lionel Hampton in the 1940s can be found on the excellent two-CD set *Hamp* (MCA, 1996). Buckner's 1970s work on both organ and piano, in a sideman role, can be heard to great advantage on a pair of fine Clarence "Gatemouth" Brown reissues, *Pressure Cooker* (Alligator, 1987, prod. Bruce Iglauer) and *Just Got Lucky* (Evidence, 1993).

what to avoid: You'd have to search pretty hard to find *Mighty High* (Argo, 1959), *Please Mr. Organ Player* (Argo, 1960), and *Midnight Mood* (Argo, 1961), but you needn't bother unless you're a completist or a big fan of mellow organ mood music.

worth searching for: Any of the French Black and Blue label 1970s releases featuring Buckner's organ are recommended, but they are hard to find. Best is *Green Onions* (Black and Blue, 1975, prod. Jacques Morgantini), which includes a wild, romping version of the title track in which Buckner sings of culinary delights and drives the point with swirling bursts of the mighty Hammond organ. Also, Illinois Jacquet's *Genius at Work* (Black Lion, 1971) is a fun, if not especially sophisticated, live set recorded at Ronnie Scott's London jazz club in 1971—a good display of the raw excitement generated by Jacquet and Buckner when they were loose. The LP *Rockin Hammond* (Capitol, 1956) collects some of Buckner's three-minute jukebox singles.

influences:

◄◄ Count Basie, Fats Waller, "Wild" Bill Davis

►► Bill Doggett, Doc Bagby, Jimmy McGriff, George Shearing, Dave Brubeck

Dan Bindert

Sonny Burgess

Born Albert Burgess, May 28, 1931, in Newport, AK.

On his Sun Records–era recordings, rockabilly singer Sonny Burgess sounds like a man trying to jump straight out of his skin. His yelping delivery (sort of Carl Perkins via Louis Jordan) and penchant for trumpet and sax solos made his records maniacally swing and jump as much as rock. Onstage, he was a mind-boggling sight. Sporting flaming red hair (dyed to match his suit, socks, shoes, and guitar), Burgess would scale a pyramid made of musicians and leap into the audience, and caterwaul on the floor while continuing to play fast, loud, and frenzied. In an era of flamboyant performers, he was one of the wildest. Burgess and his band, the Pacers, played rowdy variants of western swing and R&B in Arkansas dance halls and honky-tonks before landing at Sun Records in 1956. As with all his artists, Sun chief Sam Phillips had Burgess emphasize his fondness for black-oriented music, and a hot new rockabilly was born. His first record, "Red Headed Woman" b/w "We Wanna Boogie," featured call-and-response lyrics reminiscent of New Orleans jazz clubs, but with a pounding rock beat—it became his biggest seller. Though Ricky Nelson picked up on Burgess's excellent rockabilly version of "My Bucket's Got a Hole in It," no one else did. Burgess fashioned his greatest record, "Sadie's Back in Town" for Sun's sister label, Phillips International. Unfortunately, "Sadie," replete with manic giggles, galloping electric guitar, and a bizarre Donald Duck impression, was just too weird for the times. (Today it's considered a classic.) Burgess recorded dozens of spirited boogie and rockabilly songs at Sun; his versions of "One Night," "So Glad You're Mine," and "My Babe" top Elvis Presley's for authentic blues attitude, while "Find My Baby for Me" and "I Love You So" were distinctive, superior rockabilly performances. However, these amazing sides wouldn't even be heard until the Charly label began releasing them to rockabilly-starved Europeans during the late 1970s. Burgess left Sun in 1959 to play in Conway Twitty's band. He recorded country, rock, and some boogie for various small labels before he finally packed it in and took a regular job. He didn't fully reemerge until the '80s, when he teamed with Paul Burlison and other rockabilly musicians to form the Sun Rhythm Section. During the '90s, Burgess recorded well-reviewed solo discs with ex-Blaster Dave Alvin and a minor classic with producer Garry Tallent (of the E Street Band). No longer working a day job, Sonny Burgess tours the world.

what to buy: The concise *We Wanna Boogie* (Rounder, 1990, reissue prod. Colin Escott) includes Burgess's great early

Sun singles and such previously unreleased jumping boogie as "Mama Loochie," "Ain't Gonna Do It," and "Fanny Brown," which leer almost as much as they rock. Even better is the 25-song set *We Wanna Boogie: The Very Best of Sonny Burgess* ♪♪♪♪ (AVI, 1995/Collectables, 1999, prod. Sam Phillips, Jack Clement), which has loads of previously unreleased (in the U.S.) songs and some alternate takes that are faster and hotter than the original releases, not to mention a fine informative booklet.

what to buy next: Those wishing to check out the wild man's current style should try *Sonny Burgess* ♪♪♪ (Rounder, 1996, prod. Garry Tallent), a smartly produced set of fresh songs from Bruce Springsteen and Steve Forbert, with special guest appearances by Elvis Presley's legendary sidemen Scotty Moore and D.J. Fontana on "Bigger Than Elvis." Burgess sounds gruffer here, possessing less tonal snap than during his Sun days, but the strong material and backing musicians more than compensate.

the rest:
Tennessee Border ♪♪♪ (HighTone, 1992)
Arkansas Wild Man ♪♪♪ (Charly, 1995)

worth searching for: If you're heavily into the Sun sound (and what rational, tasteful human being isn't?), hit the import bins for *The Classic Recordings 56–59* ♪♪♪♪ (Bear Family, 1991, compilation prod. Colin Escott). This two-disc, 57-song compilation features everything Burgess cut for Sam Phillips's label, including early demos, alternate takes, instrumental sessions with Billy Lee Riley, and the inclusion of the odd country song or two. Completists should watch for the vinyl-only *The Flood Tapes 59–62* ♪♪♪ (Bear Family, 1988, compilation prod. Richard Weize), a collection of songs previously thought to have been lost in a basement flood.

solo outings:
Sun Rhythm Section:
Old Time Rock 'n' Roll ♪♪ (Flying Fish, 1987)

influences:
◄◄ Elvis Presley, Carl Perkins, Louis Jordan
►► Ricky Nelson, the Blasters, Josie Kreuzer

Ken Burke

Johnny Burnette

Born March 24, 1934, in Memphis, TN. Died August 1, 1964, in Clear Lake, CA.

Johnny Burnette went to the same high school in Memphis as Elvis Presley. He and brother Dorsey Burnette were troubled boys, sent to Catholic schools for discipline, not religion. But these two hardscrabble sometimes prize fighters—with guitarist Paul Burlison—led the Rock and Roll Trio, one of the first rockabilly outfits to emerge from local Memphis hillbilly roadhouses. Although the trio cut one of the great rock 'n' roll albums of the 1950s, the Burnettes would be left with very little to show for it; after the band broke up during an onstage fistfight between the two brothers, the Burnettes and their families moved to Los Angeles, where they showed up on Ricky Nelson's door one day, offering to write songs for the burgeoning teen idol. Such Burnette compositions as "Waitin' in School," "It's Late," and "Believe What You Say" became landmarks in the Nelson repertoire. But Johnny Burnette was destined to become best known for the sappy teen pop he himself recorded—but did not write—under the supervision of producer Snuff Garrett, especially two Top 10 hits, "You're Sixteen" and "Dreamin'." When he died in a boating accident in 1964, his career was in decline.

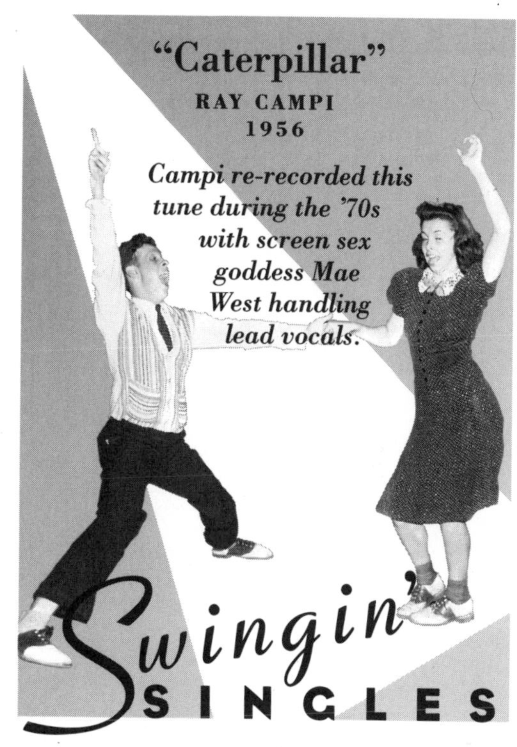
"Caterpillar"
RAY CAMPI
1956
Campi re-recorded this tune during the '70s with screen sex goddess Mae West handling lead vocals.
Swingin' SINGLES

what's available: His years at Liberty Records have been scrupulously covered with *You're Sixteen: The Best of Johnny Burnette* ♪♪♪ (EMI, 1992, prod. various), 25 songs and a 13-minute interview (huh?), although his best-known material is not necessarily his best.

worth searching for: The German import compilation of all the 1956–57 sessions by the Johnny Burnette Trio, *Rockabilly Boo-*

Don Byas **(Archive Photos)**

gie (Bear Family, 1989, prod. Bob Thiele, Paul Cohen) leaves little doubt how masterful Burnette's early recordings were.

influences:

Elvis Presley, Howlin' Wolf, Hank Williams

Eddie Cochran, Yardbirds, Stray Cats

Joel Selvin

Sam Butera

Born August 17, 1927, in New Orleans, LA.

Sam Butera made his name as the bandleader and tenor sax player for Louis Prima's band during the height of the trumpeter-singer's Las Vegas fame. He went on to record and tour under his own name, something he continues to do to this day. A native of New Orleans, Butera apprenticed under some of that city's greatest first-generation jazzmen; he claims to have even learned a few licks from Louis Armstrong. Butera's first professional gig came right out of high school with bandleader Ray McKinley; that job eventually led to his short tenures with the Tommy Dorsey and Joe Reichman big bands. Butera formed his own group in 1950, and began a four-year engagement at the 500 Club in New Orleans, which was owned by Louis Prima's brother. An appearance with Woody Herman's band led to a recording contract with RCA in 1953. Butera's early recordings feature his raucous, untamed fusion of roadhouse R&B and hard-swinging bop, but he never really caught fire on a national level. Prima first hooked up with Butera for a live date on the way to his first Vegas gig; upon arriving in Vegas, he hired Butera to lead his new backing band, which he called the Witnesses. Their act, which also featured vocalist Dorothy "Keely" Smith, was an immediate smash, and featured Prima's unique blend of risque jazz and Italiano-pop. Butera recorded seven albums with Prima over the next five years, and even appeared in a film with him called *Hey Boy! Hey Girl!* After Prima died in 1978, Butera forged ahead on his own, keeping the Prima legacy alive with interpretations of his ex-boss's most famous songs, jazz standards, and original compositions, all steeped in the loose-limbed Prima style.

worth searching for: While the music of Butera's longtime collaborator Prima is easily available—and, in fact, helped kick off the recent swing-dancing craze with Brian Setzer's version of "Jump, Jive, an' Wail" and the original's inclusion in a Gap television ad—Butera has yet to enter the CD revolution. The out-of-print classic *The Wildest* (Capitol, 1956) captures Prima and Butera at their finger-snapping, shucking-and-jiving peak. The German import *A Tribute to Louis Prima, Vols. 1 and 2* (Jasmine, 1994) is a spirited Butera run-though of some of Prima's most popular songs. And the import *By Request* (Jasmine, 1986) is a fine document of Butera's current stage act.

influences:

Louis Armstrong, Louis Jordan, Tito Puente, Benny Goodman, Glenn Miller

Cal Tjader, Perez Prado, Buddy Greco

see also: *Louis Prima & Keely Smith*

Marc Weingarten

Don Byas

Born October 21, 1912, in Muskogee, OK. Died August 24, 1972, in Amsterdam, Holland.

Tenor saxophonist Don Byas, an important figure in the jazz transition from swing to bop in the 1940s, is incredibly popular in Europe but inexplicably underrecognized in his home country. He came up in the 1930s through the bands of Lionel Hampton, Buck Clayton, Don Redman, Andy Kirk, and Count Basie. Early on, he sounded a great deal like his primary influence, Coleman Hawkins. But in the 1940s, he began shifting the sound by playing at Minton's Playhouse with Dizzy Gillespie and cutting some memorable early-bop duets with bassist Slam Stewart. In 1946 Byas went to Europe and, except for sporadic visits back home, stayed there for the rest of his life. Byas played and recorded regularly with other Americans living in Europe, with touring groups, and with local musicians. Because of his distant locale, Byas did not have the direct influence on younger tenors he might have otherwise had. But he always commanded the utmost respect for his virtuosity and individuality on his instrument.

what to buy: One of his last recordings, *A Night in Tunisia* (Black Lion, 1963/1989, prod. Alan Bates), is also one of Byas's best. Backed by a strong trio of European musicians, he stretches out in exciting form on the title track, "I'll Remember April," Tad Dameron's "Ladybird," and other standards. *Savoy Jam Party* (Savoy, 1946/1995) compiles sides Byas cut for Savoy in the mid-'40s and combines the raucous, happy energy of the best swing bands with the sophistication of early bebop. These recordings—made shortly before Byas went to Europe for good—suggest the level of jazz superstardom Byas would have encountered had he stayed in the States.

what to buy next: *A Tribute to Cannonball* (Columbia, 1962/1997, prod. Julian Adderley, reissue prod. Orrin Keepnews) is a tribute only in the very loosest sense; Cannonball Adderley's only relation to this album is his role as producer.

the rest:

Tenor Giant (Drive Archive, 1945/1996)
Walkin' (Black Lion, 1963/1992)
Don Byas 1944–1945 (Classics, 1996)
Don Byas 1945 (Classics, 1997)

worth searching for: *On Blue Star* (Verve, 1954/1991) is a 23-tune collection of mostly ballads recorded during Byas's early years (1947–52) in Europe. It was reissued on CD, but is already out of print and rather hard to find.

influences:

Coleman Hawkins

John Coltrane

Dan Keener

California Ramblers /Golden Gate Orchestra /New Jersey Casino Orchestra

Formed 1921, in OH. Disbanded 1931.

Arthur Hand, trumpet, leader; William Moore, trumpet; Arnold Brillhart, saxophone; Robert Davis, clarinet, saxophone; Ward Lay, string bass; R.F. Kitchingham, banjo, trombone; Lloyd Olsen, trombone, saxophone, cello; Adrian Rollini, saxophone, piano, xylophone; Jack Parker, violin; Bobby Davis, alto saxophone; Chelsea Quealy, trumpet; Stanley King, drums; Pete Pumiglio, clarinet; Red Nichols, cornet; Miff Mole, trumpet; Glenn Miller, trombone; other rotating members.

The California Ramblers weren't a major commercial force, but they were highly regarded by other bands, and some of the top talent of the early swing era passed through their ranks. Their best work provided an appropriate soundtrack to the days of bootleg gin, raccoon coats, and flappers. The 11-piece group derived its name from a lengthy appearance at the California Rambler's Inn in New York City. (Most of the original members were from Ohio and Pennsylvania, and the band never even played the West Coast.) But they also took many gigs under such pseudonyms as the Golden Gate Orchestra and the New Jersey Casino Orchestra. When they recorded as the California Ramblers, they expertly blended sprightly tempos with atmospheric half solos and musical asides that brought a high musical gloss to '20s-style jazz. In its rock-solid rhythm section, Adrian Rollini's fat bass sax playing provided the group's sonic signature. (So potent was Rollini's sound that when he departed, they had to replace him with a tuba player.) Stan King's light touch on the drums provided an easy feel just right for recordings, and their mix of reeds and horns foreshadowed the work of Benny Goodman.

The Ramblers never used an official arranger, they simply retweaked stock arrangements of tunes to their liking. As a result, their work, even on the most familiar of material, sounds fresh and peppy. Their recordings for several prominent record labels led to bookings at all the classiest college proms, hotels, and nightspots. They were the East Coast's "in" thing and all the heavy players of the era wanted to jam with them. At one time or another, their studio sessions featured appearances by the likes of the Dorsey Brothers, Red Nichols, Miff Mole, Glenn Miller, and Fud Livingstone (better known as the pop-eyed, mustachioed Jerry Colonna on Bob Hope's radio and TV shows). However, starting in 1927, individual members left to test the lucrative freelance market. Subsequently, an aggregation of the Ramblers stayed together (mostly as a recording unit) for a few years, but without some of their key men to shake things up, their style soon became old hat.

what's available: You'll swear you're in the middle of some old Hal Roach comedy short when you hear *Edison Laterals II* (Diamond Cut, 1994, prod. Richard Carlson, Craig Maier), a collection of 20 bouncy California Ramblers tracks c. 1928–29. Restored from rare Edison lateral discs, many of these sides are making their first appearance on record, and they provide a revealing glimpse into the hot jazz sounds of yesteryear. Such instrumental tracks as "You're the Cream In My Coffee," "Wishing and Waiting for Love," "Ain't Misbehaving," and "Me and the Man in the Moon" may sound cartoonish by today's standards, but they are quick-tempoed, full-bodied dance floor numbers featuring smooth blends and short, brilliant solos. Mole adds some tasty trumpet on "Button up Your Overcoat" (which features the forgotten line "stay away from bootleg hootch") and the soon-to-be-great Glenn Miller adds the brassy bite of his trombone to "Lady Luck" and "I'm a Dreamer (Aren't We All)."

influences:

Paul Whiteman, Bix Beiderbecke, Isham Jones, Jean Goldkette, Merry Melody Men

Dorsey Brothers, Glenn Miller, Red Nichols, Red Norvo, Beau Hunks

Ken Burke

Cab Calloway

Born Cabel Calloway III, December 25, 1907, in Rochester, NY. Died November 18, 1994, in Greenburgh, NY.

While you rarely see his name mentioned alongside the likes of Duke Ellington or Louis Armstrong, Cab Calloway was nevertheless one of the giants of 20th-century popular music—and a key touchstone for latter-day neo-swing. Purists frequently dismiss him as a novelty act, but that's about as relevant as criticizing James Brown for being repetitive and single-minded. If more people were as purely entertaining as Calloway, the world would be a much better (not to mention hipper) place. Cal-

Cab Calloway **(Archive Photos)**

loway was a key transitional figure during the '30s and '40s, when the big-band era was giving way to R&B. He was there to goose it along at every step, with acrobatic performances that predated Jackie Wilson and James Brown by decades. A consummate showman, he also more or less invented rap as a combination of jazz scat and minstrel-era "dozens" jive talk. And his popularity cut across racial lines in the South as well as the North, at a time when that was not a safe thing for a black man to do. Calloway always employed first-class bands, numbering Dizzy Gillespie, Lena Horne, Milt Hinton, Pearl Bailey, and Doc Cheatham among the notable players who passed through his orchestra. But where Calloway really made his mark was in the realm of style, contributing riffs, routines, and jive to the pop-culture lexicon that linger into the present day. His influence continues to pop up where you'd least expect it. Jim Carey's cartoonish star turn in the 1994 movie *The Mask*, for example, was little more than an extended Cab Calloway homage, right down to the moves, jive talk ("Smmmmokin'!"), and yellow zoot suit.

what to buy: The essential package is *Are You Hep to the Jive?* (Columbia/Legacy, 1994, prod. Bob Irwin), a 22-track collection drawn from Calloway's 1939–47 prime. Here is the Professor of Jive in all his hilarious glory, including "Everybody Eats When They Come to My House," "The Calloway Boogie" and the well-worn signature "Minnie the Moocher." The jokes are great and the music is absolutely killer—there ain't a bum note anywhere.

what to buy next: The 16-track *Cab Calloway—Best of the Big Bands* (Columbia, 1990, prod. Michael Brooks) broadens the picture a bit by filling in some of the gaps left by *Hep to the Jive*, with a fabulous cover of Ellington's "Take the 'A' Train" showing just how solid the Calloway Orchestra was on a purely musical level. Put this together with *Hep* and you've got a near-perfect two-disc Calloway sampler.

worth searching for: *Hi De Ho Man: Classics* (CBS, 1974, prod. Teo Macero), an out-of-print, two-record compilation, has lots of overlap with the two sets above. But it's still valuable primarily for the gatefold packaging, which includes period photos of the heart-stoppingly handsome Calloway lookin' sharp in his canary yellow zoot suit from the 1943 movie *Stormy Weather.*

influences:

◀◀ Duke Ellington, Count Basie, Louis Armstrong

▶▶ Louis Jordan, Little Richard, the Time, Joe Jackson, Phil Alvin, Squirrel Nut Zippers

David Menconi

Ray Campi

Born April 20, 1934, in New York, NY.

Ray Campi has been playing his unique brand of American roots music for more than 40 years. Whether he croons country heartbreak, boot-scooting western swing, or slap-back rockabilly, Campi gets to the heart of a song like no one else. Transplanted from New York to Austin, Texas, at an early age, Campi eagerly absorbed the area's unique cross-section of musical genres. By 1949 he and his band, Ramblin' Ray and the Ramblers, were already heating up their western swing with a little boogie on radio shows for KTAE and KNOW. So when rock 'n' roll hit during the mid-1950s, he had already mastered its root forms. Campi's first single for TNT Records ("Caterpillar" b/w "Play It Cool") is considered a genre classic today, but in 1956 it sold well only in Texas. Follow-up releases fared no better; a 1960 single on Dot earned him national exposure on *American Bandstand,* but the rockabilly rage had cooled by then.

Campi then moved to California and recorded on small labels there without much success. By the mid-'60s he had dropped out of the music business and began a teaching career in Los Angeles. Though he never really stopped recording, Campi didn't reemerge on vinyl until extreme rockabilly enthusiast Ron Weiser signed him to his label, Rollin' Rock in 1971. Campi's Rollin' Rock LP's were poorly distributed, handmade affairs, but they captured the authentic sound of true rock 'n' roll music, and were cherished by a vast underground of collectors and fans worldwide. Touring during occasional leaves from teaching, Campi eventually developed a solid fan base in Switzerland, Finland, Germany, and Spain (where his rare early records are sold for astronomical prices). On stage, Campi is the only rockabilly artist who plays a stand-up bass while singing, and he incites audiences by slapping it, standing on it, and gesturing with it as if the bulky instrument were a guitar. He gave a standout performance in the 1979 British documentary *Blue Suede Shoes,* though the film was scarcely seen in America. After several recent reissue CDs stoked interest among collectors and hardcore rockabilly fans (including singer-songwriter Rosie Flores, who occasionally performs with him) Campi seems to be finally getting the type of acclaim in America he has always had in Europe.

what to buy: Campi's style came of age at Rollin' Rock, and *Rockabilly Rebellion: The Best of Ray Campi, Vol. I* (HighTone, 1997, prod. Ron Weiser, Ray Campi) is the best of many reissues of his material there. Campi routinely crosses musical genres with playful enthusiasm and puckish good-humor on such tracks as "Rockin' at the Ritz," "Pinball Millionaire," and the Gene Snowden tribute "Quit Your Triflin'." Though available only in cassette form, *Gone Gone Gone* (Rounder, 1993, prod. Ron Weiser, Ray Campi) has many strong tracks from the end of the Rollin' Rock era, including "Wild Cat Shakeout" and "3-D Daddy."

what to buy next: An interesting overview of Campi's career, *Perpetual Stomp 1951–96* (Dionysus, 1996, compilation prod. Skip Heller), boasts the early western swing recordings "Toe Tappin' Rhythm" and "Give That Love to Me," the classic obscure rockabilly of "Caterpillar" and "Cat'n Around," and strong later versions of "Pan American Boogie" and "Guadalupe Boogie." Also, a more modified version of rockabilly and old-time country is on *Train Whistle Blue* (Sci-Fi Western/Lost Episode/Mouthpiece, 1998, prod. Skip Heller), which contains such strong rockabilly performances as "Tear It Down" and "Hot Water," but really is notable for bringing out the quieter, more expressive side of Campi's musical personality (on "Here Comes That Heartache" and "If Two Ends Meet," for example).

what to avoid: On *Rockin' around the House* (Rockhouse, 1994) the spirit is willing, but the sound is weak, and the Dutch band can't keep up.

the rest:

The Original Rockabilly Album (Magnum Force, 1990)
Ray Campi with Friends in Texas (Flying Fish, 1991)
Hollywood Cats (Part Records, 1994)
Rockabilly Rocket (Magnum, 1994)
Ray Campi 1954–68 Vol. I (Eagle, 1997)
Ray Campi 1954–68 Vol. II (Eagle, 1997)

worth searching for: The import *Taylor, Texas 1988* (Bear Family, 1988, prod. Ray Campi) features Campi making an effective return to his roots in folk and western swing. However, Campi's personal favorite is his collaboration with Rosie Flores on *A Little Bit of Heartache* (Watermelon, 1997, prod. Billy Troy, Ray Campi), a mostly acoustic tribute to Jimmy Heap and His Melodymakers first recorded in 1990. It will come as no surprise to Rollin' Rock aficionados that Campi played on recordings by a great many of his labelmates (such as Johnny Carroll, Tony Conn, and Johnny Legend), and *Rollin' Rock Got the Sock, Vol. I* (HighTone, 1998, prod. Ron Weiser), *Rollin' Rock Got the Sock, Vol. II* (HighTone, 1998, prod. Ron Weiser), and *Cat Music* (HighTone, 1998, prod. Ron Weiser) contain those recordings as well as songs by Campi not included on the his solo HighTone set. Campi also figures prominently on Jimmie Lee Maslon's *Salacious Rockabilly Cat* (HighTone, 1998, prod. Ron Weiser), 20 tracks of '70s roughhouse rockabilly recorded when Maslon was still a teenager. Finally, Campi plays Dobro on two cuts of Skip Heller's *St. Christopher's Arms* (Mouthpiece, 1998, prod. Skip Heller), an occasionally affecting alt-country disc.

influences:

◄◄ Mac Curtis, Johnny Carroll, Perk Williams, Gene Vincent, Elvis Presley

►► Rosie Flores, Dave Alvin, Col. Jim Silvers, Jackie Lee Cochran, Johnny Legend, Skip Heller

Ken Burke

Hoagy Carmichael

Born Howard Hoagland Carmichael, November 22, 1899, in Bloomington, IN. Died December 28, 1981, in Palm Springs, CA.

Cole Porter and Irving Berlin, two of America's most beloved song writers, wrote their standards purely for pop purposes, often for the movies and Broadway shows. Hoagy Carmichael, their contemporary, was a different kind of American character—he was a jazz cat who loved Dixieland music in general, cornetist Bix Beiderbecke in particular, and he really knew how to swing. In that spirit, he penned "Georgia on My Mind," "Rockin' Chair," "Heart and Soul," and dozens of others. Countless singers, from Frank Sinatra to Willie Nelson, took on his 1927 composition "Stardust," and Ray Charles made "Georgia on My Mind" a signature ballad.

Carmichael was born into a poor family, and his mother encouraged his piano-playing talent at an early age. Though he briefly considered a law career, he couldn't get jazz out of his head, and took ragtime lessons and led several Indiana University bands. In 1922 he met Beiderbecke, who recorded his first song, "Riverboat Shuffle"; he gave up law for good when he heard a Red Nichols version of his "Washboard Blues" and determined he could make more money doing something fun. Unlike Porter and Berlin, Carmichael was a prolific (if nasal-voiced) performer of his own songs. He became enough of a personality to land roles (as a pianist and singer, surprisingly enough) in *To Have and Have Not, Johnny Angel, The Best Years of Our Lives,* and a dozen other films. In the 1960s rock eliminated the need for Carmichael's jazz-pop-standard songwriting style—although it was eventually taken up in Nashville—but the composer didn't let it bother him. He retired to Palm Springs in the 1970s, where he played golf and lived the easy life until his death in 1981.

what to buy: The consummate Carmichael collection is *The Classic Hoagy Carmichael* (Smithsonian, 1994, prod. John Hasse), which, in addition to 10 solo performances, includes interpretations by Louis Armstrong, Mel Tormé, Billie Holiday, Wynton Marsalis, and many, many others. The three-disc set includes an excellent 64-page biography, and the six versions of "Stardust" demonstrate the diverse reach good songwriting can have.

Hoagy Carmichael **(Archive Photos)**

what to buy next: Though *The Classic Hoagy Carmichael* overlaps with and frequently trumps smaller collections, *Stardust & Much More* (RCA Bluebird, 1989, prod. Orrin Keepnews) is noteworthy for its original Carmichael performances. There's a 1933 version of "Stardust," for example, and a 1929 "Rockin' Chair."

what to avoid: *The Stardust Road* (MCA, 1982, prod. various) is a run-of-the-mill greatest-hits collection, rendered irrelevant by more recent CD packages.

best of the rest:
Hoagy Sings Carmichael (Blue Note, 1995)

worth searching for: *Song Is Hoagy Carmichael* (Living Era, 1992, prod. various) features Armstrong and the Mills Brothers, and the more-fun *Mr. MusicMaster* (Pearl, 1993) has Bob Hope and Bing Crosby.

influences:

◀◀ Cole Porter, Irving Berlin, Bix Beiderbecke, Duke Ellington, Louis Armstrong, Benny Goodman, Tommy Dorsey, Glenn Miller

▶▶ Ray Charles, Harlan Howard, Willie Nelson, Frank Sinatra

Steve Knopper

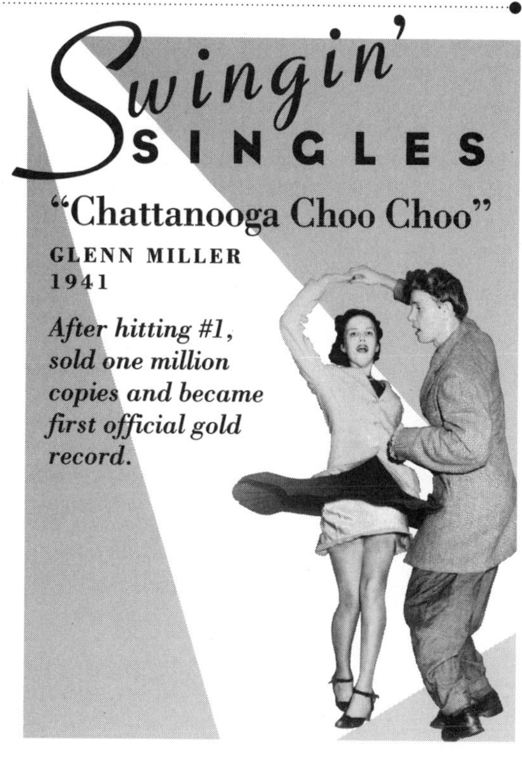

Swingin'
SINGLES
"Chattanooga Choo Choo"
GLENN MILLER
1941
After hitting #1, sold one million copies and became first official gold record.

Wynona Carr

Born August 23, 1924 in Cleveland, OH. Died May 12, 1976 in Cleveland, OH.

Wynona Carr didn't score many hits in her career, but she was an innovative force in both gospel and R&B music. A prolific and creative songwriter, Carr caused a sensation in the gospel field with "The Ball Game," a metaphor-laden account of the struggle between Jesus and Satan. While other performers mined sacred songs for pop melodies, she transformed such secular tunes as "St. James Infirmary" and "Good Rockin' Tonight" into spirituals, while retaining much of their blues and jazz flavor. Initially a soloist with the Wilson Jubilee singers, Carr also worked as a choir director for Rev. C.L. Franklin's New Bethel Baptist Church, where her emotive blues and jazz stylings made quite an impression on the minister's daughter, Aretha. Carr was dubbed "Sister Wynona" by Specialty Records boss Art Rupe to identify her in the same category as Sister Rosetta Tharpe. She hated the name, but kept it during the length of her sacred song career (c. 1949–54) to please Rupe.

Carr was too young, talented, and downright sexy to be strictly confined to gospel music. During the mid-'50s, she turned her deep, expressive contralto to the R&B market, where her bluesy ballad "Should I Ever Love Again" became a substantial hit. However, just as that record took off, a two-year bout with tuberculosis stalled her career. As a result, some wonderful, rowdy jumpers like "Jump Jack Jump!," "Boppity Bop (Boogity Boop)," "Ding Dong Daddy," and "Nursery Rhyme Rock" became little more than regional jukebox favorites. Her best work during this period helped fan the flames of the nascent soul explosion of the '60s, but Carr herself was unable to capitalize. She signed with Frank Sinatra's Reprise label in 1960, but after her only LP for the label (featuring charts by Neal Hefti) flopped, she drifted from the national music scene into obscurity. Carr coached choirs and sang in Cleveland nightspots until her death.

what to buy: The best of Carr's secular work, including her hit "Should I Ever Love Again," resides on *Jump Jack Jump!* (Specialty, 1985/1996, prod. Art Rupe, Bumps Blackwell, Sonny Bono), a 24-song helping of jump blues, R&B, and gospel-oriented rock 'n' roll recorded between 1955–59. Though this is no longer in the label's catalog, many on-line and catalog services still make it available.

what to buy next: Sister Wynona's greatest gospel recordings are on *Dragnet for Jesus* (Specialty, 1992, compilation prod. Lee Hildebrand, Opal Nations), a remarkable 26-track collection with her hit "The Ball Game." Tunes such as "I Heard the News (Jesus Is Coming Again)" and "Each Day," with stinging acoustic guitar licks, paved her entry into secular music. Among the previously unreleased tracks is the clever title track, which uses the theme from the TV show to frame a song of spiritual pleading, and "15 Rounds for Jesus," another fine sports-metaphor spiritual. Also included is a home demo of "Just a Few More Days," bookended by the singer's charming comments to label head Art Rupe.

worth searching for: If you can't get enough of Carr's scintillating salvation sound, check out Brother Joe May's *Thunderbolt of the Midwest* ♪♪♪ (Specialty, 1992, prod. Art Rupe), which has Sister Wynona dueting with May on "What Do You Know about Jesus?" and "It's All Right."

influences:

◀ Sister Rosetta Tharpe, Marie Knight, Faye Adams, Brother Joe May, LaVern Baker

▶ Aretha Franklin, Sam Cooke, Della Reese

Ken Burke

Benny Carter

Born Bennett Lester Carter August 8, 1907, in New York, NY.

A multi-instrumentalist, arranger, composer, educator, and bandleader, Benny Carter is deeply entrenched in the swing tradition, thriving successfully in a 70-year jazz career. As a soloist, he's considered, along with the revered Johnny Hodges, one of the swing-era models for alto saxophone. Many bands have performed Carter's music since the 1930s, when his arrangements appeared on recordings by seminal swing bandleaders Benny Goodman, Count Basie, Duke Ellington, Glenn Miller, Gene Krupa, and Tommy Dorsey. Carter has also provided arrangements for jazz divas Billie Holiday, Ella Fitzgerald, Sarah Vaughan, Peggy Lee, and others. His luxuriant, warm alto sax tone, flawless trumpet technique, and copious talents as composer-arranger distinguish him as one of the most important influences to rise from the jazz scene of the 1930s.

From his career start in the 1920s, Carter gained experience as a sideman in top New York bands and made his recording debut in 1927 with Charlie Johnson's orchestra, then based at the famous Harlem nightspot, Small's Paradise. After joining Fletcher Henderson's orchestra, he took over Don Redman's arranging duties, then briefly became musical director of the important Detroit-based unit, McKinney's Cotton Pickers, before returning to New York in 1932 and forming his own band. Already experienced on alto sax, Carter returned to his first instrument, the trumpet. In two years his trumpet performances rivaled his saxophone finesse. Swing stars such as Chu Berry, Teddy Wilson, Sid Catlett, and Dicky Wells passed through this band, but financial difficulties, especially during the Depression, forced the band's breakup by late 1934. During a European tour that began in 1935, Carter served as staff arranger for the BBC dance orchestra (1936–38), a role that helped spread jazz overseas. By the time Carter returned to the U.S. in 1938, the big-band sound he had helped shape was sweeping the country. He formed another splendid dance orchestra which hunkered down in Harlem's famed Savoy Ballroom during 1939 and 1940. Carter headed for Hollywood to work on the 1943 motion picture, *Stormy Weather*, his first of many film scores. He settled permanently in Southern California, working in television and forming a band there that included modernists such as Miles Davis, J. J. Johnson, Max Roach, and Art Pepper. Carter gave up full-time leadership of a big band in 1946, but continued to tour as soloist and with all-star bands.

what to buy: Carter has more than 70 albums in print, about half of which are on import labels. Many of Carter's domestic recordings are tame by today's swing standards. Yet, some, like *Live and Well in Japan* ♪♪♪♪♪ (Pablo, 1978/Original Jazz Classics, 1992, prod. Benny Carter), swing ferociously. This disc captures his jazz big band in a high-energy performance before a receptive Tokyo audience on April 29, 1977. An amusing three-tune medley, "Tribute to Louis Armstrong," features Anderson's trumpet solo and Newman's fine vocal impersonation of Satchmo on "When You're Smiling." But the romping version of Johnny Hodges's "Squatty Roo," and the definitive, grandly hip finale, an 11-minute version of Duke Ellington's "It Don't Mean a Thing (If It Ain't Got That Swing)," make this a must-own CD. *Benny Carter: The King* ♪♪♪♪♪ (Pablo, 1976/Original Jazz Classics, 1996, prod. Norman Granz), a Carter-led sextet date with revered jazz innovators, marked Carter's return to performing after years of writing and arranging. His first album as leader after a 10-year hiatus from recording, it features Carter's arrangement of tunes such as "A Walkin' Thing," "My Kind of Trouble Is You," and "Easy Money." A solidly crafted swing session, it features smartly improvised solos that add to the energy and emotion.

what to buy next: Recorded in Los Angeles in May 1994, *Elegy in Blue* ♪♪♪♪ (MusicMasters, 1994, prod. Ed Berger) is an engaging mixture of 10 ballads and hearty swingers that Carter dedicates to his late peers. Danceable tracks include medium swingers, "Did You Call Her Today?" (dedicated to the influential saxophonist Ben Webster) and "Little Jazz" (for famed trumpeter Roy Eldridge), and an up-tempo, riffing number "Good Queen Bess" (honoring Johnny Hodges). "Undecided," a hot track devoted to trumpeter Charlie Shavers, captures Carter at his best. It contains trumpeter Harry "Sweets" Edison's finest solo, and the music is light, sophisticated, and

Benny Carter **(Archive Photos)**

tastefully swinging. *Jazz Giant* (Contemporary, 1957–58/ Original Jazz Classics, 1987, prod. Lester Koenig) features Carter playing alto sax and trumpet on sessions recorded in the late 1950s with top jazz stars, including Ben Webster (tenor sax) and Barney Kessel. While most of the tunes are light to medium swingers rather than hot, danceable tracks, fine playing by Carter (especially his trumpet renderings on "I'm Coming Virginia,") and his original tunes (the deep-grooved Carter classic "A Walkin' Thing," and his bop-based swinger, "Blues My Naughty Sweety Gives to Me") make this an enjoyable armchair listen.

what to avoid: Don't be misled by the album title of *Swingin' the '20s* (Contemporary, 1958/Original Jazz Classics, 1988, prod. Lester Koenig). This disc, while perhaps worthwhile for jazz devotees and Carter collectors, is more relaxed than rabble-rousing.

best of the rest:

3-4-5 The Verve Small Group Sessions (Verve, 1955/1991)
Montreux 1977 (Pablo, 1977/Original Jazz Classics, 1989)
A Gentleman and His Music (Concord, 1985)
In the Mood for Swing (MusicMasters, 1987)
Benny Carter Meets Oscar Peterson (Pablo, 1987/Original Jazz Classics, 1995)
My Kind of Trouble (Pablo, 1988/Original Jazz Classics, 1989)
Songbook (MusicMasters, 1996)

worth searching for: The three-CD compilation from Carter's early career years, *Benny Carter: The Complete Recordings, 1930–40, Volume I* (Various, 1930–40/Charly/Affinity, 1991, prod. Francis Hood, Joop Visser) is recommended for fans who love digging for out-of-print discs. Documenting Carter's beginning years, disc one includes his performances with the Chocolate Dandies, with McKinney's Cottonpickers, with his own 1933 orchestra; it features his vocals and instrumental solos on alto sax, clarinet, and trumpet. Disc two represents Carter's work under his own name, with recording sessions in New York City, London, and Copenhagen. The third disc includes sessions recorded in London, Copenhagen, and Stockholm, and is the least interesting of the set.

influences:

◀◀ Bubber Miley, Bill Challis, Frank Trumbauer

▶▶ Miles Davis, Stan Getz, Bob Wilber, Phil Woods, Bobby Watson

Nancy Ann Lee

Casa Loma Orchestra

See: Glen Gray & the Casa Loma Orchestra

Doc Cheatham

Born Adolphus Anthony Cheatham, June 13, 1905, in Nashville, TN. Died June 2, 1997, in Washington, DC.

With a career dating to the 1920s, trumpeter Doc Cheatham was one of the few jazzmen who could say he had lived through all the major stylistic periods in jazz. When he was 15 years old, Cheatham found himself working with a traveling carnival, followed by stays with such prestigious talents as Chick Webb, Teddy Wilson, and Benny Carter. He spent a large part of the '30s as lead trumpeter with Cab Calloway's popular swing unit, and over the next several decades came into contact with many of the major soloists of the time. During a stint at Boston's Storyville, Charlie Parker sat in with the trumpeter's Dixieland group. Cheatham was also one of many musicians to appear on the historic *Sound of Jazz* TV show. In addition the early '60s found him working in a Latin vein with the ensembles of Machito, Perez Prado, and Herbie Mann. Oddly enough, it wasn't until the trumpeter was in his 70s that he actually began to hit his stride as a solo artist, recording for various labels in a bristling, brassy style and continuing to improve his range and inventiveness well into his 90s. Never content to be idle, Cheatham led a Sunday brunch session at New York's Sweet Basil for many years and performed up to the last weeks of his long and productive life.

what to buy: *The 87 Years of Doc Cheatham* (Columbia, 1993, prod. Phil Schaap) can certainly be considered the finest solo effort of the trumpeter's career. It's one of the few dates he led during his lifetime, and he fronts his working band (even singing a few chestnuts) with joy and panache. A charming and highly successful meeting of trumpeters from two distinct generations, the New Orleans session documented on *Doc Cheatham and Nicholas Payton* (Verve, 1997, prod. Andrea du Plessis, Jerry Block, George Hocutt) shows the obvious mutual admiration between the two men. An excellent cast of Crescent City players helps make this one a real keeper.

what to buy next: The seeds of the Payton-Cheatham encounter were laid in 1961 when Doc paired with Duke Ellington trumpeter Shorty Baker for the relaxed, harmonious *Shorty and Doc* (Prestige-Swingville, 1961/Original Jazz Classics, 1994, prod. Esmond Edwards).

best of the rest:

Duets and Solos (Sackville, 1976–79)
Black Beauty (Sackville, 1980)
The Fabulous Doc Cheatham (Parkwood, 1983)
Tribute to Billie Holiday (Kenneth, 1987)
Tribute to Louis Armstrong (Kenneth, 1988)
You're a Sweetheart (Sackville, 1992)
Swinging down in New Orleans (Jazzology, 1995)
At Sweet Basil (Jazzology, 1997)
Mood Indigo (Viper's Nest, 1998)

influences:

⏪ Louis Armstrong, Henry "Red" Allen, Jabbo Smith

⏩ Bobby Hackett, Yank Lawson, Billy Butterfield, Ruby Braff, Nicholas Payton

Chris Hovan

Cherry Poppin' Daddies

Formed 1989, in Eugene, OR.

Steve Perry, vocals, guitars; Dan Schmid, bass; Jason Moss, guitar; Dana Heitman, trumpet; Sean Flannery, alto saxophone; Ian Early, alto and baritone saxophones; Dustin Lanker, keyboards (1989–98); Johnny Goetchis, keyboards (1998–present).

The great swing revival of 1998 had three primary beneficiaries: the Brian Setzer Orchestra, Big Bad Voodoo Daddy, and the Cherry Poppin' Daddies, the last who had been playing horn-heavy jump blues longer than any of them. Touring for years in small clubs and theaters, the Daddies pre-dated both the *Swingers* movie and the Squirrel Nut Zippers' 1997 smash single "Hell," finally earning a hit of their own, the snappy "Zoot Suit Riot." For years before that, the Daddies' realization that the horns in early '60s ska and late '40s swing could be easily merged into modern hipster dance music was either too far ahead or too far behind the times. They toured nonstop while Big Bad Voodoo Daddy and the Royal Crown Revue received contracts from major record labels. Their mainstream success came after they suppressed their punk irreverence (like the Beastie Boys, they rolled giant phalluses on stage for a while). While the Cherry Poppin' Daddies' name doesn't exactly conjure apple-cheeked visions of the Andrew Sisters' "Boogie Woogie Bugle Boy," they've become one of the neo-swing movement's primary pillars.

what to buy: The title of *Zoot Suit Riot: The Swingin' Hits of the Cherry Poppin' Daddies* 🦴🦴🦴🦴 (Universal, 1997, prod. Steve Perry) was presumptuous when the album first came out, because the Daddies had no hits to speak of. It's terrific swing music, though, more jump blues than '30s big band. Although singer Steve Perry (no relation to the dude from Journey) lacks the drop-dead talent of great swing vocalists such as Frank Sinatra and Rudy Vallee, he compensates with enthusiasm and personality.

what to buy next: *Rapid City Muscle Car* 🦴🦴🦴 (Space Age Bachelor Pad, 1994) plays up the ska and (slightly) plays down the big-band sound, but maintains the goofiness—"Sockable Face Club" and "Hazel, South Dakota" have the sprightliest jump.

what to avoid: *Ferociously Stoned* 🦴🦴 (Space Age Bachelor Pad, 1990) has its funny bits—such as "Flovilla Thatch vs. the Garbage Man" and "Teenage Brain Surgeon"—but the sound quality is poor and it's unclear whether the Daddies want to play ska, swing, or rock.

the rest:

Kids on the Street 🦴🦴🦴 (Space Age Bachelor Pad, 1995)

influences:

⏪ Cab Calloway, Glenn Miller, David Rose, the Specials, Madness, Louis Jordan

⏩ Royal Crown Revue, the Senders, Big Bad Voodoo Daddy

Steve Knopper

Charlie Christian

Born July 29, 1916, in Dallas, TX. Died March 2, 1942, in New York, NY.

Though he was not quite the first electric guitarist in jazz (Eddie Durham beat him to it), Charlie Christian raised the electric guitar from novelty to prominence in the genre. For the first time, guitar could be heard over the other players in large ensembles (before the days of P.A. systems and mixing consoles) and thus moved from a rhythm-section instrument to an important solo role. In 1939 the great Columbia Records scout John Hammond learned of Christian's talent and hooked him up with Benny Goodman. (Most of Christian's surviving recording material comes from that time up until his death.) Christian was also among the players of the time who, like Charlie Parker and Dizzy Gillespie, rode from swing to bebop. In 1941 he came down with tuberculosis and died the next year at age 25.

what to buy: *The Genius of the Electric Guitar* 🦴🦴🦴🦴 (Columbia, 1987, prod. John Hammond) concentrates on Christian's recordings with Benny Goodman from 1939 to 1941. They include "Solo Flight," "Good Enough to Keep" (a.k.a. "Air Mail Special"), and "Honeysuckle Rose." The template for jazz guitar for the next 30 years (at least) is laid out here, though much of the music when Christian isn't playing is dated.

what to buy next: Christian is featured on the 1941 jam session recording *Swing to Bop* 🦴🦴🦴🦴 (Natasha, 1993) from the legendary New York nightclub Minton's with Thelonious Monk (piano), Kenny Clarke (drums), Joe Guy (trumpet), and Nick Fenton (bass). Its five tracks include "Swing to Bop" and "Stompin' at the Savoy." While the recording quality is primitive, the spirit of the session is of incredible historical significance.

influences:

⏪ Charlie Parker, Dizzy Gillespie, Benny Goodman

⏩ Wes Montgomery, Barney Kessel, George Benson, Herb Ellis, Pat Martino

Chris Meloche

Steve Perry of the Cherry Poppin' Daddies **(© Ken Settle)**

Cigar Store Indians

Formed in Crabapple, GA, 1992.

Ben Friedman, lead vocals, rhythm guitar; Jim Lavender, lead guitar, vocals; Keith Perissi, bass guitar, vocals; David "Pup" Roberts, drums.

If the Mavericks or Dwight Yoakam ever decided to go the Stray Cat route, they might end up sounding a lot like the Cigar Store Indians. Their catchy mix of rockabilly, Tex-Mex, and jump is often augmented with Yoakam-type harmony, and Brian Setzer–style guitar riffs. Of course, their immersion in these distinct influences doesn't mean Cigar Store Indians are a copycat or cover band. Their lead singer, Ben Friedman, writes all the songs with clever wordplay and fresh rhythmic hooks. Moreover, Friedman sings with a heartfelt southern gusto few of his contemporaries can match. Cigar Store Indians have proven to be a stellar live act, drawing both the rockabilly and swing crowds to their shows. They've opened for the likes of Merle Haggard, Squirrel Nut Zippers, and Jerry Lee Lewis. One small gripe: In their attempt to transfer the dynamics of the high-energy nightclub set to recordings, the Indians' raw vigor occasionally works against the increasingly subtle intentions of their songs.

what's available: The debut CD *Cigar Store Indians* (Landslide, 1995, prod. Rodney Mills) features danceable rockabilly rhythm that borders on modern swing, with the call-and-response ditty "Who Dat?" and the alcohol anthem "Six Sheets to the Wind" veering into Stray Cat territory. Far deeper in the groove is *El Baile de la Cobra* (Deep South, 1998, prod. Rodney Mills), 14 tracks of atmospheric jump, honky-tonk, rockabilly, and modern swing booted up a notch by the sax work of the Squirrel Nut Zippers' Ken Mosher. "Get on the Throttle," "Yi Pin," "Big Girl Blouse," and "Tossin' and Turnin'" are the top-deck dance tunes here, but the moving "Eagles Need a Push" shows the boys just might have a career waiting for them in modern country music.

worth searching for: The band sells copies of its nine-song demo cassette *Cigar Store Indians* (Ain't Records, 1994, prod. Rodney Mills) through its Web site and at live shows.

influences:

Squirrel Nut Zippers, Dick Dale, the Stray Cats, Dwight Yoakam

Ken Burke

Buck Clayton

Born Wilbur Dorsey Clayton, November 11, 1907, in Parsons, KS. Died December 8, 1991, in New York, NY.

Bandleader-arranger-trumpeter Buck Clayton began his professional career in Los Angeles leading his own bands in the early 1930s before his solo work and arrangements for the Count Basie band (1936–43) attracted attention. After an Army stint (1943–46), Clayton wrote arrangements for bands led by Basie, Benny Goodman, and Harry James. In 1946 he joined the first of many national Jazz at the Philharmonic tours organized by producer Norman Granz. During the late 1940s and 1950s Clayton worked with many notable jazz musicians, led his own groups, and toured Europe several times. In the 1950s he organized a series of *Jam Session* recordings for Columbia (compiled and reissued on the four-disc, limited edition Mosaic set), led a combo at the 1956 Newport Jazz Festival, and appeared in the Hollywood film *The Benny Goodman Story* and the prized 1959 Newport Jazz Festival documentary *Jazz on a Summer's Day.* He joined Chicago-style swing bandleader Eddie Condon for a 1959 tour of Japan and throughout the 1960s continued to tour and record. After 1969, health problems curtailed Carter's activity. Recommencing practice in 1971, Clayton toured and performed, and started teaching at Hunter College in New York City in the early 1980s. In 1983 he led a group of Basie sidemen to Europe, followed by his own big band in 1987. His autobiography, *Buck Clayton's Jazz World,* written with author/photographer Nancy Miller-Elliot, came out that same year.

what to buy: *Buck and Buddy Blow the Blues* (Swingville, 1961/Original Jazz Classics, 1995) is a seven-tune session of hearty, Basie-inspired swing. All the musicians save pianist Sir Charles Thompson are Basie-band alumni, and they consistently hit swinging grooves, whether playing well-crafted lines of a slow, aching blues ("Blue Creek") or a foot-tapping swing-blues ("A Swingin' Doll"). Spotlighting Clayton with Tommy Gwaltney's Kansas City Nine, *Goin' to Kansas City* (Riverside, 1960/Original Jazz Classics, 1990, prod. Tommy Gwaltney) contains 10 mostly swinging arrangements by producer/reeds player Tommy Newsom. Paying tribute to the swing sound that flourished in Kansas City from 1928 through 1937, Gwaltney and Newsom created new and modern arrangements without destroying the authenticity of the pieces. The session includes obscurities such as Andy Razaf and Don Redman's "An Old Manuscript," Jay McShann and Charlie Parker's "The Jumping Blues," Jelly Roll Morton's "Midnight Mama," and Count Basie's "John's Idea." Although not as hotly danceable as the Clayton-led session (above) recorded with Buddy Tate the next year, this is a wonderful swing-era tribute that still sounds fresh and vibrant.

what to buy next: On *Buck & Buddy* (Prestige/Swingville, 1960/Original Jazz Classics, 1992, prod. Esmond Edwards), Clayton's muted and open horn work stand out throughout the six selections, three of which are Clayton originals. While musicianship is superior, this set is more sedate and of shorter duration (34 minutes) than his 1961 recording with tenor saxophonist Buddy Tate.

Buck Clayton **(Archive Photos)**

what to avoid: Taken from original recordings for the H.R.S. label, the 12 selections compiled on *The Classic Swing of Buck Clayton* ♪♪♪ (Riverside, 1946/Original Jazz Classics, 1990) were restored and digitally remastered in 1990, but unless you're a die-hard jazz fan or historian, sound quality leaves a lot to be desired.

influences:

◀ Louis Armstrong, Henry "Red" Allen

▶ Harry "Sweets" Edison, Clark Terry

Nancy Ann Lee

Rosemary Clooney

Born May 23, 1928, in Maysville, KY.

Though best known as a straightforward pop singer—and many of her hits were novelty songs such as 1954's surprisingly forceful and sexy "Mambo Italiano"—Rosemary Clooney rarely strayed far from her roots in the big-band era. Even in the early '50s, when she was recording hits with schmalzy Columbia producer Mitch Miller, she worked with Benny Goodman and Woody Herman. While she doesn't communicate with quite the expression of Billie Holiday, Clooney's clear, perfect voice is a marvel—she makes "tra la la la la" sound sexy and subversive, communicates a fierce romanticism in "Invitation," and has a perfect understanding of a song's rhythm.

As teenagers, Clooney and her sister, Betty, began singing for a Cincinnati radio station; bandleader Tony Pastor heard their songs and quickly signed them up to sing for his touring orchestra. In the early 1950s Clooney signed with Columbia, then recorded 1951's bouncy, sensual "Come on-a My House." The song went to #1 and kicked off a prolific recording career, including several million-selling records and a detour into films. She starred with Bob Hope in 1953's *Here Come the Girls*, and began a life-long friendship with Bing Crosby on the set of *White Christmas*. But rock 'n' roll, especially in the 1960s, was a lousy era for both jazz and mainstream pop singers. The Beatles, among others, usurped Clooney's brand of standard-singing from the charts. Perfectly good albums, such as 1963's *Love* —delayed from release for two years because RCA was concentrating on rock, then tanking when it finally came out—

were no longer what young people wanted to hear. Clooney, frustrated, went into semi-retirement. She came back, gradually, beginning in the late '70s, recording a number of jazz-based albums, including swing tributes to songwriter Harold Arlen and arranger Nelson Riddle. Her nephew, *ER* and movie heartthrob George Clooney, has told interviewers her experience is an enduring lesson about the public's fickle taste.

what to buy: Though greatest-hits collections are more cost-effective ways of sampling Clooney's most familiar material, several of her recent CDs reflect her love for the big-band era. *Girl Singer* (Concord Jazz, 1992) is perhaps her most swing-oriented album, with songs by Duke Ellington, Cole Porter, and Antonio Carlos Jobim. Familiar standards such as "Stormy Weather" and even "Ding Dong the Witch Is Dead"—but not "Over the Rainbow," which shows she's thinking Ella Fitzgerald more than Judy Garland—dominate *Rosemary Clooney Sings the Music of Harold Arlen* (Concord Jazz, 1983). And on *Dedicated to Nelson* (Concord Jazz, 1996) Clooney returns to the sympathetic arrangements the late Nelson Riddle created for *The Rosemary Clooney Show.* It sounds like a surgeon removed Frank Sinatra's swaggering clarity from "A Foggy Day" and transplanted Clooney's deep sexuality. An excellent reissue of a '50s album, *Rosie Solves the Swinging Riddle* (Koch, 1997) finds Clooney working with Riddle's swinging arrangements for the first time.

what to buy next: Because Clooney has recorded for so many different record labels, and because she has had hits in so many different decades, there are lots of greatest-hits collections available. Aim for the songs you like: "Mambo Italiano" shows up on *The Essence of Rosemary Clooney* (Legacy, 1993, prod. various), and "Look to the Rainbow" and "Come on-a My House" are on *Greatest Songs* (Curb/MCA, 1996, prod. various). For great old stuff, there's *The Uncollected Rosemary Clooney, 1951–52* (Hindsight, 1986/Rounder, 1994, prod. Dave Dexter Jr.) and *Everything's Rosie 1952/1963* (Hindsight/Rounder, 1994, prod. various). In her post-retirement years, recording for the receptive Concord Jazz label, Clooney dedicated herself to paying tribute to big-band heroes and classic pop songwriters. Highlights include *Rosemary Clooney Sings the Music of Irving Berlin* (Concord Jazz, 1984, prod. Carl E. Jefferson), *Rosemary Clooney Sings the Music of Cole Porter* (Concord Jazz, 1982, prod. Carl E. Jefferson), and the tremendous *Here's to My Lady—Tribute to Billie Holiday* (Concord Jazz, 1979, prod. Carl E. Jefferson). One of her most interesting solo albums, though it occasionally devolves into string-heavy schmaltz, is the underrecognized *Love* (Reprise, 1963/Warner Archives, 1995, prod. Dick Peirce), which includes solemn romantic anthems like "Black Coffee" and "If I Forget You."

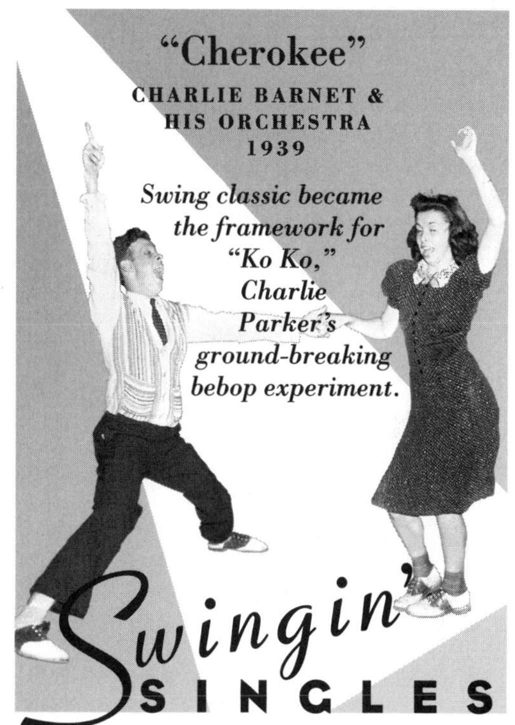

what to avoid: Clooney's orchestral Christmas album, *White Christmas* (Concord Jazz, 1996, prod. Peter Matz), is just like any other Christmas album. If you have Bing Crosby and everybody else, there's no reason to get this new album of old Christmas standards.

best of the rest:

Everything's Coming Up Rosie (Concord Jazz, 1977)
Rosie Sings Bing (Concord Jazz, 1978)
My Buddy (Concord Jazz, 1983)
Rosemary Clooney Sings Ballads (Concord Jazz, 1985)
Rosemary Clooney Sings the Music of Jimmy Van Heusen (Concord Jazz, 1986)
Rosemary Clooney Sings the Lyrics of Johnny Mercer (Concord Jazz, 1987)
Show Tunes (Concord Jazz, 1989)
With Love (Concord Jazz, 1989)
The Music of Rodgers, Hart & Hammerstein (Concord Jazz, 1990)
Rosemary Clooney Sings the Lyrics of Ira Gershwin (Concord Jazz, 1990)
For the Duration (Concord Jazz, 1991)
Tenderly (Columbia Special Products, 1992)
Do You Miss New York? (Concord Jazz, 1993)
Still on the Road (Concord Jazz, 1994)

Demi-Centennial ♪♪ (Concord Jazz, 1995)
The Best of Rosemary Clooney ♪♪♪ (Tri Star, 1996)
Mothers & Daughters ♪♪♪ (Concord Jazz, 1997)
At Long Last ♪♪♪ (Concord Jazz, 1998)
The Concord Jazz Heritage Series ♪♪♪ (Concord Jazz, 1998)

influences:

◀ Bing Crosby, Billie Holiday, Ira Gershwin, Cole Porter, Duke Ellington, Doris Day, Nelson Riddle

▶ Sinead O'Connor, Barbra Streisand, k.d. lang. Bette Midler

Steve Knopper

Clouds of Joy

See: Andy Kirk

Arnett Cobb

Born August 10, 1918, in Houston, TX. Died March 24, 1989, in Houston, TX.

Often known as the "Wild Man of the Tenor" and the "World's Wildest Tenorman," Arnett Cobb gained his first fame as a soloist in Lionel Hampton's big band from 1942–47. Cobb earned his nickname in the early days of Hampton's band, when the leader would march his musicians around the old Strand Theatre on Broadway, leading them strutting and leaping into the street. While illness and accidents plagued his career from the time he left Hamp's band, Cobb never gave up performing. His big, fat tone represents classic big-band style. His notes are filled with emotion, whether he's blowing a muscular, up-tempo solo or slowly romancing a ballad. With fellow saxman Illinois Jacquet, Cobb's colorful, stomping style defined the early Houston, Texas, tenor sound, equally at home in jazz, blues, or early R&B.

Cobb's father died of tuberculosis when he was six, and he was raised by his mother and maternal grandfather. He took up music at an early age, playing piano under the instruction of his grandmother. He tried the violin, trumpet, and C-melody sax before taking up the tenor horn. After collaborating with hometown trumpet player Chester Boone, Cobb left Boone's band to play with Milton Larkin from 1936–42. Newly married in 1939, Cobb turned down Count Basie's offer to join his horn section as the replacement for Herschel Evans. In 1942 Cobb accepted Lionel Hampton's invitation to replace Jacquet. Cobb took over not only Jacquet's slot in the band, but his famous solo on "Flyin' Home"; the famous piece was ultimately more associated with Cobb than with Jacquet, thanks to Cobb's reworking, his many live performances, and the recording of "Flyin' Home No. II." Cobb stayed with Hampton until 1947, when he left to start his own combo, which recorded for Columbia and OKeh, and occasionally backed R&B singer Ruth Brown. He was a popular figure on the New York jazz scene when a spinal operation and a period of illness sidelined him from 1948–51. On the comeback trail in the mid-'50s, a near-fatal auto accident broke both legs. Doctors told him he would not play again—but, while he was forced to walk with crutches, Cobb would not give up music. A year after the accident, Cobb was not only playing again, but recording, with *Blow, Arnett, Blow* his first in a series of excellent sessions for the Prestige label. He also did gigs in his adopted home state, New Jersey, with his small Cobb's Mob. After that, he returned to live primarily in Houston, playing nightly in a small cafe—in his words, playing "a little jazz, commercial music, and what have you."

what to buy: *Arnett Blows for 1300* ♪♪♪♪♪ (Apollo, 1947/Delmark, 1994) documents Cobb's first two recording sessions as a bandleader, recorded during his stint as a fill-in for Billie Holiday at the Baby Grand in Harlem. Cobb's chops are solid and his playing swings. Because most bandleaders retained co-composer credits for tunes written or improvised by members, "Top Flight" and "Still Flyin' " may sound familiar—they're slight revisions of Hampton-era tunes "Air Mail Special" and the classic "Flyin' Home." (Who or what 1300 refers to is unknown.) *Blow, Arnett, Blow* ♪♪♪♪♪ (Prestige, 1959/Original Jazz Classics, 1993), also known as *Go Power!!!*, is, in saxophonist Gordon Beadle's words, "the musical equivalent of a monster truck battle." The pairing of sax greats Cobb and Eddie "Lockjaw" Davis is a natural and the music is marvelous. It includes later interpretations of three Cobb standards (also found on 1947's *Arnett Blows for 1300*), "When I Grow Too Old to Dream," "Go, Red, Go," and "Dutch Kitchen Bounce."

what to buy next: *Blue and Sentimental* ♪♪♪♪♪ (Prestige, 1960/Original Jazz Classics, 1993), with the Red Garland Trio, is filled with melancholy pieces, but there is invention where you might expect cliché, and some surprising up-tempo tunes. The shining *Party Time* ♪♪♪♪ (Prestige, 1959/Original Jazz Classics, 1995) includes a jaunty, swing-infused version of "Flyin' Home." The warm, fluid, vibrant solos Cobb puts down on his mellow composition "Slow Poke" are exceptionally beautiful; the liner notes reveal this striking version was a "run-down" rehearsal take, accidentally recorded. The title track of *Smooth Sailing* ♪♪♪♪ (Prestige, 1959/Original Jazz Classics, 1995) was written by Cobb and recorded on Columbia in 1950. It was so popular in its day that Ella Fitzgerald recorded a scat vocal of Cobb's solo on Decca. "I Don't Stand a Ghost of a Chance with You" was a Cobb staple in live performance, and, recorded here for the first time, is an interesting showcase for Cobb's style, moving from moody and evocative to upbeat and wailing all in a single arrangement.

worth searching for: The box set *Hamp: The Legendary Decca Recordings of Lionel Hampton* ♪♪♪♪ (Decca Jazz, 1996, reissue prod. Orrin Keepnews) archives the Hampton band's recordings on Decca from 1942–63, and contains work by Jacquet and Cobb, as well as later tenor players. "Foot Pattin'," from *Blues Wail: Coleman Hawkins Plays the Blues* ♪♪♪♪ (Prestige/Fantasy, 1996, compilation prod. Ed Michel) features Cobb, Hawkins, Eddie "Lockjaw" Davis, and another Texan, Buddy Tate. It's taken from the out-of-print LP *Very Saxy* ♪♪♪♪ (Prestige, 1959), which finds Cobb joined by Davis, Buddy Tate, and Coleman Hawkins for an "all-star tenor sax album." *Show Time* ♪♪♪♪ (Fantasy, 1988, prod. David Thompson, Steve Williams) was recorded live in Houston with personnel including Dizzy Gillespie and Jewel Brown.

influences:

◀◀ Coleman Hawkins, Illinois Jacquet, Ben Webster, Lester Young

▶▶ King Curtis, David Newman, Sonny Rollins

B.J. Huchtemann

Eddie Cochran

Born October 3, 1938, in Oklahoma City, OK. Died April 17, 1960, in Bristol, England.

Eddie Cochran is probably the most overrated member of the early rock 'n' roll pantheon. He is remembered more for his suave, Elvis Presley–like style than the enduring quality of his songs, although a handful—"Summertime Blues," "20 Flight Rock," "Somethin' Else," "Teenage Heaven," "C'mon Everybody"—are certified classics. His influence was felt more in England, where he died in the same car crash that crippled Gene Vincent. British rock stars such as Rod Stewart, the Rolling Stones, the Who, and even the Sex Pistols have kept his songs in the book. By the time British reissue labels finished sorting through his work, the entire body looked rather less than impressive; Ricky Nelson records held up better. Some of his recordings stand up against any from his time, but just don't dig too deep.

what to buy: The 20-song collection *Somethin' Else—The Fine Looking Hits of Eddie Cochran* ♪♪♪♪ (Razor & Tie, 1998, compilation prod. David Richman) focuses on his signature driving rock sound and includes a bare minimum of schlocky ballads. It is virtually interchangeable with *Eddie Cochran: The Legendary Masters Series, Vol. I* ♪♪♪♪ (EMI, 1990, compilation prod. Ron Furmanek), which boasts the cult favorite "Pink Pegged Slacks" in addition to the hits.

what to avoid: *The Early Years* ♪♪ (Ace, 1988, prod. various) is a slapdash collection of his experiments in country music mixed with some rock. The coupling of *Singin' to My Baby* and *Never to Be Forgotten* ♪♪ (EMI, 1993, prod. various) sticks a dreadful teen pop album with a posthumous collection of worthy lesser-known rockers.

the rest:

Greatest Hits ♪♪ (Curb, 1990)

worth searching for: Airchecks from 1960 British television programs collected for one side of a major label album, *Eddie Cochran: On the Air* ♪♪♪ (EMI, 1987) gets across some of Cochran's personality that often got stifled on recordings. Who let this one out? Take a bow.

influences:

◀◀ Elvis Presley, Hank Cochran, Carl Perkins

▶▶ Ricky Nelson, Paul McCartney, Glen Campbell, Brian Setzer

Joel Selvin

Nat King Cole

Born Nathaniel Adams Coles, March 17, 1917, in Montgomery, AL. Died February 15, 1965, in Santa Monica, CA.

He was known as the King, and during his incredible, too-brief reign he actually ruled over two domains. Nathaniel Adams Cole was one of the finest jazz swing pianists in history, drawing deeply from the inspiration of Earl "Fatha" Hines. And he became one of the single most successful pop-ballad singers of the 20th century, with a voice so warm, rich, and unmistakable that it seems nearly impossible to believe he spent the early years of his career trying to make it as a piano player! After his family moved to Chicago from the Deep South, Cole began taking keyboard lessons while playing the organ and singing in church. He made his professional debut in 1936 on *Eddie Cole's Solid Swingers*, a record fronted by his brother, Eddie, with brothers Fred and Isaac accompanying. He left the group to conduct the band for *Shuffle Along*, a touring music revue; when the show closed in Los Angeles, he settled there. Struggling to find his place in the music world, Cole finally managed to organize the King Cole Trio with guitarist Oscar Moore and bassist Wesley Prince and began performing on radio. The combo became popular when they recorded Cole's "Sweet Lorraine" in 1940, and other musicians (notably Art Tatum and Oscar Peterson) formed their own trios, inspired by his sound. Johnny Miller replaced Prince and the trio rose to prominence during that decade, recording exciting jazz music, mostly for Capitol, and performing in the movies *Here Comes Elmer* and *Pistol Packin' Mama* and the first-ever Jazz at the Philharmonic concert. Along the way, Cole grew more confident in his vocal ability and became increasingly more popular as a singer. When a string of now-classic recordings, including "The Christmas Song," "I Love You for Sentimental Reasons," and "Nature Boy" culminated in a #1 hit with "Mona Lisa" in 1950, Cole be-

Eddie Cochran **(Archive Photos)**

came a pop singer fulltime. Though he continued to dabble in jazz, playing keyboards on the 1956 release *After Midnight*, Cole's vocals catapulted him to such superstardom that many of his newer fans weren't aware he could play piano. He landed his own NBC-TV series from 1956–57, an almost unheard-of accomplishment for a black man of the era. Despite being accompanied by the Nelson Riddle Orchestra and hosting many of the biggest stars of the day (Tony Bennett, Sammy Davis Jr., Peggy Lee), the show ultimately died due to lack of sponsorship and the refusal of some stations to carry it. Cole continued to be a major attraction, appearing in many movies (including *Cat Ballou* and *The Nat King Cole Story*) and becoming a musical holiday tradition at Christmas. One of the regal trademarks of the "King" was a lit cigarette in a cigarette holder, but when he died of lung cancer at the age of 47, the world mourned the loss of one of the most beloved voices of all time.

what to buy: Why it took the success of Natalie Cole's *Unforgettable* tribute to her father to prompt the release of a hit singles collection for Cole is inconceivable, but *The Greatest Hits* (Capitol/EMI, 1994, prod. various) is such a package. Covering the King's work from 1944–63 in 62 minutes and 22 tracks, the collection skips some of his famous Christmas songs but does focus on his best pop productions such as "Mona Lisa" and "Sentimental Reasons." The cuts are arranged by style and quality rather than chronology, which gives an imperfect sense of history but a better sense of the music. *Jazz Encounters* (Blue Note, 1992, prod. Michael Cuscuna) combines the great work of jazz masters like Coleman Hawkins, Benny Carter, and Dizzy Gillespie with Cole's piano and vocal stylings. Here you'll find Cole's non-trio performances and some of his best collaborations with Woody Herman and Johnny Mercer.

what to buy next: The big box set *Nat King Cole* (Capitol/EMI, 1992, prod. Lee Gillette) boasts four discs and a 60-page booklet covering 20 years in 100 different tracks. As a side dish, you'll find the previously unreleased novelty "Mr. Cole Won't Rock & Roll" as well as Leonard Feather's liner notes, complete track annotations, rare photographs, and some of the King's most inspiring jazz sets. Starting with records like *Lush Life* (Capitol/EMI, 1993) with the Pete Rugolo Orchestra, Cole was phasing out of trio work and trying to establish a vocal career over his keyboard fare. There's still jazz here, but lots of great vocals on tunes that are memorable and representative of Cole's best musical work.

what to avoid: Some musicians just could do no wrong—you didn't think they called him "King" simply because his last name was Cole, did you? His only albums worth avoiding are ones with weak or offbeat selections, such as *Greatest Country Hits* (Curb, 1990).

the rest:

Big Band Cole (EMI/Capitol, 1950)
The Billy May Sessions (EMI/Capitol, 1951)
Nat King Cole Live (A Touch of Magic)
Early American (A Touch of Magic)
(With the Nat King Cole Trio) *Hit That Jive, Jack: The Earliest Recordings (1940–41)* (Decca/MCA Jazz, 1990)
The Very Thought of You (Capitol/EMI, 1991)
The Jazz Collector Edition (Laserlight, 1991)
(With the Nat King Cole Trio) *The Trio Recordings* (Laserlight, 1991)
(With the Nat King Cole Trio) *The Complete Capitol Recordings of the Nat King Cole Trio* (Capitol/EMI, 1991)
(With the Nat King Cole Trio) *The Trio Recordings, Vol. II* (Laserlight, 1991)
(With the Nat King Cole Trio) *The Trio Recordings, Vol. III* (Laserlight, 1991)
(With the Nat King Cole Trio) *The Trio Recordings, Vol. IV* (Laserlight, 1991)
The Unforgettable Nat King Cole (Capitol/EMI, 1992)
(With the Nat King Cole Trio) *The Best of the Nat King Cole Trio: Instrumental Classics* (Capitol/EMI, 1992)
The Piano Style of Nat King Cole (Capitol/EMI, 1993)
(With the Nat King Cole Trio) *Early Years of Nat King Cole Trio* (Sound Hills, 1993)
(With the Nat King Cole Trio) *Nat King Cole & the King Cole Trio: Straighten up & Fly Right (Radio Broadcasts 1942–48)* (VJC, 1993)
(With the Nat King Cole Trio) *The Nat King Cole Trio: World War II Transcriptions* (Music & Arts Programs of America, 1994)
Spotlight on Nat King Cole (Capitol/EMI, 1995)
The Jazzman (Topaz Jazz, 1995)
To Whom It May Concern (Capitol/EMI, 1995)
Swinging Easy down Memory Lane (Skylark Jazz, 1995)
The Complete after Midnight Sessions (Capitol/EMI, 1996)
Sweet Lorraine (1938–41 Transcriptions) (Jazz Classics, 1996)
Best of: Vocal Classics 1947–50 (Blue Note, 1996)
The Vocal Classics (Capitol/EMI, 1996)
The Nat King Cole TV Show (Sandy Hook, 1996)
The McGregor Years (1941–45) (Music & Arts Programs of America, 1996)
Love Is the Thing (Gold Disc) (DCC, 1997)
Revue Collection (One Way, 1997)
A&E Biography: A Musical Anthology (Capitol, 1998)
Best of the Nat King Cole Trio (Blue Note, 1998)

worth searching for: For a fascinating insight into the performing medium and the painstaking polishing of brilliance, Cole's *Anatomy of a Jam Session* (Black Lion, 1945) with drummer Buddy Rich is especially choice. Cole attacks the keys only, no vocals, and his dynamic jams with Charlie Shavers, Herbie Hayner, John Simmons, and Rich are superb. The solos that emanate from the 12 songs, five as a quintet, make this a very

Nat King Cole **(Archive Photos)**

memorable disc and worth hunting down. Famous for his rendering of "The Christmas Song" and "Frosty the Snowman," Cole became the unofficial herald angel of Christmas. If you take the time to hunt down the reissues of *The Christmas Song* ♪♪♪♪ (Capitol, 1990, prod. Lee Gillette) and *Cole, Christmas, and Kids* ♪♪♪♪ (Capitol, 1990, prod. Ron Furmanek), you won't be sorry.

influences:

◄◄ Billy Kyle, Louis Armstrong, Louis Jordan, Duke Ellington, Teddy Wilson, Earl "Fatha" Hines

►► Johnny Mathis, Frank Sinatra, Johnny Hartman, Oscar Peterson, Bing Crosby, Mel Tormé, Billy Eckstine, Natalie Cole

Chris Tower

The Collins Kids

Lawrencine Collins (born May 7, 1942, in Tahlequah, OK), vocals; Larry Collins (born October 4, 1944, in Tulsa, OK), guitar, vocals.

As the house teen rock 'n' roll stars on the 1950s country music television program *Town Hall Party*, Larry and Lorrie Collins found their way into a lot of homes during the popular series' run on Los Angeles television and in syndication. They never experienced commensurate success with their records, although the pair produced a dazzling procession of red-hot rockabilly discs. And, despite being absent from the scene for the better part of 35 years, their reputation continues to grow. Larry Collins twanged his Mosrite double-necked guitar with the kind of ferocity that made young surf guitar king Dick Dale a disciple. His older sister belted the often puerile lyrics with a swagger and raucous bon vivance that belied her youth and apparent innocence (the act fell apart, in fact, when teen-age Lorrie Collins eloped with the much older manager of Johnny Cash). Reels of their endless hours on 1950s television and persistent reissues of their early recordings have made the Collins Kids probably better known in historical fact than they were at their height. Although guitarist Larry went on to experience some success as a country songwriter during the 1970s ("Delta Dawn" was his biggest hit), his sister gave up performing to concentrate on motherhood. But in recent years, they have emerged to headline rockabilly festivals in England and make sporadic appearances on the West Coast.

what to buy: The Collins Kids never released an album during the act's lifetime, but *Introducing Larry & Lorrie* ♪♪♪♪ (Columbia, 1983, prod. various) rectified that oversight with a blasting collection of the duo's 1950s recordings.

what to avoid: The bootlegs lifted off the *Town Hall Party* tapes sound like, well, like sound recordings from 1950s television. Stick with the studio versions.

worth searching for: The entire Columbia oeuvre was collected across two CDs titled *The Collins Kids* ♪♪♪ (Bear Family, 1991, prod. various), now available on German import, although the additional tracks hardly seem worth the freight.

influences:

◄◄ Joe Maphis

►► Dick Dale

Joel Selvin

Russ Columbo

Born Ruggerio de Rodolfo Columbo, January 14, 1908, in either San Francisco, CA, or Camden, NJ. Died September 2, 1934, in Hollywood, CA.

The circumstances of Russ Columbo's bizarre death made him larger than life, like James Dean, in the 1930s—although his name, since then, has hardly endured as a household word. Columbo, a handsome crooner with lots of personality and emotion in his low-pitched voice, was once Bing Crosby's key rival. With Crosby and Rudy Vallee, he was part of the triumvirate of pre–big-band crooning heartthrobs. But Columbo died after a shooting accident. Details remain sketchy, but Columbo was visiting a photographer friend, who allegedly lit a match on one of his souvenir antique Civil War pistols. That set off an unknown bullet, which bounced off a table and hit Columbo's head. The singer died later in a hospital.

Columbo, nicknamed "the Romeo of the Airwaves," was the son of an Italian musician and, as a young performer, worked on silent-movie sets to help actors "get in the mood" for love scenes. This work led to connections that helped Columbo score a violinist's job at a hotel and, finally, a recording contract and occasional cameo appearances in films. Unlike the more straightforward Crosby, Columbo frequently improvised with his excellent voice, stretching out the emotion in every romantic sentiment of "Prisoner of Love" and "When You're in Love."

what's available: While records by bluesman Robert Johnson, another performer of that era who died young in mysterious and violent circumstances, have resurfaced and become easily available on compact disc, Columbo's songs are comparatively hard to track down. His recorded work is still mostly out on LP, including *Russ Columbo—A Legendary Performer* ♪♪♪♪ (RCA, 1976, prod. various), which includes many of his big love-themed hits, and *Russ Columbo—Prisoner of Love* ♪♪♪ (Pelican, 1975), which documents his last-ever recording session in 1934.

influences:

◄◄ Bing Crosby, Al Jolson, Fred Astaire

►► Tony Bennett, Frank Sinatra

Steve Knopper

Commander Cody & His Lost Planet Airmen

Formed 1967, in Ann Arbor, MI.

Commander Cody (George Frayne), piano, vocals; John Tichy, guitar; West Virginia Creeper, steel guitar (1967–70); Billy C. Farlow, harmonica, vocals (1968–76); Bill Kirchen, guitar (1968–76); Bruce Barlow, bass (1968–76); Lance Dickerson, drums (1968–76); Andy Stein, fiddles, saxophone (1968–76); Bobby Black, steel guitar (1970–76); others.

A band before its time, Commander Cody & His Lost Planet Airmen can be seen as the precursor to the Austin music scene of the 1980s. In fact, the Austin kingpins first moved to San Francisco under the influence of the Cody outfit and worked clubs there as a kind of satellite of the pioneering rockabilly/western-swing revivalists. The band's first four classic albums laid the groundwork for a whole wing of retro-revisionists in country-rock, as far away stylistically as possible from the slick Los Angeles hybrid practiced by the Byrds, Poco, and others. Cody's crew specialized in a loose-jointed, rollicking brand of barroom boogie that sounded like it had been steeped in beer fumes in front of rowdy crowds as ready to fight as dance. Despite scoring a Top 10 hit ("Hot Rod Lincoln") off its debut album, Cody's band was never accorded appropriate acclaim, and the original players splintered in disarray in 1976—though the Commander continues to record and tour with an always changing squadron of Airmen.

what to buy: The first three albums have been cannibalized by an inconsistent collection, *Too Much Fun: The Best of Commander Cody & His Lost Planet Airmen* (MCA 1990, prod. various). Recently available after years of deletion, the Airmen's debut, *Lost in the Ozone* (Paramount/MCA, 1971), qualifies as a certified classic.

what to buy next: The fourth album, a jaunty concert recording, has been reissued as *Sleazy Roadside Stories* (Relix, 1995, prod. S. Jarvis), hard evidence of the original lineup's swinging brand of country and rock 'n' roll. It's available again under its original title: *Live from Deep in the Heart of Texas* (MCA, 1990, prod. S. Jarvis).

what to avoid: Without the balance of the Lost Planet Airmen personalities, Cody's solo albums have suffered from contrivance and the unmitigated dominance of his personality, none more so than *Let's Rock* (Blind Pig, 1987), despite the presence of Airmen Barlow and Kirchen.

the rest:

We Got a Live One Here (Warner Bros., 1976)
Lost in Space (Relix, 1995)
Best of Commander Cody (Relix, 1995)

worth searching for: *Hot Licks, Cold Steel, and Trucker's Favorites* (Paramount, 1972), another classic, has yet to follow its predecessor, *Lost In the Ozone*, into the CD reissue market. In the early days, the band cut a spectacular Christmas song, "Daddy's Drinking up All Our Christmas," which has been rescued from obscurity by *Hillbilly Holiday* (Rhino, 1988, prod. various).

solo outings:

Commander Cody:
Ace's High (Relix 1990)

Bill Kirchen:
Tombstone Every Mile (Black Top, 1994)
Have Love, Will Travel (Black Top, 1996)
Hot Rod Lincoln—Live! (Black Top, 1997)

influences:

◀◀ Bob Wills, Moon Mullican, Dave Dudley

▶ Asleep at the Wheel, Nick Lowe

Joel Selvin

Ray Condo & His Ricochets

Formed 1994, in Vancouver, British Columbia, Canada.

Ray Condo, rhythm guitar, saxophone, vocals; Jimmy Roy, steel guitar, second lead guitar; Stephen Nikleva, lead guitar; Clive Jackson, bass fiddle, ukulele; Steve Taylor, drums.

The musical fringe is rich these days with young bands steeped in the past, outfits that specialize in precisely duplicating the classic sounds of vintage rockabilly, western swing, honky-tonk, jump blues, and hillbilly boogie. The contingent includes California acts Big Sandy & His Fly-Rite Boys and the Dave & Deke Combo, Austin's High Noon, and Chicago's Mighty Blue Kings. At the top of the list you can safely place the neo-traditional quintet Ray Condo & His Ricochets. Led by frontman Condo, this outfit tops all comers in terms of sterling musicianship, historical knowledge, and the power to rocket the past into the future.

what to buy: The band's debut disc *Swing Brother Swing!* (Joaquin, 1996, prod. Marc L'Esperance, Stephen Nikleva, Jimmy Roy) features one original in the instrumental "Strathcona." The rest is split between classic swing and hillbilly bop numbers, including Hank Penny's 1952 "Hadicillin Boogie" and Henry "Red" Allen's "There's a House in Harlem for Sale." While all the musicians in this band are excellent, steel guitar man Roy in particular is a standout.

what to buy next: The follow-up, *Door to Door Maniac* (Joaquin, 1997, prod. Marc L'Esperance, Jeff Richardson, Stephen Nikleva, Jimmy Ray), has singer Condo hiccuping and growling through an unconventional range of cover songs, such as Billie Holiday's "Tell Me More" and cocktail-jazz blueswoman Hadda Brooks's "Jump Back, Honey, Jump Back."

worth searching for: Condo's pre-Ricochets outfit was Ray Condo & His Hardrock Goners. Two releases under that moniker, *Condo Country* ♪♪♪ (Fury) and *Hillbilly Holiday* ♪♪♪ (Fury), are well worth seeking out.

influences:
◀◀ Big Sandy & His Fly-Rite Boys
▶▶ High Noon, Dave & Deke Combo

Chris Dickinson

Eddie Condon

Born Albert Edwin Condon, November 16, 1905, in Goodland, IN. Died August 4, 1973, in New York, NY.

Eddie Condon was a well-known entrepreneur and raconteur and a possessor of a quick and acerbic wit—who had an affinity for bow ties, slicked-down hair, double-breasted suits, and, as befitted his Gallic heritage, a taste for Irish whiskey. He was also a sometime rhythm guitarist, a splendid organizer, and a champion of Chicago-styled music. The term "Chicago style" originally embraced unarranged small-group jazz improvisation performed in a direct, straight-ahead fashion, using sparsely placed notes and hot intonation and intensity, rather than slick virtuosity. Around the time of World War II and the traditional jazz revival, Chicago jazz came to be associated with solo-dominated Dixieland (a term that has since fallen out of favor) and fast-paced ensembles. Condon took part in the first jazz album ever made, producer George Avakian's 1939–40 Decca recording, *Chicago Jazz*.

Condon grew up in a musical family in which his father played violin, all four sisters were pianists, brother Cliff sang in a barbershop quartet and played alto horn, and brother Jim handed down first his ukelele and then his short-necked tenor banjo to young Eddie. By age 16, in the spring of 1922, Condon was on the road with Hollis Peavey's Jazz Bandits. Working out of the jazz mecca that was Chicago in 1924, Condon heard King Oliver and Louis Armstrong at the Lincoln Gardens, fell under the spell of cornetist Bix Beiderbecke, and hung out with young Chicago apprentice musicians like Benny Goodman, Bud Freeman, Jimmy McPartland, and Dave Tough. In 1927 he co-led the "McKenzie-Condon Chicagoans" on a groundbreaking record date for OKeh that gave definition to the term "Chicago Jazz." In 1928 Condon moved to New York City, found that work was scarce, and rode out the Depression playing banjo with the Mound City Blue Blowers and making a few record dates.

Swingin' SINGLES
"Cherokee"
CHARLIE PARKER
1942
Bird's bebop version of the Ray Noble big-band standard is said to have invented modern jazz.

As the changing sound of jazz made for subtle rhythm section alterations (tubas and banjos out, string basses and guitars in),

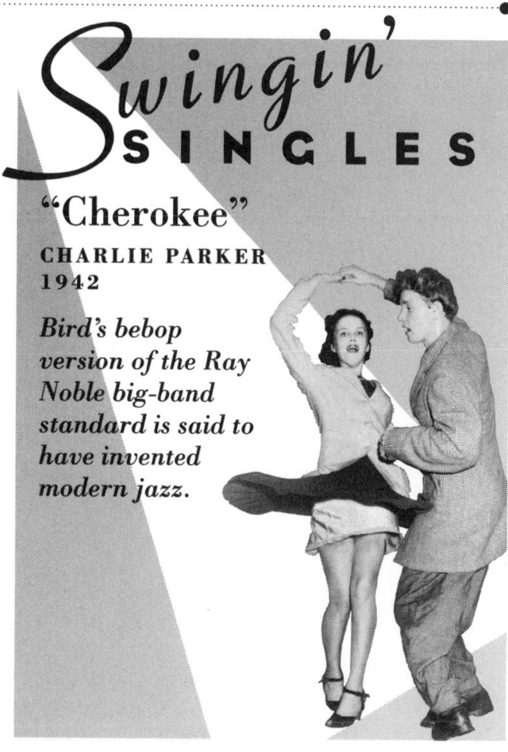

Condon chose a full-size Gibson L-5 guitar with four strings and banjo tuning, dubbed his "porkchop" because of its shape. He played along 52nd Street in the mid-1930s, co-led a band with clarinetist Joe Marsala during 1936–37, and recorded as a sideman with Bunny Berigan and Red McKenzie, among others. Condon moved to Greenwich Village in 1937 to be close to the bandstand at the famed nightspot, Nick's ("home of breaks and sizzling steaks"), where he was either leader or sideman for seven years. Condon also acted as house leader for the newly formed Commodore Records in 1938, and he organized and led many exciting sessions for that label. In 1944 Condon began a scheduled half-hour radio show on the Blue Network, which brought what announcer Fred Robbins called freewheeling "Americondon" music into New York Concert halls. The Armed Forces Radio Service transcribed 48 of the concerts and sent them around the world to U.S. troops. Amazing as it might seem now, Condon, who never soloed, won the *Down Beat* poll for jazz guitar playing in 1943 and 1944. He had well-connected publicist friends and he appeared regularly in the pages of *Time, Life, New Yorker,* and the *New York Times.* His weekly wartime concert broadcasts in the early 1940s were far-reaching at home and abroad. In 1945, Condon opened his own club at 47 West

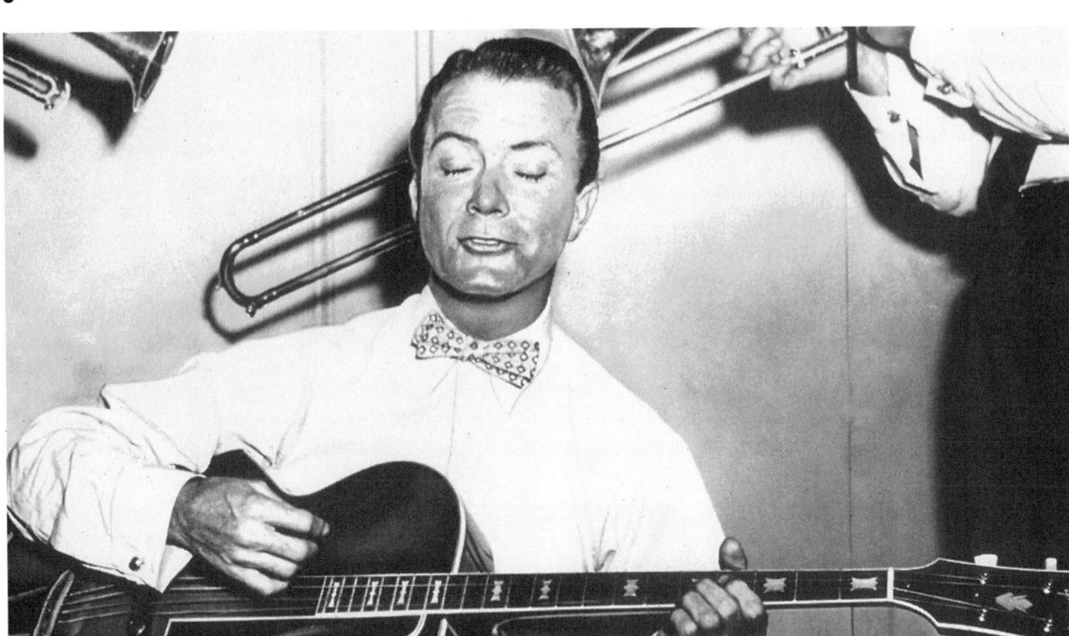

Eddie Condon **(Archive Photos)**

Third Street and played host to visiting celebrities, fellow musicians, and jazz fans galore until the lease expired in 1958 and forced a relocation to the elite East Side. Condon authored or collaborated on three books, *We Called It Music, Eddie Condon's Treasure of Jazz,* and *Eddie Condon's Scrapbook of Jazz,* which provided jazz fans with witty insights and some valuable photographic memories of Condon's life, his work, and some of his notable musical friends. Condon spent his last dozen years making occasional overseas tours and record dates.

what to buy: A generous offering of Condon-style jazz is contained in the 20-track CD *Eddie Condon, 1938–40* (Commodore, 1940/Classics, 1994, prod. various), which highlights six sessions made originally for Commodore or Decca over a 31-month span. It's hard to be glum when listening to the veteran jazzmen "swing out" on these classic jazz sides. Twenty later cuts by hardy swingsters are collected in *Eddie Condon: Dixieland All-Stars* (Decca, 1939, 1946/GRP, 1994, prod. George Avakian, Milt Gabler, reissue prod. Orrin Keepnews). The four "Chicago Jazz" sides repeated here contain two unissued alternate takes ("There'll Be Some Changes Made" and "Someday, Sweetheart"). The Condon Town Hall concert broadcasts were an absolute listening must for jazz fans who owned radios back in the 1944–45 war years. *The Town Hall Concerts, Vol. VII* (Jazzology, 1991, prod. George H. Buck Jr.) is a good place to start because it contains some fine trombone by Jack Teagarden and rare appearances by his sister, pianist Norma Teagarden, and trumpeter Wingy Manone.

what to buy next: The Associated Transcription Services is the source of a 21-tune, 33-track (including alternate takes and breakdowns) collection served up in *The Definitive Eddie Condon & His Jazz Concert All-Stars, Vol. I* (Stash, 1990, prod. Jerry Valburn, Will Friedwald). Members of the Condon mob visited the Musak Studios twice in 1944 and came up with some straight-ahead, Condon-style performances containing some very attractive solos scattered throughout. Hot Lips Page is on hand for his "Uncle Sam's Blues" ("Uncle Sam ain't no woman, but he sure can take your man"), a minor classic. Vintage Condon is in *Eddie Condon, 1927–38* (Classics, 1994, prod. Anatol Schenker), which contains classics of their genre and sound as good now as they did decades ago.

best of the rest:

Eddie Condon & His All-Stars Dixieland Jam (Columbia, 1989)
Eddie Condon Live in Japan (Chiaroscuro, 1991)
Live at the New School (Chiaroscuro, 1991)
We Dig Dixieland (Savoy, 1992)
Dr. Jazz Vol. I: Eddie Condon with Johnny Windhurst, No. I (radio air checks) (Storyville, 1993)
Eddie Condon, 1942–43 (Classics, 1994)
Ringside at Condon's (Savoy, 1994)
Eddie Condon, 1933–40 (Jazz Portraits, 1994)
Windy City Jazz (Topaz, 1995)
Dr. Jazz Vol. VIII: Eddie Condon with Johnny Windhurst, No. II (Storyville, 1995)
Dr. Jazz Vol. V: Eddie Condon with Wild Bill Davison, No. I (Storyville, 1995)
Dr. Jazz Vol. XI: Eddie Condon with Wild Bill Davison, No. II (Storyville, 1995)
Eddie Condon: Chicago Style (ASV/Living Era, 1996)
Eddie Condon, 1928–31 (Timeless, 1996)

worth searching for: *The Complete CBS Recordings of Eddie Condon & His All-Stars* (CBS, 1957/Mosaic, 1994, reissue prod. Michael Cuscuna) is a limited-edition mail-order set that seemingly transports the earth-shaking activities from Condon's Club to the recording studios.

influences:

◄◄ Louis Armstrong, King Oliver, Bix Beiderbecke, Benny Goodman

►► Marty Grosz, Ed Polcer, James Dapogny, the Original Salty Dogs

John T. Bitter

Harry Connick Jr.

Born September 11, 1967, in New Orleans, LA.

A child piano prodigy who grew up in a house and a city infused with the jazz tradition, Harry Connick Jr. has made a career mimicking the voice, swagger, and good looks of a young Sinatra—with the musical skills of the jazz masters. The result is an anachronistic sound that's often beguiling for someone his age. While his earlier work is more in a straightforward jazz tradition, Connick soon began to branch out into the big band/swing arena with mixed results. In the '90s he has alternated between showcasing his virtuoso piano playing for hard-core jazz enthusiasts and performing his often-indulgent originals with a big band to placate the masses.

After studying music intently through his teens, Connick left the Crescent City for New York City to follow in the footsteps of his friend Wynton Marsalis and sign a recording contract. Recording for Columbia, his second adult album, *20*, marking his age, brought his brand of throwback jazz to the attention of critics, but it wasn't until two years later, with the soundtrack to the immensely popular film *When Harry Met Sally,* that Connick became a sensation and an early pioneer in the mid-'90s swing resurgence. With undeniable charisma, Connick soon began a successful tour into acting, most memorably as a cocky pilot fighting the alien masses alongside Will Smith in the blockbuster *Independence Day.* (He was last seen wooing Sandra Bullock in 1998's *Hope Floats.*) With his mind occupied by the silver screen, his albums in the '90s have been uneven and somewhat tiresome. *To See You*, a collection of newly penned romantic songs, finds Connick showcasing a surprising new maturity in his arrangements and songwriting.

what to buy: Buoyed by the hit film of the same name, *When Harry Met Sally* (Columbia, 1989, prod. Marc Shaiman, Harry Connick Jr.) showcases Connick at the height of his crooning abilities as his voice soars thorough standards like "It Had to Be You" and "Let's Call the Whole Thing Off." The CD is Connick's first—and best—work with a big band.

what to buy next: As a follow-up to his film work, Connick released the mostly self-penned *We Are in Love* (Columbia, 1990, prod. Harry Connick Jr.). He does his best work when covering standards like Cole Porter's "It's Alright with Me." A return to form, *To See You* (Columbia, 1997, prod. Tracey Freeman) is Connick's endeavor to make a romantic album. With 10 original songs and a somewhat stripped-down sound, this CD could be a Valentine's Day staple for years to come.

what to avoid: With 14 (!) horns backing him up, you'd think *Blue Light, Red Light* (Columbia, 1991, prod. Tracey Freeman) would swing, but mostly it swoons. It's simply a case of talent plus hype leading directly to indulgence, as Connick hogs the spotlight and crowds out the talented players he's assembled. For a dictionary definition of excess, skip to track four, a laborious 10-minute-plus ode to his then-girlfriend (and current wife), former underwear model Jill Goodacre.

the rest:

11 (Columbia, 1978)
20 (Columbia, 1987)
Harry Connick Jr. (Columbia, 1987)
Lofty's Roach Souffle (Columbia, 1990)
25 (Columbia, 1992)
When My Heart Finds Christmas (Columbia, 1993)
She (Columbia, 1994)
Whisper Your Name (Columbia, 1995)
Star Turtle (Columbia, 1995)
Come by Me N/A (Columbia, 1999)

worth searching for: Connick's success on the silver screen proves that his charm and swagger in person can go a long way. Witness the phenomena for yourself on the video *Swing-*

ing out Live (Columbia, 1991), released as an accompaniment to *Blue Light, Red Light.*

influences:

◀◀ Frank Sinatra, Tony Bennett, Mel Tormé, Thelonious Monk, Eubie Blake, James Booker, Buster Poindexter

▶▶ Squirrel Nut Zippers, G. Love & Special Sauce, Royal Crown Revue

Alex Gordon

Chris Connor

Born November 8, 1927, in Kansas City, MO.

A prototypical song stylist from the "cool jazz" period of the 1950s, singer Chris Connor fronted many a big band during the heyday of swing and proved to be a tasteful and attractive vocalist with something important to say as well. Not as famed as June Christy or Peggy Lee, Connor's style, like that of the aforementioned ladies, has its foundations in understatement and subtlety. She delivers a song in an inviting and straight-forward manner with a resonant and sinewy voice, while avoiding any crowd-pleasing or annoying histrionics. During the late '40s, Connor worked with a variety of big bands, including those led by Bob Brookmeyer and Claude Thornhill. In 1952 she began a brief, but productive stay as the fronting vocalist with Stan Kenton's orchestra before debuting as a solo artist the following year. After cutting three sides for the Bethlehem label, Connor hooked up with Atlantic, where she would go on to record an impressive 12 vital, important albums between 1956 and 1962. Over the past decade, Connor has maintained a low profile, nonetheless recording several fine albums for various labels.

what to buy: The two-disc *Sings the George Gershwin Almanac of Song* (Atlantic, 1956–61/1989, prod. various) reissues Gershwin material from various sessions with several different accompanying groups. The choice of material is splendid and Connor's voice is in peak form. *A Jazz Date with Chris Connor/Chris Craft* (Atlantic, 1956–58/1994, prod. Nesuhi Ertegun) puts two fine albums on one CD. Connor's cool and unassuming delivery thrives in these small groups sides, exploring choice standards like "Lonely Town" and "Moonlight in Vermont."

what to buy next: *Lullabies of Birdland* (Bethlehem/Evidence, 1954/1997) contains Connor's first recordings as a leader, and even at this early date her maturity and natural appeal are evident. There's a nice mix of selections, from a big-band date with Sy Oliver to the small-group backings of Vinnie Burke and Ellis Larkins. *Two's Company* (Roulette, 1961/1996, prod. Teddy Reig) is one of a pair of sides that Connor cut with Maynard Ferguson's ensemble. Though an unlikely pairing, the opposing styles of Connor and Ferguson, with Connor as laid-back as Ferguson was incendiary, actually work well on this highlight of both artist's catalogs.

what to avoid: *Love Being Here with You* (Stash, 1983, prod. Bernard Brightman) comes from more recent times and although Connor's voice has aged well, nothing eventful occurs and the backing musicians are merely competent.

the rest:

Lover Come Back to Me (Evidence, 1981/1995)
Classic (Contemporary, 1986)
New Again (Contemporary, 1987)
As Time Goes By (Enja, 1991)

worth searching for: *Double Exposure* (Atlantic, 1961, prod. Nesuhi Ertegun) has been unavailable for quite some time but is the better of the two dates with Connor fronting the Maynard Ferguson big band.

influences:

◀◀ Anita O'Day

▶▶ Irene Krall, Morgana King

Chris Hovan

Spade Cooley

Born Donnell Clyde Cooley, February 22, 1910, in Grand, OK. Died November 23, 1969, in Oakland, CA.

Spade Cooley's tragic "extra-curricular" activities—he was convicted in 1961 for the first-degree murder of his second wife, largely on the testimony of his fourteen-year-old daughter who'd witnessed, at his insistence, her mother's fatal beating—often threaten to overshadow the King of Western Swing's abundant musical achievements. However, with a character this much larger than life, fireworks can sometimes get in the way.

Of Scots-Irish and Cherokee descent, both Cooley's father and grandfather were fiddlers of renown, and young Cooley's first musical instrument, not surprisingly, was the cello. As so many did during the Depression, the Cooleys headed west in 1931, and Hollywood beckoned: Soon Spade was hired by Republic Pictures as a stand-in for the latest Singing Cowboy sensation, Roy Rogers. So impressed was Rogers by Cooley's fiddling ability that he quickly hired the would-be thespian to tour with his band between pictures. Later, Spade joined Cal Shrum's combo, and made his first-ever trip to the recording studio with them in 1941. It was really only a matter of time, though, before Cooley formed his own band: a monstrous (up to 22 members at times) aggregation that brought a blend of country, jazz, and pure wartime dance music to the booming Southern California ballroom circuit, drawing crowds of 5,000 a night in Santa Monica. His first session for Columbia Records in December of 1944

Spade Cooley **(Archive Photos)**

produced his biggest-ever hit, "Shame on You," and Cooley found time to appear in several motion pictures—even playing host to his own highly rated local television series well into the '50s. A long-time investor in California real estate, his plan to develop a mammoth recreational park called Water Wonderland in the middle of the Mojave Desert (go figure) was derailed when he discovered his wife bragging of an affair with old pal Roy Rogers. Roy survived this incident relatively unscathed; Spade, however, didn't let his wife off so easy. On August 22, 1961, the King of Western Swing was sentenced to life imprisonment for the murder of young Ella Mae Cooley. Due to be paroled for good behavior from Vacaville Prison in 1970, he died of a massive heart attack several weeks prior to his release—following a benefit performance he'd just given for the Alameda Deputy Sheriff's Association.

what's available: Although he later recorded for RCA and Decca, Cooley's legend rests with his OKeh and Columbia recordings from the mid-'40s, the best of which are lovingly restored, annotated, and compiled on *Spadella!: The Essential Spade Cooley* ♪♪♪ (Sony/Legacy, 1994, prod. various). Although the biggest hits, crooned for the most part by vocalist Tex Williams, are somewhat lackluster, the instrumentals jump and cook as few others of their ilk did, or could, in their day. *Radio Broadcasts 1945* ♪♪♪½ (Country Routes, 1998) contains 22 examples of his pioneering sound exactly as it went out over the airwaves in Spade's prime.

influences:

◀ Cass County Boys, Riders of the Purple Sage, Jimmy Wakely

▶ Western Caravan, Dan Hicks & His Hot Licks, Ray Condo & His Ricochets

Gary Pig Gold

Creole Jazz Band

See: Joe "King" Oliver

Crescent City Maulers

Formed 1993, in NJ.

Tony "Scams" Salimbene, saxophone, vocals; "Big Al" Sagnella, guitar, vocals; Kevin "Where's the Bar" McCarthy, upright bass; "Crusher" Carmean, bass (1993–97); Lenni "Boom Boom" Zaccaro, drums.

This East Coast jump/jive band of thirty-something musicians climbed in two years from virtual obscurity to playing to large crowds at New Jersey nightspots. Named after the energetic vintage music forged in Louisiana gin joints, the Crescent City Maulers released their debut CD, *Screamin'*, in April 1996. It was eventually repackaged and released by Slimstyle Records to rave reviews and return invitations to appear on the USA Network show, *Up All Night*, hosted by Gilbert Gottfried. Although the band is a cooperative venture, Tony Salimbene is the unofficial leader and Al Sagnella sings most of the vocals. The band now performs in clubs scattered around New York, New Jersey, and Pennsylvania and, to fulfill the enthusiastic craze for their dance music, most gigs are preceded by swing dance lessons.

what's available: Just as it will satisfy neo-swing fans, the rousing 14-tracks of the studio-recorded CD *Screamin'* ♪♪♪♪ (Slimstyle, 1997, prod. Don Sternecker, Crescent City Maulers) will remind long-time jump-jazz and jitterbug fans of the honking sax-vocals led, bar-walking bands of the 1940s and 1950s. These four cats create more consolidated, raucous energy and a bigger sound than any larger ensemble. Salimbene's gritty, raw tenor saxisms are reminiscent of 1950s Chicago saxophonist Tab Smith's full-bodied sound. You'll dig CCM's takes on familiar tunes popularized by jump-swing master Louis Jordan ("Reet, Petite, and Gone" and "Caledonia.") as well as classics (often with hilarious lyrics) originally forged by Louis Prima and Cab Calloway.

influences:

◀ Cab Calloway, Louis Jordan, Louis Prima

Nancy Ann Lee

Bing Crosby

Born Harry Lillis Crosby, May 3, 1903, in Tacoma, WA. Died October 14, 1977, in Madrid, Spain.

It's hard to speculate what the swing era would have been like without Bing Crosby to pave its way as a popular force. His 50-year recording career spawned more than 200 hit records and was the launching pad for equally successful forays into radio, motion pictures, and television. From a base of jazz and swing, he effortlessly reinterpreted cowboy, Hawaiian, boogie-woogie, polkas, and religious material into his own cool-cat style and achieved a now-unheard-of longevity in the face of changing musical trends.

Crosby began his career in 1925 singing and playing drums for Al Rinker's orchestra, the Musicaladers. The following year, Rinker and Crosby recorded their first Columbia single, "I've Got the Girl," as a duet, just before joining bandleader Paul Whiteman's orchestra. Whiteman teamed them with Harry Barris, dubbed his new trio the Rhythm Boys, and recorded dozens of hits with them, including "Side by Side," "I'm Coming Virginia," and "My Blue Heaven." The Rhythm Boys left Whiteman in 1930 to establish themselves as a solo act and constant chart presence. Crosby's increasingly popular solo spots, combined with union problems (concerning missed bookings), broke up the act, and he signed with Brunswick in 1931. Under the direction of Jack Kapp, Crosby's recording career exploded. His clean, jazz-influenced phrasing and casual, erudite manner led to major hits, such as "Just One More Chance," "I Surrender Dear," and "Where the Blue of the Night" (where he whistles and scats the immortal phrase "boo-boo-boo-boo"), and established him as a household name. Crosby's concurrent rise as a radio and motion picture star dovetailed into a publicity bonanza, and he became King of the Crooners, biggest star of the Depression era. However, his enormously busy schedule was not without consequences: After severely straining his vocal chords, Crosby had to lower his pitch and undergo coaching on proper breathing technique. The result was the warmer, more intimate style most people now associate with him.

When Kapp left Brunswick for Decca Records in 1934, Crosby went with him and continued to dominate the charts with such classics as "Pennies from Heaven," "Sweet Leilani," "I'm an Old Cowhand." Kapp was instrumental in expanding Crosby's style to other genres, and paired him with the Mills Brothers, Connee Boswell, Louis Armstrong, Judy Garland, and the Andrews Sisters for a series of amazingly popular discs. Crosby insisted upon working with the top jazz and swing artists of the day, regardless of skin color, and his influence provided exposure for many artists who otherwise would not have broken the color line of the times. If Crosby was hot in the '30s, he supernovaed in the '40s. He became Hollywood's leading box office draw (with and without his *Road Picture* partner, Bob "ol' Ski-nose" Hope), had one of the highest rated radio shows in the country, and recorded the biggest-selling single of all time, "White Christmas" (from the 1942 movie *Holiday Inn*). Decca pressed so many copies of "White Christmas" that the company damaged the master recording and had to re-record the tune in 1947. Perhaps Crosby's absolute peak as a multimedia star was in 1944 when he won a best-actor Oscar for *Going My Way*, as well as scoring seven #1 hit records ("Swinging on a Star," "Don't Fence Me In," and "I'll Be Seeing You" among them). Crosby also weathered the rise of a new crooner who threatened his popularity—Frank Sinatra, of whom he said, "A voice like that comes along once in a generation. Why did it have to be mine?" Despite Sinatra's sudden fame, Crosby consistently sold more records. Crosby's enormous popularity extended well past the war years into television's golden age, but his amazing string of hit records dried up after 1951. His final Top 10 hit, "True Love" (a duet with Grace Kelly from the film *High Society*), came in 1956 for MGM. In the 1950s, as a freelance artist, Crosby returned to his jazz roots, cut some swing and standards, and released movie soundtracks and remakes; throughout the '60s, he generally attempted to update his pop style for Sinatra's Reprise Records and other labels. By the '70s a "semi-retired" Crosby hosted occasional TV specials and golf tournaments, made commercials, took feature parts in movies, recorded two LPs for United Artists (one with Count

"Cow Cow Boogie"
ELLA MAE MORSE
1942
After failing in Jimmy Dorsey's band—she forgot lyrics on a national radio broadcast—Morse was hired by Dorsey pianist Freddy Slack for his first hit.
Swingin' SINGLES

Basie), and profited handsomely from his many entertainment business interests.

what to buy: As a starting point, *Greatest Hits* ♪♪♪♪♪ (MCA, 1995, prod. various) is an inexpensive 12-song collection featuring such hits as "Too-Ra-Loo-Ra-Loo-Ral," "Ac-cent-tchu-ate the Positive," "White Christmas," and "Don't Fence Me In." However, the mid-priced *Bing's Gold Records* ♪♪♪♪♪ (Decca, 1997, compilation prod. Andy McKaie) has 21 songs and encompasses the best of those two releases.

what to buy next: The epiphany of true Bing-ness can be achieved by purchasing *Bing Crosby: His Legendary Years, 1931–57* ♪♪♪♪♪ (MCA, 1993, compilation prod. Steve Lasker, Andy McKaie), a four-CD, 101-track box set culled from his great years with Decca that includes Crosby's hit collaborations with the Andrews Sisters, Judy Garland, Louis Armstrong, Louis Jordan, and his son, Gary, as well as a comprehensive 68-page booklet. Those who dig Der Bingle as a Christmas-crooner will truly give thanks for *The Voice of Christmas: The Complete Decca Songbook* ♪♪♪♪ (Decca, 1998, compilation prod. Steve Lasker), a two-disc set with Crosby's previously unreleased first take of "White Christmas."

what to avoid: They're OK for completists, but don't be misled: *Christmas through the Years* (Laserlight, 1995) and *White Christmas* (Laserlight, 1993) do not feature Crosby's original Decca renditions of his famous seasonal offerings. Also, there's too much Mitch Miller and the Golden Orchestra and not enough of "The Old Groaner" on *How Lovely Is Christmas* (Drive Archive, 1998), an anemic seasonal offering.

the rest:
Blue Skies (Sandy Hook, 1946/1996)
Best of Bing Crosby & Fred Astaire: A Couple of Song & Dance Men (Curb, 1975/1993)
Bing Crosby's Christmas Classic (Capitol/EMI, 1977/1997)
Bing Crosby Sings Again (MCA, 1986)
Radio Years–20 Songs (GNP/Crescendo, 1987)
Radio Years–25 Songs (GNP/Crescendo, 1988)
Pocketful of Dreams (Pro Arte, 1989)
Pennies from Heaven (Pro Arte, 1989)
The Radio Years, Vol. I (GNP/Crescendo, 1990)
The Radio Years, Vol. II (GNP/Crescendo, 1990)
The Radio Years, Vol. III (GNP/Crescendo, 1990)
The Radio Years, Vol. IV (GNP/Crescendo, 1990)
All-Time Best of Bing Crosby (Curb, 1990)
That's Jazz (Pearl, 1991)
Bing Crosby & Some Jazz Friends (Decca Jazz, 1991)
The Movie Hits (Pearl, 1992)
On the Sentimental Side (ASV, 1992)
Here Lies Love (ASV, 1992)
16 Most Requested Songs (Columbia/Legacy, 1992)
The Jazzin' Bing Crosby 1927–40 (Affinity, 1992)
Original Soundtrack Sessions: Holiday Inn & Blue Skies (Vintage Jazz Classics, 1993)
Merry Christmas (MCA, 1993)
The Great Years (Pearl, 1993)
That Christmas Feeling (MCA Special Products, 1993)
On Treasure Island (JSP, 1993)
Sings Christmas Songs (MCA Special Products, 1993)
Classic Bing Crosby 1931–38 (DRG/ABC, 1994)
World War II Radio (Laserlight, 1994)
Bing Crosby 1927–34 (Mobile Fidelity Lab, 1995)
Swingin' on a Star (Flapper, 1995)
I'm an Old Cow Hand (Living Era, 1995)
Bing Crosby with Paul Whiteman (Chanson's Cinema, 1995)
Bing Crosby & Friends (Living Era, 1995)
Greatest Hits on the Radio, Vol. I (Enterprise/Radio Years, 1995)
Bing Crosby in Hollywood 1930–33 (Chansen's Cinema, 1995)
Bing Crosby in Hollywood, Vol. III (Chansen's Cinema, 1995)
Duets 1947–49 (Viper's Nest, 1996)
Bing Crosby/Andrews Sisters: Their Complete Recordings (MCA, 1996)
Top o' the Morning: His Irish Collection (MCA, 1996)
Bing Sings whilst Bregman Swings (Mobile Fidelity, 1996)
My Favorite Cowboy Songs (MCA, 1996)
On the Radio in the '30s (Enterprise/Radio Years, 1996)
A Little Bit of Irish (Atlantic, 1996)
Love Songs (MCA Special Products, 1997)
My Favorite Hymns (MCA Special Products, 1997)
American Legends # Seven (Laserlight, 1997)
My Favorite Hawaiian Songs (MCA Special Products, 1997)
That Christmas Feeling: Bing Crosby & Frank Sinatra (Unison, 1997)
The EP Collection (See for Miles, 1997)
WWII Christmas Shows (Laserlight, 1997)
WWII Radio: Special Christmas Show (Laserlight, 1997)
The Revue Collection (Revue Collection, 1997)
(With Louis Armstrong) *Havin' More Fun* (Jazz Unlimited, 1997)
The Complete United Artists Sessions (EMI, 1997)
My Favorite Irish Songs (MCA Special Products, 1998)

worth searching for: Crosby's early years as a young sensation with a high, hard vocal technique are on *The Crooner: The Columbia Years 1928–34* (Columbia, 1988, prod. various), which has 67 tracks, including his work as part of the Rhythm Boys, with Paul Whiteman, and his first solo efforts.

influences:
◀◀ Rudy Vallee, Mildred Bailey, Al Jolson, Louis Armstrong, Ethel Waters

▶▶ Russ Columbo, Dick Haymes, Frank Sinatra, Dean Martin, Frankie Laine, Perry Como, Roy Brown, Eddie Fisher

Ken Burke

Bob Crosby

Born George Robert Crosby, August 25, 1913, in Spokane, WA. Died March 9, 1993, in La Jolla, CA.

He lived his entire life in the shadow of brother Bing, but Bob Crosby's big bands in the '30s and '40s flung horns in every swinging direction and racked up a long list of hits—some with the most famous singers of the era, from Connee Boswell to, yes, Bing Crosby. Crosby, a skilled bandleader with a natural feel for swing music, was never much of a singer, so he suffered from harsh critical comparisons to his brother his whole career. But in retrospect, the Dixieland-influenced songs he left behind—"South Rampart Street Parade" and "Wolverine Blues," among many—hold up as fun, jittery, horn-rich standards. Orchestra leader Anson Weeks invited the 18-year-old Crosby to join his orchestra, and another opportunity quickly opened up. Several musicians in Ben Pollack's popular band got tired of arguing with their feisty bandleader, so they declared a mutiny and labored briefly under skilled businessman but not-so-personable Gil Rodin until Crosby, with his love of Dixieland and family connections, won the helm. With these players—saxophonist Eddie Miller and trumpeter Yank Lawson among them—Crosby's big band and its smaller, tighter incarnation, the Bobcats, went on to huge commercial success; the fame led to singing engagements for Crosby, plus small roles in films such as *Two Tickets to Broadway* and *Let's Make Music*. The band's popularity waned as rock 'n' roll took over the music industry, but despite the bandleader's death in 1993 and legal hassles with the name, Crosby's late-career saxophonist, Bobby Levine, continues to lead the Bob Crosby Orchestra on tours of the U.S.

what to buy: The most comprehensive Crosby CDs, unfortunately, are only available on British import, but some domestic record companies have released his material in dribs and drabs. *The Bobcats Play 22 Original Big Band Records* (Hindsight, 1987/1994) captures many of Crosby's popular early '50s recordings with his small Dixieland revival combo, including "March of the Bobcats," "March of the Mustangs," "Jazz Me Blues," and "In a Sentimental Mood." *Uncollected* (Hindsight, 1992) reissues the orchestra's early 1940s hits, and *Uncollected, Vol. I* (Hindsight, 1992) continues into the early 1950s.

what to buy next: *South Rampart Street Parade* (Decca, 1989) is a jazzier sampling of Crosby's prolific days with Decca Records; it includes "Dixieland Shuffle," "Air Mail Stomp," "Wolverine Blues," and several others in which the horns jump around like characters in a cartoon. With singing guests June Christy and Polly Bergen, *The Bob Crosby Orchestra with Guests* (Hindsight, 1990, prod. Tom Gramuglia) features snappy, slightly exotic, songs like "Ostrich Walk," "Song of the Islands," and the crooning standard, "Willow Weep for Me."

best of the rest:

The Bob Crosby Orchestra and the Bobcats (Living Era, 1992)
1939–42 Broadcasts (Jazz Hour, 1995)
Eye Opener (Topaz Jazz, 1996)

worth searching for: The best way to delve into Crosby's overshadowed career is via English imports: several are available, the most thorough being *Complete Discography 1939–40* (Halcyon, 1997, prod. various). For more context, Crosby's hits show up on several big-band compilation boxes, including the excellent *Swing Time! The Fabulous Big Band Era, 1925–55* (Columbia/Legacy, 1993, prod. various), which contains Crosby's hit "South Rampart Street Parade" among tracks by Claude Thornhill, Bunny Berigan, Benny Goodman, Duke Ellington, Cab Calloway, and many others.

influences:

◀◀ Bing Crosby, Duke Ellington, Louis Armstrong

▶▶ Fats Domino, the Boswell Sisters, Guy Lombardo, Buddy Greco

Steve Knopper

Xavier Cugat

Born Francisco de Asis Javier Cugat Mingall de Bru y Deulofeo, January 1, 1900, in Gerona, Spain. Died October 27, 1990, in Barcelona, Spain.

Latin music has always been malleable enough to fit a wide range of American pop tastes, and few made rumbas and cha-cha-chas easier to stomach than Xavier Cugat and his orchestra. He's still best known, to an extent, as the swarthy Cuban womanizer who made the beautiful singer Abbe Lane his third wife. But in addition to his easy-listening trailblazing for '60s Latin-pop artists such as Herb Alpert's Tijuana Brass and Serigo Mendes's Brazil 66, Cugat, early in his career, led a swinging big band and appeared on landmark radio shows with Benny Goodman.

Originally a child-prodigy classical violinist, Cugat lived with his family in Cuba before moving to New York City around 1918. To get by during the Depression, he became a well-known cartoonist with the King Features Syndicate, his work running in newspapers around the country. He immediately established connections in the Latin community, befriending actor Rudolph Valentino, who encouraged him to start a tango band. Cugat also wound up in such movies as *In Gay Madrid* and *Bathing Beauty*—he was the playboy, in many MGM musicals, who spoke while cradling a chihuahua. But his passion was music, and the more popular, the better. He and Perez Prado were among the first performers to add Latin touches to U.S. pop music, and Cugat sired a young Desi Arnaz in his orchestra. (Eventual celebrity Charo, then a folk guitarist, was one of many Latinos who first got a break with Cugat.) Cugat adapted easily to all the Latin crazes, first the rumba, then the samba, the mambo, the cha cha cha, and the tango. His light, easy orchestra featured prominent tinkly percussion and strong, loud horns, with the occasional electric guitar or organ to spice up a verse, but it never became even as heavy as Alpert's later smash "The Lonely Bull." Rock 'n' roll and younger, more marketable artists like Alpert forced Cugat to change his approach. He spent most of the 1960s and 1970s re-recording movie music, from "Chim, Chim Cher-ee" (from *Mary Poppins*) to *Thunderball*). He appeared on several hip cocktail compilations during the early-1990s lounge-music comeback.

what to buy: Cugat's big-band roots are mostly on British imports (such as *On the Radio: 1935–42* (Harlequin, 1997), which explores his early big-band phase and is pretty easy to find). To fully experience his tinkly brand of easy-listening music, you'll need a sampling of his earlier sambas and cha cha chas and his film music of the '60s. *Cugie a-Go-Go* (MCA, 1966/1997, prod. Harry Meyerson) reprints the space-villain femme fatale, complete with ray gun and dark blue glasses, on the cover, and includes such swinging horn music as "Judith,"

John Barry's James Bond anthem "Goldfinger" and the Disney standard "Zip-a-Dee-Doo-Dah."

what to avoid: Though MCA has reissued several of Cugat's '60s albums on CD, there's no real point to adding anything beyond *Cugie a Go-Go* to your library. So don't bother with *Xavier Cugat Today!* (Decca, 1967).

best of the rest:
Feeling Good! (Decca, 1965)
Bang Bang (Decca, 1966)
De Colleccion (PolyGram Latino, 1994)
Say Si! Si! (Pair, 1994)

worth searching for: *Waltzes—But by Cugat!* (Columbia) and *Cugat Caricatures* (Mercury) are excellent finds, and a decent representative of the bandleader's Columbia and Mercury years. And, while the pairing isn't exactly Frank Sinatra and Nelson Riddle, the Cugat–Dinah Shore collaborative CD *1939–45* (Harlequin, 1994) will look hilarious and sound decent in any respectable record collection.

influences:
◀◀ Dizzy Gillespie, Duke Ellington, Benny Goodman, Glenn Miller

▶▶ Perez Prado, Tito Puente, Charo, Desi Arnaz, Juan Garcia Esquivel, Abbe Lane, Herb Alpert, Sergio Mendes

Steve Knopper

Chris Daniels & the Kings

Formed March 18, 1984, in Denver, CO.

Chris Daniels (born September 30, 1952), vocals and guitar; Forrest Means, trumpet; Carlos Chavez, alto and tenor saxophones; Dean Ledoux, keyboards; Bones Jones, guitar; Randy Amen, drums; Kevin Lege, bass; Fly McClard, tenor saxophone.

In Amsterdam, where Chris Daniels and the Kings have had two # 1 albums, Jip Golsteijn of *De Telegraaf* has written: "Chris Daniels: Ik ben leider omdat ik niet kan volgen." Who can disagree with that? Who can understand that? The scoop is Daniels was inspired to make music a career back in 1969 and hit the road to work with artists like Kate Taylor, David Johansen (pre-New York Dolls and Buster Poindexter), and Russell Smith (post-Amazing Rhythm Aces). Daniels studied at the Berkelee College of Music in Boston before recording an LP, *Definitely Live*, as guitarist and singer in a Denver band called the Spoons. That and his 1983 solo album *Juggler* laid the groundwork for a stint playing stringed instruments for Smith with several other musicians who would form the first version of the Kings. The general style of the Kings' first six records was horn-based R&B, in the mode of Little Feat and Tower of Power. Via Armed Forces radio exposure, Daniels gained a (wooden) toe-hold in Holland and a record deal that made the Kings actual stars in the land of dikes and tulips. In the U.S., the Kings work constantly, and their pockets of converts follow the band's new/old direction, to the swing era. Daniels is executive director of the Swallow Hill Music Association, which organizes Denver-area folk, bluegrass, and Cajun concerts.

what to buy: For fans of swing, the only Kings' disc to buy is *Louie Louie* (Moon Voyage, 1998, prod. Chris Daniels). The title doesn't allude to the frat-rock classic by the Kingsmen, it pays homage to the triumvirate of Louis: Prima, Armstrong, and Jordan. Songs include "If You're So Smart, How Come You Ain't Rich" and "Is You Is Or Is You Ain't My Baby."

what to buy next: The only other Kings' release with swing is *Is My Love Enough* (Flying Fish, 1993, prod. Chris Daniels), which is mostly R&B, but features a red-hot cover of the Benny Goodman (and Prima-penned) rave-up "Sing Sing Sing." The Neon Park cover, with a duck in a provocative nude Marilyn Monroe–like pose, is a true classic.

what to avoid: On *That's What I Like about the South* (Redstone, 1990, prod. Al Kooper), Blues Project founder and former Bob Dylan sideman Al Kooper's production is not as dynamic as what would come later. But the cover of the Tom Petty/Mudcrutch song "Depot Street" is a winner. Finally, there is nothing the matter with the out-of-print LP by Spoons *Definitely Live* (Sunshine, 1981, prod. John Aldridge, Leigh Kutchinsky), but it bears little resemblance to the Daniels we recognize in the Kings' releases.

the rest:
In Your Face (Flying Fish, 1992)
Live Wired (Flat Canyon, 1996)

worth searching for: Out of print are *When You're Cool* (Moon Voyage, 1987, prod. Jim Mason, Chris Daniels & the Kings), *Has Anyone Seen My Keys* (Harmony, 1985, prod. Bob Barnham, Chris Daniels) (with a cool version of the soul standard "634-5789"), and *Juggler* (Next Coast, 1983, prod. Jim Mason). Some of Daniels's hard-to-find albums can be obtained at http://www.ChrisDaniels.com or by writing Moon Voyage, 2035 Jasmine, Denver, CO 80207.

influences:
◀◀ Little Feat, Tower of Power, Louis Jordan, Louis Prima, Randy Newman

▶▶ Dem Rite, Hot Skillet

George W. Krieger, D.D.S.

Bobby Darin

Born Walden Robert Cossoto, May 14, 1936, in Bronx, NY. Died December 20, 1973, in Los Angeles, CA.

When discussing the decline of rock 'n' roll music in the late '60s/early '70s, the great Jerry Lee Lewis remarked, "One day I looked around and there was a whole flock of Bobbys on the radio! Bobby Vee, Bobby Vinton, Bobby Rydell, Bobby Darin." Certainly that statement rings with truth, but let it be declared for good and all: Darin was the main Bobby. Intense, creative, and deeply talented, Darin assumed many identities in his career: Brill Building songwriter, '50s teen idol, Frank Sinatra heir apparent, hipster, actor, folkie, political activist, and all-round Vegas-style entertainer. He was successful at nearly every phase of his career, but had he narrowed his scope he might have been much bigger than he was. Several childhood bouts with rheumatic fever left Darin with damaged heart valves and the painful knowledge that his life would be short. So he attempted to cram as much into his career as possible. A versatile musician (piano, drums, guitar, and vibes) and a prolific composer, Darin got his start writing commercial jingles and pitching songs with future pop mogul Don Kirschner. In 1956 he signed with Atco Records and released a series of high-profile bombs that would've destroyed the career of a less determined artist. Finally, in 1958 he and disc jockey Murray the K cobbled together the quintessential rock 'n' roll novelty, "Splish Splash." Upon cementing his Top 10 status with "Queen of the Hop" and the teen masterpiece "Dream Lover," Darin switched directions, and (against the advice of Dick Clark) recorded an unquestionably swinging, Sinatra-style version of "Mack the Knife," his biggest hit ever.

For a time, Darin was able to successfully court both adult and teen audiences (not to mention movie audiences) by alternating brassy remakes of standards with occasional sidesteps to Ray Charles-inspired rock and teen pop. Darin left Atco for Capitol Records in 1963, and wrote two of his finest records, the country flavored "You're the Reason I'm Living," and "18 Yellow Roses," both major pop hits. During the mid-'60s, the combination of the British Invasion and a string of lame film vehicles rendered his singing career irrelevant. Darin tried to rebound by raising his social consciousness, eschewing his toupee and tuxedo, dressing in denim, and in 1966 returned to Atlantic to record folk music. His version of Tim Hardin's "If I Were a Carpenter" is definitive and was a solid Top 10 hit, but despite worthy follow-ups, the public could not reconcile its image of the finger-snapping Sinatra wannabe with the new ultra-serious folk singer "Bob" Darin. Robert Kennedy's death in 1968 totally unhinged Darin: He abandoned show business, moved into a trailer in the Big Sur, and spent his fortune writing, producing, directing, and starring in an unreleasable film about a heroic folk singer. His career seemed over until his old protégé, Wayne Newton, got him to come back and perform live in Las Vegas. Darin's comeback was highlighted by a hit summer variety series on NBC, where he proved to be as deft a comedian as he was a singer. Darin recorded his final chart entry, "Happy (Lady Sings the Blues Love Theme)," for Motown before dying, at age 37, during heart-valve replacement surgery.

what to buy: Darin's fertile hit years at Atco/Atlantic are well represented on several fine solo discs. *Splish Splash: The Best of Bobby Darin, Vol. I* (Atco, 1991, compilation prod. Greg Geller) highlights the best of his teen material. *Mack the Knife: The Best of Bobby Darin, Vol. II* (Atco, 1991, compilation prod. Greg Geller) contains 21 tracks from his Sinatra period. *Bobby Darin Story* (Atlantic, 1989, prod. Ahmet Ertegun) and *The Ultimate Bobby Darin* (Warner Bros. Special Products, 1986, prod. Ahmet Ertegun) are nice varied compilations as well. However, if your budget can stand the strain, the four-disc set, *As Long as I'm Singin'* (Rhino, 1995, prod. Ahmet Ertegun), features the very best of Darin's recorded work for Atco, as well as 11 previously unreleased songs and alternate takes.

what to buy next: Darin unsuccessfully fought the British Invasion at Capitol Records, where he alternated retro-Sinatra sounds with smart country-pop. *Bobby Darin: Capitol Collector's Series* (Capitol/EMI, 1996/Gold Rush, 1998, compilation prod. Ron Furmanek) contain "You're the Reason I'm Living," "18 Yellow Roses" (which Darin wrote for his wife, Sandra Dee), and swinging takes on such standards as "Hello, Dolly." Darin made his move from teen idol to all-around adult entertainer on *Darin at the Copa* (Atlantic, 1960/1994, prod. Ahmet Ertegun, Nesuhi Ertegun), a 17-track reissue of the LP recorded live at Frank Sinatra's old stomping grounds, the Copacabana. Those wishing to partake of the full range of Darin's abilities should definitely check out Capitol's new *A&E Biography* edition of *Bobby Darin: A Musical Anthology* Capitol, 1998, compilation prod. Cheryl Pawelski, Steve Blauner). On this smart package, the artist can be heard effortlessly entertaining live audiences with his blend of comedy, brassy pop, and folk. In addition to his big Capitol hits "You're The Reason I'm Living" and "Hello, Dolly!" the studio tracks include such juiced-up standards as "Call Me Irresponsible," "Don't Rain on My Parade", and the previously unreleased "Love Look Away."

what to avoid: Darin's post–Bobby Kennedy assassination depression asserts itself most gloomily on *Born: Walden Robert Cosotto* (Direction, 1968, prod. Bobby Darin), a folk protest LP Darin believed in so strongly he refused to wear his toupee while recording it. Steer clear of the budget-rack mongrel *The Best of Bobby Darin* (Curb, 1990, prod. various), a thin-sounding hodgepodge of recordings from various labels.

Bobby Darin **(Archive Photos)**

the rest:
Bobby Darin (Atlantic, 1958/1994)
That's All (Atlantic, 1959/1994)
This Is Darin (Atlantic, 1960/1994)
As Long As I'm Singin' Vol. I (Jass, 1993)
Two of a Kind: Bobby Darin & Johnny Mercer (Atlantic, 1994)
Greatest Hits (Classic, 1994)
Spotlight on Bobby Darin (Capitol/EMI, 1995)
Say Willie (MCA Special Products, 1996)
Bobby Darin (A Touch of Class, 1997)
You're the Reason I'm Living/I Wanna Be Around (EMI, 1997)

worth searching for: Darin's cocky vocal style is oddly appealing on *25th of December* (Atco, 1991, prod. Ahmet Ertegun), a true lounge lizard's idea of how to make holiday fare really swing. Also, four of Darin's mid-to-late '60s LPs are combined for *If I Were a Carpenter/Inside Out* (Atlantic 1966/1967/Diablo, 1998, prod. various) and *Shadow of Your Smile/In a Broadway Bag* (Atlantic, 1966/Diablo, 1998, prod. various).

influences:
◄◄ Frank Sinatra, Ray Charles, Tim Hardin
►► Bobby Rydell, Wayne Newton, Harry Connick Jr.

Ken Burke

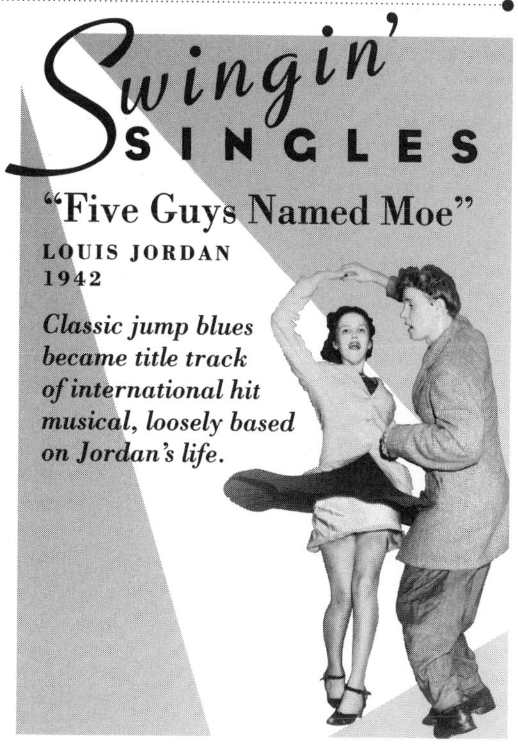

Swingin' SINGLES
"Five Guys Named Moe"
LOUIS JORDAN
1942
Classic jump blues became title track of international hit musical, loosely based on Jordan's life.

Eddie "Lockjaw" Davis

Born March 2, 1922, in New York, NY. Died November 3, 1986, in Culver City, CA.

Taking his cue from swing-jazz notables Ben Webster and Coleman Hawkins, tenor saxophonist Eddie "Lockjaw" Davis was a rough-and-tumble player with an immediately recognizable sound and attack. He would first make a name for himself in the 1940s while with the bands of Cootie Williams, Lucky Millinder, and Andy Kirk. He also would be a star soloist with Count Basie's orchestra on many occasions, first from 1952 to 1953, then during 1957, and from 1964–1973. On any of the many Basie albums of those periods, you're likely to find Davis's jubilant soloing, usually brief and sometimes short on melodic development, but always delightfully alive with an aggressive swagger and sway. One of Davis's most memorable associations was with organist Shirley Scott during the late '50s, with their famous "Cookbook" sessions virtually defining the organ/tenor combo. A true heavyweight in every manner, Davis most benefited from the quintet he co-led with Johnny Griffin during the 1960s.

what to buy: *The Eddie "Lockjaw" Davis Cookbook, Vol. I*, *The Eddie "Lockjaw" Davis Cookbook, Vol. II*, and *The Eddie "Lockjaw" Davis Cookbook, Vol. III* (Prestige, 1958/Original Jazz Classics, 1991, prod. Esmond Edwards), all essential classics with organist Shirley Scott, find Lockjaw in top form. *Live at Minton's* (Prestige, 1961/1998, prod. Esmond Edwards) is the best of the many recordings produced by the pair of Davis and Griffin. With the exception of two cuts, this single CD, when taken in tandem with the reissue of *The Tenor Scene* (Prestige, 1961/Original Jazz Classics, 1997, prod. Esmond Edwards), presents the entire output of a 1961 club appearance that catches Davis and Griffin in peak form.

what to buy next: *Trane Whistle* (Prestige, 1960/Original Jazz Classics, 1990, prod. Esmond Edwards) finds "Jaws" in the company of Oliver Nelson's large ensemble and the results are truly explosive. As good as Davis's small combo work is, he's just a natural when placed in front of a big band. *Afro-Jaws* (Riverside, 1961/Original Jazz Classics, 1989, prod. Orrin Keepnews) has Davis fronting a large trumpet and percussion section and producing spirited versions of "Tin Tin Deo" and "Alma Alegre," among others.

what to avoid: *Gentle Jaws* (Prestige, 1960/1997, prod. Esmond Edwards) pairs two late '50s sessions for Prestige's Moodsville subsidiary and while there's some fine ballad work to be heard, the predominance of ballad tempos ultimately wears thin.

best of the rest:

Jaws (Prestige, 1958/Original Jazz Classics, 1994)
Smokin' (Prestige, 1958/Original Jazz Classics, 1991)
Jaws in Orbit (Prestige, 1959/Original Jazz Classics, 1992)
Streetlights (Prestige, 1962/Original Jazz Classics, 1995)
Straight Ahead (Pablo, 1976/Original Jazz Classics, 1991)
Montreux '77 (Pablo, 1977/Original Jazz Classics, 1989)
The Heavy Hitter (Muse/32 Jazz, 1979/1998)

worth searching for: *Save Your Love for Me* (Bluebird, 1988, reissue prod. Ed Michel) has been deleted from print, but it's a fine compilation of Davis's mid-'60s RCA dates—including a big-band set and a pairing with Paul Gonsalves.

influences:

◀◀ Coleman Hawkins, Ben Webster

▶▶ Eddie Chamblee, Harry Warren, Tad Shull

Chris Hovan

Sammy Davis Jr.

Born December 8, 1925, in New York, NY. Died May 16, 1990, in Los Angeles, CA.

Sammy Davis Jr. was the ultimate cabaret performer. Onstage he was intensely dramatic, comic, physically expressive, and a peerless dancer, but recordings seldom conveyed the full depth of his abilities. He was also a key member of the Rat Pack, that gang of entertainers that included Frank Sinatra, Dean Martin, Peter Lawford, and Joey Bishop. After leaving the Will Mastin Trio, Davis began recording with Decca Records in 1954 and established a pattern of reinterpreting Broadway show tunes and movie hits, and jazzing up standards, à la Billy Daniels and Frank Sinatra. During the mid-1950s he scored hits with "Hey There" (also a hit for Johnnie Ray), "Something's Gotta Give," "Love Me or Leave Me," "That Old Black Magic," "I'll Know," "Earthbound," and "New York Is My Home." Rock 'n' roll's popularity knocked Davis's efforts off the charts, though he continued to record prolifically for Decca. After signing with Sinatra's Reprise Records in 1961 he was able to exert much more creative control over his musical output, though his recording career would continue to take a back seat to his fabulously successful work in Broadway musicals, films, TV shows, and nightclubs. Later, the Rat Pack showcased their swaggering, cocktail-in-hand, doll-on-each-arm, hipper-than-thou attitude in such films as *Ocean's Eleven* and *Robin and the Seven Hoods*, with Davis's sensational singing and dancing usually stealing the show. In 1962 "What Kind of Fool Am I?" (from the musical *Stop the World I Want to Get Off*) became Davis's first million-selling record and crystallized his persona as an artist who sang less about romance than about being a heartbroken man facing impossible odds. "As Long as She Needs Me" and "The Shelter of Your Arms" were sung with similar dramatic intensity and were sizable hits, but once again musical tastes changed, this time towards the British Invasion, and Davis's chart momentum stalled.

Davis recorded several highly regarded jazz, pop, and musical variety LPs throughout the 1960s, but he didn't have another big hit single until 1968. With "I've Gotta Be Me" (from the musical *Golden Rainbow*), Davis was doing what he always had done—but this time the burgeoning baby-boomer culture, grappling with changing identities, responded positively and adopted the record as a pop anthem. This began Davis's let's-get-down-and-be-groovy-love-children phase, where he dressed in psychedelic clothes, spouted peace-and-love rhetoric, and began experimenting with drugs. Musically, however, little changed, and soon his hippie garb and "peace, love, and brotherhood" raps became fodder for comedians and impressionists. Davis's only #1 hit, 1972's frivolous smash "Candy Man" (inspired by the film *Willy Wonka and the Chocolate Factory*), briefly re-energized his career, but his follow-up, "People Tree," let him down. Afterwards, Davis recorded sporadically for Motown, EMI, and Columbia without much success or enthusiasm. However, even in his last sickly years, during any given concert, he could still lay claim to the title "World's Greatest Entertainer."

what to buy: Davis personally culled his best-selling singles and most memorable cuts for *His Greatest Hits, Vols. I & II* (DCC, 1990, reissue prod. Sammy Davis Jr.) and *Greatest Hits, Vol. III* (DCC, 1990, reissue prod. Sammy Davis Jr.) brilliantly chronicling his years with Decca, Reprise, and MGM. The Marty Paich Dek-Tette bring out the best in Davis on *The Wham of Sam: Sammy Davis Jr.* (Warner Archives, 1994, compilation prod. Greg Geller), a stirring example of contemporary jazz with the singer really going to town on such standards as "A Lot of Livin' to Do," "Too Close for Comfort," "Begin the Beguine," and "Bye Bye Blackbird." This just may be Davis's finest solo studio album and the booklet is superb.

what to buy next: The singer cut his most consistent material for Frank Sinatra's Reprise label, and *I've Gotta Be Me: The Best of Sammy Davis Jr. on Reprise* (Reprise Archives, 1996, compilation prod. Greg Geller) features the cream of his work there. These moody sides challenge such great Sinatra Capitol LP's as *No One Cares* and *Only the Lonely* for the most introspective performances ever recorded on a commercial record. Also, Davis is obviously having a ball jamming live with legendary drummer Buddy Rich on *The Sounds of '66: Sammy Davis Jr./Buddy Rich* (DCC Jazz, 1966/1996 prod. Jimmy Bowen), and the digitally remastered sound is gorgeous.

what to avoid: Davis is really out of his element on *From Nashville with Love* (EMI/Capitol Special Products, 1994, prod. various), a belated stab at high-gloss country crossover music that seldom sounds convincing.

the rest:

Sammy Davis Jr. Sings, Laurindo Almeida Plays ♪♪♪♪ (DCC Jazz, 1966/1997)
The Great Sammy Davis Jr. ♪♪♪ (Columbia, 1989)
Capitol Collector's Series ♪♪♪ (Capitol/EMI, 1990)
Sammy Davis Jr. ♪♪♪ (MCA Special Products, 1990)
Greatest Songs ♪♪♪ (Curb, 1990)
The Decca Years 1954–1960 ♪♪♪ (MCA, 1990)
Best of Sammy Davis Jr. ♪♪♪ (Curb, 1991)
What Kind of Fool Am I? ♪♪♪♪ (Pair, 1993)
That Old Black Magic ♪♪♪ (MCA Special Products, 1995)
Greatest Hits Live ♪♪ (Curb, 1995)
What I've Got in Mind ♪♪♪ (Charly, 1995)
All the Things You Are ♪♪♪ (Pair, 1996)

worth searching for: One of the best recorded examples of Davis performing live in a nightclub can be found on *Sammy Davis Jr. at the Coconut Grove* ♪♪♪♪ (Reprise, 1961), a free-wheeling set featuring Broadway medleys, 1950s rock and country segues, some hits, and 17 of his best celebrity impersonations.

influences:

◄◄ Frank Sinatra, Billy Daniels, Frankie Laine, Nat King Cole, George Kirby

►► Gregory Hines, Ben Vereen, Billy Crystal

Ken Burke

Wild Bill Davison

Born January 5, 1906, in Defiance, OH. Died November 14, 1989, in Santa Barbara, CA.

Cornetist Wild Bill Davison was among the most forceful voices of Chicago-style jazz in the 20th century. Deserted by his parents, he was raised by his grandparents who ran the Defiance Public Library. Condemned to spend much of his childhood in silence in the library's basement, he would later practice his cornet in the middle of a lake. In Chicago in the 1920s, Davison became associated with young Chicagoans Frank Teschemaker and Eddie Condon, who were under the sway of the many New Orleans musicians in the city, such as Joe "King" Oliver, Jimmy Noone, brothers Baby and Johnny Dodds, and, especially, Louis Armstrong. Davison's initial inspiration was the subtle approach of Bix Beiderbecke, but the impact of Louis Armstrong erased this early influence. He had found a style that suited his own brash personality, and he would remain true to it, and the cornet, for the next six decades. Unfortunately, his career was frequently derailed by bad luck. He was injured in the 1932 car accident that killed Teschemaker and, later moving to Wisconsin, he suffered a serious lip injury from a flying beer mug in Milwaukee. In the 1940s he was in New York, playing regularly with Condon at the guitarist's club and elsewhere, and making distinguished records with Sidney Bechet and Art Hodes. Whether leading his own band or working as a visiting soloist in Dixieland revival bands, Davison worked steadily in the later decades of his life. His style was particularly popular in Europe, and he spent the 1970s residing in Denmark. *The Wildest One: The Life of Wild Bill Davison* by Hal Willard (Avondale Press, 1996), is an excellent full-length account of the cornetist's colorful life and career.

what to buy: Davison's finest moments in the studio came during his 1943 sessions—on *Commodore Master Takes* ♪♪♪♪♪ (Commodore/GRP, 1997, prod. Milt Gabler)—which epitomize Chicago-style jazz with his strident horn perfectly complemented by a band that includes Pee Wee Russell on clarinet and Eddie Condon on guitar. For swing enthusiasts, *Jazz Giants* ♪♪♪♪♪ (Sackville, 1968/1997, prod. John Norris, Bill Smith) is an excellent performance with Davison in a band of veteran peers more oriented to swing than the Dixieland that Davison often played. It's vital and swaggering, serene and profound, filled with wit and high spirits—one of the great later incarnations of the small-band swing idiom.

what to buy next: There's more swing-oriented play on *Solo Flight* ♪♪♪♪ (Jazzology, 1994, prod. George Buck), which provides a late and engaging look at Davison in an unusual context, displaying his still-strong trumpet in a 1981 quartet. *Wild Bill Davison with the Alex Welsh Band* ♪♪♪♪ (Jazzology, 1997, prod. George Buck), recorded in England in 1966, features aggressive sparring between Davison's cornet and Alex Welsh's trumpet.

best of the rest:

Showcase ♪♪♪♪ (Jazzology, 1994)
AfterHours ♪♪♪♪ (Jazzology, 1994)
Lady of the Evening ♪♪♪ (Jazzology, 1994)
'S Wonderful ♪♪♪ (Jazzology, 1994)

influences:

◄◄ Bix Beiderbecke, Louis Armstrong.

►► Tom Saunders, Alex Welsh

Stuart Broomer

Ronnie Dawson

Born Ronald Monroe Dawson, August 12, 1939, in Dallas, TX.

There isn't much Ronnie Dawson doesn't do well. He was a teen-age rockabilly singer with an unusually strong taste for the blues, he can warble western swing and folk, and as a mature artist he belts flat-out rock 'n' roll and jump blues with authority. Of all the obscure rockabilly artists to emerge after Elvis Presley's death, Dawson is clearly the best. The youngest of the 1950s rockabilly performers, like Jerry Lee Lewis (they both attended the Southern Bible Institute) he eschewed a career in religion to make music with a beat. His first band, Ronnie Dee and the D Men, played R&B and rockabilly to enthusiastic crowds in Waxahachie, Texas, where they won the Big D Jamboree talent contest 10 weeks in a row. In 1957 Dawson signed with Gene Vincent's manager, Jack Rhodes, who wrote his first two singles, "Rockin' Bones" and "Action Packed." These two remarkable singles should've made Dawson a star; he was talented, fresh-faced and energetic, and his peroxide blonde crewcut provided a distinct and recognizable image. Yet these discs sold poorly outside of his hometown. After an unsuccessful stint at Dick Clark's Swan label, Dawson played western swing with the Light Crust Doughboys, sang with the Levee Singers, recorded under different names and did session work for eccentric Texas producer Major Bill Smith (Dawson played drums on Bruce Channel's "Hey Baby" and Paul and Paula's "Hey Paula"). During the mid-1960s, he entered a career in radio and TV advertising, writing commercial jingles and doing voiceover work (he was the voice of "Hungry Jack"). But more than a decade later, his early sides began to fetch high prices at auctions, while the Cramps and other neorockabillies recorded "Rockin' Bones" and "Action Packed." Rhino Records stirred further interest by including the latter on its *Rock This Town* anthology. During the late 1980s Dawson finally reemerged, touring overseas to enthusiastic audiences and recording a series of well-received albums. More than just a well-preserved legend from rock's golden era, Dawson (like Sleepy LaBeef) has actually improved with age. His vegetarian diet keeps him looking surprisingly youthful, he has become an exciting lead guitarist, and he displays honest joy and intensity on stage.

what to buy: All of Dawson's 1950s work, including 20 previously unreleased tracks, bluesy demos, songs released under the name Commonwealth Jones, and sides with the Lightcrust Doughboys are on *Rockin' Bones: The Legendary Masters 1957–1962* ♪♪♪♪ (No Hit, 1993/Crystal Clear, 1996, prod. David Dennard), a two-CD set featuring an informative booklet with some great photos. A first class piece of rock archaeology, this one will have you shaking your head and wondering "How come THIS guy wasn't a major player during the '50s?"

what to buy next: The guitars snarl and the horns jump almost as much as Dawson does on *Just Rockin' & Rollin'* ♪♪♪♪ (Upstart, 1996, prod. Ronnie Dawson, Liam Watson, Barnie Koumis), a smoking set of guitar-based R&B, Tex-Mex, and flat-out rockers that are more entertaining and danceable than 90 percent of the stuff you'll hear on radio these days. Also, *More Bad Habits* ♪♪♪♪ (Yeprock, 1999, prod. Ronnie Dawson) is as good a rockabilly album as you're going to find in the modern era. Dawson's country flavor combined with his burbling electric rhythm and twangy-ass guitar riffs produce a definitive artistic moment for the Blonde Bomber.

the rest:
Rockinitis ♪♪♪♪ (No Hit, 1993/Crystal Clear, 1996)

worth searching for: For those who want more Rockin' Ronnie for their buck, the 23-song *Monkey Beat* ♪♪♪ (No Hit/Crystal Clear, 1994, prod. Liam Watson, Barney Koumis, Boz Boorer) includes two complete LPs previously unavailable in the U.S. with backing provided by the Planet Rockers, Big Sandy's Fly-Rite Boys, and Tin-Star.

influences:
◀◀ Gene Vincent, Johnny Carroll, Mac Curtis
▶▶ Johnny Dollar, the Cramps, Big Sandy & His Fly-Rite Boys, Marc Bristol

Ken Burke

Doris Day

Born Doris Mary Anne von Kappelhoff, April 3, 1924, in Evanston, OH.

Before becoming a perennial top box-office draw in major motion pictures, Doris Day was one of the finest big-band singers of the '40s. With her sultry style and clean phrasing she could swing, scat, emote, and even seduce. Day's best recordings brought shades of complex emotion and sensuality to a wide variety of jazz- and pop-oriented songs. She was only 15 years old, and still known as Doris Kappelhoff, when she began appearing with Barney Rapp's band on Cincinnati radio. One of her songs, "Day after Day," proved so popular that she became known as "the Day after Day Girl," then just Doris Day. A short stint with Bob Crosby's swing band attracted the attention of orchestra leader Les Brown. With him, Day developed her intimate approach to a song, singing as if to one person, not a mass audience. "My Dreams Keep Getting Better All the Time" and the classic "Sentimental Journey" were major hits from this period, as were her duets with Buddy Clark, "Love Somebody" and "Confess." Day's string of hits and sexy, youthful looks helped make Brown's orchestra a major force during the war years, and their fame spread even further when they appeared in several motion picture "soundies."

At her early peak, Day almost quit the business after a failed marriage, but an opportunity to replace the pregnant Betty Hutton in the film *Romance on the High Seas* opened a new career avenue and supplied the million-seller "It's Magic." Bringing the same tender persona to the big screen that made her recordings so special, Day turned in some top-quality dramatic performances before appearing in the Rock Hudson bedroom farces that unjustly tarred her cinematic reputation. The movies also supplied two classic songs that most people identify with Doris Day: "Secret Love" and "Que Sera Sera (Whatever Will Be Will Be)." At Columbia, Day's work fell under the supervision of the aesthetically challenged Mitch Miller, who had her record such cutesy stuff as "I Said My Pajamas (and Put on My Prayers)," "Hoop De Doo," "A Guy Is a Guy," and "A Bushel and a Peck." The fact that these records were hits and still listenable is a testament to Day's remarkable charm, interpretive skills, and star power. Day also recorded hit duets with such other top Columbia acts as the Four Lads, Frankie Laine, and Johnnie Ray, which helped further their respective careers. Despite the rock 'n' roll siege of the '50s, Day continually charted with movie themes and Miller-produced novelties well into the '60s. Her son, Terry Melcher (who would later work with the Byrds), co-wrote and produced her last big hit, "Move over Darling." The death of her husband, Martin Melcher (and the resultant mess concerning the state of their finances), stopped work on what became Day's final LP, *The Love Album*. After that, according to her son, she just didn't want to record "one minute past her prime."

what to buy: You could quench your thirst for such luminescent standards as "Que Sera Sera," "It's Magic," and "Secret Love" with *Greatest Hits* ♪♪♪♪ (Columbia, 1987, prod. various), but the skillful mixing of Day's big-band work with her movie hits on *16 Most Requested Songs* ♪♪♪♪♪ (Legacy, 1992, compilation prod. Didier C. Deutsch) and *16 Most Requested Songs: Encore!* ♪♪♪♪♪ (Columbia, 1996, compilation prod. Didier C. Deutsch) are more exhilarating. Some of Day's finest work ever resides on the soundtrack to the Ruth Etting biopic *Love Me or Leave Me* ♪♪♪♪ (Legacy, 1993, reissue prod. Didier C. Deutsch). Her torchy, mature delivery is deeply satisfying on this set of Etting's tunes, and the package contains a detailed booklet and previously unreleased alternate takes.

what to buy next: Day is unusually jivey on *Best of the Big Bands* ♪♪♪♪ (Legacy, 1990, prod. various), with 16 tracks recorded with Les Brown and His Band of Renown. It's worthwhile to hear Day bounce through the inspired sass of "Tain't Me" and the sensual "Dig It." Some may want to skip right to *Complete Doris Day with Les Brown* ♪♪♪♪ (Collectors' Choice, 1997, prod. various), a two-disc set with all her great early work. Almost as interesting, *It's Magic: Her Early Years at Warner Bros.* ♪♪♪♪ (Rhino Movie Music, 1998, compilation prod. George Feltenstein) contains songs intended for the motion pictures *Romance on the High Seas, My Dream Is Yours,* and *It's a Great Feeling*.

what to avoid: As tempting as it may be to get the two queens of nice on one budget disc with *Merry Christmas from Doris Day & Dinah Shore* ♪♪ (Laserlight, 1992), you could get fuller, more satisfying solo collections by either artist for the same price. Better sound, too.

"Flying Home"
LIONEL HAMPTON
& HIS ORCHESTRA
1940
Used in many films, and most recently in a television commercial for khakis.
Swingin'
SINGLES

the rest:

Hooray for Hollywood, Vol. I ♪♪♪ (Columbia, 1958/1988)
(With Andre Previn) *Duet* ♪♪♪♪ (Columbia Special Products, 1962/1996)
A Day at the Movies ♪♪♪ (Columbia, 1988)
Doris Day Christmas Album ♪♪♪ (Columbia, 1964/1989)
Sings 22 Original Big Band Hits ♪♪ (Hindsight, 1992)
Personal Christmas Collection ♪♪♪ (Legacy, 1994)
Sentimental Journey ♪♪♪ (Hindsight, 1994)
Live It Up ♪♪♪ (Sony Special Music, 1995)
Magic of Doris Day ♪♪♪ (Sony Special Music, 1995)
Uncollected Doris Day, Vol. I: 1953 ♪♪♪ (Hindsight, 1995)
(With the Page Cavanaugh Trio) *Uncollected Doris Day, Vol. II: 'S Wonderful* ♪♪♪ (Hindsight, 1995)
Golden Hits ♪♪♪ (ITC Masters, 1996)
16 Very Special Songs ♪♪♪ (Prism, 1997)
Blues Skies ♪♪ (MSI, 1997)
Day by Day/Day by Night ♪♪♪♪ (MusicRama, 1997)
Love Album ♪♪♪ (Vision Music, 1997)
Cuttin' Capers/Bright & Shiny ♪♪♪♪ (Columbia, 1997)

Doris Day **(Archive Photos)**

Sentimental Journey (Musketeer, 1997)
Day in Hollywood/Showtime (MusicRama, 1997)
Latin Lovers/Love Him (MusicRama, 1997)

worth searching for: In the event you want everything Doris Day cut from the '40s to the '60s, some import shops and catalog services carry *It's Magic* (Bear Family, 1993, prod. Richard Weize), a six-disc set covering 1947 to 1951 with a 91-page booklet; *Secret Love* (Bear Family, 1995, prod. Richard Weize), a five-disc set of her work from 1952 to 1955; *Que Sera Sera* (Bear Family, prod. Richard Weize), a five-disc set from 1956 to 1959; and *Move over Darling* (Bear Family, 1997, prod. Richard Weize), which extensively covers her work well into the next decade. Finally, Day actually sings "Que Sera, Sera" on Sly and the Family Stone's *Fresh* (Epic, 1973/Legacy, 1991, prod. Sly Stone). Insert your own joke here.

influences:

◄◄ Ella Fitzgerald, Connee Boswell, Jo Stafford, Betty Hutton

►► Debbie Reynolds, Rosemary Clooney, Betty Bonney, Lucy Ann Polk, Tracey Ullman

Ken Burke

The Delmore Brothers

Formed around 1926, in Elkmont, AL.

Alton Delmore (born December 25, 1908, in Elkmont, AL; died June 8, 1964), vocals, guitar; Rabon Delmore (born December 3, 1916, in Elkmont, AL; died December 4, 1952), vocals, guitar.

The Delmore Brothers melded the close harmonies common to brother acts with intricate, syncopated guitar and tenor guitar instrumental accompaniment to create a new and highly influential duet sound. Combining traditional country music with fast-paced blues-boogie rhythm, the Delmores captured the spirit of western swing music, especially on their later recordings. Their 1930s-era Bluebird recordings featured such timeless numbers as "Brown's Ferry Blues," "Gonna Lay down My Old Guitar," and "Weary Lonesome Blues." On their later records for King, they featured blues-influenced rhythms and lyrics, electric guitar, and Wayne Raney's harmonica accompaniment, creating many classics, including "Freight Train Boogie," "Hillbilly Boogie," and "Pan American Boogie," along with many other standards, including "Blues Stay away from Me." They also recorded as members of the Brown's Ferry Four, a gospel quartet, along with Grandpa Jones and Merle Travis or Red Foley. The Delmore Brothers were early members of the Grand Ole Opry and remain an important influence in the music to this day.

what to buy: *Brown's Ferry Blues* (County, 1995, reissue prod. Gary B. Reid) is full of classic Bluebird material from 1933 to 1940, including "Blue Railroad Train," "Gonna Lay down My Old Guitar," "The Weary Lonesome Blues," and "Brown's Ferry Blues." On *Sand Mountain Blues* (County, 1986, reissue prod. Dave Freeman) early King recordings find the Delmores in a transitional mode between the pristine brother harmony duets they'd cut for Bluebird and the later, more raucous King boogies.

worth searching for: *When They Let the Hammer Down* (Bear Family, 1984, prod. Richard Weize), a German reissue, features 18 tracks performed by the great country harmonica player Wayne Raney alongside the Delmores—classic stuff. There is some duplication with the Ace King compilation, but they're both well worth having. Twenty classic blues and boogies are included on *Freight Train Boogie* (Ace, 1993), an English reissue of the Delmores' King material. This disc features topnotch instrumentalists of the day, including Wayne Raney, Homer and Jethro, Merle Travis, and others.

influences:

◄◄ Blue Sky Boys, Jimmie Rodgers

►► Louvin Brothers, O'Kanes

Randy Pitts

Paul Desmond

See: Dave Brubeck

Jimmy Dorsey

Born February 29, 1904, in Shenandoah, PA. Died June 12, 1957, in New York, NY.

Of the two swinging Dorsey brothers, Jimmy was more committed to jazz. A lover of fast tempos and blaring brass, his high technical skill on both the clarinet and alto saxophone is still admired by musicians today. Dorsey was only 17 years old when he turned pro with the Scranton Sirens. As in most of his early band affiliations, Dorsey would join and then later persuade the other members to include younger brother Tommy on trombone. Popular session musicians for the likes of Red Nichols, the Boswell Sisters, and Ben Pollack, the Dorseys were also part-time recording stars in their own right until 1934 when they formed the Dorsey Brothers Orchestra. After the brothers went their separate ways, Jimmy Dorsey was not immediately successful, even though his band featured some of the finest talent of his era (Ray McKinley, Dave Matthews, Freddie Slack, Charlie Teagarden, and so on). It wasn't until the '40s that Dorsey's Orchestra became popular on the strength of big hits sung by Helen O'Connell ("Green Eyes," "Tangerine") and

Bob Eberle ("Amapola"). At its peak, the Jimmy Dorsey Orchestra appeared in such films as *I Dood It, Four Jills in a Jeep,* and *Hollywood Canteen.* Success often breeds forgiveness, and the Brothers patched up their differences long enough to make the 1947 turkey *The Fabulous Dorseys,* in which the pair ineptly played themselves. (At least the music was good.) During the post-war years, Jimmy Dorsey added Maynard Ferguson to his group and began embracing modern bop (something his brother never did), but the stylistic adaptation wasn't enough to reduce his declining fortunes. Jimmy reteamed with his brother Tommy and his band in 1953, billed simply as the Tommy Dorsey Orchestra featuring co-leader Jimmy Dorsey. The brothers' comeback bid was given a big boost when they signed to do *Jackie Gleason's Stage Show*—at the time, the only bandstand series on TV. After Tommy died in 1956, Jimmy carried on with his brother's band. Their 1957 recording of "So Rare" became the last hit from a major big band, just as Jimmy Dorsey was dying of cancer.

what to buy: Big hits and hot instrumental moments reside on *Best of Jimmy Dorsey & His Orchestra* (Curb, 1992, compilation prod. Don Ovens), which has Helen O'Connell's "Tangerine" and "Green Eyes," Bob Eberle's "Amapola," and Dorsey's swan song, "So Rare." As budget discs go, this is a great one.

what to buy next: The largely instrumental LP *Contrasts* (Decca Jazz, 1993, prod. Dave Grusin, Larry Rosen, Orrin Keepnews) features Jimmy Dorsey's strongest orchestra lineup with Ray McKinley and piano-boogie legend Freddy Slack on a mix of cool jams and jazz jumpers.

what to avoid: The sound quality leaves a lot to be desired on *Jazz Collector's Edition* (Laserlight, 1991), an easy-to-find budget disc with few engaging performances. Worse still is *Giants of the Big Band Era: Jimmy Dorsey* (Pilz, 1992), which skimps on tracks as well. Others worth skipping are *Plays His Greatest Hits* (Hollywood/Rounder, 1987) and *Best of the Big Band* (Hollywood, 1994)—cheapies for completists only.

the rest:

Pennies from Heaven (ASV, 1992)
1939–1940 (Hindsight, 1993)
1940 (Circle, 1993)
1939–1940 (Circle, 1993)
Uncollected Jimmy Dorsey (Hindsight, 1993)
22 Original Recordings (Hindsight, 1994)
Perfidia (Laserlight, 1994)
At the 400 Restaurant 1946 (Hep, 1994)
Don't Be That Way (Aerospace, 1995)
Jimmy Dorsey (Empire, 1995)
Tangerine (MCA Special Products, 1995)
America Swings—The Great Jimmy Dorsey (Hindsight, 1996)
Mood Hollywood (Hep, 1996)
A Kiss to Build a Dream On (Sony Music Special, 1996)
Dorsey Itis (Drive Archive, 1996)
So Rare: Jimmy Dorsey's Boogie Woogie (Richmond, 1996)
Jimmy Dorsey & Orchestra (Members Edition, 1997)
1938–39 Broadcasts in Hi-Fi (Jazz Hour, 1997)
I Remember You (Empire, 1998)
Jimmy Dorsey/Woody Herman: Live at the Edgewater (Jerden, 1998)
America's Premier Dixieland Jazz Band Live, 1950 (Jazz Crusade, 1998)
Jimmy Dorsey & His Orchestra (Rhino, 1998)

worth searching for: Among the many live radio transcriptions available, the import *Frolic Club, Miami 7/16/44* (Canby, 1995) stands out as especially atmospheric, musically complete, and somewhat historically important.

influences:

◀◀ Red Nichols, Paul Whiteman, Ben Pollack, Jimmie Noone

▶▶ Ray McKinley, Freddy Slack, Maynard Ferguson, Lester Young

see also: *Tommy Dorsey*

Ken Burke

Tommy Dorsey /The Dorsey Brothers

Born November 19, 1905, in Manahoy City, PA. Died November 26, 1956, in Greenwich, CT.

Whether teamed with brother Jimmy as part of the Dorsey Brothers, or leading his own band, Tommy Dorsey was one of the most successful and important figures of the big band era. (His orchestra was also the first to truly develop the young Frank Sinatra as a vocalist.) A trombone player possessing an amazing command of tone, Dorsey could let out all the stops on hot swing or play sweet and cozy on the sentimental ballads he preferred. During the early '20s, Dorsey and older brother Jimmy co-led such groups as Dorsey's Novelty Six and Dorsey's Wild Canaries before hiring on with Jean Goldkette's orchestra and then with Paul Whiteman. Billed as featured soloists with Whiteman, the brothers began cutting popular swing records as the Dorsey Brothers in 1928, but didn't form their own outfit until 1934. Packed with talent (Bunny Berigan played trumpet, Glenn Miller wrote arrangements and played in the horn section), the Dorsey Brothers Orchestra was wildly popular with swing fans and musicians alike. However, the intense sibling rivalry between the Dorseys (hot-headed Tommy and perfectionist Jimmy) resulted in creative disputes, constant quarrels, and even fistfights. Their 1935 split was inevitable. Jimmy kept their established band, and Tommy took over an excellent orchestra

Tommy and Jimmy Dorsey **(Archive Photos)**

from retiring band leader Joe Haymes. (He also appropriated their joint hit "In a Sentimental Mood" as his theme song.)

The Tommy Dorsey Orchestra employed several top jazz musicians through the years (Alex Stordahl, Buddy Rich, Yank Lawson, Charlie Shavers, and Bud Freeman among them), but it is best known for its famous vocalists. Sy Oliver, Jack Leonard, Jo Stafford, and Connie Haines all cut hits with Dorsey, but with young Frank Sinatra at the mike, his orchestra truly hit the big time. Sinatra had already hit with the Harry James Orchestra, but it was with Dorsey's outfit that he developed his unique breathing technique—which led to the sensual interpretive style that drove bobbysoxers wild. With a string of monster hits, Sinatra and Dorsey established each other as major stars. When Sinatra left in 1942 Dorsey replaced him with Dick Haymes, causing fans to argue over which was the greater vocalist. (It's a moot point today.) During the war years, Dorsey expanded his orchestra to include string sections and vocal choirs for his increasingly ballad-heavy style, though he didn't forsake swing entirely. Dorsey's popularity continued into the post-war years, but during the early '50s, the big-band decline began affecting him, too. In a stroke of publicity genius, he reunited with brother Jimmy (whose own band had folded in 1953) to play nostalgic dance-band music. Their reunion earned much publicity and resulted in their hosting *Jackie Gleason's Stage Show,* where they introduced the nation to yet another singer destined to become a pop icon, Elvis Presley. After Tommy Dorsey died in 1956, brother Jimmy followed seven months later. Subsequent editions of the band, billed as the Tommy Dorsey Orchestra under the direction of Sam Donahue, toured with another familiar name, Frank Sinatra Jr. Dorsey's catalog is glutted with popular and sentimental numbers, some of which haven't aged well, but his brand of classic swing is as hot as ever.

what to buy: The Dorsey Brothers are joined by Bunny Berigan and Glenn Miller on *The Dorsey Brothers: Best of the Big Bands* (Legacy, 1992, compilation prod. Michael Brooks), a strong set of their early recordings featuring vocals by Mildred Bailey and Johnny Mercer. As an introduction to Tommy as a solo artist, *Best of Tommy Dorsey* (RCA, 1992, compilation prod. John Snyder), *Greatest Hits* (RCA, 1996, compilation prod. Hank Hoffman), and *The Homefront 1941–1945* (RCA, 1998, prod. various) are all pretty solid, mid-priced hits compilations featuring such vocalists as Jack Leonard, Charlie Shavers, and the Pied Pipers. Or, you can get a full disc of Dorsey and that skinny kid from Hoboken with *Tommy Dorsey/Frank Sinatra: Greatest Hits* (RCA, 1996, reissue prod. Chick Crumpacker), a 15-song collection with Ol' Blue Eyes crooning "Night and Day," "Once in Awhile," and his early theme, "Polka Dots and Moonbeams."

what to buy next: The five-disc, 120-track *This Song Is for You* (RCA, 1994, compilation prod. Paul Williams) contains every note of Dorsey and Sinatra's work together on one set. The analytical booklet, gorgeous sound quality, and six previously unreleased performances make this a must-have for serious collectors of both artists.

what to avoid: The poorly assembled *Golden Hits* (ITC Masters, 1997) won't improve your collection one iota. Also, even at budget prices, for the money you spend on a split disc such as *Tommy Dorsey Orchestra & David Rose String Orchestra* (Laserlight, 1994), you could get a full disc by either artist (although Rose's CDs are largely out of print). There's nothing new here. And both the Dorseys had been dead for several years by the time *Live 1962 at Villa Venice Chicago* (Jazz Hour, 1994) was recorded, so don't even bother with this Sam Donahue-led curio.

the rest:

(With the Clambake Seven) *Having a Wonderful Time* (RCA, 1958/1995)
One and Only (RCA Camden, 1988)
Best of the Big Bands (Columbia, 1988)
(With Frank Sinatra) *All-Time Greatest Hits, Vol. I* (RCA Bluebird, 1988)
(With Frank Sinatra) *All-Time Greatest Hits, Vol. II* (RCA Bluebird, 1988)
(With Frank Sinatra) *All-Time Greatest Hits, Vol. III* (RCA Bluebird, 1989)
Well Get It! The TD CD (Jass Records, 1989)
Best of Tommy Dorsey (MCA, 1989)
Sentimental (MCA Jazz, 1989)
The 17 Number Ones (RCA Bluebird, 1990)
(With Frank Sinatra) *Oh! Look at Me Now & Other Big Band Hits* (RCA Bluebird, 1990)
The Great Tommy Dorsey (Pearl, 1991)
Jazz Collector's Edition, Vol. I (Laserlight, 1991)
Jazz Collector's Edition, Vol. II (Laserlight, 1991)
Best of Tommy Dorsey & His Orchestra (Curb, 1991)
1942 War Bond Broadcasts (Jazz Hour, 1992)
Boogie Woogie (Pro Arte, 1992)
Radio Days (Star Line, 1992)
Live in Hi-Fi at Casino Gardens (Jazz Hour, 1992)
(With Frank Sinatra) *Stardust* (RCA Bluebird, 1992)
The Post-War Era (RCA Bluebird, 1993)
Stop, Look & Listen (Living Era, 1993)
Great Tommy Dorsey (Pearl/Flapper, 1993)
New York Jazz in the Roaring Twenties (Biograph, 1994)
Tommy Dorsey & His Greatest Band (Jasmine, 1994)
At the Fat Man's 1946–48 (Hep, 1994)
The Carnegie Hall V-Disc Session—April 1944 (Hep, 1994)
All-Time Hit Parade Rehearsals 1944 (Hep, 1994)
1936–1938 (Jazz Archives, 1994)

(With Frank Sinatra) *I'll Be Seeing You* &&&v (RCA, 1994)
1942 War Bond Broadcasts &&v (Jazz Hour, 1994)
November 26, 1940—Hollywood Palace &&& (Jazz Hour, 1994)
Sheik of Swing &&& (Drive Archive, 1995)
1935–1936 &&& (Jazz Chronological Classics, 1995)
Vol. 15 Masterpieces && (Jazz Archives, 1995)
His Best Recordings 1928–1942 &&& (Best of Jazz, 1996)
1936 &&v (Jazz Chronological Classics, 1996)
Irish American Trombone &&& (Avid, 1996)
Dance with Dorsey &&& (Parade/Koch International, 1996)
The Sentimental Gentleman of Swing &&v (Music Memories, 1996)
Masterpieces 15 &&& (EPM, 1996)
Tommy Dorsey, Vol. I && (Laserlight, 1997)
Tommy Dorsey, Vol. II && (Laserlight, 1997)
Tommy Dorsey && (Eclipse, 1997)
Tommy Dorsey: Members Edition && (United Audio, 1997)
1936–1937 &&v (Jazz Chronological Classics, 1997)
(With the Clambake Seven) *Best of Tommy Dorsey & the Clambake Seven 1936–38* &&& (Challenge, 1997)
1937 &&v (Jazz Chronological Classics, 1997)
Vol. II—1937 && (Jazz Chronological Classics, 1997)
1936–41 Broadcasts &&& (Jazz Hour, 1997)
1938–1939 in Hi-Fi Broadcasts &&& (Jazz Hour, 1997)
Frank Sinatra & the Tommy Dorsey Orchestra: Love Songs &&& (BMG, 1997)
Vol. I Popular Frank Sinatra && (BMG, 1997)
1936–41 Broadcasts &&& (Jazz Hour, 1998)

worth searching for: With his band-within-a-band, the Clambake Seven, Dorsey's group (featuring the great Max Kaminsky on trumpet), really lets loose on *Panic Is On* &&& (Viper's Nest, 1994), a set of sparkling up-tempo radio transcriptions. Many of these numbers were not recorded for release by the group and are appearing on disc, with complete information, for the first time. You can get this little gem through the Jazz Classics catalog. Also, *Yes, Indeed!* &&&&v (RCA Bluebird, 1990, compilation prod. Orrin Keepnews) focuses more on hot jazz (c. 1939–1942) than sentimental pop, and is well worth tracking down.

solo outings:

The Dorsey Brothers:
I'm Getting Sentimental over You && (Pro Arte, 1990)
Harlem Lullaby &&& (Hep, 1994)
Live in the Big Apple &&v (Magic, 1994)
NBC Bandstand 8/2/56 &&v (Canby, 1995)
Live in the Meadowbrook && (Jazz Hour, 1995)
Mood Hollywood &&& (Hep, 1996)
Opus No. 1 &&v (K-Tel, 1996)
Dorsey-itis &&&v (Drive Archive, 1996)
Stage Show &&& (Jazz Band, 1996)
Dorsey Brothers, Vol. I—New York 1928 &&&v (Jazz Oracle, 1997)
Dorsey Brothers, Vol. II—New York 1929–1930 &&& (Jazz Oracle, 1997)
Swingin' in Hollywood &&& (Rhino Movie Music, 1998)
Tommy & Jimmy Dorsey: Go Their Separate Ways &&v (Empire, 1998)

influences:

« Paul Whiteman, Joe Haymes, Jean Goldkette

» Glenn Miller, Ziggy Elman, Sam Donahue

see also: *Jimmy Dorsey, Frank Sinatra*

Ken Burke

Bob Eberly

See: Helen O'Connell

Billy Eckstine

Born William Clarence Eckstine, July 8, 1914, in Pittsburgh, PA. Died March 8, 1993, in Pittsburgh, PA.

Often considered a groundbreaker for black vocalists, the immortal "Mr. B." cut a racial swath through America even before Nat King Cole came to the scene. Billy Eckstine was one of the very first African-American matinee idols, singing for Earl Hines's orchestra, then veering off with his own band in 1943. Besides making a name for himself, he helped launch the careers of Charlie Parker, Sarah Vaughan, and Dizzy Gillespie by recommending that Hines hire them for the band. Eckstine is normally credited with reviving the jazz ballad as a vocal medium, so as a result, the "swing" aspects of his music are generally overlooked. His deep baritone is immediately arresting, and he was also known for his ability to play trumpet, guitar and trombone—which he often did on his many tours of Europe and Australia. Between 1949 and 1952, he had a dozen tunes hit the charts—some in the top 10—and soon thereafter secured a lucrative contract with MGM. In the meantime, he became well known for being a keen scout of young talent; he gave jobs to a young Miles Davis, Art Blakey, Dexter Gordon, and Lena Horne, among others, paving the way for a generation of bop performers to surface. Eckstine's mass appeal wore off in the mid-1950s, although he continued his career overseas, doing all-star jazz gigs and club acts.

what to buy: *At Basin Street East* &&&&v (Mercury, 1962/1990) is a terrific re-release of some original sessions with Eckstine and a young Quincy Jones. If for nothing else, buy it for the superb recordings of "Caravan" and "Sophisticated Lady." Eckstine resurfaced in the 1980s with *Billy Eckstine Sings with Benny Carter* &&&&v (Verve, 1986, prod. Kiyoshi Koyama), a sur-

Billy Eckstine **(Archive Photos)**

prisingly energetic album that took jazz observers by surprise and even snagged a Grammy nomination. Eckstine is likely to appeal to lovers of robust swing ballads—in the mode of Johnny Hartman—and is unlikely to disappoint.

what to buy next: *Mister B and the Band* (Denon, 1947/1995, prod. Herb Abramson) puts Eckstine alongside Miles Davis and Dexter Gordon, just as the two bop players were hitting their stride—a can't-miss purchase. *No Cover, No Minimum* (Blue Note, 1992), a nice collection of jazz standards, like "Lush Life" and "Till There Was You," makes a perfect introduction into Eckstine's world.

worth searching for: The British import *Boppin with B* (Indigo, 1997) isn't a bad album by any means, but it's not on a par with other available Eckstine albums. It features a more obscure mix of songs.

influences:

◀◀ Louis Armstrong

▶▶ Nat King Cole, Sarah Vaughan, Frank Sinatra, Joe Williams, Johnny Hartman

Carl Quintanilla

Harry "Sweets" Edison

Born October 10, 1915, in Columbus, OH.

One of the most distinctive trumpeters in jazz history, Harry "Sweets" Edison can say more with one note than most can say in five choruses. A master of understatement with a wry, backhanded sense of humor and a blues-drenched sensibility, Edison is also one of the few trumpeters from his generation influenced by the younger bebop innovator Dizzy Gillespie. Since the '80s his style has grown even more concise as his chops have diminished, but he is still an inimitable improvisor who places notes with surgical precision. First influenced by Louis Armstrong, whom he heard play at a neighborhood dance hall, Edison was raised by his aunt and uncle in Kentucky, and he credits his uncle with giving him a solid musical education. He toured widely with some of the best territory bands, including Jeter-Pillars and Earl Hood, and landed a job with Lucky Millinder when he arrived in New York in 1937. Fired by Millinder in favor of Gillespie, Edison was quickly hired in early 1938 by Count Basie, where he was dubbed "Sweets" by Lester Young. Featured on many of Basie's greatest recordings, he stayed with the classic band until Basie broke it up in 1950. In the second phase of his career Edison toured with Jazz at the Philharmonic, served as Josephine Baker's music director, and began a long association with Frank Sinatra, with whom he performed and recorded for years. His contributions to Sinatra's classic Nelson Riddle albums on Capitol—*Songs for Swingin' Lovers!*, *Swing Easy*, and *A Swingin' Affair*—can't be overrated. Edison settled in Los Angeles in the early '50s and became one of the first black musicians to break into the studios, where he worked too much to keep up a jazz profile. He reunited with Basie numerous times for concerts and recording dates (many documented on Pablo) and often worked with Benny Carter and tenor saxophonist Eddie "Lockjaw" Davis.

what to buy: A two-CD set that contains three Verve records, including Edison's *Gee Baby, Ain't I Good to You*, *The Soul of Ben Webster* (Verve, 1958/1995, prod. Norman Granz) is a treasure trove featuring long-out-of-print sessions by three jazz giants. The Edison album pairs his witty, hide-and-seek trumpet with the robust, breathy tenor of Ben Webster. *Jawbreakers* (Riverside, 1962/Original Jazz Classics, 1990, prod. Orrin Keepnews) is a rambunctious session featuring the two former Basie-ites: Edison and tough tenor Eddie "Lockjaw" Davis. Steeped in the blues but hardly trapped in the swing era, Edison and Davis make a timeless duo. At first glance *Oscar Peterson and Harry Edison* (Pablo, 1975/Original Jazz Classics, 1992, prod. Norman Granz) might seem like a highly unlikely pairing, but such are the mysteries of jazz. The combination of one of the most prodigious players with one of the great minimalists produces an album for the ages, a set full of thrilling interplay and fascinating improvisational contrasts. Though *Edison's Lights* (Pablo, 1976/Original Jazz Classics, 1994, prod. Norman Granz) once again unites Edison with the great "Lockjaw" Davis, it's the presence of Count Basie that makes this an event. Their joy at working together again is reflected directly into the music.

what to buy next: Not one of the greatest sessions with Edison and "Lockjaw" Davis, *Simply Sweets* (Pablo, 1978/Original Jazz Classics, 1996, prod. Norman Granz) features the two swinging veterans on a program of five blues and a few ballads, including the unfortunate "Feelings." A solid session with a strong band, *For My Pals* (Pablo, 1988/1997, prod. Eric Miller) has Sweets showing off his lyrical side, especially on "There Is No Great Love." He really cuts loose on the concluding 11-minute "Blue for the Cats," which was added to the CD reissue. A hard-driving album recorded live in Tokyo by the Frank Wess-Harry Edison Orchestra, *Dear Mr. Basie* (Concord Jazz, 1991, prod. Carl E. Jefferson) isn't really a Basie tribute. Which isn't a complaint, because this all-star session swings like mad and features some strong solos, including Edison's on "I Wish I Knew."

best of the rest:

'S Wonderful (Pablo, 1982)
Just Friends (Pablo, 1983)
Swing Summit (Candid, 1991)

Harry "Sweets" Edison (© Jack Vartoogian)

worth searching for: Recorded live at the legendary Lighthouse in Hermosa Beach, the out-of-print *The Inventive Mr. Edison* ♪♪♪♪♪ (Pacific Jazz, 1953, prod. Richard Bock) features a top-flight West Coast band and Edison stretching out in one of his first small group recordings after leaving Basie.

influences:

◀◀ Louis Armstrong, Rex Stewart

▶▶ Bobby Hackett, Miles Davis

Andrew Gilbert

Jonathan & Darlene Edwards

See: Jo Stafford

8½ Souvenirs

Formed 1994, in Austin, TX.

Olivier Giraud, guitar, vocals; Glover Gill, piano, kazoo, vocals; Adam Berlin, drums, percussion; Todd Wulfmeyer, bass (1994–98); Kevin Smith, bass (1998–present); Kathy Kiser, vocals (1994–96); Juliana Sheffield, vocals (1996–97); Chrysta Bell, vocals (1998–present).

Cowboy hats, not berets, are the rule in Texas, but don't tell that to this defiantly Euro-retro group, which somehow has the mistaken impression that their hometown of Austin is on the left bank of the Seine, not the Colorado. In truth, guitarist and group leader Olivier Giraud is a Frenchman who relocated to Austin in the late '80s. Eventually the other members of the group signed on to help realize Giraud's vision of a contemporary band playing '30s- and '40s-era cosmopolitan jazz. Their success helped to foster the swing scene in Austin, where they held forth at a regular gig at that town's Continental Club. They recorded their debut album there, and it was released through the club's label, and later reissued when the band signed with RCA. Named after the classic Fellini movie *8½*, the group is not without its pretensions or its troubles in keeping the vocalist slot filled, so it'll be interesting to see how far they can go with all this. But for now, listening to 8½ Souvenirs creates a powerful craving for some 30-weight coffee, strong tobacco, and a depressing French novel.

what to buy: *Happy Feet* (Continental, 1995/RCA Victor, 1998, prod. 8½ Souvenirs, Jack Hazzard) is a reissue of the group's indie debut, but with a twist. Rather than a straight-ahead repackaging, the album features new vocals by new band member Chrysta Bell, replacing those of original singer Kathy Kiser. The song selection offers a tasty mix of covers by Italian crooner Paolo Conte, legendary instrumentalists Django Reinhardt and Stephane Grappelli, and lounge lizard king Serge Gainsbourg, plus a couple of originals of a piece with the older numbers.

what to buy next: *Souvonica* (Continental, 1997, prod. 8½ Souvenirs, Jack Hazzard) emphasizes originals over covers, and features guest vocal performances by Austin luminaries Kelly Willis, Kris McKay, Toni Price, and recently departed group member Juliana Sheffield.

worth searching for: It seems a tad obsessive, but if you can find a copy of the original version of *Happy Feet* (Continental, 1995, prod. 8½ Souvenirs, Jack Hazzard), you can A-B the vocals by Kathy Kiser and Chrysta Bell.

influences:

◀◀ Nino Rota, Django Reinhardt, Serge Gainsbourg, Paolo Conte

Daniel Durchholz

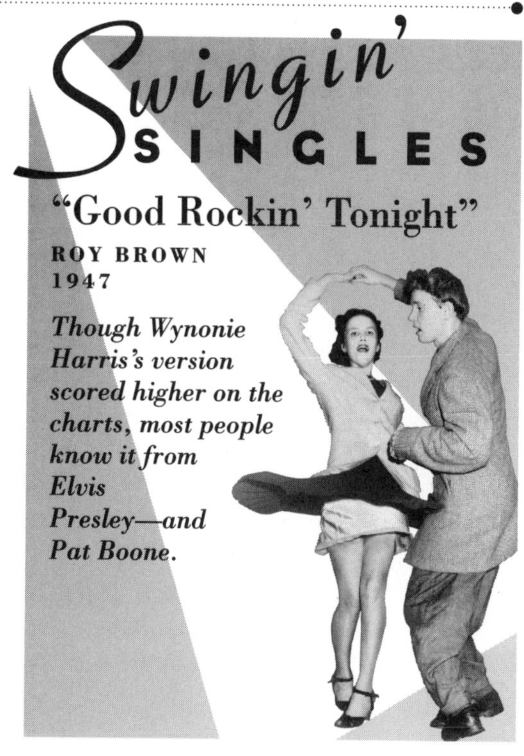

Swingin' Singles
"Good Rockin' Tonight"
ROY BROWN
1947
Though Wynonie Harris's version scored higher on the charts, most people know it from Elvis Presley—and Pat Boone.

Roy Eldridge

Born January 30, 1911, in Pittsburgh, PA. Died February 26, 1989, in Valley Stream, NY.

Trumpeter Roy Eldridge is often considered a bridge between jazz greats Louis Armstrong and Dizzy Gillespie, but his innovation and virtuosity prove he deserves mention as an equal. Eldridge began playing with territory bands in the Mideast in the early 1930s, but his big musical break came when he hooked up with Teddy Hill's group in 1935. He also backed Billie Holiday, played with Fletcher Henderson, and by the end of the 1930s was probably the most important trumpeter in jazz. The early 1940s saw Eldridge, who had gained the nickname "Little Jazz," presented with lucrative offers to join the popular bands of Gene Krupa and Artie Shaw. But by the end of the 1940s Eldridge's playing had gone out of style, and he went to Europe for a couple of years. He returned to the United States in 1951 with renewed confidence and was embraced as part of the resurgence in mainstream jazz. Eldridge went on to make many stimulating recordings—mostly for Norman Granz's labels Verve, Clef, and Pablo—in the 1950s, 1960s, and 1970s. Eldridge's style, like that of any trumpeter of the era, was profoundly influenced by Armstrong. But he also assimilated the longer lines and fluid articulation of prominent reed players, especially Coleman Hawkins and Benny Carter, and in this way had a major influence on bop trumpeters. These influences, combined with Eldridge's own ebullient nature, combined to make him one of the most exciting jazz soloists of his era, or any other.

what to buy: *Little Jazz* (Columbia, 1989, prod. Michael Brooks) is an incredible collection of early Eldridge recorded from 1935–40 featuring many exciting cuts made with Teddy Hill, Billie Holiday, and Fletcher Henderson. But the real gems are the records made under Eldridge's own leadership as part of the "Heckler's Hop" session of 1937; these are important documents in the career of a trumpet giant. Producer Norman Granz was famous for bringing together formidable musicians in interesting settings. On *Roy and Diz* (Verve, 1955/1994, prod. Norman Granz), he teams the combative Eldridge with the jazz giant who looked up to him as a mentor. Rarely did Granz's machinations work this wonderfully. Sometimes this CD sounds like a cutting contest, sometimes like a mutual admiration society—but it always sounds like great jazz. Also worth noting is the wonderful backing provided by the Oscar Peterson Trio. Eldridge called all the shots on *The Nifty Cat* (New World, 1970/1986, prod. Bill Weilbacher), made rather late in his life—he chose the tunes (all his own),

Roy Eldridge (r) and Flip Phillips **(Archive Photos)**

hired the musicians, and just about everything else. The result is reminiscent of a self-portrait by an aging painter; it is as personal a statement as Eldridge would ever make.

what to buy next: *After You've Gone* (GRP Decca, 1991, prod. Orrin Keepnews) is another excellent CD compilation of early Eldridge recorded from 1936–46 featuring quite a few tracks with Gene Krupa and Anita O'Day. *Montreux '77* (Pablo, 1978/Original Jazz Classics, 1989, prod. Norman Granz) is the last recording Eldridge would make, and it's also one of his best. How a musician in his late 60s with fading chops could still sound so incandescent and exuberant is a marvel. The last two tunes, "Perdido" and "Bye Bye Blackbird," provide a fitting testament to a brilliant career.

what to avoid: *Jazz Maturity . . . Where It's Coming From* (Pablo, 1978/Original Jazz Classics, 1994, prod. Norman Granz) is a second meeting between Eldridge and Gillespie that doesn't even come close to creating the fireworks of the first meeting. It's not bad music, but after the 1955 record it's a bit of a disappointment.

best of the rest:

Roy Eldridge in Paris (Vogue, 1950/1995)
Little Jazz: The Best of the Verve Years (Verve, 1951–60/1994)
Count Basie & Roy Eldridge (Pablo, 1972/Original Jazz Classics, 1988)
Happy Time (Pablo, 1975/Original Jazz Classics, 1991)
What It's All About (Pablo, 1976/Original Jazz Classics, 1995)
Just You, Just Me—Live in '59 (Stash, 1990)
(With Gene Krupa & Anita O'Day) *Uptown* (Columbia, 1990)
Heckler's Hop (Hep, 1993)
Eldridge, 1935–1940 (Classics, 1993)
The Big Sound of Little Jazz (Topaz, 1995)

worth searching for: The two-LP set *Dale's Wail* (Clef, 1954, prod. Norman Granz) has yet to be reissued on CD, but the music is certainly deserving. Although he's backed by such stars as Oscar Peterson and Buddy Rich, Eldridge is alone, front and center throughout.

influences:

◀◀ Louis Armstrong, Coleman Hawkins

▶▶ Dizzy Gillespie, Howard McGhee, Fats Navarro

Dan Keener

Larry Elgart

See: Les Elgart

Les Elgart

Born August 3, 1918, in New Haven, CT.

In the context of big bands, Les Elgart was a talented role player, a lead trumpeter with personality who also knew exactly how to plug into a swinging horn section. But after playing in the early 1940s with such band leaders as Harry James and Woody Herman, he formed his own band and really developed a style. Elgart and his saxophonist brother, Larry, played swing music rooted in the pop-jazz tradition but were playfully willing to adapt to popular dance fads, most notably the twist. The Les Elgart Band, formed in 1953 and intensely popular on college campuses, produced lounge-ready, finger-tapping music like "Frenesi-Twist" well into the 1960s.

what to buy: Though Elgart's many studio albums haven't quite seen the reissue renaissance of such better-known forebears as Benny Goodman and Harry James, *Best of the Big Bands: Sophisticated Swing* ♪♪♪♪ (Sony, 1992, prod. George Avakian) is an excellent recollection of the band leader's 1953 and 1954 New York City sessions. Among the twisty gems: "The Weasel Pops Off," "Sophisticated Lady," and "Senior Hop."

the rest:

Elgart Touch/For Dancers Also ♪♪♪ (Collectors Choice, 1996)

worth searching for: The 18-song collection *Cocktail Mix, Vol. II: Martini Madness* ♪♪♪♪ (Rhino, 1996, prod. Janet Grey) unites big-band, mambo, cha-cha-cha, classic pop, and R&B within the "martini music" context; Elgart's lightheaded "Frenesi-Twist" fits snugly among Perez Prado's bouncy Latin jazz and Connie Francis's sophisticated bossa nova.

influences:

◀◀ Duke Ellington, Benny Goodman, Glenn Miller, Nelson Riddle, Chubby Checker

▶▶ Ray Conniff, Louis Prima

Steve Knopper

Duke Ellington

Born Edward Kennedy Ellington, April 29, 1899, in Washington, DC. Died May 24,1974, in New York, NY.

Duke Ellington is quite possibly the greatest musician and composer of the 20th century—certainly one of the top five. As a composer, he wrote thousands of songs and arranged and rearranged those and others during his lifetime. He wrote his songs for the individual musicians in his orchestra and not for "sections." As a band leader, he performed nearly constantly for most of his career. As a musician, he was a giant, considered one of the best pianists of his era. And unlike most of his contemporaries, he was able to update his work, modernizing it to blend into the sound of the decade in which he was creating. Ellington's orchestra was his main vehicle, and he worked with his orchestra—though it changed constantly—throughout his career, recording more than 200 albums. New collections and reissues of his work continue to appear, making it seem as if he didn't die in 1974.

Ellington started studying the piano at the age of seven, adopting the nickname "Duke" around the same time. Drawn by the ragtime music of the time, he joined the music world in 1917 with the biggest ad in the telephone yellow pages and a desire to be a band leader despite his then-limited repertoire. The ad worked, and he was soon heading up several Washington, D.C.-area bands. He worked on his technique by analyzing fingering from slowed-down piano rolls. In 1923 he ventured to New York City and formed the Washingtonians with friends. He landed the band a job at the Hollywood Club, where they began to play regularly and where Bubber Miley helped Ellington create the "jungle sound" that made his group distinct. After some struggles to find the right sound or breakthrough music, Duke Ellington and His Orchestra was born around 1926 with hot numbers like "East St. Louis Toodleoo" and "Birmingham Breakdown." The very next year, the group scored its break, earning a permanent spot at the Cotton Club on the strength of numbers such as "Black and Tan Fantasy" and "Creole Love Call." From there, Ellington and crew began radio broadcasts and became famous throughout the country. Fortunately for the band leader, he had found success by the time the Great Depression struck, and never lacked work or suffered through hard times. During the 1930s he built his band up with eight soloists—most bands didn't even have three. Leaving the Cotton Club in 1931, the Ellington Orchestra hit the road and became a big act throughout the country and soon throughout the world, touring Europe and Sweden in 1933 and 1939. By 1940 Duke Ellington's Orchestra was the greatest in the world, featuring newly acquired musicians like Ben Webster on tenor sax, Jimmy Blanton on bass, and Billy Strayhorn as an arranger and composer—all of whom, like many of the musicians who worked with Ellington, would go on to become some of the greatest names in jazz music. His 1940–42 band was one of his best, and Ellington added many songs to his repertoire during those years that would become lifelong standards—"Take the 'A' Train," "Perdido," and "The 'C' Jam Blues," among others. Ellington gave his first performance at Carnegie Hall in 1943, debuting "Black, Brown, and Beige." As the 1940s killed the big bands and bebop rose to prominence, Ellington continued to perform, tour, and record with his orchestra. The 1950s was his "slump" decade, even though his artistic output was never stronger. In 1956 Duke soared back into the spotlight at the Newport Jazz Festival. During the 1960s, he dabbled in religious music and collaborated with jazz greats who had not started under his wing, including Charles Mingus, Max Roach, Count Basie, John Coltrane, and Louis Armstrong. Ellington continued to tour and record extensively throughout the 1960s despite his age and received the recognition he so richly deserved. He outlasted many of his closest working partners, including Billy Strayhorn and Johnny Hodges, and continued making music despite the deaths of his associates and friends, updating the orchestra, and persevering until 1974 when, stricken with cancer, he died a month after his 75th birthday. Ironically, though Ellington was a widely known artist, much about the man remains unknown. Reticent to speak about his life, he is conspicuously absent as a character in his own autobiography, *Music Is My Mistress*. Ellington was an even-tempered man, some said almost saintly in demeanor. Even in the face of obvious prejudice—for example, when the Pulitzer Prize committee of 1965 denied him a special lifetime achievement award, overruling its own official judges—Ellington took it in stride, saying, "Fate doesn't want me to be famous too young." He was 66 years old at the time.

what to buy: Ellington and his orchestra performed all over the world, and though each performance couldn't be the greatest ever, there were nights when the crew reached a unique level of inspiration and craft. *All Star Road Band Vol. II* (Signature, 1957/CBS Special Products, 1990) is one such occasion. At a dance one evening in Chicago in 1964, Ellington and his orchestra rocked the hall and tried out some new arrangements of the standards. He got superb solo work from trumpeters Cootie Williams and Cat Anderson, trombonists Lawrence Brown and Buster Cooper, and the entire saxophone section. This is a great one. Ellington revitalized his career with *Ellington at Newport* (Columbia, 1956/1987, prod. George Avakian), a big commercial comeback for the musician. "Diminuendo and Crescendo in Blue" was one of the concert's most intense tunes, and the 27-chorus blues marathon solo by Paul Gonslaves drove the audience wild, so much so that there was nearly a riot. Ellington made worldwide news as a result and was back on top of the music world.

what to buy next: *All Star Road Band* (Signature, 1964/1989) is not as wild as Vol. II, but it's enjoyable and fun and includes such Ellington standards as "Take the 'A' Train," "Mood Indigo," and "Sophisticated Lady." This is an all-star orchestra and an all-star performance. Then, if you're looking for a good sampler of the Duke's works, try *Compact Jazz: And Friends* (Verve, 1987, prod. Norman Granz), a hot collection with a variety of the best of jazz and blues musicians working with Ellington, including Ella Fitzgerald, Ben Webster, Johnny Hodges, Oscar Peterson, and Dizzy Gillespie. *The 1952 Seattle Concert* (RCA, 1954/1995, prod. Jack Lewis) is another fine live recording, with great back-up and impressive versions of "Skin Deep," "Sultry Serenade," "Sophisticated Lady," and "Perdido," not to mention a sublime rendering of "Harlem Suite."

what to avoid: There's really no bad Ellington. But when it comes to collections, there are some that are clearly not the best places to start. *16 Most Requested Songs* (Columbia/Legacy, 1994, prod. various) is just too incomplete to serve as an introduction to his career.

best of the rest:

Piano Duets: Great Times with Billy Strayhorn (Riverside/Original Jazz Classics, 1950/1995)
Duke Ellington Presents . . . (Bethlehem, 1956/1995)
Ellington Jazz Party (Columbia, 1959)
The Great Paris Concert (Atlantic, 1963/1989)
(With Ray Brown) *This One's for Blanton—Duets* (Original Jazz Classics, 1972/1994)
Duke's Big Four (Pablo, 1973/1988)
Duke Ellington: The Blanton-Webster Band, 1939–1942 (Bluebird, 1986)
(With Coleman Hawkins) *Duke Ellington Meets Coleman Hawkins* (MCA, 1986)
(With Johnny Hodges) *Side by Side* (Verve, 1986)
Money Jungle—1962 (Blue Note, 1986)
(With Count Basie) *First Time: The Count Meets the Duke–1961* (Columbia, 1987)
Uptown—Early 1950s (Columbia, 1987)
The Duke Ellington Orchestra: Digital Duke (GRP, 1987)
Walkman Jazz/Compact Jazz (Verve, 1988)
Black, Brown & Beige 1944–46 (Bluebird, 1988)
Blues in Orbit—1960 (Columbia, 1988)
(With John Coltrane) *Duke Ellington & John Coltrane* (MCA/Impulse!, 1988)
The Piano Album (Capitol, 1989)
Braggin' in Brass: The Immortal 1938 Year (Portrait Masters, 1989)
Ellington Indigos: Sept.–Oct. 1957 (Columbia, 1989)
The Private Collection, Vols. I–IV (Saja, 1989)
The Private Collection, Vol. V: "The Suites" 1968 (Saja, 1989)
The Private Collection, Vols. VI–X: Dance Dates, California, 1958 (Saja, 1989)
The Best of Duke Ellington (Signature, 1989)
New Mood Indigo (Signature, 1989)
Solos, Duets, and Trios (Bluebird, 1990)
The Jungle Band: The Brunswick Era, Vol. II (1929–31) (Decca Jazz, 1990)
The Intimacy of the Blues 1967 & 1970 (Fantasy, 1991)
1924–1927 (Classics, 1991)
Up in Duke's Workshop—1969–72 (Fantasy, 1991)

The Essence of Duke Ellington: I Like Jazz (Columbia, 1991)
Duke Ellington's My People (Red Baron, 1992)
Sophisticated Lady: Masters of the Big Bands (Bluebird, 1992)
Duke Ellington & His Orchestra: Jazz Cocktail: 1928–31 (ASV Living Era, 1992)
Live at the Blue Note—1952 (Bandstand, 1992)
Duke Ellington Vol. IV: 1928 (MA Recordings, 1992)
The Pianist: 1966, 1970 (Fantasy, 1992)
(With Chick Webb) *1937* (Classics, 1993)
Original Hits, Vol. I: 1927–31 (King Jazz, 1993)
Original Hits, Vol. II: 1931–38 (King Jazz, 1993)
The Great London Concerts—1964 (MusicMasters, 1993)
Duke Ellington & His Orchestra—1938, Vol. II (Classics, 1993)
Duke Ellington & His Orchestra—1938, Vol. III (Classics, 1993)
In the 20s—Jazz Archives No. 63 (EPM, 1993)
Things Ain't What They Used to Be (LRC, 1993)
Things Ain't What They Used to Be/S.R.O. (LRC, 1993)
Live at the Rainbow Grill (Moon/FTC, 1993)
Mood Indigo (EPM Musique, 1994)
Live at the Blue Note (Roulette Jazz, 1994)
Black, Brown, and Beige—Mastersound Series (Columbia, 1994)
Duke Ellington, 1938–1939 (Classics, 1994)
Duke Ellington, Vol. II: Swing 1930–38 (ABC Music, 1994)
Duke Ellington & His Orchestra Live at Newport—1958 (Columbia/Legacy, 1994)
Uptown Downbeat with His Orchestra: Cotton Club, Jungle Band 1927–40 (Empire/Avid, 1995)
Satin Doll, 1958–59 (Jazz Time, 1995)
Duke Ellington, 1924–30 (Classics 6, 1995)
From the Blue Note—Chicago 1952 (Musicdisc, 1995)
In a Mellotone—1940–44 (RCA, 1995)
70th Birthday Concert—Nov. 1969 (Blue Note, 1995)
Live at the Whitney: April 10, 1972 (MCA/Impulse!, 1995)
The Cornell University Concert—December 1948 (MusicMasters, 1995)
New York Concert: In Performance at Columbia University—1964 (MusicMasters, 1995)
Duke Ellington & His Great Vocalists (Legacy, 1995)
The Best of Duke Ellington (Blue Note, 1995)
Duke Ellington & John Coltrane with Jimmy Garrison, Aaron Bell etc., Recorded September 1962 (MCA/Impulse!, 1995)
Duke Ellington: Greatest Hits (RCA, 1996)
Ellingtonia (Fat Boy, 1996)
This Is Jazz (Columbia, 1996)
Vol. IV: The Mooche, 1928 (EPM Musique, 1996)
Vol. V: Harlemania, 1928–29 (EPM Musique, 1996)
Vol. VI: Cotton Club Stomp (EPM Musique, 1996)
Vol. IX: Mood Indigo, 1930 (EPM Musique, 1996)
Vol. X: Rockin' in Rhythm, 1930–31 (EPM, 1996)
Sophisticated Lady—1941–49 (Vocal Jazz, 1996)
Ellington at Basin Street East: The Complete Concert of 14 January 1964 (Music & Arts, 1996)

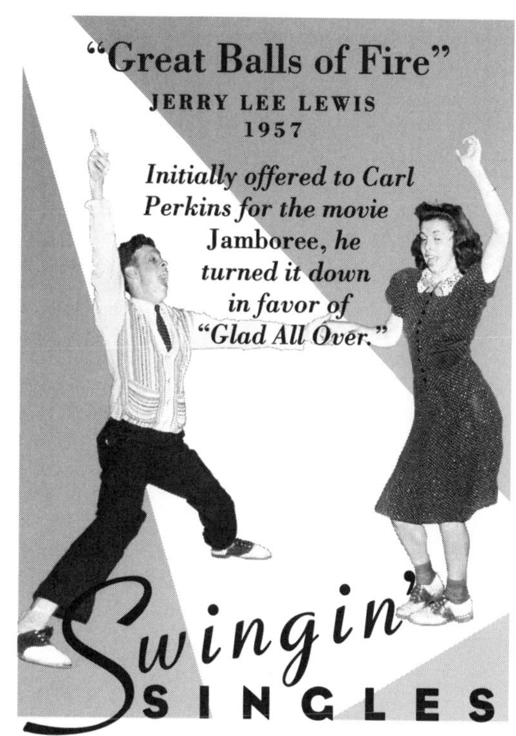

"Great Balls of Fire"
JERRY LEE LEWIS
1957
Initially offered to Carl Perkins for the movie Jamboree, he turned it down in favor of "Glad All Over."
Swingin'
SINGLES

Rockin' in Rhythm, 1958–59 (Jazz Hour, 1996)
Best of Early Ellington (Decca, 1996)
Duke Ellington & His Famous Orchestra: Fargo, North Dakota, Nov. 7, 1940 (Vintage Jazz Classics, 1940/1996)
The Great Duke Ellington (Hindsight, 1996)
Cornell University Concert (MusicMasters, 1996)
Cornell University: Second Set (MusicMasters, 1997)
Duke Ellington's Greatest Hits (Sony, 1997)
Jazz Profile (Blue Note, 1997)
Revue Collection (One Way, 1997)
Priceless Jazz (GRP, 1998)
This Is Jazz: Duke Ellington Plays Standards (Sony, 1998)
Duke Ellington at the Cotton Club—1938, Band Remotes from Harlem (Sandy Hook)
1941: The Jimmy Blanton/Ben Webster Transcriptions (Vintage Jazz Classics)
Duke Ellington & His Famous Orchestra: Hollywood, CA—Jan-Dec. 1941 (Vintage Jazz Classics)
The Complete Capitol Recordings of Duke Ellington, 1953–55 (Mosaic)
Second Sacred Concert–1968 (Prestige)
New Orleans Suite–1970 (Atlantic)
Lullaby of Birdland (Intermedia)

Duke Ellington **(Archive Photos)**

worth searching for: Ellington didn't do very much work with the movies, but his out-of-print soundtrack for *Anatomy of a Murder* (Anadisq, 1959/Rykodisc, 1987) fit the story and movie perfectly and is one of the very best soundtracks of the era, as well as a good stand-alone album. Dave Grusin's *Homage to Duke* (GRP, 1993) is a great collection of different interpretations of Ellington tunes by one of the masters of contemporary light jazz.

influences:

◀◀ Fats Waller, James P. Johnson, Sidney Bechet, Willie "The Lion" Smith

▶▶ Thelonious Monk, Benny Goodman, Cecil Taylor, Count Basie, Quincy Jones, Gil Evans, Fletcher Henderson, Sun Ra, Maurice White

Chris Tower

Mercer Ellington

Born March 11, 1919, in Washington, DC. Died February 8, 1996, in Copenhagen, Denmark.

Mercer Ellington could never escape the overwhelming shadow of his father, Duke Ellington, but, then again, he never really tried. Instead, he strove to perpetuate his father's legacy after his death. Mercer learned music in Washington, D.C., while growing up. After moving to New York he tried to start up a succession of his own bands in the late 1930s and early 1940s. He was ultimately unsuccessful, despite having sidemen such as Billy Strayhorn and Carmen McRae. During this time he also made notable contributions to the Duke Ellington songbook, writing "Things Ain't What They Used to Be" and "Blue Serge" (among others). Through the next few decades, Ellington would work in many capacities within the music industry, trying his hand at managing, sales, disc jockeying, and trumpet work for his father and Cootie Williams. After Duke's death in 1974 Mercer took over his band, making some enjoyable, but not very important, music in that capacity. He also wrote a biography of his father titled *Duke Ellington in Person.*

what to buy: For the enjoyable *Digital Duke* (GRP, 1987, prod. Michael Abene, Mercer Ellington), Mercer's group mixed such Ellington alumni as trumpeter Clark Terry, altoist Norris Turney, and trombonist Britt Woodman with other talented musicians, including saxophonist Branford Marsalis and pianist Sir Roland Hanna.

what to buy next: *Only God Can Make a Tree* (MusicMasters, 1995, prod. Steve Fox) has a worldly, environmental theme and features interesting arrangements of such Ellington standards as "Caravan" and "Sophisticated Lady." It's rather run of the mill, but still a good example of what Mercer did with the band after his father's passing.

what to avoid: *Take the Holiday Train* (Special Music, 1992, prod. Mercer Ellington) is the kind of lazy, commercial album Mercer's father never would have made, relying more on cliches and a few big names than on originality. The Duke-ish renditions of Christmas tunes are worth skipping.

the rest:

Continuum (Fantasy, 1975)
Hot and Bothered (Doctor Jazz, 1984)
Music Is My Mistress (MusicMasters, 1988)

worth searching for: With a cast including tenorman Ben Webster, altoist Johnny Hodges, pianist Strayhorn, and trumpeter Terry, one would hardly know the strong *Black and Tan Fantasy* (Coral, 1958, prod. Mercer Ellington) was an album by Mercer and not his father's orchestra.

influences:

◀◀ Duke Ellington

▶▶ Quincy Jones, T.S. Monk Jr.

Dan Keener

Bill Elliott Swing Orchestra

Formed 1993, in Los Angeles, CA.

Bill Elliott heads up a genuine 15-piece big band capable of alternating the cozy, sweet sounds of Sammy Kaye with the too-hot-to-handle jazz of Benny Goodman. However, that doesn't mean his outfit is a cover band. Nearly everything his orchestra pumps out is written by Elliott himself, a triple threat of the old school (arranger, pianist, writer) who crafts swing-era tunes rife with modern allusions. Every now and then he even exercises the "band leader's prerogative" and takes a whack at singing. However, for the most part, he employs quartets such as Vocalworks or Bill's Lucky Stars to handle the vocal chores, à la the Pied Pipers and Modernaires. Elliott got his foothold in the music business composing and conducting music for such TV programs as *Northern Exposure* and *Relativity,* among many others. After writing "Pep, Vim, and Verve" for the *Dick Tracy* soundtrack, he decided to focus on conjuring original music with a vintage sound. An avid student of the genre, Elliott says he modeled his orchestra on Tommy Dorsey, but his outfit can deftly evoke the sounds of any number of bands, from Chick Webb and Artie Shaw to Jimmie Lunceford and Duke Ellington. This versatility has earned Elliott and his group plenty of soundtrack work in such feature films as *Independence Day* and *That Darn Cat.*

what's available: Elliott's first disc, *Swing Fever* (Wayland, 1994, prod. Bill Elliott), consolidates his early TV and motion picture contributions ("Alaskan Nights," "Pep, Vim, and Verve") with eerily accurate and inspired homages to the past masters of big band ("Azure," "Wham-Rebop," "The Best Things Happen When You Dance"). Though the orchestra is top-notch throughout, Elliott relies too heavily on the his singers Vocalworks and Amy Weston, who seldom achieve a consistent blend. The best numbers are the instrumentals ("Struttin' with Kate," "Bill's Bounce") which indicate the band leader might've been holding back a little too much. Elliot's second disc, *Calling All Jitterbugs!* ☊☊☊ (Wayland, 1997, prod. Bill Elliott), plays more to the band's strengths and audience expectations. Vocalist Weston ("The Guy I Met This Evening") sounds more authentic and his new group, the Lucky Stars ("I Dreamed about You"), achieve richer harmonies. On some tunes composed for the big and small screen ("My Baby Said She's Marry Me," "Tonight I'm Going out with You") the orchestra proves to be an excellent mimic of the muted-trumpet, Vo-de-oh-do sound of '20s and '30s jazz. The band leader himself takes an inoffensive vocal on a few cuts and turns in a stunning and sweet instrumental ("Oh Vicky!") on the piano. However, it's on the flat-out dance numbers ("Mildred, Won't You Behave," "Bill's Bounce," "12 Cylinders") where Elliott and company really catch fire.

influences:

◀◀ Benny Goodman, Tommy Dorsey, Johnny Mercer, White Heat Band, the Pied Pipers, the Modernaires

Ken Burke

Esquerita

Born Eskew Reeder Jr. in Greenville, SC. Died October 23, 1986, in Harlem, NY.

Was Esquerita the original version of Little Richard or merely a Penniman wannabe? Richard himself has said Esquerita (a.k.a. The King of Voola) taught him how to play in the frenzied, cracked treble-note style that drove "Good Golly Miss Molly," "Slippin' and Slidin'," and so many others up the charts. Yet Esquerita did not emerge until after Little Richard "retired" from show business in 1957. According to legend, Richard gave his old mentor much of his wardrobe and sincere blessings on a career. Yet it was Paul Peek (of Gene Vincent's Blue Caps) who discovered the singer/pianist playing under the name Professor Eskew Reeder, and brought him to the attention of Capitol Records. The label's producers set him up with a studio band that wailed much like Little Richard's group the Upsetters, and the singer fashioned many tunes similar to Richard's, such as "I'm Battie over Hattie," "Hey Miss Lucy," and "Good Golly, Annie Mae." Though as flamboyant as Richard with his extremely high pompadour, flashy clothes, and wild-ass stage demeanor, Esquerita couldn't quite imitate the voice. He had the falsetto "woooooo" down pat, but if he tried to mimic Richard's gospel shout too fully, his voice would break up, and the music lost momentum. His piano work was frenzied, yet jazzy, and his best sides achieved a fast, danceable groove. Esquerita never had anything close to a hit record or a substantial fan base. Capitol dropped the high-haired singer after 1959; his one bright spot during the '60s came when Little Richard himself covered "Dew Drop Inn"—included as the B-side of the Reprise hit "Freedom Blues." Esquerita vanished during the '70s. It wasn't until the '80s that Billy Miller and Miriam Linna began singing his praises in *Kicks* magazine, and thus a cult was born.

what to buy: Formerly titled *Believe Me When I Say Rock 'n' Roll Is Here to Stay, Rockin' the Joint* ☊☊☊♭ (Capitol, 1990/Collectables, 1998, compilation prod. Ron Furmanek) features 28 of the King of Voola's best Capitol sides. Esquerita does a credible job as an R&B/blues singer on "She Left Me Crying," "Laid Off," and "I Live the Live I Love," but the rocking jump blues of "Hole in My Heart," "Hey Miss Lucy," "Katie Mae," and "Baby Come Back" will convince you of his power as a performer. Even the Georgia Peach never did anything as sonically weird as "Esquerita and the Voola."

what to buy next: The running time is a little short on *Vintage Voola* ☊☊♭ (Norton, 1997, compilation prod. Billy Miller), but fans will absolutely dig this set of Esquerita odds and ends. His first Capitol demo sessions featuring members of Gene Vincent's Blue Caps are included, along with the piano pounder's contributions to Peek's first solo outing. Such tracks as "Sweet Skinny Jenny" and "Sarah Lee" make this disc a solid companion to the Collectables set, and the color photos are gorgeous.

worth searching for: Completists might want the import *Sock It to Me Baby* ☊☊ (Bear Family, 1993, prod. Herb Abramson), which features a Little Richard interview and 13 tracks of just Esquerita and his piano from 1965. Love him or hate him, it's hard to resist the rhythmic appeal of "Dew Drop Inn," "Mississippi Goddamn," "Wig Wearin' Baby," and the title track.

influences:

◀◀ Roy Brown, Billy Wright

▶▶ Little Richard

Ken Burke

Ruth Etting

Born November 23, 1896, in David City, NE. Died September 24, 1978, in Colorado Springs, CO.

Ruth Etting was Queen of the Torch Singers. Her Depression-era classics "10 Cents a Dance," "Mean to Me," and "Love Me or Leave" permanently fixed her image as a woman who is scorned no matter how well she loved her man. That image was a little closer to the truth than Etting liked to acknowledge. Initially a chorus girl in a 1920s Chicago revue, she married gangster Martin "Moe the Gimp" Snyder, who used his influence to get her bookings in top nightspots and secure a contract with Columbia Records. An insanely jealous man, Snyder levied all sorts of abuse on Etting and never let the singer forget he "made" her. Talentwise, Etting didn't really need him. She could wring emotion from the tritest pop lyric, groove with the jazz cats, and even raise a smile with a novelty song. Modern critics tend to dismiss her work, but Etting's ability to change tempos to increase a song's dramatic effect was innovative for the times, and she worked with some of the finest swing and pop musicians of the era. The singer's major breakthrough came on Broadway in such shows as *Ziegfield Follies of 1927, Whoopee, Simple Simon,* and *Ziegfield Follies of 1931,* which supplied many of her greatest songs. Between 1926 and 1937 Etting recorded more than 60 major hit records. During the same time period, she starred in early musical motion picture shorts and feature films, and had her own network radio program. As a multi-media star, only Bing Crosby was bigger, but it all came tumbling down in 1937. Tired of the abusive Snyder, Etting finally sought a divorce so she could marry pianist Myrl Alderman. Her enraged husband shot Alderman and ended up going to jail for attempted murder. Though Alderman survived (the two would eventually wed), the sordid publicity killed Etting's career. She resurfaced during the war years as a frequent guest on radio, and briefly starred on her own program, but by then her melodramatic style was considered old hat. The 1955 James Cagney-Doris Day vehicle *Love Me or Leave Me* was based on Etting's story, and while some aspects are fictitious, the tone is accurate and it struck a nerve with audiences. The Oscar-nominated film rekindled interest in Etting, but she declined to capitalize. Her first brush with fame had been rough enough.

what to buy: There are plenty of classic hits on *Love Me or Leave Me* (Pearl Flapper, 1996, compilation prod. David Lennick), a 25-song collection featuring "10 Cents a Dance," "Button up Your Overcoat," and the title track. Jazz buffs will be pleased to note the aural presence of Eddie Lang and Joe Venuti, as well as the redoubtable Ted "Is Everybody Happy?" Lewis. The equally fine *10 Cents a Dance* (Living Era, 1994, compilation prod. Kevin Daly), is a 20-track disc that has all the same hits, plus several different melodramatic tunes of heartbreak not on the Pearl Flapper set.

what to buy next: *America's Greatest Songstress: 24 Recordings from 1926–37* (GSE Claremont, 1997 prod. various) features such old-time delights as "Ain't Misbehavin'," "Were Your Ears Burnin' Baby," and "All of Me."

the rest:

Goodnight My Love (1930–37) (Take Two, 1994)

(With Helen Morgan) *More Than You Know* (Encore Productions/Original Cast, 1996)

worth searching for: Vintage songs from Etting's early movie career can be found on *Glorifier of American Song* (Take Two, 1998, restoration prod. George Morrow), a 20-track disc featuring "Were You Sincere?" "Can We Talk It Over," "It's a Sin to Tell a Lie," and two private recordings from 1958.

influences:

◀◀ Nora Bayes, Mildred Bailey

▶▶ Annette Hanshaw, Fanny Brice, Helen Morgan

Ken Burke

Charlie Feathers

Born June 12, 1932, in Hollow Springs, MS.

Though never blessed with any real commercial acceptance, Charlie Feathers nonetheless made his mark as one of the most singular and respected practitioners of 1950s rockabilly. Hooking up with Sam Phillips's Sun Records during the early part of that decade, Feathers made the transition from straight country to rock 'n' roll by the time Elvis Presley began cutting sides (Feathers supposedly co-wrote Presley's "I Forgot to Remember to Forget"). Feathers made his most enduring music with King Records, including the tough "One Hand Loose" as well as other rockabilly staples like "I Can't Hardly Stand It" and "Tongue-tied Jill." He has remained active through the years, surfacing here and there with the verve of his 1950s recordings intact.

what to buy: *Get with It: Essential Recordings (1954–69)* (Revenant, 1998, prod. various) is a thorough career retrospective, including Sun material, a bluesy 1956 version of the standard "Frankie and Johnny," and demos with the late Mississippi bluesman Junior Kimbrough. *Tip Top Daddy* (Norton, 1991, prod. various) and *Uh Huh Honey* (Norton, 1992, prod. various) both contain essential Feathers tracks from 1958–73, including "Bottle to the Baby," "This Lonesome Feeling," and "Fireball Mail."

what to buy next: Feathers returned to the studio for *Charlie Feathers* (Elektra, 1991, prod. Ben Vaughn), which shows the man in fine form after all this time, teamed with former Sun cohorts Stan Kesler and Roland Janes.

worth searching for: Feathers recorded a pair of late-1970s albums, the out-of-print *Charlie Feathers, Vol. I* (Feathers

Records, 1979, prod. Charlie Feathers) and *Charlie Feathers, Vol. II* (Feathers Records, 1979, prod. Charlie Feathers), with more than a few choice moments of rockabilly fever.

influences:

Elvis Presley, Hank Williams

Al Anderson, Dave Edmunds

David Simons

Ella Fitzgerald

Born April 25, 1917, in Newport News, VA. Died June 14, 1996, in Beverly Hills, CA.

Many critics consider Ella Fitzgerald "the First Lady of Song," the best female jazz singer ever, though in her customary modesty Fitzgerald hailed Sarah Vaughan as the finest vocalist of all time. Regardless, there can be no debate that Fitzgerald belongs in that select pantheon of incomparable voices (Vaughan, Billie Holiday) that could transform the weakest material into a masterpiece, making any song uniquely her own. She could swing with the best of them, is credited with creating the free-form singing style known as "scat," and interpreted every number with spectacularly clear diction and a powerful, versatile voice. The perpetually cheerful lilt in that voice stood in sharp contrast to an early life spent in abysmal poverty; she was a homeless 16-year-old in 1933, but turned her fortunes around the following year. Fitzgerald showed up at an amateur talent contest at Harlem's Apollo Theater and won the $25 first prize by singing an impromptu version of "Judy" in the style of her main influence, Connee Boswell. Jazz great Benny Carter was in the audience and soon landed Fitzgerald a spot singing with Chick Webb's orchestra; by 1937, she was the featured attraction. Her first successful recordings included "Love and Kisses," "Undecided," and "A-Tisket, A-Tasket," the last created, so legend goes, as a nonsensical ditty to lift the spirits of Webb, who was critically ill at the time. Webb died in 1939 and Fitzgerald took over as leader of his orchestra until 1941 when she broke up the band to go solo. In the '40s Fitzgerald collaborated with acts like the Ink Spots and the Delta Rhythm Boys, eventually finding a home with Norman Granz's Jazz at the Philharmonic. She began performing more jazz and bop numbers, teaming with Dizzy Gillespie and doing raucous, scat-filled numbers in her sets. She hit the charts with "Lady Be Good" and "Flying Home," married bassist Ray Brown in 1948 (a union that would last only four years), appeared in the films *St. Louis Blues* and Jack Webb's *Pete Kelly's Blues*, and made many TV appearances starting in the '50s and continuing throughout her career. All these events were concurrent with her signing to Granz's Verve label and beginning her project of making her seminal and very popular "songbook" recordings. Fitzgerald achieved the pinnacle of her career in 1960 with her European concert tour, notably the Berlin show featuring her scat-heavy spoof of "Mack the Knife." Her radiance lost some luster in the late '60s as she tried to cash in on the popular music of the day, but she rebounded with live recordings in the '70s, working with Count Basie, Oscar Peterson, and Joe Pass. In the 1980s, however, Fitzgerald began to fade. Her health declined and she lacked the "verve" she had displayed so effortlessly in her younger years. Heart and eye trouble prevented her from performing or recording for long stretches, and by 1994 she had completely retired. She died in the spring of 1996, though her legacy lives on in more than 100 available recordings and a reputation that has made her name synonymous with great singing, great jazz, and scat coolness.

what to buy: In 1956 Fitzgerald signed with Verve Records and undertook a massive project: A series of "songbooks" featuring the works of the greatest composers of the 20th century. Though not her finest jazz performances, the best of these albums is *The Cole Porter Songbook* (Verve, 1956/DCC, 1995, prod. Norman Granz), and it serves as a wonderful introduction to Fitzgerald if you prefer not to drop a quarter of a grand for *The Complete Ella Fitzgerald Song Books* (Verve, 1993, prod. Norman Granz). Her Porter offering was the best-received of all the "songbooks," and features Fred Astaire, Bing Crosby, Marlene Dietrich, Billie Holiday, Gene Kelly, Judy Garland, Ethel Merman, and Porter himself teaming with her talent. A solid companion piece to the Porter disc is Fitzgerald's *The Complete Duke Ellington Songbook* (Verve, 1956, prod. Norman Granz), though this Verve offering is a two-volume box set and priced accordingly. If the Porter set is Fitzgerald at her vocal best, the Ellington sessions find Ella at her jazz singing best, backed by jazz music's best: Gillespie, Johnny Hodges, Oscar Peterson, Billy Strayhorn, and, of course, Sir Duke. Predictably, a flood of new recordings and reshuffled compilations have hit the market since Fitzgerald's death. The wide-ranging collection *The Best of the Songbooks* (Verve, 1996) is certainly worthy, but has the disadvantage of moving the songs far away from their original context.

what to buy next: By 1960 Fitzgerald had reached the pinnacle of her dazzling career. She carried the experience 30 years of singing brings, along with the energy and intensity she had when she began. *Mack the Knife: The Complete Ella in Berlin Concert* (Verve, 1993, prod. Phil Schaap) is an example of Fitzgerald at her best. Her hilarious and legendary take on "Mack the Knife" made this concert perhaps her most memorable. This disc combines the concert tracks with several rare and previously unreleased recordings, as she sparkles on her rendition of Sarah Vaughan's "Misty," her own scat-filled "How High the Moon," and standards like "The Lady Is a Tramp" and

Ella Fitzgerald **(Archive Photos)**

"Too Darn Hot." For all-around collections, there are none better than *75th Birthday Celebration* (Decca, 1993, compilation prod. Orrin Keepnews), a two-CD set charting 39 songs from the first half of her career. Fitzgerald swings and scats here as both a big band and jazz vocalist.

what to avoid: There's nothing inherently wrong with K-Tel, except that their TV ads are annoying. But *Ella Fitzgerald* (K-Tel, 1996, prod. various) is a weak assortment compared to all the others competing with it. Should you get the urge to order by phone at 3 a.m., resist the temptation by strapping yourself in bed until you can get to the CD store the next day and purchase a truly good compilation.

best of the rest:

Gershwin Songbook (Verve, 1950)
Ella Fitzgerald Sings the George & Ira Gershwin Songbook (Verve, 1959/1998)
Clap Hands, Here Comes Charlie (Verve, 1961/1989)
Ella & Basie (Verve, 1963)
The Johnny Mercer Songbook (Verve, 1964)
Ella & Louis (Verve, 1972)
Ella in London (Fantasy, 1974/Original Jazz Classics, 1998)
Dream Dancing (Pablo, 1978/1987)
Ella Fitzgerald & Joe Pass: Speak Love (Pablo, 1983)
Silver Collection: The Songbooks (Verve, 1984)
The Jerome Kern Songbook (Verve, 1985)
These Are the Blues (Verve, 1986)
Ella Fitzgerald at the Opera House (Verve, 1986)
The Irving Berlin Songbook Vols. 1 & 2 (Verve, 1986)
Fine and Mellow (Pablo, 1987)
Ella Fitzgerald & Louis Armstrong, "Compact Jazz" series (Verve, 1988)
The Harold Arlen Songbook Vol. I (Verve, 1988)
The Harold Arlen Songbook Vol. II (Verve, 1988)
Fitzgerald and Pass ... Again (Pablo, 1988)
Ella Fitzgerald/Count Basie/Joe Pass: Digital III at Montreux (Pablo, 1988)
Ella Fitzgerald & Count Basie: A Classy Pair (Pablo, 1989)
Ella Fitzgerald & Joe Pass: Easy Living (Pablo, 1989)
Ella Fitzgerald & Count Basie: A Perfect Match (Pablo, 1989)
Ella Fitzgerald/Tommy Flanagan, Montreux 1977 (Original Jazz Classics, 1989)
Ella Fitzgerald & Duke Ellington: The Stockholm Concert, Feb. 7, 1966 (Pablo, 1989)
Ella: Things Aren't What They Used to Be: And You Better Believe It (Reprise, 1989)
The Best of Ella Fitzgerald (Pablo, 1989)
The Intimate Ella (Verve, 1990)
Ella & Louis Again (Verve, 1990)
Ella a Nice (Original Jazz Classics, 1990)
Ella Live! (Verve)
Ella Fitzgerald/Count Basie/Benny Goodman Jazz Collector Edition Vol. II (Laserlight, 1991)
Ella Fitzgerald & Joe Pass: Take Love Easy (Pablo, 1991)
Returns to Berlin (Verve, 1991)
Like Someone in Love (Verve, 1991)
Ella Fitzgerald & Oscar Peterson: Ella & Oscar (Pablo, 1991)
Ella Swings Lightly (Verve, 1992)
The Essential Ella Fitzgerald: The Great Songs (Verve, 1992)
Ella Swings Gently with Nelson (Verve, 1993)
Ella Swings Brightly with Nelson (Verve, 1993)
At the Montreux Jazz Festival, 1975 (Original Jazz Classics, 1993)
First Lady of Song (Verve, 1993)
Compact Jazz—Ella & Duke (Verve, 1993)
The Best of Ella Fitzgerald (Curb, 1993)
The Best of Ella Fitzgerald: First Lady of Song (Verve, 1994)
The Best of the Songbooks: The Ballads (Verve, 1994)
Jazz 'round Midnight (Verve, 1994)
Jazz 'round Midnight Again (Verve, 1994)
The War Years (Decca Jazz, 1994)
Pure Ella (Decca Jazz, 1994)
The Concert Years (Pablo, 1994)
Verve Jazz Masters 6 (Verve, 1994)
Verve Jazz Masters 24 (Verve, 1994)
The Jazz Sides: Verve Jazz Masters 46 (Verve, 1995)
Ella: The Legendary Decca Recordings (Decca Jazz, 1995)
Live from the Roseland Ballroom—New York 1940 (Musicdisc, 1995)
Newport Jazz Festival/Live at Carnegie Hall (Classics, 1995)
Ella Fitzgerald/Billie Holiday/Dinah Washington, Jazz 'round Midnight: Three Divas (Verve, 1995)
The Early Years, Pt. 1 & 2 (Decca Jazz, 1995)
Let No Man Write My Epitaph (Classic, 1995)
Lady Time (Pablo, 1995)
Dreams Come True (Drive Archive, 1995)
Daydream: The Best of the Duke Ellington Songbook (Verve, 1995)
Love Songs: Best of the Verve Songbooks (Verve, 1996)
The Best of Ella Fitzgerald with Chick Webb & His Orchestra (Decca Jazz, 1996)
Oh, Lady Be Good! Best of the Gershwin Songbook (Verve, 1996)
Ella & Friends (Decca Jazz, 1996)
Sunshine of Your Love (Verve, 1996)
Ella Fitzgerald (Dove Audio, 1996)
Bluella: Ella Fitzgerald Sings the Blues (Pablo, 1996)
You'll Have to Swing It (Eclipse, 1996)
Rock It for Me (Eclipse, 1996)
The Best Is Yet to Come (Pablo, 1996)
Sings the Rodgers & Hart Songbook (Verve, 1997)
Rhythm and Romance (Living Era, 1997)
A-Tisket, A-Tasket (ITC Masters, 1997)
The Best of Ella Fitzgerald & Louis Armstrong on Verve (Verve, 1997)

The Complete Ella Fitzgerald & Louis Armstrong on Verve ♪♪♪♪♪ (Verve, 1997)
Ella Fitzgerald/Sarah Vaughan/Carmen McRae: Ladies of Jazz ♪♪♪♪ (Laserlight, 1997)
Ella Fitzgerald with the Tommy Flanagan Trio ♪♪♪ (Laserlight, 1997)
Priceless Jazz Collection ♪♪♪♪ (GRP, 1997)
Priceless Jazz Collection: More Ella Fitzgerald ♪♪♪♪ (GRP, 1998)

worth searching for: Christmas albums are not always easy to find, since they're usually only big in the bins during the season to be jolly. But Fitzgerald's Christmas offerings, *Ella Fitzgerald's Christmas* ♪♪♪♪ (Capitol/EMI, 1996, prod. Ron Furmanek) and *Wishes You a Swinging Christmas* ♪♪♪♪ (Verve, 1993, prod. Norman Granz), are worth tracking down. Once you get in the spirit, you'll be jolly to have Ella's swinging versions of timeless Christmas standbys.

influences:
◀◀ Maxine Sullivan, Connee Boswell, Billie Holiday, Bessie Smith

▶▶ Sarah Vaughan, Lena Horne, Betty Carter, Mel Tormé, Carmen McRae, Joe Williams, Shirley Horn, Diana Ross, Whitney Houston, Gladys Knight, Bette Midler, Barbra Streisand

Chris Tower

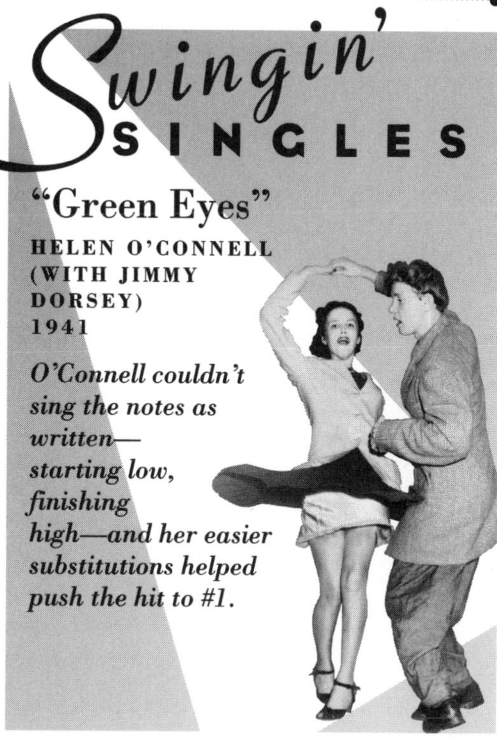

Swingin' SINGLES
"Green Eyes"
HELEN O'CONNELL (WITH JIMMY DORSEY)
1941
O'Connell couldn't sing the notes as written—starting low, finishing high—and her easier substitutions helped push the hit to #1.

Flattop Tom & His Jump Cats

Formed January 1992, in Los Angeles, CA.

"Flattop Tom" Hall, vocals, harmonica; Bruce "Dr. Time" King, drums; "Brother" Bob Robles, guitar; Steve "the Professor" Soloman, baritone sax, piano; "Jumpin'" George Pandis, trumpet, flugelhorn; Jotty Johnson, upright bass; Taryn Donath, piano, vocals; Tina Stevens, vocals.

"Flattop" Tom Hall has certainly lived the swinger lifestyle. During the 1980s he frequented Los Angeles rockabilly clubs to see the likes of the Stray Cats and the Blasters. His tastes turned to blues and, after attending the 1987 Topanga Canyon Blues Festival, he decided to become a musician. Harpist William Clarke, who was on the Topanga bill, taught Hall his trade. Meanwhile, Hall continued to dance. His resume includes the films *Shout* (with John Travolta in 1991) and the big-band-reviving cult classic *Swingers*. Then he formed Flattop Tom and His Jump Cats.

what's available: Hall, who plays the diatonic and chromatic harmonicas, and his Jump Cats released two CDs, *Jumping Blues for Your Dancing Shoes* and *Rockin' and Jumpin' the Blues*, before distributing *Swing Dance Party* around the U.S. and Europe. *Swing Dance Party* ♪♪ (Palamar, 1998, prod. Flattop Tom & His Jump Cats) is a weak effort that could serve as a "Swing 101" course. Doing his best Elvis impersonation, Hall sings of all the stereotypical swing topics—his baby, his favorite hang, and himself. It's impossible to tell from Hall's vocal style if he's laughing or trying to sing vibrato in "Rocket 88." One reviewer said the CD "would make Louis Jordan proud." Or not.

influences:
◀◀ Glenn Miller, Benny Goodman, Paul Butterfield, William Clarke, the Blasters

▶▶ Big Bad Voodoo Daddy, Cherry Poppin' Daddies

Christina Fuoco

Myron Floren

Born November 5, 1919, near Webster, SD.

With his bright, toothy smile and those fast-moving fingers across his huge accordion keys, Myron Floren became the biggest star of the Lawrence Welk Orchestra in its prime, and he continues to keep the Welk family tradition alive under his own name. A musical prodigy—he could play the family pump organ at age seven—Floren was already on the radio at age 19. He moved to St. Louis in 1946 to join the Buckeye Four, where he was hired on the spot after delighting the Welk band with a career-making solo during an audition at the Casa Loma Ballroom. It was the perfect arrangement for both: Welk no longer had to rely on his own limited accordion skills, and Floren, a natural showman and consummate professional, got the center stage he deserved. Floren worked with Welk for 32 years and still performs regularly with the Stars of the Lawrence Welk Show, where his self-deprecating humor and easy-going style have made him a kind of Bruce Springsteen for the geriatric set.

what to buy: You can always find Floren's latest work for sale after his concerts, in both cassette and compact discs, and you can get your picture taken with the entire cast, too. If you're not so lucky, *The Polka King* (Ranwood, 1993) and *Polka Favorites* are worthy collections of this accomplished accordion master.

best of the rest:

22 of the Greatest Polkas (Ranwood, 1992)
22 Great Accordion Classics (Ranwood, 1993)
22 Dance Party Favorites (Ranwood, 1993)
Inspirational Songs (Ranwood, 1993)
22 Great Polka Hits, Vol. II (Ranwood, 1993)
Dance Little Bird (Ross, 1997)

influences:

Lawrence Welk

"Weird Al" Jankovic

see also: *Lawrence Welk*

Leland Rucker

Rosie Flores

Born September 10, 1950, in San Antonio, TX.

Dwight Yoakam's *Guitars, Cadillacs, Etc., Etc.* was often held up as the "alternative" linchpin of the late 1980's new-traditionalist movement, but the real dust was kicked up by Rosie Flores's self-titled 1987 solo debut. A sassy southern California-based Texan who had apprenticed in an all-woman rock band called the Screamin' Sirens, Flores sings with a raspy authority and a fiery grace capable of straddling Tex-Mex, blues, rockabilly, and even girl-group pop. After Warner Bros. dropped her in 1988 Flores moved to Austin, Texas, and eventually signed with Oakland, California-based HighTone. Despite living in a city that helped trigger the '90s alternative-country boom, Flores has forsaken country-rock in favor of exploring the rawer rockabilly roots she flaunted in a late-1970s bar band called Rosie and the Screamers. She collaborated with childhood heroes Wanda Jackson and Janis Martin on 1995's *Rockabilly Filly* and Ray Campi on 1997's *A Little Bit of Heartache*.

what to buy: *A Honky Tonk Reprise*, a.k.a. *Rosie Flores* (Warner Bros., 1987/Rounder, 1996, prod. Pete Anderson), is a reissue of her stunning 1987 self-titled Warner Bros. debut, which ranges from such neo-traditional romps as "Crying over You" and "Heartbreak Train" to such sobering ballads as "Somebody Loses, Somebody Wins" and "God May Forgive You (But I Won't)." The latter—a Harlan Howard/Bobby Braddock composition that eclipses Lyle Lovett's similar "God Will"—has been resurrected as a Flores-inspired fixture in Iris DeMent's live show. The Rounder reissue comes with six bonus tracks, including a heartmelting cover of Skeeter Davis's "End of the World."

the rest:

After the Farm (HighTone, 1992)
Once More with Feeling (HighTone, 1993)
Rockabilly Filly (HighTone, 1995)
(With Ray Campi) *A Little Bit of Heartache* (Watermelon, 1997)

worth searching for: Rosie's faithful cover of "My Own Kind of Hat" appears on the Merle Haggard tribute *Tulare Dust* (HighTone, 1994, prod. Tom Russell, Dave Alvin).

influences:

Wanda Jackson, Brenda Lee, Patsy Cline

Iris DeMent, k.d. lang

David Okamoto

Helen Forrest

Born April 12, 1918, in Atlantic City, NJ.

Though largely forgotten today, Helen Forrest was one of the finest vocalists of the big-band era. Her ability on lush romantic numbers as well as hot swing earned her the respect of the top orchestra leaders of the '30s and '40s. She was the star vocalist in Artie Shaw's band during its greatest years—beginning in 1938, when she replaced Billie Holiday. Attractive and sensual, Forrest's renditions of "I Don't Want to Walk without You Baby," "What's New," and others added an intimate dimension Shaw's band had previously been lacking. When the mercurial Shaw suddenly disbanded his outfit (he was never at ease with public life), Forrest signed on briefly with Benny Goodman. She didn't really get along with the King of Swing, but cut fine sides such as "I'm Nobody's Baby" and "It Never Entered My Mind" before departing. Brief stints with Nat King Cole's trio and Lionel Hampton led to big hits with Harry James and His Orchestra, "I Had the Craziest Dream" and "I've Heard That Song Before" among them. Feature films followed, with appearances in *Springtime in the Rockies, Bathing Beauty,* and *You Came Along.* After leaving James's orchestra, Forrest teamed with singer Dick Haymes for a series of solid hit singles and radio appearances. After disappearing in the '50s, she resurfaced for a tour with Tommy Dorsey's Orchestra during 1961–62, and again in 1983 when she recorded an LP for Stash Records. Two years later she reunited on film with one of her old bosses in

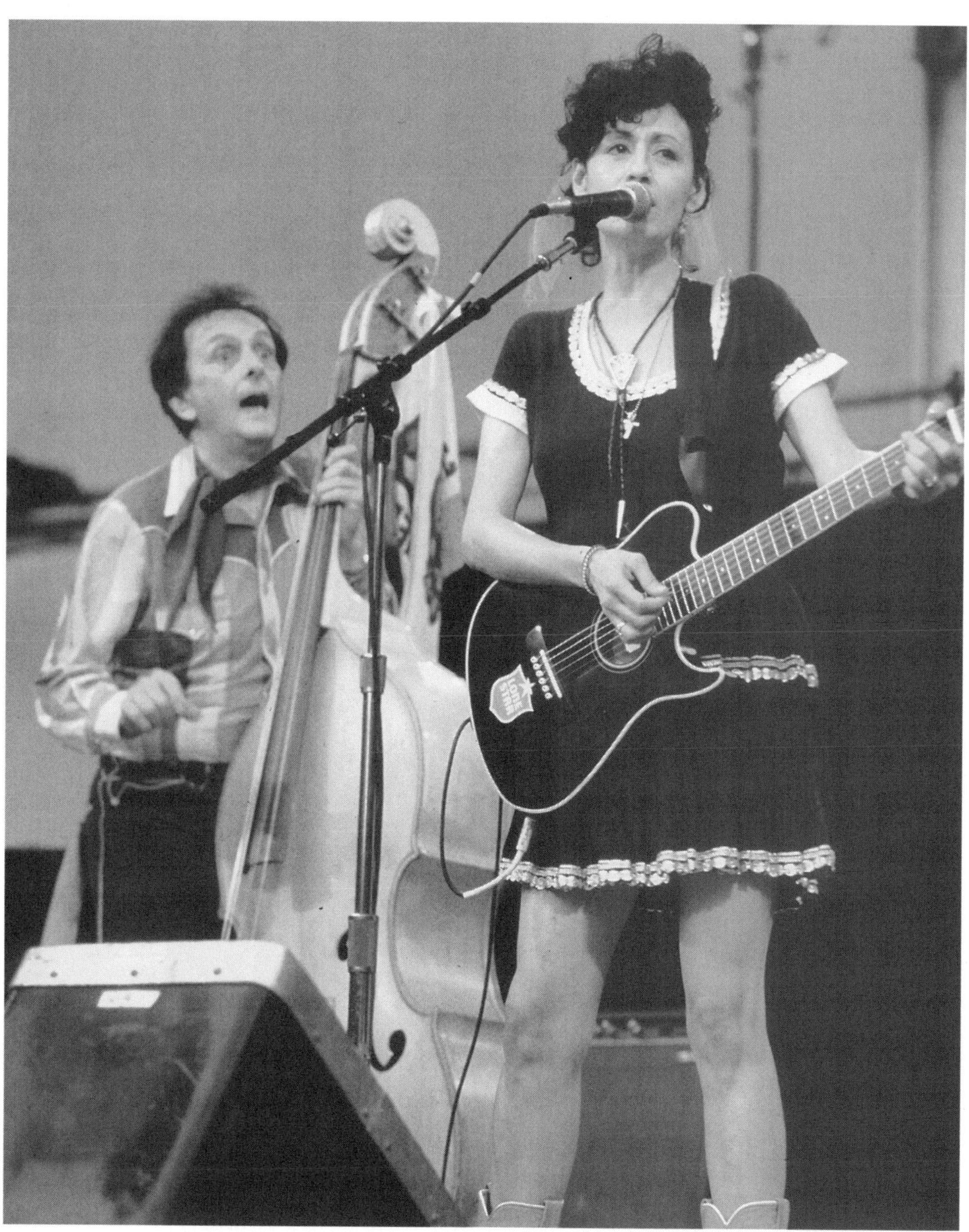

Rosie Flores (© Jack Vartoogian)

Helen Forrest **(Archive Photos)**

Artie Shaw: Time Is All You've Got and followed up with a solid appearance in another documentary, *Symphony of Swing.*

what to buy: Some of Forrest's better moments with the Artie Shaw, Benny Goodman, and Harry James orchestras are on *Voice of the Big Bands* (Jasmine, 1997, prod. various), a fine introduction to this underrated vocalist, with the hits "I Had the Craziest Dream," "I've Heard That Song Before," and "The Devil Sat Down and Cried," with Haymes.

what to buy next: From late in the big-band era (1949–50), *I Wanna Be Loved* (Hindsight, 1993, prod. Thomas Gramuglia) offers excellent performances with the Harry James Orchestra, including "Bill," "Too Marvelous for Words," "I Hadn't Anyone 'till You," and the hit title track.

the rest:

On the Sunny Side of the Street (Audiophile, 1994)
Embraceable You (Hindsight, 1995)
Sentimental Swing (Sony Music Special, 1996)
Them There Eyes (Mr. Music, 1996)
Now and Forever: The 1983 Studio Sessions (Viper's Nest, 1996)
The Cream of Helen Forrest (Flapper, 1996)

worth searching for: You can find more work by Forrest scattered over discs by her famous bandleaders. On Benny Goodman's *Benny and the Singers* (Memoir Classics, 1996), Forrest sings "It Never Entered My Mind," "Oh Look at Me Now," and "When the Sun Comes Out," on a disc with tracks by Peggy Lee, Louise Tobin, Martha Tilton, and Helen Ward. Artie Shaw's *Best of the Big Bands* (Legacy, 1990, compilation prod. Michael Brooks) features Forrest singing "I Don't Want to Walk without You Baby," and "I've Heard That Song Before." Forrest also guests with Artie Shaw on *Artie Shaw—22 Original Big Band Recordings* (Hindsight, 1993), *Begin the Beguine* (RCA Bluebird, 1988), *The Uncollected Artie Shaw & His Orchestra 1938, Vol. II* (Hindsight, 1979/1994); with Harry James on *Harry James & His Orchestra: Jump Sauce* (Viper's Nest, 1995), *Harry James—Yes Indeed!* (ASV, 1993), and *Harry James & His Orchestra 1943–46* (Hindsight, 1994); and on Benny Goodman's *Vol. II Clarinet à la King* (Columbia, 1988).

influences:

Billie Holiday, Mildred Bailey, Ella Fitzgerald, Kitty Kallen

Peggy Lee, Martha Tilton, Anita O'Day, Helen Ward

Ken Burke

Pete Fountain

Born July 3, 1930, in New Orleans, LA.

Pete Fountain identifies strongly with New Orleans: He was born there, learned to play there, and continues to perform there in a nightclub in the Hilton hotel, complete with red velvet on the walls, that bears his iconic name. Although he borrowed a great deal from Benny Goodman, Fountain's most enduring influence on clarinet was his teacher and early mentor, Irving Fazola. By 1950, after playing with various New Orleans-based Dixieland combos, Fountain made his recording debut with Phil Zito's International Dixieland band. In the '50s, he led his own combo, and toured Chicago with the Dukes of Dixieland. From 1957 to 1959, Fountain achieved widespread popularity during a stint with the *Lawrence Welk Show,* on which he played Dixieland numbers. After leaving Welk Fountain returned to New Orleans, purchased his first nightclub, and began a productive association with the Decca subsidiary Coral Records. Little else has changed since then—Fountain is still a New Orleans monument, he still plays with the same warm tone and Dixieland style, and he still wanders into the studio every now and then.

what to buy: *Do You Know What It Means to Miss New Orleans?* (Decca, 1996, prod. Orrin Keepnews), a two-CD compilation subtitled "Playing Dixieland Classics and Louis Armstrong Favorites," is a well-conceived, enjoyable program collecting the best of Fountain's Coral recordings from the '60s.

what to avoid: *A Touch of Class* (Ranwood, 1995, prod. Owen Bradley) has nothing new to offer. The accompanying musicians are sub par, and Fountain sounds bored on a lazy set of ballads.

the rest:

The Blues (Coral, 1959)
Pete Fountain Day (Coral, 1960)
Pete Fountain's French Quarter (Coral, 1961)
Standing Room Only (Coral, 1965)
Swingin' Blues (Ranwood, 1990)
Live at the Ryman (Sacramento, 1992)
Cheek to Cheek (Ranwood, 1993)
Country (Ranwood, 1994)
The Best of Pete Fountain (Decca, 1996)
Dixieland King (Tradition, 1998)

worth searching for: *Pete Fountain's New Orleans* (Coral, 1959/MCA, 1993) is one of the few individual albums Fountain cut for Coral that has actually been reissued on CD, but it is out of print. Many New Orleans favorites are included, like "When the Saints Go Marching In" and "When It's Sleepy Time Down South."

influences:

Irving Fazola, Benny Goodman, Johnny Dodds, Louis Armstrong

Michael White, Al Hirt

Dan Keener

The Frantic Flattops

Formed 1992, in Rochester, NY.

"Frantic" Frank DeBlase, vocals, guitar; "Too Tall" Paul, percussion; Sid Baker, stand-up bass.

"Frantic" Frank DeBlase, who stands 6'5'' tall, banged away at the piano for 10 years before moving onto guitar after hearing the Ramones for the first time. A former member of the Pharoahs, DeBlase met "Too Tall" Paul, a former punk player, at a Rochester, New York, club. Bassist Sid Baker was inspired by English punk, having been born in Scotland and raised in Canada. An award-winning freelance journalist, Baker began his musical career playing the bagpipes. The Frantic Flattops, who once toured in a hearse, are road warriors, traveling about 3,000 miles per month and packing houses with little airplay.

what's available: *Cheap Women, Cheap Booze, Cheaper Thrills* (Pravda, 1998, prod. Andy Babiuk, Greg Prevost) is a tribute to raw 1950s rock 'n' roll. It begins on a weak note, with rockabilly legend Ronnie Dawson introducing the band over canned live sounds. Wading past the goofy taped applause reveals the highlight of the album, "Sweeter 17," a dirty, sweaty, 100-miles-an-hour rocker. DeBlase hiccups his way through Dawson's "Boy Next Door," and also covers Link Wray's "The Black Widow."

influences:

Jerry Lee Lewis, Ronnie Dawson, Stray Cats

Twistin' Tarantulas

Christina Fuoco

Slim Gaillard

Born Bulee Gaillard, around 1915, in Detroit, MI. Died February 26, 1991, in London, England.

One of jazz music's most inventive humorists, "Slim" Gaillard was truly *sui generis*, a pianist, guitar player, and drummer who fashioned positively surreal musical concoctions using his own twisted syntax and mongrel vernacular; non-words like "voit," "voutee," and "reenie" frequently cropped up in his work. Gaillard grew up in Detroit and began his musical career as a guitar-playing, tap-dancing novelty act. In 1937 he hooked up with bassist Slam Stewart to form the duo Slim and Slam, whose biggest hit was "Flat Fleet Floogie" (as in "the flat fleet floogie with a floy joy"). After a brief stint in the army, Gaillard moved to California in 1944, where he found steady work on various radio shows and attracted the attention of Charlie Parker and Dizzy Gillespie, who toured with him in 1945. Gaillard continued to tour the jazz circuit until the mid-'50s, but his career lost momentum by the end of the decade. He made a reunion album with Stewart in 1958, and appeared in the film *Absolute Beginners* in 1985.

what to buy: *Laughing in Rhythm: The Verve Years* (Verve, 1994, prod. Norman Granz) is all the Slim you'll ever really need. Sample tracks: "Boip! Boip!," "Mashugana Mambo," "Chicken Rhythm" . . . you get the idea.

what to buy next: While a little recorded Slim goes a long way, it's possible to collect most of his *oeuvre* with *1937–38* (Jazz Chronological Classics, 1994); *1939–40* (Jazz Chronological Classics, 1994); *1940–42* (Jazz Chronological Classics, 1994); *1945* (Jazz Chronological Classics, 1996); and *1945, Vol. II* (Jazz Chronological Classics, 1997).

the rest:

Anytime, Anyplace, Anyday (Hep, 1994)
Slim's Jam (Drive, 1996)

influences:

Charlie Parker, Dizzy Gillespie, Al Jolson, Louis Armstrong

Stan Freberg, Mickey Katz, Eddie Fisher

Marc Weingarten

Cecil Gant

Born April 6, 1913, in Nashville, TN. Died February 4, 1951, in Nashville, TN.

Cecil Gant was one of the great one-hit wonders of 1940s R&B, a singer who riveted the entire blues-buying public with his 1944 smash, "I Wonder," but was unable to repeat his phenomenal success. "I Wonder" stayed on the R&B charts for 28 weeks, turning Gant, an Army private who had sung at Los Angeles war bond rallies, into the "G.I. Sing-Sation." Gant's mellow blues and laid-back boogie hearkened back to Leroy Carr, and though Gant couldn't keep his own fortunes afloat, his brief fame influenced the early careers of cocktail-and-riff pianists like Charles Brown and Amos Milburn. Gant followed the melancholy "I Wonder" with a string of lesser hits, but he disappeared from the charts after 1949.

worth searching for: Neither "I Wonder" nor the rest of Gant's gilt-edge recordings are on the British import *Cecil Gant* (Krazy Kat, 1989/Flyright, 1997), but the 20 cuts from the late 1940s that do appear are pretty representative of Gant's talents, divided almost evenly between mopey ballads and light boogies. Buying *Mean Old World: The Blues from 1940–94* (Smithsonian, 1996, prod. Bruce Talbot, Lawrence Hoffman), a costly, well-annotated four-CD survey of American blues (including jump blues, of course), is the only way to find "I Wonder" in the digital realm. Worth getting if you want the rest of the set's expansive blues view (Billie Holiday to Tutu Jones), but otherwise "I Wonder" is at best a historical curiosity.

influences:

⏪ Leroy Carr

⏩ Charles Brown, Amos Milburn, Ray Charles

Steve Braun

Erroll Garner

Born Erroll Louis Garner, June 15, 1921, in Pittsburgh, PA. Died January 2, 1977, in Los Angeles, CA.

Erroll Garner is famous for three things: 1) being one of the most technically skilled jazz pianists to record since Art Tatum; 2) writing "Misty," a jazz standard that has been covered to the hilt; and 3) never having learned to read music. In any case, Garner cannot be dismissed as a serious contributor to jazz piano—or to swing. His playing style was unique—perhaps because he wasn't bounded by notes on the page—and the results are in his astonishingly textured performances. As the liner notes on one of his CDs suggest, "If you can't pat your foot or feel his beat, you need a doctor." Garner was a locally famous musician in Pittsburgh in the 1940s when he moved to New York and began playing clubs. Then, in 1946, an *Esquire* poll picked him as the year's New Star, propelling him into the recording studio with the likes of Charlie Parker. Making numerous television appearances in the 1950s, by decade's end Garner was one of the best-selling jazz pianists in the world—touring regularly overseas and toting his signature tune, "Misty," which has become not only a standard but an iconic American song (evidence of which is its central place in Clint Eastwood's 1971 film, *Play Misty for Me*).

what to buy: Thankfully, Garner's work has been steadily reissued on CD, so listeners are likely to find what they're looking for the first time out. But one record should be kept in mind: *Concert by the Sea* (Columbia, 1970/1987), perhaps his single finest recording and an album that captures the complex technique of his syncopated piano voicings. Any other album in which he plays "Misty," such as *Erroll Garner Plays Misty* (EmArcy, 1954/Verve, 1987), is highly recommended.

Perhaps the most straight-ahead swing of any Garner recording, *Closeup in Swing* (Telarc, 1997) staples in swing music: "Back in Your Own Backyard" and "A New Kind of Love."

what to buy next: *Long Ago and Far Away* (Columbia, 1951) is a great recording of Garner in his prime—however, without the sound quality to back it up. *Plays Gershwin & Kern* (EmArcy, 1968) is a reissue of recordings from the mid-1960s, conveniently packaged from a variety of old record labels; it's also available as a package with *Magician* as the CD *Magician & Gershwin & Kern* (Telarc, prod. Martha Glazer).

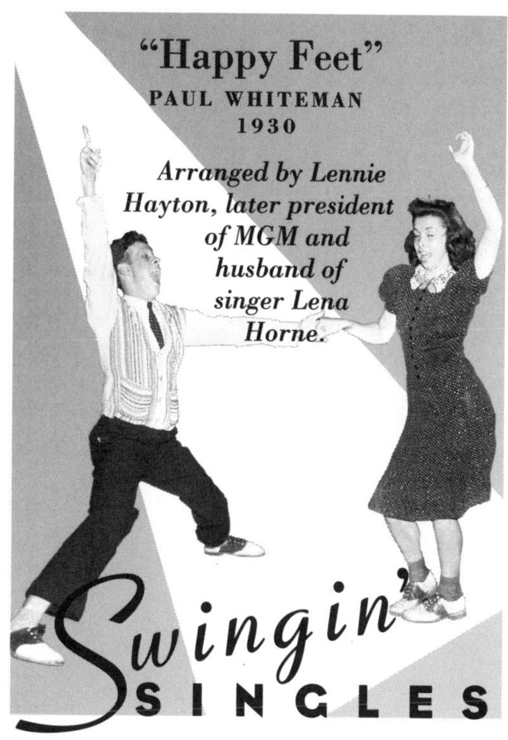

best of the rest:
Original Misty (Mercury, 1954/EmArcy, 1988)
Dancing on the Ceiling (EmArcy, 1989)
Body and Soul (Columbia/Legacy, 1991)
Complete Savoy Mastertakes (Savoy, 1998)

worth searching for: *Afternoon of an Elf* (Mercury, 1955) is a strange album of solo piano works in which Garner disassembles jazz standards and puts them back together with his own tempo and pace. For completists only.

influences:

⏪ Fats Waller, Art Tatum, George Gershwin

⏩ Bill Evans, Kenny Barron, George Shearing

Carl Quintanilla

George Gee & His Make-Believe Ballroom Orchestra

Formed 1990, in New York, NY.

George Gee, leader; Carla Cook, vocals; Ed Pazant, lead alto sax; Cleave Guyton, alto sax, piccolo flute; Lance Bryant, tenor sax; Marshall McDonald, tenor sax; Al Acosta, baritone sax, bass clarinet;

Erroll Garner **(Archive Photos)**

Charles Stephens, lead trombone; Eddie Bert, trombone; Joe Fiedler, trombone; Wayne Coniglio, bass trombone; Joe Cowherd, piano; Daryl Hall, bass; Richard Lieberson, guitar; Dave Gibson, drums.

Charismatic band leader George Gee says: "Wherever we play—that's the Make Believe Ballroom." Certainly his orchestra sounds like a throwback to the days of big-band jazz, uptown dance halls, and men who actually wore hats. His sound, largely based on that of Count Basie, is bolstered by several of the Count's ex-sidemen and the arrangements and special material of Frank Foster. Gee, who feels his own musicianship doesn't meet with his orchestra's high standards, does a hep-cat variation on the old-style baton-waving band leaders. While introducing soloists, or egging the dancers on, he gives out with the type of jive-talk and patter that wouldn't seem out of place in an old Warner Bros. gangster flick. Gee became entranced with the sound of Count Basie while attending college during the late '70s. As his interest mushroomed, he became an authority on all aspects of big-band styles and began to lead his own popular band in Pittsburgh. Once in New York, Gee's orchestra played a wide variety of classy venues, drawing crowds of all ages and backgrounds who just wanted to dance. Gee has had guest shots on TV programs like *Live with Regis and Kathie Lee* and his orchestra had a feature role in *The Fantastic Four—The Movie*. In between tours and special engagements, the Make-Believe Ballroom Orchestra settles in at the Swing46 Jazz and Supper Club, where they astound the regulars with their ever-growing playlist of '40s-referenced dance numbers.

what's available: You'll swear Count Basie was leading his old road band again on Gee's *Swingin' Live* (Swing46, 1998, prod. George Gee), 12 tracks recorded at the Swing46 Jazz and Supper Club in New York. The Make-Believe Ballroom Orchestra's renditions of "Come on In," "Down for the Count," and "Shiny Stocking" swing in the Basie tradition, and Carla Cook is truly fine singing "Let the Good Times Roll." However, Cook has only two numbers, the rest being instrumentals in a similar style, which becomes monotonous after awhile. Plus, the group's versions of "Where or When" and "Here's That Rainy Day" seem unfocused and discordant at times. They're a good band, and for a live recording, the sound quality is great, but Gee could stand to mix things up a bit.

influences:

Count Basie, Lionel Hampton, Chick Webb, Tommy Dorsey

Ken Burke

The Ray Gelato Giants

Formed as Ray Gelato & His Giants of Jive, 1988, in England. Became the Ray Gelato Giants in 1994.

Ray Gelato, tenor sax, vocals; Enrico Tomasso, trumpet; Andy Baker, trombone; Alex Garnett, alto and tenor saxes; Richard Busiakiewicz, piano; Clark Kent, acoustic bass; Steve Rushton, drums.

Americans best know Ray Gelato as the male voice in the Dockers ad featuring the song "Tu Vuo'Fa l'Americano." In England he's known as one of the artists who helped kick-start the European version of the swing revival more than 15 years ago. During the early '80s, Gelato honked Bill Haley–style rock for a band called Dynamite before he got the jazz bug and helped form the Chevalier Brothers. This seminal neo-swing group played loud, fast, and funny while earning a reputation as one of England's top show bands. But transferring its vibe-oriented sound to the recording studio was an arduous task. As a result, the Brothers' most successful projects were recorded in a live setting, which best caught their zany interplay and manic energy. After the Chevalier Brothers broke up, Gelato took bassist Clark Kent (so dubbed because of his strong resemblance to Christopher Reeve in *Superman*) and formed a new outfit. Though Gelato is perfectly capable of writing a good song the majority of his band's playlist comes from the swing era. The Giants champion Louis Jordan's leering R&B, Nat King Cole's urbane jazz, and Benny Goodman's jungle rhythms—but mostly they dig Louis Prima. They replicate his gleeby rhythm so well you'd swear Prima was still alive and playing Vegas with Keely Smith. Gelato, a top sax man, imitates his idol (as well as Cole) to perfection, sometimes more than is good for the integrity of his music. Gelato also fronts a side band called Three Tough Tenors, plays sax with the Echoes of Ellington Orchestra, has collaborated with the Good Fellas on two discs which have proven extremely popular in Italy, and has sung on soundtracks for British films and TV shows. With the Ray Gelato Giants, he has played most of the top jazz festivals in Europe and is planning to tour here.

what to buy: Showcasing the band's finest line-up to date, *The Men from Uncle* (Double Scoop, 1998, prod. Peter Tomasso) boasts a strong assortment of Louis Prima-esque shuffles ("Josephine Please No Lean on the Bell," "I'm Confessin' That I Love You," "If You Were the Only Girl in the World"), Louis Jordan jumpers ("Chicky Mo"), Nat King Cole confections ("L-O-V-E," "The Great City"), and their new version of the tune from the Levi's Dockers ads. Though not exactly original in approach, the band convincingly delivers in all styles, making this an entertaining introduction to its sound.

what to buy next: Their first disc as the Ray Gelato Giants, *The Full Flavour* (Linn, 1995, prod. Calum Malcolm) shows improvement from strong jazzy piano and much-needed creative discipline. Some wild instrumental jams ("Dark Eyes," "Apple Honey"), a funny original tune ("Forget about Livin'"), and a bluesy duet with Claire Martin ("Under a Blanket of Blue") are standouts that make the Louis Prima homages ("Undecided,"

"Up a Lazy River," "That's Amore") much more effective by contrast.

what to avoid: Though it has some nice moments, *Gelato Espresso* ♪♪ (K-Tel, 1994, prod. Pete Thomas) depends too heavily on Gelato's vocal imitation of Prima and recycles its strongest cuts from an earlier LP.

the rest:
Ray Gelato's Giants of Jive ♪♪ (Blue Horizon, 1989)
A Taste of Gelato ♪♪ (High Five, 1992)

worth searching for: Gelato's early work with the Chevalier Brothers can be found on *Live and Still Jumping* ♪♪♪ (Westside, 1998, digital prod. Duncan Cowell), which issues their original live LP, plus several previously unreleased tracks. The Chevalier Brothers bring more than a hint of punk energy to such standards of swing and jive as "Five Guys Named Moe," "Fat Sam from Birmingham," and "Jumpin' at the Jubilee."

solo outings:
Echoes of Ellington Orchestra:
Rockin' in Ronnie's ♪♪♪ (Jazz House, 1997)

Ray Gelato:
(With the Good Fellas) *Gelato All' Italiana* ♪♪♪ (Durium, 1998)
(With the Good Fellas) *Gangsters of Swing* ♪♪ (Durium, 1998)

influences:
◀ Bill Haley, Louis Prima, Louis Jordan, Nat King Cole
▶ The Good Fellas, the Big Six

Ken Burke

Banu Gibson

Born October 24, 1947, in Dayton, OH.

One of the '90's best singers and performers of 1920s and 1930s jazz, guitarist/banjoist Banu Gibson has spent most of her life on stage. Her vivacious and ebullient singing style harkens to the golden age of American music, when pop and jazz were often the same. Growing up in Hollywood, Florida, Banu started dancing by age three, and was taking voice lessons by age nine. She performed professionally while in her teens, and graduated from college with a degree in music and theater. She played briefly at Disneyland, where she appeared in a Roaring '20s-style show, then moved to New Orleans, where she formed her own band in 1981. Various TV appearances boosted her visibility. With her Hot New Orleans Jazz Band, Gibson tours extensively.

what to buy: "Santa Claus Blues" (a classic early 1920s jazz tune) and "Christmas Night in Harlem" (from the early 1930s) from *'Zat You, Santa Claus* ♪♪♪♪♪ (Swing Out, 1995, prod. Banu Gibson) showcase the Hot New Orleans Jazz Band's many talents across jazz periods and styles. *Livin' in a Great Big Way* ♪♪♪♪♪ (Swing Out, 1994, prod. Banu Gibson) features Gibson's effervescent voice in a more intimate setting, with just piano accompaniment. Her tune selections are excellent samples from an encyclopedia of well-written songs produced from the mid-1920s to the mid-1930s. "It's Been So Long," "About a Quarter to Nine," and "I'll See You in My Dreams" are some of the stand-out tracks.

what to buy next: *Jazz Baby* ♪♪♪ (Stomp Off, 1990, prod. Bob Erdos) has fine singing by Gibson, but the band is not as coherent as it would become.

worth searching for: *Battle of the Bands: San Antonio vs. New Orleans* ♪♪♪♪♪ (Pacific Vista, 1994, prod. Margaret Pick, Lynne Cruise), volume four in Texas Public Radio's "Riverwalk Live at the Landing Vintage Jazz Collection" series, features the Jim Cullum Jazz Band playing against Gibson's group. Highlights include wonderful vocals by Gibson on "Down-Hearted Blues" and "Wrap Your Cares in Rhythm and Dance" (where she also tap dances along with Savion Glover) as well as a sizzling instrumental version of the Chocolate Dandies' "Krazy Kapers."

influences:
◀ Chocolate Dandies, Jelly Roll Morton, Sidney Bechet, Louis Armstrong, King Oliver

Jim Prohaska

Harry "The Hipster" Gibson

Born Harry Raab, 1914, in New York, NY. Died May 9, 1991, in CA.

Harry "The Hipster" Gibson is one the weirdest, funniest characters to come out of the '40s jazz and swing movement. His irreverent bop-talk and surreal hip attitude forever imprinted the persona of the zoot-suit hep cat in the minds of generations to follow. Gibson's gravelly vocals and masterful boogie and jazz pianistics caused many to assume he was a black performer—until they saw him. According to legend, the zoot-suited Gibson would manically scramble through a crowded nightclub audience to hit the stage. Once there, he would proudly display a Benzedrine inhaler and yell "Skoal!" Then, after taking a mighty sniff, he'd commence to pound mad, hyper boogie and jazz from his piano while singing eccentric, comic songs. He was mostly an in-joke, a favorite among jazz cats in small after-hours clubs. Yet somehow, in 1944 one of his freaky compositions, "Who Put the Benzedrine in Mrs. Murphy's Ovaltine," became a major hit. Gibson began appearing in motion picture "soundies" and touring with big-name outfits. Though he never had another hit, he continued to record some of the hippest, funniest sides of his era, such as "Zoot Gibson Rides Again" and "Stop That Dancing." Novelty acts with a penchant for self-destruction don't usually last long, and a series of drug arrests (he generally used what he sang about) ruined Gibson's career on records and in cabarets. By the early '50s, he had returned to the small-time, finding work in strip-clubs and as a session pianist when he was lucky. He was nearly forgotten until, during the early '70s, Dr. Demento's syndicated radio program began featuring Gibson's one great hit. Soon a whole new generation (and drug culture) was laughing along with "The Hipster." He never made the big time again, but Gibson did write and record again in the years before his death, exhibiting much of the topical bite he displayed in the '40s.

what to buy: Gibson's original version of "Who Put the Benzedrine in Mrs. Murphy's Ovaltine" can be found on *Reefer Songs: 23 Original Jazz & Blues Vocals* (Stash, 1975/Mojo, 1996, compilation prod. Bernard Brightman), an amusing set of decidedly politically incorrect tunes that also includes the star power of Cab Calloway, Ella Fitzgerald, Trixie Smith, Benny Goodman, and Chick Webb. The best solo collection presently available is *Who Put the Benzedrine in Mrs. Murphy's Ovaltine* (Delmark, 1996, prod. Robert G. Koester, Jeff Silvertrust), which includes a strong 1989 remake of his most famous song in addition to such funny new tunes as "I Flipped My Wig in San Francisco," "Get Hip to Shirley MacLaine," and the R&B standard "I Got Framed." This spirited reissue is bulked up with six live tracks recorded in 1976 with a blues-rock band. Gibson's voice breaks up at times, but he's playing hard boogie and jazz throughout.

what to buy next: Gibson waxed one of the most eccentric seasonal offerings ever with *Harry the Hipster Digs Christmas* (Viper's Nest, 1974/1994). This wildly uneven set features great jazz and boogie piano work from Gibson, and rather inspired versions of "Rudolph the Red Nosed Reindeer," "I Saw Mommy Kissing Santa Claus," and the self-penned "I Wish My Mother-in-Law Don't Visit Us for Christmas." However, the artist's tendency towards self-parody renders other numbers virtually incoherent. Also included are two bonus tracks recorded for Dr. Demento in honor of the U.S. Bicentennial.

worth searching for: Gibson's original 1940s hits have been collected on the out-of-print *Boogie Woogie in Blue* (Musicraft, 1988/1994, prod. Albert Marx), which includes "Who Put the Benzedrine in Mrs. Murphy's Ovaltine" plus the period humor of "Zoot Gibson Rides Again," "Stop That Dancing up There," and "Get Your Juices at the Deuces." For a compelling visual overview of Gibson's life and times, check out the video *Boogie in Blue* (Rhapsody Films, 1992), which mixes "soundies" from the '40s with interviews with the artist in the years before he died.

influences:

◀◀ Fats Waller, Slim Gaillard, Babs Gonsalez

▶▶ Lord Buckley, Lenny Bruce, Dick Shawn

Ken Burke

Dizzy Gillespie

Born John Birks Gillespie, October 21, 1917, in Cheraw, SC. Died January 7, 1993, in Englewood, NJ.

Dizzy Gillespie packed so many accomplishments into his 76 years on earth that his creation of the last great big bands is often overlooked among them all. The man who was Charlie Parker's accomplice in the creation of bebop, one of the first to champion Latin strains in jazz, a showman as beloved as Louis Armstrong, and a trumpeter second only to Armstrong in skill also happened to be a band leader on the order of Duke Ellington, Count Basie, and Cab Calloway. Gillespie's 1947–49 big band was an airstreamed unit capable of playing at impossibly breakneck tempos, yet its sound was always propulsively danceable—as long as your feet could move at the speed of light. Gillespie brought forth a second big band in the late 1950s, and while it wasn't as hellbound as the first, still produced swing and bop of the first order, toured the world and introduced Lee Morgan, Quincy Jones, and Benny Golson to jazz fans.

Gillespie came into the music world with an impeccable swing pedigree, playing in big-band brass sections led by Teddy Hill, Lucky Millinder, Benny Carter, Calloway, Earl Hines, and Billy Eckstine. He was bounced from Calloway's band after the band leader wrongly accused him of chucking a spitball at him during a performance and Diz responded by nicking the Hi De Hi man with a blade. Gillespie met up with Parker in Hines's unit and the two briefly co-led a small band that released bop's first classics. When Parker was waylaid in Los Angeles by his heroin habit Gillespie returned to New York and set about creating his own big band. Hiring young bopsters like bassist Ray Brown, drummer Kenny Clarke, future Modern Jazz Quartet members John Lewis and Milt Jackson, and even a green John Coltrane, Gillespie drilled them in rapid-paced charts with trumpet lines that snaked out in a thicket of movement. Their tunes became bebop standards: "Things to Come," "Two Bass Hit," "Emanon," "Woody 'n' You," "Oop-Pa-Pa-Da." But their avant-garde sound didn't bring in the dough and Gillespie closed shop, retreating for the next decade into tours, quintet recordings and mugging onstage. He tried again in 1957, this time finding more applause and financial backing for a second big band that mixed old Gillespie standards like "Tin Tin Deo" and "Umbrella Man" with cutting-edge hard bop tunes like Benny Golson's "Stablemates" and "I Remember Clifford." Gillespie never left the limelight afterwards, always filling clubs and jazz festival grounds from the 1960s through the 1990s, even occasionally reprising the glory days of his big bands. When he died in 1993 his tributes rivaled those accorded jazz's first great trumpeter, Louis Armstrong.

what to buy: When dancers try to impress you with their floorwork, insist they first take a few spins to *Dizzy Gillespie—The Complete RCA Recordings* (RCA Bluebird, 1995, prod.

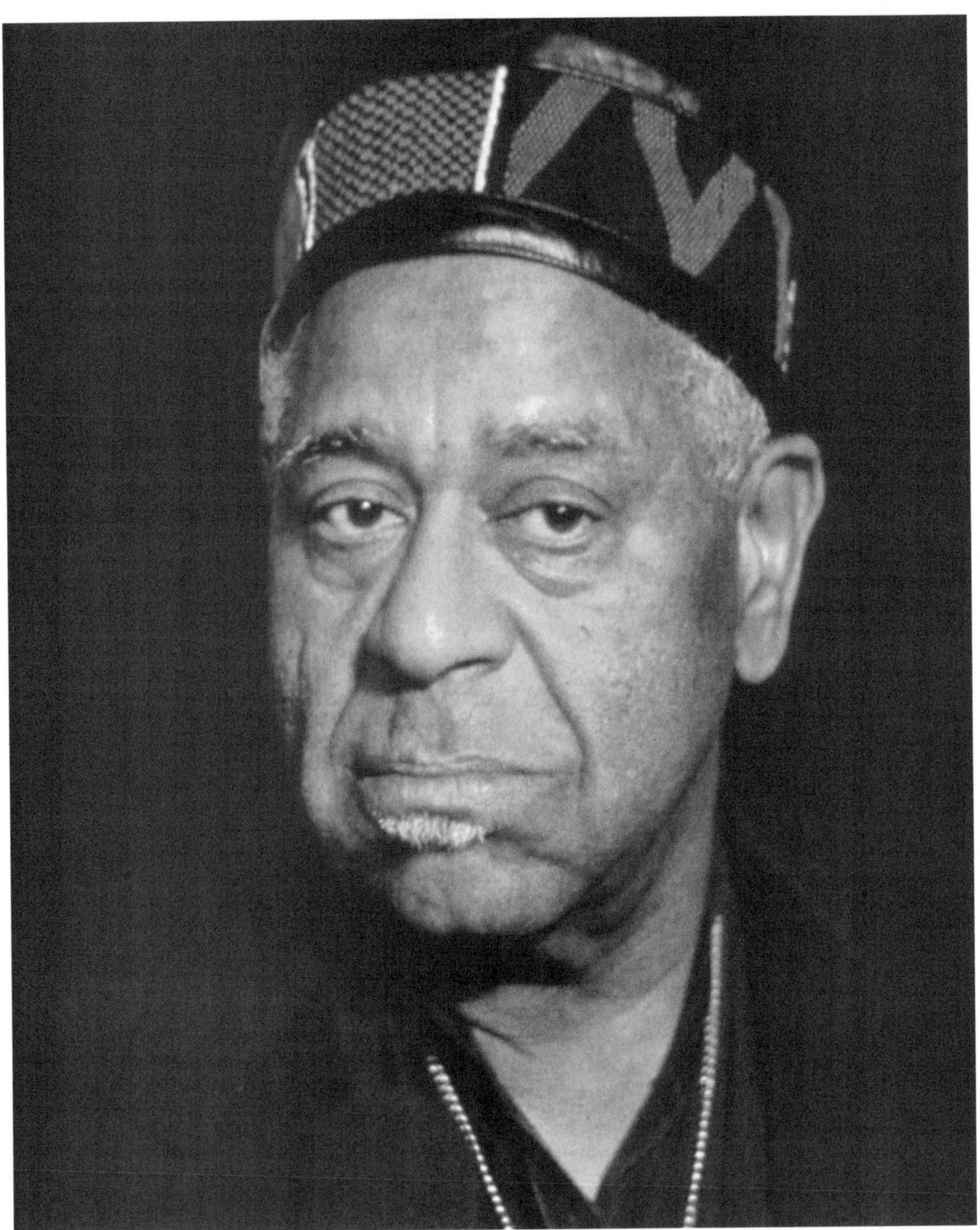

Dizzy Gillespie **(Archive Photos)**

Orrin Keepnews). If they're truly heroic, they might make it through "Two Bass Hit," but will be breathless by "Stay on It." This two-CD set has all of the RCA big band work of the 1940s and it steams like a bullet train. Its complement is *Shaw Nuff* (Discovery, 1988, prod. Albert Marx), which culls all of Gillespie's Musicraft and Guild sides from the 1940s and adds 11 essential small-group takes with illustrious cohorts such as Charlie Parker, Sonny Stitt, Dexter Gordon, and Milt Jackson.

what to buy next: *Birks Works: The Verve Big-Band Sessions* (Verve, 1995, prod. Norman Granz) pulls in Gillespie's late 1950s big band material, all of it as tempered as German steel and smooth as aged French brandy. The same group also plays on *Dizzy Gillespie at Newport* (Verve, 1992, prod. Norman Granz), a 1957 concert of Gillespie standards and even a slightly pretentious "Zodiac Suite."

best of the rest:

Dee Gee Days (Savoy, 1985)
Dizzy's Diamonds (Verve, 1993)
Roy & Diz (Verve, 1995)
Duets (Verve, 1997)
Dizzy Gillespie 1945 (Classics, 1996)
Dizzy Gillespie 1945–46 (Classics, 1997)

worth searching for: Gillespie's big-band roots are on the out-of-print *Most Important Recordings of Dizzy Gillespie* (Official, 1989), a Danish import that spans his career from his days as a young trumpeter to the flowering of the 1957 big band. There are snapshots of Diz in big bands led by Hill, Millinder, Calloway, and Eckstine, then a bevy of bop originals, followed by tracks from both of Gillespie's big-band experiments. The sound is not sterling, but this is the only place you can get a wide-ranging glance at Gillespie's river of a career.

influences:

Louis Armstrong, Roy Eldridge, Teddy Hill, Benny Carter, Charlie Parker

Fats Navarro, Kenny Dorham, Miles Davis, the Modern Jazz Quartet, John Coltrane, Jon Faddis, Tito Puente

Steve Braun

Golden Gate Orchestra

See: California Ramblers

Benny Goodman

Born May 30, 1909, in Chicago, IL. Died June 13, 1986, New York, NY.

"King of Swing" Benny Goodman, the first great clarinetist in the history of jazz, perfected a style of playing that is still the dominant influence on the instrument. It is a style based on clearly articulated, hard-swinging melodic lines, played with a very centered, clear, clarinet tone. It was the incredible excitement and clarity of his playing that made it great, rather than any profound harmonic or rhythmic invention. His work was remarkably free of gratuitous musical posturing, and he limited his use of clichés to where they were effective in many of his, and his audience's, favorite tunes. Although Goodman became fantastically popular, and performed a good deal of classical music, he remained first and foremost a jazzman throughout his career. His classic "Sing, Sing, Sing" (written by Louis Prima) still packs wedding dance floors all around the world.

Perhaps because of Goodman's enigmatic personality—he tended to be interested in music above all else, even basic social civility—his role as a jazz explorer has been underappreciated. In the mid-1930s it was Goodman who first brought the music of the Harlem jazz bands to the general public through his purchase and presentation of the compositions and arrangements of Fletcher Henderson and others. He didn't do this to steal anyone's music, and he freely credited his sources, though sometimes adding his own name, as was the questionable custom of the time. He simply wanted the best charts he could get his hands on. Also in the mid-1930s, Goodman premiered the high profile presentation of racially mixed ensembles with his inclusion of African-American pianist Teddy Wilson and vibraphonist Lionel Hampton in his trio and quartet. (Goodman included these musicians simply because he liked the way they played, rather than to make any social statement.) While Goodman himself was never an effective bop soloist, he made sure his bands of the 1940s included, at various times, boppers Fats Navarro, Wardell Grey, and others. After that, he never again jumped head first into bop, but he often returned to bop principles, especially with the 10-piece band he led in 1959 and 1960. Goodman's groups were great talent incubators, giving their first prominent exposure, in person or on records, to Billie Holiday, Harry James, Gene Krupa, Teddy Wilson, Lionel Hampton, Charlie Christian, Peggy Lee, Stan Getz, Roland Hanna, Zoot Sims, and many others.

what to buy: There are hundreds of Goodman studio performances and live dates on CD from his peak years, 1937–39. The Victor studio sessions reveal well-rehearsed, precise ensembles and were well recorded, although they have not always been well-remastered for reissue. The best of the live dates are a little muddier, but still sound fine and reveal a much more exciting band, mistakes and all. The live sessions have the edge. Duplicating the 1950s LPs titled *Jazz Concert No. 2*, the two-CD set *On the Air, 1937–1938* (Columbia, 1993, reissue prod. Michael Brooks) offers a fine set of 14 remastered tracks. Most tracks are up-tempo, but Fletcher Henderson's sensuous arrangement of "Sometimes I'm Happy" rivals any of the faster songs. The apogee of Goodman's career was his 1938 Carnegie

Benny Goodman **(Archive Photos)**

Hall concert, which was privately recorded, surprisingly quite well. The positive tension felt by the Goodmanites conquering Carnegie in 1938 came through on the LPs, as it does on the two CDs of *Benny Goodman Carnegie Hall Jazz Concert* (Columbia, 1987). "Sing, Sing, Sing" was the concert's high point, with an solo by pianist Jess Stacy, and a crowd-pleasing tom-tom solo by Krupa. The fine three-CD set *Benny Goodman/The Birth of Swing* (Bluebird, 1991, prod. Orrin Keepnews) documents the start of the swing era, and includes the sides Bunny Berigan made as a Goodmanite, as well as a session with a very young Ella Fitzgerald. Delights are found in superior versions of pop songs of the day, as well as in the "killer-dillers." The Goodman trio and quartet of the 1930s was important for sociological (it was the first high-profile racially integrated jazz ensemble) as well as musical reasons. The entire Victor studio output of these Goodman small groups, including previously unissued alternate takes, was recently released on a three-CD set, *The Complete RCA Victor Small Group Recordings* (RCA, 1997, reissue prod. Orrin Keepnews) incorporated the following LPs: *The Original Trio & Quartet Sessions, Vol. I* (Bluebird, 1987) and *Avalon: The Small Bands, Vol. II* (Bluebird, 1990).

what to buy next: In 1939 Goodman added Charlie Christian (the first significant electric guitarist in jazz) to his entourage. The resulting recordings, many of which are found on *Featuring Charlie Christian* (Columbia, 1989), provided much inspiration for the beboppers coming just around the corner. Columbia has not reissued their wonderful early 1940s Goodman catalog, but until they do, *Featuring Peggy Lee* (Columbia, OKeh 78s/Columbia, 1993, prod. Michael Brooks) provides great insight into the "let's play beautiful music without getting cutesy or worrying about the jitterbuggers" side of Goodman. Lee, brand new on the scene, sings very well, and the Eddie Sauter and Mel Powell arrangements can be equated to early, very good Gil Evans. On the limited edition, four-CD set *Benny Goodman: Complete Capitol Small Group Recordings* (Mosaic, 1993, prod. Michael Cuscuna), Goodman displays incredible clarinet technique and seems bound by few stylistic limitations. Among the many highlights are the angular "Hi 'Ya Sophia" (from 1947) and a slashing "Air Mail Special" (from 1954). Goodman's 10-piece (1959–60) band has been largely forgotten. Too bad—it was one of his loosest, most swinging bands. Several recent CDs have rectified the band's two commercial recordings (one on MGM and one on Columbia), which didn't capture it at its best. A concert from Basil, Switzerland, is documented on the single-CD *Legendary Concert* (TCB, 1993, prod. Gino Ferlin), as well as on the four-CD set *B.G. World-Wide* (TCB, 1993, prod. Gino Ferlin).

what to avoid: A number of out-of-print LPs (which may eventually be released on CD), such as *Hello Benny* (Capitol, 1964, prod. Dave Cavanaugh), *Made in Japan* (Capitol, 1964, prod. Dave Cavanaugh), and *Let's Dance Again* (Mega, 1969, prod. John Franz), should interest completists.

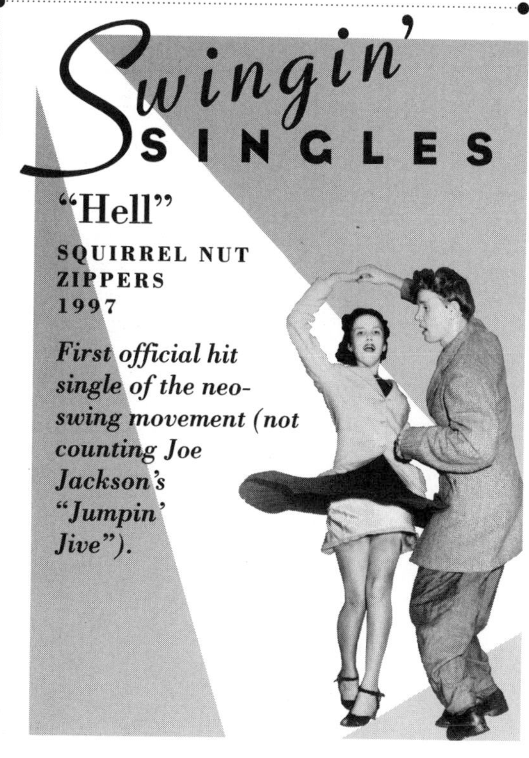

best of the rest:

B.G. in Hi-Fi (Capitol, 1954/1989)
Together Again (RCA Victor, 1964/Bluebird, 1996)
Let's Dance (MusicMasters, 1986)
Benny Goodman's 1934 Bill Dodge All-Star Recordings Complete (Melodeon/Circle, 1987)
Air Play (Signature, 1989)
Best of the Big Bands (Columbia, 1990)
Solo Flight (VJC, 1991)
B.G. & Big Tea in NYC (Decca, 1992)
The Harry James Years, Vol. I (Bluebird, 1993)
Swing, Swing, Swing (MusicMasters, 1993)
The Alternative Goodman (Phontastic, 1993–94)
Swing Sessions (Hindsight, 1994)
Wrappin' It Up: The Harry James Years, Part 2 (Bluebird, 1995)
Undercurrent Blues (Capitol, 1995)
Benny Goodman Plays Eddie Sauter (Hep, 1996)
The King of Swing (MusicMasters, 1996)

worth searching for: If you still have a turntable, the three-LP box set (also issued as single LPs) *Treasure Chest Series* (MGM, 1959) is about as good as the previously noted *On the Air, 1937–1938* recordings. These peak-era big band and combo air-checks find Harry James, Gene Krupa, and the rest of the Goodman firmament exhibiting the spontaneity that is the essence of jazz. The best concert by Goodman's 1959–60 10-piece band is on the separate LPs *Session* (Swing House, 1981, prod. Christopher A. Pirie) and *Jam* (Swing House, 1983, prod. Christopher A. Pirie). Vocalist Anita O'Day was still with the band for this Berlin concert. Goodman fired her shortly thereafter.

influences:

◀◀ Fletcher Henderson, Chick Webb, Casa Loma Orchestra, Tommy Dorsey, Jimmy Dorsey

▶▶ Frank Sinatra, Billy May, Nelson Riddle, Louis Prima, Buddy Greco

John K. Richmond

Robert Gordon

Born 1947, in Bethesda, MD.

Robert Gordon emerged on the New York City club scene of the 1970s as a contemporary artist whose dress and stylistic approach were rooted deep in rockabilly and country. After a stint fronting the glam-punk group the Tuff Darts, Gordon resumed his pursuit of music that owed nothing to current trends. He recorded a string of albums during the 1970s and 1980s for Private Stock and RCA, accompanied by respected guitarists such as Link Wray, Chris Spedding, and Danny Gatton. Gordon has never laid claim to significant commercial success, though he did record early versions of Bruce Springsteen's "Fire" and Marshall Crenshaw's "Someday, Someway," songs that later reached the pop Top 40 for other artists. His influence can be seen in later acts like the Stray Cats and, by extension, the Brian Setzer Orchestra.

what to buy: Private Stock and RCA haven't seen fit to release CD versions of Gordon's original albums, such as *Fresh Fish Special* or *Rock Billy Boogie*, but *Red Hot 1977–1981* (Razor & Tie, 1995, prod. various) gives a great overview of Gordon's best recordings ("Fire," covers of Conway Twitty's "It's Only Make Believe" and Roy Orbison's "Uptown").

what to buy next: *King Biscuit Flower Hour Presents Robert Gordon* (King Biscuit, 1996) is a previously unreleased concert from 1979 that captures Gordon and Spedding promoting *Rock Billy Boogie* with ferocious live interpretations of rock 'n' roll and country classics, as well as Gordon's trademark songs. The sound quality is pretty good for a live recording and showcases the quality that made Gordon a cult hero.

what to avoid: *All for the Love of Rock 'n' Roll* (Viceroy, 1994, prod. Robert Gordon) doesn't live up to Gordon's previous work. Marred by uneven material, it lacks the earlier albums' spontaneity and raucousness.

worth searching for: *Greeting from New York City* (New Rose), a French release of a 1989 live recording from New York's Lone Star Roadhouse, contains 14 songs, mostly covers.

influences:

◀◀ Elvis Presley, Gene Vincent, Carl Perkins

▶▶ Stray Cats, Blasters, Brian Setzer Orchestra

Judy Rabinovitz

Stephane Grappelli

Born January 26, 1908, in Paris, France. Died December 1, 1997, in Paris, France.

Stephane Grappelli is considered one of the greatest jazz violinists, matching the contributions to jazz by violin swing-masters Joe Venuti, Eddie South, and Stuff Smith. Mostly self taught from the age of 12, Grappelli received some formal training at the Paris Conservatory, but dropped out after he heard his first jazz recordings and never returned. Instead, he eked out a living playing violin in the street and for silent films at a local movie theatre. In the mid-1920s Grappelli abandoned violin and learned piano to get work with dance bands but resumed in the late 1920s. In 1933 he teamed up with the now famous Belgian gypsy jazz guitarist Django Reinhardt to form the Quintette Du Hot Club De France. During a London engagement in 1939, war broke out. Reinhardt, reportedly annoyed with Grappelli's growing popularity, abruptly left the group to return to Paris. Grappelli remained behind, establishing a base and working throughout the war years with the elegant jazz pianist George Shearing.

Grappelli returned to Paris in 1946, and worked sporadically with Reinhardt from 1947–49. During the next two decades, he performed regularly in clubs and at music festivals throughout Europe, but was less active as a leader and made fewer albums as sideman. Grappelli remained largely unknown to American audiences until his appearance at the 1969 Newport Jazz Festival won him wider appeal in the U.S. Other international festival performances followed, and a series of successful swing-oriented albums from the 1970s into the 1990s boosted his visibility and popularity. His last performance was in September at French President Jacques Chirac's palace, where he performed from a wheelchair.

what to buy: Start with the late-career recording *Stephane Grappelli Live* (Justin Time, 1998, prod. Marie-Claude

Sirois). Impeccably performed at a 1994 Montreal concert, the lively 10-tune set contains sublimely executed improvisations on swing classics Grappelli performed many times throughout his career. It includes dance-friendly versions of "I Thought about You," "Makin' Whoopee," "Sweet Georgia Brown," and other up-tempo gems, as well as a couple of ballads. Grappelli, 85 years old at the time of this recording and unable to perform standing up, is in prime form. His early-career hot-and-sweet swinging historic recordings with the Quintette Du Hot Club De France (under Django Reinhardt's name as leader) begin with *Shades of Django* (Verve, 1975/1989, prod. Mike Hennessey). It includes sweet versions of "Sweet Lorraine," "Ain't Misbehavin'," and more lightly swinging sprees designed for armchair fans.

what to buy next: On *Live at the Blue Note* (Telarc, 1996) Grappelli is in fine form, especially on the up-tempo gems "Blue Moon," "Lady Be Good," and his signature tune, "Sweet Georgia Brown." Although most of the tunes are artsy and slow-paced, some fervent swing numbers are on *Flamingo* (Dreyfus Jazz, 1995, prod. Yves Chamberland, Francis Dreyfus). Highlights include up-tempo sprees on "Sweet Georgia Brown" and "I Got Rhythm," which will challenge the best dancers.

what to avoid: An 11-tune studio session, *Vintage 1981* (Concord, 1981/1992, prod. Carl E. Jefferson) finds Grappelli heading a strings band that plays viable swing standards, but with a lack of spirit. *Stephane Grappelli: Jazz Masters 11* (Verve, 1966–92/1994), a 14-tune compilation from the Verve vaults, could have been better assembled. Selections are all over the map and come off as a hastily thrown together, jumbled mess. Containing ballads, string-orchestra backed performances, live-recorded tracks, and even a crummy vocals-led piece, the disc features only one real danceable number, the famous "Djangology."

best of the rest:

Afternoon in Paris (MPS, 1971/Verve, 1994)
Live in London (Black Lion, 1973/1992)
Just One of Those Things (EMI Classics, 1973/Angel, 1988)
(With Philip Catherine, Larry Coryell, Niels-Henning Orsted Pedersen) *Young Django* (PolyGram/MPS, 1979)
Tivoli Gardens (Original Jazz Classics, 1979)
At the Winery (Concord, 1981/1994)
Stephanova (Concord, 1983/1989)
(With Yo-Yo Ma) *Anything Goes* (CBS, 1989)
One on One (Milestone, 1990)

worth searching for: Recorded during the same 1979 period as *Tivoli Gardens*, the live *Skol* (Original Jazz Classics, 1982/1990, prod. Norman Granz) features Oscar Peterson as leader and ranks among Grappelli's best collaborations. The out-of-print *Souvenirs* (1938–46/London, 1988, prod. various) compiles original versions of 20 swinging sides recorded for various labels, capturing Grappelli and Reinhardt with the Quintet of the Hot Club of France. The import *Bringing It Together* (Cymekob, 1984/1995, prod. Andrew Kulberg) captures the relaxed collegial spirit between co-leaders Grappelli and Belgian-born harmonica master Toots Thielemans on nine medium-to-hot swing standards.

influences:

A.J. Piron, Joe Venuti, Eddie South

Stuff Smith, Ray Nance, John Frigo, Vassar Clements, Matt Glaser, Randy Sabien, Tom Morley

Nancy Ann Lee

Wardell Gray

Born February 13, 1921, in Oklahoma City, OK. Died May 25, 1955, in Las Vegas, NV.

One of the most natural swingers and creative improvisors in jazz saxophone history, Wardell Gray was, in the words of Count Basie bio discographer Chris Sheridan, "one of the two or three most articulate tenor players in the band's *50-odd* year history." Raised in the fertile Detroit jazz scene of the late 1930s and early 1940s, Gray's earliest name-band work was with the great New Orleans boogie-woogie and jazz pianist Earl Hines. Though Gray briefly played with the Billy Eckstine band, he rejoined the Hines band and, with it, relocated to Los Angeles in 1946. Until the end of 1947 he was a major figure in the vibrant Central Avenue scene of club and concert jam sessions. He spent 1948–49 with Benny Goodman's septet and the big bands of Goodman and Count Basie. When Basie's band broke up in early 1950 Gray returned to Detroit. When Basie reformed his big band in late 1951, Gray chose to remain in Los Angeles, where he was based until his unexplained death. During a 1955 sojourn in Las Vegas with a band led by Benny Carter, his body was found in the nearby desert.

what to buy: *Wardell Gray Memorial Album, Vol. II* (Prestige, 1950/1952/OJC, 1992) consists of three different dates. The first 10 tracks (master and alternate takes of four tunes, two blues, a piece based on the chords of "Blue Moon," and the fairly obscure ballad, "A Sinner Kissed an Angel") find Gray in fine form in Detroit between the demise of Basie's big band and the formation of his septet. Among the standouts are his beautiful ballad treatments of "Sweet and Lovely" and "Lover Man."

what to buy next: *Wardell Gray Memorial Album, Vol. I* (Prestige, 1950–53/Original Jazz Classics, 1992, prod. Bob Weinstock, Teddy Charles) consists of a 1949 Gray-led quartet session with Charlie Parker's rhythm section of that period, and a 1953 session led by vibist Teddy Charles. The first four tracks are the master and three alternates of one of Gray's most famous pieces, "Twisted." With one exception, *How High the Moon* ♪♪♪♪ (Moon, 1950–52/1997, prod. various) contains television and radio broadcast material by the Basie septet. The last track is a live club jam with Criss and Chet Baker. *Stan Hasselgard with Benny Goodman* ♪♪♪♪ (1948/Phontastic, 1990) is a series of broadcasts by the Goodman septet boasting an unusual front line of two clarinets and Gray's tenor.

what to avoid: *Wardell Gray: One for Prez* ♪♪♪ (Jazz Selection, 1946/Black Lion, 1988, prod. Eddie Laguna, reissue prod. Alan Bates) is notable for the presence of Dodo Marmarosa, legendary pianist on the California bop scene of the mid-1940s. If this were a 10-inch LP consisting only of the master takes of the five tunes, the rating would be higher, but the alternate takes become repetitive. Not the place to start.

worth searching for: *The Chase!* ♪♪♪♪ (Giants of Jazz, 1992), a famous 1947 live recording, contains one of Gray's greatest performances, "Blue Lou," with Erroll Garner on piano. Another important track is "Little Pony"—with Gray at full speed from start to finish, booted on by a Count Basie-organized big band. The disc also contains their rendition of Charlie Parker's "Steeplechase." "Groovin' High" and "Hot House" are on *An Unforgettable Session* ♪♪♪♪ (Giants of Jazz, 1992), most of which comes from California concert jams of that period, but not, contrary to the implication of the liner notes, from the one legendary concert. Gray recorded with leader Dexter Gordon on *The Chase!* ♪♪♪♪♪ (Dial, 1947/Stash, 1995, prod. Ross Russell); the title track, the only one on which Gray appears, is the all-time best-seller in the Dial catalog (including Charlie Parker's work for the label).

influences:

◄◄ Lester Young, Charlie Parker

►► Frank Foster

Mark Ladenson

Glen Gray & the Casa Loma Orchestra

Formed as the Orange Blossom Band, 1924, in Detroit, MI. Renamed the Casa Loma Orchestra in 1927. Disbanded 1950.

The Casa Loma Orchestra played on the ground floor of the swing revolution in the late '20s and early '30s. Though its style might seem stiff and overly regimented by today's standards, during its heyday the orchestra was immensely popular, and Gene Gifford's catchy arrangements were considered quite innovative. Initially a subgroup within Jean Goldkette's orchestra called the Orange Blossom Band, Casa Loma (named after its first proposed gig, at Toronto's never-opened Casa Loma hotel), became the big-band era's first cooperative, electing officers and sharing in the profits. Though saxophonist Gray was elected president, the orchestra's first leaders were Henry Biagini and later Mel Jenssen. Filled with such able sidemen as Billy Rausch, Pee Wee Hunt, Herbie Ellis, and Red Nichols, the Casa Loma Orchestra quickly became one of the most successful outfits in the country. Recordings on various big record labels spawned a string of hits, including "Smoke Rings," "Blue Moon," "Sophisticated Lady," "No Name Jive," and "It's the Talk of the Town." Radio programs such as *The Burns and Allen Show* and *The Camel Caravan* (where the hit "Smoke Rings" became the show's official theme) spread the group's fame further, and led to recordings with the likes of Louis Armstrong, the Boswell Sisters, and Hoagy Carmichael. The group voted Gray in as its official leader in 1937, the same year Decca Records began putting his name in front of the orchestra's. Always better at "sweet" band rhythm than swing, the group began relying more on singers Kenny Sargent, the LeBrun Sisters, Eugenie Baird and others during the '40s. By decade's end, Casa Loma sounded like just another dance band with too many voices coming in and out of its sound. Gray belatedly retired the orchestra in 1950. A few years later, he recreated his group's sound with studio musicians for a series of nostalgic Capitol LPs, not one of which possessed the heart or originality of the group's '30s sides.

what to buy: The band's late '20s sides for the OKeh label are collected on *Best of the Big Bands* ♪♪♪♪ (Columbia, 1990, compilation prod. Michael Brooks), a 16-song set with the hits "Smoke Rings" and "Casa Loma Stomp," as well such standards as "I Got Rhythm" and "Ol' Man River."

what to buy next: Hit the online services for the 26-song import *Maniac's Ball* ♪♪♪♪ (Hep, 1996, reissue prod. John R.T. Davies), which showcases some of the orchestra's finest instrumental moments. Renditions of the Casa Loma hits "Blue Jazz," "Black Jazz," "White Jazz," and the title track make this a must-have item for swing fans.

what to avoid: There's just not much to get excited about on *Glen Gray & the Casa Loma Orchestra 1940* ♪ (Circle, 1994, compilation prod. George Buck Jr.), a collection of radio transcriptions mainly focused on the ballad style of vocalist Kenny Sargent.

the rest:

The Uncollected Glen Gray & the Casa Loma Orchestra: 1939–40 ♪♪ (Hindsight, 1992)

The Uncollected Glen Gray & the Casa Loma Orchestra: 1943–46 ♪♪ (Hindsight, 1992)

Glen Gray & the Casa Loma Orchestra: Mostly 1939 ♪♪ (Circle, 1994)

1929–30: The Casa Loma Stomp ♪♪♪♪ (Jazz Archives, 1994)

Live at the Rainbow Room (Jazz Hour, 1995)
Moonglow: 1930–36 (Aero Space, 1995)
Essence of Swing (Drive Archive, 1997)
Continental (Hindsight, 1995)

worth searching for: As usual, some of the best U.S. music is in the import racks, where you'll find more strong selections from the orchestra's hot, creative period from 1929–36 on *Boneyard Shuffle* (Hep, 1998, compilation prod. John R.T. Davies, Alastair Robertson), with guest appearances by Louis Armstrong and Hoagy Carmichael, and *1930–1934* (EPM Musique, 1996), a collection comparable to the Columbia set.

influences:

Jean Goldkette, Henry Biagini

Red Nichols, Frankie Carle, Sunny Dunham, Pee Wee Hunt

Ken Burke

Buddy Greco

Born August 14, 1926, in Philadelphia, PA.

Buddy Greco's name looks funny in small print—it's much more at home in giant capital letters on the late, lamented Sands or the modern Caesar's Palace marquees in Las Vegas. Along with Steve and Eydie, Tom Jones, Jack Jones, and a few of the other surviving showroom singers, Greco has come to epitomize Vegas showmanship and culture. Though he's not nearly as talented a singer as Frank Sinatra or Dean Martin, Greco has impeccable swing credentials, having revered Nat King Cole as a child and having direct experience in Benny Goodman's band. The singer-pianist's biggest hit, the finger-snapping 1960 "The Lady Is a Tramp," hipsterized from Sinatra's well-known version of a few years earlier, solidified his commercial cachet in the Emerald City. A superb pianist, Greco began playing at age four and was already making public appearances at age 16, when Benny Goodman spotted him. The swing king hired Greco to tour the world with his band; the collaboration lasted four years, then Greco went solo and embarked on a long hitmaking career. The '90s found him and his fourth wife, singer Lezlie Anders, selling out concerts in Vegas and beyond, and Greco continues to add to his list of 65-plus recorded albums.

what to buy: Wouldn't you know it? Most of Greco's dozens of albums are out of print, but he's popular enough to merit a few excellent greatest-hits CD sets. Start with *16 Most Requested Songs* (Sony, 1993, compilation prod. Didier C. Deutsch), which of course has "The Lady Is a Tramp," but also swing-pop standards such as "My Kind of Girl."

what to buy next: Greco indulges his lifelong Nat King Cole fascination with *Route 66: A Personal Tribute to Nat King Cole* (Candid, 1995), which doesn't quite match Cole's masterful phrasing or pure soul, but, as a more-fun alternative to the inescapable Natalie Cole tribute, includes impeccably played renditions of "Smile" and "Unforgettable."

what to avoid: Like Jack Jones and Andy Williams, Greco can also embody the schmaltzy, almost unlistenable side of lounge culture: *MacArthur Park* (Candid, 1996) has its charms, including a romantic "My Funny Valentine," but it gets old real fast.

the rest:

Walk a Little Faster (USA Music Group, 1996)
Movin' On (USA Music Group)

worth searching for: *Jackpot! The Las Vegas Story* (Rhino, 1996, compilation prod. James Austin, Richard Foos, Will Friedwald, Tony Natelli), in addition to including Greco's "The Lady Is a Tramp," is the ultimate Vegas-music collection. Liberace's "Cherry Hill Park/MacArthur Park/Echo Park" suite is not to be missed, and Dean Martin, Sammy Davis Jr., Vic Damone, and Ann-Margret show up to swingify the standards.

influences:

Benny Goodman, Frank Sinatra, Dean Martin, Sammy Davis Jr., Russ Columbo, Bing Crosby, Nat King Cole

Jack Jones, Liza Minnelli, Tom Jones, Ann-Margret, Jerry Vale, Liberace

Steve Knopper

Merle Haggard

Born April 6, 1937, in Bakersfield, CA.

Merle Haggard, a 1994 Country Hall of Fame inductee, is one of the greatest songwriters ever. He has amplified his reputation by consistently going his own way, keeping his distance from Nashville's power structure, paying eloquent tribute to his favorite predecessors in a business that's often uncomfortable with its past and, for a long time, keeping his music about as pure as country gets. A one-time hellraiser who served nearly three years in San Quentin for burglary, he's ironically best known to mainstream America for the ultra-conservative, anti-hippie "Okie from Muskogee" and "The Fightin' Side of Me." And he also used his considerable clout in country music to record a superb tribute to Bob Wills and generally keep the western-swing tradition alive.

In the beginning of his remarkable career Haggard was known for criminal portrayals ("The Legend of Bonnie and Clyde,"

Merle Haggard **(© Jack Vartoogian)**

"Branded Man," "The Fugitive"), but he eventually became seen as a spokesman for the working class ("Workin' Man Blues," "A Working Man Can't Get Nowhere Today"). At first glimpse he seems easy to sum up, but Haggard is actually full of depth and contradictions—an ironic iconoclast. One thing he's always had a knack for is songs of plainspoken heartbreak. From his first hit, "Sing a Sad Song," to his classic "Today I Started Loving You Again" to his prototype drinking songs "The Bottle Let Me Down" and "I Threw Away the Rose," Haggard knows how to express despair. He only slips over the line into bathos, ironically, in his nostalgic family songs, such as "Daddy Frank (The Guitar Man)," where he lays on the tear-jerking details to excess. The secret of Merle's success may be that no matter what the subject, even being a bum ("I Take a Lot of Pride in What I Am"), he projects an inner nobility.

what to buy: *A Tribute to the Best Damn Fiddle Player in the World (or, My Salute to Bob Wills)* 🦴🦴🦴🦴🦴 (Capitol, 1970/Koch, 1995, prod. Earl Ball) might be the most musically and historically successful tribute album ever made. Certainly the excitement of the performances, while not equal to Wills's western-swinging originals, is tangible and enhanced by the improved sonics. *Down Every Road* 🦴🦴🦴🦴🦴 (Capitol, 1995, prod. various) is an altogether exemplary career overview that covers his Tally and Capitol years on three CDs and his subsequent stays at MCA (10 tracks), Epic (nine tracks) and Curb (one track) on the last CD. This may be all the post-Capitol Hag most people will need—and enough of a taste for fanatics-to-be to decide that for themselves. A few previously unreleased tracks surface, so even fans with all the albums (like anybody has that many!) will find it worth getting. *The Lonesome Fugitive: The Merle Haggard Anthology (1963–77)* 🦴🦴🦴🦴🦴 (Razor & Tie, 1995, prod. various) is for those who only want the essential material but can't be satisfied with a one-CD set. The well-chosen collection's first CD entirely overlaps the Capitol box, but the second diverges plenty. Those who own no Hag and want to explore could find no better starting point.

what to buy next: *Same Train, a Different Time: Merle Haggard Sings the Great Songs of Jimmie Rodgers* 🦴🦴🦴🦴 (Capitol, 1969/Koch, 1995, prod. Ken Nelson) doesn't have quite the assurance and natural fit of the Wills tribute, but Haggard clearly loves the music. Such Rodgers classics as "Waitin' for a Train" even sound like Haggard could have written them. The five between-songs narrations can be easily skipped on repeat listening.

what to avoid: At least on his mediocre 1980s material there's a sense that many of the songs are good and the production is annoying. But on the next decade's *1996* 🦴 (Curb, 1996, prod. Merle Haggard, Abe Manuel Jr.), the songs are annoying and built around generalities. And Haggard's singing, on a long downward decline for years, is so throaty it hardly seems like the same man. There is one great song amid the dreck: Hag's original version of "Untanglin' My Mind," which Clint Black later revised. The rest is as unimaginative and repetitive as the recycled album title.

"Hootie Blues"
JAY McSHANN ORCHESTRA
1939
McShann still plays this familiar blues, which once featured Charlie Parker, with its "hello little girl" introduction.
Swingin' SINGLES

the rest:
Strangers 🦴🦴🦴🦴 (Capitol, 1965/Koch, 1995)
Land of Many Churches 🦴🦴🦴½ (Capitol, 1972/Razor & Tie, 1997)
Serving 190 Proof 🦴🦴🦴 (MCA, 1979)
The Way I Am 🦴🦴🦴½ (MCA, 1980)
Greatest Hits 🦴🦴🦴½ (MCA, 1988)
Big City 🦴🦴🦴½ (Epic, 1981)
Going Where the Lonely Go 🦴🦴🦴 (Epic, 1982)
(With George Jones) *A Taste of Yesterday's Wine* 🦴🦴🦴 (Epic, 1982)
That's the Way Love Goes 🦴🦴 (Epic, 1983)
Epic Collection 🦴🦴🦴½ (1983 live) (Epic, 1983)
(With Willie Nelson) *Pancho & Lefty* 🦴🦴🦴 (Epic, 1983)
It's All in the Game 🦴🦴½ (Epic, 1984)
Kern River 🦴🦴🦴½ (Epic, 1985)
A Friend in California 🦴🦴½ (Epic, 1986)
Chill Factor 🦴🦴½ (Epic, 1987)
(With Willie Nelson) *Seashores of Old Mexico* 🦴🦴 (Epic, 1987)
5:01 Blues 🦴🦴🦴½ (Epic, 1989)
Greatest Hits of the 1980s 🦴🦴🦴½ (Epic, 1990)

His Epic Hits: The First 11/To Be Continued ♪♪♪ (Epic, 1984)
Blue Jungle ♪♪♪ (Curb, 1990)
A Christmas Present ♪♪♪ (Curb, 1992)
1994 ♪♪ (Curb, 1994)
Super Hits/Super Hits, Vol. II/Super Hits, Vol. III ♪♪♪♪ (Sony, 1997)
16 Biggest Hits ♪♪♪ (Sony, 1998)
This Is Merle Haggard ♪♪♪ (Music Club, 1998)

worth searching for: *Untamed Hawk* ♪♪♪♪♪ (Bear Family, 1995, prod. various) contains all Haggard's work on Tally and Capitol from 1962–68 with the exception of the Rodgers tribute album. If you can find this import from Germany and have $140 available, you can have every track from his most important period on five jam-packed CDs.

influences:

◀ Jimmie Rodgers, Bob Wills & His Texas Playboys, Lefty Frizzell, Woody Guthrie, Hank Williams, Marty Robbins, Buck Owens

▶ James Talley, Stoney Edwards, Vince Gill, Dwight Yoakam, George Strait, Jayhawks, Five Chinese Brothers

Steve Holtje

Bill Haley

Born July 6, 1925, in Highland Park, MI. Died February 9, 1981, in Harlingen, TX.

It's kind of cute how the history books depict Bill Haley's "Rock around the Clock" as inciting teenagers to riot, rip up theater seats, flash knife blades, you name it. Try imagining the chunky singer, with his goofy ever-present grin and greased curly-Q hair, putting fear in the hearts of the religious right today. On the contrary, he'd be lauded as wholesome family entertainment. But in 1954 the former country & western singer's lumpen tunes were at the helm of rock 'n' roll's birth and thus brought with them the air of revolution. His songs were plodding, his arrangements barely existent, he was fat, and he was already 30. Yet he still managed to drive the kids nuts. Why? Because there was no one else on the playing field. When the sex-drenched Elvis Presley and the lunatic Little Richard burst upon the American public, Haley was revealed as the square he always was and lost his teenage cachet as quickly as he found it. As a country singer with a fondness for cutting R&B songs, Haley first dabbled in cultural miscegenation with a 1951 recording of the Jackie Brenston R&B hit "Rocket 88"; he was Bill Haley & the Saddlemen then. The first record by the renamed Bill Haley & the Comets, "Crazy Man Crazy," on the independent Essex Records label, became the first rock 'n' roll record to make the nationwide Top 20. After signing to Decca Records in 1954, Haley recorded the epochal "Rock around the Clock," which failed on its initial release but scorched up the charts after a film, *The Blackboard Jungle,* used the song as a theme the following year. Haley's records tended toward the cutesie ("Skinny Minnie") and novelty ("Mambo Rock"), but Decca producer Milt Gabler, a savvy veteran, sagaciously styled Haley's sound after another one of his charges, the rollicking Louis Jordan, and came up with some stunning, underrated pieces. Haley's "Rip It Up," for instance, may actually out-rock the Little Richard original. Ultimately, however, his career amounted to little more than "Rock around the Clock," and he spent many years living in Mexican exile before settling in Texas, where a bitter, deranged Haley would show strangers his driver's license to prove who he was.

what to buy: All compilations on the market have nearly identical song listings, but *From the Original Master Tapes* ♪♪♪ (MCA, 1985, prod. Milt Gabler, compilation prod. Steve Hoffman) is the most thorough and provides adequate detail for most libraries. A good boost in sound quality finds the congenial Haley remastered for the modern age.

what to buy next: Haley's evolution from a country singer to the first rock 'n' roll star is examined in fine-point detail on *Rock the Joint! The Original Essex Recordings, 1951–54* ♪♪♪ (Schoolkids, 1994), an historic 24-song collection that hews closely to Haley's developing rock 'n' roll style.

what to avoid: An unilluminating late '60s interview with Haley, interspersed with snatches of music, *The Haley Tapes* **woof!** (Jerden, 1995, prod. Red Robinson) does not make an interesting or rewarding CD.

the rest:

Greatest Hits ♪♪♪ (MCA, 1968/1991)
Shake, Rattle & Roll ♪♪♪ (Drive, 1994)
Rock 'n' Roll Scrapbook ♪♪ (Sequel, 1994)
Later Alligator ♪♪ (Chicago, 1995)
Vol. 20—American Legends ♪♪♪ (Laserlight, 1996)
Rock around the Clock ♪♪ (ITC Masters, 1997)

worth searching for: The German reissue specialists, Bear Family, produced a five-disc box set called *The Decca Years & More* ♪♪♪♪ (Bear Family, 1990, compilation prod. Richard Weize), although that may be overkill in this case.

influences:

◀ Big Joe Turner, Bob Wills, Louis Jordan

▶ Pat Boone, Bruce Springsteen, the Ramones

Joel Selvin and Allan Orski

Lionel Hampton

Born April 20, 1908, in Louisville, KY.

Lionel Hampton, founding father of jazz vibes since he first emerged in the early 1930s, is an exuberant, swing-based improviser, a tremendously successful band leader, and one of the keenest talent scouts in jazz history. He learned his first instrument, drums, from a Dominican nun while he attended Holy Rosary Academy in Kenosha, Wisconsin. When Hampton moved to Chicago he joined the *Chicago Defender* Newspaper Boys Band, where he learned percussion and marimba. His first major inspiration was drummer Jimmy Bertrand, who also occasionally played the xylophone. Hampton moved to Los Angeles around 1927 and worked steadily in various bands, but his big break came when he joined Les Hite's band, which backed Louis Armstrong at Sebastian's Cotton Club in Culver City. The gig marked another turning point for Hamp, as he met and soon married Cotton Club dancer Gladys Riddle. She became his business manager and profoundly helped shape his career, encouraging him to practice the vibes and to study theory at the University of Southern California. Hampton started his own band in order to feature himself on the vibes, and in 1936 landed a job at the Paradise Cafe in Los Angeles. Benny Goodman came in one night and soon Hamp found himself on stage with Goodman, drummer Gene Krupa, and pianist Teddy Wilson. Goodman recorded the group and began featuring Hampton with his quartet on the *Camel Cigarette* program, making the vibraphonist a star. RCA Victor gave Hampton wide latitude to assemble all-star bands in the late 1930s, resulting in 90 sides that mark the high point of the swing era.

Hampton stayed with Goodman through 1940, including a featured role in the legendary 1938 Carnegie Hall concert, and then left to start his own big band. The group was a tremendous success, and has never strayed far from the formula established with the huge 1942 hit "Flying Home"—potent screaming brass over an insistent, driving rhythm section. Tenor saxophonist Illinois Jacquet's classic "Flying Home" solo was an essential element in the emergence of R&B, a style Hampton's orchestra incorporated effectively into its hard-charging, extroverted sound. By the mid-'40s, the orchestra had adopted elements of bebop, though Hampton's style remained grounded in swing. Over the decades, the band also became known as one of jazz's most fertile proving grounds for young talent. The list of musicians who paid early dues with Hampton is prodigious, starting with Dinah Washington, Betty Carter, Charles Mingus, Dexter Gordon, Clark Terry, Illinois Jacquet, Art Farmer, Fats Navarro, Wes Montgomery, Clifford Brown, and Johnny Griffin. Hamp's other ventures have also been successful, running from a publishing house and two record labels (Glad Hamp and Who's Who) to the Lionel Hampton Development Corp., which built two apartment complexes in Harlem. By the 1970s he was an important figure in New York and Republican politics. In 1988 the Lionel Hampton Center for Performing Arts opened in Idaho and there is now also an annual Lionel Hampton Jazz Festival in the state. Despite suffering from a stroke and other health problems in the 1990s, Hampton continues to record for MoJazz and Telarc, and tour with his big band and his all-star group the Golden Men of Jazz, featuring such relative youngsters as Clark Terry, Sweets Edison, James Moody, and Al Grey.

what to buy: Until all Hampton's Decca sessions are reissued on CD, *Midnight Sun* ♪♪♪♪♪ (Decca, 1946–47/1993, prod. Milt Gabler) is the best place to start. These 20 tracks capture one of the most advanced, bop-influenced big bands of the mid-'40s, sessions featuring both up-and-coming jazz stars (such as Johnny Griffin and Charles Mingus), and fine, lesser-known players such as powerhouse trumpeters Jimmy Nottingham and Leo Sheppard. These are consistently excellent, high-spirited recordings and, though Hamp retains his swing style, some tracks (such as "Mingus Fingers") are amazingly bop-oriented. Containing 16 Decca tracks alternating between Hampton's septet and orchestra, *Flying Home* ♪♪♪♪ (MCA, 1942–45/1990, prod. Milt Gabler) includes the original 1942 hit "Flying Home" with Illinois Jacquet's classic tenor solo (and a 17-year-old Dexter Gordon, on his first major gig). Milt Buckner, Cat Anderson, and Earl Bostic are some of the other young talents featured here, as well as a 19-year-old Dinah Washington, backed by some gritty Arnett Cobb tenor work on "Blow Top Blues." Although this is a good introduction to Hamp's extroverted style as an improviser and bandleader, the album loses a bone for slipshod presentation. The first disc in RCA's frustrating, incomplete Bluebird reissue series of Hampton's classic all-star sessions, *Hot Mallets, Vol. I* ♪♪♪♪ (Bluebird, 1937–39/1987) contains the four master tracks from the legendary date with Coleman Hawkins, Ben Webster, Chu Berry, Benny Carter, and a young Dizzy Gillespie still under the sway of Roy Eldridge. Forget about their ages and allegedly contrasting styles, swing veteran Hampton and cool tenor saxophonist Stan Getz find plenty of common ground on *Hamp and Getz* ♪♪♪♪♪ (Verve, 1955, prod. Norman Granz), a session featuring some take-no-prisoners jousting.

what to buy next: An excellent concert album recorded at the Pasadena Civic Auditorium, *Lionel Hampton with the Just Jazz All-Stars* ♪♪♪♪ (MCA/GNP, 1947/1993, prod. Gene Norman) features a host of jazz stars. The material—"Flying Home," "Hamp's Boogie Woogie," and "Perdido"—is from Hamp's standard repertoire, and the solos are consistently strong. *You Better Know It!!!* ♪♪♪♪½ (Impulse!, 1965/1994, prod. Bob Thiele) is a wonderful small group session with tenor saxman Ben Webster and trumpeter Clark Terry. The third and final installment in RCA's scattered reissue series of Hampton's classic all-star swing sessions, *Tempo and Swing* ♪♪♪♪ (Bluebird, 1939–40/1992) contains 23 tracks featuring Webster, Benny Carter, Coleman Hawkins, and

Lionel Hampton **(Archive Photos)**

the Nat King Cole Trio. There's no excuse for RCA dividing up sessions between discs, but Hamp knew how to create excitement and inspire his players and the music here is at an extremely high level. Most of *Reunion at Newport 1967* (RCA/Bluebird, 1967/1993, prod. Brad McCuen, Bill Titone) features a big band of Hampton alumni assembled for the Newport Festival. Illinois Jacquet reprises his classic "Flying Home" solo.

what to avoid: Despite the presence of many fine musicians, *For the Love of Music* (MoJazz, 1995, prod. Gary Haase, Stevie Wonder, Israel Sinfonietta) is an over-produced mess that rarely comes to life. A banal, funkified version of "Flying Home" with keyboardist Patrice Rushen is one low point, while Chaka Kahn is wasted on the piffle of "Gossamer Wings." Hampton clearly has fun sitting in with Tito Puente's band on "Mojazz" and "Don't You Worry 'bout a Thing," two rare high points on this weak effort to package a musician who needs no help from clever producers.

best of the rest:
I'm in the Mood for Swing (Living Era, 1930–38/1992)
In Paris (Vogue Disques, 1953/1995)
Rare Recordings, Vol. I (Telarchive, 1977/1992)
Mostly Blues (MusicMasters, 1989)
Mostly Ballads (MusicMasters, 1990)
Live at the Blue Note (Telarc, 1991)
Just Jazz: Live at the Blue Note (Telarc, 1992)
Swing-Sation Series: Lionel Hampton (GRP, 1998)

worth searching for: Some of the most thrilling small-group sessions in jazz history, *After You've Gone: The Original Benny Goodman Trio and Quartet Sessions, Vol. I* (Bluebird, 1935–37/1987) covers 10 tracks by the Benny Goodman Trio, with pianist Teddy Wilson and drummer Gene Krupa, and the first 12 tracks recorded by the Benny Goodman Quartet, which added Hampton's irrepressible vibes to the trio. This is timeless music by the first racially mixed bands to work regularly in public.

influences:
◀◀ Jimmy Bertrand, Louis Armstrong
▶▶ Red Norvo, Tyree Glenn, Milt Jackson

Andrew Gilbert

Sir Roland Hanna

Born February 10, 1932, in Detroit, MI.

Technique and a well-developed sense of jazz performance history make Sir Roland Hanna an enormously respected solo and ensemble performer in many different jazz genres, from swing to bop. He studied at Juilliard and at the Eastman School, receiving a firm grounding in the classics to go along with his ever-developing piano skills. His first gigs of renown came with Benny Goodman and Charles Mingus, but he has led his own trios since 1959, in addition to serving a long stint in the Thad Jones/Mel Lewis Jazz Orchestra (replacing Jones). Hanna has also served as an accompanist to Sarah Vaughan and performed extensively with the New York Jazz Quartet, which he helped form in 1974. During a solo tour of Africa in 1969, Hanna was knighted by President Tubman of Liberia for his humanitarian work, raising money for the education of African youth.

what to buy: One of the best solo piano recitals in Hanna's catalog, *Perugia* (Freedom, 1975, prod. Alan Bates, Michael Cuscuna) is a live recording from the Montreux Jazz Festival in 1974. Including Duke Ellington classics such as "Take the 'A' Train" and "I Got It Bad and That Ain't Good" to Hanna originals "Wistful Moment" and the album's eight-minute centerpiece, "Perugia," there are no slack moments, whether he's quoting blues phrases or classical composers such as Satie or Debussy.

what to buy next: Despite Hanna's undeniable gifts as an accompanist, solo piano performances are where this gifted pianist really shines. While not the same kind of beautiful performance heard on *Perugia*, *Sir Roland Hanna at Maybeck, Vol. 32* (Concord Jazz, 1994, prod. Nick Phillips) is yet another distinguished entry into the Maybeck Hall Recital series. The material dips heavily (three songs and a three-tune medley) into the Gershwin catalog with stopovers for Romberg, Rogers, Strayhorn, and Rollins. About the only disappointment is the lack of Hanna originals.

the rest:
Walkin' (Jazz Hour, 1975)
Glove (Storyville, 1978)
Bird Tracks: Remembering Charlie Parker (Progressive, 1978)
(With the New York Jazz Quartet) *Oasis* (Enja, 1981)
Persia My Dear (DIW, 1987)
(With Jesper Thilo) *This Time It's Real* (Storyville, 1988)
'Round Midnight (Town Crier, 1990)
Duke Ellington Piano Solos (MusicMasters, 1991)
Roland Hanna Plays Gershwin (LRC, 1993)
(With the New York Jazz Quartet) *Surge* (Enja, 1993)

worth searching for: *Swing Me No Waltzes* (Storyville, 1980, prod. Rune Ofwerman) is another wonderful solo album, showcasing Hanna the composer more than any of his other titles. He writes seven of the nine tunes on the record (not yet available on CD) and adds a fine rendition of Duke Ellington's "Everything but You" and an amusing arrangement of "I Hear You Knockin' but You Can't Come In."

influences:
◀◀ Bud Powell, Teddy Wilson, Art Tatum, Erroll Garner
▶▶ Craig Taborn

Garaud MacTaggart

Phil Harris

Born January 16, 1904, in Linton, IN. Died August 11, 1995, in Rancho Mirage, CA.

Modern audiences know Phil Harris best as the voice of Baloo the Bear in Walt Disney's animated 1967 classic *The Jungle Book*, but he was also a top bandleader in the 1930s and 1940s, as well as a beloved radio comedian. Harris began his career as a drummer for Francis Craig's band in the early 1920s, then co-founded the Lofner-Harris Orchestra with Carol Lofner in 1928. Four years later, the singer formed his own band and broadcast live shows from the Coconut Grove over NBC radio. His stints there led to a popular short subject film about him, which in turn earned his orchestra the house band slot on *The Jack Benny Program* in 1936. On radio, Harris developed his wisecracking, soused band-rat character years before Dean Martin came up with the same idea, and he routinely garnered big laughs and applause with his zoot-suit greetings of Jack Benny and Mary Livingstone. ("Hiya Jackson!" he shouted. "Hello Livvy . . . you doll, you!") When he and his band weren't backing Dennis Day or some special guest star, Harris sang such ditties as "That's What I Like about the South," "G.I Jive," and "Smoke! Smoke! Smoke! That Cigarette," all of which became substantial hits. Harris wasn't a great vocalist, but as his recordings attest, his phrasing was hep-cat cool and his style was instantly identifiable. In 1946 Harris and his wife, Alice Faye, started their own sitcom on CBS radio that lasted eight years. Tired of touring, he eventually disbanded his orchestra; Harris's early '50s youth-oriented hits "The Thing" (a purposefully vague novelty that still gets airplay on Dr. Demento's radio show) and "I Know an Old Lady" were his last chart entries. He remained in demand as a nightclub entertainer, TV guest, supporting player in movies, and voice for feature-length cartoons. His last major voiceover role, in 1992's *Rock-a-Doodle,* featured an 88-year-old Harris singing "Life Is Just like Tying Your Shoes" with the philosophic verve of a lifelong southern-fried hipster.

what to buy: Harris's best tracks from the 1930s through the early 1950s, including his jaunty novelty hits are collected on *The Thing about Phil Harris* ♪♪♪♪ (Living Era, 1996, prod. various), featuring the wonderfully vague hit "The Thing."

what to buy next: Harris's first blush of fame with his own band is neatly documented on *Echoes from the Coconut Grove* ♪♪♪½ (Take Two Records, 1996, prod. various), with radio transcriptions from 1932–33.

the rest:

The Jungle Book ♪♪♪½ (Original Soundtrack) (Disney, 1967/1997)
1933–Phil Harris & His Orchestra ♪♪♪ (Hindsight, 1992)

worth searching for: Some catalogs carry *That's What I Like about the South* ♪♪♪♪ (Good Music, 1997, prod. various), which contains 24 tracks of fun-loving jive such as "Smoke! Smoke! Smoke! That Cigarette," "Ain't Nobody Here but Us Chickens," and "Preacher and the Bear." Also, some old-time radio catalogs have *The Phil Harris–Alice Faye Show* ♪♪♪♪ (Adventures in Cassettes, 1997, prod. various), *Phil Harris-Alice Faye Show "What's a Rexall?"* ♪♪♪♪ (Adventures in Cassettes, 1996, prod. various), and *Movie Star* ♪♪♪ (Adventures in Cassettes, 1998, prod. various), all tape compilations from radio's golden age.

influences:

◄◄ Francis Craig, Carol Lofner, Bert Williams

►► Kay Kyser, Tex Beneke, Dean Martin

Ken Burke

Wynonie Harris

Born August 24, 1915, in Omaha, NE. Died June 14, 1969, in Los Angeles, CA.

The rowdy jump blues and smoky vocal bravado of Wynonie Harris clearly set the stage for rock 'n' roll. Between 1945–52, no blues shouter (not even Harris's idol and mentor, Big Joe Turner) rocked harder. Harris began his career as a comedian and hoofer (he danced in the film *Harlem Hit Parade 1943*) before he taught himself to play drums and formed his own band. His big break as a vocalist came with Lucky Millinder's Orchestra in 1944. Their Decca recordings of "Hurry Hurry" and "Who Threw the Whiskey In the Well" were solid hits, but Harris was unsatisfied with the financial arrangements and quickly departed. After recording several hits for various labels, his incendiary 1948 reworking of Roy Brown's "Good Rockin' Tonight" established him as a major star. Though most of Harris's King hits were about sex ("All She Wants to Do Is Rock," "I Like My Baby's Puddin'") or liquor ("Rot Gut," "Drinkin' Wine Spo-Dee-Oh-Dee"), artistically Harris was more than just a whiskey-guzzling sex fiend. (Off-stage is another story, however.) On songs such as "Grandma Plays the Numbers," "I Feel Old Age Coming On," and others, he displays comic timing unique among blues shouters. Even at his peak, Harris was sometimes too racy for the race charts, but around 1952, smoother, less suggestive sounds began to dominate and his string of hits ended. Later he ended up tending bar in some of the joints he used to play. During his glory years, trade publications denounced Harris's music as vulgar. Nowadays, they refer to these same recordings as classics.

what to buy: All of Harris's big ground-breaking hits for the King label show up on *Bloodshot Eyes—The Best of Wynonie Harris* ♪♪♪♪♪ (Rhino, 1994, compilation prod. James Austin), an 18-track slug of essential hot and sweaty R&B. This is driving, danceable stuff, and such licentious tracks as "Keep on

Phil Harris **(Archive Photos)**

Churnin' ('Till the Butter Comes)," "Lovin' Machine," and "Git to Gittin' Baby" make this a highly enjoyable adults-only item.

what to buy next: A potent sample of Harris's earlier work for Apollo can be found on *Everybody Boogie* (Delmark, 1996, compilation prod. Robert G. Koester, Steve Wagner), which includes the hits "Playful Baby" and "Young & Wild." Not as raw and frantic as the later King sides, these overtly sensual rhythms will have you undulating your hips with the willing partner of your choice. Rock 'n' roll started right here, folks.

what to avoid: There's not a thing wrong with *Battle of the Blues* (King, 1986), *The Battle of the Blues, Vol. II* (King, 1989), or *Battle of the Blues, Vol. IV* (King, 1989), which also contain tracks by Roy Brown and Eddie "Cleanhead" Vinson, but a full disc by any of these artists costs the same as a mixed disc.

the rest:

Laughing but Crying (Route 66, 1991)
Good Rockin' Tonight (King, 1996)
More Blues Rockin' (King, 1996)
1944–45 (Jazz Chronological Classics, 1996)
1945–47 (Jazz Chronological Classics, 1998)
Good Rockin' Tonight (See for Miles, 1998)

worth searching for: Completists will definitely want the import *Women, Whiskey & Fishtails* (Ace, 1993, compilation prod. Ray Topping), which contains 21 previously unreleased tracks and alternate takes from Harris's fertile King records period. The still-available *Atlantic Blues Vocalists* (Atlantic, 1986, prod. various) has two of Harris's Atco sides, including "Destination Love," an absolute killer.

influences:

◀◀ Louis Jordan, Big Joe Turner, Jimmy Rushing, Buddy Johnson

▶▶ Roy Brown, Screaming Jay Hawkins, Esquerita, Elvis Presley

Ken Burke

Coleman Hawkins

Born November 21, 1904, in St. Joseph, MO. Died May 19, 1969, in New York, NY.

The first giant of the tenor saxophone, Coleman Hawkins defined swing music's direction in the first half of the century. He gigged with Louis Armstrong, Billie Holiday, and Fletcher Henderson, taking his show to Europe, where he sat in with Belgian guitar legend Django Reinhardt, then returned stateside and created the swing ballad with his superhuman 1939 performance, "Body and Soul." He projected elegance even when the bebop revolution stopped him briefly—Hawk listened hard to the rebels, then played even with them. Discovered in a Kansas City theater pit by blues singer Mamie Smith, Hawk soon played his way into Fletcher Henderson's first great swing band of the mid-1920s. He learned from his bandmate, trumpeter Louis Armstrong, sticking with Henderson until 1934, then heading to Europe, where he spent five years experimenting with British and continental bands, dueling with Reinhardt and violinist Stephane Grappelli. Challenged on his return by the popular smooth-toned saxophonist Lester Young, Hawk responded with the ethereal "Body and Soul," the ultimate jazz solo. He veered between swing and bop units during the war years, then spent the 1950s touring with the Jazz at the Philharmonic shows and playing small clubs with trumpeter Roy Eldridge. Age and dissolution caught up with Hawkins by the mid-1960s, and his final recordings are sad and ghostly.

what to buy: Hawkins's undying "Body and Soul" can be found on several compilations of his Victor recordings, but the best is *The Indispensable Coleman Hawkins (1927–56)* (BMG, 1992, prod. Jean-Paul Guiter), which picks the cream from four decades. *The Complete Coleman Hawkins* (Mercury, 1987, prod. Harry Lim), a four-CD opus, culls Hawkins's 1940s-era sides for the New York Keynote label, but they are all sublime, made with a cabal of swing's top session men. Perhaps the best representation of Hawk's 1950s bouts with Roy Eldridge, *At the Opera House* (Verve, 1994, prod. Norman Granz) is filled with solid blues and ballads, backed by three-fifths of the Modern Jazz Quartet.

what to buy next: Hawk's fling with the bopsters does him good on *Hollywood Stampede* (Capitol, 1989, prod. Michael Cuscuna). Included are "Rifftide" and "Stuffy" and Hawkins's appropriations of Thelonious Monk's "Hackensack" and "Stuffy Turkey." His players include a young Miles Davis, Howard McGhee, and Max Roach.

best of the rest:

Rainbow Mist (Delmark, 1992)
The Hawk in Paris (RCA/Bluebird, 1993)
Coleman Hawkins Encounters Ben Webster (Verve, 1997)
The Genius of Coleman Hawkins (Verve, 1997)

worth searching for: *The Jazz Scene* (Verve, 1994, prod. Norman Granz) is a lavish two-CD book that reproduces a 1949 classic that includes cuts from Hawk, Charlie Parker, Duke Ellington, Lester Young, and Willie Smith. Amid these giants, Hawkins stands out for "Picasso," an unaccompanied saxophone solo that rendered the jazz world breathless and continues to inspire sax giants like Sonny Rollins.

influences:

◀◀ Fletcher Henderson, Louis Armstrong

▶▶ Lester Young, Don Byas, Ben Webster, Charlie Parker, Sonny Rollins, Chu Berry, Wardell Gray, Eddie "Lockjaw" Davis, Gene Ammons

Steve Braun

Erskine Hawkins

Born July 26, 1914, in Birmingham, AL. Died November 11, 1993, in Willingboro, NJ.

Leading a blues-charged outfit associated with the Kansas City riffing style of Bennie Moten and Count Basie, trumpeter Erskine Hawkins was responsible for two huge swing-dance hits, 1939's "Tuxedo Junction" and 1940's "After Hours" (credited to arranger Avery Parrish). Glenn Miller's later version of "Tuxedo Junction" became one of the most played recordings of the '40s, and Hawkins's commercial successes allowed his band to endure far longer than most big bands of the swing era. The Hawkins band adapted to R&B, surviving well into the '50s before the leader downsized to a sextet. Hawkins's first instruments were drums and trombone, before he took up the trumpet at age 13. As a student at the Alabama State Teachers' College in Montgomery, he became leader of the a college band, the 'Bama Sate Collegians. Initially fronted by J.B. Sims, the band travelled to New York in 1934 to generate money to keep the college afloat during the Depression. The band stayed in New York, with Hawkins gradually emerging as the leader. The band started recording in 1936 and frequently appeared at the Savoy Ballroom, where it first won tremendous popularity with dancers, then the public at large. What began as a student band turned into a first-class professional unit, with a talented pianist and arranger in Parrish and excellent soloists in trumpeter Dud Bascomb and tenorist Paul Bascomb. Hawkins specialized in high-note trumpet effects, billing himself as the "20th-Century Gabriel," but at his best he was a powerful and expressive soloist in the Louis Armstrong mold.

what to buy: For original hits and a good sense of the Erskine Hawkins band's range and power, the best choice is *The Original Tuxedo Junction* (BMG, 1989, reissue prod. Orrin Keepnews), which contains "Tuxedo Junction" and "After Hours."

what to buy next: *Erskine Hawkins 1938–39* (Jazz Chronological Classics, 1992, prod. various) has the original "Tuxedo Junction" and excellent versions of "King Porter Stomp" and Hawkins's own "Gin Mill Special."

what to avoid: *The Original Tuxedo Junction* is not to be confused with the inferior *Tuxedo Junction* (MCA, 1991, prod. various), which has a short playing time and includes later remakes of original tunes with different personnel.

best of the rest:

Original Broadcast Performance, 1945 (Musidisc, 1992)
Erskine Hawkins & His Orchestra 1939–40 (Jazz Chronological Classics, 1992)
Erskine Hawkins & His Orchestra 1936–38 (Jazz Chronological Classics, 1992)
Erskine Hawkins & His Orchestra 1940–41 (Jazz Chronological Classics, 1993)
Erskine Hawkins & His Orchestra 1941–45 (Jazz Chronological Classics, 1996)

worth searching for: The hard-to-find *From Alabama to Harlem 1938–40* (Black & Blue, 1995, prod. various) has generous playing time and track selection.

influences:

◀◀ Bennie Moten, Count Basie, "Hot Lips" Page

▶▶ Louis Jordan, Joe Morris, Ray Charles

Stuart Broomer

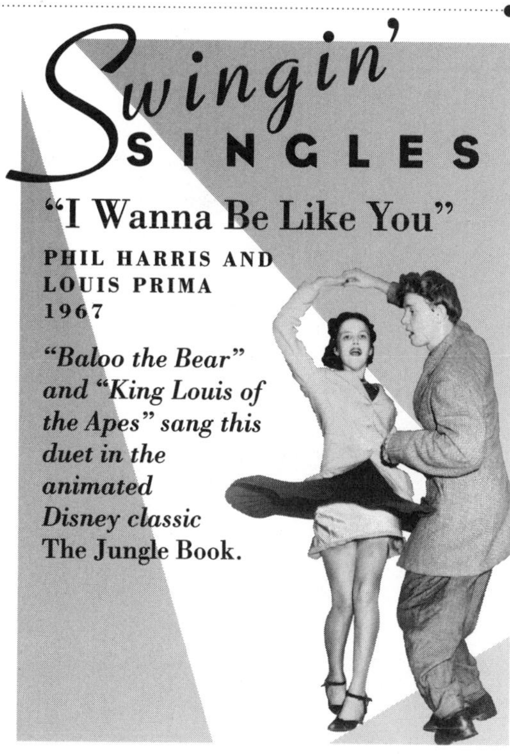

Swingin'
SINGLES
"I Wanna Be Like You"
PHIL HARRIS AND LOUIS PRIMA 1967
"Baloo the Bear" and "King Louis of the Apes" sang this duet in the animated Disney classic The Jungle Book.

Dick Haymes

Born Richard Benjamin Haymes, September 13, 1916, in Buenos Aires, Argentina. Died March 28, 1980, in Los Angeles, CA.

Though Dick Haymes was a terrific crooner and a suave, long-faced hunk in a bow tie, he's most frequently remembered as the guy who replaced Frank Sinatra in Harry James's swing band. In his time, though, Haymes was far more than an answer to a pop-music trivia question: his trademark songs, such

Erskine Hawkins **(Archive Photos)**

as "My Silent Love," "For You, for Me, Forevermore," and "It Might As Well Be Spring" were big hits, and he briefly rivaled Sinatra and Bing Crosby in the 1940s. Born to an Englishman and an Irishwoman, Haymes emulated his concert-singing mother in his teens, catching on with the Johnny Johnson band at age 16 and becoming a Hollywood songwriter and movie extra throughout the 1930s. James was receptive to Haymes's song-selling pitches, and hired him as a singer in 1940; that led to higher-profile gigs with the Benny Goodman and Tommy Dorsey bands. Haymes's smooth, smooth voice was perfect for romantic balladeering, but he wasn't suited for the faster numbers (which gave the more versatile Sinatra a competitive edge). By 1941 Haymes was a bona fide solo star, and he successfully transferred his charisma to film, from 1943's *Dubarry Was a Lady* to 1948's *Up in Central Park*. Haymes, who was born in Argentina, managed to avoid the World War II draft by registering as a "resident alien." When he returned to the U.S. from a trip abroad with Rita Hayworth (one of his seven wives), the government tried to deport him as an "undesirable alien." The deportation papers were later revoked. Surviving that, plus two later declarations of bankruptcy, he became a reasonably popular touring singer in England, the U.S., Ireland, and Spain through the 1970s.

what to buy: The two-disc *Complete Columbia Recordings* (Collectors' Choice, 1998, prod. various) collects Haymes's work with the Harry James and Benny Goodman big bands, and he croons nicely on slow ballads such as "I Never Purposely Hurt You" and "I Guess I'll Have to Dream the Rest." But it's easy to see why Sinatra's appeal has endured longer than the Muppetish voice of Haymes.

what to buy next: Though *Complete Columbia Recordings* and another thorough compilation, *The Very Best of Dick Haymes, Vols. I & II* (Taragon, 1997, prod. various), have recently outpaced it, *The Best of Dick Haymes* (Curb, 1991, prod. various) has long been the consummate Haymes set. It shows off his vibrato-less voice as he croons like Nat King Cole on "Our Love Is Here to Stay," "Where or When," and "Love Walked In."

best of the rest:

For You, For Me, Forevermore (Audiophile, 1994)
Serenading with the Big Bands (Sony Special Products, 1995)
Star Eyes (Jazz Classics, 1996)

Soft Lights and Sweet Music (Hindsight, 1997)
You'll Never Know (ASV, 1997)

worth searching for: Haymes was already a mature, confident singer when he joined James's big band in the early 1940s, and two British import sets, *Dick Haymes with Harry James: How High the Moon* (Memoir Classics, 1994, prod. Gordon Gray) and *Dick Haymes with Harry James: It Had to Be You* (Memoir Classics, 1995, prod. Gordon Gray), prove that. The latter includes "Fools Rush In" and "All or Nothing at All."

influences:

◀◀ Frank Sinatra, Harry James, Russ Columbo, Bing Crosby, Al Jolson, Louis Armstrong

▶▶ Vic Damone, Jack Jones, Rudy Vallee, Buddy Greco

Steve Knopper

Horace Heidt

Born May 21, 1901, in Alameda, CA. Died December, 1, 1986, in Los Angeles, CA.

The rap on Horace Heidt was "great showman, corny band"—and there's truth to that assessment. Coming out of vaudeville, Heidt stocked his orchestra (known as the Brigadiers, later His Musical Knights) to appeal to mainstream audiences, not jazz purists. Though he had plenty of fine players, they were all expected to be entertainers, not just musicians. As a result, audiences were treated to all sorts of on-stage antics, not the least of which were Alvino Rey and his "singing" electric guitar, Frankie Carle masterfully playing piano with his hands behind his back, and even a performing dog named Lobo. At one point, Heidt carried only 14 musicians but had 16 vocalists, among them Gordon MacRae, the King Sisters, and Donna and Her Don Juans, the latter featuring Art Carney years before he co-starred in *The Honeymooners.*

Heidt's recordings were mostly the "sweet" band variation of swing, filled with fluttering trumpets, goopy slide trombones, and weeping strings. During the late '30s through the mid-'40s, his outfit scored dozens of bonafide smashes such as "Gone with the Wind," "It's the Natural Thing to Do," and every hand-clapper's favorite, "Deep in the Heart of Texas." A large amount of this success was due to the band's regular appearances on two enormously popular network radio game shows, *Pot of Gold* and *Treasure Chest.* When Glenn Miller entered the armed services in 1942, Heidt sharpened his own group's swing chops by hiring several of Miller's key men, including arranger Bill Finegan. This hot new approach only lasted a year. A dispute with his management at MCA provoked Heidt to retire at the peak of his popularity. He returned three years later with *The Youth Opportunity Show,* a popular radio talent show that made it onto early network TV. Heidt, one of the wealthiest men to ever wave a baton, continued to dabble in music and broadcasting until he began devoting his full attention to real estate during the late '50s. These days, his music is preserved by his son Horace Heidt, whose All-Stars were the official band of the Oakland Raiders from 1982 until 1995.

what to buy: The best of Heidt's work on Columbia with future band leaders Alvino Rey, Frankie Carle, and Frank DeVol is on *The Hits and More* (Collectors' Choice, 1998, prod. various). This superior 24-song set includes such hits as "Gone with the Wind," "Tipi-Tin," and "This Can't Be Love." It's corny stuff, but well-executed, sometimes even danceable, corny stuff. To hear the band in a live setting, the cassette-only *The Uncollected Horace Heidt & His Musical Knights, Vol. II 1943–45* (Hindsight, 1992, prod. Wally Heider) is a collection of old-time radio transcriptions.

what to avoid: Though it's by no means a bad album, be aware *New Heidts* (Quicksilver, 1995) contains a mix of standards and new songs as recorded by Horace Heidt Jr. and His All-Star Band.

worth searching for: You can view Heidt and his latter-day band on the home video *Horace Heidt & His Musical Knights* (Quicksilver, 1995), a collection of vintage TV performances from the '50s hosted by his son.

influences:

◀◀ Fred Waring, Guy Lombardo, Glenn Miller

▶▶ Alvino Rey, Frank DeVol, Frankie Carle, Dick Contino, Mitch Miller, Horace Heidt Jr.

Ken Burke

Fletcher Henderson

Born December 18, 1897, in Cuthbert, GA. Died December 29, 1952, in New York, NY.

Big bands, featuring brass, sax, and rhythm sections, have been around since the early 1900s. But prior to the emergence of the Fletcher Henderson band in the 1920s, few had more than a passing flirtation with jazz. Henderson, a pianist, led the first great jazz-focused big band, an ensemble through which passed many greats on their way to fame, including trumpeters Louis Armstrong, Cootie Williams, Red Allen, and Roy Eldridge; trombonists Charlie Green, Jimmy Harrison, and J.C. Higginbotham; saxophonists Coleman Hawkins, Benny Carter, Chu Berry, and Ben Webster; clarinetist Buster Bailey; bassists John Kirby and Israel Crosby; and drummer Sid Catlett. Serious jazz-band arranging appears to have begun with the charts Don Redman wrote for Henderson in the early 1920s. Shortly thereafter, Benny Carter, Edgar Sampson, and Fletcher's younger brother Horace also contributed to the book. It wasn't until the early 1930s that, on a bet, Fletcher started arranging, but he soon became the dominant style-setter of the era. He arranged not only for his own band, but for many others as well. He sold more than 200 charts to Benny Goodman, who readily acknowledged that Henderson's work was a major factor in Goodman's becoming the "King of Swing."

Though Henderson pioneered the Harlem big-band movement, his band was dogged by bad luck, much brought on by Henderson's own lax leadership. (Because Henderson originally studied to be a chemist, biographers have speculated he never learned enough discipline to be a bandleader, and a serious car wreck in Kentucky further blunted his ambition.) Among musicians, especially those who played with Henderson, the story long persisted that the band was great on the job, but froze up in the recording studio. Henderson's recorded legacy does reveal a frequent lack of ensemble precision, but just as often finds the band's soloists turning in performances that set high standards. The bad luck, combined with Henderson's phenomenal success arranging for others, led him to disband on June 8, 1939, just when many other big bands were on the verge of fame. Some of Fletcher's musicians went with his brother Horace's band. Fletcher himself took over the piano chair with Benny Goodman's small groups; then, when Jess Stacy left in a huff, he took over in Goodman's big band as well. Henderson led another band from 1941 through 1947, but it was never very successful, either commercially or artistically. After 1947 Henderson played piano accompaniment for various singers, arranged and played for a review, *The Jazz Train,* and finally led a swing sextet at a New York club, Cafe Society, where his final performance was recorded as an air check the night of December 21, 1950, mere hours before he suffered a debilitating stroke. Henderson spent his last two years as an invalid.

what to buy: Intended to be a complete set, 17 separate CDs form the Fletcher Henderson series on the Jazz Chronological Classics label. Compiled from original 78-rpm recordings on many labels, these CD reissues, released in the 1990s, present in chronological order virtually all of Henderson's work as a leader from 1921 through 1941. The sides including Louis Armstrong, as he showed New Yorkers how to swing, are on *Fletcher Henderson: 1924, Vol. III* (Jazz Chronological Classics, prod. Gilles Petard), and *Fletcher Henderson: 1924–25* (Jazz Chronological Classics, prod. Gilles Petard). "Everybody Loves My Baby," with Armstrong's first vocal on wax, and the classic "Sugarfoot Stomp," on which Louis plays a solo later copied by innumerable trumpeters, are just a couple of the Armstrong/Henderson gems. *Fletcher Henderson: 1932–34* (Jazz Chronological Classics, prod. various) is a great selection of mature Henderson, including a number of charts later recorded by Benny Goodman, including Fletcher's "King Porter Stomp," "Down South Camp Meetin'," and "Wrappin' It Up," as well as brother Horace's "Big John's Special." There's more meat to Henderson's readings, and the soloists, especially trumpeter Red Allen, tell more convincing stories. But the Goodman band out-swings Henderson. It's no wonder there was mutual admiration between Henderson and Goodman.

what to buy next: The last Henderson CD on Classics, *Fletcher Henderson: 1940–41* (Jazz Chronological Classics) is not particularly notable for the 1941 sides by Fletcher, but more for the 1940 output of the Horace Henderson band, which features many of Fletcher's former sidemen and a few of Fletcher's arrangements. This was a great overlooked band. Trumpeter Emmett Berry was its most notable soloist, producing particularly hot work on "Flinging a Whing Ding." But for a broad look at Fletcher Henderson's recorded output, *A Study in Frustration* (Columbia, 1994, prod. Frank Driggs) is the set to buy. This three-CD reissue of a four-LP set chronicles the band from 1923 through 1938. The notes and discography are excellent, but if you can find the LP set, the booklet contains many fine early photos of the band.

worth searching for: The LP *Fletcher Henderson's Sextet 1950* (Alamac, 1950) is pretty low-key, with tenor saxophonist Lucky Thompson providing the most interest. Despite the low rating, this recording is significant because it is Henderson's last LP, recorded the night of his debilitating stroke.

influences:

◀◀ Art Hickman, James Reese Europe

▶▶ Sy Oliver, Edgar Sampson, Jimmy Mundy, Ernie Wilkins, Benny Goodman

John K. Richmond

Horace Henderson

See: Fletcher Henderson

Woody Herman

Born Woodrow Charles Thomas Hermann, May 16, 1913, in Milwaukee, WI. Died October 29, 1987, in West Los Angeles, CA.

Woody Herman was the consummate orchestra leader, a "road father" to many of his musicians, and a durable jazzman whose lengthy, difficult career as leader spanned more than 50 years. A versatile reedman, he recorded as clarinetist and alto/soprano saxophonist, and was an above-average band vocalist. Like his famous contemporary Duke Ellington, whose first love was his band, Herman often downplayed his instrumental skills, concentrating instead on keeping his top-flight musical aggregations on the road and one step ahead of the competition. The old "Woodchopper" was responsible for unleashing

Fletcher Henderson **(Archive Photos)**

some of the best sidemen and arrangers in the dance-band business. He had a knack for setting the right tempos, discovering fresh, young talent, and keeping abreast of an ever-changing jazz scene. With all the financial and health problems that confronted him near the end of his life, Herman was able to fall back on what he called "the great escape," his love of jazz music.

Herman did some vaudeville song-and-dance routines at an early age and worked the old Orpheum circuit as the "Boy Wonder of the Saxophone." At age 16, still in high school, he played as sideman in Joey Lichter's band at Eagles Million Dollar Ballroom in Milwaukee. In February 1931, Herman entered Brunswick recording studio in Chicago to cut his first records with bandleader Tom Gerun, and in 1932, waxed his first vocals. Leaving Gerun in 1934, he returned to Milwaukee, joined Harry Sosnik's band, and later, while touring with Gus Arnheim, met his next employer, famous composer-bandleader Isham Jones. Herman remained with Jones until September 1936 when Jones sought retirement. A hot contingent from the defunct Jones organization formed the nucleus for the band billed as Woody Herman & the Band That Plays the Blues. Originally a cooperative unit, the band employed a quasi-Dixieland style, struggling at the outset but eventually landing a Decca recording contract. Herman had the support of his new wife, Charlotte, and after scuffling for almost three years, had a big hit single with "Woodchopper's Ball," which really got things moving. The band landed in several movies, started playing major locations, and adopted a new theme song, "Blue Flame."

Tremendous personnel changes occurred in the Herman big band ranks during the early World War II years. By the end of 1944 Herman had assembled the orchestra that eventually became known as the First Herd. Broadcast via ABC-Radio every Saturday night, the orchestra featured wild ensembles, unison brass passages, and arrangements by Ralph Burns and Neal Hefti that were destined to become lasting big-band classics. Due to Herman family problems, the First Herd disbanded at the height of its popularity, after having won the 1946 Best Band awards in *Billboard* and *Metronome,* and Best Swing Band in *Down Beat.* In mid-1947, Herman reemerged with the Second Herd, also known as the Four Brothers Band. Keeping the Herds straight is difficult, but the leader himself dubbed his early 1950s band of swingers the Third Herd, which featured a more conservative, danceable style. By the summer of 1955 it was becoming increasingly grueling to maintain a big band, and Woody opted for taking an octet into the Las Vegas gig at the Riviera Hotel. The Herd that formed going into 1956 was a different group in personnel and conception, and by mid-1959 had been identified in an album title as the Fourth Herd. This gang made a U.S. State Department tour of South America, Central America, and the Caribbean in 1958, and upon return went into the recording studios with Tito Puente and a group of his Latin percussionists. The next year jobs were erratic and Herman, experiencing difficulties booking the big band, was often forced to work with smaller groups. The early 1960s saw the birth of the Swingin' Herd and a resurgence of interest in the Woody Herman Band. In the late 1960s and early 1970s the Herd of the moment experimented with electric piano and bass and entered into an era of fusion that lasted for approximately a decade. Tenor saxophonist Frank Tiberi joined in 1969 and remained for years as acting leader during Herman's illnesses and after his death in 1987. Herman and the New Thundering Herd celebrated the leader's 40th anniversary with a noteworthy Carnegie Hall concert on November 20, 1976 that featured some famous alumni along with younger Herdsmen. By the late 1970s the band was returning to a more swinging, straight-ahead approach. Herman's health was in a downward spiral, however, and his personal problems mounted, with pressure from the IRS relating to management problems over the years and the death of his wife. Like his characteristic Herdsmen, he was still full of thunder and enthusiasm and celebrated his 50th anniversary as a bandleader in 1986. Herman was in and out of hospitals until his death.

what to buy: The roar and bite of the First Herd is captured in *The Thundering Herds, 1945–47* (Columbia, 1988, prod. Michael Brooks), which allocates 14 tracks to the explosive 1945–46 band and two tracks to the Second Herd (a.k.a. the Four Brothers Band). Titles include Herman classics "Apple Honey," "Northwest Passage," "Wildroot," and "Your Father's Mustache," which, 50 years later, remain the ultimate in swinging big-band fare. The blues-tinged "Goosey Gander" and Neal Hefti's well-constructed "The Good Earth" (originally "Helen of Troy") are welcome additions to the mix. Al Cohn's "The Goof and I" and Jimmy Guiffre's well-known "Flour Brothers" are Second Herd selections featuring such Herman luminaries as Zoot Sims, Stan Getz, Herbie Steward, and Serge Chaloff in a powerhouse sax section. *The First Herd* (Le Jazz, 1996) is a generous set offering 17 tunes from the full orchestra's 1945–46 Columbia masters and six exciting Woodchopper-like Keynote sides. There is some overlap with the Columbia set, but this one includes some obscure minor classics like "Let It Snow" and "Put That Ring on My Finger." The First Herd collection *Woody Herman, the V-Disc Years, Vols. I & II, 1944–46* (Hep, 1994, prod. various) offers extended versions of many Herman delights ("Apple Honey," "Wildroot," and "Blowin' up a Storm"), plus songs never recorded commercially ("Red Top" and "Jones Beachhead"). The 19 tunes on *Keeper of the Flame: Complete Capitol Recordings of the Four Brothers Band* (Capitol, 1992, prod. Pete Welding, Michael Cuscuna) contain some of the best tracks by Herman's Second

Herd, which had a decided bop flavor. The lovely "Early Autumn" and "Tenderly" are here amidst the wacky "Lemon Drop" and swingers like "The Great Lie," "More Moon," and "Not Really the Blues."

what to buy next: A newly discovered treasure for Herman fans, *Jantzen Beach Oregon 1954* (Status, 1996, prod. Dave Kay) offers previously unissued live material and brings the Third Herd to the forefront in a 15-tune collection for a dance date. "Moten Swing" is handled neatly under the guise of "Moten Stomp," and charts for "Prez Conference," "Mulligantawny," and "Cohn's Alley" swing in a very relaxed groove as they pay tribute to legendary jazz performers such as Count Basie. *Verve Jazz Masters 54: Woody Herman* (Verve, 1996, prod. Jack Tracy) is a compilation of 13 driving examples by the 1960s band known as the Swingin' Herd. Herman's alto sax generates some exceptional moments on "Body and Soul" and "Deep Purple," and the entire band has a funky approach on "Sister Sadie," "Camel Walk," and "Better Git It in Your Soul." The live *Woody's Winners* (Columbia, 1965, prod. Teo Macero) highlights a slightly later edition of the band tearing it up. *The Best of Woody Herman & His Big Band: The Concord Years* collects 12 selections from nine earlier Concord Jazz albums recorded from September 1979 through March 1987. From the 1979 *Woody and Friends* comes "Woody 'n' You" (spotlighting guests Woody Shaw and Dizzy Gillespie along with arranger-trombonist Slide Hampton), and "What Are You Doing the Rest of Your Life?" (featuring gorgeous tenor saxisms by Herman alumnus Stan Getz). Excerpts from *Live at the Concord Jazz Festival 1981* spotlight tenor saxist Al Cohn on "Things Ain't What They Used to Be" and Getz on Bill Holman's arrangement of "The Dolphin," and offer a reprise of "Lemon Drop," a wacky bop tune from the Second Herd library.

best of the rest:

Live in Stereo at Marion, June 8, 1957 (Jazz Hour, 1957/1994)
Live at Peacock Lane, Hollywood 1958 (Jazz Hour, 1958/1994)
The Fourth Herd/New World of Woody Herman (Ultradisc, 1959–62/Mobile Fidelity, 1995)
The Raven Speaks (Original Jazz Classics, 1972)
Giant Steps (Original Jazz Classics, 1973/1996)
The Thundering Herd (Original Jazz Classics, 1974/1995)
Woody Herman Presents, Vol. I, A Concord Jam (Concord, 1981/1990)
Woody & Friends (Concord, 1981/1992)
Woody Herman Big Band Featuring Stan Getz Live at the Concord Jazz Festival (Concord, 1981/1997)
Woody Herman Presents, Vol. III, A Great American Evening (Concord, 1983)
World Class (Concord, 1984/1987)
50th Anniversary Tour (Concord, 1986)
Woody's Gold Star (Concord, 1987/1989)

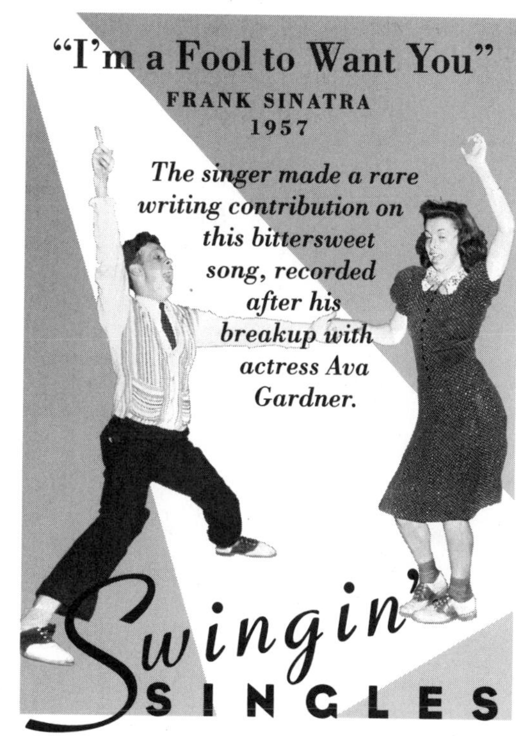

"I'm a Fool to Want You"
FRANK SINATRA
1957
The singer made a rare writing contribution on this bittersweet song, recorded after his breakup with actress Ava Gardner.
Swingin'
SINGLES

The Sound of Jazz (Cleopatra, 1988/1996)
Best of the Big Bands: Woody Herman (Sony/Columbia, 1990)
The Best of Woody Herman & His Orchestra (Curb/Capitol, 1990)
Blues on Parade (Decca/GRP, 1991)
The Herd Rides Again (Evidence, 1992)
Herman's Heat and Puente's Beat (Evidence, 1992)
Crown Royal (Laserlight, 1992)
(With Stan Getz) *Early Autumn* (RCA/Bluebird, 1992)
Blowing up a Storm (Drive, 1994)
The Essence of Woody Herman (Columbia/Legacy, 1994)
(With Tito Puente) *Blue Gardenia* (Laserlight, 1994)
At the Woodchopper's Ball (ASA/AJA, 1995)
Woody Herman & the Band That Plays the Blues (Circle, 1995)
At Lake Compounce 1959/Jantzen Beach '54 (Status, 1995)
Blues and the First Herd, Vol. I (Jazz Archives, 1996)
Amen 1937–42 (Aero Space, 1997)
Blues on Parade, 1938–41 (Aero Space, 1997)
This Is Jazz 24: Woody Herman (Sony/Columbia, 1997)
The Second Herd (Storyville, 1997)
Feelin' So Blue (Original Jazz Classics, 1997)
Concord Jazz Heritage Series (Concord Jazz, 1998)

worth searching for: *The 1940s—The Small Groups: New Directions* (Columbia, 1988, prod. Michael Brooks) contains

Woody Herman **(Archive Photos)**

selections from the Gene Krupa Trio, a Harry James octet, and 10 tracks (all jewels) from Woody Herman & the Woodchoppers, a small unit drawn from the First Herd. *Woody Herman Presents, Vol. II—Four Others* ♪♪♪♪ (Concord, 1982, prod. Carl E. Jefferson) features four of Woody Herman's stellar tenor sax players from separate, distinctive band periods forming a section and offering individual solos. Woody himself was on hand to set the tempos and approve the final takes, adding his sonorous alto to "Tenderly." Johnny Mandel's "Not Really the Blues," Al Cohn's "The Goof and I," and "Woody's Lament" sail along nicely with solid rhythm from pianist John Bunch, drummer Don Lamond, and bassist George Duvivier. Singer Rosemary Clooney headlines with the Woody Herman big band on *My Buddy* ♪♪♪♪ (Concord, 1983, prod. Carl E. Jefferson), working well with the band and Woody on an eight-tune set.

influences:

◀◀ Johnny Hodges, Benny Goodman, Barney Bigard, Duke Ellington, Jimmie Noone, Pee Wee Russell, Frank Teschemacher

▶▶ Stan Getz, Zoot Sims

John T. Bitter

Harriet Hilliard

See: Ozzie Nelson

Earl "Fatha" Hines

Born December 28, 1903, in Duquesne, PA. Died April 22, 1983, in Oakland, CA.

In addition to fronting a Chicago big band for 10 years and helping lay the swing era's foundation, pianist Earl "Fatha" Hines was an important player in several key jazz phases. He adapted Louis Armstrong's solo style to the piano, establishing the keyboard as an important central instrument even in big bands, and continued to innovate at the dawn of bebop. Singer Sarah Vaughan and saxophonist Charlie Parker were among the notables to pass through Hines's band, and the great bebop pianist Bud Powell drew heavily from Fatha's ideas.

Hines's first paying gigs were in Pittsburgh with vocalist Lois Deppe, and his move to Chicago in 1923 found him working with some of the city's top bands. It was while working for Carroll Dickerson in 1926 that Hines and Armstrong became associates. After some abortive attempts at a musical and commercial partnership (they ran a nightclub together with Zutty Singleton for less than a year), the two finally hooked up in 1928 for some primal jazz recordings, including their pivotal duet on a King Oliver tune, "Weather Bird." Few people played piano the way Hines did in the 1920s, with his right hand handling single-note improvisations as his left hand picked out counter-rhythms. It also fit Armstrong's vision for accompaniment—a loosening of the rhythmic straitjacket he had been playing in with his earlier Hot Five and Hot Seven groups. In 1928 Hines started his own band at the Grand Terrace, a gig that provided a steady base of income for the leader through the 1930s. During the early and mid-'40s, budding beboppers such Dizzy Gillespie, Parker, and Billy Eckstine passed through the band on their way into the history books. By the end of the decade however, the Grand Terrace well was starting to dry up and Hines folded his operation as a bandleader and joined Louis Armstrong's All-Stars for a four-year stint. During the 1950s Hines's career appeared to be in decline. He still fronted small groups after leaving Armstrong, but time seemed to be passing him by in pursuit of bop and cool jazz. By the time the 1960s rolled around, Hines was contemplating retirement. What changed all this was a series of 1964 concerts organized by jazz writer Stanley Dance. The Little Theater Concert of March 7, 1964, is often considered the turning point in Hines's later career. Playing solo and within a trio, Hines whipped through an assortment of medleys, covers, and originals that reminded the critics he was still a force. After that the pianist was in demand for solo and small group concerts around the world. In 1965 Hines played to enthusiastic audiences at the Newport, Monterey, and Berlin Jazz Festivals in addition to being elected to *Down Beat* magazine's Hall of Fame.

what to buy: *Earl Hines Plays Duke Ellington* (New World, 1988, prod. Bill Weilbacher) and *Earl Hines Plays Duke Ellington, Vol. II* (New World, 1997, prod. Bill Weilbacher) represent an Olympian nod to the greatest jazz composer from one of the idiom's most important pianists. Familiar classics such as "Sophisticated Lady," "Satin Doll," and "It Don't Mean a Thing" receive fresh treatments while lesser-known gems ("Heaven," "All Too Soon," and "Black Butterfly") shine with a similar glow. Hines could vamp forever on "Tea for Two" and never repeat the same idea, impressing listeners with his fecund imagination and wide harmonic palette, and *Tour de Force* (Black Lion, 1973/1990, prod. Stanley Dance, Alan Bates) and *Tour de Force Encore* (Black Lion, 1973, prod. Stanley Dance, Alan Bates) include a healthy dose of previously unreleased masterpieces. The periods covered in *1932–34* (Jazz Chronological Classics, 1995, prod. various), *1939–40* (Classics, 1996, prod. various), and *1941* (Jazz Chronological Classics, 1996, prod. various) document the high points in Hines's career as a big-band leader. This was the era when "Jelly, Jelly" and "Grand Terrace Shuffle" were hits and Hines's solo piano skills and concepts proved years ahead of his contemporaries in the eerily titled "Child of a Disordered Brain."

what to buy next: *Piano Solos* (Laserlight, 1992, prod. Dave Caughren), a compilation of 1974 recordings, is probably the best-bang-for-the-buck Hines CD around. Mostly covers of chestnuts ("I Want a Little Girl," "She's Funny That Way"), it also includes Hines singing like a cross between Charles Brown and Louis Armstrong on his own "So Can I." Hines did a lot of live recording at New York City's Village Vanguard, and *Grand Reunion* (Verve, 1995, prod. David A. Himmelstein, Don Schlitten), documenting a spring night in 1965, is up to his usual high standards, in some cases surpassing them. With jazz giants Roy Eldridge and Coleman Hawkins, the collection has a ton of Fats Waller, a few tastefully chosen Duke Ellington classics, and the usual batch of Broadway chestnuts. *Live at the Village Vanguard* (Columbia, 1988, prod. Frank Driggs) offers more well-chosen selections circa 1965. *Four Jazz Giants* (Solo Art, 1997, prod. E.D. Nunn) combines these classic tribute albums from the vinyl era into a two-CD set. Hines's solo recitals were always marvels of economy and thought no matter what high-flying pianistic riffs were bouncing off studio walls. While the W.C. Handy and Louis Armstrong dates got the most press, the swing-ready Hoagy Carmichael tunes such as "Rockin' Chair," "Stardust," and "Georgia on My Mind" suit Hines's sense of musical adventure even more.

best of the rest:

Earl Hines at Home (Delmark, 1969/1996)
Live at the New School (Chiaroscuro, 1973/1995)
(With Louis Armstrong) *Louis Armstrong and Earl Hines* (Columbia, 1989)
Earl Hines & the Duke's Men (Delmark, 1994)
Earl Hines Plays Cole Porter (New World, 1996)

worth searching for: The high-powered *The Legendary Little Theater Concert of 1964* (Muse, 1983, prod. Gary Giddins) generated the buzz that put Hines back into currency after decades of decreasing presence on the jazz scene. *Here Comes Earl Fatha Hines: Spontaneous Explorations* (Sony/Red Baron, 1982, prod. Bob Thiele) are part of *The Indispensable Earl Hines, Vols. V & VI: The Bob Thiele Sessions* (RCA/France, 1982, prod. Bob Thiele). Incredible solo piano playing combines with a trio date featuring a rhythm section of (then) young lions, bassist Richard Davis and drummer Elvin Jones. While the solo performances generate major heat, the versions of "Shoe Shine Boy" and "The Stanley Steamer" are album highlights.

influences:

◀◀ James P. Johnson

▶▶ Mary Lou Williams, Bud Powell, Nat King Cole, Jaki Byard

Garaud MacTaggart

Milt Hinton

Born June 23, 1910, in Vicksburg, MS.

A towering jazz figure for more than 65 years, bassist Milt Hinton's direct contributions to swing music came primarily during his 15 years in Cab Calloway's band—and, after 1951, with Bing Crosby, Louis Armstrong, Count Basie, and many other important figures. When he was a 13-year-old Chicago high school student, Hinton began playing violin, but soon discovered he could get more work as a bassist. After working with several well-known musicians, in 1936 he joined Calloway's band, and supplied the backbone for such seminal jives as "Minnie the Moocher" and "Are You All Reet?" Hinton has appeared on countless records as a sideman, including recordings with Ethel Waters, Billie Holiday (during her early years and again on 1958's *Lady in Satin*), Louis Armstrong, Eubie Blake, and many others. With Jackie Gleason's help, he broke into work as a studio musician in the 1950s, which allowed him to be at home with his family. In 1954, as a staff musician for CBS, Hinton became the bassist in a group that came to be known as the "New York Rhythm Section"—with pianist Hank Jones, guitarist Barry Galbraith, and drummer Osie Johnson—backing many of the popular entertainers of the era. Throughout the 1970s, 1980s, and 1990s Hinton traveled extensively, entertaining audiences around the world with his warmth and vitality, and continuing to exhibit his expertise at "slapping that bass." In 1988 he published the book *Bass Lines*, followed by *Overtime* in 1991.

what to buy: The Milt Hinton Trio's *Back to Bass-ics* (Progressive, 1984/1989, prod. Jane Jarvis, George H. Buck) contains a wide spectrum of tunes, including the swinging original "Cut Glass," written in collaboration with the masterful pianist Jane Jarvis. "Fascinatin' Rhythm" features Hinton "slapping the bass," an art he works at preserving. Jean Bach, who was responsible for the film *A Great Day in Harlem*, wrote the liner notes. Hinton and Jarvis sometimes perform together at Zinno, a club in New York City's Village.

what to buy next: Hinton, 85 years old when he recorded *Laughing at Life* (Columbia, 1995, prod. Frank Zuback), demonstrates his delightfully personal and intimate style.

best of the rest:

Old Man Time (Chiaroscuro, 1992)

worth searching for: Recorded as part of a National Public Radio series, Marian McPartland's *Piano Jazz with Guest Milt Hinton* (Concord/Jazz Alliance, 1995, prod. Shari Hutchinson) opens with Hinton's "rap poem," in which he charmingly describes his musical life.

influences:

◀◀ Jimmy Blanton

▶▶ Niels-Henning Orsted Pedersen, Brian Torff, Bob Haggart

Susan K. Berlowitz

Hipster Daddy-O & the Handgrenades

Formed 1997, in Tucson, AZ.

Mike Edwards (born Michael Edward Piek), vocals, guitars; Ty Lebsack, bass; Grant Lange, trumpet; Andrew Sternberg, saxophone; Daryl Seymour, drums; Kris Wiedeman, trombone.

A hybrid of swing, ska, and rockabilly, Hipster Daddy-O & the Handgrenades played their first gig at the Arizona Music Awards—and received an encore. After selling out shows across their home state, the group signed with Slimstyle Records.

what's available: With the mafia as its shtick, Hipster Daddy-O & the Handgrenades call themselves "America's most wanted band: the gangsters of swing." Playing off of that, the band uses a man with a horrific mafia accent to introduce them on their debut CD *Armed and Swingin'* (Slimstyle, 1998, prod. Mike Edwards): "Hey, yous, yeah, the one who just bought this CD, congratulatschkins on the most worthwhile investments you've ever made." The pain quickly goes away with the song "Daddy-O"—but pull out the Tums, it only goes downhill. Edwards uses gruff vocals, similar to Tim Armstrong of the punk band Rancid, to sound like an intimidating gangster. Be prepared to pull out the CD around the fourth song, "Cigar Smoke," during which Edwards sings "Got my cigar/Smokin' it/it's what I do/I'll blow my smoke in little circles/and make you blue/Smell the scent/let it overcome you." Ouch!

influences:

◀◀ Mustard Plug, the Pilfers

Christina Fuoco

Al Hirt

Born Alois Maxwell Hirt, November 7, 1922, in New Orleans, LA. Died April 27, 1999, in New Orleans, LA.

Wherever you hear the sound of Al Hirt's trumpet, a barbecue or block party can't be far behind. The top exponent of Dixieland jazz over the last 40-plus years, Hirt was an enormously gifted musician whose detractors complained he would rather play popular tunes than stretch the boundaries of his talents

Milt Hinton (© Jack Vartoogian)

on more challenging material. They obviously missed the point. Hirt was no supercilious bebopper too proud to take the bandstand with musicians of a lesser genre. He was an entertainer! He was the last of the old-style singing trumpeters with an unerring instinct for what his audiences wanted. He also played to please himself, which resonated with fans but infuriated purists. Perhaps he made it seem too easy; in a blindfold test, Miles Davis once lavishly praised Hirt's technique, but that only increased the ire of his critics.

A classically trained musician, Hirt divided the early part of his career between playing in symphony orchestras and working in the trumpet sections of the Tommy Dorsey, Jimmy Dorsey, Horace Heidt, and Ray McKinley bands. An eight-year stint as the leader of the house band at a New Orleans radio station led to Hirt's first recordings; he subsequently teamed with legendary clarinetist Pete Fountain. After Fountain left the combo in the late '50s to become a regular on *The Lawrence Welk Show,* Hirt signed with RCA. Under the guidance of Steve Sholes (who tamed Elvis Presley's sound for the mass market), Hirt released a series of top-selling singles, including "Java," "Cotton Candy," and "Fancy Pants," which drew inspiration from country-pop and gospel as much as Dixieland. Using his own Crescent City club as a base, Hirt's sound and bearded visage became synonymous with New Orleans. Throughout his peak years in the '60s, Hirt recorded extensively both as a solo act and in pairings with such singing celebrities as Brenda Lee and Ann-Margret, with more than three dozen of his LPs hitting the charts. Hirt's many TV appearances and high-profile concerts with major pops and symphony orchestras showcased his spectacular technique and won him new fans well into the '70s. In his later years, Hirt's weight-related health problems and a lip injury kept his name in the news more frequently than his trumpet playing. His best-selling singles still receive airplay on jazz and adult-contemporary radio stations worldwide.

what to buy: An outstanding introduction, *The Al Hirt Collection: Featuring Beauty and the Beard with Ann-Margret* (Razor & Tie, 1997, compilation prod. Mike Ragogna) has both Hirt's instrumental hits "Java," "Cotton Candy," and "Sugar Lips," and a complete reissue of his 1964 duet LP with Ann-Margret. Hirt's gruff-and-easy vocals perfectly accent the Hollywood sex-kitten's purring on such tracks as "Tain't What You Do," "Mutual Admiration Society," and "Personality," creating an irresistible chemistry.

what to buy next: If you want Hirt and nothing but Hirt, check out *That's a Plenty* (Pro Jazz, 1988/1996, compilation prod. Steve Vining) and *Al Hirt's Greatest Hits* (Pro Arte, 1990, compilation prod. Steve Vining), with all his adult-contemporary hits and finest instrumental moments from the early to late 1960s.

what to avoid: It's bad karma to knock a Christmas LP, but despite the generous 22-track lineup, *The Sound of Christmas* (RCA, 1992, prod. Steve Sholes) is an unusually weak seasonal LP, featuring bloated, sugary arrangements and a by-the-numbers approach from Hirt. Muzak from hell? Maybe so.

the rest:

Al Hirt/Pete Fountain: Super Jazz (Columbia, 1988)
Jazzin' at the Pops (Pro Arte, 1989)
All-Time Great Hits (RCA, 1989)
Cotton Candy (Pro Jazz, 1989/1993)
Al Hirt & the Alliance Hall Band: Dixieland's Greatest Hits (Pro Arte, 1991)
Raw Sugar, Sweet Sauce & Banana Pudd'n' (Monument, 1991)
Al Hirt & Guests: Dixieland's Greatest Hits (Intersound, 1994)
Brassman's Holiday (Hindsight, 1996)
Rainy Night in Georgia (Sony Special Products, 1996)
Best of Al Hirt (EMI/Capitol, 1996)
Al Hirt Live! (Laserlight, 1996)

worth searching for: A little corny, a little slick, and occasionally brilliant, the out-of-print *Our Man in New Orleans* (RCA, 1962, prod. Steve Sholes) is the quintessential Al Hirt LP. With the Anita Kerr singers providing occasional lyrical interludes, Hirt's trumpet embraces moods sassy and sensitive, wacky and warm. Many fans received their introduction to Hirt via this LP.

influences:

Harry James, Roy Eldridge

Herb Alpert, Doc Severinsen, the Baja Marimba Band

Ken Burke

Johnny Hodges

Born July 25, 1907, in Cambridge, MA. Died May 11, 1970, in New York, NY.

It's impossible to overemphasize the importance of Johnny Hodges's supremely lyrical but searingly hot alto saxophone sound to the Duke Ellington Orchestra, where he spent almost his entire career. Hodges was masterful on up-tempo flag wavers and could play supremely soulful blues, but his ballad work has never been surpassed. Only Benny Carter comes close to challenging Hodges for the title of greatest alto saxophonist of the '30s, and Hodges's influence is widespread today.

Hodges began playing soprano sax at age 14, modeling himself after his idol, Sidney Bechet, though he soon switched to alto and by 1940 had given up the smaller horn entirely. He developed his style early and never really changed it. Before he joined Ellington in 1928 he had played with Bechet, Chick Webb, Lucky Roberts, and Willie "the Lion" Smith, but it was a fateful day when he replaced Otto Hardwicke in Ellington's sax-

Johnny Hodges **(Archive)**

ophone section. Hodges soon became one of the orchestra's most important stars, a dependably brilliant improviser who inspired Ellington (and later Billy Strayhorn) to write countless pieces for him. His sound was a central element in the Ellington orchestra during its greatest decades of the '30s and '40s. The jazz world was shocked when Hodges left the orchestra to lead his own band in 1951, but the sax player had long felt underappreciated with Ellington. His group, which included a young John Coltrane, met some success, but ultimately Hodges decided to return to the security of the Ellington orchestra in 1955. He continued to record his own sessions, mostly on Verve, and remained with the Ellington band until his death. Though Hodges isn't exactly overlooked, neither is he as celebrated a figure as his music deserves.

what to buy: Recorded between 1938–39, *Hodge Podge* ♪♪♪♪♪ (Legacy/Epic, 1995, prod. Frank Driggs) brings together some of Hodges's classic small-group sessions. Featuring players from the Ellington orchestra, including Cootie Williams (trumpet), Lawrence Brown (trombone), and Ellington himself at the piano, the recordings were conceived as vehicles to highlight the overwhelming beauty of Hodges's alto (and some of his last tunes on soprano). An excellent introduction to this singular artist, *Passion Flower: 1940–46* ♪♪♪♪♪ (Bluebird, 1995, reissue prod. Orrin Keepnews) brings together two of Hodges's great small-group sessions with Ellington, performing such classics as Strayhorn's "Day Dream" and "Passion Flower" and Hodges's own "Good Queen Bess" and "Squaty Roo." *Everybody Knows Johnny Hodges* ♪♪♪♪♪ (Impulse!, 1964, prod. Bob Thiele) combines two records, the title one and *Inspired Abandon* by the Lawrence Brown All-Stars featuring Hodges.

what to buy next: A two-disc set recorded in 1961, *Johnny Hodges at Sportpalast, Berlin* ♪♪♪♪♪ (Pablo, 1993, prod. Norman Granz) features Hodges with a small Ellington-style group. The program mostly consists of short arrangements of Ellington's greatest hits, with the occasional standard thrown in, and Hodges sails through the tunes with his glorious tone as perfect as ever. Hodges is actually only present on the first half of *Caravan* ♪♪♪♪♪ (Prestige, 1992, reissue prod. Ed Michel), but the 12 previously rare tracks from 1947 are classics with gorgeous Billy Strayhorn arrangements (he's also at the piano).

best of the rest:

Triple Play ♪♪♪♪♪ (Bluebird, 1967/RCA Victor, 1996)
Complete Johnny Hodges Sessions: 1951–55 ♪♪♪♪♪ (Mosaic, 1989)
The Duke's Men: Small Groups, Vol. 1 ♪♪♪♪♪ (Columbia/Legacy, 1991)
The Duke's Men: Small Groups, Vol. 2 ♪♪♪♪♪ (Columbia/Legacy, 1993)

worth searching for: *A Smooth One* ♪♪♪♪♪ (Verve, 1979, prod. Norman Granz) features two big-band sessions from 1959–60 that went unreleased at the time. Hodges wrote almost all the material, but with a host of past and present Ellington members (Ben Webster, Jimmy Hamilton, Ray Nance, and Lawrence Brown, for starters) the music is familiarly Duke-ish. This double-LP has yet to be reissued on CD.

influences:

◄◄ Sidney Bechet

►► Charlie Parker, Marshal Royal, Norris Turney, Bobby Watson, Steve Wilson

Andrew Gilbert

Billie Holiday

Born Eleanora Fagan, April 7, 1915, in Baltimore, MD. Died July 17, 1959, in New York, NY.

Despite a tragic career that took her from the spotlight too soon, Billie Holiday ranks with Ella Fitzgerald as the greatest female vocalist in the history of jazz. Her unmistakable sound—a thin, airy voice and an ability to stretch lyrics into a completely unique style—made her the popular sensation of her day. Drugs, abusive relationships, and financial strains finally took their toll, but not before Holiday influenced entire generations of female vocalists—both in and out of the jazz world. Although she's remembered as a jazz icon and brilliant interpreter of pop standards, Holiday's career intersected many times with swing music: Her first recording dates were with Benny Goodman; she sang for Count Basie and Artie Shaw; she collaborated frequently with bandleader Teddy Wilson and saxophonist Lester Young; and her father, who abandoned her at an early age, was a guitarist in Fletcher Henderson's band.

Not much is known about Holiday's childhood, despite decades of investigation by jazz historians. We know she was abandoned by her father at an early age, and that he resurfaced only after she had become famous. Her mother moved to New York early on and left Holiday with relatives, whom Holiday later said abused her. Holiday began singing in Harlem nightclubs as a teenager, and was discovered in the 1930s by pioneering Columbia scout John Hammond, who set up recording dates between her and Benny Goodman. She also recorded with Teddy Wilson, establishing herself as a serious vocalist and eventually sealing a long-lasting partnership with Lester Young, the saxophonist who gave her the nickname "Lady Day." (Because, he said, her mother must have been a duchess.) Holiday and Young were a huge sensation in the late 1930s. Soon thereafter, she began singing for Count Basie and Artie Shaw, becoming one of the first black vocalists to sing for a white band. In 1939 she recorded her first rendition of "Strange Fruit," Lewis Allen's haunting song about a black lynching, and her career hit a fever pitch: she became known for specializing in sad ballads about hurtful relationships and love gone awry.

Swingin' Singles
"In the Mood"
GLENN MILLER
1939
Melody "borrowed" from Fletcher Henderson's "Hot and Anxious" (itself taken from "Tar Paper Stomp").

But that's when Holiday was introduced to opium and heroin by her first husband, James Monroe. She tried to beat the habit but eventually was jailed in 1947. Worse, her cabaret card—the license that allowed her to perform—was revoked, leaving her at the mercy of club owners who continued to book her but shortchanged her salary. Addicted to heroin, she continued to perform through the early 1950s, going on disastrous tours with Red Norvo and Charles Mingus. Finally, after her voice had deteriorated to the point where bad reviews were flowing in, Holiday went into isolation in the spring of 1959. After attending Lester Young's funeral in March, she went into a coma. Laid up in the hospital with liver and heart trouble, she finally suffered one last indignity: being fingerprinted and arrested—in bed, while dying—for drug possession. She died weeks later. Holiday's biography, while tragic, doesn't illustrate the impact she had on jazz vocalists, however. The unabashed emotional attachment she had with her lyrics, no matter what the song, hasn't been recreated in the 40 years since her death.

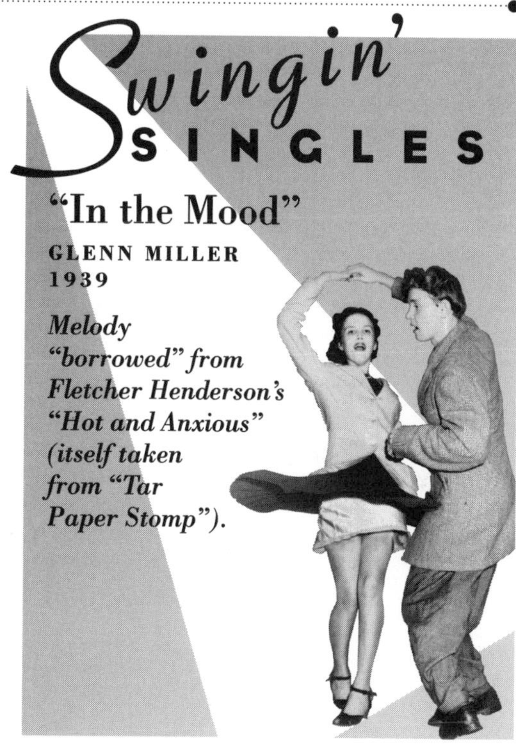

what to buy: Holiday's work is documented on more than 80 CDs and collections, but thanks to the archival genius of the CD age, it's very easy to reduce that number to a core, must-have collection. First of all, the title of Columbia's nine-volume retrospective series, *The Quintessential Billie Holiday* (Columbia, 1987–91, prod. John Hammond, Bernie Hanighen, reissue prod. Michael Brooks) is not far off the mark. In this chronological series of her work for the Columbia, Brunswick, and Vocalion labels, even the most dispensable set, *Vol. I, 1933–35*, contains great performances—"Miss Brown to You," "If You Were Mine"—as the new recording artist finds her sea legs. By the last CD, *Vol. IX, 1940–42*, Holiday's character and style are completely formed and she sings with absolute certainty on such definitive numbers as "God Bless the Child," "Solitude," and "Gloomy Sunday." For listeners who want to delve deeply into her creative process in the studio, *The Complete Commodore Recordings* (GRP, 1997, prod. Milt Gabler, reissue prod. Orrin Keepnews, Joel Dorn) is a two-CD set full of alternate takes (including a second take of "Strange Fruit") that give insight into her evolution from the jazz band-oriented style to full-blown pop. *The Complete Decca Recordings* (GRP, 1991, prod. Milt Gabler, reissue prod. Steven Lasker, Andy McKaie) covers Holiday's best performing period in only two CDs. She recorded only 36 sides for the label, and the definitive "Lover Man" sets the collection's tone. It includes a number of alternate takes but isn't as heavy with them as the Commodore collection. This is the most satisfying and consistent listening experience in Holiday's catalog. After her vacation in the reformatory, producer Norman Granz returned Holiday to jazz-oriented sessions. Her voice was raspier, and sometimes you can hear her struggle for the breath to finish a phrase, but there's a soulfulness that the ravages of abuse bring out in her voice that makes her stint with Granz nearly as memorable as her Decca years. Hence, the 10-CD *The Complete Billie Holiday on Verve 1945–49* (Verve, 1995, prod. various) is an indispensable collection of the work she did as she collapsed upon herself, including "Lady Sings the Blues," the tune written to capitalize on the title of her autobiography.

what to buy next: *Lady in Satin* (Columbia, 1986, prod. Ray Ellis, reissue prod. Michael Brooks) is based on the template of the original 1958 album that paired Holiday, at her request, with the easy-listening orchestral sounds of Ray Ellis. Technical wizardry creates a stereo take of *The End of a Love Affair*, which previously existed only in a mono master. The juxtaposition of her soulful but nearly shot voice and Ellis's extremely sweet strings gives the project a character it couldn't have had when she was younger. *Billie's Blues* (Blue Note, 1988) features Holiday's top concert recording, from a 1954 date in Europe.

what to avoid: Recorded early in 1959, *Last Recordings* (Verve, 1988, prod. Ray Ellis) is another date with Ellis, absent the triumph of *Lady in Satin*. Besides, you'll get the complete Verve set, right?

best of the rest:
Masters of Jazz, Vol. III ♪♪♪♪ (Storyville, 1987)
At Storyville ♪♪♪♪ (Black Lion, 1988)
Fine and Mellow ♪♪♪♪ (Collectables, 1990)
Lady in Autumn: The Best of the Verve Years ♪♪♪♪ (Verve, 1991)
Greatest Hits ♪♪♪ (Sony, 1998)

worth searching for: Issued by a now-defunct Italian bootleg label, *Live and Private Recordings in Chronological Order* ♪♪♪♪ (Jazz Up/New Sound Planet, 1989, prod. various) fills in a number of gaps. This set of 12 CDs (available in four boxes of three CDs each and also issued in a highly limited edition single box in Japan) features Holiday's only recording with Duke Ellington, "Big City Blues (The Saddest Tale)," plus recordings from radio and television and other sources such as private parties. With the first box covering 1935–45, the second 1949–53, the third 1954–56, and the fourth 1956–59, there's an obvious tilt towards the more uneven period of her career, and a few favorite songs recur with great frequency, so this is most suited to fanatical collectors. Some interviews with Holiday are scattered throughout.

influences:
◀◀ Bessie Smith, Louis Armstrong
▶▶ Frank Sinatra, Carmen McRae, Betty Carter, Madeline Peyroux

Carl Quintanilla and Salvatore Caputo

Claude Hopkins

Born August 24, 1903, in Alexandria, VA. Died February 19, 1984, in New York, NY.

Overshadowed by contemporaries throughout much of his career, pianist and bandleader Claude Hopkins's musical life is full of deferred dreams and missed opportunities. During the 1930s swing era, Hopkins and his big band often played such noted venues as the Roseland Ballroom and the Cotton Club, yet they recorded a scant few times and disbanded before they really developed a staunch audience. In addition to his big-band work, Hopkins served as musical director for Josephine Baker and also worked in a number of modest combos. A masterful stride pianist, Hopkins had the talent to play sophisticated lines and chords with his right hand while providing bass notes and outlining the chords with his left. During the '60s and '70s, Hopkins worked with such masters as Red Allen and Wild Bill Davison while occasionally fronting his own small groups.

what to buy: All Hopkins's big-band recordings from the '30s are on three CD reissues: *1932–34* ♪♪♪♪♪ (Jazz Chronological Classics, 1994), *1934–35* ♪♪♪♪ (Jazz Chronological Classics, 1994), and *1937–40* ♪♪♪♪ (Jazz Chronological Classics, 1994). The first set is the most essential, with some refined Jimmy Mundy arrangements and such imaginative soloists as clarinetist Edmund Hall.

worth searching for: *Yes Indeed* ♪♪♪♪ (Prestige-Swingville, 1960, prod. Esmond Edwards), *Let's Jam* ♪♪♪ (Prestige-Swingville, 1961, prod. Esmond Edwards), and *Swing Time* ♪♪♪♪ (Prestige-Swingville, 1963, prod. Esmond Edwards) are the three '60s sides Hopkins cut for Prestige—and it's a shame none of them have been reissued on CD.

influences:
◀◀ Jelly Roll Morton, Lil Hardin
▶▶ Earl Hines, Teddy Wilson, Jess Stacy, Dick Wellstood, Art Hodes

Chris Hovan

Hot Club of Cowtown

Formed 1997, in New York, NY.

Whit Smith, guitar, vocals; Elana Fremerman, fiddle, vocals; Billy Horton, upright bass, vocals.

One of the nice things about the revival of big-band swing is that it has also opened the doors for highly proficient western-swing outfits like Hot Club of Cowtown. Remarkably fluid, the drummerless Austin-based trio achieves a surprisingly full sound while synthesizing early pop, jazz, and country music into a danceable mix. Their clomping, chunky country rhythm gives solid support to free-flowing solos, and helps highlight understated, old-timey vocals. Hot Club pays homage to the likes of Bob Wills and His Texas Playboys, guitar wizard Django Reinhardt, and even fiddlemasters Joe Venuti and Johnny Gimble, without sacrificing their own unique stamp. Initially, Whit Smith and Elana Fremerman worked together in an 11-piece outfit called the Western Caravan. The club's early efforts to revitalize the genre's authentic sounds weren't fully appreciated in New York City; however, after moving to Texas and adding rock-solid bassist Billy Horton, Hot Club's sound jelled and audiences have been growing ever since.

what's available: You'll swear Bob Wills is alive when you hear *Swingin' Stampede* ♪♪♪♪ (HighTone, 1998, prod. Hot Club of Cowtown), which has such fine Wills remakes as "My Confession" and "End of the Line" (complete with a Tommy Duncan trademark, "Ahhh"), and guest fiddling from the legendary Johnny Gimble. This strong 14-track debut also features stunning versions of the old chestnuts "Chinatown, My Chinatown" and "Somebody Loves Me"—plus terrific instrumentals, "Snowflake Reel," "Red Bird," and "Sweet Jenny Lee."

influences:
◀◀ Bob Wills & His Texas Playboys, Milton Brown, Django Reinhardt, Joe Venuti, Johnny Gimble

Ken Burke

Hot Rize /Red Knuckles & the Trailblazers

Formed 1978, in Boulder, CO. Disbanded 1990.

Tim O'Brien, vocal, mandolin, fiddle; Pete Wernick, banjo; Nick Forster, bass; Charles Sawtelle, guitar. Former members include Mike Scap, guitar, vocals.

Hot Rize and their zany alter-egos, Red Knuckles & the Trailblazers, walked a fine line between folk, country, pop, jazz and bluegrass, and, surprisingly, rarely alienated anyone in the process. The group's lineup changed only once in nearly 15 years, even as they continued to diversify. Led by Tim O'Brien's folksy vocals and supplemented by the skillful playing of Pete "Dr. Banjo" Wernick, Hot Rize (named for the secret ingredient in Martha White flour, long associated with bluegrass music) first recorded in 1979. Three years later they introduced their counterparts, the Trailblazers (the name comes from Martha White's brand of dog food!) with "Waldo Otto" (Wernick) on steel guitar, "Wendell Mercantile" (Forster) playing lead guitar, "Slade" (Sawtelle) on bass, and the devilishly charming "Red Knuckles" (O'Brien) on lead vocals and rhythm guitar. Veering from bluegrass to explore more honky-tonk music and to showcase their gifts for humor, the Trailblazers were as much in demand (if not, they frequently joked, as well-treated) as Hot Rize. O'Brien had a Top 10 country hit in 1990, a duet with Kathy Mattea on "Battle Hymn of Love," and earlier, in 1986, Mattea had hit the Top 10 with O'Brien's "Walk the Way the Wind Blows." O'Brien also released solo albums and recorded duet albums with sister Mollie throughout the years Hot Rize was in existence. After the group broke up, Forster picked up a guitar and went on to host *E-Town,* the long-running National Public Radio music-and-environment variety show based in Boulder. In 1996 the band held a short reunion tour that was highlighted by their appearance on the Martha White Bluegrass Series at Nashville's historic Ryman Auditorium. Once again, Red Knuckles & the Trailblazers threatened to steal the show, but all ended well as fans were reminded why Hot Rize will be remembered as one of the most innovative and important bluegrass/traditional bands of the 1980s.

what to buy: *Untold Stories* (Sugar Hill, 1987, prod. Hot Rize) is an absolutely beautiful record with some solid bluegrass picking and O'Brien in fine voice.

what to buy next: The immensely entertaining *Take It Home* (Sugar Hill, 1990, prod. Hot Rize) is a thoroughly satisfying collection, and sadly, the band's last.

the rest:

Hot Rize (Flying Fish, 1979)
Radio Boogie (Flying Fish, 1981)
Red Knuckles & the Trailblazers/Hot Rize in Concert (Flying Fish, 1982/1984)
Hot Rize Presents Red Knuckles & the Trailblazers: Shades of the Past (Sugar Hill, 1988)
Traditional Ties (Sugar Hill, 1988)

solo outings:

Tim O'Brien:

Hard Year Blues (Flying Fish, 1991)
Odd Man In (Sugar Hill, 1991)
Rock in My Shoe (Sugar Hill, 1995)
Red on Blonde (Sugar Hill, 1996)
When No One's Around (Sugar Hill, 1997)

Pete Wernick:

(With others) *Dr. Banjo Steps Out* (Flying Fish, 1978/1992)
On a Roll (Sugar Hill, 1993)
I Tell You What! (Sugar Hill, 1996)

influences:

◀◀ Bill Monroe, Del McCoury, Bob Wills

▶▶ Sam Bush, Bela Fleck & the Flecktones, BR5-49, Jeff White

Stephen L. Betts

Hot Rod Lincoln

Formed 1992, in San Diego, CA.

Chris "Buzz" Campbell, vocals, guitar; Johnny G. d'Artenay, vocals, upright bass; Ty Cox, backing vocals, drums.

The rockabilly trio Hot Rod Lincoln has been courting both swing and roots-rock audiences since its inception. The band's bop-cat song stylings easily mesh with jazzier selections, and its rapid tempos appeal to both the saddle-shoe crowd and cowboy-boot contingent. The dominant characteristic of the group's sound is Buzz Campbell's Eddie Cochran/Brian Setzer-inspired electric guitar, which rings and wavers with vibrato and sway bar. Johnny G. d'Artenay can slap a bass as well as Elvis Presley sideman Bill Black ever did, and there is a decidedly heavy, big-band feel to Ty Cox's drumming. Wildly popular in San Diego, Hot Rod Lincoln has also toured top nightspots throughout the country and shared a stage with such acts as Jerry Lee Lewis, the Brian Setzer Orchestra, Chuck Berry, and Commander Cody & the Lost Planet Airmen. The LP *Blue Cafe* won the 1998 San Diego Music Award for Best Local Recording.

what's available: Many catalogs and online services still carry the group's debut *The Boulevard* (Dionysus, 1996. prod. Chris "Buzz" Campbell, Johnny G. d'Artenay), which contains 20 tracks of faithful rockabilly covers, solid original tunes, and a potent live version of "Swing Tango." Easier to find is *Blue Cafe* (Hep Cat, 1997, prod. Lee Rocker), produced by ex-

Stray Cat Lee Rocker with the title song written by Setzer. This interesting mix of such rockabilly standards as "Flying Saucers Rock 'n' Roll" and "Lonesome Train" with solid originals as "One More Part" and "Cattin' Around" is somewhat diffused by thin lead vocals, but the musicianship is excellent. The group makes overtures to the swing crowd with "Saddle Shoe Stomp" and "Please Please Please." Both discs are eminently danceable and fun, but Hot Rod Lincoln's best work likely hasn't made it on to record yet.

worth searching for: Hot Rod Lincoln provides all the excellent back-up on Josie Kreuzer's *Hot Rod Girl* (She Devil, 1997, prod. Josie Kreuzer), which features 12 of the rockabilly singer-songwriter's best tracks to date, including "Dead Man Walking," "Ball That Jack," and "Honey Pie."

influences:

⏪ Eddie Cochran, Johnny Cash, Johnny Burnette, Blasters, Stray Cats

⏩ Josie Kreuzer

Ken Burke

The Hucklebucks

Formed late 1990s, in Sacramento, CA.

Doug James, vocals, harp, saxophone; Bill La Rock, drums; Ken Marchese, guitar (1997); Greg Roberts, bass, vocals (1997); Robert Sidwell, guitar, vocals (1998–present); R.W. Grigsby, bass, vocals (1998–present).

Sort of a third-generation Roomful of Blues, the jump band the Hucklebucks clearly takes its cues from R&B shouter Big Joe Turner more than the complex horn patterns of swing-era stars like Benny Goodman. Using Doug James's horn and Robert Sidwell's rhythm-guitar backbone to nice effect on fast-paced originals like "Jive Train" and the standard "Cherry Wine," the band's primary strength is its rhythm section. But because James is a better saxman than singer, the Hucklebucks' CDs aren't hugely distinguishable from the other jump-blues/neo-swing glutting the market these days.

worth searching for: The band's two self-produced albums, *Coastin'* (1997, prod. the Hucklebucks) and *Everybody's in the Mood* (1998, prod. the Hucklebucks), mostly circulate at concerts and around the Sacramento area. At their strongest, the Hucklebucks combine harp, sax, and guitar solos for a squawking noise that nicely complements their fast-paced R&B backbone. But the band is still developing, and judging from the Hawaiian shirts and leis they wear on *Everybody's in the Mood*, we're betting they sound much crazier live than in the studio.

influences:

⏪ Roomful of Blues, Big Joe Turner, Ray Charles, Bill Haley, Ruth Brown, Rod Piazza, Stick McGhee

Steve Knopper

Helen Humes

Born June 23, 1913, in Louisville, KY. Died September 13, 1981.

Of all the Helens who recorded in the swing era, Helen Humes was more admired by her peers than, say, Helen Forrest or Helen O'Connell. Humes's skillful expressionism and supple ebullience could put across double-entendre blues, light pop, R&B, and sophisticated big-band jazz with equal skill and feeling. Humes first began recording at age 13, cutting racy novelty sides for the OKeh label, which her girlish voice infused (ever so slightly) with youthful innocence. She made the transition from bawdy blues to big-band swing working with orchestras led by Victor Andrade, Al Sears, and Stuff Smith. Humes cut her first sides as an adult with the Harry James Orchestra in 1937, but her work with Count Basie brought the initial blush of fame. Humes replaced Billie Holiday when Lady Day left Basie's outfit to join Artie Shaw. Basie then used Humes as a pop-singing counterpoint to the great blues shouter Jimmy Rushing, and recorded several well-received (if not high-selling) specialty numbers with her. She broke away to record freelance during the '40s, mixing raucous jump blues with tender, heartfelt balladry for a variety of bands and labels. So great was her command of genres that Humes was considered the perfect replacement for Lena Horne at a ritzy, sophisticated nightspot in 1941.

Humes never stuck with one trend for very long. Her two solo hits "E-Baba-Le-Ba" and "Million Dollar Secret" (a.k.a. "Helen's Advice") melded jazz and blues sass with the burgeoning R&B scene, but she was never comfortable being strictly labeled as a blues singer. She returned to jazz during the late '50s, cutting highly acclaimed LPs for the Contemporary label, and touring with Red Norvo before retiring to take care of her sickly mother. Humes reemerged at the Newport Jazz Festival in 1973. The overwhelmingly positive response resulted in fresh tours with Count Basie, and strong new LPs on various record labels. Humes's voice remained clear and youthful, and she experimented with variants of her style until she could sing no more.

what to buy: There's some mighty risque stuff on *1927–45* (Classics, 1996, prod. various), a 22-song set featuring her earliest recordings, and some swingy sides with Bill Doggett and Wild Bill Moore (a couple featuring Dizzy Gillespie). Some of the first rhythm and blues rumblings can be felt here. Equally fine is the import *Blues Prelude* (Pearl, 1998, compilation prod. Colin Brown, Tony Watts), a 24-song set with some of the Classics tracks, plus the hit "E-Baba-Le-Ba" and some tasty numbers with Count Basie.

what to buy next: Midway through her career Humes recorded some fine jazz discs, the best of which, *Songs I Like to Sing* (Contemporary, 1960/Original Jazz Classics, 1992, prod. Lester Koenig) and *Swingin' with Humes* (Contemporary, 1961/Original Jazz Classics, 1991, prod. Lester Koenig), have her wailing standards in a youthful, effervescent style.

the rest:

Tain't Nobody's Biz-ness If I Do (Contemporary, 1959/Original Jazz Classics, 1990)
On the Sunny Side of the Street (Black Lion, 1993)
Deed I Do (Contemporary, 1995)

worth searching for: From later in her career, the out-of-print *Helen Humes & the Muse All Stars* (Muse, 1994) is a strong jazz set boasting duets with Eddie "Cleanhead" Vinson and some fine small combo jams. It was her last shining moment.

influences:

◀◀ Ethel Waters, Ivie Anderson, Mildred Bailey, Billie Holiday

▶▶ Lena Horne, Esther Phillips, Dinah Washington, Ruth Brown

Ken Burke

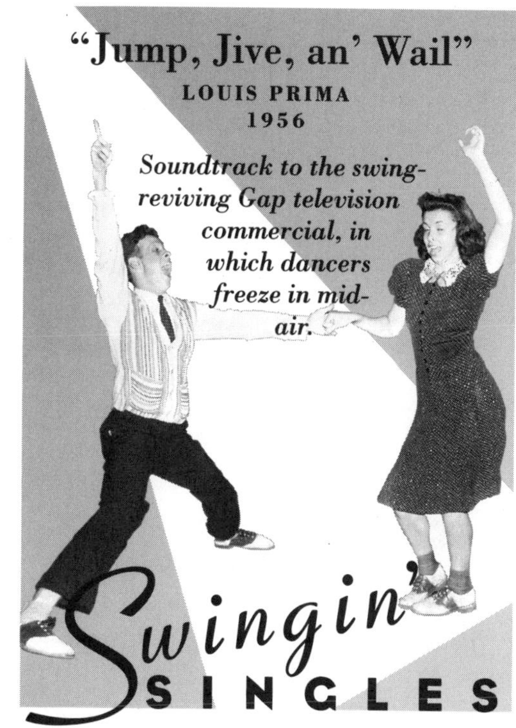

"Jump, Jive, an' Wail"
LOUIS PRIMA
1956
Soundtrack to the swing-reviving Gap television commercial, in which dancers freeze in mid-air.
Swingin' SINGLES

Betty Hutton

Born Elizabeth June Thornburg, February 26, 1921, in Battle Creek, MI.

With the ability to convincingly condense a four-hour Shakespearean epic into less than three minutes, the gall to hawk up a spit-glob in mid-song, and the balance to turn around and croon a straight standard, Betty Hutton's allure came as much from her honesty and versatility as it did her voice. Known primarily as a silver-screen blonde bombshell for her roles in films such as 1950's *Annie Get Your Gun* and 1952's *The Greatest Show on Earth,* the bulk of Hutton's hits in the '40s and '50s came from her movies. Though some were dismissed at the time as novelties, she refused to treat them as throwaways. Owing to Hutton's full-bore interpretations, the songs on both available CD compilations still stand strong. With a Rosie the Riveter-meets-Lucille Ball candidness, Hutton had the capacity to transform herself from sultry to silly, all the while remaining undeniably sexy. Considering she got her start singing for the customers of her mother's speakeasy (her father left the family when she was two years old), her blue-collar, street-smart attitude almost always rings true. Still, she could pull off an edgy vulnerability. Hutton regained a modicum of fame with a new generation in the '90s when Björk covered the swing-band Hanslang/Reisfeld number "It's Oh So Quiet," with the lyrics: "You blow a fuse/zing boom/the devil cuts loose/zing boom/so what's the use/wow bam/of falling in love?" In her version on 1995's *Post*, Björk remains faithful to Hutton's famous take, right down to the bordering-on-psychotic screams that accompany Hutton's inevitable charm. Hutton's life would hardly follow her rendition of Irving Berlin's uplifting "Blue Skies"—she lost all her millions, ran into problems with alcohol, and watched as her marriages failed. Recently, she has bounced back, cleaning up physically and mentally, even earning an acting degree. In the words of a certain rebel: "I Wake up in the Morning Feeling Fine."

what to buy: *Betty Hutton: Best of the RCA Years* (One Way, 1996, compilation prod. Terry Wachsmuth), released after Björk's version of "It's Oh So Quiet" returned the song to radio, begins with the "Shhh" that becomes more than a warning for Hutton's original whisper-to-a-screech. *RCA Years* includes some of Hutton's early work with bandleader Vincent Lopez. Unfortunately, the album's design is bare-bones, offering nowhere near the elaborate liner notes of the Columbia collection (it doesn't even list songwriters). The songs, however, fill in Hutton's story well, from the self-imposed stuttering on the ragtime-like "Who Kicked the Light Plug (Out of the Socket)" to the growls of "Murder, He Says" and the squeaks that punctuate "On the Other End of a Kiss." The collection does a fine job

Dick Hyman **(Archive Photos)**

of highlighting Hutton's usually smart, always expansive, range.

what to buy next: *Spotlight on Great Ladies of Song—Betty Hutton* (Capitol, 1994, compilation prod. Brad Benedict), with the song "A Square in the Social Circle," has Hutton singing "Take your blue blood and stick it in your fountain pen/She'll not only tell you she's got a muscle of steel/she'll go on to shout, anyone here wanna feel?" Nearly half of the songs are penned by Frank Loesser, including "Hamlet," a stripped-down, just-the-basics version of the Bard's classic. In contrast to the RCA collection, *Spotlight* contains detailed liner notes on each song, including take numbers.

influences:

◀◀ Jo Stafford, Billie Holiday, Bessie Smith, Frank Sinatra, Perry Como, Bing Crosby

▶▶ Björk, Rosemary Clooney

Jim Sheeler

Dick Hyman

Born Richard Roven Hyman, March 8, 1927, in New York, NY.

An impressively hard-working pianist and arranger, Dick Hyman is mostly known for his solo piano work and for scoring many Woody Allen films, including *The Purple Rose of Cairo* and *Radio Days*. Hyman studied classical music as a child and, while a student at Columbia University, won a set of music lessons with pianist Teddy Wilson through a radio station contest. Besides playing with Charlie Parker, Dizzy Gillespie, and Benny Goodman, Hyman served for years as a studio musician during the 1950s—and even did time as NBC's staff pianist from 1952 to 1957. While technically brilliant, Hyman arguably brings little to lounge music that listeners couldn't get from another, more innovative musician, and he rarely breaks out into the kind of swing music that inspires dancing. Still, his CDs serve as wonderful retrospectives of *other* pianists, from Duke Ellington to Jelly Roll Morton. It's in this role as jazz historian that Hyman has really made his name in the jazz world.

what to buy: While *The Great American Songbook* (MusicMasters, 1994, prod. Gregory K. Squires) features Hyman's solo work, it also highlights his ability to swing without the benefit of a rhythm section. The songs are some of the greatest hits by American composers: Cole Porter, George Gershwin, Irving Berlin, and Harold Arlen.

Hyman, with his trademark attention to detail, painstakingly recreates the music of Duke on *Plays Duke Ellington* (Reference, 1993, prod. J. Tamblyn Henderson Jr.). It's more of an homage than a true jazz album, but Hyman still knows his subject. "Prelude to a Kiss" is the highlight. On *Plays Fats Waller* (Reference, 1990), another fine tribute to a grandfather of the piano, Hyman pays respects to Waller—with songs like "Ain't Misbehavin'" and "Honeysuckle Rose"—while also making his own voice heard.

what to buy next: On *Music of Jelly Roll Morton* (Smithsonian, 1978), Hyman explores the artistry of maybe his greatest musical influence.

what to avoid: *Themes and Variations on "A Child Is Born"* (Chiaroscuro, 1977) is a strange and unfortunate album in which Hyman takes "A Child Is Born" and plays it in the style of 11 other pianists—from Jelly Roll Morton to George Shearing.

the rest:

Manhattan Jazz (MusicMasters, 1985)

worth searching for: *Stride Piano Summit* (Milestone, 1991) is a fun look at the style of stride piano, in which the left hand bounces up and down the keyboard, creating a bassy, swing feel. Hyman gets to show off a few technical skills in the process.

influences:

◀◀ Scott Joplin, Jelly Roll Morton, James Johnson, Fats Waller, Duke Ellington, Teddy Wilson.

▶▶ Marcus Roberts, Ralph Sharon, John Campbell

Carl Quintanilla

I

Indigo Swing

Formed 1994, in San Francisco, CA.

Johnny "The Swing Lover" Boyd, vocals; Baron Shul, tenor sax; William Beatty, piano; Bowen Brown (1995–present), drums; "Big Jim" Overton (1997–present), drums; Josh Workman, guitar (1996–present); Vance Ehlers (1997–present), stand-up bass.

Indigo Swing prides itself on reviving swing in the San Francisco Bay area. Instead of infusing pop and rock into swing, Indigo Swing stays true to the roots of the 1940s-inspired sound. Singer Johnny Boyd founded the band in 1994 and remains the only original member. Soon after hooking up with Baron Shul a year later, Indigo Swing played as a five-piece until solidifying the line-up with the current members. In the band's infancy, Boyd's vocal style leaned toward crooning, but he now prefers a more natural approach.

what to buy: *All Aboard!* (Time Bomb, 1998, prod. Bill Elliott, Indigo Swing) is an apropos name for Indigo Swing's sophomore effort. There are plenty of train references here among the boogie-woogie piano, double-shuffle drums and '40s-style swing. Unlike many of its contemporaries, Indigo Swing recorded mostly original material for *All Aboard*, with the exception of the cover of Willie Dixon's "Violent Love." The sweet, earnest ballad "How Lucky Can One Guy Be?" and the tongue-in-cheek-titled "(Today's the Day) I'm Glad I'm Not Dead" are stand-out tracks.

worth searching for: *Indigo Swing* ♪♪ (Welt & Placket, 1995, prod. Indigo Swing) shows the musical progression the band has made from 1995 to 1998—most notably because of Jim Overton's addition.

influences:

◀◀ Louis Jordan, Willie Dixon

▶▶ Atomic Fireballs

Christina Fuoco

J

Bullmoose Jackson

Born Benjamin Jackson, April 22, 1919, in Cleveland, OH. Died July 31, 1989, in Cleveland, OH.

To look at boogie saxophonist Bullmoose Jackson, you'd hardly peg him for a sex symbol. A lantern-jawed, bulbous-nosed giant, Jackson appealed to ladies with a voice like a bellows, a teasing swing with his tenor sax, and some of the most salacious songs ever written. His "Nosey Joe" outdoes Digital Underground's hip-hop classic "The Humpty Dance" for nasal nookie and his "Big Ten-Inch Record" has yet to be surpassed for its sheer virile audacity. Bullmoose indeed. Yet Jackson came to the fore not as an X-rated lungsman, but as a singer of dreamy swinging postwar melodies whose lilting version of "I Love You, Yes I Do" caused women to wilt in city after city. When the ballads stopped selling, King label head Syd Nathan turned Jackson's booming vocals to nastier items, and the change worked into the mid-1950s. When rock 'n' roll displaced him, Jackson became a janitor, his anonymity interrupted by one last splurge of musicianship in the late 1970s when a Pittsburgh jump band took him on tour.

what's available: *Badman Jackson, That's Me* ♪♪♪♪ (Charly, 1991, prod. Syd Nathan) contains most of the Moose's adult-oriented boogies and a few of the softer, swinging ballads. Aided by songwriters like Jerry Leiber, Mike Stoller, and Henry Glover, the Moose rampages on with "Ten Inch," "I Want a Bow-legged Woman," and "Big Fat Mamas are Back in Style Again." Not for kids or apostles of virtue.

influences:

◀◀ Wynonie Harris, Trevor Bacon

▶▶ Aerosmith, Taj Mahal

Steve Braun

Joe Jackson

Born August 11, 1954, in Burton-on-Trent, England.

Few artists have ever had a more wrongheaded assessment of their own relative strengths and weaknesses than this modestly talented journeyman pianist, whose early-'80s work foreshadowed the '90s swing revival. In hindsight, Jackson's first four albums sound like blueprints of the elements that went into his fifth album, 1982's brilliant lounge masterpiece *Night and Day*. Tying together the jittery new wave of *Look Sharp!* and *I'm the Man* with *Beat Crazy*'s third-world rhythms and the old-school jump blues of *Jumpin' Jive*, *Night and Day* plays as a seamless whole. It remains Jackson's commercial, conceptual, and aesthetic high point. Unfortunately, Jackson's stubbornness began to get the better of him shortly afterward. While he contented himself with flaky gimmicks like applause-free, three-sided live albums (1986's *Big World*) and the occasional soundtrack venture, his indulgences remained at least intermittently entertaining. But then he started hiring orchestras, succumbing to his own worst tendencies with a series of pointless and ill-conceived stabs at classical music. Although admirable in a to-thine-own-self-be-true way, Jackson's adamant refusal to be pigeonholed would count for more if better music came out of it.

what to buy: *Night and Day* ♪♪♪♪♪ (A&M, 1982, prod. David Kershenbaum, Joe Jackson) is a marvelous record, one that no civilized household should be without. With salsa and jazz flavorings added to Jackson's warmest-ever set of songs, *Night and Day* plays like a love letter to New York City. Equally warm is *Jumpin' Jive* ♪♪♪♪ (A&M, 1981/1999, prod. Joe Jackson), an all-covers homage to Louis Jordan and Cab Calloway. At the time of its release, *Jumpin' Jive* seemed like a one-off lark. But it hinted at the magnum opus to come with *Night and Day*, and today seems downright prescient in light of the punk-to-swing pipeline that opened in the '90s.

what to buy next: Although they have nothing to do with swing or lounge, Jackson's first three albums are all worthwhile, especially the debut *Look Sharp!* ♪♪♪♪ (A&M, 1979, prod. David Kershenbaum). There's not a weak cut anywhere, and for pure adrenaline rushes it's tough to beat the two "time" bookends (the opening "One More Time" and the closing "Got the Time").

Joe Jackson (© Ken Settle)

Although its reception was mixed at the time of its release, *Body and Soul* ♪♪♪♪ (A&M, 1984, prod. David Kershenbaum, Joe Jackson) has held up well. It reprises much of what made *Night and Day* so outstanding, but with material that isn't quite as strong.

what to avoid: Jackson's first major misstep was the all-instrumental *Will Power* ♪♪ (A&M, 1987, prod. Joe Jackson). Given an orchestra to work with, all he comes up with is stupefying sub-Stravinsky noodling. *Night Music* ♪♪ (Virgin, 1994, prod. Joe Jackson, Ed Roynesdal) is similarly dull, with chamber pop boring enough to induce narcolepsy. But the absolute low point is *Heaven & Hell* ♪ (Sony Classical, 1997, prod. Joe Jackson, Ed Roynesdal), an excruciatingly pretentious song cycle about the Seven Deadly Sins. Listening to Jackson hold forth on the subject of "pride"—on "Song of Daedalus," which concludes with him bellowing, "Call me God!"—might be the silliest listening experience this side of Spinal Tap's "Stonehenge."

the rest:
I'm the Man ♪♪♪♪ (A&M, 1979)
Beat Crazy ♪♪♪♪ (A&M, 1980)
Mike's Murder ♪♪♪ (Original Soundtrack) (A&M, 1983)
Big World ♪♪♪ (A&M, 1986)
Live 1980/86 ♪♪♪♪ (A&M, 1987)
Tucker: The Man and His Dream ♪♪♪ (Original Soundtrack) (A&M, 1988)
Blaze of Glory ♪♪♪ (A&M, 1989)
Laughter & Lust ♪♪♪ (Virgin, 1991)
Greatest Hits ♪♪♪♪ (A&M, 1996)

worth searching for: The import collection *This Is It: The A&M Years 1979–1989* ♪♪♪♪ (A&M U.K., 1997, prod. David Kershenbaum, Joe Jackson) is a pricey yet well-chosen two-disc sampler, much more complete than the 1996 U.S. single-disc *Greatest Hits*. Jackson also does a fine job covering "'Round Midnight" on *That's the Way I Feel Now: A Tribute to Thelonious Monk* ♪♪♪♪ (A&M, 1984, prod. Hal Wilner).

influences:
◄◄ Cole Porter, Cab Calloway, Louis Jordan, Randy Newman, Elvis Costello
►► Ben Folds Five

David Menconi

Wanda Jackson

Born October 20, 1937, in Maud, OK.

Whether rasping out gems of frustrated sensuality like "Mean Mean Man," sexual braggadocio à la "Fujiyama Mama," or joyously whooping through "Let's Have a Party," rockabilly heroine Wanda Jackson competed with male artists on her own terms. Her hot-tempered sexuality leaked through every fast song she ever recorded. Jackson was still a teenager when she first began crooning on her own radio show over KPLR in Oklahoma City during the early '50s. Discovered by country star Hank Thompson, she toured with his band, the Brazos Valley Boys, but his label wouldn't sign her because of her tender age. As a result, her 1954 hit duet with Billy Gray, "You Can't Have My Love," was released through Decca, where her sound was more or less modeled after Kitty Wells. Two years later, she was touring the South with up-and-comer Elvis Presley. When she complained about her lack of chart action, the King suggested she try recording rock 'n' roll and allowed her to browse through his blues collection. When Presley's popularity exploded, Jackson got the message loud and clear, and she began to growl out sexually aggressive rock 'n' roll from the female perspective. At Capitol Records, where she recorded with top musicians including guitarist Buck Owens, Jackson told producer Ken Nelson (who also worked with Gene Vincent & the Blue Caps) she wanted her records to sound just like Vincent's, echo chamber and all. Her first single in the new direction, "I Gotta Know," hit the country Top 20, but such truly great records as "Honey Bop," "Hot Dog! That Made Him Mad," and "Baby Loves Him" scared the bejeesus out of country and pop radio programmers. She didn't score a really big hit until, thanks to an Iowa disc jockey, her version of Presley's "Let's Have a Party" (recorded in 1958) became a surprise Top 40 entry in 1960. However, real rock 'n' roll was pretty much dead by then. After a full LP of fresh sounds failed to spawn hits, she concentrated on the country crossover market. Warbling sweet and pure on the ballads "Right or Wrong" and "In the Middle of a Heartache," Jackson finally achieved her niche in country music, where she became a constant chart presence until the early '70s. Although she sang the usual moralistic odes country crowds preferred (e.g., "Tears Will Be the Chaser for Your Wine" and "A Girl Don't Have to Drink to Have Fun"), Jackson often asserted the fiery, sometimes violent persona of her rockabilly sides. Her hits "The Box That It Came In" and "Big Iron Skillet" threatened death and/or brutal assault upon her lying, cheating spouse. Jackson found religion during the '70s and stopped recording secular material. She released several LPs of sacred songs on the Myrrh and Word labels and hosted her own religious program on cable TV. As with many of her contemporaries, the death of Elvis Presley renewed interest in her early sides. As the rockabilly revival built momentum, she began touring the world again, giving fans live renditions of her old hits mixed in with a little preaching.

what to buy: You could flip a coin and be equally satisfied with *Rockin' in the Country: The Best of Wanda Jackson* ♪♪♪♪♪ (Rhino, 1990, compilation prod. James Austin) or *Vintage Collection Series* ♪♪♪♪♪ (Capitol, 1996, compilation prod. John

Johnson). Both contain Jackson's sassy run of rockabilly records as well as her big country hits. With its inclusion of such politically incorrect country classics as "My Big Iron Skillet" and "The Box That It Came In," and the openly erotic "Savin' My Love," the Rhino set has the zingier edge. The Capitol collection has a couple more tracks and concentrates mainly on her fine rockers, including "Rock Your Baby," "I Gotta Know," and "Hard-Headed Women."

what to avoid: Recorded in Sweden, *Rock 'n' Roll Away Your Blues* ♪♪ (Varrick, 1986, prod. Kenth Larsson) contains mostly re-recordings of rock 'n' roll standards that sound canned and uninspired. For completists and fanatics only.

the rest:
Greatest Hits ♪♪♪ (Curb, 1979/1990)
Let's Have a Party ♪♪♪♪ (Charly, 1986/1992)

worth searching for: The German import *Right or Wrong* ♪♪♪♪ (Bear Family, 1993, compilation prod. Richard Weize), a four-disc, 124-song set, contains all her early recordings with Billy Gray on Decca and hot-boppin' numbers on Capitol. Every great rockabilly side Jackson ever barked out is here, as are her forays into pop and country crossover. Those deeply into Jackson's career as a mature country singer will want *Tears Will Be the Chaser for Your Wine* ♪♪♪ (Bear Family, 1997, compilation prod. Richard Weize), an eight-CD set of all her later Capitol recordings from 1963 to 1973. There's some real oddities here; songs sung in other languages, live tracks, and rare B-sides. It's all topped off with a brilliant booklet written by Colin Escott. Jackson also guests on Rosie Flores's *Rockabilly Filly* ♪♪♪ (HighTone, 1995), although their duet on "Rock Your Baby" is somewhat brief.

influences:
◀◀ Rose Maddox, Kitty Wells, Elvis Presley, Gene Vincent

▶▶ Loretta Lynn, Pam Tillis, Jan Browne, Rosie Flores, Kim Lenz

Ken Burke

Illinois Jacquet

Born Jean Baptiste Jacquet, October 31, 1922, in Broussard, LA.

Tenor saxophonist Illinois Jacquet was raised in Houston, Texas, which influenced the biting, full-bodied sound that often stretches into the instrument's upper range and came to be known as the "Texas tenor" style. Jacquet grew up on the stage as the youngest of the four Jacquet Brothers, a tap-dance team with the family orchestra led by father Gilbert. Jacquet began playing drums as a teenager before learning soprano and alto saxophone. In the late 1930s he performed in various bands before picking up the tenor sax in vibist Lionel Hampton's band. That's where Jacquet gained wider fame on May 26, 1942, for his legendary 64-bar honking solo on the original Hampton band single, "Flying Home." After his Hampton stint, Jacquet joined the Cab Calloway band (1943–44), and from 1945 to 1946 he worked with the Count Basie Orchestra, while occasionally leading his own groups. From 1950 he toured with Norman Granz's renowned Jazz at the Philharmonic bands as a principal soloist. Jacquet settled in New York and continued to tour Europe with the Texas Tenors, a group that included influential blues-based saxophonists Arnett Cobb and Buddy Tate. Jacquet worked as sideman to various groups and occasionally participated in all-star reunion bands with Hampton from the late 1960s through 1980. From 1984 into the 1990s, Jacquet led his own Jazz Legends big band. He became a less aggressive player, mellowing over the years, and his later playing took on the warm-toned, silken, mainstream influences of Coleman Hawkins and Lester Young.

what to buy: *The Soul Explosion* ♪♪♪♪♪ (Prestige, 1969/Original Jazz Classics, 1991, prod. Don Schlitten) is exactly what its title implies. Leading a 10-musician band, Jacquet delivers swinging, early R&B-influenced, soul-jazz arrangements enhanced by Milt Buckner's piano and organ playing. Whether waxing seductive on ballads such as the nine-minute "I'm a Fool to Want You" (performed as a quartet with Buckner, guitarist Wally Richardson, drummer Al Foster) or delivering the pulsating, full-band, title tune of equal duration, Jacquet's playing is fervid, full-bodied, and facile. Recorded five months later, *The Blues: That's Me!* ♪♪♪♪♪ (Prestige, 1969/Original Jazz Classics, 1991, prod. Don Schlitten) is not completely swinging, but dance fans will find suitable tempos in the romping Frank Foster tune, "Still King," and the shuffle-blues "Everyday I Have the Blues." A gorgeous bonus is the leader's exceptional (and rare) deep-toned bassoon solo on the smoky ballad standard "'Round Midnight," one of the best-ever covers of this song.

what to buy next: *Jacquet's Got It!* ♪♪♪♪♪ (Atlantic/Rhino, 1988, prod. Bob Porter), Jacquet's big-band album, is especially notable for swinging versions of Benny Goodman's "Stompin' at the Savoy" and the classic "Three Buckets of Jive." Jacquet coaxes raspy tones from his tenor and swinging tempos from his team on *Bottoms Up* ♪♪♪♪♪ (Prestige, 1968/Original Jazz Classics, 1989). Jacquet masters his original jumper, "Jivin' with Jack the Bellboy," with his deep-toned, sturdy sound and driving rhythms. The reissued CD adds a previously unissued take of the ballad "Don't Blame Me."

best of the rest:
Flying Home: The Best of the Verve Years ♪♪♪♪♪ (Verve, 1951–58/1994)
Flying Home ♪♪♪♪ (RCA Bluebird, 1962/1992)
The Comeback ♪♪♪♪ (Black Lion, 1971/1992)

Illinois Jacquet (© Jack Vartoogian)

influences:

◀◀ Herschel Young, Ben Webster, Coleman Hawkins

▶▶ Arnett Cobb, Willis "Gator Tail" Jackson, Joe Newman, Clark Terry, Houston Person, Stanley Turrentine, Buddy Tate, King Curtis, Scott Hamilton

Nancy Ann Lee

Harry James

Born March 15, 1916, in Albany, GA. Died July 5, 1983, in Las Vegas, NV.

Considering how we've deified Count Basie, Duke Ellington, and even Benny Goodman, it might come as some surprise that the top big-band leader between 1942 and 1946 was none other than Harry James. It was a glamorous time for the trumpet player, who was only 19 when he made his recording debut with Ben Pollack's big band, and just 21 when he joined Goodman's band. In 1939, James took his own group on the road. For a stretch, he was romantically involved with the band's sensuous vocalist, Helen Forrest (then he met Betty Grable, appeared in several films, and eventually married the Hollywood pin-up). The bebop era, which killed off most swing musicians' livelihoods, didn't end James's career. He simply cut his string section and continued to tour as the greatest white big-band trumpeter of his time. His final recording, done in 1979 for the specialty label Sheffield Labs, includes one of the strangest big-band covers ever, the theme from *Sanford and Son.*

what to buy: To truly get a taste of James you need to hear both his instrumentals and his work with vocalists like Dick Haymes and Helen Forrest. The three-disc *Bandstand Memories 1938–48* ♪♪♪♪ (Hindsight, 1994, prod. Pete Kline) is the best place to start. If you're interested in a smaller sampling, try *Best of the Big Bands* ♪♪♪♪ (Columbia, 1990, prod. Michael Brooks). The only difference between this and *Great Vocalists* ♪♪♪♪ (Columbia/Legacy, 1995) is more instrumentals.

what to buy next: Listening to *Jump Sauce 1943–44* ♪♪♪♪ (Viper's Nest, 1994) and *Always* ♪♪♪½ (Viper's Nest, 1994) is like stepping back in time. These radio shows were recorded in 1943, when James was at the peak of his popularity but couldn't put out a single 78 because shellac was needed for World War II. Thankfully, these acetates were recorded.

best of the rest:

Best of the Big Bands: Harry James and His Great Vocalists ♪♪♪½ (Columbia/Legacy, 1995)

Featuring Frank Sinatra ♪♪♪ (Columbia/Legacy, 1995)

worth searching for: *The Small Groups: New Directions* ♪♪♪♪ (Columbia, 1988, prod. Michael Brooks) features James on only two of the compilation's 17 songs, but it's worth getting if only to hear how the big-band era's stars—Woody Herman, Gene Krupa, and James—reacted to the new wave of bebop jazzmen. James's sextet swings so hard it almost bops.

influences:

◀◀ Louis Armstrong, Joe "King" Oliver

▶▶ Louis Belson, Buddy Rich, Harry Connick Jr.

Geoff Edgers

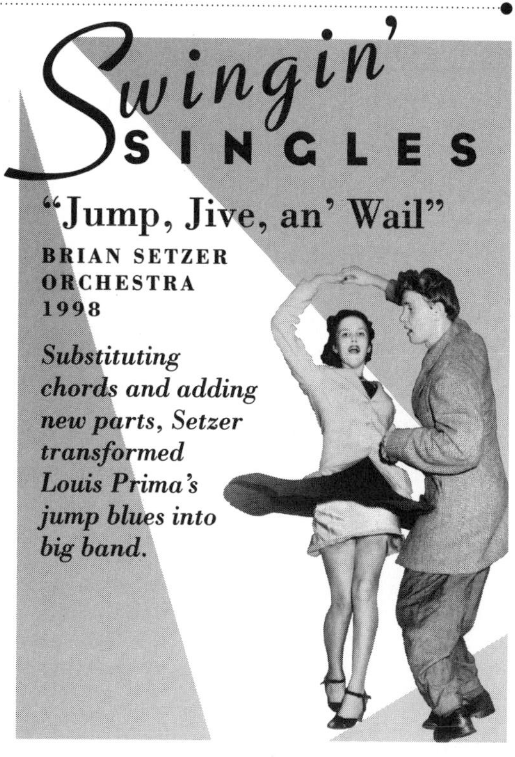

Swingin' SINGLES
"Jump, Jive, an' Wail"
BRIAN SETZER ORCHESTRA 1998
Substituting chords and adding new parts, Setzer transformed Louis Prima's jump blues into big band.

Gordon Jenkins

Born May 12, 1910, in Webster Groves, MO. Died May 1, 1984, in Malibu, CA.

One of the finest composers and arrangers of the big-band era, Jenkins brought semi-classical sounds to mainstream pop in the '50s. His expressionistic use of strings brought high drama to his own works and to works by such top vocalists as Judy Garland, Frank Sinatra, Nat King Cole, Eartha Kitt, and Peggy Lee. During the '30s, Jenkins's multi-instrumental ability gave him a special edge as an arranger, and the charts he supplied to bandleaders Isham Jones, Woody Herman, Vincent Lopez, and Benny Goodman heightened their respective sounds. A respected songwriter as well, Jenkins wrote or co-wrote such big hits as "Blue Prelude," "You Have Taken My Heart," "Homesick, That's All," "San Fernando Valley," and others. Jenkins conducted on Broadway and was the musical director of radio's *Dick Haymes Show* before he became a staff conductor at Decca Records in 1943. With his own orchestra, he recorded the hits "My Foolish Heart," "Bewitched," "Don't Cry Joe," and "I Don't See Me in Your Eyes Anymore," among others. Jenkins's greatest achievement as a composer/conductor was his symphonic ode to New York City, *Manhattan Tower,* an extended work released in a set of four 78 rpm records. At Decca, Jenkins was the first to recognize the potential of the Weavers, who scored massive hit versions of "Goodnight Irene" and "So Long, It's Been Good to Know Ya." After Jenkins left Decca for Capitol, his output as a solo artist and conductor slowed, although he continued arranging for the biggest names in the business. His relationship with Frank Sinatra was especially enduring. Not only did Jenkins arrange and conduct for two of Sinatra's most devastatingly moody LPs at Capitol (*No One Cares* and *All Alone*), but for his best LPs at Reprise as well. When Sinatra starred in his final film (*The First Deadly Sin*), he would let no one else but Jenkins compose the musical score.

what's available: Jenkins's original 1946 four-part series, *Manhattan Tower,* and "The Nightmare" from his *Seven Dreams* LP, are on *Collection* ♪♪♪♪ (Razor & Tie, 1997, prod. various), a definitive compilation of his most influential work as a composer, arranger, and hit producer. Also included are Jenkins's solo hits "I'm Forever Blowing Bubbles," "Bewitched," and "I Don't See Me in Your Eyes Anymore," as well as hit singles featuring the Weavers ("Tzena Tzena Tzena," "So Long, It's Been Good to Know Ya"), Billie Holiday ("God Bless the Child"), and Judy Garland with Dick Haymes ("For You, For Me, For Evermore"), among others.

worth searching for: Jenkins won a Grammy award for his work on Frank Sinatra's *September of My Years* ♪♪♪♪♪ (Capitol, 1965). His sensitive string arrangements encase Sinatra's melancholy with sweeping poignancy. Also, you can hear much more of Jenkins work with the Weavers on *Best of the Decca Years* ♪♪♪♪ (MCA, 1996, compilation prod. Marty Wesker), a solid compilation with Jenkins collaborations on eight of their biggest hits. Finally, Jenkins's later expanded version of his best conceptual piece is on *Gordon Jenkins's Complete Manhattan Tower* ♪♪♪♪ (Capitol, 1955), which is well worth owning for its superior fidelity.

influences:

◀◀ Isham Jones, George Gershwin, Andre Kostelanetz

▶▶ David Rose, Nelson Riddle

Ken Burke

Jet Set Six

Formed as Beat Positive, 1989, in New York, NY.

John Ceparano, vocals, guitar; Joseph Pelletier, bass, vocals; David Berger, drums, vocals; Steve Gluzband, trumpet; Jim Jedeikin, tenor sax; J. Walter Hawkes, trombone.

In a neo-swing world where who came first is as important as who sings the best, Jet Set Six has even more credibility than its more-celebrated peers, Royal Crown Revue and the Cherry Poppin' Daddies. Beginning in the late '80s as an experimental trio called Beat Positive, the band of punk-rock graduates tinkered with loungey, horn-enhanced songs from long-gone jazz eras. Recognizing the rebellious connections between Dean Martin and Johnny Rotten, the band performed as part of New York's ultrahip "cocktail nation" scene, wearing zoot suits and skinny ties. After one CD and a wave of personnel changes, the band finally accepted its swinging, dance-oriented identity and renamed itself Jet Set Six, after Tony Bennett's *Song for the Jet Set* album. They play regularly in New York City, Philadelphia, Florida, and other East Coast hotspots.

what to buy: *Livin' It Up* ♪♪♪♪ (Mutiny, 1998, prod. Dae Bennett), compared to similar-sounding 1998 releases by Big Bad Voodoo Daddy and Royal Crown Revue, barely registered on the heavily hyped swing movement's publicity scale. That's too bad, because Jet Set Six is consistently tighter than either of those bands, staking everything on a talented horn section and a strong sense of rhythm. Ceparano isn't much of a singer—there's a lot of that going around the neo-swing movement these days—but he tries really hard and sometimes sounds like the charismatic rock singer Freedy Johnston.

worth searching for: Beat Positive's sole CD, *Come Out Swingin'* ♪♪♪ (1994), came out before the band underwent personnel changes and the scattered swing bands around the country coalesced into a "scene."

influences:

◀◀ Frank Sinatra, Nelson Riddle, Tony Bennett, Dean Martin, Harry James, Glenn Miller

▶▶ Royal Crown Revue, Cherry Poppin' Daddies, Brian Setzer Orchestra, Big Bad Voodoo Daddy

Steve Knopper

Buddy Johnson

Born Woodrow Wilson Johnson, January 10, 1915, in Darlington, SC. Died February 9, 1977, in New York, NY.

Pianist, songwriter, vocalist, and bandleader Buddy Johnson led a very popular and influential swing band, which, after World War II, played a major role in the rise of R&B. His outfit's characteristic walking rhythm made it a favorite for dancers—and superb members, such as saxophonist Purvis Henson, vocalist Ella Johnson (his sister), and the great R&B singer Arthur Prysock, provided the strong solos. Johnson recorded for Decca from 1939 to 1952, when he signed with Mercury, and he continued to have hit recordings even in the early rock 'n' roll days. His big band,which served as the house band for Allan Freed's legendary early-rock dance parties, survived well into the 1950s, playing countless one-nighters. A number of Johnson's songs have become pop standards and have been recorded by such diverse artists as AnnieLaurie (with Paul Gayten), Lou Rawls, Ruth Brown, and Muddy Waters. Johnson retired from music in the early 1960s and devoted his remaining years to church activities. He became a minister before dying from cancer in 1977.

worth searching for: The British import *Walk 'Em: The Decca Sessions* (Decca, 1941–1952/Ace, 1996, prod. various, compilation prod. Richard Tapp, John Broven) is a wonderful collection of 24 performances, such as "Since I Fell for You," "Baby You're Always on My Mind," and "Satisfy My Soul." The four-disc German box *Buddy and Ella Johnson 1953–1964* (Bear Family, 1992, reissue prod. Richard Wieze) contains all the recordings Johnson made after leaving Decca, including plenty of terrific instrumentals and ballads from Ella Johnson. Even the in-print stuff is hard to find: *The Chronological Buddy Johnson 1939–1942* (Jazz Chronological Classics, 1998); *Go Ahead & Rock* (Collectables, 1991), also with Ella Johnson; and *Rockin' 'N' Rollin'* (Collectables, 1995).

influences:

Count Basie, Fletcher Henderson, Benny Goodman

Arthur Prysock, Ruth Brown, Bill Haley

Ron Weinstock

Pete Johnson

Born March 24, 1904, in Kansas City, MO. Died March 23, 1967, in Buffalo, NY.

Along with Albert Ammons and Meade Lux Lewis, bluesman Pete Johnson was the greatest of the boogie-woogie pianists. Initially a drummer who learned piano from his uncle, Johnson, with his firm left hand, became one of Kansas City's busiest solo pianists. He met blues shouter Joe Turner in the early 1930s, and the pair began their long residence at Sunset Crystal Palace. Producer John Hammond heard them and invited them to New York, where Johnson participated in Hammond's famous "From Spirituals to Swing" concerts at Carnegie Hall; he backed Turner and played with Ammons and Lewis as the Boogie Woogie Trio. Johnson moved to the West Coast from 1945 to 1950, then to Buffalo, New York, working often outside the music business.

what to buy: Two compilation albums contain some of Johnson's finest playing and historic performances from his Kansas City musical associates. *The Chronological Pete Johnson 1938–1939* (Jazz Chronological Classics, 1992, prod. various) combines his early Vocalion and Decca recordings, and *The Chronological Pete Johnson 1939–1941* (Jazz Chronological Classics, 1992, prod. various) contains sides from his Blue Note, Decca, and Victor recordings. The 1938–39 sides include Johnson piano solos from Don Whaley's Solo Art label, the Vocalion recordings of Joe Turner's "Roll 'Em Pete," and a jump-band session featuring Joe Turner's classic first recording of "Cherry Red" backed by trumpeter Hot Lips Page.

what to buy next: Joe Turner, with Pete Johnson's orchestra, appears on *Tell Me Pretty Baby* (Swingtime, 1949/Arhoolie, 1992, prod. Jack Lauderdale, Chris Strachwitz), which gathers classic recordings, including four Johnson instrumentals from the seminal black-owned label Swingtime. *The Boogie Woogie Trio,Vol. 1* (Storyville, 1994) is another valuable reissue with 10 recordings by the Boogie Woogie Trio originally on McGregor transcriptions, four 1947 concert tracks by Johnson with a rhythm section, and eight tracks by Meade Lux Lewis from radioair checks. Turner's *Boss of the Blues* (Atlantic, 1956/1981, prod. Nesuhi Ertegun, Jerry Wexler) reunited Johnson and Turner with a terrific group of swing-band veterans. Johnson is superb, particularly on "Roll 'Em Pete" and "Cherry Red."

the rest:

Pete's Blues (Savoy, 1946)
Central Avenue Boogie (Delmark, 1994)
The Chronological Pete Johnson 1944–1946 (Classics, 1997)
Radio Broadcasts, Film Soundtracks (1939–1947) (Document, 1998)

worth searching for: The invaluable British reissue *Boogie Woogie Boys 1938–1944* (Magpie, 1994) includes seven previously unissued Johnson (with Ammons and Lewis) tracks taken from acetate recordings of the Carnegie Hall "From Spirituals to Swing" concerts, the eight Victor duets by Johnson and Ammons, and 10 duets by Ammons and Johnson recorded originally for McGregor transcriptions.

influences:

Scott Joplin, Jelly Roll Morton

Jay McShann, Big Joe Duskin, Sammy Price

see also: *Big Joe Turner*

Ron Weinstock

Al Jolson

Born Asa Yoelson, on or about May 26, 1886, in Seredzius, Lithuania. Died October 23, 1950, in San Francisco, CA.

Al Jolson introduced popular music to swing. His delivery was syncopated and jazzed up, and it made him a musical-theater

Pete Johnson **(Archive Photos)**

sensation and pop's first recording star. The Shubert Theater Organization billed him as the "World's Greatest Entertainer." Today, listening to his affected, leathery "Mammy" voice overwhelming the mechanical recording horn, we might laugh at our ancestors' naïveté. Then again, how will future listeners who never had a chance to see performances by Elvis Presley, Michael Jackson, or Bruce Springsteen rate them based on recordings and videos?

Jolson brought to white American pop the first transition away from Europe's hold on performance styles. Influenced by a familiarity with jazz, he was never entirely comfortable with swing as a serious means of expression. His rhythmic tunes pulse with campy humor and an eye-rolling caricature of sexuality. When he gets "serious," his singing becomes decidedly more Old World. Jolson's audiences loved him, and the word from commentators who saw him live is that none of his recordings or movies captured the magic of his performances. He was born into a world where movies, radio, and recording did not yet exist, and he developed a love-hate relationship with those media. (That didn't keep his records from being hits, though.) Only on stage could Jolson tear down barriers between performer and audience. The humor of his ad-libs and asides rested on being able to step out of the "performance" into the world where the audience lived while still being part of the performance on stage. His dancing and humor also had a sexual brashness that was Elvis-like in scope but rarely comes across in the artifacts he left behind. Jolson's exuberant personality carried many a thin script and tune. He set up the world in which pop singers, by dint of their personality, could be stars. Still, when listening to Jolson it's important to remember that he wasn't a pop-music star but a musical-theater star. In fact, he was thought of mostly as a comedian until he began making movies. He sang to the back of the house and never learned how to be intimate with microphones and movie cameras. That task would be left to the next generation of singers, such as Bing Crosby and Judy Garland, whom Jolson influenced mightily.

Insecure and driven, Asa Yoelson was about 8 years old when he saw his mother screaming in the childbirth that killed her. An egotist who publicly was the brashest man on earth, Jolson sought constant reassurance. Yoelson became Jolson when he and his brother Harry were working in vaudeville in the early 1900s. That's also when he donned blackface (today an embarrassing reminder of America's racial troubles), which helped him overcome stage jitters and unleashed his overpoweringly sexy alter-ego. Jolie, as he called himself, recorded successively for the Victor, Columbia, Brunswick, American, and Decca record labels, starting in 1911 with two tunes from his stage vehicle, *Vera Violetta.* Despite unsympathetic orchestral backing, virtually everything he put out for Columbia was a hit in the years from 1913 to 1923. He was similarly successful at Brunswick from 1924 to 1930. However, a dispute with a Brunswick executive led Jolson to stay out of the recording studio until 1945, except for five songs he cut for American in 1932. Shortly before he began recording again, Jolson had a major part of his left lung removed—but you'd never know it from his full-voiced, powerful recordings. Listen through the leather, and you'll hear that Jolson could carry a tune beautifully and that he possessed a richly shaded voice and a fresh, spontaneous sense of phrasing. His return to recording can't be separated from the 1946 movie *The Jolson Story.* Jolson, 60, sang all the songs and did a remarkable job of coaching star Larry Parks to mimic his performances. It's one of the best jobs of lip-synching ever, and the mesmerizing tandem gives some clue to Jolson's on-stage power and appeal. After the movie, Jolson shook off a career decline, staying in the forefront of the show-business world until his death in 1950, by a heart attack brought on by a typically hard-driving schedule. He had only recently returned from performing 42 shows in seven days for U.S. troops in Korea.

what to buy: *The Best of the Decca Years* (MCA, 1992, compilation prod. Tony Natelli) is a thoroughly satisfying collection of songs associated with every phase of Jolson's career, including remakes of "Swanee," "April Showers," "Rock-a-Bye Your Baby with a Dixie Melody," "Anniversary Song," and a lively duet with Bing Crosby on the hoary "Alexander's Ragtime Band." Best of all, you don't have to listen "through" the recording process to really hear him; his voice comes bounding out of the speakers with all the salacious zest (if not all of the bottom) that he had in live performance. To top it off, orchestras by the postwar era had learned to play pop songs with a much more sympathetic and lively feel that perfectly supports Jolson's singing. This will do until a box set comes along containing all 71 titles he recorded for Decca. The most complete collection of Decca recordings is on cassette but not CD: *The Best of Al Jolson* (MCA, 1962).

what to buy next: *Let Me Sing and I'm Happy: Al Jolson at Warner Bros., 1926–1936* (Turner Classic Movies/Rhino, 1996, prod. Ian Whitcomb) fills in Jolson's big recording gap by culling songs from eight of his Warner Bros. movies, including *The Jazz Singer,* which was hailed then and is known today as "the first talkie" and the film that ended the silent movie age (it wasn't really). The performances, especially up-tempo numbers such as "I'm Sitting on Top of the World" and "There's a Rainbow Round My Shoulder," are winning, in stark contrast to Jolson's hammy "acting" in these flicks. A special treat is Jolson's interplay with Cab Calloway, who gives no hint of being uncomfortable with the former blackface performer on "I Love to Sing-A." *You Ain't Heard Nothin' Yet: Jolie's Finest Columbia*

Recordings ♪♪♪♪ (Columbia/Legacy, 1994, prod. Didier C. Deutsch) is more of historical interest than musical interest. The modern ears of all but the most extreme Jolson fanatics will need a special dose of imagination to hear the real Jolie in the relatively staid readings of such jumpers as "Swanee." Still, there's a thrill in hearing the original recordings, especially "naughty" novelties such as "O-Hi-O (O My! O!)," in which he opines "a country girl, you know, is just like a Ford/they're not so stylish/but the service, oh Lord!" This disc opens a window on musical scenes nearly 90 years gone.

the rest:

You Ain't Heard Nothin' Yet ♪♪♪♪ (ASV/Living Era, 1992)
The First Recordings, 1911–1916: You Made Me Love You ♪♪♪ (Stash, 1993)
Volume 1: Stage Highlights, 1911–1925 ♪♪♪ (Pearl Flapper, 1993)
Volume 2: The Salesman of Song 1911–1923 ♪♪♪ (Pearl Flapper, 1993)
The Jolson Story: Rock-a-Bye Your Baby ♪♪♪♪ (MCA, 1995)
Live ♪♪♪ (Laserlight, 1995)
Rainbow 'Round My Shoulder ♪♪♪♪ (MCA, 1995)
American Legends, Vol. 11 ♪♪♪ (Laserlight, 1996)
Legends of Big Band: Al Jolson ♪♪♪ (Intersound, 1996)
Volume 3: The Twenties—From Broadway to Hollywood ♪♪♪ (Pearl Flapper, 1996)
Al Jolson on Broadway ♪♪♪ (Intersound, 1997)
Golden Collection ♪♪♪ (IMG, 1997)
Great ♪♪♪ (Goldies, 1997)
Hits ♪♪♪ (Public Music, 1997)
Very Best of Al Jolson ♪♪♪ (Prism, 1997)
Barry Gray Show (1946) ♪♪♪ (On Stage DNA, 1998)
First Choice: Best of Al Jolson ♪♪♪ (Intersound, 1998)

influences:

◄◄ Bert Williams, Eddie Leonard

►► Bing Crosby, Judy Garland, Jerry Lee Lewis

Salvatore Caputo

Isham Jones

Born January 31, 1894, in Coalton, IA. Died October 19, 1956, in Hollywood, CA.

Isham Jones was one of the most successful and influential bandleaders of the '20s and '30s. He refined the "sweet" style of swing: reed-heavy, sentimental music perfect for the less demanding steps of dance-floor romance. Jones and his men could also wail hot and heavy, and their later recordings paved the way for Benny Goodman and Glenn Miller. Jones started his first band in 1912 and immediately established himself as a triple threat. Not content to just smile and wave a baton, he played saxophone, co-wrote arrangements (with Gordon Jenkins, Victor Young, and Joe Bishop), and most importantly, wrote songs, including "I'll See You in My Dreams," "When My Dream Boat Comes Home," and "It Had to Be You." His arrangement of Hoagy Carmichael's "Stardust" transformed the tune into the familiar romantic classic. His group was recognized as the best sweet band in the country, and its radio broadcasts were considered must-listen events. During the mid-'30s, with swing music well-established and his band at its popular peak, Jones suddenly retired due to illness. That's when a musician in his band, Woody Herman, hired several key men and began his long career as a bandleader. Jones came back the following year, but his career had lost considerable momentum, although appearances in such Hollywood features as *The Roaring Twenties* and *Incendiary Blonde* gave him a brief boost. By the mid-'40s, bandleading had become something of a hobby, and he tended to his interests in publishing, which had made him enormously wealthy.

what's available: Taken from ultra-crisp radio transcriptions, *Centennial Album* ♪♪♪♪ (Viper's Nest, 1994) features Jones's great bands from 1935 and 1937 playing a hotter blend of jazz than on earlier records. After Jones introduces a medley of his most famous compositions in the slower, sweet style, he allows his band to let fly on such brassy ditties as "King Porter Stomp," "Restless," and "Crazy Rhythm."

worth searching for: The out-of-print *Swingin' Down the Lane 1923–1930* ♪♪♪♪ (Memphis Archives, 1995, prod. Richard James Hite, Eddie Dattel) features a strong line-up of Jones's early sweet orchestras from the Brunswick era. Big hits such as "I'll See You in My Dreams," "That Certain Party," and "Nobody's Sweetheart" make this a must-have item for fans of the genre.

influences:

◄◄ Paul Whiteman, New Orleans Rhythm Kings

►► Gordon Jenkins, Kay Kyser, Sammy Kaye, Woody Herman, Benny Goodman

Ken Burke

Jo Jones

Born October 7, 1911, in Chicago, IL. Died September 3, 1985, in New York, NY.

With a career spanning 50 years, peaking with a long, influential stint in Count Basie's swing band, Jo Jones leads the short list of the most influential jazz drummers. His most significant innovation—marking rhythm on the cymbals while using the bass drum for occasional accents to drive the beat—was the inspiration for the early bebop drummers. He spent most of his career driving Basie's band, but found himself left behind when beboppers such as Charlie Parker and Dizzy Gillespie shifted jazz's focus from dance music to art music.

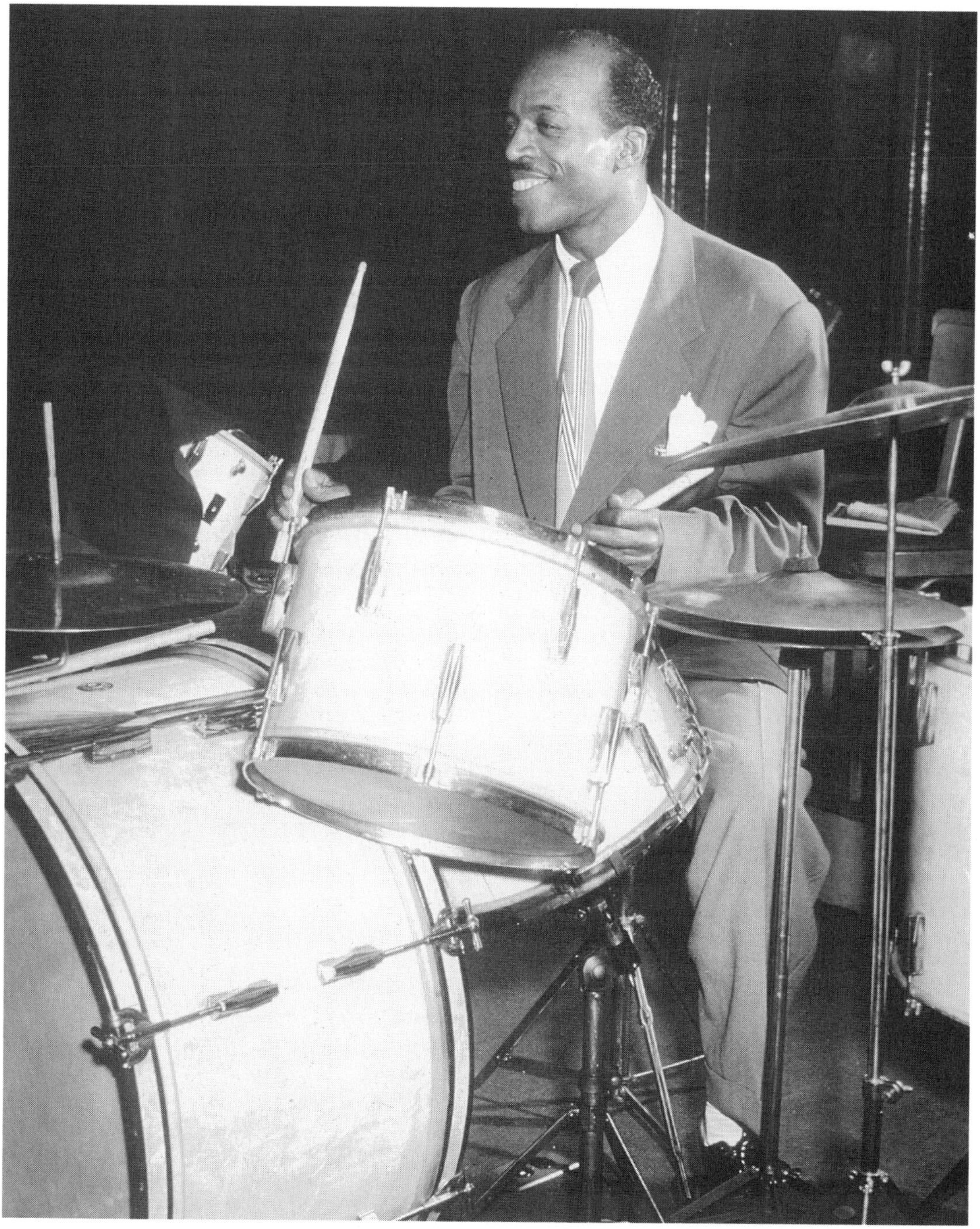

Jo Jones **(Archive Photos)**

Jones's long career began with a brief but formative experience as a tap dancer. His first appearances as a drummer were in the 1920s with territorial bands like Bennie Moten's. Beginning in 1934, Jones keyed the great Basie rhythm session of Jones, bassist Walter Page, guitarist Freddie Green, and Basie himself on piano. This group produced a rhythmic pulse unlike any heard before, propulsive but never over-driven. Throughout the 1930s and 1940s, Jones's fame and influence were at a peak, and he found the opportunity to record with virtually every significant jazz artist of the era. Despite these side ventures, Jones remained on staff with the Basie band for 14 years, until leaving for good in 1948. By the 1950s, he was a dinosaur of the swing era, revered for both his drumming and his famous and ever-present grin. Producers Norman Granz and John Hammond matched Jones with other swing veterans for some memorable sessions, but only a few with Jones as the front man. Unsurpassed as a timekeeper, he was at his best playing rhythm behind the band. But Jones also came to be known for his distinctive drum solos, which never fail to bring the rhythms of tap dance to mind. Despite failing health in his last years, "Papa" Jones remained on the jazz scene as a performer and storyteller up until the time of his death in 1985.

what to buy: Jones recorded two LP albums for Vanguard in the 1950s, now reissued together as *The Essential Jo Jones* ♪♪♪♪ (Vanguard, 1977/1995, prod. John Hammond). The first album, *The Jo Jones Special*, a longtime favorite of Basie fans, reunites Jones with Walter Page, Freddie Green, and (on one track) Basie himself. Soloists include the under-recorded trumpeter Emmett Berry and tenor saxophonist Lucky Thompson, both in good form. The sleeper, however, is the second album, *The Jo Jones Trio*. There are no fireworks here, just a well-drilled trio (which features the young Ray Bryant on piano) and some of the finest small-ensemble drumming anywhere.

what to buy next: *The Main Man* ♪♪♪ (Original Jazz Classics, 1976/1995, prod. Norman Granz) finds Jones in the friendly company of swing-era veterans such as Roy Eldridge, Harry Edison, Eddie "Lockjaw" Davis, and his old Basie partner, Freddie Green. The aging bandmates may have lost some of their fire, but fans of these artists will appreciate this good-natured session.

worth searching for: Jones's association with Verve in the 1950s resulted in many fine sessions with such greats as Ben Webster, Johnny Hodges, Coleman Hawkins, Roy Eldridge, and Benny Carter. A sentimental favorite would have to be the Lester Young/Teddy Wilson album *Pres and Teddy* ♪♪♪♪ (Verve, 1956/1986, prod. Norman Granz). The ravaged beauty of Lester Young's late work is not to all tastes, but true "Pres" fans will want this great quartet session.

influences:

◀◀ Baby Dodds

▶▶ Max Roach, Shadow Wilson, Kenny Clarke

Will Bickart

Johnny Jones

Born November 1, 1924, in Jackson, MS. Died November 19, 1964, in Chicago, IL.

Every retrospective of this well-connected and hugely talented artist takes on a sad "if only . . . " tone. Boogie master "Little Johnny" Jones, the piano-playing equal of Otis Spann (who was possibly his cousin), Floyd Dixon, and Charles Brown, moved from Mississippi to Chicago in 1946 and almost immediately found work in the guitarist Tampa Red's band. What made him famous, though, was the octane he added to Elmore James's legendary band and classic 1950s singles; he had powerful fingers and could quickly bring a lackluster song to life. If he had lived, he could have been one of the most famous backup pianists in blues history, but he died far too young of lung cancer.

what's available: There are a few essential boogie-woogie piano records, and the underheralded *Johnny Jones with Billy Boy Arnold* ♪♪♪♪ (Alligator, 1979, prod. Norman Dayron) is clearly one of them; recorded at Chicago's Fickle Pickle club in 1963, it's a terrific document of Jones's deceptively smooth piano style (backed sparsely by harpist Arnold). At first, on Lowell Fulson's straightforward two-fister "I Believe I'll Give It Up," Jones sounds too clunky, like he's trying to bash his way through the song, but when the rhythm clicks it's as smooth as anything Nat King Cole has ever done.

influences:

◀◀ Charles Brown, Jimmy Yancey, Otis Spann, Ray Charles, Professor Longhair

▶▶ Dr. John, Little Richard, Jerry Lee Lewis

Steve Knopper

Quincy Jones

Born March 14, 1933, in Chicago, IL.

Despite Quincy Jones's numerous contributions to jazz, he's probably still best known as the man who gave Michael Jackson his *Thriller* and the only man respected enough by his peers to have pulled off the "We are the World"studio session. He was also heavily influenced by the swing era, working with the Count Basie Orchestra when it backed Frank Sinatra in the '60s, and coming up with jumping singles such as 1962's marriage of soul, Latin, and big-band music, "Soul Bossa Nova."

Jones started his career as a jazz trumpeter, forming a band with Ray Charles at age 14 and playing with Lionel Hampton before he was old enough to drive. After winning a scholarship in his teens and attending Boston's Berklee School Music, he was invited to write arrangements for Oscar Pettiford and began hobnobbing with the likes of Miles Davis, Charlie Parker, Dizzy Gillespie, and Thelonious Monk. Returning to New York in 1961, he became one of the first African Americans to become a music industry executive, as a vice president for Mercury Records (for whom he recorded "Soul Bossa Nova" with Lalo Schifrin and jazzman Rahsaan Roland Kirk). He began producing and playing on other people's sessions and continued to arrange, winning Grammy awards for his 1963 arrangement of the Basie orchestra's "I Can't Stop Loving You" and Frank Sinatra's "Fly Me to the Moon." He cemented his producing preeminence in the '70s with his work for Aretha Franklin, the *Roots* miniseries soundtrack, and Michael Jackson's monster hits *Off the Wall* and *Thriller*. Jones was at the center of some of the most important projects of the '80s, producing "We Are the World" as well as Steven Spielberg's film *The Color Purple*. In the 1990s, Jones was honored with a Grammy Legend award; saw the release of his film biography, *Listen Up: The Lives of Quincy Jones*; produced the hit TV sitcom *Fresh Prince of Bel-Air*; launched the hip-hop music magazine *Vibe* and a spinoff television version; and released *Miles and Quincy Live at Montreux*, a document of Miles Davis's final recording. On an astounding variety of fronts, "Q" continues to prove he is one of the essential cogs of the entertainment industry machine.

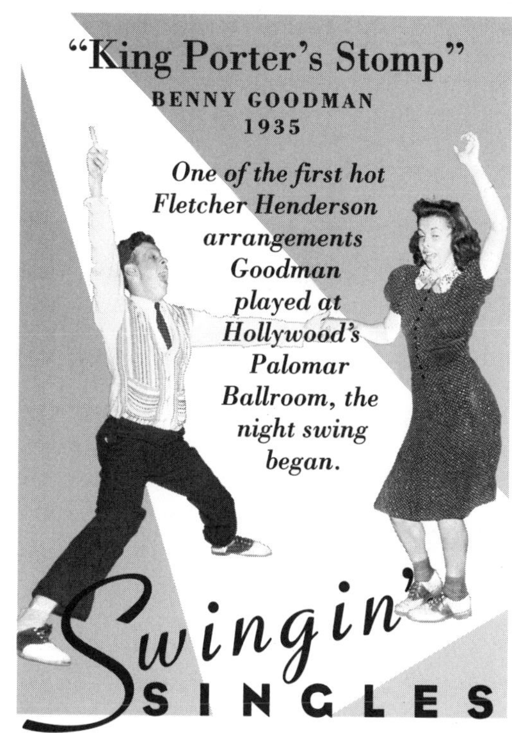
"King Porter's Stomp"
BENNY GOODMAN
1935
One of the first hot Fletcher Henderson arrangements Goodman played at Hollywood's Palomar Ballroom, the night swing began.
Swingin'
SINGLES

what to buy: Of Jones's several greatest-hits packages, *The Best of Quincy Jones* (A&M, 1981, prod. Quincy Jones) is the standout, combining his best efforts for A&M ("Killer Joe," "Smackwater Jack") with key tracks off his blistering pop albums, like 1974's *Body Heat*. *The Best, Vol. 2* (Rebound, 1988) celebrates Q's TV themes, like the streetwise *Sanford and Son* music and the kooky "Hikky-Burr" scat from *The Bill Cosby Show*.

what to buy next: The best feature of *Back on the Block* (Qwest, 1989), like many projects from Quincy the Great, is a guest list that reads like a Who's Who of the music world: Sarah Vaughan, Dionne Warwick, George Benson, Ray Charles, Miles Davis, Ella Fitzgerald, Dizzy Gillespie, Luther Vandross, Ice T, Sheila E, Take 6,Chaka Khan, James Moody, and Kool Moe Dee. Some nitpicky music critics with horns for brains complain that Q steers clear of jazz and instead puts together a buffet of run-of-the-mill urban pop. What do they know? The LP was still a huge Grammy-winning hit and features some the best work Jones has ever done. *Pawnbroker/Deadly Affair* (Verve, 1996, prod. Quincy Jones) is a recently re-released double dip soundtrack that features some scintillating Quincy Jones compositions, particularly "Main Theme to the Pawnbroker."

what to avoid: Too much of a good thing can sometimes be a bad thing, and *Q's Jook Joint* (Qwest, 1995) proves that adage true. This dispassionate rehashing of old formulas shows Q must constantly guard against letting his power spin out of control. There are brief cameos by literally hundreds of superstar performers, but all that's not enough to keep *Jook* from being a gyp.

the rest:

This Is How I Feel About Jazz (UNI/Impulse!, 1957/1992)
In the Heat of the Night/They Call Me Mister Tibbs! (Original Soundtracks) (MGM, 1967/1970/Rykodisc, 1998)
Roots (A&M, 1977/1997)
The Quintessence (MCA Jazz/Impulse!, 1986)
Quincy Jones: Compact Jazz Series (Verve, 1989)
Sarah Vaughan/Quincy Jones, "Misty" (Mercury, 1990)
Miles Davis & Quincy Jones Live at Montreux (Warner Bros., 1993)
Pure Delight: The Essence of Quincy Jones and His Orchestra, 1953–1964 (Razor & Tie, 1995)
Greatest Hits (A&M, 1996)
Q Live in Paris Circa 1960 (Qwest, 1996)
Jazz 'Round Midnight (Verve, 1997)
From Q, with Love (Qwest/Warner Bros., 1999)

worth searching for: With Jones at his artistic and career peak, the out-of-print *Walking in Space* (A&M, 1969) is a return to the big-band styles with contemporary flair that resurrected Q's rep as a bandleader and artist after a long spell of hacking for Hollywood. Mindful of the modern era, Jones merges old styles with new, blending in electric instruments and pop music while making a sizzling version of "Hair" (from the hit Broadway show) the album's hallmark. At the same time, he gathered some of the best jazz musicians of his age—Freddie Hubbard, Roland Kirk, Hubert Laws, J.J. Johnson, Jimmy Cleveland—to add their expertise.

influences:

◀◀ Clark Terry, Dizzy Gillespie, Ray Charles, Lionel Hampton

▶▶ Thad Jones, Gil Evans, Benny Carter, Mel Lewis, the Brothers Johnson, George Benson, Michael Jackson, James Ingram, Patti Austin, Patrice Rushen, Luther Vandross, Prince, Maxwell

Chris Tower and Steve Knopper

Spike Jones

Born Lindley Armstrong Jones, December 14, 1911, in Long Beach, CA. Died May 1, 1965, in Bel Air, CA.

Among Spike Jones's many musical accomplishments over his 30-plus-year career, perhaps his biggest was introducing such instruments as the latriophone (a toilet seat strung with wire) and the burpaphone (self-explanatory) to the lexicon of American popular music. Much more than a novelty act, Jones was a musical visionary. "I'm the dandruff in longhair music," Jones has said about his comical presence in the world of more serious bandleaders in the '50s and '60s. In fact, a lot of the over-the-top elements in modern swing can be traced to Jones's wacky antics and inspired vision. Like some of today's top swing bands, Jones had the gift of never taking himself too seriously. He began his career as a studio musician drummer, playing on Bing Crosby's monster hit "White Christmas." Bored by conventional music, Jones began to add unusual instruments to his drum set and set out to form a band to fulfill his zany vision. In the early '40s, he formed the City Slickers, and Jones turned the world of popular music on its ear with crazy parodies and bizarre musical collages. The band's unlikely first hit was 1942's Hitler spoof "Der Fuehrer's Face," on the basis of which the band successfully toured the country. By the late '40s Jones had expanded the band's live shows to include midgets, jugglers, and other loony acts, while scoring on the charts with song interpretations like "Cocktails for Two"—replete with a hiccuping chorus. Jones and the band appeared in several films and brought their brand of musical folly to TV in the '50s and early '60s with four versions of *The Spike Jones Show.* Jones died of emphysema in 1965, but not before establishing himself as one of the true musical pioneers of the 20th century, and easily the most hilarious.

what to buy: Among the numerous greatest-hits packages is an inspired sampling of Jones's lunacy on *Musical Depreciation Revue: The Spike Jones Revue* (Rhino, 1994, prod. various), which features 40 classics, including the funniest song ever written about Hitler, "Der Fuehrer's Face," his famous gargling rendition of "William Tell's Overture," and the swinging "Hotcha Cornia." Jones is at his hilarious best on *Radio Years, Volume 1* (Rhino, 1993, prod. Ken Greenwald), which features two complete post–World War II radio shows with plenty of impromptu music and comedy, and special guests Boris Karloff and Peter Lorre to boot.

what to buy next: You'll have trouble listening to straight renditions of classic carols after hearing *Let's Sing a Song for Christmas* (MGM, 1978, prod. various).

the rest:

Riot Squad (Harlequin, 1989)
Louder & Funnier (Harlequin, 1994)
Corn's a-Poppin' (Harlequin, 1995)
Cocktails for Two (Pro Arte, 1997)

worth searching for: With a cover by cartoonist Art Spiegelman, liner notes by author Thomas Pynchon, and some previously unreleased tracks, *Spiked!* (Catalyst, 1994, prod. Paul Williams) is a fantastic alternative overview of Jones's career.

influences:

◀◀ Al Jolson, Harmonica Frank, Emmett Miller

▶▶ "Weird Al" Yankovic, Allan Sherman, Phillip Glass, the Beatles, Jerry Lewis, Frank Zappa, Big Six, Big Bad Voodoo Daddy, Cherry Poppin' Daddies

Alex Gordon

Thad Jones /The Thad Jones/Mel Lewis Orchestra

Born March 28, 1923, in Pontiac, MI. Died August 20, 1986, in Copenhagen, Denmark.

With enviable abilities as both a trumpeter and composer/arranger, Thad Jones, co-founder of the great Thad Jones/Mel Lewis Orchestra, is one of the few jazz talents who can accurately be called a "complete" musician. Along with his brothers, drummer Elvin and pianist Hank, Thad was part of a vital jazz scene in Detroit, where he worked with Sonny Stitt and Billy Mitchell during the '40s and '50s. Following a short stint with Charles Mingus, Jones became a star soloist with Count Basie's Orchestra, where he remained in the trumpet section for several years

Spike Jones **(Archive Photos)**

(1954–63). This very productive period had Jones writing a good number of arrangements and originals for the band, not to mention his famous solo on "April in Paris." His own Blue Note recordings of the mid-'50s reveal a trumpet player of great agility and melodic invention, his sound tart and razor-sharp.

In 1965 Jones embarked on one of his most significant endeavors, teaming with drummer Mel Lewis to form a big band comprised mainly of New York's top-shelf studio musicians. With several exceptional recordings cut for the Solid State label and a regular Monday night gig at New York's Village Vanguard (which continues to this day, albeit under different leadership and with a rotating cast of players), the Thad Jones/Mel Lewis Jazz Orchestra went on to become one of the most influential and popular big bands of its time. Jones contributed many of his finest pieces to the band's book, including "A Child Is Born," "Kids Are Pretty People," "Fingers," and "Little Pixie." In 1978 Jones inexplicably left the band and headed for Denmark, where he found work as an arranger. A comeback as leader of the Count Basie band in 1984 was short lived, with his ill health ultimately leading to his death two years later.

what to buy: *Fabulous Thad Jones* (Debut, 1955/Original Jazz Classics, 1991), one of the few early Jones recordings still in print, is notable for band members Charles Mingus (on bass) and Kenny Clarke and Max Roach (both on drums).

what to avoid: *Suite for Pops* (A&M Horizon, 1972, prod. John Snyder) has yet to appear as a CD reissue, but even if it does, it's not all that memorable.

best of the rest:
Live at Montmartre, Copenhagen (Storyville, 1978/1993)

worth searching for: *The Complete Solid State Recordings of the Thad Jones/Mel Lewis Orchestra* (Mosaic, 1970/1994, reissue prod. Michael Cuscuna, Charlie Lourie) is a five-disc (or seven-LP) box set with the historic and long out-of-print original recordings of this big band complete with improved fidelity and bonus tracks. *The Complete Blue Note/UA/Roulette Recordings of Thad Jones* (Mosaic, 1956–59, reissue prod. Michael Cuscuna, Charlie Lourie) contain small group settings that reveal his great talents as a trumpeter. His three Blue Note sides, *Detroit–New York Junction*, *The Magnificent Thad Jones*, and *The Magnificent Vol. 3*, are worth the price of admission alone and have been sought out by collectors for years. Taken in tandem with the Solid State set, this three-disc boxed edition gives us the most complete look at Jones to date. Quantities are limited, and you must order by mail. *Presenting Joe Williams with the Thad Jones/Mel Lewis Jazz Orchestra* (Solid State/Blue Note, 1966/1994, prod. Sonny Lester) and *Ruth Brown with the Thad Jones/Mel Lewis Orchestra* (Solid State/Capitol Jazz, 1968/1993, prod. Sonny Lester) pair two accomplished blues crooners with the big band and singular arrangements by Jones. *New Life* (A&M Horizon, 1975, prod. John Snyder) was briefly available on CD in the late '80s, but then quickly disappeared.

influences:
◄◄ Harry "Sweets" Edison, Bobby Hackett, Roy Eldridge

►► Don Goldie, Marvin Stamm, Conte Candoli, Virgil Jones

see also: *Mel Lewis*

Chris Hovan

Louis Jordan

Born July 8, 1908, in Brinkley, AR. Died February 4, 1975, in Los Angeles, CA.

Louis Jordan's jumping novelty music bridged the gap from old-school R&B and big-band music to Little Richard and Chuck Berry's fast-paced rock 'n' roll. But more importantly, today his songs still swing—maybe that's why the musical *Five Guys Named Moe*, loosely based on Jordan's life and music, has had so much staying power around the world. Among Jordan's classics, which are both party-happy and aware of poverty, racism, and other social problems, are: "Caldonia," "Let the Good Times Roll," "Beans and Corn Bread," and "What's the Use of Getting Sober (When You're Gonna Get Drunk Again)." Son of an Arkansas bandleader, Jordan left town in his 20s to play in Philadelphia with Charlie Gaines and in Harlem with drummer-bandleader Chick Webb and then-unknown singer Ella Fitzgerald. Soon, after Webb's sudden death, the alto sax player built on his musical talent and fun-loving sense of humor to create a more popular, accessible version of Louis Armstrong and Duke Ellington's jazz. "What makes your big head so hard?" he wondered of "Caldonia," the subject of which had "great big feet." On "Beans and Corn Bread," a subtly disguised social commentary about racial conflict, the beans fight at a party with the corn bread. Countless artists, from Ray Charles to B.B. King, heard Jordan's records on the radio and tried to copy his style. Years after Jordan's peak, Chuck Berry stepped up the old blues beat, added humorous lyrics about dances and teenagers and sounded uncannily like Jordan's famed seven-member Tympani Five—only with guitar solos where the sax bits used to be. In 1981, British rocker Joe Jackson's *Jumpin' Jive* paid further homage.

what to buy: *The Best of Louis Jordan* (MCA, 1975, prod. Milt Gabler) has all his 1940s hits, including "Choo Choo Ch'-Boogie," "Caldonia," and "School Days (When We Were Kids)," and it remains the most thorough Jordan retrospective.

what to buy next: Slowly, the rest of Jordan's material has seeped into other sets: although they're not essential, fans will find different, jazzier perspectives on *I Believe in Music*

Louis Jordan **(Archive Photos)**

(Evidence, 1973/Classic Jazz, 1980, prod. various) and *Just Say Moe! Mo' of the Best of Louis Jordan* ꝏꝏꝏ (Rhino, 1992, prod. Milt Gabler). *Rock 'N' Roll* ꝏꝏꝏ (Mercury, 1989, prod. various), with re-recorded 1956–57 versions of older hits, features conductor-arranger Quincy Jones.

what to avoid: *No Moe! Decca Recordings* ꝏꝏ (MCA, 1992, prod. various) is deceptively advertised: despite a few original Jordan tracks, the bulk of it is actors' versions of songs from *Five Guys Named Moe. Rock 'n' Roll Call* ꝏꝏ▽ (RCA Bluebird, 1993, prod. John Snyder) reissues Jordan's 1950s recordings even though they sound just as good on earlier collections.

the rest:

One Guy Named Louis ꝏꝏ▽ (Blue Note, 1954)
No Moe! Louis Jordan's Greatest Hits ꝏꝏ▽ (Verve, 1992)

worth searching for: *At the Cat's Ball—the Early Years* ꝏꝏꝏ (JSP, 1991, prod. various), an import, is a nice historical look into the big-band swing sound that led up to Jordan's seminal 1940s recordings.

influences:

◀ Louis Armstrong, Duke Ellington, Bessie Smith, Charlie Christian, Cab Calloway

▶ Elmore James, Chuck Berry, B.B. King, Ray Charles, Robert Jr. Lockwood, Joe Jackson, Royal Crown Revue, Squirrel Nut Zippers

Steve Knopper

Jumpin' Jimes

Formed 1995, in Los Angeles, CA.

Michael "Mojo" Jones, bass, vocals; Bob "Crazy Legs" Smith, guitar, vocals; Mark Anthony Tortorici, vocals; Tomas Sanderson, trumpet, vocals; Neal Tabachnick, alto/baritone sax; Gusta vo Bulgach, tenor sax; Charles "Spanky" Lake, drums.

Combining the sound and style of swing, jazz, and rockabilly, the Jumpin' Jimes are part of the recent swing revival celebrating the 1940s and 1950s. Although they have not achieved the commercial success of similar-sounding bands such as Royal Crown Revue, Big Bad Voodoo Daddy, or Squirrel Nut Zippers, the Jumpin' Jimes are known for a raucous West Coast live show, regularly filling the Derby in Hollywood. Leaning on the jump-blues end of the swing spectrum, the band's main strengths are Mark Anthony Tortorici's baritone vocals and the tight clarity of the horn and percussion sections. The question remains whether the band will merely ride out the current swing revival, or remain versatile enough to sustain its unique brand of swingabilly.

what's available: The band's sole CD, *They Rock! They Roll! They Swing!* ꝏꝏꝏ▽ (Galaxy Records, 1998, prod. Earl Mankey, the Jumpin' Jimes), features covers of such classics as "Brutha Can You Spare a Dime," "I Wanna Be Somebody," and "Rock and Roll All Night," plus a number of original tracks. The toe-tapping, ebullient "Swing Shift" and a more subdued "St. Louis Blues" demonstrate the talented band's range and energy.

influences:

◀ Cab Calloway, Louis Prima, Louis Jordan, Gene Krupa, Bill Haley

Ajay Mehrotra

Candye Kane

Born in Los Angeles, CA.

Bad girls and the blues have gone together since the time of Ma Rainey, and so it is today with Candye Kane, a former stripper who's not ashamed of her past and whose, um, assets should afford her a worthwhile future. Vocally, Kane is a belter, which suits her predominantly bluesy style. But she can take it sweet and soft for one of her folkier numbers or add some Patsy Cline twang for some country honk. She's extremely versatile, even if her voice isn't the first thing you notice about her. She's also a songwriter of note, whose work often carries a none-too-subtle political or social commentary. She's an outspoken supporter of feminist issues and organizations from NOW to COYOTE, but the music still comes first. Kane is anything but a one-dimensional performer.

what to buy: "Play to your strengths" is advice artists don't take nearly enough. But that's what Kane does on *Diva La Grande* ꝏꝏꝏ▽ (Antone's/Discovery, 1997, prod. Dave Alvin, Derek O'Brien, Candye Kane). Kane embraces her role as a hefty blues-belting mama intent on shaking her moneymaker, consequences be damned. Randy and raucous, Kane is sexy and assertive on the originals "You Need a Great Big Woman," "The Lord Was a Woman," and—yikes—"All You Can Eat (And You Can Eat It All Night Long)." There's also a spicy Cajun-flavored version of Nancy Sinatra's "These Boots Are Made for Walkin'." *Swango* ꝏꝏꝏ▽ (Sire, 1998, prod. Mike Vernon, Andy Paley), which features big-band arrangements and more covers than her previous albums, seems somewhat calculated to draw in the Gap-ad swing set, but there's some fine material here, too, including Kane's own randy "200 Lbs. of Fun," a coy remake of the Mama Cass hit "Dream a Little Dream of Me," and the swing/tango-inspired title track, "Swango."

the rest:
Home Cookin' (Antone's, 1994)
Knockout (Antone's, 1995)

influences:
Ma Rainey, Bessie Smith, Mae West

Daniel Durchholz

Sammy Kaye

Born March 13, 1910, in Rocky River, OH. Died June 2, 1987, in Ridgeway, NJ.

"Swing and sway with Sammy Kaye" was this bandleader's famous tag-line, and while he didn't swing particularly hard, his popular "sweet" band racked up nearly 100 chart records between 1937 and 1953. In addition to writing and arranging tunes for his own band, Kaye was a respected songwriter who penned hits for Perry Como ("A—You're Adorable") and Nat King Cole ("My Sugar Is So Refined," "Too Young"), among others. Unique among bandleaders, Kaye didn't serve an apprenticeship with any other band; he made a name for himself leading an orchestra at Ohio University, and simply turned pro after graduation. After successful stints on Cincinnati and Pittsburgh radio, Kay and his orchestra hit the big time with a series of network radio programs such as *The Old Gold Cigarette Program, The Chesterfield Supper Club*, and *So You Want to Lead a Band.* For the latter, Kaye offered fans the opportunity to come on stage, lead his band, and win a band baton, an immensely successful gimmick. This potent exposure resulted in such major hit records as "Until Tomorrow," "Remember Pearl Harbor," "Wanderin'," "Rosalie," and many others. Among Kaye's many vocalists, Tommy Ryan and Don Cornell were able to establish an especially large fan base, and their mellow crooning was responsible for a large portion of Kaye's success. Most of the big bands died out in the '50s, yet Kaye was able to keep his orchestra's sweet, reed-heavy style popular throughout the decade via his TV version of *So You Want to Lead a Band* and his later show, *The Manhattan Shirt Program.* The 1964 instrumental "Charade" was Kaye's final Top 40 hit. Afterwards, Kaye cut an LP of brassy Dixieland, which drew positive reviews but few sales, and he began slowly phasing himself out of the business. In 1986, he handed the baton to Roger Thorpe, who toured with a new lineup of the Sammy Kaye Orchestra, although Kaye maintained creative and quality control until his death.

what to buy: Kaye's run of big hits at Columbia is on *Sammy Kaye: Best of the Big Bands* (Columbia, 1990, compilation prod. Nedra Neal), with #1 songs "Daddy," "Tennessee Waltz," and "Harbor Lights," among many others. An even bigger helping of the baton-master's work is *Swing & Sway with Sammy Kaye: 21 of His Greatest Hits* (Collectors' Choice, 1998), a fine disc available through the label's mail order catalog, featuring many of the same tracks as the Columbia disc.

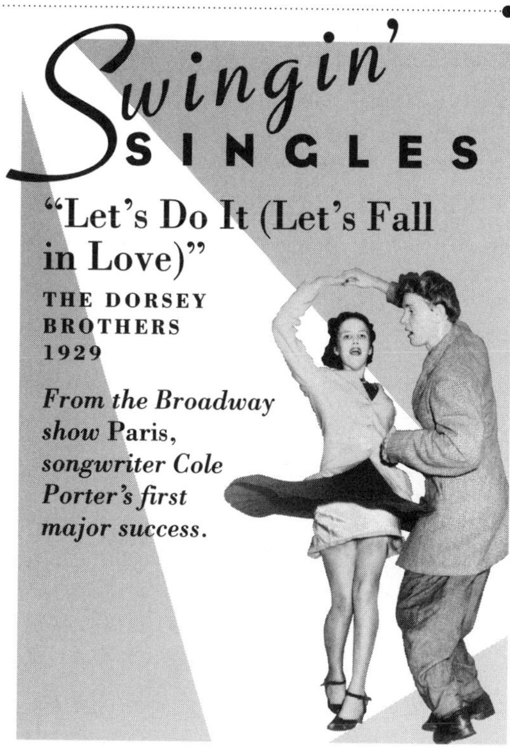

what to buy next: Taken from live radio transcriptions, *Sammy Kaye & His Orchestra: 22 Original Big Band Recordings, 1941–44* (Hindsight, 1987/1993, prod. Wally Heider) has thin sound but is a nice piece of history.

the rest:
Vocalion Hits (Sony, 1998)

worth searching for: The out-of-print *Sammy Kaye* (RCA Special Products, 1993) and *Best of Sammy Kaye* (MCA Jazz, 1974) cover Kaye's big hits and finest moments from his era with those respective labels.

influences:
Isham Jones, Guy Lombardo, Kay Kyser
Eddy Howard, Roger Thorpe, Ralph Flanagan

Ken Burke

Hal Kemp

Born James Harold Kemp, March 27, 1905, in Marion, AL. Died December 21, 1940, in Madera, CA.

Hal Kemp led of one of the more popular sweet bands of the '30s. His relaxed, casual style and southern charm blended well with the romantic showtunes and occasional novelty songs his orchestra excelled at playing. Aided by arrangers John Scott Trotter and Hal Mooney, his outfit conjured warm, sophisticated tones accentuated by muted trumpets and gentle reeds, and their best work embraced a sophistication that eluded competing bands. Initially, Kemp ran a full-fledged swing band featuring Bunny Berigan and Jack Pettis on trumpets. Although not particularly popular in America, Kemp's early line-up won favor in Europe, and Prince George of England was an ardent admirer. At home, bandleader Fred Waring was so taken with Kemp's outfit that he provided financial support and secured a New York engagement. After transforming his group into a "sweet" band, Kemp began featuring such vocalists as Skinnay Ennis, Bob Allen, and Maxine Gray, and the group scored hits with "Lamplight," "Got a Date with an Angel," "You're the Top," and many others. Kemp's tenor sax man Saxey Dowell sang the novelty numbers and authored the perpetually silly "Three Little Fishes," with its immortal refrain "Boop-boop, diddum daddum waddum chew."

Live radio broadcasts from the Blackhawk Cafe in Chicago and the Waldorf-Astoria in New York boosted their popularity and led to short-subject films and lucrative tours. As the '30s progressed, Kemp felt the need to compete with the emerging hot swing bands, and he began to incorporate fuller brass sounds into his band's arrangements. This change in direction, combined with the departure of Ennis and several key members, stopped the orchestra's career momentum cold. Subsequently, Kemp brought in new personnel (including a young singer who would soon be known as actress Janet Blair), but nothing helped. The affable bandleader was planning to restaff with fresh talent when complications from an auto accident took his life in 1940.

what's available: The band's theme, "Got a Date with an Angel," plus such deftly rendered standards as "The Way You Look Tonight," "It's D'Lovely," and "Mood Indigo," reside on *Hal Kemp and His Orchestra, 1934 and 1936* (Circle, 1994, reissue prod. George H. Buck Jr.), a solid 24-song compilation. Vocalists Skinnay Ennis and Bob Allen along with Kay Thompson and Her Rhythm Singers are heavily featured, although Kemp's band does sneak in its trademark riffs here and there. Some online services and catalogs still list the out-of-print *Got a Date with an Angel* (Pro Arte, 1992, prod. various), with "Lamplight," "Dodging a Divorcee," "It's Only a Paper Moon," and several more rhythmic goodies from the Kemp group's mid-'30s peak with Brunswick.

worth searching for: Kemp's finest early sides for Columbia are on *Best of the Big Bands* (Legacy, 1990), an out-of-print release that includes a fine booklet with informative notes about this great "lost" bandleader and his work.

influences:

Fred Waring, Paul Specht

Henry Jerome, Porky Dankers, Kay Kyser, Skinnay Ennis

Ken Burke

Sid King & the Five Strings

Formed 1952, in Denton, TX. Disbanded 1958.

Sid King, vocals, guitar (born Sid Erwin, October 15, 1936, in Denton, TX); Billy King (born Billy Erwin), lead guitar; Mel Robinson, steel guitar, sax; Ken Massey, bass; Dave White, drums, vocals.

During the immediate postwar years, the American Southland was positively teeming with musical visionaries blindly adapting what they'd hear on late-night "race radio" to their daytime country-western pursuits. As early as 1952, Dallas station KDNT was sponsoring a show featuring one such combo busy mixing Lefty Frizzell with Fats Domino. Named the Western Melody Makers, the group's brave devotion to R&B and jump blues, highly unusual for a Texas band at the time, won them a contract with the then-fledgling Starday label in 1953. Their lone release, a bizarre Harry Gibson parody entitled "Who Put the Turtle in Myrtle's Girdle?," not surprisingly failed to garner much airplay. But it did bring the band, newly rechristened Sid King & the Five Strings, to the attention of Don Law and Columbia Records. Over the next three years they cut dozens of sides together, running the gamut from western swing to what would soon be called rockabilly. Although their startling originality probably did more to harm than help sales and airplay at the time, to hear this material today is absolutely revelatory. Under Law's firm but lenient hand, the Five Strings were free to indulge their every musical whim, from Hank and Elvis to the Drifters, Spike Jones and beyond, and the body of work they created is without equal in both its polish *and* its perversity. However, it was most likely this very eccentricity that caused confusion and ultimately indifference among the record-buying public, to say nothing of Columbia's top brass, eventually leading to the band's unfortunate, inevitable dissolution. However, Sid and brother Billy continue performing to this day (when not tending to their barber shop in Richardson, Texas), recently touring the Orient fronting a Japanese rockabilly band called the Rollin' Rocks.

worth searching for: The exemplary German import *Gonna Shake This Shack Tonight* (Bear Family, 1991, compilation prod. Sid King, Richard Weize) contains literally every note the Five Strings recorded, including the initial Columbia A-side, King's own "I Like It," which sounds as if Frank Zappa had hijacked a Bob Wills session. *Rockin' on the Radio* (Schoolkids, 1996) presents two live broadcasts from 1954–55 that fully capture the evolution of the Five Strings' sound from accomplished western cut-ups to trail-blazing proto-rockabillies. *Let's Get Loose* (Rockhouse, 1987, prod. Jim Colegrove) contains an interesting selection of cuts recorded in 1979 and 1980 by the King Brothers & Friends—ironically, just as the rockabilly revival was about to rear its immaculately coiffed head.

influences:

◄◄ Milton Brown, Dewey Phillips, Bill Haley

►► Buddy & Bob, Merrill Moore, Commander Cody, Ray Condo & His Ricochets

Gary Pig Gold

Andy Kirk

Born Andrew Dewey Kirk, May 28, 1898, in Newport, KY. Died December 11, 1992, in New York, NY.

Andy Kirk & His Clouds of Joy were one of the finest bands to come out of the Southwest during the late 1920s. His well-dressed and well-rehearsed band represented some of the best in Kansas City big-band jazz; Mary Lou Williams's hot piano, in particular, made Kirk a favorite among ballroom dancers and jukebox listeners alike. As a child growing up in Denver, Kirk received music lessons from Wilberforce Whiteman, father of the popular early-century bandleader Paul Whiteman. By 1918 Kirk was playing bass sax, baritone sax, and tuba, and touring professionally. In 1925 he joined Terence Holder's Band, which he eventually took over as leader in 1929. Because Decca Records, one of Kirk's many labels, was priced well (35 cents per disc, or three for $1), the danceable Kirk band sold many, many records. The success of Kirk's Decca recordings was bolstered by the sophisticated and silken voice of singer Pha (pronounced "Fay") Terrell. He made hits of "What's Your Story Morning Glory," "Until the Real Thing Comes Along," and others. Kirk kept the band together until 1948, when he semi-retired from the music business. (He then ran a hotel in Harlem for many years.) He was also responsible for organizing a local for the Musician's Union in New York City.

what to buy: By far, the "jazziest," or hottest, recordings by Andy Kirk & His Clouds of Joy were their earliest recordings for Brunswick, which make up *Andy Kirk, 1929–31* (Jazz Chronological Classics, 1994, prod. Gilles Petard). Titles such as the jaunty "Mess-a-Stomp" and "Sumpin' Low and Slow" showcase the band's popular swinging Kansas City style. For a cross section of the band's better instrumental prewar titles and showcases for Williams, check out Andy Kirk and Mary Lou Williams on *Twelve Clouds of Joy* (ASV, 1929–49/1993), and *Mary's Idea* (Decca, 1936–41/1993, prod. Jack Kapp).

what to buy next: The later the band progresses in the 1930s, the more ballad-oriented it becomes. The Classics CDs provide the complete prewar output of the band, starting with the first Decca recordings, *Andy Kirk, 1936–37* (Jazz Chronological Classics, 1994, prod. Gilles Petard). Especially good performances of "Christopher Columbus" and "Froggy Bottom" (a reworked, "modern" arrangement of the band's original 1929 recording) are fine examples of the Kirk band of this period. Also included is Pha Terrell's performance of "Until the Real Thing Comes Along" that sucked up so many jukebox nickels in 1936.

what to avoid: Although the band's late period of ballads produced some gems, few of them are on *Andy Kirk, 1940–42* (Jazz Chronological Classics, 1995).

the rest:

Kansas City Bounce (Black & Blue, 1992)
A Mellow Bit of Rhythm (RCA, 1993)
Andy Kirk, 1937 (Jazz Chronological Classics, 1994)
Andy Kirk, 1937–38 (Jazz Chronological Classics, 1994)
Andy Kirk, 1939–40 (Jazz Chronological Classics, 1994)

worth searching for: The Clouds of Joy's 1938 song "Dunkin' a Doughnut" not only inspired a fast-food chain, but it was also a huge dance-band hit and shows up on *An Anthology of Big Band Swing 1930–1955* (Decca/GRP, 1993, reissue prod. Orrin Keepnews), among Fletcher Henderson, Count Basie, Glenn Miller, Duke Ellington, and Artie Shaw.

influences:

◄◄ Wilberforce Whiteman, Paul Whiteman, Benny Goodman, Glenn Miller

►► Guy Lombardo, Bob Crosby

Jim Prohaska

Rahsaan Roland Kirk

Born Ronald Theodore Kirk, August 7, 1936, in Columbus, OH. Died December 5, 1977, in Bloomington, IN.

Rahsaan Roland Kirk could play three horns at once, carried a siren whistle to mark the end of a solo, and broke into a jubilant scat whenever the moment moved him. Which is why, during his prime, Kirk was overshadowed by "serious" players of the day: John Coltrane, Miles Davis, and Thelonious Monk. He didn't compromise a note. He could play and compose with anyone, from hard-bop to pop, electric funk to strange, twisting saxophone symphonies. And he could swing, both literally—check out *Boogie-Woogie String Along for Real* or his live, double-saxed version of "Satin Doll"—and more importantly, in spirit. Kirk's two-line croon on his version of "My Cherie Amour" is one of the funniest, most joyful moments in music. Even though he only recorded for 20 years, Rahsaan left a rich legacy of happy songs, political songs, and lonely songs. *Case*

Andy Kirk **(Archive Photos)**

of the 3-Sided Dream in Audio Color, recorded late in his life, is considered the *Sgt. Pepper* of jazz by many Kirkophiles.

Although Kirk's professional career began in the early '50s, it wasn't for another decade, during a stint with bassist Charles Mingus, that he began to make a name. During the '60s, he recorded a wealth of material for Mercury, stretching out from bop and playing almost anything: tenor, manzello, stritch, flute, trumpet, clarinet, and harmonica. What Rahsaan couldn't play he invented, building instruments with electrical tape, homemade pipes, and his imagination. A master of circular breathing, he often blew three horns at once and reportedly set the world record for longest unbroken note. (He never got credit, which to this day rankles his longtime producer, Joel Dorn.) And what a sight on stage! With so many horns to play, Rahsaan tended to look more like a fly fisherman than a musician, straps hanging from his jacket, hands groping for pipes, brass, and nose flutes. Unlike many of his contemporaries, Rahsaan cared only about the sound, not the look. Can you imagine Miles Davis playing a horn through his schnauzer?

what to buy: The safe bet is always Rhino's double-disc best of *Does Your House Have Lions* (Rhino, 1993, prod. Joel Dorn). The downside is that none of the Mercury material is included. That problem is easily solved with *We Free Kings* (PGD/Verve, 1961), Kirk's great quartet album, a bare, hard-bop rhythm section behind his thick, piercing lines. He turns Charlie Parker's "Blues for Alice" into a rave, "We Free Kings" into his "My Favorite Things." *The Inflated Tear* (Atlantic/Rhino, 1968, prod. Joel Dorn) kicked off a string of more conceptual/spiritual/political albums. And it is moody, with dissonant ballads, skipping, carefree flute-bop, and the occasional shout-out. In the '70s, Kirk added to his canon. *Aces Back to Back* (32 Jazz, 1996, prod. Joel Dorn) is a great start, bringing together *Left & Right*, *Rahsaan, Rahsaan*, *Prepare Thyself to Deal with a Miracle*, and *Other Folks' Music*.

what to buy next: *Rahsaan—The Complete Mercury Recordings* (Mercury, 1961–65/PolyGram, 1990)is a no-brainer. Still in print, this set is nearly perfect, starting with *We Free Kings* and winding up to the Atlantic years. *A Standing Eight* (32 Jazz, 1998, prod. Joel Dorn) offers Rahsaan's final three albums: *The Return of the 5000-lb Man*, *Kirkatron*, and *Boogie-Woogie String Along for Real*. All three are worth hearing, but the emotional highlight is *Boogie-Woogie*, recorded after the 1975 stroke that left Rahsaan partially paralyzed. No more triple horns runs; he had to learn to play without the use of his right hand. There's no way to forget those circumstances when listening to the album, especially the seven-minute version of "Make Me a Pallet on the Floor." His sad clarinet feels strangely connected to Jelly Roll Morton's "I Thought I Heard Buddy Bolden Say," done in 1939 just before his death. It is as if both men—unappreciated masters in their own times—had come to terms with the end. For one last time, they wanted nothing more than to be heard.

the rest:

Introducing Roland Kirk (GRP, 1960/Chess, 1998)
(With Jack McDuff) *Kirk's Work* (Original Jazz Classics, 1961/1990)
Reeds and Deeds (Mercury, 1963)
I Talk with the Spirits (Verve, 1964/1998)
Rip Rig & Panic & Now / Please Don't You Cry, Beautiful Edith (Verve/Emarcy, 1965–67/1990)
Volunteered Slavery (Atlantic/Rhino, 1969/1993)
Blacknuss (Atlantic/Rhino, 1972/1993)
Bright Moments (Atlantic/Rhino, 1974/1993)
Case of the 3-Sided Dream in Audio Color (Atlantic, 1975/1987)
Verve Jazz Masters 27 (Verve, 1994)
Simmer, Reduce, Garnish & Serve (WEA/Warner Bros., 1995)
(I, Eye, Aye) Live at the Montreaux Jazz Festival, Switzerland, 1972 (Atlantic/Rhino, 1996)
Talkin Verve: Roots of Acid Jazz (Verve, 1996)
Years in the Fourth Ring (32 Jazz, 1997)

influences:

◀◀ Don Byas, Dexter Gordon, Charles Mingus, Yusef Lateef

▶▶ Anthony Braxton, John Stubblefield, James Carter

Geoff Edgers

Diana Krall

Born November 16, 1964, in Nanaimo, British Columbia, Canada.

Perhaps it was as simple as trading parent company GRP's logo for the expectation-raising Impulse! imprint. Maybe it was a backhanded bonus of the lounge-music craze. Or maybe it was that there just aren't that many blonde, female singer-pianists working in traditional jazz. Whatever the reason, Diana Krall's third album, *All for You*, a loving tribute to the Nat King Cole Trio, jettisoned the young Canadian toward the top of the jazz charts in 1996 after almost a decade of club-hopping obscurity. Schooled at Berklee and mentored by pianist Jimmy Rowles and bassist Ray Brown, Krall is certainly a dexterous, economical player. But her smoky contralto—a bluesy testament to the emotional wallop of nuance—has developed into one of the decade's most inviting, invigorating vehicles for standards, a reputation solidified with the romantic repertoire of 1997's gorgeous *Love Scenes*, which ranges from the sultry "Peel Me a Grape" to a delightfully intimate reading of "They Can't Take That Away from Me."

what to buy: A tribute to the lighthearted swing of the Nat King Cole Trio, *All for You* (Impulse!, 1996, prod. Tommy LiPuma) remains faithful to the piano-bass-guitar arrangements of such Cole classics as "I'm an Errand Girl for Rhythm," "Gee Baby, Ain't I Good to You," and "Frim Fram Sauce." Krall's

Gene Krupa **(Archive Photos)**

singing adds a sense of seductive mischief to what could easily have been a cabaret cakewalk.

the rest:

Stepping Out (Justin Time, 1993/Impulse!, 1998)
Only Trust Your Heart (GRP, 1995)
Love Scenes (Impulse!, 1997)
Have Yourself a Merry Little Christmas (GRP EP, 1998)
When I Look in Your Eyes N/A (Verve, 1999)

worth searching for: The import version of *All for You* (Impulse!, 1996, prod. Tommy LiPuma) boasts an extra track: "When I Grow Too Old to Dream"

influences:

Carmen McRae, Nat King Cole, Shirley Horn

David Okamoto

Gene Krupa

Born January 15, 1909, in Chicago, IL. Died October 16, 1973, in Yonkers, NY.

Just about every drummer working today owes a massive debt to Gene Krupa. The most exciting and energetic drummer of his time, he transformed the drums from a mere time-keeping device into a full-fledged solo instrument. Whether he played jivey and fast with wire brushes or pounded the toms with heavy hands and sticks, he conveyed loads of unabashed rhythmic energy with intense showmanship.

At age 16, Krupa helped establish the Chicago style of jazz with the Frivolians and Eddie Condon's Austin High School Gang. With the McKenzie/Condon Chicagoans in 1927, Krupa became the first musician to use a full drum kit in a recording studio. A popular session man, Krupa also played in bands fronted by Russ Columbo, Buddy Rogers, and Red Nichols, before joining Benny Goodman's orchestra in 1934. The King of Swing made the most of Krupa's extroverted, highly visual style, and before long Goodman's orchestra was not only perceived as the best, but also as the most popular. Krupa's pneumatic drum solo on the classic "Sing, Sing, Sing" created a popular sensation, and his spotlight-stealing performance at Goodman's 1938 Carnegie Hall concert made him a household name. Krupa split with Goodman and formed his own band in 1938. Hits like "Wire Brush Stomp," "Drummin' Man," and

"Drum Boogie" propelled the handsome drummer's individual popularity to even greater heights and led to appearances in more than a dozen Hollywood movies. Krupa's band (featuring Roy Eldridge and Anita O'Day, among others) peaked in the early '40s with hits such as "Bolero at the Savoy," "Let Me Off Uptown," "After You've Gone," "Rockin' Chair," and "Thanks for the Boogie Ride."

But it all came crashing down in 1943. After a drug bust and the resultant waves of bad publicity, Krupa disbanded his orchestra. Once cleared of the charges, he publicly rehabilitated himself in stints with Goodman and Tommy Dorsey. In 1944 Krupa started another band, which allowed the bebop arrangements of Gerry Mulligan to seep into the swing-band style (an artistic and commercial risk at the time). Krupa backed a few more hit records and kept various lineups of his orchestra going until 1951. By then, the big bands were dying, and Buddy Rich's superior technical skill eclipsed Krupa's in the minds of fans. Always a workhorse, Krupa continued recording LPs with trios and quartets throughout the '50s and was a featured star of Norman Granz's "Jazz at the Philharmonic" tours. Interest in his career resurged after the 1959 film *The Gene Krupa Story*, a largely inaccurate biopic and a vehicle for Sal Mineo with Krupa's work on the soundtrack. Krupa recorded with small jazz groups and in big-band reunion settings throughout the '60s and early '70s until his death.

what to buy: Krupa's best orchestra lineup (1941–42) and biggest hits are on *Drum Boogie* (Legacy, 1993, compilation prod. Michael Brooks), an essential introductory collection, with "Drum Boogie," "No Name Jive," "How About That Mess," and "Rum Boogie."

what to buy next: *Drummer* (Pearl 1993, compilation prod. Colin Brown, Tony Watts), a 22-track disc culled from his 1935 to 1941 output, contains the amazing "Wire Brush Stomp." A good mix of hits and percussion pyrotechnics is on *Drummin' Man* (Charly, 1989, prod. various), an import collection with "Bolero at the Savoy," "Leave Us Leap," "After You've Gone," and more jumping jive.

what to avoid: The sound quality is poor on the budget-rack perennial *Giants of the Big Band Era* (Pilz, 1992).

the rest:

Krupa & Rich (Verve, 1955/1994)
Drummer Man (Verve, 1956/1996)
Compact Jazz (Verve, 1988/1992)
1946 Live! (Jazz Hour, 1994)
Gene Krupa 1935–38 (Jazz Chronological Classics, 1994)
Gene Krupa—1938 (Jazz Chronological Classics, 1994)
Gene Krupa—1939 (Jazz Chronological Classics, 1995)
Gene Krupa 1939–40 (Classics, 1995)
Gene Krupa & His Orchestra (Jazz Hour, 1995)
Hollywood Palladium 1/18/45 (Canby Records, 1995)
It's Up to You; 1946, Vol. 2 (Hep, 1995)
The Legendary Big Bands (Sony Music Special Products, 1995)
Radio Days (CACD, 1995)
Radio Years; 1940 (Jazz Unlimited, 1995)
What's This? 1946, Vol. 1 (Hep, 1995)
1940, Vol. 2 (Classics, 1996)
Drummer Man (Hindsight, 1996)
Leave Us Leap (Vintage Jazz Classics, 1996)
Swings with Strings (Vintage Jazz Classics, 1996)
Volume 3: Hop, Skip, & Jump (Hep, 1996)
Vol. 13—Masterpieces (EPM Musique, 1996)
1940 (Jazz Chronological Classics, 1997)
1941 (Jazz Chronological Classics, 1997)
Gene Krupa & His Orchestra: Members Edition (United Audio, 1997)
Vol. 2 1941 (Jazz Chronological Classics, 1997)
V-Disc Recordings (Collectors' Choice, 1998)

worth searching for: Krupa's sextet delivers some effective hard bop on *Leave Me Off Uptown* (Drive, 1996), recorded at three live performances circa 1949.

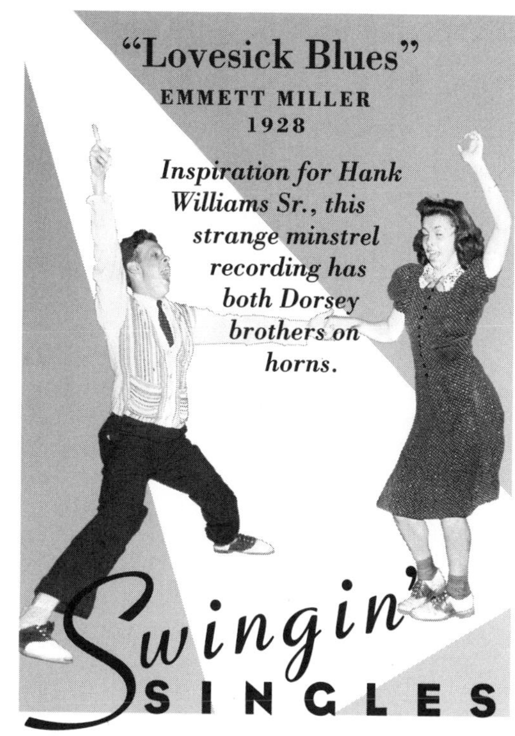

influences:

⏪ Roy C. Knapp, Edward B. Straight, Chick Webb

⏩ Big Sid Catlett, Buddy Rich, Louis Belson, Keith Moon

see also: *Tommy Dorsey, Benny Goodman*

Ken Burke

Kay Kyser

Born James King Kern Kyser, June 18, 1906, in Rocky Mount, NC. Died July 23, 1985, in Chapel Hill, NC.

Dressed in professorial attire and addressing his faithful listeners as "students," Kay Kyser's use of southern-fried hep-talk and singing song titles helped him stand out in an era of colorful musical figures. Kyser, who could neither write nor read music, formed his first band in the mid-'20s, shifting to jazz later in the decade. Sensing a shift in popular music, Kyser adopted the "sweet" band style and began prominently featuring a series of vocal groups and singers on a variety of catchy (sometimes gimmicky) pop tunes. His career really took off when NBC Radio hired him to fill a hole in its Monday night lineup. In an attempt to fit as much music as possible into his 15-minute time slot, Kyser developed the technique of having his vocalists sing a song title, with his orchestra vamping while he introduced them. Kyser's radio popularity expanded further when he added a quiz-show format, with audience participation, to his college-themed program, *Kay Kyser's Kampus Klass,* later retitled *Kay Kyser's Kollege of Musical Knowledge.* Recording for Columbia, Kyser and his band notched 20 Top 10 hits, including "(I Got Spurs) That Jingle Jangle Jingle," "Ole Buttermilk Sky," "The Old Lamplighter," "Woody Woodpecker," and their classic "Slow Boat to China." Among the many singers featured in Kyser's band were Hollywood star-in-training Jane Russell, future talk-show host Mike Douglas, and Kyser's wife, Georgia Carroll. Kyser's popularity led to appearances in 10 feature films, with 1939's *That's Right, You're Wrong* based on one of his many zany catch-phrases. The war years were Kyser's peak, and despite recording bans and shellac shortages, his orchestra sold millions of records. Soldiers especially appreciated his band's playful sound, and Kyser returned the compliment by tirelessly raising money for the war effort and playing free shows for the troops. (During this time, his band hit with "Praise the Lord and Pass the Ammunition.") Despite the postwar big-band decline, Kyser was still popular and had successfully transformed his radio show into an early TV hit, when chronic arthritis forced him to retire.

what to buy: Kyser's biggest hits, "Slow Boat to China," "(I Got Spurs) That Jingle Jangle Jingle," "There Goes That Song Again," "Woody Woodpecker," the perennial saber-rattler "Praise the Lord and Pass the Ammunition," and many more are on *Kay Kyser: Best of the Big Bands* ♪♪♪♪ (Legacy, 1990, prod. Michael Brooks), an easy-to-find budget disc. Ginny Simms, Georgia Carroll, the Glee Club, the Campus Kids, Gloria Wood, and Mike Douglas do the singing.

what to buy next: There's a generous selection of songs on *Songs of World War II, Vol. 2: I'll Be Seeing You* ♪♪♪½ (Vintage Jazz Classics, 1993, prod. various), a fine representation of Kyser's radio years featuring guest stars the King Sisters, the Town Criers, and fellow big-bandleader Phil Harris.

what to avoid: Kyser doesn't appear at all on *Kay Kyser's Greatest Hits* ♪½ (Capitol, 1962/1989), which features his original band (fronted by Billy May) re-recording its best-known songs with comedian Stan Freberg imitating the voice of Kyser. It's out of print, but some CDs may still be in stores; despite having Kyser's picture on the cover, it's not the real thing.

the rest:

Kay Kyser's Kollege of Musical Knowledge ♪♪½ (Jazz Hour, 1996)
Music Maestro Please ♪♪♪ (Empire, 1998)

worth searching for: The "'Ol Perfesser" is at his ever lovin' best in the video version of the 1941 film *Playmates* ♪♪ (Theatre Communications Group, 1990), wherein Kyser and his band really put the moves on a swing version of "Romeo and Juliet."

influences:

⏪ Hal Kemp, Isham Jones, Phil Harris

⏩ Sammy Kaye, Eddy Howard, Sully Mason, George Duning

Ken Burke

L

Sleepy LaBeef

Born Thomas Paulsley LaBeef, July 20, 1935, in Smackover, AR.

Though his degree of stardom has never come close to matching his gargantuan talents, Sleepy LaBeef is one of the most amazing musicians in America. A dramatic singer with a big, booming baritone voice and a guitarist of dazzling versatility, LaBeef broke into the Houston country/rockabilly scene of the early 1950s, recording for Wayside and other obscure labels before moving on to Plantation, Sun, Columbia, and, beginning in 1980, Rounder. Despite a couple of minor hits, LaBeef's records have never really captured his true genius, which is revealed only on stage. It is there that LaBeef, who's blessed with an encyclopedic knowledge of American music, gives free rein to his muse, combining the collective histories of country,

Sleepy LaBeef (© Jack Vartoogian)

blues, gospel, bluegrass, rockabilly, R&B, and whatever else catches his fancy into a unique genre-straddling LaBeefian stew he calls "goosebump music." The music comes out in guitar-driven torrents, often in extended stream-of-consciousness medleys that leave listeners gaping in astonishment. Anyone who has ever witnessed one of those shows understands just what *The New York Times* meant when it called Sleepy LaBeef a "national treasure."

what to buy: *Nothin' but the Truth* ♪♪♪½ (Rounder, 1987, prod. Scott Billington) has the right idea; instead of trying to capture the magic in a studio, record LaBeef in his natural element, on stage at a smoky, sweaty honky-tonk. It's not perfect, but it does a good job of explaining LaBeef's musical worldview, in which Hank Williams, Howlin' Wolf, Nancy Sinatra, Chuck Berry, Bill Monroe, and the Five Blind Boys not only exist as equals, but also share space in the same medley. High points include smoking versions of "Tore Up Over You" and "Let's Talk about Us" and the droll, autobiographical "Boogie at the Wayside Lounge."

what to buy next: *Strange Things Happening* ♪♪♪ (Rounder, 1994, prod. Jake Guralnick, Peter Guralnick) is a pretty apt title for a LaBeef album, as this one veers from nods to Ernest Tubb ("Waltz Across Texas") to Muddy Waters ("Young Fashioned Ways"), with stops along the way for Sister Rosetta Tharpe (the title song) and Elvis ("Trying to Get to You"). *I'll Never Lay My Guitar Down* ♪♪♪ (Rounder, 1996, prod. Jake Guralnick), while a bit uneven and restrained, has its moments, ranging from the "Mystery Train" shuffle of "Treat Me Like a Dog" to the swampy "Roosevelt & Ira Lee" to the closing "The Open Door," which sounds like Brother Claude Ely updated for the late 1990s.

the rest:

It Ain't What You Eat . . . It's the Way How You Chew It ♪♪♪ (Rounder, 1980/1995)
Electricity ♪♪♪ (Rounder, 1995)
Human Jukebox ♪♪♪ (Sun, 1995)
Flying Saucers Rock & Roll ♪♪♪ (Collectables, 1999)

worth searching for: Though it's big and pricey, the German import *Larger Than Life* ♪♪♪♪ (Bear Family, 1996, prod. various) spreads LaBeef's prolific career over six CDs.

influences:

◀◀ Sister Rosetta Tharpe, Elvis Presley, Hank Williams

▶▶ John Fogerty, The Blasters

Jon Hartley Fox

Frankie Laine

Born Francesco Paul LoVecchio, March 30, 1913, in Chicago, IL.

Best known for his definitive whip-cracking version of the *Rawhide* television-show theme, Frankie Laine was also one of the most phenomenally successful recording artists from the late 1940s through the mid-1950s. With his soaring baritone, Laine mixed jazz phrasing, gospel-flavored sentiments, showbiz standards, blues and folk rhythms, and western themes with utter joy and abandon. Laine scuffled in jazz clubs for most of his early career. There, he developed his unique ability to use swing rhythm and jazz phrasing to distinguish songs from many different genres. When he finally achieved success with a goosed-up version of "That's My Desire" in 1947, he also earned the ire of old-guard popular singers—particularly Frank Sinatra. According to columnist Earl Wilson, while Laine's "The Cry of the Wild Goose" was topping the charts, a jealous, career-slumping Chairman of the Board hit the stage of the Copacabana wearing a coonskin cap, cracking a whip, and sarcastically honking like a goose.

Laine, who prided himself on his 1,000-song repertoire, soon delegated song-selection duties to the label's new A&R man, Mitch Miller. Noting the "universality" in the singer's voice, the unabashedly schmaltzy producer found powerful hit ballads for Laine, such as "Lucky Old Sun." When Miller left Mercury for Columbia in 1951, Laine brought his hitmaking power with him. The singer expanded upon his remarkable chart consistency by appearing in several movies, recording prolifically with the likes of Jo Stafford, Johnnie Ray, Jimmy Boyd, and the Four Lads, and hosting both a syndicated and network TV show. Though rock 'n' roll diminished Laine's profile considerably, he recorded one last chart smash, 1956's "Moonlight Gambler," and remained a popular LP artist throughout the decade. In 1959, Laine's boisterous version of the *Rawhide* television theme exposed the singer's voice to a large audience every week. Benefiting from the late-1960s nostalgia movement, Laine began hitting the easy-listening charts with reworked oldies such as "I'll Take Care of Your Cares" and "Making Memories." In 1987, his collaboration with the Cincinnati Pops Orchestra Round-Up made it to # 4 on the classical album charts. Despite heart problems, Laine still performs one or two concerts a month and releases new albums on a fairly regular basis.

what to buy: Laine's first great jazz-tinged pop hits ("That's My Desire," "Shine") and his early western and folk classics ("Mule Train," "The Cry of the Wild Goose") are packaged on *The Frankie Laine Collection: The Mercury Years* ♪♪♪♪½ (Mercury, 1991, compilation prod. Ron Furmanek). The hits keep coming with *16 Most Requested Songs* ♪♪♪♪ (Columbia/Legacy, 1989, compilation prod. Michael Brooks), an inexpensive collection of his best-known Columbia sides ranging from the torrid "Jezebel," through the steel-tonsil dramatics of "High Noon," to the devoutly inspirational "I Believe."

what to buy next: Laine's last volley of hits for ABC makes up *The Very Best of Frankie Laine* ♪♪♪½ (Tarragon, 1996, prod.

Jimmy Bowen, Bob Thiele, Eliot Goshman), with "Laura, What's He Got That I Ain't Got," "You Gave Me a Mountain," and the cult classic "Dammit Isn't God's Last Name."

what to avoid: Late in his career Laine rerecorded his big hits and mixed them with unlikely modern selections, such as Creedence Clearwater Revival's "Proud Mary" and Bill Anderson's "Po' Folks," on *16 Greatest Hits* (Trip, 1978, prod. various). Stick with the original hit versions.

the rest:

You Gave Me a Mountain (MCA Special Products, 1990)
The Uncollected Frankie Laine, Vol. 2 (Hindsight, 1992)
Best of Frankie Laine (Curb, 1993)
The Essence of Frankie Laine (Columbia/Legacy, 1993)
The Uncollected Frankie Laine—1947 (Hindsight, 1994)
Frankie Laine & Friends (Classic, 1994)
Return of Mr. Rhythm: 1945–1948 (Hindsight, 1995)
Greatest Hits (Columbia, 1995)
Dynamic (ITC Masters, 1996)
Portrait of a Legend (After 9, 1997)
High Noon: 20 Greatest Hits (Remember, 1997)
Wheels of a Dream (After 9, 1998)
Young Master (Flapper, 1998)

worth searching for: Laine's robust vocal style was never put to better use than on *On the Trail* (Bear Family, 1990, compilation prod. Richard Weize) and *On the Trail Again* (Bear Family, 1992, compilation prod. Richard Weize), which contain all his great whip- cracking, cowboy-flavored classics, including "High Noon," "Moonlight Gambler," and "Rawhide." Also, one of the undisputed highlights of Laine's career was his wonderfully straight rendition of the title song to Mel Brooks's raunchy western parody *Blazing Saddles* (1974), included on *High Anxiety* (Asylum, 1978, prod. various), a collection of songs from Brooks's best comedy features. (Laine claims to have not known the song was a put-on, which is why it works so well.)

influences:

◀◀ Bing Crosby, Louis Armstrong, Al Jolson, Carlo Buti, Nat King Cole

▶▶ Anita O'Day, Johnnie Ray, Guy Mitchell, Marty Robbins, Charlie Gracie

Ken Burke

Lester Lanin

Born August 26, 1911, probably in Philadelphia, PA.

Lester Lanin's name is synonymous with big-band "society music"—by his own recollection, he had his orchestras booked at more than 10,000 weddings, 3,000 debutante parties, and 1,500 proms. He followed in the footsteps of his father and grandfather as a bandleader—the youngest of 10 boys, he originally studied to be a criminal attorney, but his father became ill and he assumed one of his commitments. His father told him to be as individual as he could, so Lanin sang the phrasing he wanted to the men in the band. His career ended up spanning four decades, and he eventually performed for the high society element in every major American city—the DuPonts, the Rockefellers, the Fords, the Whitneys, the Vanderbilts, and the Chryslers, as well as members of international royalty. He was most proud of having played at seven presidential inaugural balls; he had 13 White House performances in all.

what to buy: While other big-band leaders played by the books, never varying from their routine, Lanin always adapted to the times, adding Dixieland, Latin, and rock music. He didn't even have sheet music up on the bandstand—his orchestras had memorized thousands of songs, and they were always learning new standards. *This Is Society Dance Music* (Columbia/Legacy, 1956/1993), a reissue, is a live mono recording made during the Monte Carlo Ball in New York circa 1956.

the rest:

Best of the Big Bands (Sony, 1990)
1960–62 (Hindsight, 1992)

worth searching for: Lanin and his orchestra contributed the song "Christmas Night in Harlem" to the compilation *Big Band Christmas* (Sony, 1987), which also features Artie Shaw, Red Norvo, and Les Brown.

influences:

◀◀ Glenn Miller, Tommy Dorsey

▶▶ Frank Sinatra Jr.

G. Brown

Peggy Lee

Born Norma Delores Engstrom, May 26, 1920, in Jamestown, ND.

Peggy Lee's renaissance talents as singer, composer, arranger, and lyricist kept her on top of the music world from the 1940s through the 1960s. A consummate jazz/R&B stylist with a husky, quiet voice and smoky onstage delivery, Lee starred in and scored musicals and films, and recorded more than 60 albums of jazz, blues, swing, Latin, and pop. Though never considered a great vocalist in a classical sense, Lee's calm, cuddle-up delivery—she made sexy sound so *easy*—and chartbusting singles ("Big Spender," "Fever," "Mañana," and "Is That All There Is?" among them, the last three among her many compositions) made her an enormous crossover star. Like contemporary Frank Sinatra, she was instrumental in the shift to more earthy, emotional vocalization techniques, creating a cast of unforgettable female characters in her songs that appealed to

Peggy Lee **(Archive Photos)**

both sexes. It wasn't always easy. Lee left Capitol for Decca Records in a dispute over "Lover," a Rodgers and Hart tune she jump-started with an innovative mambo rhythm arrangement that became one of her biggest hits in 1952. The next year, her moody, intensely bluesy montage, *Black Coffee*, was a "concept" album 15 years before the term became popular with the release of the Beatles' *Sgt. Pepper's Lonely Hearts Club Band*.

Lee left North Dakota for Hollywood after graduating from high school, but wound up in Minneapolis, where she broke in and toured with the Will Osborne Band. Her first break came when Benny Goodman picked her to replace Helen Forrest in 1941. Dave Dexter Jr. talked her into a Capitol contract in 1944, a company for which she recorded during most of her career. Lee starred in several films and was nominated for an Academy Award for her work in *Pete Kelly's Blues*, and her songs and voice are all over Disney's animated *Lady and the Tramp*. In recent years Lee has produced books of verse, worked in painting and design, and written her autobiography, *Miss Peggy Lee* (Donald J. Fine, 1989).

what to buy: Casual listeners might want to invest in something like the generous, 26-song *Capitol Collector's Series: Vol. 1, the Early Years* ♪♪♪♪ (Capitol, 1990/Gold Rush, 1996, compilation prod. Ron Furmanek). But you just can't beat *Miss Peggy Lee* ♪♪♪♪ (Capitol, 1998, compilation prod. Brad Benedict), an exhausting, four-disc overview that spans almost her entire career. With the exception of the Decca exile period, this is pretty much the full remastered Lee enchilada—a versatile package with all the big hits (including "Fever," "Why Don't You Do Right," and "Is That All There Is"), excursions into Latin ("Mañana," "You Stepped Out of a Dream"), country ("Riders in the Sky"), movies ("I'm Gonna Go Fishing" with Duke Ellington for *Anatomy of a Murder*), blues (Leiber and Stoller's "I'm a Woman"), jazz, duets, pick-of-the-litter album tracks, and even a few obscurities getting their first release. *Best of the Decca Years* ♪♪♪♪ (MCA, 1997, compilation prod. Andy McKaie) includes orchestra work with Bing Crosby recorded between 1952 and 1956 and representative songs from *Black Coffee* and *Lady Is a Tramp*. It includes the inventive "Lover," the classic on which Capitol passed.

what to buy next: *Best of Peggy Lee* ♪♪♪♪♪ (Capitol Jazz/Blue Note, 1997) gathers recordings with Benny Goodman, Quincy Jones, Benny Carter, Billy May, and George Shearing. A quiet, small-combo, 1961 session recorded in a New York club became *Basin Street East Proudly Presents* ♪♪♪♪ (Blue Note, 1995). *Peggy Lee Sings with Benny Goodman* ♪♪♪♪ (Sony Special Products, 1994) captures her early raw appeal.

what to avoid: Watch out for the many budget discs that offer one hit (usually "Fever") amid a short list of mediocre material; *If I Could Be with You* ♪ (Jasmine, 1992) or *Fever & Other Great Hits* ♪♪ (Capitol Special Products, 1994) offer little Lee for the loot.

the rest:
Christmas Carousel ♪♪♪♪ (Capitol, 1960)
Close Enough for Love ♪♪♪ (DRG, 1989)
(With George Shearing) *Beauty and the Beat* ♪♪♪♪ (Cema/Capitol, 1990)
Sings the Blues ♪♪♪♪ (Musicmasters, 1990)
Moments Like This ♪♪♪♪ (Chesky Jazz, 1992)
Live—1947 & 1952 ♪♪♪ (Jazz Band, 1993)
The Uncollected Peggy Lee with the David Barbour and Billy May Bands, 1948 ♪♪♪♪ (Hindsight, 1994)
Peggy Lee, Vol. 1: The Early Hits ♪♪♪♪ (Alliance, 1997)
Fever ♪♪♪ (Golden Sounds, 1998)

worth searching for: *Black Coffee & Other Delights: The Decca Anthology* ♪♪♪♪ (Decca, 1994, prod. Tony Natelli) extends *Best of the Decca Years* into two discs and 46 total tracks.

influences:
◀◀ Count Basie, Bennie Moten, Jo Stafford, Billie Holiday, Sarah Vaughan, Mildred Bailey, Benny Goodman, Doris Day, Frank Sinatra, Dick Haymes

▶▶ Johnny Mathis, Marlene Dietrich, k.d. lang, Dakota Staton, Elvis Costello, Madonna, Carmen McRae, Nancy Wilson

Leland Rucker

Lee Press-On & the Nails

Formed 1994, in San Francisco, CA.

Lee Press-On, vocals, vibes; Stuart Sperring, stand-up bass; Beau Faw, drums; Taylor Cutcomb, piano; Matt Cohen, trumpet; Todd Grady, trumpet; David Kraczek, trombone; Bob Thies, trombone; Mark Donelly, alto saxophone, clarinet; Bobby Rogers, tenor saxophone, clarinet; Leslie Presley, vocals.

Sure, Lee Press-On & the Nails walk the walk, talk the talk, and swing those crazy cats and kittens on dance floors all over the West Coast. But these jivers have an unusual twist: They jump with the devil. "Swing or die!" is the band's war cry, as well as the name of its Web site; "Jump Swing from Hell" is its self-described sound and the name of its lone album. Others call it "goth-swing," and Press-On, with his coal-ringed eyes, slicked-back hair and sinister leer, often earns comparisons to Gomez Addams. Fortunately, the band is more than the sum of its gimmick: It quite capably cruises through the standards—with witty deliveries and delicious surprises such as a cover of Van Halen's "Hot for Teacher," in full sassy, brassy glory. Press-On & the Nails also do a number of originals, all played with the same irresistible sense of fun. Press-On says the band is based on the premise that swing was the punk rock of its day, the scandalous outlaw music of Prohibition-era flappers and zoot-suiters. Press-On's stage persona is derived mainly from the Joker, with plenty of other influences blended in (from Groucho to *Beetlejuice*).

what's available: *Jump Swing from Hell* ♪♪♪♪ (Irascible Records, 1997, prod. Amazing Larry, Lee Press-On) is high swing at high speed, with supercool selections such as They Might Be Giants' "Istanbul (Not Constantinople)" and Van Halen's "Hot for Teacher."

influences:

◀ Cab Calloway, Louis Prima, Woody Herman, Glenn Miller, Dean Martin, Frank Sinatra, Stan Kenton, Billy May, James Brown, Frank Zappa, Fishbone, Oingo Boingo, The Damned

Lynne Margolis

Johnny Legend

Born Martin Marguiles, October, 3, 1949, in San Fernando, CA.

Hey! Don't scan to the next entry! Johnny Legend is neither a Las Vegas Elvis imitator nor an old star of TV westerns who cut a few country tunes to cash in on his fame. Dubbed the "Rockabilly Rasputin" (because of his long pointy beard), Legend has turned his irreverent obsession with white-trash schlock and low-rent rhythms into some way out, authentic-sounding music, and oddly, a career in Hollywood films.

Initially a folk rocker, Legend and his band, the Seeds of Time, recorded a version of "Across the Universe" that actually made it into stores ahead of the Beatles' disc. The lure of the '50s revival, combined with his interests in low-budget exploitation films, doo-wop, and rockabilly eventually led him to Ron Weiser's Rollin' Rock Records. A prolific writer with an ability to find totally unique hooks, Legend covered up his vocal deficiencies through the judicious use of slapback echo, which, with his speedy, hiccuping delivery, helped keep profanity and impure notions hidden—at least until the second or third listen. Few of his songs received much attention in America, but in Sweden, Legend's "Soakin' the Bone" is quite a collectors' favorite.

Legend's life is filled with colorful sidelines. He has shamelessly promoted professional wrestling matches, managed wrestlers, produced and appeared in the first X-rated rockabilly movie, directed Andy Kaufman's last film, *My Breakfast with Blassie*, and written the Dr. Demento favorite "Pencil Neck Geek" for wrestler Freddie Blassie. His Something Weird video company has rediscovered and re-released dozens of obscure low-budget films to enthusiastic trash-culture audiences worldwide. He has appeared in several horror flicks, most memorably as the lead zombie in *Bride of the Re-animator*, and has a role in Jim Carrey's Andy Kaufman biopic *The Man on the Moon*. Because he doesn't seem to take music too seriously, his recent work evokes a quirky "who gives a damn" spirit—which is hard not to admire.

what to buy: Legend recorded his most energetic and amusing sides for Ron Weiser's Rollin' Rock label; they show up on *Rockabilly Bastard: The Best of Johnny Legend Vol. None* ♪♪♪½ (HighTone, 1996, prod. Ron Weiser). The Rockabilly Rasputin is given ample instrumental support from Ray Campi, Jimmie Lee Maslon, Lewis Lymon (from the '50s doo-wop group the Teenagers), and the pre-X Billy Zoom on some of the best productions to come from that label. Throughout *Rockabilly Bastard*, Legend walks the fine line between rockabilly parody ("Are You Hip To It?," "Guess Who Ain't Getting Laid Tonight"), propagandist schlock ("Stalin Kicked the Bucket," "The South Is Gonna Rise Again,"), and honest tribute (Bo Diddley's "Crackin' Up," Hank Williams's "Ramblin' Man").

what to buy next: Nowhere near as provocative as the cover or inside flap (which features Legend wrestling with topless women), *Bitchin'* ♪♪½ (Dionysus, 1998. prod. Tim Horrigan, Johnny Legend) is proof that Legend is a pretty good vocalist when he wants to be. Amid the horror movie odes ("Teenage Caveman," "House of Frankenstein"), wrestler tributes ("Santos Street"), politically incorrect doo-wop ("Crack the Whip," "Don't Say She's Gone"), and tales of the truly psychotic ("Teachers," "Psycho Rock"), lives a Marty Robbins clone dying to get out.

worth searching for: Though Legend has only one tune on *The Big Monster Bash, Vol.1* ♪♪½ (Mouthpiece, 1998, prod. not listed), his demented spirit is carried on by the likes of the Hillbilly Varmints, the Swing Rays, the Vibro Champs, and El Vez (the Mexican Elvis impersonator) on a set of 21 decidedly strange themes for would-be monster movies. Also, one of the funniest doo-wop parodies ever is on Rhino's video series *Teenage Theater*, a collection of lovable grade-Z exploitation movies from the '50s. Legend sings the theme with David Starns and its lyrics brilliantly sum up his skewed vision.

influences:

◀ Elvis Presley, Gene Vincent, Little Richard, Fats Domino, Marty Robbins, Hank Williams, Johnny Burnette, the Three Stooges

▶ Billy Zoom, Jimmie Lee Maslon, the Blasters, "Classy" Freddie Blassie

Ken Burke

Kim Lenz

Born November 1, 1969, in San Diego, CA.

Dallas-based rockabilly singer Kim Lenz brings a lot of '50s style to her stage show and convincing roadhouse energy to her recorded music. An exceptional songwriter, Lenz deftly creates ear-catching hook songs, chronicling deep thirsts for barroom rhythm and rowdy sensuality. An avid rockabilly fan as well as performer, Lenz's playlist of cover versions is drawn more from archival flea-market finds than from the genre's big stars. The sassy redhead cites such legendary figures as Barbara Pittman, Janis Martin, and Charlie Feathers (among many others) as her chief influences. Indeed, she cops Pittman's brooding sexuality while interpolating all manner of hiccups, growls, and vocal wallops into every song. Occassionally, her throaty, sexually charged style works against her modest range, so some drawn-out notes rail flat, and she reaches for vocal effects which just aren't there. But the chemistry, drive, and spontaneity she creates with her group, the Jaguars, more than compensates. A tight three-man unit of snare drum, slap-bass, and vintage lead guitar, her band effortlessly combines the echoey slapback of the Sun Records and manic-twang, rimshot appeal of Gene Vincent's Capitol sides.

what's available: Recorded live with no overdubbing, *Kim Lenz and her Jaguars* ♪♪♪♪ (HighTone, 1998, prod. Wally Hersom) features top-notch revivals of Ray Smith's "You Made a Hit," Johnny Carroll's "The Swing," and the Miller Sisters' "Ten Cats Down" with stylish verve and gusto. When the Jaguars, no mere revival act, light into such originals as "Devil on My Shoulder," "You Ain't Seen Nothin'," and "I Swear I Was Lyin'," they achieve the whiskey-drenched, white-trash perfection of true rockabilly music. Lenz also demonstrates some convincing '50s country music dramatics on "Thinkin' about You," an affecting change-of-pace heartbreaker.

influences:

◀◀ Ella Mae Morse, Janis Martin, Barbara Pittman, Big Sandy & His Fly- Rite Boys

Ken Burke

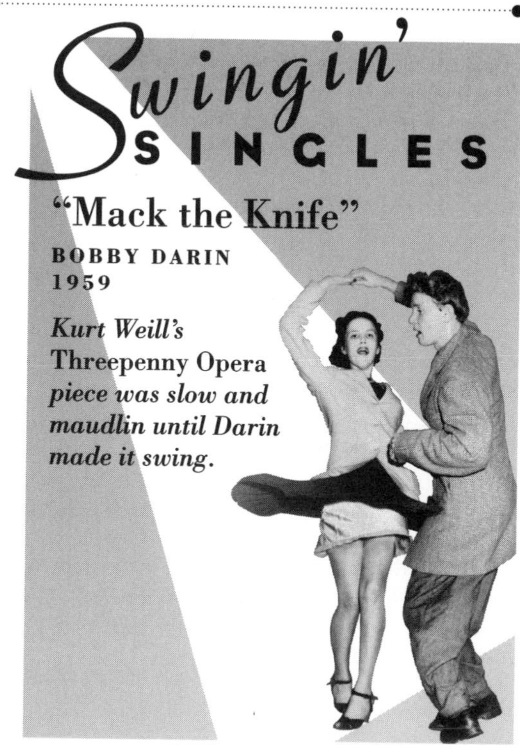

Swingin' SINGLES
"Mack the Knife"
BOBBY DARIN
1959
Kurt Weill's Threepenny Opera piece was slow and maudlin until Darin made it swing.

Sonny Lester

Birthdate and birthplace unknown.

This mysterious character did the heavy lifting for a then-sexist but now-camp LP series titled *How to Strip for Your Husband*. (Thus fulfilling two of the three definitions of "swing"—as far as we know, a children's swingset has nothing to do with this.) Though those two albums, with wonderful drawings of an unzipped '50s woman posing seductively for her pleased, leering husband, have long been collectors' treasures, the bulk of the music within has been reissued on a funny Rhino CD. In liner notes for the reissue, New York DJ Eddie Gorodetsky offers this biography: "To be honest, I don't know who Sonny Lester is. He could have been a journeyman horn player who hung around Birdland. . . . Or perhaps he was a fictitious creation given a name melded from two great sax players—Sonny Stitt (or perhaps Rollins) and Lester Young. On a number of cuts Sonny Lester's alto sax seems influenced by Lester Young's tenor." Either way, as Rhino's *Take It Off! Striptease Classics* proves, Lester's curvy, horny big-band music is the perfect complement for David Rose's classic "The Stripper" in any of your town's most unsavory establishments.

what to buy: *Take It Off! Striptease Classics* ♪♪♪♪ (Rhino, 1997, compilation prod. Andrea Kinloch, Jill Ruzich, James Austin) compiles 18 tracks by Lester, all with the same va-va-voom big-band arrangements, and all operating on both campy and quality-music levels (this stuff is really, really cheesy—it's also really, really well performed). Standouts include a version of Irving Berlin's "A Pretty Girl Is Like a Melody" and Bill Grundy's more-salacious "Lonely Little G-String." The liner notes, holographic cover photo, and seductive pictures of ladies stripping are not to be missed.

worth searching for: As the Rhino collection explains, the original LPs—*Ann Corio Presents: How to Strip for Your Husband/Music to Make Marriage Merrier* ♪♪♪♪♪ (Roulette, 1962, prod. Sonny Lester) and *Ann Corio Presents: More How* *to Strip for Your Husband, Vol. 2/Music to Make Marriage Merrier* ♪♪♪♪ (Roulette, 1963, prod. Sonny Lester)—are long out of print. If you happen upon them in a record store or a collectors' convention, don't hesitate to buy.

influences:

◀◀ David Rose, Raymond Scott, Duke Ellington

▶▶ Every strip joint in America, Combustible Edison, Love Jones

Steve Knopper

Jerry Lee Lewis

Born September 29, 1935, in Ferriday, LA.

Boogie-woogie was a vital component to both swing and rock 'n' roll. Indeed, many of the great early rock musicians were pianists (Fats Domino, Little Richard, Amos Milburn) in the Pete Johnson mold. Even Chuck Berry depended heavily on piano men like Johnnie Johnson and Lafayette Leake. However, there is no better place to experience the transformation of swing-era boogie into cathartic rock 'n' roll than the Sun-era recordings of Jerry Lee Lewis. The greatest of the '50s rockers, Lewis's blues-drenched bravado, combined with his dramatic feel for country music and sexually charged boogie-woogie, effortlessly created the impression he was living every moment of each song on a grand scale. Moreover, he has left behind a richer, more varied catalog of recordings than any of his contemporaries. On stage, he raised rock 'n' roll showmanship to a high, nearly Pentecostal art. After bopping the keyboards with his fists, elbows, feet, and ass (somehow always hitting the right note), he would triumphantly kick back his stool, suggestively corkscrew into an upright position while playing one last run, and then vault onto the piano top. Then, with his long, peroxide-blonde hair hanging in his eyes, he would exhort his ecstatic followers to "Shake it, baby, shake it!" Rebellious kids seeking rhythmic freedom and release loved him. Their parents hated his freaking guts.

Lewis absorbed his stark, personal country style from his father's Jimmie Rodgers and Hank Williams records and experienced the liberating forces of the blues at Haney's Big House. On his own, he learned to transform everything from the cowboy songs of Gene Autry to the overwrought pop of Al Jolson into thrilling cut-time boogie and moving honky-tonk ballads. A masterful self-taught pianist, Lewis could attack the keys with frightening energy and power, or softly caress them cocktail-time style. In the years before the epiphany of rock 'n' roll, he played his music in bloody buckets and honky-tonks where variety and drive mattered as much as style. After the emergence of Elvis Presley, Lewis made a beeline for Memphis, and demanded (and received) an audition at Sun Records. Once signed, he picked up eating money by playing on sessions for lablemates Carl Perkins, Johnny Cash, Billy Lee Riley, and others. Initially banned for being lewd, his hit "Whole Lotta Shakin' Goin' On" broke through to a national audience when Lewis performed it on NBC's *The Steve Allen Show*. It became the biggest hit in Sun Records' history. His wild R&B-flavored follow-ups "Great Balls of Fire" and "Breathless" put him in line to become rock's new king once Presley was inducted into the Army. It never happened. Just as his theme to the 1958 movie *High School Confidential* was scaling the charts, the furor over his marriage to his 13-year-old cousin resulted in the banishment of his records from most radio playlists. Some great singles such as "Lovin' Up a Storm" and "Let's Talk about Us" were adversely affected by the blackout. He even cut a pounding instrumental version of Glenn Miller's "In the Mood" under the name "The Hawk," but programmers knew who it was at the keyboard instantly, and Lewis wouldn't have another national hit until his ballsy remake of Ray Charles's "What'd I Say" hit the Top 30 in 1961. Lewis switched to Smash/Mercury Records in 1963. Aided in no small part by producer/guitarist Jerry Kennedy, he recorded several fine LPs of country, rock, and even soul, but only the concert disc *Greatest Live Show on Earth* sold well nationally. Finally, late in 1968, as a favor to his old friend Eddie Kilroy, Lewis cut the honky-tonk classic "Another Place, Another Time." The record became a major country smash and a string of hits, including "She Still Comes Around," followed. On these sides, Lewis revealed a deeper, more mature voice which resonated with the emotional power of the blues. After crossing over to the pop charts with his Memphis-beat version of "Me and Bobby McGee" and the Grammy-nominated "Chantilly Lace," Lewis returned to rock 'n' roll full force with the double LP *The Session*. Recorded in London with such superstar rock pickers as Peter Frampton and Alvin Lee, it became his biggest-seller of all time. At this point, it was Lewis's intention to cut a rock LP for every country disc, but excessive drinking, pill-popping, and complex personal tragedies too numerous to mention took their toll on his productivity and sound. Touring up to 300 days a year, Lewis fried his throat, and often recorded while audibly drunk. In the meantime, his soundalike cousin Mickey Gilley usurped his place on country playlists. Despite a few great singles for various labels, most of Lewis's subsequent country albums were sloppy affairs, and his gun-wielding studio antics so disgusted Elektra chief Jimmy Bowen that he paid the Killer's manager to "make him go away." Battling chronic health problems, substance abuse, and the IRS, Lewis hoped the 1989 movie *Great Balls of Fire!* would revive his sagging fortunes, but the soundtrack (provided by JLL himself) was the best aspect of that box-office bomb. He didn't appear on record again until his 1995 debut on Sire, where he proved he could still transform a stunning array of American musical genres into pulse-pumping, heart-wrenching Jerry Lee Lewis music. Though racked by ill health, which has

Jerry Lee Lewis **(Archive Photos)**

rendered him ghostly white and (at times) feeble, the Killer continues to tour the world, rocking his life away.

what to buy: To hear why Jerry Lee Lewis was among the first inductees to the Rock and Roll Hall of Fame, check out the 19-song *Original Sun Greatest Hits* ♪♪♪♪♪ (Rhino, 1984, compilation prod. Art Fein), which not only contains his legendary '50s hits, but remarkably wild lesser-known tunes such as "Drinkin' Wine Spo-dee-o-dee," "Put Me Down," and the infamous "Big Legged Woman." The 20-song *Sings the Rock 'n' Roll Classics* ♪♪♪♪♪ (Eagle, 1998, prod. Jack Clement, Sam Phillips) is every bit as impressive with such swinging boogie as "Mean Woman Blues," "Little Queenie," and 10 others not on the Rhino disc. Those wishing to baby-step into Lewis's vast country catalog should find *Killer Country* ♪♪♪♪♪ (Mercury, 1995, compilation prod. Colin Escott), a 20-song collection with some of the finest honky-tonk performances of this or any other era. He brings forth a lot of punk energy for the must-have *Live at the Star Club, Hamburg* ♪♪♪♪♪ (Rhino, 1992, compilation prod. Siggi Loch), the finest live performance ever captured on tape by any of the original rockers.

what to buy next: The two-disc, 42-song set *The Jerry Lee Lewis Anthology: All Killer, No Filler* ♪♪♪♪ (Rhino, 1993, compilation prod. James Austin) contains nearly every major chart record from his eras with Sun, Smash, Mercury, and Elektra.

what to avoid: The Killer has never cut a completely bad LP, but there are several discs out there you should be wary of, such as *Duets* **woof!** (Sun Entertainment, 1979/1996, prod. Shelby Singleton), a deceptive package that has Jimmy "Orion" Ellis overdubbing his imitation of the King onto several of Lewis's Sun-era tracks in a cynical attempt to trick fans into believing Elvis recorded extensively with Jerry Lee. Disgraceful stuff like this should not be encouraged with your purchase. *The Golden Rock Hits of Jerry Lee Lewis* ♪♪♪ (Smash, 1967/1987, prod. Jerry Kennedy, Shelby Singleton) features slick re-recordings of his Sun material taped during his first months at Smash/Mercury. *Great Balls of Fire* ♪♪♪ (Original Motion Picture Soundtrack) (Polydor, 1989, prod. T-Bone Burnett) also contains re-recordings of his classic Sun material (albeit potent ones) for the film of the same name. *Great Balls of Fire!* ♪♪ (Columbia River, 1997), *Great Balls of Fire Live!* ♪♪ (Pilz, 1993), and *Whole Lotta*

Shakin' Goin' on Live! (Pilz, 1993) all use colorized photos of Lewis from the '50s on their covers, but the music inside (which is pretty good though the sound is a bit thin) is drawn from various TV concerts during the '70s and '80s. *Roots of Rock 'n' Roll* (Prime Cuts, 1995/Direct Source, 1997) and *Live in Concert* (Tring/Double Play, 1998) sound as if they were recorded with a hand-held tape recorder, which is a shame because Lewis really burns through this late-'70s concert set. *Ladies & Gentlemen . . . Live* (Master Tone, 1998) draws from many of the sets listed above, with despicably muddy sound. Also, with all the hits compilations available, you don't really need *Back to Back* (K-Tel, 1996, prod. various) unless you also want cuts by Mickey Gilley.

the rest:

Jerry Lee Lewis (Sun, 1958/Rhino,1989)
Jerry Lee's Greatest! (Sun,1961/Rhino,1989)
The Greatest Live Shows on Earth (Smash, 1964, 1967/Bear Family, 1994)
(With Johnny Cash and Carl Perkins) *The Survivors* (Columbia, 1982/Razor & Tie, 1995)
Silver Eagle Presents Jerry Lee Lewis Live (Silver Eagle, 1984/1997)
Milestones (Rhino, 1985)
Live at the Vapors Club (SCR, 1985/Ace, 1993)
(With Carl Perkins, Roy Orbison, and Johnny Cash) *Class of '55* (America/Smash/Mercury, 1986)
20 Classic Jerry Lee Lewis Hits (Original Sound Entertainment, 1986)
(With Elvis Presley and Carl Perkins) *The Complete Million Dollar Session* (Charly/Sun, 1987)
Rare and Rockin'—Original Sun Recordings (Charly, 1987)
Rare Tracks: Wild One (Rhino, 1989)
Killer: The Mercury Years, Volume One: 1963–1968 (Mercury, 1989)
Killer: The Mercury Years, Volume Two: 1969–1972 (Mercury, 1989)
Killer: The Mercury Years, Volume Three: 1973–1977 (Mercury, 1989)
Rocket 88 (Tomato, 1989/1992)
Heartbreak (Tomato, 1989/1992)
The Complete Palomino Club Recordings (Tomato, 1989/1991)
The EP Collection (See For Miles, 1991)
Best of Jerry Lee Lewis (Curb, 1991)
Rockin' My Life Away: The Jerry Lee Lewis Collection (Warner Bros., 1991)
Live in Italy (Magnum, 1991)
Great Balls of Fire! (Charly, 1992)
Good Rockin' Tonight (Charly, 1992)
The Alternate Collection (Charly, 1992)
Rockin' My Life Away (Tomato, 1992)
Honky Tonk Rock 'n' Roll Piano Man (Ace, 1992)
Pretty Much Country (Ace, 1992)
The EP Collection, Vol. 2 (See For Miles, 1994)
Rocket '88 (Tomato, 1992)
Greatest Hits—Finest Performances (Sun, 1995)
Young Blood (Sire, 1995)
Best of the Best of Jerry Lee Lewis (Federal, 1996)
Mercury & Smash Recordings (Collectables, 1997)
The Hits (Mercury, 1997)
Whole Lotta Shakin' Goin' On—The Very Best of Jerry Lee Lewis, Vol. 1 (Collectables, 1999)
Invitation to Your Party—The Very Best of Jerry Lee Lewis, Vol. 2 (Collectables, 1999)

worth searching for: Box sets were made for someone as prolific as the Killer and *Classic Jerry Lee Lewis (1956–1963)* (Bear Family, 1989/1992, reissue prod. Colin Escott) is one of the best ever. This enormously satisfying and listenable eight-CD, 247-song set collects everything cut at Sun including off-the-cuff jams, alternate takes, and his famous argument with Sam Phillips concerning religion and "Great Balls of Fire." Fair warning: Once you become addicted to the Sun sound, everything else sounds hideously overproduced and phony. The oddly titled *Locust Years . . . And the Return to the Promised Land* (Bear Family, 1994, reissue prod. Richard Weize) is an eight-CD set that encapsulates all of Lewis's mid-to-late '60s work for Smash Records, including his three brilliant live LPs, experiments in soul, pop, and modern country music. For his later Mercury material, the vinyl-only sets *The Killer 1969–1972* (Bear Family, 1989, compilation prod. Richard Weize) and *The Killer 1973–1977* (Bear Family, 1989, compilation prod. Richard Weize) will have to do until Bear Family reissues them on CD. The former contains his work as a leading hit country artist and a remarkable gospel recording cut live in a church. The latter documents his briefly successful return to rock and slow slide off the country charts. *Rocket* (Bellaphon, 1988, prod. Bob Moore) is a decent mix of rock and country marred by incomplete production values and some of the most prominent basslines ever heard on a Lewis record (which makes sense because the producer is his bass player). *Jerry Lee Lewis Jokes and Sings Mona Lisa* (Flash, 1991) is a vinyl-only release documenting Lewis's struggle to record "It Was the Whiskey Talkin' (Not Me)" for the *Dick Tracy* movie. Lewis's comments about Mickey Gilley, Jimmie Lee Swaggert, and his hit "Breathless" ("I hated that song from day one") are revealing and frequently hilarious. *The Killer's Private Stash* (Electrovert, 1991) is an amazing piece of musical archaeology featuring Lewis's very first recordings from 1954, rehearsal tapes for the play *Catch My Soul* in 1968, and outtakes from the film soundtrack of *Great Balls of Fire*. *That Breathless Cat* (Stomper Time, 1992, compilation prod. Dave Travis) contains two amazing live performances from '50s TV shows and 17 tracks from the early '80s of Lewis talking, noodling around on the piano, and singing snatches of old hits, old-time country, pop standards, and new songs made up on the spot. *At Hank Cochran's* (Trend, 1995, prod. Hank Cochran, Mack Vickery) is the weirdest thing Lewis has ever done (which is why it's so interesting), 14 tracks of old-time country, gospel, and Al Jolson tunes recorded with a synthesizer and preloaded effects which could have been subtitled "The Killer Sings Karaoke." *Old-Time Rock 'n' Roll* (Killer, 1997) is blurry sounding evidence that much of Lewis's best work at Elektra went unreleased. The video *Shindig! Presents Jerry Lee Lewis* (Rhino Home Video, 1992) contains powerful vintage performances from the classic mid-'60s TV show.

influences:

Amos Milburn, Little Richard, Fats Domino, Hank Williams, Jimmie Rodgers, Big Joe Turner, George Jones, Ray Charles, Bob Wills, B.B. King, Chuck Willis, Professor Longhair

Carl Mann, Charlie Rich, Mickey Gilley, Jimmie Lee Swaggert, Tom Jones, Hank Williams Jr., Gary Stewart, Elton John, Billy Joel, Preacher Jack, Marcia Ball.

see also: *Billy Lee Riley, Warren Smith*

Ken Burke

Meade "Lux" Lewis

Born Meade Anderson Lewis, September 4, 1905, in Chicago, IL. Died June 7, 1964, near Minneapolis, MN.

"Milkcow Blues Boogie"
ELVIS PRESLEY
1954
Contains the immortal aside "Hold it, fellas; that don't move me; let's get real, real gone for a change."
Swingin'
SINGLES

One of the great boogie-woogie pianists, the powerful Meade "Lux" Lewis had less technique but more creativity than his two famous contemporaries, Pete Johnson and Albert Ammons. He's responsible for "Honky Tonk Train Blues," released in 1929, a piano classic that predated the boogie-woogie craze of the late '30s. Lewis became enamored of piano blues in Chicago, when he heard his neighbor, the influential Jimmy Yancey, playing in 1921. He worked odd jobs and performed with little national fame until 1935, when Columbia Records scout John Hammond discovered Lewis and his housemate Albert Ammons washing cars and driving a taxi for a living. Hammond got Lewis into the studio in November of that year to re-record "Honky Tonk Train Blues." The great boogie-woogie craze that started with the Hammond-organized 1938 Spirituals to Swing concert in Carnegie Hall jump-started Lewis's career again, and he began recording and performing in concerts, sometimes with fellow pianists Ammons and Pete Johnson as the Boogie Woogie Trio. After the craze died down in the '40s, he continued recording, then moved to Los Angeles, where he did nightclub and television work. He was driving back from a concert in Minneapolis when he died from injuries sustained in an auto accident.

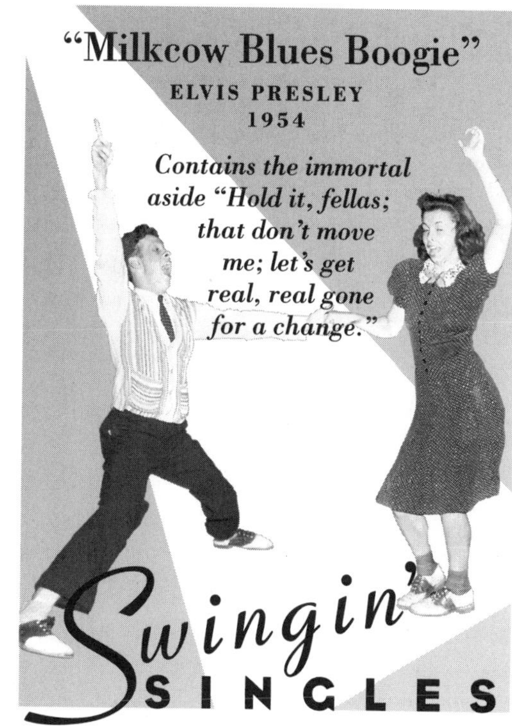

what to buy: Among the 18 songs that make up *The Chronological Meade Lux Lewis: 1927–1939* (Jazz Chronological Classics, 1993) are three versions of "Honky Tonk Train": the original from 1927, John Hammond's recording from 1935, and one cut in 1937. The recording of "Boogie Woogie Prayer Parts 1 & 2" by the piano trio of Lewis, Ammons, and Johnson can be found only on this set. *The First Day* (Blue Note, 1992, prod. Alfred Lion) is split between some fine Lewis solo tunes, two duets with Ammons, and solo material from Ammons.

what to buy next: *The Blues Piano Artistry of Meade Lux Lewis* (Original Jazz Classics, 1962/1991, prod. Chris Albertson) is unadulterated piano playing by Meade Lux Lewis, without vocals or other instruments clamoring for attention. The whole session was recorded in less than three hours because Lewis had made an appointment to be somewhere else at the end of the date. Results bear out Lewis's calm assurance at the beginning of the session: "Don't worry, we'll make it." In addition to some wonderfully inventive boogie-woogie piano playing on his own originals, it's interesting to hear him take off on Duke Ellington's "C-Jam Blues." Lewis also improvises with the celeste's bell-like tones on three songs, making the most of this novelty.

the rest:
Tidal Boogie (Tradition, 1954/1996)
Meade Lux Lewis: 1939–1954 (Story of the Blues, 1991)
Meade Lux Lewis: 1939–1941 (Jazz Chronological Classics, 1994)
Meade Lux Lewis: 1941–1944 (Classics, 1994)
Meade Lux Lewis: Alternate Takes, Live Performances, Soundies, Etc.: 1939 to Late 1940s (Document, 1998)

influences:
◀◀ Jimmy Yancey, Charles "Cow Cow" Davenport, Cripple Clarence Lofton

▶▶ Lafayette Leake

Garaud MacTaggart

Mel Lewis

Born Melvin Sokoloff, May 10, 1929, in Buffalo, NY. Died February 2, 1990, in New York, NY.

A legendary big-band drummer, Mel Lewis also led one of the most respected big bands as well, the Thad Jones/Mel Lewis Big Band, which played Monday nights at the Village Vanguard for 23 years, until Lewis's death, and continues to this day as the Vanguard Jazz Orchestra. The son of a professional drummer, Lewis began his career at age 14 working with dance bands in his hometown of Buffalo. By 1948 he had played with some of the better dance bands in jazz, including the Boyd Raeburn Orchestra and the bands of Alvino Rey, Tex Beneke, and Ray Anthony. In 1954 he joined the Stan Kenton Orchestra and immediately gained a reputation as a drummer who understood the nuances of working with a big band, swinging the cumbersome Kenton orchestra as never before. After several years on the road with Kenton, he moved to Los Angeles in 1957 and worked with big bands led by Gerald Wilson and Terry Gibbs, as well as in the combos of Hampton Hawes and Frank Rosolino. By the 1960s he was back on the road with Dizzy Gillespie and Benny Goodman. Relocating to New York in the mid-'60s, he was active in the studio scene and in 1965 formed his group with trumpeter Thad Jones. When Jones fled to Europe in the late 1970s, much to the surprise of everyone, including Lewis, the drummer became the orchestra's sole leader. In the 1980s he maintained a busy recording schedule, performing with his own groups, as well as the American Jazz Orchestra.

what to buy: After the departure of Jones in 1978, Lewis kept his band book fresh by commissioning new arrangements. *Live at the Village Vanguard* (DCC, 1980/1991, prod. Norman Schwartz) features the compositions and charts of valve trombonist/arranger Bob Brookmeyer, a charter member of the Jones/Lewis band at its inception in 1965. Where Jones's writing had its roots in Count Basie, Brookmeyer's concept is informed by modern classical music. Nevertheless, this is one swinging session, thanks to Lewis's driving percussion. A decade after Jones's departure, Lewis pulled out some of Jones's first charts once again and recorded them on *Definitive Thad Jones, Volume 1* (MusicMasters, 1989, prod. John Snyder) with an edition of his famed big band. Although this was done in the studio, it has the feel of a live date because the solos really stretch out. Gems like "Three in One," which runs 13 minutes, and "Little Pixie" at 15 minutes showcase the soloists and also Jones's intelligent, challenging writing, as well as the finesse of the band's section work. When Lewis did *Mel Lewis* (VSOP, 1957/1995, prod. Red Clyde), in Los Angeles, he was a busy studio player best known for his work with Stan Kenton. It's hard bop with a West Coast feel, more laidback and not as intense as its New York counterpart. Rather than just a blowing session, Lewis and his group work hard to create something original, with "Brookside," "Charlie's Cavern," and "Grey Flannel" as examples of peerless musicianship and distinctive improvisations. *Lost Art* (MusicMasters, 1990, prod. John Snyder), a sextet session, was one of Lewis's last recordings and it includes a group of musicians from his big band, notably pianist Kenny Werner, whose compositions and arrangements are featured. Lewis never lost his touch, as shown on "4/4."

the rest:
Definitive Thad Jones, Volume 2 (MusicMasters, 1990)

influences:
◀◀ Chick Webb, Gene Krupa, Jo Jones, Buddy Rich, Louis Bellson, Shelly Manne, Tiny Kahn, Max Roach

▶▶ Duffy Jackson, Butch Miles, Frank Capp, Dennis Mackrell, Jeff Hamilton, Peter Erskine

see also: *Thad Jones*

Bret Primack

Ted Lewis

Born Theodore Leopold Friedman, June 6, 1892, in Circleville, OH. Died August 25, 1971, in New York, NY.

An icon of the Depression era, Ted Lewis brought dramatic style and showmanship to his role as a big-band leader. His famous catch-phrase "Is everybody happy?" was less a rally cry for partiers than a reminder to put on a brave face and forget one's troubles, if only for a while. Initially, he played clarinet in bands fronted by Bessie Clayton and Earl Fuller. Lewis's visual style (really hamming it up on the bandstand) made him a crowd favorite and led to the formation of his own five-piece group in 1916. Billed as Ted Lewis & His Nut Band, he played the vaudeville circuit until the early '20s, when he expanded the size of his orchestra and began tackling dance music. Though Lewis's own musicianship was frequently dismissed as corny or too sentimental, his choice of back-up musicians more than compensated. Among his band regulars included Muggsy Spainer on trumpet and George Brunies on trombone, and his recordings included the likes of Fats Waller, Jack Teagarden, Jimmy Dorsey, Red Nichols, Benny Goodman, and supreme vocalist Ruth Etting. Dubbed the "High Hat Tragedian of Song," the bandleader talked or acted his way through such songs as "When My Baby Smiles at Me," "Just a Gigolo," and his pathos-laden smash "Me and My Shadow." His flair for stage histrionics made a hard-to-match impact on live audiences, and his outfit often drew bigger crowds than other, more musically adventurous bands. Lewis's successful recordings for various big record labels led to such network radio series as *The Valspar Paint Program* and the *Van Merritt Beer Program*, then several Hollywood films, including *Here Comes the Band*. Though his brand of jazz was passe by the '40s, he scored a few typically nostalgic and charming post-war hits ("Blue Skies," "My Blue Heaven," "King for a Day").

what's available: Fats Waller shares the vocal chores with Lewis on *Is Everybody Happy Now* (Take Two, 1998, digital prod. Robert Vosgien), a 20-song collection featuring Lewis's famous catch-phrase and theme, along with the jivey "I'm Crazy 'Bout My Baby" and "Darktown Strutter's Ball." Music archaeologists may prefer *Jazzworthy 1929–33* (Challenge, 1998, compilation prod. Chris Ellis), a 22-song set of Depression-era recordings that made the bandleader a household name. This set is loaded with blues and razzmatazz jazz, showing Lewis's heart was in the right place, and he knew how to make good commercial use of budding talent (such as Jimmy Dorsey, Jack Teagarden, and Benny Goodman).

worth searching for: Completists might want *Last Recordings* (Starline, 1998), a Lewis-led collection of syrupy sweet nostalgic recordings.

influences:

Earl Fuller, Bessie Clayton, Buster Bailey

Muggsy Spanier, Red Nichols, Benny Goodman, Ruth Etting, Leon Redbone

see also: *Fats Waller*

Ken Burke

Jimmy Liggins

Born October 14, 1922, in Newby, OK. Died July 18, 1983, in Durham, N.C.

Though jump-blues star Jimmy Liggins briefly tried to make it as a boxer and a disc jockey, his lineage made it impossible for him to stay away from the R&B world for long. His older brother, Joe Liggins, bandleader and singer of the well-known R&B group the Honeydrippers, hired Jimmy as his chauffeur—and before long Jimmy was fronting his own band, the Drops of Joy. Liggins's subsequent string of hits, including 1948's "Tear Drop Blues" and 1953's hilariously blunt "Drunk," just barely predated rock 'n' roll. Later hits by Little Richard, Elvis Presley, and Ike Turner drew heavily from jumping R&B sides by both Liggins brothers—as well as Big Joe Turner, Ivory Joe Hunter, and Elmore James.

worth searching for: Both collections of Liggins's 1940s and 1950s sides are excellent (they include "Drunk," of course): The Drops of Joys *Legends of Specialty Series* (Specialty, 1989) and the slightly jazzier *Vol. 2: Rough Weather Blues* (Specialty, 1992) are important transitional documents of the years between jumping blues and swinging rock 'n' roll.

influences:

Louis Jordan, Joe Liggins, Ivory Joe Hunter, Ruth Brown, Ray Charles

Little Richard, Chuck Berry, Bill Haley, Elvis Presley

Steve Knopper

Joe Liggins

Born 1915, in Guthrie, OK. Died July 26, 1987, in Los Angeles, CA.

Joe Liggins came to the fore at the dividing line between early 1940s swing and the harder-driving urban R&B of the late 1940s, and while he tends to be claimed by the latter era, his music often strayed into the earlier period. Liggins was Mr. Dependable compared to his guitar-stroking brother, Jimmy, who led a wilder-booting band until he was shot in the face by a demented fan. Joe was tamer and more avuncular, but he owned the R&B charts in the immediate post-war era, racking up 13 Top 10 hits on Exclusive and Specialty from 1945 until 1951. His sound was unmistakable—arcing, rubbery horns over a light back beat and pleasing vocals. It was a recipe he used on classics like "The Honeydripper" and "Pink Champagne" until he finally wore out his welcome at the dawn of the rock 'n' roll era in the early 1950s. Soon after his family moved to San Diego in 1932, Liggins joined Texas sax honker Illinois Jacquet, then started up his own unit, breaking out with 1945's "The Honeydripper," which sold 2 million copies. Label-hopping to Specialty worked, but by the end of the 1950s, Liggins was back to playing weddings and small clubs in Los Angeles. He reintroduced a new generation of Angelenos to his smooth R&B in the mid-1980s and even headed a few West Coast festivals before his untimely death.

what to buy: The place to start is with the cream of Liggins's Exclusive Records repertoire, collected on *The Honeydripper* (Night Train, 1996, prod. Leon Rene). Unfortunately, there

Guy Lombardo **(Archive Photos)**

is teeth-gritting fluff here, like the obnoxious "Darktown Strutters Ball."

what to buy next: Liggins's driving Specialty sessions are on *Joe Liggins and the Honeydrippers* (Specialty, 1990, prod. Art Rupe), a 25-track survey of his best from the early 1950s. "Pink Champagne" and the giddy "Rhythm in the Barnyard" are just two of his classics, all recorded with punchy, clear sound.

what to avoid: *Darktown Strutters Ball* (Jukebox Lil, 1990) offers a few scant hits, but mostly the dregs of the Exclusive sides. The leftovers of Liggins's Specialty years are on the feeble *Dripper's Boogie* (Specialty, 1992, prod. Art Rupe).

influences:

◀◀ Illinois Jacquet, Louis Jordan

▶▶ Jimmy Liggins, Little Willie Jackson

Steve Braun

Lightcrust Doughboys

See: Bob Wills

Guy Lombardo

Born Gaetano Lombardo, June 19, 1902, in London, Ontario, Canada. Died November 5, 1977, in Houston, TX.

"Enjoy Yourself," the name of Lombardo's trademark 1949 hit, was also the durable bandleader's musical philosophy. He could produce dramatic, swing-heavy pop like Frank Sinatra, but his best-known songs tended to come out like Sinatra's goofy, playful "High Hopes." His singing brother, Carmen, dribbled such phrases as "cuckoo like a cuckoo in a clock" as if to insist that listeners not take themselves so seriously. Lombardo's longtime radio show turned the band's version of "Auld Lang Syne" into a New Year's Eve ritual, like today's Dick Clark TV broadcasts and Times Square ball-dropping. Even when the big bands died out, Lombardo's "sweet music" perservered and he continued performing until his death.

Lombardo's Italian-born father, a closet musician, advised his son at an early age to "don't forget the melody and choose songs people can sing, hum, or whistle," according to 1996 liner notes. He and his two brothers, singer-songwriter Carmen and squawky, lyrical trumpeter Lebert, formed a swing band and built their sound so straightforwardly that they refused to change keys during a song. In 1927, after naming themselves the Royal Canadians, they landed an influential Chicago radio gig, then converted that into a longtime broadcast at New York City's Roosevelt Grill. Thanks to the radio exposure—plus recurring movie roles for both Guy and Carmen—the Lombardo band began an impressive string of hits that lasted through the mid-1950s. A speedboat racer who won a late-1940s national championship, Lombardo wound up selling more than 200 million records. Most of his 1940s singles, including "Boo Hoo," "Coquette," "What's the Reason (I'm Not Pleasin' You)," were big hits; the string let up only when a different type of up-tempo music, rock 'n' roll, began to dominate the pop charts. Late in his life, Lombardo organized revues at his Marine Theatre in New York—but the essence of "The Sweetest Music This Side of Heaven" really died when Carmen Lombardo succumbed to cancer in 1971. Guy Lombardo suffered a fatal heart attack six years later.

what to buy: The most impressively organized Lombardo package, *Enjoy Yourself: The Hits of Guy Lombardo* (Decca/MCA, 1996, prod. Marty Wesker), has excellent liner notes and a ready-for-New-Year's version of "Auld Lang Syne." Plus, the opening songs "Enjoy Yourself (It's Later Than You Think)" and "It's Love-Love-Love" are refreshing lessons on how to live life to the fullest. But the collection lacks some of Lombardo's biggest hits, including "Boo Hoo," which shows up instead on the Royal Canadians' *The Best of Guy Lombardo* (Curb/Capitol, 1990, prod. various) and on *16 Most Requested Songs* (Sony/Legacy, 1989, prod. various).

what to buy next: Though it doesn't show off the great strengths of either band, the Lombardo-Mills Brothers collaboration *Christmas* (MCA, 1993) is a high-class holiday collection, lacking the corny nature of most pop artists' dutiful, moneymaking showings of spirit.

what to avoid: Because Lombardo recorded for several different record labels, it's easy to pick up redundant greatest-hits packages. We recommend the aforementioned instead of *Sweetest Music This Side of Heaven* (Living Era, 1995), although it does include a few collaborative cameos by Bing Crosby.

the rest:
Auld Lang Syne (MCA, 1990)
All Time Favorites (MCA Special Products, 1998)

worth searching for: Lombardo's band takes on several blues songs, including "Frankie and Johnny" and "St. Louis Blues," on the hard-to-find *The Best of Guy Lombardo* (MCA, 1977, prod. various).

influences:
◀◀ Louis Armstrong, Duke Ellington, Frank Sinatra, Isham Jones

▶▶ Tony Bennett, Dean Martin, Gordon MacRae, Paul McCartney, Rosemary Clooney

Steve Knopper

The Lost Continentals

Formed 1993, in Atlanta, GA.

Amy Pike, vocals; Jeff Passifiume, guitars, six string bass, accordion, vocals; Johnny Cowan, double bass, vocals; Michael "Hammer" Wray, drums, vocals.

The Lost Continentals combine elements of lounge, jump blues, rockabilly, and swing to forge an appealing, never-forced small combo sound. Vocalist Amy Pike is the chief asset, emoting sensual and cool bop, belting with a bluesy vibrato, and even growling a little rock. In addition, she's a promising songwriter whose work contains no hint of hipster nostalgia or performance art irony. (If this swing revival is going to truly succeed, it needs more vocalists and writers of Pike's caliber.) Winners of awards for Best Rockabilly Band and Best Swing Band in Atlanta, the Lost Continentals have toured with Brian Setzer, made appearances on local TV, and their first disc has been in regular rotation on more than 100 radio stations. Thus far, they haven't caused much of a stir beyond the southeastern seaboard, but the potential is there. The band plans to release a new disc in late 1999.

what's available: Few debuts are as fully formed artistic statements as *Moonshine & Martinis* (Landslide, 1997, prod. Jeff Bacos), which combines some truly inspired reworkings of obscure oldies ("Love Rollercoaster," "Kiss Me Big," "5 Months 2 Weeks 2 Days") with first-rate original material ("Notorious," "Dirty Daddy," "Natty Nat," "I Can't Imagine") neatly and simply done. Jazz and lounge fans will find the band's intimate small-combo sound appealing; rockabilly and jump cats will appreciate Passifiume's atmospheric guitar leads, and all should dig the hot and cool vocals of Amy Pike.

influences:
◀◀ Louis Prima, Big Joe Turner, Anita O'Day, Esquivel, Nat King Cole, Julia Lee & Her Boyfriends

Ken Burke

The Love Dogs

Formed 1994, in Boston, MA.

Ed Duato Scheer, vocals, percussion; Alizon Lissance, keyboards, vocals; Steve Brown, drums; Jesse Williams, bass; Myanna, alto and tenor sax; Glenn Shambroom, sax, guitar.

The Love Dogs have what most of the trendy '90s swing bands lack—style. Instead of cashing in on the all-too-common finger-snapping sound, the band mixes New Orleans–style blues with swing and soul. Scheer's bluesy vocals are captivating over the sax- heavy sound.

what to buy: The hard-to-find Love Dogs' debut *I'm Yo Dog* (Tone Cool, 1996, prod. Ed Duato Scheer) was a satisfactory introduction, but *Heavy Petting* (Tone Cool, 1998, prod. Ed Duato Scheer) is the band at its best. Humor is key, with covers of Chuck Willis's "Wrong Lake to Catch a Fish" and Louis Prima's "Oh Babe." "Lock You Up" is a high-energy, Latin-style swing romp. The energy continues through the CD, with the exception of "Something's Wrong," an out-of-place, soulful R&B ballad.

influences:

◀◀ Louis Prima, Gene Krupa, Los Lobos, Dr. John

▶▶ Big Bad Voodoo Daddy

Christina Fuoco

Steve Lucky & the Rhumba Bums

Formed 1993, in Oakland, CA.

Steve Lucky, vocals, piano; Carmen Getit, vocals, guitar; Pee Wee Magee, saxophones; Ben Whalen, saxophones; Professor Humphrey Bottoms, bass; Michael Berry, drums.

The brainchild of keyboardist Steve Lucky, the high-energy Rhumba Bums have become sparkplugs of the swinging Bay Area jump scene. Originally from Ann Arbor, Michigan (where he started a swing/jump/blues band, the Blue Front Persuaders, in 1979), Lucky took a job in New York with blues singer Johnny Copeland's touring band in 1987. For the next five years he worked in Europe and in Gotham with Earl King and Lowell Fulson, among others, before he and future guitarist Carmen Getit moved to the West Coast. He formed the Rhumba Bums as a Professor Longhair-heavy New Orleans R&B band, but swing soon became a focal point, especially after the arrival of guitarist and singer Getit, whose onstage presence is as fiery as her name suggests.

what's available: *Come Out Swingin'* (Rumpus Records, 1998, prod. Steve Lucky, Carmen Getit) is a high-energy, well-produced potpourri of swing. Lucky's "Jumptown" celebrates the Bay Area scene, and his "Rumpus Room Honeymoon" and "Play It Cool" (the latter co-written with Getit) slip in nicely alongside classic swing covers like T-Bone Walker's "Bye Bye Baby" and Hadda Brooks's "Jump Back."

influences:

◀◀ Pete Johnson, Professor Longhair, Amos Milburn, T-Bone Walker, Tiny Grimes, Rusty Zinn, Otis Spann, Roy Milton, Big Joe Turner, Ray Charles, Ruth Brown, Smiley Lewis

Leland Rucker

The Lucky Strikes

Formed 1992, in Austin, TX.

Craig Marshall, vocals, guitar; David Levy, drums; Milan Moorman, trumpet, fluglehorn; Freddie Mendoza, trombone; Elias Haslanger, tenor saxophone; Dave Miller, string bass.

The Lucky Strikes are one of the few modern lounge and swing bands to exclusively record original material. Guitarist Craig Marshall pens all the tunes in the style of such legendary tunesmiths as Cole Porter, James Van Heusen, and Johnny Mercer. Both the compositions and the group's arrangements refuse to acknowledge any aspect of the modern era—surprising for a group whose members come from the ranks of power pop, funk, and rock bands. Their arrangements are creative, if not always well executed. The group's press kit mentions both Tony Bennett and Frank Sinatra as vocal influences, but let's not mince words here—with the exception of an occasional foggy note, Marshall outright mimics the Rat Pack's deceased leader. Though imitation has been called the sincerest form of flattery, Marshall repeatedly risks crossing the fine line between paying homage and exploiting Sinatra's memory. Regardless, in Austin, Texas, the Lucky Strikes' sophisticated blend of '40s-style ballads and sprightly love paeans has gone over extremely well with both nostalgia and neo-swing crowds.

what's available: The debut, *Twelve Past Midnight* (Lazy S.O.B., 1996, prod. David Sanger), is more of a lounge album than a swing-fest. Written in the style of Frank Sinatra's great moody Capitol recordings, the 12 original songs concentrate exclusively on expositions of romantic love in mostly downbeat tempos. The tunes and small combo are fine (though many tracks are too long), but lead singer Marshall never lets you forget he's aping the Chairman of the Board's phrasing and tone. (Even Matt Monro's Sinatra imitation wasn't this painstakingly humorless.) As a result, Marshall unnecessarily bleeds a lot of energy and sincerity away from such promising material as "Is This Happening?" and "Time Flies." The group's sophomore effort, *Song and Dance* (Lazy S.O.B., 1998, prod. David Sanger, Craig Marshall), features the bouncier tempos and jazzier rhythms that swing crowds prefer. Romantic hook songs such as "Things Are Looking Up," "Let's Make the Rounds," "Swing, Let's Swing," and "If You Could Be Me" have an energetic, appealing Las Vegas feel. The songs are also shorter and better focused, which heightens the effectiveness of the solos (especially special guest Floyd Domino's).

influences:

◀◀ Frank Sinatra, Nat King Cole, Billy May, Nelson Riddle

Ken Burke

Jimmie Lunceford

Born James Melvin Lunceford, June 6, 1902, in Fulton, MO. Died July 12, 1947, in Seaside, OR.

Jimmie Lunceford led a powerhouse swing band in the 1930s and 1940s. He was a highly skilled musician, playing trombone, all of the saxophone family, clarinet, flute, and guitar, but he rarely performed as a soloist on his recordings. The Lunceford Orchestra, in its peak years from about 1934 through 1942, was a brilliant musical unit, a great dance band, and a visual treat, with the members impeccably dressed in different uniforms for each show. The sections performed physical "shtick" with their instruments—trumpets pointing skyward, saxophones swaying, trombones rotating in circles—all the while remaining a high-precision jazz machine executing wildly original charts. Lunceford grew up in Denver, where he studied music with Wilberforce J. Whiteman (Paul Whiteman's father) and played alto sax with George Morrison's orchestra in 1922. He earned a bachelor of music degree at Fisk University, where he met fellow students Willie Smith, Ed Wilcox, and Henry Wells, all of whom later joined his band. From 1926 to 1929 he taught music at Manassa High School in Memphis, until a band he had formed turned professional—touring in Cleveland, Ohio, and Buffalo, New York, before moving to New York City in 1933. Lunceford's group had a highly successful six-month stay at the celebrated Cotton Club in Harlem starting in January of 1934. Nightly broadcasts served to enhance the band's reputation; they soon landed a Decca recording contract and began touring extensively, achieving a following and notoriety comparable to that of Duke Ellington and Count Basie. In 1939 the band switched to Columbia/Vocalion, lost arranger Sy Oliver to Tommy Dorsey, gained trumpeters Gerald Wilson and Snooky Young, and added a 22-year-old arranger, Billy Moore. In 1941 they recorded Wilcox's "Yard Dog Mazurka," which showed up years later in Stan Kenton's band as "Intermission Riff." The Lunceford Orchestra appeared in the film *Blues in the Night* and returned to Decca for a big hit record of the same title. As players like Wilson and Young left in the early 1940s, the quality of the band deteriorated, and the once-glorious unit became just another band, lasting until just after Lunceford's death in 1947.

what to buy: *Stomp It Off* ♪♪♪♪♪ (Decca, 1992, reissue prod. Orrin Keepnews) offers 21 tracks of auditory proof that 1934–35 was a banner period for the Lunceford organization. There are four interesting nods toward Duke Ellington with "Sophisticated Lady," "Mood Indigo," "Black and Tan Fantasy," and "Solitude" in the program. But the adventurous arrangements show that Willie Smith and Sy Oliver had their own original approaches to the material. An unidentified trio of band members introduce a familiar Lunceford device, the unison vocal, with spirited versions of "Rain," and the delightful "Since My Best Girl Turned Me Down." *For Dancers Only* ♪♪♪♪♪ (Decca, 1994, reissue prod. Orrin Keepnews) is a continuation of MCA/Decca's chronological Lunceford series that brings back 21 classic swing sides from September 1935 through June 1937. Included are Sy Oliver-arranged gems such as "Swanee River," "My Blue Heaven," "Organ Grinder's Swing," "Linger Awhile," and the title tune. This band really swung and these compilations are wonderful introductions to big-band swing and the Lunceford powerhouse.

Swingin' SINGLES
"Minnie the Moocher"
CAB CALLOWAY
1931
Calloway scat-sang famous "Hi-de-hi-de-hi-de-ho/ho-de-ho-de-ho-de-hee/oodlee-odlye-odlyee-oodlee-doo" when he suddenly forgot the lyrics in concert.

the rest:

Jimmie Lunceford and His Orchestra, 1940 ♪♪♪♪ (Circle, 1940/1994)

The Uncollected Jimmie Lunceford & His Harlem Express Live at Jefferson Barracks, Missouri, 1944 ♪♪♪ (Hindsight, 1994)

Jimmie Lunceford and His Orchestra, 1930–1934 ♪♪♪♪ (Jazz Chronological Classics, 1994)

Jimmie Lunceford and His Orchestra, 1934–1935 ♪♪♪♪♪ (Jazz Chronological Classics, 1994)

Jimmie Lunceford and His Orchestra, 1935–1937 ♪♪♪♪♪ (Jazz Chronological Classics, 1994)

Jimmie Lunceford and His Orchestra, 1939 ♪♪♪♪ (Jazz Chronological Classics, 1994)

Jimmie Lunceford and His Orchestra, 1939–1940 (Jazz Chronological Classics, 1994)
Jimmie Lunceford and His Orchestra, 1940–1941 (Jazz Chronological Classics, 1994)
Jimmie Lunceford, 1927–1934, Volume 1, No. 12 (Masters of Jazz, 1994)
Jimmie Lunceford, 1934, Volume 2, No. 18 (Masters of Jazz, 1994)
Jimmie Lunceford, 1935–1936, Volume 3, No. 57 (Masters of Jazz, 1995)
Jimmie Lunceford, 1935–1937, Volume 4, No. 71 (Masters of Jazz, 1995)
Jimmie Lunceford, 1937–1939, Volume 5, No. 84 (Masters of Jazz, 1995)
Jimmie Lunceford, The Quintessence, 1934–41 (Freemeaux & Associates, 1995)
Jimmie Lunceford, 1939, Volume 6, No. 98 (Masters of Jazz, 1996)
Jimmie Lunceford and His Orchestra, 1941–1945 (Jazz Chronological Classics, 1996)
Jimmie Lunceford and His Orchestra, 1937–1939 (Jazz Chronological Classics, 1997)
Swing-Sation Series: Jimmie Lunceford (GRP, 1998)

influences:

◀◀ Wilberforce J. Whiteman, George Morrison, Don Redman, Fletcher Henderson, Casa Loma Orchestra, Zack Whyte's Band

▶▶ Stan Kenton, Sam Donahue, Sonny Dunham, Tommy Dorsey

John T. Bitter

The Maddox Brothers & Rose /Rose Maddox

Formed 1937, in Modesto, CA. Disbanded 1957.

Cliff Maddox, vocals, guitar, mandolin; Cal Maddox, vocals, guitar, harmonica; Fred Maddox, vocals, bass; Don Maddox, vocals, fiddle; Henry Maddox, vocals, mandolin, guitar; Rose Maddox (born August 15, 1925, in Boaz, AL), vocals, bass, snare drum.

Favorites in California, the Maddox Brothers & Rose were a raucous bunch who billed themselves as "the most colorful hillbilly band in America." They played a loud, infectious mix of country boogie, rockabilly, western swing, honky-tonk and even gospel, were famous for their outrageous outfits, and recorded for 4 Star Records and Columbia. When the band broke up, Rose, who was a mere 11 years old when the family formed its band as an alternative to the itinerant fruit-tramp life that had been their lot since they had emigrated to California from Alabama, continued to perform as a soloist, a path she continues to this day. She is popular in the U.S. at bluegrass festivals and has quite a reputation in rockabilly circles in Europe. Ill health has slowed Rose down, but hasn't kept her from touring and recording extensively.

what to buy: *America's Most Colorful Hillbilly Band—Their Original Recordings, 1946–1951* (Arhoolie, 1993, prod. Chris Strachwitz) and *Maddox Brothers & Rose, Volume Two* (Arhoolie, 1995, prod. Chris Strachwitz) offer the most comprehensive overview of the band at its peak.

what to buy next: *On the Air: The 1940s* (Arhoolie, 1996, prod. Chris Strachwitz) presents intriguing live broadcasts from 1940 to 1949, including the band's 1949 appearance on the Grand Ole Opry. *A Collection of Standard Sacred Songs* (King, 1960/1994) reissues Starday gospel material.

worth searching for: *Rockin' Rollin' Maddox Brothers & Rose* (Bear Family, 1981, prod. Richard Weize) is a German reissue of the band's more rockabillyish material. *Columbia Historic Edition* (Columbia, 1985) is an excellent reissue of the band's Columbia material.

solo outings:

Rose Maddox:

Rose of the West Coast Country (Arhoolie, 1990)
Thirty-Five Dollars and a Dream (Arhoolie, 1994)
Live—On the Radio (Arhoolie, 1998)

influences:

◀◀ Hoosier Hotshots, Patsy Montana

▶▶ Ranch Romance, BR5-49

Randy Pitts

Big Joe Maher

See: Big Joe & the Dynaflows

Henry Mancini

Born Enrico Nicola Mancini, April 15, 1924, in Cleveland, OH. Died June 14, 1994, in Los Angeles, CA.

Best known for the terrific hit singles spawned by his immensely popular, high-profile movie scores, Henry Mancini had a lifelong affection for swing music, which helped to shape his career and influence his entire body of work. Mancini's greatest strength was in the variety of film genres in which he not only performed, but in some cases set the standard. Mancini's most prominent influence was Benny Goodman. Max Adkins, Mancini's musical mentor in Pittsburgh, introduced Mancini to

Henry Mancini **(Archive Photos)**

the master of big-band swing. Goodman encouraged the young arranger to study at the Juilliard school. He was accepted, but the year was 1942. After serving overseas, he moved to New York, went to work for Tex Beneke's band as arranger and pianist, and met Ginny O'Connor, a singer with the vocal group the Mellolarks and the woman he would marry. Henry and Ginny, who were solid with the young crowd in Hollywood (including Mancini's partner-to-be, Blake Edwards), gravitated to California. At Universal, Mancini's work included writing bits of music for films like *The Creature from the Black Lagoon* and *Ma and Pa Kettle at Home.* His big break was his assignment to score Orson Welles's *Touch of Evil* in 1958. He broke the mold set by the Europeans: *Touch of Evil* was subtle, flavored with jazz brass, and distinctly American. He always considered it among his best film scores. His career soared with *Peter Gunn,* a brilliant blend of atmospheric West Coast jazz with shimmering pop ("Dreamsville"), and there was even a touch of big-band aggressive swing in cuts like "Fallout." Mancini found time in between film and television assignments to record other music.

His best swing album—and one of the best records he's ever made—is 1960's *The Blues and the Beat*, which features versions of "Big Noise from Winnetka" and a groovy take on Louis Prima's classic "Sing, Sing, Sing." In that same year, Mancini assembled a stellar swing contingent for *Combo!*, with Shelly Manne, Ronny Lang, and Art Pepper. Mancini revisited swing only occasionally as composing became his full-time vocation. When he did come back to the genre, he tended to have fun with it: Witness "The Swing March" from the 1966 film *What Did You Do in the War, Daddy?* When he crossed that Big Moon River, Mancini left the rest of us a legacy of light popular music as mountainous as the riches he accrued, scoring nearly 80 films, plus about two dozen television shows and series, and recording more than 80 albums.

what to buy: Among the many compendiums of Mancini's hits (and some misses) is the three-disc *Days of Wine and Roses* ♪♪♪♪ (RCA, 1995, prod. various), which captures the Mancini magic spanning several decades. It's a terrific Mancini 101 course, collecting enough of the composer's greatest hits (starting with "Peter Gunn") to satisfy most beginners. The hard-to-find "Soldier in the Rain" theme is included. Mancini buffs should seek out the reissued score to the classic Orson Welles film *Touch of Evil* ♪♪♪♪ (1958/Varese Sarabande, 1993, reissue prod. Robert Townson, Tom Null), which contains many cues of what was to come. It's dark, moody, typically Mancini, and sounds, like so much of his work, strikingly modern even 40 years after the fact.

what to buy next: *Breakfast at Tiffany's* ♪♪♪ (RCA, 1962/1988, prod. Dick Peirce) was among Mancini's most facile scores, and certainly among the easiest to lay on the turntable and let play over and over. Some of it is too familiar—"Moon River" is probably the "Stairway to Heaven" of pop instrumentals—but much of it is just so endearing. *Cinema Italiano* ♪♪♪ (RCA, 1991, prod. John McClure) is one of Mancini's rare excursions on record into other film composers' works. There are some lovely treatments here of Ennio Morricone's theme to *The Untouchables* and his lyrical suite for *Cinema Paradiso*. It's a rare chance to hear Nino Rota's chirpy music from Fellini's *Boccaccio 70* as well as a Mancinified version of Rota's haunting waltz from *The Godfather.*

what to avoid: *The Best of Mancini* ♪♪ (RCA, 1980/1987, prod. Simon Rady, Dick Peirce, Steve Sholes, Joe Reisman) is the condensed version of the superior *Days of Wine and Roses* collection. It has all the predictable hits in one place (including "Peter Gunn," "Moon River," and the title track), but really skims the surface of Mancini's output. Also, Mancini fills out *Music from the Films of Blake Edwards: The Film Composers Series, Vol. IV* ♪♪ (RCA, 1991, prod. Simon Rady, Dick Peirce, Steve Sholes, Joe Reisman) with some marginal cues from his many film collaborations with director Edwards. The usual suspects are in place—"Peter Gunn," "Pink Panther," "Victor/Victoria"—but do we really need bits from *The Party* and yet another "Moon River" track?

best of the rest:
Collection ♪♪♪ (Pair, 1987)
Legendary Performer ♪♪ (RCA, 1987)
Academy Award Collection ♪♪♪ (Pair, 1988)
All Time Greatest Hits ♪♪♪ (RCA, 1988)
Premier Pops ♪♪ (Denon, 1988)
Mancini Rocks the Pops ♪♪♪♪ (Denon, 1989)
"As Time Goes By" and Other Classic Movie Love Songs ♪♪♪ (RCA Victor, 1992)
"The Pink Panther," "Baby Elephant Walk," "Moon River" and Other Hits ♪♪♪ (RCA Victor, 1992)
Top Hat: Music from the Films of Astaire and Rogers ♪♪♪ (RCA Victor, 1992)
Love Story ♪♪ (Pair, 1992)
Mancini Country ♪♪♪ (RCA, 1992)
Theme from "The Godfather" ♪♪♪ (RCA Victor, 1993)
Martinis with Mancini ♪♪♪ (RCA, 1997)
Merry Mancini Christmas ♪♪♪ (RCA, 1997)

worth searching for: The Grammy Awards debuted in 1958, and Mancini had the honor of receiving the first Album of the Year award for the now-out-of-print LP *The Music from "Peter Gunn"* ♪♪♪♪♪ (RCA Victor, 1958, prod. Simon Rady). Few would disagree that the classic status of "Peter Gunn" has only appreciated over the years, and it sounds as fresh today as it did 40 years ago. Another out-of-print collectors' treasure, *Hatari!* ♪♪♪♪ (RCA, 1962, prod. Dick Peirce), was one of the many superior Mancini scores that accompanied a rather mediocre pic-

The Manhattan Transfer (© Jack Vartoogian)

ture. The opening cut, "Sounds of Hatari," with its ominous brass and stunning percussion, is a *tour de force* of rushing percussion. The scores to *Charade* ♪♪♪ (RCA, 1963, prod. Joe Reisman) and *Arabesque* ♪♪♪ (RCA, 1966, prod. Joe Reisman) both have their moments.

influences:

◀◀ Shorty Rogers, Benny Goodman, Tex Beneke, Glenn Miller, Nino Rota

▶▶ John Barry, James Newton Howard, Sergio Mendes, Michael Kamen, Herb Alpert

Stephen Williams

The Manhattan Transfer

Formed 1969, in New York, NY.

Tim Hauser, vocals (1969–present); Laurel Masse, vocals (1972–79); Cheryl Bentyne, vocals (1979–present); Alan Paul, vocals (1972–present); Janis Siegel, vocals (1972–present).

Weaving their voices in and out of each other's with exquisite precision, the heavily swing-influenced Manhattan Transfer nail harmonies so effortlessly it sounds like anyone could do it. Amateur choirs spend hours trying to work out vocal arrangements by the Manhattan Transfer, in the end making the inevitable conclusion: there's gold in them there voices—eight Grammys' worth, to date. Beginning as a down-home jug band, the original Manhattan Transfer disintegrated in 1972, with remaining member Tim Hauser putting together the vocal ensemble that quickly found a cult following on the New York cabaret circuit. The band's 1975 self-titled record charted on both sides of the Atlantic, starting what was to become a tradition in global appeal. Working from the Louis Armstrong–Ella Fitzgerald scat-singing tradition, the group has covered pop, swing, jazz, and rock.

what to buy: *Swing* ♪♪♪♪ (Atlantic, 1997, prod. Tim Hauser) sets the group loose on swing-era orchestral numbers. "A Tisket, a Tasket," an arrangement inspired from a 1938 Chick Webb recording, morphs Ella Fitzgerald's talent with Webb's orchestral style and results in one of the best numbers the band has ever recorded. *Vocalese* ♪♪♪♪ (Atlantic, 1985, prod. Tim Hauser), the word for a style that sets lyrics to previously recorded jazz instrumentals, racked up 12 Grammy nominations and won two. On it, the group rocks up Ray Charles's soulful piano stomp "Ray's Rockhouse," along with the catchy "That's Killer Joe," and the intricately playful "Another Night in Tunisia," with Man of 10,000 Sounds Bobby McFerrin joining on vocals. All the lyrics were penned by vocalese master Jon Hendricks. *The Manhattan Transfer* ♪♪♪♪ (Atlantic, 1975/1987, prod. Tim Hauser, Ahmet Ertegun) offers "Java Jive," an easy-listening tribute to coffee, as well as the down-on-your-knees gospel number "Operator," and the swinging "Tuxedo Junction." This record captures the group in straightforward confidence before it became hugely popular and started experimenting with the entire musical spectrum.

what to buy next: *Anthology: Down in Birdland* ♪♪♪♪ (Rhino, 1992, prod. various) offers the span of hits—from "Trickle Trickle" to "Baby Come Back to Me (The Morse Code of Love)"—in a two-CD package. It's a good introduction, given that some Transfer albums can be sketchy in between the gems, dabbling in the latest sound of the times. *Very Best of Manhattan Transfer* ♪♪♪ (Rhino, 1994, prod. various) is more compact, skimming the cream from the top of the *Anthology* and pouring it onto one CD. *Mecca for Moderns* ♪♪♪ (Atlantic, 1981, prod. Jay Graydon) includes the pop number "Boy from New York City." Finally, any jazz vocal group worth its weight in lung power is expected to sing "Route 66," and the Manhattan Transfer offers its groovy take on it on *Bop Doo Wopp* ♪♪♪♪ (Atlantic, 1985, prod. Tim Hauser).

what to avoid: On *Tonin'* ♪ (Atlantic, 1995, prod. Arif Mardin), an exercise in pop horror, the group attempts to jazz up pop standards, featuring guest vocalists like Frankie Valli and Phil Collins. Smokey Robinson probably didn't even keep his copy of the CD, on which he sang a flat remake of his classic "I Second That Emotion." "The Thrill Is Gone" (and it really is) when the group sings behind blues greats B.B. King and Ruth Brown.

the rest:
Jukin' ♪♪ (Capitol, 1971)
Coming Out ♪♪♪ (Atlantic, 1976)
Pastiche ♪♪♪♪ (Atlantic, 1978)
The Manhattan Transfer Live ♪♪♪ (Atlantic, 1978)
Best of the Manhattan Transfer ♪♪♪ (Atlantic, 1981)
Bodies and Souls ♪♪ (Atlantic, 1983)
Live in Tokyo ♪♪ (Atlantic, 1987)
Brazil ♪♪♪ (Atlantic, 1987)
The Offbeat of Avenues ♪♪ (Columbia, 1991)
The Christmas Album ♪♪♪ (Columbia, 1992)
The Manhattan Transfer Meets Tubby the Tuba ♪♪ (Summit, 1994)
Man Tora! Live in Tokyo ♪♪♪ (Rhino, 1996)

worth searching for: The jazz-fusion rendition of Weather Report's "Birdland" on *Extensions* ♪♪♪♪ (Atlantic, 1979, prod. Jay Graydon) has become the group's trademark song, a modern classic that will leave you wanting to drop everything and sing for a living. (Although the same album's disco-new wave "Twilight Zone/Twilight Tone" is more reminiscent of the werewolf howls in Michael Jackson's *Thriller* than a showcase of musicianship.)

solo outings:
Janis Siegel:
Experiment in White ♪♪ (Atlantic, 1982)
At Home ♪♪♪ (Atlantic, 1987)

influences:
◀◀ Jon Hendricks, Louis Armstrong, Ella Fitzgerald, Judy Garland, Benny Goodman, Count Basie, the Supremes, Nat King Cole, Bette Midler, Weather Report

▶▶ Take 6, Al Jarreau, Bobby McFerrin, Juan Luis Guerra, Matt Bianco

Jack Jackson

Dean Martin

Born Dino Paul Crocetti, June 17, 1917, in Steubenville, OH. Died December 25, 1995, in Beverly Hills, CA.

Dean Martin could swing, even when the music didn't. Essentially a crooner in the Bing Crosby mold, swing for Martin was an aphrodisiac that made his ballads effective. His biggest hit, "Everybody Loves Somebody," is done in a big-budget crossover country style that was big in the years immediately after Ray Charles's breakthrough country records. Martin's sly, lightly swinging vocals give the song the wings to fly. Swing is but a syncopation in his vocals on the records he made after that as he became more "countryfied." Martin sang well but never was as serious as his Rat Pack buddy, Frank Sinatra. At his best, on "Ain't That a Kick in the Head," he could match Sinatra swing for swing. However, he hardly ever aimed for the fences like Sinatra, recording many stinkers throughout his long career. He did so with a wink, though. In fact, it seems as though Martin was never serious about anything. His school days established his pattern of doing only what came easily to him. Everything he ended up doing for a living—acting, comedy, singing—essentially was a con game.

Fortunately for him, his voice was not a con. Singing is a staple among Italian families, and this son of Italian immigrants was about as Italian as an American can get. Martin began working in Steubenville's underground gambling dens as a high schooler, had a short career as a boxer, and moved on to singing in nightclubs. With his good looks (aided by a nose job) and a devil-may-care sensuousness in his singing, Martin was first a hit with women. The con in his singing was that he could make the girls think he was crooning exclusively to them, even though he was not interested in anyone exclusively. Still, his career was at the third-tier level at best in 1946, when he and Jerry Lewis met up in Atlantic City. The team began tearing audiences apart with madcap comedy routines, becoming one of the biggest comedy phenomena of the late '40s and early '50s. They appeared in movies, radio, and TV series. Their egos ultimately crashed the partnership in 1956 after 16 flicks. Even though he was a natural at comedy, Martin focused more on singing, and his first real hit, "Memories Are Made of This," came as the partnership with Lewis was on its last legs. There was considerable speculation that Martin would fade away without Lewis, but the singer kept getting movie roles, even when his recording career stalled in the early '60s.

When "Everybody Loves Somebody" knocked the Beatles' "A Hard Day's Night" out of *Billboard*'s #1 singles spot on August 15, 1964, Martin won a new audience. He charted more (11 times) than Sinatra did (eight times) in the subsequent three years. (Sinatra's own biggest hit of the period, "Strangers in the Night," relied on Martin's behind-the-scenes guys, producer Jimmy Bowen and arranger Ernie Freeman.) Martin's new hits were spurred at least in part by the popularity of his TV variety series on NBC from 1964 to 1975. He also continued to play Vegas and make middle-of-the-road records. From the end of his TV series until his death in 1995, Martin's story was one of slow dissolution. Never one to work too hard, he was more likely to be found wearing his jeans for a solitary dinner after work than decked out for a night on the town. Martin was married three times and had seven kids. In 1987, Dean Jr., a captain in the Air National Guard, died when his jet fighter crashed. Martin, set to start a Rat Pack reunion tour in 1988 with Sinatra and Sammy Davis Jr., was devastated. While Sinatra and Davis basked in the glory of hitting the stage together one last time, to Martin it was nothing but ashes—and too much work. Citing health problems, he left the tour early. He was quickly back doing Vegas shows, reportedly soaked in Percodan. He was a loner until he died.

what to buy: There are two must-own choices, depending on how deep you want to go with Dino. *Greatest Hits: King of Cool* (Capitol, 1998, executive prod. Mickey Kapp) is the first collection to gather songs from his entire career, which was divided between stints at Capitol and Reprise. Although it's tough to summarize a career in just 16 songs, Mickey Kapp and crew have for the most part chosen well, covering 15 genuine hits, including "That's Amore" and "Everybody Loves Somebody," as well as the swinging *Oceans 11* number "Ain't That a Kick in the Head," which went nowhere when it was banned by radio for being "too suggestive" (1960 was a different world). What this non-chronological CD offers in scope, it lacks in context. The liner notes are quick bullet points of his career. That's what makes *Dean Martin: Capitol Collector's Series* (Capitol, 1989, compilation prod. Ron Furmanek) worth getting, even though there's quite a bit of repetition between this set and *King of Cool*. This chronological set from Martin's Capitol years, 1948–1961, begins with his first recorded tune, "That Certain Party," a duet with Jerry Lewis, and lets listeners hear Martin maturing in the studio. "That's Amore" was rightfully Dino's breakthrough. Before it, he sounded stiff, as if his tie was strangling him, but this cut loosened the tie. Originally, Martin didn't want to do the pidgin Italian tune, but it took off to #2. (Listen to the background singers mess up the pronunciation of the rolling Italian "r," while Martin glides through it liquidly.) The other big hits of his Capitol years—"Memories Are Made of This" and "Return to Me"—are also included here. Martin's "Volare," while not as big a hit as these others, shows him at his best. The song is about the heady loss of control as infatuation hits, and Martin's "whoa-oh" captures the exact feeling of a heart taking off into the sky. Italian-American Martin understood and performed this song better than any Italian tenor of the time.

what to buy next: *The Capitol Years* (Capitol, 1996, compilation prod. Bob Furmanek) is a two-CD set that features nine of the 20 cuts from *Capitol Collector's Series*. *Capitol Years* tries to flesh out what rockers would call "the album cuts" side of Dino; the rarities, unreleased tracks, and extra songs don't add much. Still, it's pretty cool to hear him dueting with Nat King Cole on "Open up the Dog House (Two Cats Are Coming In)." A team-up with Peggy Lee on "You Was" lets both play off their languorous sensuality. *That's Amore: The Best of Dean Martin* (Capitol, 1996, prod. various) covers much of the same ground, but this one is weighted toward the Italian songs. Such staples as "Volare" and "That's Amore" act as the iceberg tip for "Return to Sorrento," "Vieni Su," and "Arrivederci Roma." That last track is a must. Martin's "eat, drink, and be merry" approach meshes perfectly with a tune from the *La Dolce Vita* era of Italy. *Sleep Warm* (Capitol, 1959, prod. Lee Gillette) is the only CD issue of an original Martin album left in print (the rest are compilations). A fairly average record for its time, *Sleep Warm* 's most notable feature is that Frank Sinatra conducted the orchestra. The Sinatra-like concept album featured songs about sleep and dreaming—from the title cut to the closing "Brahms' Lullaby."

the rest:

Best of Dean Martin (Capitol, 1990)
All-Time Greatest Hits (Curb, 1991)
Season's Greetings from Dean Martin (Capitol, 1992)
Collection (Castle, 1992)
Spotlight on Dean Martin (Capitol, 1995)
Solid Gold (Madacy, 1995)
Sings Italian Favorites (Capitol, 1995)

You're Nobody Till Somebody Loves You ♪♪♪ (Capitol, 1995)
I Wish You Love ♪♪♪ (Great Hits, 1996)
Love Songs by Dean Martin ♪♪♪ (Ranwood, 1997)
Making Spirits Bright ♪♪♪ (Capitol, 1998)

worth searching for: *The Best of Dean Martin: 1962–1968* ♪♪♪♪ (Charly, 1996, prod. Jimmy Bowen) is a comprehensive collection of Martin's Reprise Records singles, many of which are not available on CD in the United States. These songs dovetailed with Dino's weekly TV persona as a singing Hugh Hefner. The distinctive slurs, which, in his early career, added a casual *bon vivant* vibe to the proceedings, become the dominant element in his singing here, as if he were perpetually buzzed. *Memories Are Made of This* ♪♪♪♪ (Bear Family, 1997, prod. various) deserves a mention because it's an eight-CD collection of everything Martin recorded for Capitol.

influences:
◄◄ Bing Crosby, Al Jolson
►► Elvis Presley

Salvatore Caputo

Freddy Martin

Born December 9, 1906, in Cleveland, OH. Died September 30, 1983.

During the '30s, saxophonist-bandleader Freddy Martin led a run-of-the-mill society band, which played smooth music at such elite venues as the Waldorf Astoria. In 1941, along with pianist Jack Fina, he stumbled upon the gimmick of transforming classical music themes into sweet, sentimental pop. His big instrumental hits, "Tonight We Love" and "I Look at Heaven" (taken from Tchaikovsky's B-flat Piano Concerto and Grieg's Piano Concerto, respectively), virtually created the concept of commercial "beautiful music," and still receive airplay today. Martin also had a good ear for vocalists, employing the likes of Russ Morgan, Gene Vaughn, Buddy Clark, Helen Ward, and future talk-show host Merv Griffin (who scored a big hit with the bouncy novelty "I've Got a Lovely Bunch of Coconuts"). At their peak, Martin and his orchestra hosted their own network radio shows and appeared in the movie musicals *Stage Door Canteen, What's Buzzin', Cousin?*, and *The Mayor of 44th Street*. A perennial guest on early '50s TV, Martin hosted his own network show for two years, plus several local ones on the West Coast. Never lacking work, Martin and various incarnations of his band played top nightspots into the late '60s. After a bout with semi-retirement, Martin and fellow bandleaders Bob Crosby and Frankie Carle formed the Big Band Cavalcade, which toured with great success in the early '70s.

what to buy: The best of a skimpy lot, *Freddy Martin & His Orchestra: 1950–52* ♪♪♪ (Collectors' Choice, 1996) showcases some nice selections, such as "Once in Love with Amy," "You Do Something to Me," "Please Mr. Sun," "Heaven Drops Her Curtains," and the hit "Early in the Morning." You can find this one in the Collectors' Choice mail order catalog.

the rest:
Uncollected Freddy Martin & His Orchestra, Vol. 2: 1944–1946 ♪♪ (Hindsight, 1992)
Uncollected Freddy Martin & His Orchestra, Vol. 3: 1952 ♪♪ (Hindsight, 1992)
Uncollected Freddy Martin & His Orchestra, Vol. 4: 1948–52 ♪♪ (Hindsight, 1992)

worth searching for: It's worth the extra trouble to find *Hits of Freddy Martin* ♪♪♪♪ (Capitol/EMI, 1989), which features "Tonight We Love," "Bye Lo Bye Lullabye," and Merv Griffin's early claim to fame, "I've Got a Lovely Bunch of Coconuts." Though out of print, it's a much more powerful collection of hits than the Collectors' Choice disc.

influences:
◄◄ Guy Lombardo, Arnold Johnson, Jack Albin
►► Frankie Carle, Mort Lindsey, Merv Griffin

Ken Burke

Billy May

Born William E. May, November 10, 1916, in Pittsburgh, PA.

May arranged one of the biggest big-band hits ever, Charlie Barnet's version of "Cherokee"—later a key inspiration for Charlie Parker, who styled his bebop classic "Koo-Koo" after it—then became an indispensable behind-the-scenes arranger and bandleader for many, many musicians and record labels. Beginning in the early '40s, May worked with Glenn Miller, Bing Crosby, Paul Weston, Nat King Cole, Yma Sumac, and Frank Sinatra. His squawking-horn music swung hard, but it never carried quite the trailblazing weight of past bandleaders such as Duke Ellington or Benny Goodman; May's style was much more playful, which explains his work on the Arthur Murray dance-instruction series and his enduring kids' song "I Tawt I Taw a Puddy Tat."

May, who always claimed to be self-taught, was a tuba player in high school, then turned out to be good at arranging. Never an astounding visionary, May's fast, workmanlike qualities impressed first Barnet, then Miller, who invited him to join his influential swing band. Later, as Capitol's musical director, his personal habits—such as knocking down vodka during sessions—only enhanced his reputation as a fun-loving, fast-working party animal. Naturally, Sinatra was drawn to him, and he employed May's orchestra on his classic *Come Fly with Me* album. In the '60s May scored several television series themes, including *The Mod Squad* and *Emergency.* Though his intense lifestyle slowed him down, he continued working with Sinatra and on movie soundtracks through the '80s and '90s.

what to buy: Though May recorded his most influential music with other people, two volumes of his instrumental big-band work—*Best of Billy May, Vol. I* ♪♪♪ (Aerospace, 1990, prod. various) and *Best of Billy May, Vol. II* ♪♪♪ (Aerospace, 1990, prod. various)—are fast, playful, and almost intimidatingly brassy. On standards like "Little Brown Jug" and "Makin' Whoopee," both from *Volume II*, the "slurping saxophones" play melodies as thick as syrup, and the rhythm chugs along like a whistle-blowing train. *Volume I* is loaded with more familiar songs, such as "Charmaine," "Unforgettable," and "All of Me."

what to buy next: Originally two LPs, *Sorta May/Sorta Dixie* ♪♪♪ (Creative World, 1996) includes lesser-known May-slurped standards like "Deep Purple," "Soon," and "Thou Swell."

worth searching for: May, like Nelson Riddle before him, helped transform Sinatra from a stiff-shirted crooner to a hipster swing cat. The arranger also encouraged Sinatra to express his sense of humor and swaggering confidence; the result of these sessions, *Come Fly with Me* ♪♪♪♪♪ (Capitol, 1957, prod. Voyle Gilmore), includes the classics "Blue Hawaii," "Isle of Capri," and the title track. Further evidence of May's style is on Nat King Cole's *Billy May Sessions* ♪♪♪♪ (Capitol/EMI, 1993).

influences:

◀ Charlie Barnet, Nelson Riddle, Ray Noble

▶ Leroy Anderson, Mantovani, Charlie Parker, Frank Sinatra, Nat King Cole, Bing Crosby

Steve Knopper

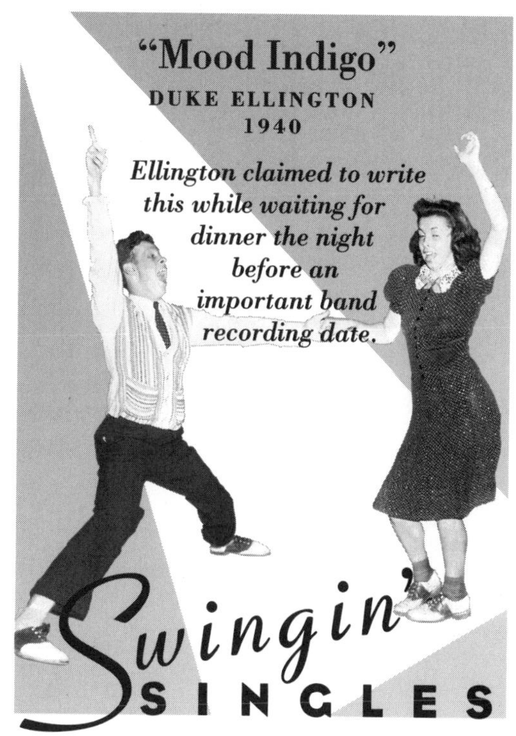

"Mood Indigo"
DUKE ELLINGTON
1940
Ellington claimed to write this while waiting for dinner the night before an important band recording date.
Swingin'
SINGLES

Floyd McDaniel

Born July 21, 1915, in Athens, GA. Died July 23, 1995, in Chicago, IL.

Blues veteran Floyd McDaniel had this whole jump blues/swing thing down cold. Whether playing with small jazz groups or traditional blues bands, his guitar work tastefully mixed the shuffle boogie of T-Bone Walker and the eloquent jazz riffs of Charlie Christian. As a vocalist, McDaniel got every ounce of feeling and soul from a lyric without ever resorting to shouting. And, like a really good bottle of whiskey, he just got better with age. McDaniel became a solo performer rather late in life. During the '20s, he had performed in high school bands with Nat King Cole, singing for the then-too-shy leader. With the Rhythm Rascals, McDaniel played and sang material by the Mills Brothers, Count Basie, and the Ink Spots on Chicago streets. An appearance at the 1933 Chicago World's Fair led to a lengthy gig at the Cotton Club in Harlem, where they opened for the likes of Cab Calloway, Duke Ellington, and Lionel Hampton. However, McDaniel was part of a far more successful group during the '40s and '50s, Lindsey Holt & the Four Blazes, which added the jumping sounds of Louis Jordan to the Rhythm Rascals' mix. A popular club attraction, the Four Blazes eventually hit the charts with "Raggedy Ride," "Mary Jo," and "My Hat's on the Wrong Side of My Head." When rock 'n' roll killed the market for blues shuffle, McDaniel semi-retired from music. He ran a bar, worked construction, and took occasional gigs with Jump Jackson's band and a rock group called the Y-Nots. He didn't fully reemerge until the '70s, when he joined an Ink Spots revival group that prospered for more than a decade. A 1986 appearance with Willie Dixon at the Chicago Blues Festival reignited McDaniel's love for the blues, inspiring him to become a headliner in his own right. Though well past retirement age, McDaniel sounded smooth and assured, and his fully formed style quickly earned him fans overseas. Americans awakening to the swing and jump blues revival were just beginning to rediscover McDaniel around the time of his death.

what to buy: Big-band brass, jazz, and blues come together with style to spare on *Let Your Hair Down* ♪♪♪♪ (Delmark, 1994, prod. Robert G. Koester), a potent 17-song collection featuring

McDaniel's vivid guitar playing and the exemplary horn arrangements of the Blues Swingers. Particularly fine are their swinging renditions of "Mary Jo," "St. Louis Blues," "Sent for You Yesterday," and "Caldonia." Younger acts have revisited this type of material, but not with McDaniel's ease and unerring sense of taste.

what to buy next: Dave Specter & the Bluebirds aid McDaniel for *West Side Baby* ♪♪♪ (Delmark, 1997, prod. Dave Specter), which tracks a solid live show in Germany. Together they pay tribute to Gene Ammons ("Red Top"), Nat King Cole ("Route 66"), T-Bone Walker ("Mean Old World"), and Bessie Smith ("Backwater Blues").

worth searching for: *Floyd McDaniel & Erwin Helfer: 100 Days from Today* ♪♪♪ (CMA, 1995, prod. Rolf Schubert) is out of print. *Mary Jo* ♪♪♪ (Delmark, 1998), a collection of tunes by the early '50s R&B group the Four Blazes, features McDaniel's sparkling guitar work.

influences:

◀◀ T-Bone Walker, Charlie Christian, Joe Williams, Nat King Cole, Louis Jordan.

▶▶ Dave Specter, the Blues Swingers

Ken Burke

McKinney's Cotton Pickers

Formed c. 1926, in Paducah, KY. Disbanded c. 1934.

William McKinney, bandleader, drums; John Nesbitt, trumpet; Don Redman, arranger, alto saxophone, vocals; Prince Robinson, clarinet; Claude Jones, trombone; Fathead (George) Thomas, vocals; Dave Wilborn, vocals.

Originally a quartet, McKinney's Cotton Pickers were one of the great swinging bands of the late 1920s and early 1930s. Formed by former big-band drummer William McKinney around 1926, it originated as the Sinco Septet, then evolved into the 10-piece Cotton Pickers, a show band that performed the funny-hat routines and regularly played the Arcadia Ballroom in Detroit. Nearby at the Greystone Ballroom, where the Fletcher Henderson band performed, McKinney wooed away Henderson arranger Don Redman and made him musical director. Redman drilled his new crew regularly until they mastered his intricate, swinging charts and put together a competitive band of black musicians that matched Henderson's band and the up-and-coming Duke Ellington orchestra. After building up a strong national reputation, they began a series of single recordings, including the RCA Victor hits, "If I Could Be with You One Hour Tonight" and "Baby, Won't You Please Come Home," featuring fine instrumental solos, excellent Redman arrangements, and all-star sessions with soloists Coleman Hawkins, Fats Waller, Lonnie Johnson, and others. When Redman departed from the band in 1931 to form his own unit, saxophonist Benny Carter took over as musical director and hired fine players such as Doc Cheatham and Hilton Jefferson. But the band never achieved its former musical heights and made only one more recording before the Depression forced it to fold in 1934.

what to buy: The only domestic album available by McKinney's Cotton Pickers, *The Band Don Redman Built (1928–1930)* ♪♪♪♪ (Bluebird, 1990) contains 22 of the Pickers' best classic Dixieland-to-swing-style recordings after Redman became the unofficial leader. It includes popular favorites aimed more at a general audience than the fervid collector: "I've Found a New Baby," "Gee Baby, Ain't I Good to You," "I Want a Little Girl," and others, with performances from band members such as Benny Carter, Coleman Hawkins, Fats Waller, and others.

the rest:

McKinney's Cotton Pickers: 1928–1929 ♪♪♪♪♪ (Jazz Chronological Classics, 1994)
McKinney's Cotton Pickers: 1929–1930 ♪♪♪♪♪ (Jazz Chronological Classics, 1994)

influences:

◀◀ Fletcher Henderson, Duke Ellington

▶▶ Count Basie, Jay McShann

see also: *Don Redman*

Nancy Ann Lee

Big Jay McNeely

Born Cecil McNeely, April 29, 1927, in Los Angeles, CA.

Jay McNeely has never been shy about his claim to fame; he simply will not be blown off the stage. Neither a disciplined stylist like King Curtis, an urbane swingmaster like Benny Carter, or a bomb-thrower like Charlie Parker, McNeely became a legend for his ability to deliver a never-ending spray of honks, bleats, and squeals, all designed to get wallflowers out on the floor to dance. He blew on his knees, on his back, standing on his head. (One story has it that during one lengthy solo, McNeely left the stage, went to the men's room, relieved himself, zipped up and returned, blowing all the while.) A fan of the mainstream early swing bands of Earl Hines and the Los Angeles hepster outfits led by Jack McVea, McNeely began by playing the clubs in the 1940s heyday of black L.A.'s Central Avenue strip and later claimed to have briefly taken the stage during an appearance by Bird. Recording for the New York Savoy label, McNeely hit with "Deacon's Hop," a sax-and-handclap classic that set the pace for the rest of his career. Taking his cue from audience pleasers like Illinois Jacquet and Arnett Cobb, McNeely barnstormed through the chitlin circuit. Label-hopping with Exclusive, Atlantic, Federal, and Aladdin, McNeely prospered even at the dawn of the soul era, igniting with the 1959 ballad "There Is Something on Your Mind." He cut back on his touring through most of the 1960s, but the 1980s and 1990s found him undimmed, releasing a slew of new records and even showing up on TV as—what else?—the leader of a hard-blowing combo.

what to buy: The packaging on *Swingin' Golden Classics* ♪♪♪♪ (Collectables, 1990) is as sparse as a wish sandwich, but all you need is the front cover—a grainy shot of Jay contorted on his back, blowing to the heavens—to know what's contained inside. Here are 16 steamers, not only the fine "Something on Your Mind," but wild ravers like "Back . . . Shack . . . Track" and the even more manic "Psycho Serenade." More honks than a runaway tugboat.

what to buy next: A survey of Big Jay in the 1950s would not be complete without the giddy "Nervous, Man, Nervous," a Federal smash that featured a wigged-out chorus chanting the title behind Big Jay's wails. It's included on *Nervous* ♪♪♪♪ (Saxophile, 1995), which also collects several takes from a pristine recording of a 1957 Big Jay live blowing marathon. *Live at Birdland: 1957* ♪♪♪♪ (Collectables, 1990) has the complete version of that show live from Seattle's now-defunct Birdland. Big Jay vaults into the stratosphere with churners like "Insect Ball" and the Illinois Jacquet chestnut "Flying Home."

the rest:

Big Jay in 3-D ♪♪♪ (King)
Az Bootin' ♪♪♪ (Big J, 1993)

influences:

◀◀ Earl Hines, Illinois Jacquet, Jack McVea, Arnett Cobb, Charlie Parker

▶▶ King Curtis, Gene Barge

Steve Braun

Carmen McRae

Born April 8, 1922, in New York, NY. Died November 10, 1994, in Beverly Hills, CA.

In the pantheon of jazz singers, Carmen McRae doesn't rank with Ella Fitzgerald, Sarah Vaughan, or Billie Holiday, but she isn't too far beneath them, and her renditions of standards are classics in their own right. After working with swing bandleaders Benny Carter, Count Basie, and Mercer Ellington through the '40s, McRae debuted as a leader in 1954 and quickly established her relaxed vocal style. Over the course of her long career, which lasted into the '90s despite emphysema, McRae recorded more than 50 albums, including numerous collections of standards, collaborations with Dave Brubeck and George Shearing, and a series of tributes to performers and composers such as Holiday, Vaughan, Nat King Cole, and Thelonious Monk.

what to buy: *The Great American Songbook* ♪♪♪♪♪ (Atlantic, 1992) is McRae's finest album, with standards like "Days of Wine and Roses," "I Only Have Eyes for You," "At Long Last Love," and a superb "It's Like Reaching for the Moon."

what to buy next: *Sings Great American Songwriters* ♪♪♪♪♪ (Decca, 1993, reissue prod. Orrin Keepnews) is another winning collection of standards, including "My Funny Valentine," "My Foolish Heart," "Basin Street Blues," "Love Come Back to Me," and "Ev'ry Time We Say Goodbye." And *The Collected Carmen McRae* ♪♪♪♪ (RCA, 1998) is a nice greatest-hits overview, with "Dear Ruby," "Tenderly, " and "Misty. "

what to avoid: *Can't Hide Love* ♪♪♪ (Pausa, 1976) manages to hide McRae's prodigious skill behind poor song selection and fussy arrangements.

best of the rest:

Here to Stay ♪♪♪♪ (Decca, 1959)
You're Looking at Me: A Collection of Nat King Cole Songs ♪♪♪♪ (Concord Jazz, 1984)
Sings Lover Man & Other Billie Holiday ♪♪♪♪ (Sony, 1997)

worth searching for: *Live in Robbie Scott's* ♪♪♪♪ (DRG, 1977, prod. Peter King) captures McRae live at the British jazz club, performing "If You Could See Me Now," "Evergreen," and "Weaver of Dreams," among others.

influences:

◀◀ Sarah Vaughan, Billie Holiday, Ella Fitzgerald

▶▶ Betty Carter, Dinah Washington, Nancy Wilson, Cassandra Wilson, Holly Cole

Ben Greenman

Jay McShann

Born January 12, 1916, in Muskogee, OK.

One of the last living survivors of the swing era, Jay McShann's musical journey continues unabated; the same "Hootie" McShann who hired the embryonic teenager Charlie Parker as his saxophonist in 1939 fronted the Duke Robillard Band at the 1997 Kansas City Blues and Jazz Fest. McShann, who began playing the piano as a child, had his own band in Kansas City by 1938, and by the early 1940s his enlarged group, fronted by singer Walter Brown, greased by cocky saxman Parker, and catapulted by the huge hit "Confessin' the Blues," could hold its ground against any big band of the period. Led by McShann's powerful piano pumping, his bands always struck a balance between blues and jazz—and they swung like crazy. After he got out of the service and the Basie and Andy Kirk bands went

Carmen McRae **(Archive Photos)**

nationwide, McShann recorded in Hollywood with singer Julia Lee before returning to Kansas City, still his base of operations today. Whether playing with big bands or the smaller groups he used in the 1940s (including a nascent R&B combo that included singer Crown Prince Waterford, Numa Lee Davis, and, in his debut recording, Jimmy Witherspoon), McShann remains a powerful pianist, vocalist, and performer, not yet content to rest on his considerable laurels.

what to buy: *Hootie's Jumpin' Blues* ♪♪♪♪ (Stony Plain, 1997, prod. Duke Robillard, Holger Peterson) pits the 80-ish pianist with a hard-swinging contemporary group. *The Early Bird Charlie Parker* ♪♪♪♪♪ (MCA, 1982, prod. various) has the studio recordings of the early McShann powerhouse, including "Swingmatism," "Hootie Blues," and "Confessin' the Blues." McShann is the main force behind *Kansas City Blues 1944–49* ♪♪♪♪ (Capitol, 1997, prod. Billy Vera), an exhaustive three-disc look at post–World War II KC lineups. Besides introducing Witherspoon, he sings up a storm of his own—you wonder why McShann ever let other singers front the band—alongside equally noteworthy tracks by Julia Lee & Her Boyfriends, Bus Moten & His Men, Tiny Kennedy, and Walter Brown.

what to buy next: The historical "Wichita Transcriptions" and live performances on *Early Bird* ♪♪♪♪ (Stash, 1991, prod. various) capture young gun Charlie Parker at a significant moment in his development and offer more proof that the McShann band could swing anybody's ass off any stage. The much more recent *Swingmatism* ♪♪♪ (Sackville, 1990) offers up a tasty choice of updated material, including the gems "Night in Tunisia" and "The Mooche."

best of the rest:
Hootie's Vine Street Blues ♪♪♪ (Black Lion, 1974/1994)
Some Blues ♪♪♪ (Chiaroscuro, 1993)
Vine Street Boogie ♪♪♪ (Black Lion, 1994)
Piano Playhouse ♪♪♪ (Night Train, 1996)
Just a Lucky So and So ♪♪♪ (Sackville, 1996)
1941–1943 ♪♪♪ (Melodie Jazz Classic, 1996)
My Baby with the Black Dress On ♪♪♪ (Chiaroscuro, 1998)
After Hours ♪♪♪♪ (Storyville, 1998)
1944–1946 ♪♪♪♪ (Melodie Jazz Classic, 1998)

worth searching for: Jazz giants Herbie Mann, Gerry Mulligan, and John Scofield get down to some serious, late-night jazz business with McShann on *The Big Apple Bash* ♪♪♪♪ (Atlantic, 1979, prod. Ilhan Mimaroglu), but only if you can find it on vinyl.

influences:
◀◀ Bennie Moten, Andy Kirk, Harlan Leonard
▶▶ Louis Jordan, Tommy Douglas, Wynonie Harris, Roy Brown, Jimmy Witherspoon, Walter Brown, Duke Robillard

Leland Rucker

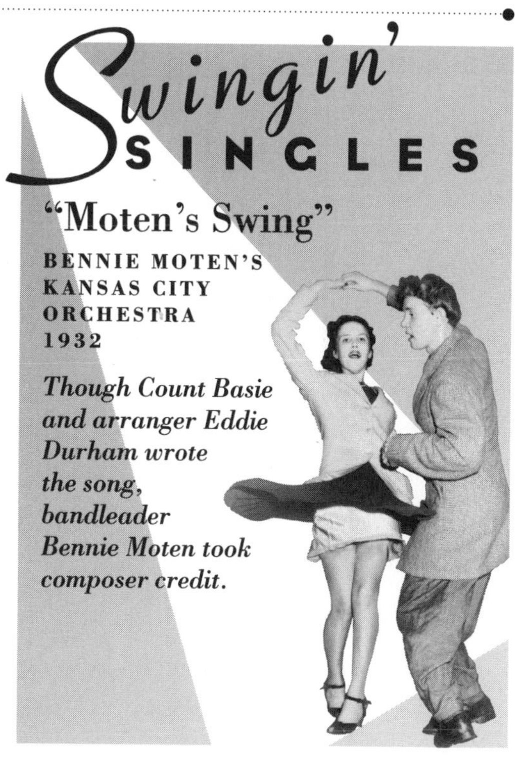

Swingin' SINGLES
"Moten's Swing"
BENNIE MOTEN'S KANSAS CITY ORCHESTRA 1932
Though Count Basie and arranger Eddie Durham wrote the song, bandleader Bennie Moten took composer credit.

Bette Midler

Born December 1, 1945, in Patterson, NJ.

Sassy and brassy, witty and wily, Bette Midler is a pure entertainer. Among the divas who emerged in the past few decades, her voice doesn't rank near the top. Her taste in material, however, and her preservation of the most shameless vaudeville traditions, distinguishes her as one of the best all-around performers. Her 1972 revival of the Andrews Sisters' "Boogie Woogie Bugle Boy" got America swinging again, and she has continued to demonstrate affection for the music of the 1940s throughout her careers in film (*One for the Boys*) and recording (*Bathhouse Betty*).

Born in New Jersey and raised in Hawaii, Midler moved to New York in the 1960s. She soon won a Broadway role in *Fiddler on the Roof.* By the early 1970s, she had developed a nightclub act incorporating pop standards, choreography, and comedy; her creative partners included Barry Manilow and Melissa Manchester. After signing to Atlantic Records and making a nationwide splash with her brand of nostalgia, her career slowed somewhat. In 1979, she came back with her starring role and soundtrack for *The Rose,* a loose adaptation of Janis Joplin's life. She's

Jay McShann (© Jack Vartoogian)

the author of a book, *A View from a Broad,* and continues to please crowds with her films, recordings, and concerts.

what to buy: *The Divine Miss M* ♪♪♪♪ (Atlantic, 1972, prod. Barry Manilow, Ahmet Ertegun, Joel Dorn) is Midler's swinging debut, with the Top 40 hits "Friends," "Do You Want to Dance?" and the Andrews Sisters update "Boogie Woogie Bugle Boy." *Experience the Divine: Greatest Hits* ♪♪♪♪ (Atlantic, 1993, prod. Arif Mardin, Bette Midler) gathers those hits as well as her heartfelt if overexposed ballads "Wind Beneath My Wings" (winner of the 1989 Grammy for Record of the Year), "From a Distance," and her most-played hit, "The Rose."

what to buy next: *The Rose* ♪♪♪♪ (Atlantic, 1979, prod. Paul A. Rothchild) soundtrack includes the title track and Joplin-esque rockers. *Divine Madness* ♪♪♪♪ (Atlantic, 1989, prod. Dennis Kirk) is a fine document of one of her bawdy live shows. After too much time spent in the middle of the road, with *Bathhouse Betty* ♪♪♪♪ (Warner Bros., 1998, prod. Ted Templeman, Arif Mardin, Brock Walsh, Marc Shaiman, Chuckii Booker, David Foster) Midler dances with the one that brought her on this saucy return to form. It includes a fun collaboration with 1990s swingers Royal Crown Revue, "One Monkey Don't Stop No Show."

what to avoid: Midler is a wonderful comedienne, but *Mud Will Be Flung Tonight!* ♪♪ (Atlantic, 1985, prod. Bette Midler), her only all-comedy album, is too much of a good thing.

the rest:

Bette Midler ♪♪♪ (Atlantic, 1973)
Songs for the New Depression ♪♪♪ (Atlantic, 1976)
Broken Blossom ♪♪♪ (Atlantic, 1977)
Live at Last ♪♪♪ (Atlantic, 1977)
Thighs and Whispers ♪♪♪ (Atlantic, 1979)
No Frills ♪♪♪ (Atlantic, 1983)
Beaches ♪♪♪ (Atlantic, 1988)
Some People's Lives ♪♪♪ (Atlantic, 1990)
For the Boys ♪♪♪ (Atlantic, 1991)
Gypsy ♪♪♪ (Atlantic, 1993)
Bette of Roses ♪♪ (Atlantic, 1995)

worth searching for: The Disney compilation *For Our Children* ♪♪♪♪ (Disney, 1991, prod. various) is a compilation of comfort songs, including Midler's "Blueberry Pie" (plus kids' songs by Bruce Springsteen, Brian Wilson, Meryl Streep, Barbra Streisand, Paul McCartney, and others).

influences:

◀◀ Barbra Streisand, Liza Minnelli, the Andrews Sisters, Ethel Merman, Judy Garland, Janis Joplin, Dionne Warwick

▶▶ Whitney Houston, Barry Manilow, Melissa Manchester, Linda Eder

Jay Dedrick

Mighty Blue Kings

Formed 1994, in Chicago, IL.

Ross Bon, vocals; Gareth Best, guitar; Jimmy Sutton, bass (1994–97); Jonathan Doyle, saxophone; Jerry DeVivo, saxophone; Samuel Burckhardt, tenor saxophone (1994–96); Jimmy Olson, drums; Bob Carter, drums (1994–97); Donny Nichilo, piano (1994–97); Clark Sommers, bass (1997–present); Simon Sweet, keyboards (1997).

After debuting at Chicago's famous Buddy Guy's Legends, opening for the great blues harpist Junior Wells, this contemporary swing band moved on to a weekly residency at the Green Mill jazz club a few miles north. Since then, the band has slowly amassed a huge local following and spread its effervescent "jump-jive" sound of the '40s and '50s to various clubs around the United States. The Kings' résumé now includes dates opening for rocker Pete Townshend at Chicago's House of Blues, and for soul singer Tina Turner at a TV industry party Oprah Winfrey threw at her Harpo Studios. They also earned a song on the soundtrack to the David Schwimmer movie *Since You've Been Gone*; the exposure led to a 1997 deal with Sony Records' Work label.

what to buy: On its debut, *Meet Me in Uptown* ♪♪♪ (R-Jay Records, 1996, prod. Wally Hersom, Mighty Blue Kings), the Mighty Blue Kings pay tribute to their infancy with "Jumpin' at the Green Mill," and include blues and jazz covers by Percy Mayfield, Jimmy Lunceford, and Sonny Rollins. Buoyed by a tight, talented horn section, the Kings also refurbish "Cadillac Boogie" and "Pink Cadillac," and the nicely titled "Grinnin' Like a Cheesy Cat."

what to buy next: There aren't too many live albums worth the $17 price, but *Live from Chicago* ♪♪♪ (R-Jay Records/Red Ink, 1998, prod. Mighty Blue Kings) is one exception. The CD captures the charm of the Mighty Blue Kings' live shows—charismatic vocalist Bon sings along with the fervent crowd, especially on Lunceford's "Buzz, Buzz, Buzz"—featuring top-notch musicianship and between-song banter. While it's a worthwhile purchase, the cover of Jimi Hendrix's "Manic Depression" leaves little to be desired. *Come One, Come All* ♪♪♪ (R-Jay Records, 1997, prod. Mighty Blue Kings), dedicated to the late Junior Wells, includes the bouncy "Go Tell the Preacher," which chides a woman who is mistreating her lover; on "Put Your Hand in Mine," Bon begs a woman to stay. Typically creative cover versions include "No Blow, No Show" by soul man Bobby "Blue" Bland, and "Green Grass Grows All Around" by jump-blues pioneer Louis Jordan.

influences:

◀◀ The Treniers, Wynonie Harris, Joe Williams, Count Basie, Jimmy Liggins, Louis Jordan, Squirrel Nut Zippers

▶▶ The Senders, Royal Crown Revue, Big Bad Voodoo Daddy

Christina Fuoco

Amos Milburn

Born April 1, 1927, in Houston, TX. Died January 3, 1980, in Houston, TX.

Amos Milburn stomped out the piano-boogie and sang the virtues of whiskey and sex in an unashamed, seductive manner. After signing with Aladdin Records in 1946, Milburn began recording his great string of drinking records ("Bad Bad Whiskey," "One Scotch, One Bourbon, One Beer," "Let Me Go Home, Whiskey"), influential and danceable boogie songs ("Down the Road Apiece," "Chicken Shack Boogie," "Let's Rock Awhile," "Roomin' House Boogie"), smooth, emotive blues ("Walkin' Blues," "Empty Arms Blues"), and intimate R&B ballads ("Bewildered," "Tears, Tears, Tears"). As a pianist, Milburn could bang the boogie hard like Cecil Gant or tickle the ivories light and jazzy like Johnnie Johnson, and his band the Chickenshackers could play burbling hot or icy cool behind him. As a vocalist, he could be velvety smooth like his friend Charles Brown (with whom he cut a few duets) or playful like Louis Jordan. As good as Milburn was, his music was too adult in nature to make it out of the R&B joints into the teen-oriented rock 'n' roll scene of the mid-1950s—which is probably why it sounds so good today. After 1954's "Good Good Whiskey," Milburn's string of big hits ended, though he kept a high professional profile, playing top night spots and appearing in the films *Harlem Jazz Festival* (1955), *Rhythm & Blues Revue* (1955), and *Basin Street Revue* (1956). Milburn's last legitimate shot at a comeback came with Motown in 1962; Berry Gordy Jr. tried hard to update Milburn's sound, but their LP *Boss of the Blues* flopped. Always a heavy drinker, Milburn's health went sour during the 1960s, but he played club dates until a series of strokes and the amputation of one of his legs retired him from the business. His last recordings were weak affairs made for the Blues Spectrum label, not long before he died in 1980. It's better to remember Milburn through his early sides, which helped set the stage for the joyous, soulful throb we all came to know as rock 'n' roll.

what to buy: *The Best of Amos Milburn—Down the Road Apiece* 𝅘𝅥𝅮𝅘𝅥𝅮𝅘𝅥𝅮𝅘𝅥𝅮𝅘𝅥𝅮 (Alliance, 1997, prod. various) contains a generous sampling of Milburn's greatest boogie anthems, whiskey tributes, and romantic ballads. This, and a similarly titled release on EMI (now out of print), contains essential music from one of the true greats of the pre-rock era.

what to buy next: Though no longer in Capitol's catalog, some stores and online services still carry *Blues Barrelhouse & Boogie Woogie* 𝅘𝅥𝅮𝅘𝅥𝅮𝅘𝅥𝅮𝅘𝅥𝅮½ (Capitol/EMI, 1996, compilation prod. Pete Welding). This powerful compilation contains 66 songs on three discs from his hot period on the Aladdin label. *All* the hot boogie, hits, and drinking songs are here. Once you've heard this set you'll become an honorary Chickenshacker for life.

what to avoid: *Johnny Otis Presents . . .* 𝅘𝅥𝅮 (Laserlight, 1993, prod. Johnny Otis, Tom Morgan) features remakes of big hits by Milburn, Joe Turner, Joe Liggins, Charles Brown, and Louis Jordan, cut through the years for Otis's Blues Spectrum label. Milburn could only play with one hand at this point in his career (Otis played the other parts), and he doesn't sound like he's in very good shape. Sad.

the rest:
Ace Story, Vol. 2 𝅘𝅥𝅮𝅘𝅥𝅮½ (Ace Records, 1994)

worth searching for: Check the import racks and collector's catalogs for *The Complete Aladdin Recordings of Amos Milburn* 𝅘𝅥𝅮𝅘𝅥𝅮𝅘𝅥𝅮𝅘𝅥𝅮 (Mosaic, 1994, prod. various), a seven-CD, 155-song compilation that includes every decent note Milburn laid down at Aladdin. This is a tremendous example of music archaeology and great music besides. Also, the recently deleted *Motown Years 1962–64* 𝅘𝅥𝅮𝅘𝅥𝅮½ (PolyGram, 1996, compilation prod. Andre Williams) features Berry Gordy's attempt to apply elements of Motown magic to the ol' Chickenshacker's potent barroom sound. Completists will find this quite rewarding in spots.

influences:
◀◀ Charles Brown, Louis Jordan, Ivory Joe Hunter
▶▶ Fats Domino, Jimmy Liggins, Rosco Gordon

Ken Burke

Emmett Miller

Born February 2, 1900, in Macon, GA. Died March 29, 1962 in Macon, GA.

A little-known figure said to have taught Hank Williams his first hit, "Lovesick Blues," and given Bob Wills his entire western swing style, Emmett Miller first gained notoriety via Nick Tosches's 1977 book *Country*. Miller was a minstrel performer who cut some rare OKeh 78s during 1927 and 1928 in New York with the Dorsey brothers and some other respected swing bandleaders of the time. It's one of the few examples, however obscure, of crossover between western (country) swing and big-band (pop) swing at the time. Bootleg editions of Miller's recordings fueled his legend and fostered more disciples, notably Leon Redbone, who based a considerable part of his act on Miller's unnatural, guttural sound. Biographical details are thin, and Miller disappeared into the ether of history without so much as a fare-thee-well. But his cult continues.

what's available: *Emmett Miller: The Minstrel Man from Georgia* 𝅘𝅥𝅮𝅘𝅥𝅮𝅘𝅥𝅮𝅘𝅥𝅮 (Columbia/Legacy, 1996, compilation prod. George Morrow, Lawrence Cohn) is a masterpiece in musical archaeology, a collection of 20 selections from those long-ago sessions—many of which feature Jimmy Dorsey on clarinet and alto sax, Tommy Dorsey on trumpet, and Jack Teagarden on

Amos Milburn **(Archive Photos)**

trombone. While falling somewhat short of establishing Miller conclusively as this great missing link in country music (too often the songs are little more than trite exercises in racial slander that passed as humor at the time), these recordings do show Miller to be a stylist of great originality and a vocalist with singular vitality—an altogether fascinating and rewarding unrevealed chapter in music history.

influences:

◀◀ Al Jolson

▶▶ Hank Williams, Bob Wills, Merle Haggard, George Jones, Bob Dylan

Joel Selvin

Glenn Miller

Born March 1, 1904, in Clarinda, IA. Reported missing December 15, 1944, on a flight from England to France.

For many people Glenn Miller's name is synonymous with big bands and the swing era. While he was never more than a mediocre trombonist, as an arranger he developed perhaps the most distinctive of all the big-band sounds, and his band provided the soundtrack for a generation.

Miller grew up poor in Iowa, Nebraska, and Colorado. There were no musicians in his family and he connected with the trombone only when he found an old one in the basement of a butcher's shop where he was working as an errand boy. The butcher gave him his first lessons. By 1916 he was playing in the Grant City (Missouri) Town Band. After leaving high school he joined a now-unknown band in Laramie, Wyoming, and when it broke up after a year, Miller entered the University of Colorado, where he continued playing and took up arranging. After only two years of college he joined the Ben Pollack Orchestra in California, then returned with Pollack to his base in New York and stayed with him until 1928 (Benny Goodman was a fellow band member). In September 1926 Pollack made the first known recordings using Miller's arrangements ("When I First Met Mary" and "'Deed I Do"). As a freelancer in New York Miller worked as an arranger, played on many studio recordings (including nearly 100 with the Dorsey Brothers Orchestra, for whom he provided at least half the arrangements), was in the pit for several Broadway shows, and on the side studied arranging with Dr. Joseph Schillinger. In 1935 he helped organize and wrote arrangements for the first American band organized by Ray Noble, and it was during his stint with Noble that he wrote what later became his theme song, "Moonlight Serenade." In 1936 he became an arranger for Glen Gray's famous Casa Loma Orchestra.

In January of 1937 Miller formed his own band, and in 1938, after a short hiatus, the re-organized band slowly became popular. At its peak it was one of the highest-paid bands in the nation, with an instantly recognizable sound that sold millions of recordings. The band had a wonderful way with finely arranged ballads, but Miller's biggest hits were instrumental riff tunes such as "Little Brown Jug" (Miller's first swing hit), "In the Mood," "Tuxedo Junction," and "Pennsylvania 6-5000." The Miller arrangements (including many by Jerry Gray, Bill Finegan, and Billy May) were the basic strength of the band, but good soloists were not lacking. Bobby Hackett was the featured trumpet soloist on many of Miller's best-known jazz charts, most famously on "String of Pearls." Tex Beneke handled most of the tenor sax jazz solos (Al Klink, a better soloist, was kept somewhat in the background), and though he was far from being in a class with Hawkins or Webster (or even Klink), Beneke was enormously popular with the band's audiences, probably for his vocals. Miller and the band were featured in two major films, *Sun Valley Serenade* and *Orchestra Wives.*

In mid-1942 Miller volunteered for service in the army, where he put together an all-star service personnel band that first toured the United States on recruiting drives and then, in 1944, was posted to England. On December 15 he was flying ahead of his band to a session in Paris, when his small plane disappeared; a year later he was declared dead. Hollywood honored him with a posthumously released film, *The Glenn Miller Story,* in 1953. A Miller "ghost band," currently fronted by Jack O'Brien, is still on the road playing his arrangements, as are other bands around the world. There are recurrent Glenn Miller festivals; music scholarships have been established in his name; and Miller, though gone at age 40, is anything but forgotten.

what to buy: *Glenn Miller: A Memorial* (Bluebird, 1992, prod. Steve Backer) gives an excellent overview of the band's offerings between 1939 and 1942 (and includes one track by the Miller Army Air Force Band), with a good mixture of the band's sweet and swing styles. Almost all of the big hits are here, plus some lesser known but equally engaging arrangements, such as "Song of the Volga Boatmen," "Anvil Chorus," and "Kalamazoo." The ballad style is represented in "Stairway to the Stars," "Sunrise Serenade," "Star Dust," and "Danny Boy." This CD is a re-release of an album from 1969 that sold more than a million copies in its LP format. *The Spirit Is Willing (1939–42)* (Bluebird, 1995, prod. Orrin Keepnews) is a different and welcome take on the Miller band, focusing on "its substantial jazz content," limited to instrumentals, and avoiding the Miller favorites included everywhere else. Some of the early efforts are "King Porter Stomp," "Rug Cutter's Swing" (by Fletcher Henderson's brother Horace), and "Bugle Call Rag," while the band's later style is reflected in "I Dreamt I Dwelt in Harlem," "Boulder Buff," and "Caribbean Clipper." Billy May's conception of "Take the 'A' Train" as a ballad will surprise you.

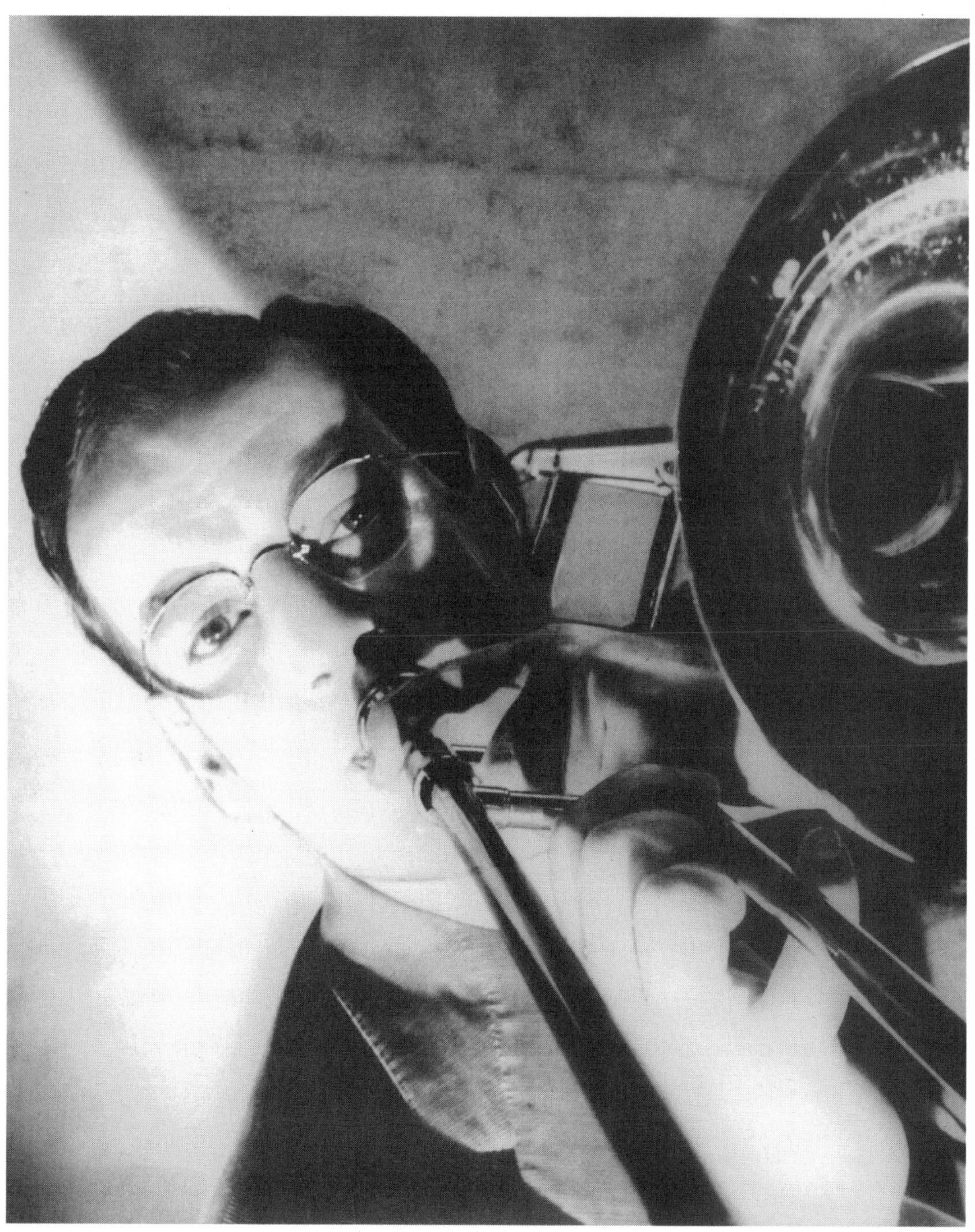

Glenn Miller **(Archive Photos)**

Lucky Millinder (r) and Rosetta Tharpe **(Archive Photos)**

what to buy next: For avid fans who want quantity as well as quality, there is the three-disc set *Glenn Miller: The Popular Recordings 1938–1942* (Bluebird, 1989). Miller fans with an historical bent ought to consider *Glenn Miller: The Lost Recordings* (RCA, 1995, prod. Alan Dell), which contains 45 tracks on two discs and performances by Miller's air force band intended for broadcast to a German audience (to undermine their will to fight). This band maintained—and in some ways surpassed—the high standards of the civilian band (Miller's civilian band never had the likes of Mel Powell on piano, for example), and the sound quality is excellent (recorded in the famous Abbey Road studios in London).

what to avoid: *In the Digital Mood* (GRP, 1983, prod. Dave Grusin) presents fairly recent re-recordings of the most popular Miller arrangements by anonymous studio musicians. They are certainly competent, but unless you have a passion for the latest in digital recording technology you're better off with reissues of the original work.

best of the rest:
Pure Gold (Bluebird, 1988)
Classic Glenn Miller: Original Live Recordings (Pair, 1989)
The Collector Edition: Glenn Miller (Laserlight, 1991)
Chattanooga Choo Choo: The Number One Hits (Bluebird, 1991)
A Legendary Performer (Bluebird, 1991)
Best of the Big Bands: Evolution of a Band (Columbia/Legacy, 1992)
Miller Plays Mercer (RCA Victor, 1998)
Operation: Build Morale (RCA Victor, 1998)
The Best of the Lost Recordings and the Secret Broadcasts (RCA Victor, 1998)

worth searching for: Miller's "In the Mood," which must rank with Benny Goodman's "Sing, Sing, Sing" as one of the most popular wedding songs ever, is one of the many swing-orchestra classics on *Swing Time! The Fabulous Big Band Era 1925–1955* (Columbia/Legacy, 1993). Miller, Benny Goodman, Fletcher Henderson, and Count Basie are among the towering figures throughout the four CDs.

influences:
Benny Goodman, Ray Noble, Duke Ellington, Tommy Dorsey, Jimmy Dorsey, Fletcher Henderson, Count Basie

▶▶ Nelson Riddle, Billy May, Frank Sinatra, Louis Armstrong, Louis Prima, Buddy Greco, Dean Martin, Tony Bennett, Charlie Parker, Miles Davis, Bob Wills, Raymond Scott

Jim Lester

Lucky Millinder

Born Lucius Venable, August 8, 1900, in Anniston, AL. Died September 28, 1966, in New York, NY.

Lucky Millinder led one of the great dance bands of the swing era and eventually sharpened the idiom's edges with touches of gospel, blues, and modern jazz. He began his career as a tap dancer in Chicago, before becoming a non-playing bandleader. His dancing background and acrobatic showmanship contributed to his vigorous conducting style. After leading an orchestra in France, he assumed the leadership of a major New York swing band, the Mills Blue Rhythm Band, in 1934. Originally used by Irving Mills as a substitute group for the Duke Ellington and Cab Calloway bands, the Blue Rhythm Band had already developed its own charging, joyous identity under the direction of Baron Lee. The Blue Rhythm Band broke up in 1938 and Millinder declared bankruptcy. After working with Bill Doggett, Millinder formed a new band under his own name in 1940. The best years for Millinder's band came during the early '40s, when it became an incubator for both bop and R&B. Dizzy Gillespie provided the signs of the bop to come, while the band's blues-based drive pointed to R&B, with such future stars as singers Sister Rosetta Tharpe and Wynonie Harris, pianist/organist Doggett, and tenor saxophonist Sam "The Man" Taylor. Millinder broke up his band in 1952, later working as a liquor salesman and disc jockey.

what to buy: An excellent introduction, the 24-track *Back Beats* ♪♪♪♪½ (Pearl, 1996, prod. Tony Watts, Colin Brown) ranges from the classic swing of "Ride, Red, Ride," a 1935 feature for trumpeter Red Allen when Millinder led the Mills Blue Rhythm Band, to the proto-bop of Dizzy Gillespie's solo on "Little John Special." Also included are the band's hits, "I Want a Tall Skinny Papa," sung by Rosetta Tharpe, and "Who Threw the Whiskey in the Well," featuring blues shouter Wynonie Harris.

what to buy next: For the complete recordings of Millinder's own band in its greatest period, go for *Lucky Millinder 1941–42* ♪♪♪♪½ (Jazz Chronological Classics, 1993, prod. various). Also, *Ram Bunk Shush* ♪♪♪♪ (Charly, 1992, prod. various) provides a fine overview of the later band as it moved toward R&B.

worth searching for: Millinder's best years with the Mills Blue Rhythm Band are on *Mills Blue Rhythm Band 1934–36* ♪♪♪♪ (Jazz Chronological Classics, 1993, prod. various), with tight ensembles and plenty of spots for distinguished soloists, including Red Allen, clarinetist Buster Bailey, and trombonist J.C. Higginbotham.

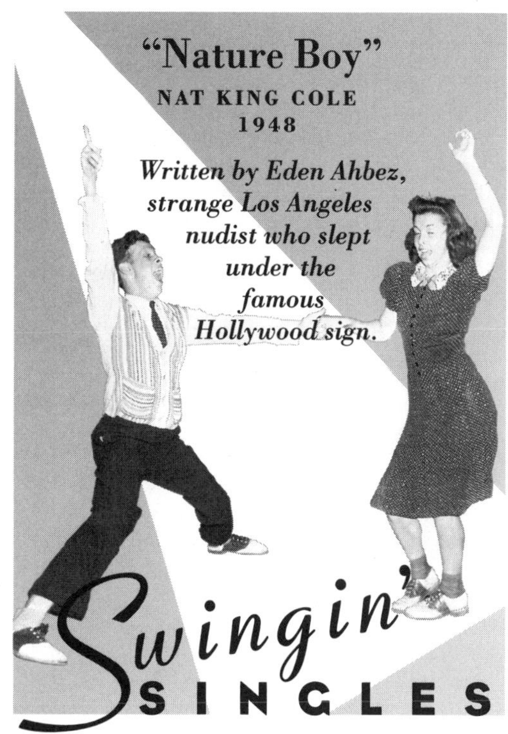
"Nature Boy"
NAT KING COLE
1948
Written by Eden Ahbez, strange Los Angeles nudist who slept under the famous Hollywood sign.
Swingin' SINGLES

influences:

◀◀ Don Redman, Duke Ellington, Cab Calloway, Count Basie

▶▶ Dizzy Gillespie, Joe Morris

Stuart Broomer

Mills Blue Rhythm Band

See: Lucky Millinder

Roy Milton

Born July 31, 1907, in Wynnewood, OK. Died September 18, 1983, in Los Angeles, CA.

A fine drummer, excellent composer, and first-rate bandleader, jump-blues star Roy Milton emerged from the rich Oklahoma music community that produced Charlie Christian, Jay McShann, Jimmy Rushing, Oscar Pettiford, and other pioneers of modern music. Milton worked with the Ernie Fields Orchestra, a popular territory band, and migrated to Los Angeles in the 1930s. He was first recorded by Lionel Hampton and then signed with producer Art Rupe, who was starting up JukeBox records in 1945.

Milton's second release for Rupe, "R.M. Blues," was a smash R&B hit and put both the bandleader and the fledgling label (soon to become Specialty Records) on the musical map. Milton and his band, the Solid Senders, featuring pianist Camille Howard, contributed an unending stream of great singles to the Specialty catalog over the next 10 years. Milton helped define the small-band R&B idiom with records like "Milton's Boogie," "True Blues," "Keep a Dollar in Your Pocket," "Hop, Skip & Jump" and "Information Blues." Howard was featured on a series of singles issued under her own name, including the classic "X-Temperaneous Boogie," recorded in the waning moments of New Year's Eve 1947, just before the recording ban of 1948 took effect.

what to buy: Milton and his band can be heard in all their glory in the "Legends of Specialty Records" series, meticulously produced and annotated by Billy Vera. *Roy Milton & His Solid Senders* ♪♪♪♪♪ (Specialty, 1990) reprises most of *R.M. Blues* ♪♪♪♪ (Specialty, 1988)—from the first batch of Specialty CDs before the catalog was purchased by Fantasy—and contains the hits cited above plus "The Hucklebuck," "Porter's Love Song," and a cover of Louis Prima's "Oh Babe!" *Volume Two: Groovy Blues* ♪♪♪♪ (Specialty, 1992) continues to mine the vaults, turning up seven unissued sides and excellent singles like "Groovy Blues," "Pack Your Sack, Jack," and "Short, Sweet, and Snappy." *Volume Three: Blowin' with Roy* ♪♪♪♪ (Specialty, 1994) continues with another dozen unissued sides and more fine singles such as "Train Blues," "New Year's Resolution," and more.

what to buy next: Milton can be heard in concert with the Johnny Otis Show on *Live at Monterey* ♪♪♪♪ (Sony, 1993), a 1970 performance that also featured Esther Phillips, Roy Brown, and other R&B pioneers reassembled by Otis for modern listeners.

worth searching for: A recent Billy Vera–produced sampler is a fantastic collection of jump blues and jazz from the Golden Age. *Jumpin' and Jivin'* ♪♪♪♪ (Specialty, 1997) digs out another five Roy Milton Specialty singles—including "Tell It Like It Is" and "Baby Don't Do That to Me"—and another unissued side to tantalize Milton completists. The Swedish collection *Grandfather of R&B* ♪♪♪♪♪ (Mr. R&B, 1994) samples Milton's Specialty hits in a one-disc set.

influences:

◀ Jay McShann, Count Basie

▶ Johnny Otis, Ray Charles, Dave Bartholomew

John Sinclair

Mr. & Mrs. Swing

See: Mildred Bailey, Red Norvo

Matt Monro

Born Terry Parsons, December 1, 1932, in London, England. Died February 7, 1985, in London, England.

Matt Monro was England's answer to Frank Sinatra. A talented soundalike, he brought his own warm, sentimental tone to a variety of standards and movie themes in the '60s. Under the name Al Jordan, he sang with Harry Leader's band in the mid-'50s. As Matt Monro his first taste of fame came as the singer of a Camay soap commercial, but he earned his real break when producer George Martin hired him to contribute to the Peter Sellers comedy LP *Songs for Swingin' Sellers*. Using the name Fred Flange, Monro's "You Keep Me Swingin'" was such a convincing imitation of Frank Sinatra, many fans believed they were hearing Ol' Blue Eyes himself.

Later, Monro became a constant chart presence in the U.K. with such hits as "Portrait of My Love" and "Why Not Now/Can This Be Love." Once his records were distributed in the United States, he actually scored a couple of Top 40 hits with the swinging "My Kind of Girl" and the over-the-top ballad "Walk Away." By this time, Sinatra had left Capitol Records, so his old label started importing Monro's discs in an effort to fill the void. The Beatles era, combined with Sinatra's own commercial resurrection on Reprise, blunted Monro's chart momentum, though his versions of "Yesterday" and "Softly as I Leave You" received some airplay. Monro moved permanently to the United States in 1965 and recorded fine versions of movie themes, including "From Russia with Love" and "Born Free." On his later efforts, Monro tried to temper his Sinatra stylings with a more velvety, personal tone, but comparisons remained inevitable. (For the record, Monro thought he sounded more like Perry Como.) He remained a popular nightclub performer well into the '70s, and recorded some well-regarded (though low-selling) big-band jazz versions of contemporary tunes until ill health forced him to retire. He died of cancer in 1985, but his son, Matt Monro Jr., carries on.

what to buy: The best available domestic collection of Monro's big Capitol/EMI hits, *Spotlight on Matt Monro* ♪♪♪♪ (Gold Rush, 1996/Alliance, 1997, compilation prod. Brad Benedict) includes some choice LP tracks and Sinatraesque versions of Cole Porter and Hoagy Carmichael standards. "Portrait of My Love" and the hit title track light up the romance-oriented *My Kind of Girl* ♪♪♪♪ (Warwick, 1961/Collectables, 1995, prod. George Martin), an exact reissue of Monro's first U.S. LP, which also features sterling versions of "Let's Face the Music and Dance" and "Cheek to Cheek." Sinatra's influence is keenly felt in the song arrangements and the singer's phrasing and tone, yet Monro's own stylistic warmth shines through.

what to buy next: You'll have to hit the import racks and catalog services to get *The Very Best of Matt Monro* ♪♪♪♪ (Musicrama, 1995) and *Born Free—His Greatest Hits* (Musicrama, 1997), similar offerings with a greater emphasis on his run of British chart singles. They're both fine introductions to this nearly forgotten artist.

the rest:

Softly as I Leave You (Musicrama, 1995)
This Is Matt Monro (Musicrama, 1997)
Love Is the Same Anywhere (Musicrama, 1997)
Hollywood & Broadway (Musicrama, 1997)
Through the Years (Musicrama, 1997)
Time for Love (Musicrama, 1997)
This Is the Life/Here's to My Lady (EMI, 1997)
Matt Monro En Espanol (Best, 1998)

worth searching for: Monro's best regarded LP and finest work is *Matt Monro Sings Hoagy Carmichael* (EMI, 1962, prod. George Martin), a concept LP that showcases his warmest, most affecting vocals. Also, you can hear Monro under the name Fred Flange on *A Celebration of Sellers: The Comedy Recordings of Peter Sellers 1953–1979* (Angel, 1994, prod. George Martin, Derek Lawrence, Walter J. Ridley), a four-CD set of perpetual zaniness and comedic brilliance.

influences:

⏪ Frank Sinatra, Frankie Vaughn, Perry Como, Vic Damone

⏩ Engelbert Humperdinck, Harry Connick Jr., Matt Monro Jr.

Ken Burke

Russ Morgan

Born April 28, 1904, in Scranton, PA. Died August 8, 1969, in Las Vegas, NV.

Russ Morgan was one of the most consistent hitmakers of the big-band era. A singing bandleader in the Rudy Vallee mode, he was also an accomplished trombonist who popularized the muted wah-wah-wah sound and a prolific songwriter with several standards to his credit. Morgan left the coal mines of Pennsylvania to play piano in the silent movie houses of the early '20s. His abilities on several instruments (guitar, saxophone, vibraphone, organ, trombone) helped him understand the intricacies of orchestral sound early on. As a result, after his first band failed, Morgan was able to find steady work as an arranger for Victor Herbert, John Phillips Sousa, Jean Goldkette, Fletcher Henderson, Chick Webb, Louis Armstrong, and the Dorsey Brothers. Freddy Martin gave Morgan's career a boost when he hired him as both arranger and trombonist, but it was Rudy Vallee who backed Morgan when he formed his own orchestra in 1935. Morgan's sound wasn't too different from Martin's—mostly easy dance material, perfect for hotel ballrooms and society outings. As a vocalist and emcee, his smooth, light, and elegant style made him quite popular with radio audiences and he hosted several network programs. In addition to writing such hit songs as "Does Your Heart Beat for Me" and "Somebody Else Is Taking My Place," Morgan had an uncanny knack for choosing songs the public would buy. The likes of "Dance with the Dolly (with a Hole in Her Stocking)," "The Merry-Go-Round Broke Down," and "I'm Looking Over a Four Leaf Clover" sound exceedingly corny today, but way back when, they were very big hits. Morgan continued to court popular tastes by adding such singing groups as the Skylarks and the Ames Brothers (who eventually became stars in their own right) to his lineup. Subsequently, in 1949, while all his contemporaries were facing difficult changes in the music business, Morgan became the country's top recording artist. The hits dried up in the '50s, but numerous radio and television appearances helped retain his band's popularity, and he toured with a full 17-piece unit into the early '60s.

what's available: Morgan's sound hasn't aged particularly well, so there's very little in print by this major hitmaker. The most comprehensive collection of his most popular numbers from the '40s through early '50s can be found on *The Best of Russ Morgan* (GNP, 1972/MCA, 1989, prod. Milt Gabler), a two-LP reissue with 24 tracks featuring vocals from the Skylarks, the Ames Brothers, and the bandleader himself. The more concise *1941–1954: Music in the Morgan Mood* (Circle, 1997, prod. George Buck Jr.) showcases vocalists Phyllis Lynn and Clarence Miller and may be slightly more enjoyable because it contains less fluff.

worth searching for: Live versions of Morgan's biggest hits from the '40s are on *22 Original Big Band Recordings* (Hindsight, 1990, prod. Wally Heider) and *America Swings—Russ Morgan* (Hindsight, 1989, prod. Wally Heider), two sets of radio transcriptions for the nostalgia crowd.

influences:

⏪ Jean Goldkette, Freddy Martin, Ted Fio Rito, Rudy Vallee

⏩ Will Bradley, Eddie Bush, Jack Morgan

Ken Burke

Ella Mae Morse

Born September 12, 1924, in Mansfield, TX.

Ella Mae Morse just may have been the first female rock 'n' roller. Her 1942 rendition of "Cow Cow Boogie" was Capitol Records' first million-selling single, and a stone gas besides. A white hipchick who flirtatiously belted a roadhouse mix of boogie, jazz, R&B, and country, Morse was only 14 years old when she joined Jimmy Dorsey's band in 1939. After Dorsey replaced her with Helen O'Connell three years later, boogie-piano legend Freddie Slack recruited her for his orchestra, and they produced some of the bawdiest jive of the pre-rock era: "Mister Five by Five," "Milkman Keep Those Bottles Quiet," "Patty Cake Man," and "The House of Blue Lights" (the latter featuring some hep jive-talk between Morse and Don Raye). It's worth noting that her biggest hits scored better on the "race" charts than the pop listings, and, until he met her, even Sammy Davis Jr. thought Morse was an African-American. Indeed, in Morse's voice lay the seeds of the cross-cultural pollination that would explode to fruition in the Elvis Presley era. At her peak in the '40s, Morse recorded dozens of great sides with the Nelson Riddle and Billy May orchestras, and was featured in motion pictures such as *Reveille with Beverly* (1943) and *South of Dixie* (1944). After a four-year hiatus from recording to start a family, Morse returned in 1951 and employed her lusty blues chops on the type of pop and country boogie material that made Tennessee Ernie Ford famous. She also covered R&B tunes such as "Money Honey" and "Lovey Dovey" with a credibility few singers of her era could match. She made her final vinyl appearance in 1957, just as the rock era was hitting fever pitch. Even today, Morse's music seems startling in its boldness.

what to buy: Rockabillies and swingheads alike will dig *The Very Best of Ella Mae Morse* ♪♪♪♪♪ (Collectables, 1998), 21 tracks of lusty rocking, years before it was fashionable. Freddie Slack lays down the hardest boogie this side of Jerry Lee Lewis, the horns are punchy and hot, the beat is low-down, and Morse sings everything like a seductive R&B chanteuse in an after-hours club. All her greatest boogie and big-band hits are here, as well as her wonderfully sly takes on "Tennessee Saturday Night" and "Oakie Boogie."

what to buy next: Morse has four songs (three not on the Collectables disc) on the remarkable *Jumpin' Like Mad: Cool Cats & Hip Chicks* ♪♪♪♪♪ (Capitol Blues, 1996, compilation prod. Billy Vera), a two-disc set filled with the hot pre-rock boogie and jump blues of Joe Liggins, T-Bone Walker, Louis Jordan, Peggy Lee, Kay Starr, and many more. Morse saucily belts several tunes live on *Radio Days* ♪♪♪♪ (Moon Records, 1995, prod. various), a compilation of radio appearances with tracks by Louis Armstrong and Frank Sinatra, c. 1944.

worth searching for: Every blessed note the "Cow Cow Boogie Girl" cut at Capitol records is on *Barrelhouse, Boogie, and Blues* ♪♪♪♪♪ (Bear Family, 1997, reissue prod. Richard Weize), a five-disc, 134-song box set with 20 previously unreleased tracks and some rocking duets with the old pea-picker, Tennessee Ernie Ford.

influences:

◀◀ Bessie Smith, Margaret Whiting, Freddie Slack

▶▶ Rose Maddox, Kay Starr, Wanda Jackson, Kim Lenz

Ken Burke

Jelly Roll Morton

Born Ferdinand Joseph Lementhe (some sources say La Menthe, Lemott, LaMothe), October 20, 1890, in New Orleans, LA. Died July 10, 1941, in Los Angeles, CA.

Few musicians in the history of jazz were as colorful or gifted as Jelly Roll Morton. A pool hustler, pimp, and notable self-mythologizer, he was also the first great jazz composer and a pianist and vocalist of immense skill. Morton grew up in New Orleans, where he was playing piano in brothels as early as 1902. Around 1904 he became an itinerant musician and traveled the country from New York City to Los Angeles. He worked in a variety of settings, including long stints in minstrel shows, and added regional piano styles to his already impressive command of the ragtime, French quadrilles, light classics, blues, and Caribbean syncopations (all of which became the foundation of swing) that he had originally picked up in New Orleans. By the mid-1920s he was living in Chicago, where he recorded with his Red Hot Peppers from 1926 to 1928. These sides are his finest small ensemble recordings, the first recorded examples of real jazz composition-arrangement, and enduring masterpieces of early jazz. Ironically, they were recorded just as Louis Armstrong was changing the shape of jazz, and Morton's greatest works—with their emphasis on New Orleans collective improvisation and polyphony, as opposed to the virtuoso soloist and the homophony of the emerging big bands, never brought Morton the fame he deserved. In 1928 he moved to New York, and while he made some more impressive recordings there, he was considered out of date, and drifted into an embittered obscurity. He settled in Washington, D.C., where Smithsonian musical folklorist Alan Lomax found him and recorded a remarkable series of his solo piano performances and reminiscences at the Library of Congress in 1938. These recordings led to renewed interest in Morton and a handful of new recordings, but, in a final cruel irony, he died in 1941 and was again cheated of the recognition he was due.

what to buy: *The Jelly Roll Morton Centennial: His Complete Victor Recordings* ♪♪♪♪♪ (RCA, 1926/1990, reissue prod. Orrin Keepnews) is a five-CD set containing all the Red Hot Peppers sessions, including dazzling masterpieces like "Grandpa's Spells," "Black Bottom Stomp," and "The Pearls." The later work never equaled these sessions, but there are flashes of brilliance throughout and other New Orleans greats like Henry "Red" Allen, Barney Bigard, and Sidney Bechet appear as sidemen, which alone makes the music worth a listen. The remastering doesn't do justice to the music, but it's essential stuff. All four volumes of Morton's Library of Congress musings are worth owning, but if you have to limit yourself, get *The Pearls: The Library of Congress Recordings, Volume 3* ♪♪♪♪♪ (Rounder, 1993, prod. Alan Lomax) for its stellar versions of "King Porter Stomp," "The

Jelly Roll Morton **(Archive Photos)**

Pearls," and "Bert Williams." For some real insight into how Morton might have entertained audiences in the seamier establishments he worked, this CD restores the previously censored "Murder Ballad" to its sexually explicit full length. *Winin' Boy Blues: The Library of Congress Recordings, Volume 4* (Rounder, 1993, prod. Alan Lomax) contains "Creepy Feeling," a superbly paced performance over a slinky tango rhythm (the Spanish tinge that Morton championed) that is perhaps the single best track of these epic recording sessions.

what to buy next: *Kansas City Stomp: The Library of Congress Recordings, Volume 1* (Rounder, 1993, prod. Alan Lomax) reveals a fascinating and profound portrait of American music on the verge of jazz. Morton plays rags, gospel tunes, blues, parlor ballads, and light classics, transforming them into jazz before your ears. Immensely exciting music that is both history lesson and art. *Anamule Dance: The Library of Congress Recordings, Volume 2* (Rounder, 1993, prod. Alan Lomax) offers an ironic, nostalgic version of "Mr. Jelly Lord," an unflaggingly imaginative "Original Jelly Roll Blues," and another R-rated (and pretty misogynist) blues, "Make Me a Pallet on the Floor."

best of the rest:

Jelly Roll Morton: 1923–24 (Milestone, 1993)
Last Sessions: The Complete General Recordings (Commodore/GRP, 1997)
Jelly Roll Morton: The Piano Rolls (Nonesuch, 1997)

worth searching for: *Jelly Roll Morton, Volume 1* (JSP, 1990, prod. John R.T. Davies) covers the same Red Hot Peppers material as the RCA Centennial collection, but producer John R.T. Davies's remastering is infinitely better. If sound quality is really important to you and you don't mind paying the extra money and or hunting for British imports, JSP reissues of Morton's entire Victor catalog are worth it.

influences:

◀◀ Buddy Bolden

▶▶ Earl "Fatha" Hines, Charles Mingus, Dick Hyman, James Dapogny

Ed Hazell

Bennie Moten

Born November 13, 1894, in Kansas City, MO. Died April 2, 1935, in Kansas City, MO.

Bennie Moten's band was significant to the history of jazz because the core of Count Basie's early swing band evolved from Moten's orchestra. Until Basie took over, Moten's band enjoyed a reputation as the best band throughout Kansas, Oklahoma, and Missouri.

A skilled, driven pianist, Moten first recorded on the OKeh label with a small group in 1923, and again in 1926 with a larger ensemble. Musicians in his band included "Hot Lips" Page, Jimmy Rushing, Count Basie on second piano, Booker Washington, Eddie Durham, Eddie Barefield, Ben Webster, and Walter Page, among others. When the band was on the road, and playing in Kansas City, Moten often let Basie sit in for most of the performance. In 1932 the band recorded its most famous sides for Victor, including the classic "Moten Swing." When Moten passed away from a bungled tonsillectomy operation in 1935, his brother took over for a short time, and then the band passed into the hands of Count Basie.

what to buy: *Basie Beginnings (1929–1932)* (RCA, 1929–32, compilation prod. Orrin Keepnews), which documents three sessions in Chicago, Kansas City, and Camden, New Jersey, captures brilliant and exciting moments. Trumpeter Oran "Hot Lips" Page had, by the Kansas City sessions, joined the band, along with vocalist Jimmy Rushing, who sings five tunes, including "Won't You Be My Baby," "That Too, Do Blues," "Liza Lee," "When I'm Alone," and "Now That I Need You," while Basie adds vocals to "Somebody Stole My Gal." By 1932, as the last session illustrates, Moten's continuous revisions and refinements gave the orchestra a more sophisticated and smooth swinging sound. Seven tunes recorded at the 1932 session include the debut of Bennie and Buster Moten's "Moten Swing," as well as "Toby," "The Blue Room," "New Orleans," "Milenberg Joys," and "Lafayette."

the rest:

Bennie Moten 1923–1927 (Jazz Chronological Classics, 1994)
Bennie Moten 1927–1929 (Jazz Chronological Classics, 1994)
Bennie Moten 1929–1930 (Jazz Chronological Classics, 1994)
Bennie Moten 1930–1932 (Jazz Chronological Classics, 1994)

influences:

◀◀ Jelly Roll Morton

▶▶ Count Basie, Duke Ellington, Big Joe Turner

Susan K. Berlowitz

Moon Mullican

Born Aubrey Mullican, March 29, 1909, in Corrigan, TX. Died January 1, 1967, in Beaumont, TX.

A spiritual forebear of rock 'n' roll and a direct, obvious influence on Jerry Lee Lewis, pianist Moon Mullican remains a little-known country music pioneer. Bald and overweight, he hardly looked like the father of rock 'n' roll, but his 1956 classic "Seven Nights to Rock" captured the exact feel of the burgeoning idiom with ease for the master of hillbilly boogie. He was a Grand Ole Opry regular in the wake of his 1949 hit "I'll Sail My Ship Alone," and he co-wrote "Jambalaya" with none other than Hank Williams, although his contributions went uncredited. Mullican's barrelhouse style fell from favor in the country world and he suffered health problems. He described his own style in a self-effacing bit of hillbilly hyperbole: "You got to make those bottles bounce on the table."

what to buy: Mullican recorded more than 100 sides for the King Records label during his 10 years with the Cincinnati-based company. The collection of his vintage recordings currently available is a reissue of an old album, *Sings His All-Time Hits* (King, 1958/1994).

what to avoid: The German reissue specialists Bear Family have compiled a pricey set of his post-King recordings, *Moon's Rock* (Bear Family, 1994), but these were not his finest hours.

the rest:

22 Greatest Hits (Deluxe, 1991)

worth searching for: The compilation album *Seven Nights to Rock: The King Years 1946–56* (Western, 1981) captures Mullican's roughneck-roadhouse, whiskey-belting best.

influences:

◄◄ Milton Brown & His Brownies, Big Joe Turner

►► Hank Williams, Jerry Lee Lewis, Gary Stewart, Asleep at the Wheel

Joel Selvin

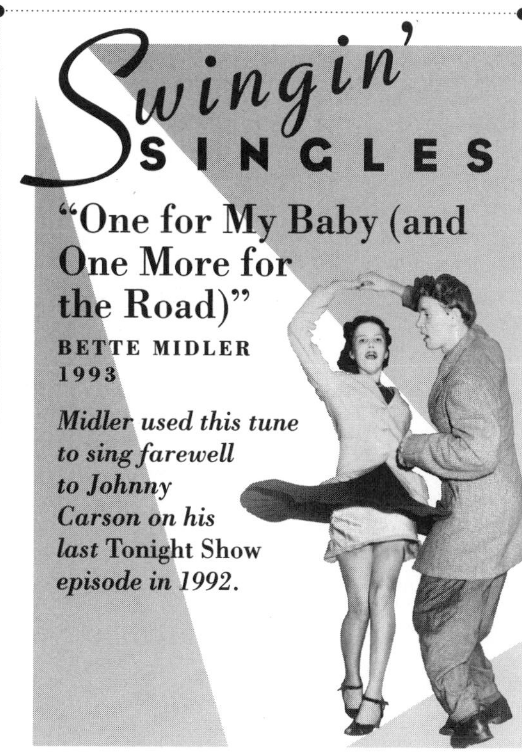

Swingin' SINGLES
"One for My Baby (and One More for the Road)"
BETTE MIDLER
1993
Midler used this tune to sing farewell to Johnny Carson on his last Tonight Show episode in 1992.

Musical Knights

See: Horace Heidt

Ozzie Nelson

Born Oswald George Nelson, March 20, 1906, in Jersey City, NJ. Died June 3, 1975, in Hollywood, CA.

You didn't know Ozzie Nelson used to head up a swing band? It's true. Long before he brought us television's *The Adventures of Ozzie and Harriet* (with sons David and "the irrepressible" Ricky), Nelson waved the baton for his own successful orchestra, wrote songs, and sang. A first-string quarterback and aspiring cartoonist at Rutgers University, Nelson was finishing up law school when he and some classmates bluffed their way onto a local radio show in 1930. Nelson did his best imitation of Rudy Vallee and the band played the same tunes and arrangements they'd heard others do. Surprisingly, they were quite a hit, and became regulars on *Roemer's Homers Radio Hour.* Host Milton Roemer was an important factor in Nelson's quick rise. His flair for publicity (and stuffing contest ballot boxes) was instrumental in Nelson's surpassing the "King of Jazz," Paul Whiteman, in a newspaper popularity poll, and moving the orchestra into the classier venues of the day. Nelson and his orchestra racked up nearly 40 hit records from 1931 to 1944. His band played it safe, tackling mostly the white bread commercial aspects of big-band jazz. Yet such instrumentals as "Rigamarole," "Swamp Fire," and "Riff Interlude" were respectable swing, with the latter winning the praise of Count Basie. Nelson's 1935 version of "In a Sentimental Mood" even out-sold Duke Ellington's. Other hits such as "The Kid in the Three-Cornered Pants" and "I'm Looking for a Guy Who Plays Alto and Doubles on Clarinet and Wears a Size 37 Suit" exploited Nelson's coy sense of humor to big effect. During its peak years, Nelson's orchestra featured two pianos, rich brass and sax sections, arrangements by Glenn Miller and Billy May, and a pretty singer named Harriet Hilliard. Initially, Hilliard chased a career in feature films and on Broadway before becoming Nelson's wife and full-time stage partner. Their easy chemistry and Harriet's superb comedic timing made them particular favorites on radio where they became regulars on *The*

Baker's Broadcast, starring Joe Penner, *The Bob Ripley Show*, and *The Red Skelton Show*.

The Nelsons, tired of lengthy touring, pulled their band off the road for good in 1944 to concentrate on their family-oriented radio sitcom, *The Adventures of Ozzie and Harriet*. Once the show became a hit (eventually moving into TV and films), the orchestra disbanded. But that wasn't the end of Nelson's involvement in music. During the '50s, when son Ricky became interested in making music Elvis Presley–style, Ozzie Nelson produced sessions, helped select material, and masterminded all the business aspects of the young rocker's career.

what to buy: None of Nelson's studio recordings are available; however, *Ozzie Nelson & His Orchestra, 1937: With Vocals by Eddy Howard & the Trio* ♪♪♪ (Circle, 1981/1994, compilation prod. George H. Buck Jr.) is a fine radio transcription that reveals the band's true style and flavor. These recordings accentuate Nelson's lighter moments with such novelties as "The Girl on the Police Gazette," "Swing, Swing Dear Mother-in-Law," and his tribute to son David, "The Kid in the Three-Cornered Pants."

what to buy next: Ozzie and Harriet sound easy and smooth on *Head Over Heels in Love* ♪♪½ (Hindsight, 1995, compilation prod. Pete Kline), a collection of duets via radio transcription. The duo sounds especially cozy on such numbers as "I've Got My Love to Keep Me Warm," "Let's Have Another Cigarette," and "Two Sleepy People."

worth searching for: One of the better collections of radio transcriptions, *Nelson Touch: 24 Band Hits 1931–1941* ♪♪♪½ (ASV/Living Era, 1996, compilation prod. David Lennick) features live versions of such popular Nelson numbers as "Rigamarole," "Jersey Jive," and "Central Avenue Shuffle." Nelson and his wife Harriet share the vocal chores on this superior collection.

influences:

◀◀ Rudy Vallee, Paul Whiteman, Isham Jones

▶▶ Woody Herman, Eddy Howard, Billy May, Ricky Nelson

Ken Burke

New Jersey Casino Orchestra

See: California Ramblers

The New Morty Show

Formed 1995, in San Francisco, CA.

Neal "Morty" Okin, trumpet/bandleader; Larry "Vise Grip" (a.k.a. "Bald Guy") Castle, lead vocals; Kat Starr (Kathleen Thomas), lead vocals (1997–present); "Papa" Van Hughes, trombone; Dan Andrews, bass (1995–97); Dave Rubin, drums (1995–97); Kevin Stevens, drums; Whitney Wilson, guitar; John Quam, piano; David Murotake, tenor sax; Tom Griesser, baritone sax; Tom Beyer, bass (1997); Andrew Higgins, bass (1998).

Riding the zoot-suited wave of new swingers, the New Morty Show boasts a high-energy sound that blows the roof off venues from Vegas to Virginia. With a schmaltz-filled act as full of yuks as it is brass, the New Morty Show puts the emphasis on Show. You know they've gotta have a sense of humor when they pull out swing versions of Billy Idol's "White Wedding" and Metallica's "Enter Sandman"—and they sound better than the originals. Morty claims he was meant to play Vegas; from the band's debut album, *Mortyfied*, it sure sounds that way. The band has appeared in the Francis Ford Coppola flick *Jack*, starring Robin Williams, and Vise Grip showed up in *The Game*, with Michael Douglas and Sean Penn.

what's available: A rousing disc in the classical jump-swing mode, the band's debut, *Mortyfied* ♪♪♪½ (Slimstyle, 1998, prod. Mark Eastwood), nonetheless offers a twist or two—specifically, the jazzed-up cocktail-hour cha-cha of "White Wedding (Rebel Yell) Medley" and "Enter Sandman" (followed by "Caldonia"!) and the torchy chanteuse vocals and sublime jazz piano of "Blue Martini."

influences:

◀◀ Louis Prima, Woody Herman, Keely Smith, Sam Butera, Count Basie, Burt Bacharach

Lynne Margolis

Joe Newman

Born September 7, 1922, in New Orleans, LA. Died July 4, 1992, in New York, NY.

One of the finest trumpeters to emerge during the big-band era, Joe Newman's style was all about thrill and exhilaration. He had a broad and brassy tone that cut through any trumpet section and his melodic ideas set him aside from the typical session player.

His first important work came in the early '40s as a member of Lionel Hampton's big band, followed by his initial stint with the Count Basie orchestra from 1943 to 1947. During this period, Newman was a sideman with various groups, including those of Illinois Jacquet and J.C. Heard. In 1952, Newman rejoined the Basie band for a fruitful period of nearly a decade. Part of Basie's "atomic period," Newman appeared on several of the group's momentous '50s Roulette sessions. The next few decades found Newman working as a session musician, leader of his own groups, educator, and jazz advocate. Newman's trips overseas included a 1962 Russian tour with Benny Goodman and a 1975 European jaunt with the New York Repertory Orchestra.

what to buy: *Jive at Five* ♪♪♪♪ (Swingville, 1960/Original Jazz Classics, 1990, prod. Esmond Edwards) pairs Newman with his

Basie bandmate Frank Wess and pianist Tommy Flanagan. Underpinned by the solid bass work of Eddie Jones and inspired by the small-group swing of Basie, Newman and crew provide the best and most relaxed jazz of the period. *Good 'n' Groovy* (Swingville, 1961/Original Jazz Classics, 1994, prod. Esmond Edwards) features Joe working alongside his other Basie partner, tenor saxophonist Frank Foster. The tunes range from swing classics to hard-bop delights—and even a children's nursery rhyme.

what to buy next: *The Best of Count Basie—The Roulette Years* (Roulette, 1957–1962/Roulette/Blue Note, 1991, prod. Teddy Reig) is a Basie-band sampler from the '50s.

what to avoid: *Hangin' Out* (Concord, 1984, prod. Carl Jefferson) comes from more recent times and finds Newman's work lacking a bit in comparison with his earlier triumphs.

the rest:
I Feel Like a Newman (Black Lion, 1956/1992)

worth searching for: Newman's third album for Prestige's Swingville subsidiary has yet to appear as an Original Jazz Classics reissue. That's a shame, because *Joe's Hap'nin's* (Prestige/Swingville, 1961, prod. Esmond Edwards), a stellar quartet date with pianist Tommy Flanagan, puts Newman out front, where his warm and brassy tone is heard on an agreeable selection of standards, ballads, and blues.

influences:
◀◀ Louis Armstrong, Harry "Sweets" Edison
▶▶ Marvin Stamm, Virgil Jones, Conte Candoli

Chris Hovan

Ray Noble

Born November 17, 1903, in Brighton, England. Died April 3, 1978, in London, England.

Ray Noble, who wrote the big-band standard "Cherokee," is best known for his 1930s work with singer Al Bowlly, but his orchestras were always smoother and more romantic than the jittery swing of Benny Goodman or Glenn Miller. "Goodnight, Sweetheart" was one of his first compositions in 1931, and in addition to becoming his trademark showstopper, it led to a lucrative career writing film music and collaborating with the lovey-dovey singer Alan Murray. At an early age, Noble won a dance-arrangement competition sponsored by *Melody Maker*, and that led to a high-level music director position at the record company His Master's Voice, and later EMI, where he led the house band. In 1935, his first U.S. tour was a fiasco; because of British union rules, he could only bring Bowlly with him, and the musicians Glenn Miller helpfully dug up were talented but totally undisciplined, and they got into all sorts of trouble. Abruptly, the impatient Noble disbanded the orchestra and shifted to a film career, where he took on many stereotypical roles as the goofy Englishman. Despite occasional returns to orchestra leading in the late 1930s and 1940s, he achieved his greatest U.S. prominence as a comedian on the George Burns–Gracie Allen and Edgar Bergen radio shows. Television crushed even that career, and Noble moved to a Mediterranean island where he lived for most of the rest of his life.

what's available: One of the few historical documents of Noble's highly respectable big-band career is the short *The Very Thought of You* (Living Era, 1993), which includes "Love Is the Sweetest Thing" and, of course, "Goodnight, Sweetheart." Some imports exist, including *1935–36 for Radio Only* (Jazz Band, 1994), released only in England.

influences:
◀◀ Duke Ellington, Benny Goodman, Glenn Miller, Tommy Dorsey, Coleman Hawkins
▶▶ Nelson Riddle, Les Elgart, Frank Sinatra

Steve Knopper

Sugar Ray Norcia

Born June 6, 1954, in Westerly, RI.

Sugar Ray Norcia has spent more than two decades honing his distinctive, velvet-smooth vocals and tasteful harmonica technique. As a member of the Bluetones, beginning in 1979, then with Ronnie Earl & the Broadcasters and later with Roomful of Blues, this Rhode Island native has performed and recorded across a wide spectrum of roots-based music. Norcia often played a supporting role in these ensembles, but he clearly has found his niche with his solo release, *Sweet & Swingin'*, which separates him from a generation of indistinguishable blues/R&B hopefuls stuck in the same generic rut.

what to buy: *Sweet & Swingin'* (Bullseye Blues and Jazz, 1998, prod. Carl Querfurth, Ray Norcia) is a glorious collection of eclectic late '40s/early '50s R &B, swing, and blues drawn from such impeccable sources as Percy Mayfield, Lonnie Johnson, Jimmy Witherspoon, Hank Williams, and Big Walter Horton. With vocal backing from the Jordanaires, a tasteful garnish of horns, and a decidedly light production touch, *Sweet & Swingin'* is Norcia's finest hour and unabashedly recommended.

what to buy next: Norcia is prominently featured on Roomful of Blues' *Roomful of Christmas* (Bullseye Blues, 1997, prod. Carl Querfurth), which mixes traditional and R&B holiday tunes. He also shines on Roomful's *Dance All Night* (Bullseye Blues, 1994, prod. Carl Querfurth). *Don't Stand in My Way* (Bullseye Blues, 1991, prod. Ron Levy) features Norcia with the

Ray Noble **(Archive Photos)**

Bluetones in a setting of mostly original blues. It's well-done, but with little swing feel. It does feature horns, however.

what to avoid: Even farther from Norcia's swing/R&B persona is Sugar Ray & the Blue Tones' *Knockout* (Varrick, 1989, prod. Ron Levy). It's an effective straight dose of raw, rocking electric blues, but there's no swinging here.

the rest:

(With Ronnie Earl & the Broadcasters) *I Like It When It Rains* (Antone's, 1990)
(With Ronnie Earl & the Broadcasters) *Surrounded By Love* (Black Top, 1991)
(With Ronnie Earl & the Broadcasters) *Test of Time* (Black Top, 1992)
(With Roomful of Blues) *Turn It On! Turn It Up!* (Bullseye Blues, 1995)
(With Roomful of Blues) *Under One Roof* (Bullseye Blues, 1997)

influences:

◄◄ Jimmie Rodgers, Jimmy Witherspoon, Percy Mayfield, Big Joe Turner, Joe Williams, Ray Charles, Wynonie Harris, Little Walter Jacobs, Big Walter Horton

see also: *Roomful of Blues*

Bryan Powell

Red Norvo

Born Kenneth Norville, March 31, 1908, in Beardstown, IL. Died April 6, 1999, in Santa Monica, CA.

Red Norvo's career spanned some of the most exciting developments in jazz—he not only swung with the hottest names in big-band music, but jammed with the legendary innovators who would deconstruct swing and make it bop. After starting out on the piano, the young Norvo was eventually inspired to pick up the mallets and tackle the xylophone. In the '30s he was the first musician to introduce the instrument to the jazz world. By the early '40s he had moved from xylophone to the vibraphone. Throughout the '40s and '50s he worked with some of the greatest names in jazz, playing in big bands led by Benny Goodman and Woody Herman, then assembling small combos that included Charlie Parker, Charles Mingus, and Dizzy Gillespie. Though he put together groups as large as seven, he seemed to prefer trios, and the Norvo catalog is dominated by various configurations of three. He was married for a time to jazz singer Mildred Bailey, and the couple (affectionately known as "Mr. & Mrs. Swing") recorded several albums together.

what to buy: Though *Red Norvo Septet featuring Charlie Parker and Dizzy Gillespie* (Stash, 1995, reissue prod. Tony Williams, Will Friedwald) isn't really an album proper—more like an EP of four tunes plus alternate takes—and the recording technology of the day (June 1945) makes for a rather flat sound fidelity, this interlude in jazz history nonetheless lives up to the title "Red Norvo's Fabulous Jam Session." Featuring Charlie Parker and Dizzy Gillespie, this combo really cooks. *Music to Listen to Red Norvo By* (Original Jazz Classics, 1957), a sextet recording, is a combination of shorter pieces plus clarinetist Bill Smith's 20-minute-plus "Divertimento." Though the group never loses its relaxed, swinging demeanor, there are enough bop-ish spikes here and there to give it an edge. *The Red Norvo Trios with Jimmy Raney or Tal Farlow and Red Mitchell* (Prestige, 1995) compiles sessions recorded over a two-year period from September 1953 through October 1955, plus two albums, *The Red Norvo Trio* and *The Red Norvo Trios* (though one track from the former, "Puby La Keg," was deleted). In order to make the original double album *The Red Norvo Trio with Tal Farlow and Charles Mingus* (Denon/Savoy, 1995, prod. Richard Bock) fit onto one CD, five tracks were omitted from this collection—so if you are a completist, your only option may be to track down the vinyl version.

worth searching for: On occasion, compilers omit a track or two to make two or three albums fit on a single CD, so tracking down the individual albums depends on how much of a completist you are. All the tracks on *Move!* (Savoy/Denon, 1992, prod. Ozzie Cadena) were compiled onto *The Red Norvo Trio with Tal Farlow and Charles Mingus. Red Norvo Trio* (Original Jazz Classics, 1991, prod. Marvin Jacobs) works its way through eight numbers—originals plus standards by Cole Porter, Duke Ellington, and others.

influences:

◄◄ Duke Ellington, Fletcher Henderson, Scott Joplin

►► Lionel Hampton, Dave Brubeck

see also: *Mildred Bailey*

Sandy Masuo

Tim O'Brien

See: Hot Rize

Helen O'Connell

Born May 23, 1920, in Lima, OH. Died September 9, 1993.

Jazz purists hated her singing style, but without Helen O'Connell's string of hits and dazzling stage presence, Jimmy Dorsey's orchestra likely would have struggled much longer

Red Norvo **(Archive Photos)**

than it did. Admittedly, O'Connell did not have great vocal range, but she worked hard to find ways to sing around notes she couldn't hit. In the process, she became a distinctive performer, both as a solo artist and in tandem with the pre–Frank Sinatra swoon crooner Bob Eberly. O'Connell sang for Larry Funk & His Band of a Thousand Melodies before replacing Ella Mae Morse in Dorsey's band. Up to that point, Jimmy Dorsey's outfit had not been as successful as brother Tommy's, even though the former was considered the better jazzman. (Great chops and snob appeal can only take a band so far.) Once O'-Connell came on board in 1939, that changed. She sang straight on her hit versions of "All of Me" and "Embraceable You," but she established herself with such novelties as "Six Lessons from Madam La Zonga" and "The Bad Humor Man." O'Connell's flirty, wacky sense of humor and drop-dead good looks brought something fresh to the sometimes-lifeless art of big-band singing. The career momentum of both Jimmy Dorsey and O'Connell shifted into high gear once handsome vocalist Bob Eberly joined the mix. Dorsey arranged their duets in a unique fashion. He alternated Eberly's ballad style, the band's jazz solos, a slow passage, and a spirited, big finish from O'-Connell—all in the course of the same tune. Masterful variations on this formula brought Eberly and O'Connell a string of classic hits such as "Amapola," "Yours," "Tangerine," and "Green Eyes" (the latter featuring her sexy pronouncement "cool and limpid"). Movies, radio shows, and live gigs made her a very big star, but at her (and the band's) peak in 1943, O'-Connell temporarily retired to start a family. She re-emerged during the early days of television, co-hosting the *Today Show* with Dave Garroway and starring in her own network variety program. She resumed recording as well, finally silencing her critics with a series of confident, well-crafted pop albums. In the years before her death, O'Connell toured with Rose Marie, Kay Starr, and Rosemary Clooney as part of the extremely popular traveling revue *Four Girls Four.*

what's available: Sadly, there are no solo albums of O'Connell's studio work in print—only collections of radio performances that have fallen into the public domain. The cassette-only *With Irv Orton's Orchestra* (Hindsight, 1992, prod. Wally Heider) is drawn from the mid-'50s and sports thin sound and an uninspired orchestra. The superior *The Sweetest Sounds: 1953–1963* (Southport, 1994, prod. Pete Kline) showcases 16 public radio appearances and includes live renditions of many of her hits from the '40s and '50s. The latter is a nice piece of history for collectors and longtime fans, but not exactly the best place to start.

worth searching for: O'Connell's original versions of "Green Eyes," "Amapola," and "Brazil," with the great Bob Eberly, can be found on the mail-order-only *18 Hits with the Jimmy Dorsey Orchestra* (Good Music, 1998), a set of Eberly's finest duet and solo performances.

influences:

◀ Martha Tilton, Kay Weber

▶ Betty Engels, Marion Hutton, Kitty Kallen

see also: *Jimmy Dorsey*

Ken Burke

Anita O'Day

Born Anita Belle Colton, October 18, 1919, in Chicago, IL.

Even though she may not have invented the form, Anita O'Day certainly perfected the art of scat singing. Her crisp enunciation, rhythmic energy, and creative delivery heightened the bebop aspect of big-band jazz. While O'Day was starting out with the Erskine Tate Orchestra as a marathon dancer and part-time singer, she constantly quizzed one of her partners, Frankie Laine, about phrasing, pitch, and song selection. After failing auditions with bandleaders Benny Goodman and Raymond Scott, O'Day was hired by drummer extraordinaire Gene Krupa for his band in 1941. She and trumpeter Roy Eldridge were key components in making Krupa's band one of the best of that era. O'Day's string of hits ("Let Me off Uptown," "Alreet," "Bolero at the Savoy") propelled the group to its popular peak just before Krupa was arrested on a drug charge and forced to temporarily fold the band. After a brief stint with Woody Herman, O'Day recorded hits with Stan Kenton's band ("And Her Tears Flowed Like Wine," "The Lady in Red") before returning to Krupa's orchestra. O'Day went solo in 1946, but didn't find the right label until she signed with Norman Granz's Verve Records in 1952; there she became a highly respected LP artist, collaborating on great sides with Billy May and Oscar Peterson, among others. O'Day's filmed 1958 appearance at the Newport Jazz Festival, *Jazz on a Summer's Day* (where she scats up a storm on "Tea for Two"), is considered her career high-water mark. O'Day cut top-notch discs and toured worldwide well into the '60s, until her longstanding addiction to heroin nearly took her life. Drug-free, she rebounded in the '70s with a smash appearance at the Berlin Jazz Festival. In 1997, the National Endowment for the Arts presented O'Day with the American Jazz Masters Award.

what to buy: Backed by the Oscar Peterson Quartet, O'Day never sounded better than on *Anita Sings the Most* (Verve, 1957/1990, prod. Norman Granz), a remarkable collaboration with inspired versions of "Them There Eyes," "Bewitched, Bothered, and Bewildered," and "They Can't Take That Away from Me." Equally fine, though less cohesive as an LP, *Verve Jazz Masters 49* (Verve, 1995, prod. Norman

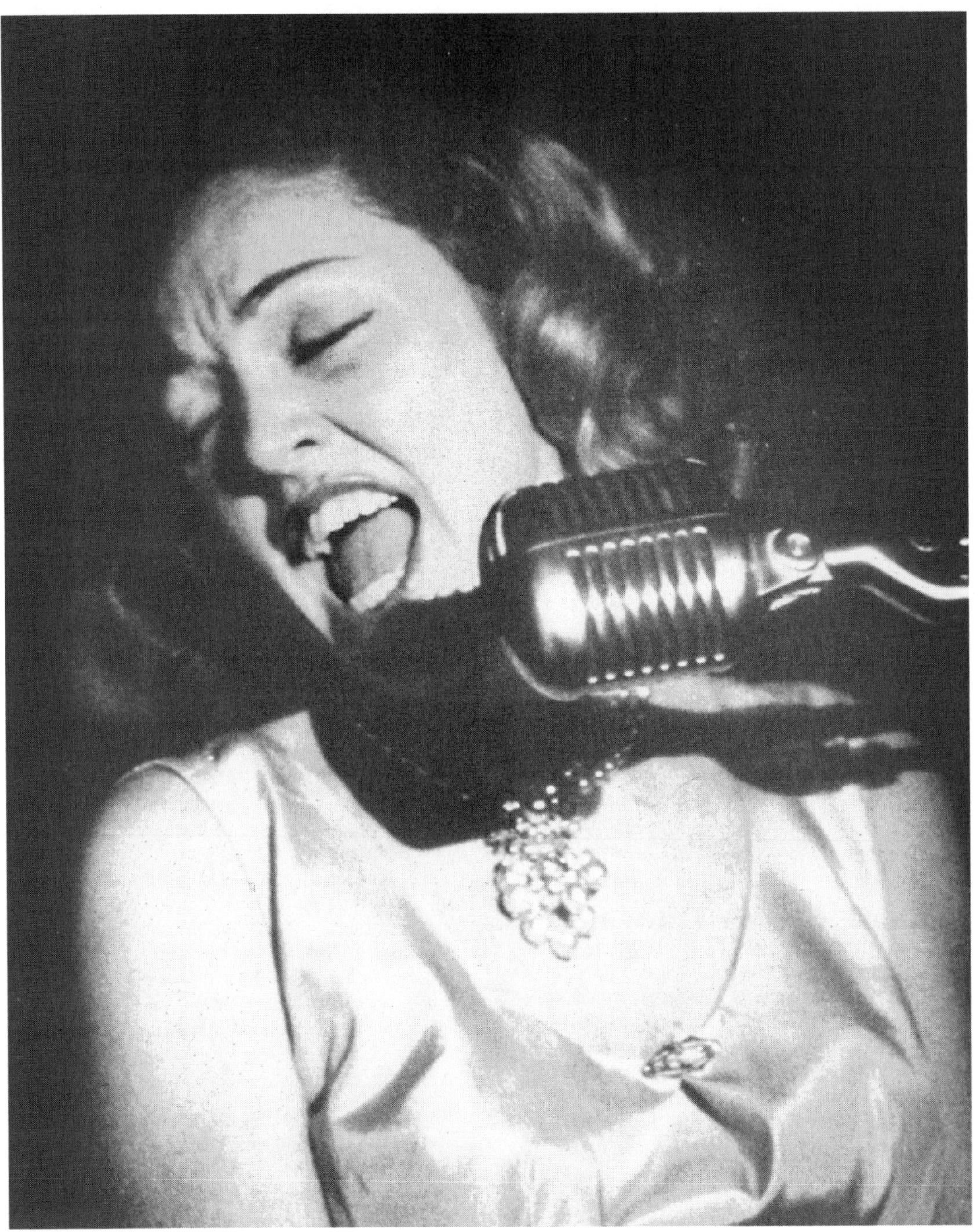

Anita O' Day **(Archive Photos)**

Granz) offers "A Nightingale in Berkeley Square," "Angel Eyes," and "I Can't Get Started."

what to buy next: The Verve era was O'Day's hot period as a solo act, so you could just as easily be satisfied with *Compact Jazz* (Verve, 1993, prod. Norman Granz), with tracks recorded between 1952 and 1962 with the Gene Krupa, Buddy Bregman, Billy May, and Marty Paich orchestras. *Pick Yourself Up* (Verve, 1956/1992) and *This Is Anita* (Verve, 1956/1990) are great reissues of her original LPs, fattened up with previously unreleased alternate takes. Also, O'Day is at her cool, introspective best on *All the Sad Young Men* (Verve, 1961/1998, prod. Creed Taylor), a superior reissue featuring the Gary MacFarland Orchestra (which includes Doc Severinsen, Hank Jones, and Phil Woods) on a mix of '40s standards and original tunes.

what to avoid: O'Day was well past her prime when she recorded *At Vine Street Live* (DRG, 1991, prod. Hugh Fordin) and *Rules of the Road* (Pablo, 1993, prod. Buddy Bregman). On both of these albums, her voice sounds shot as she sings new versions of old classics.

the rest:
Jazz 'Round Midnight (Verve, 1954/1997)
Anita (Verve, 1954/1987)
I Get a Kick out of You (Evidence, 1975/1993)
Live in Person (Starline, 1976/1993)
In a Mellow Tone (DRG, 1989)
Sings the Winners (Verve, 1990)
(With Billy May) *Swings Cole Porter* (Verve, 1991)
I Told Ya I Love Ya, Now Get Out (Signature, 1991)
Mello Day (GNP/Crescendo, 1992)
Wave: Live at Ronnie Scott's (Castle, 1993)
Meets the Big Bands (Moon, 1994)
That's That (Moon, 1995)
Let Me off Uptown (Pearl, 1996)
Anita O'Day, Vol. 19: 1941–46 (L'Art Vocal, 1997)
Complete Recordings (Baldwin, 1998)
Let Me off Uptown: The Best of Anita O'Day N/A (Columbia/Legacy, 1999)

worth searching for: O'Day's early years swinging with Gene Krupa's big band are chronicled on *Sings with Gene Krupa* (Tristar, 1994, prod. various), which contains many of their biggest hits from the early '40s. *Drummer Man* (Verve, 1956/1996, prod. Norman Granz) is another solid Krupa disc featuring strong later work with and without O'Day.
Jazz 'Round Midnight (Verve, 1997)

influences:
◀◀ Mildred Bailey, Billie Holiday, Connee Boswell, Frankie Laine
▶▶ June Christy, Chris Connor, Helen O'Connell, Peggy Lee

Ken Burke

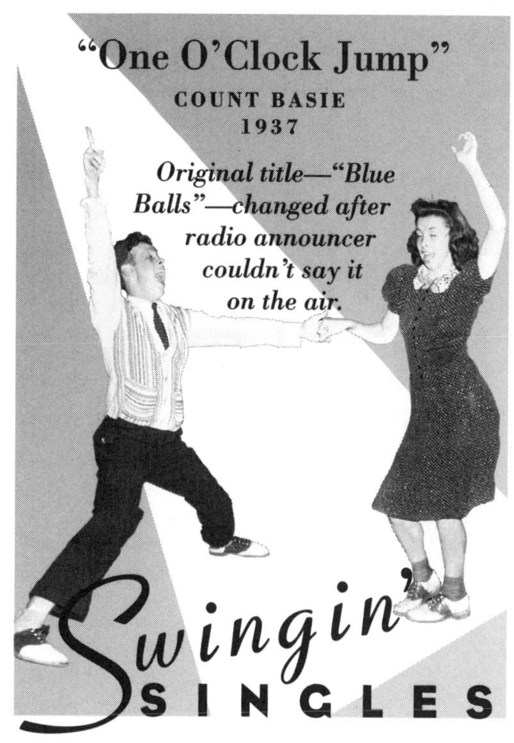

"One O'Clock Jump"
COUNT BASIE
1937
Original title—"Blue Balls"—changed after radio announcer couldn't say it on the air.
Swingin'
SINGLES

Joe "King" Oliver

Born Joseph Oliver, May 11, 1885, in Abend, LA. Died April 8, 1938, in Savannah, GA.

Cornetist Joe "King" Oliver was a titanic figure who straddled the worlds of early New Orleans jazz and its rapid spread through recordings in the 1920s. He created a wealth of new sounds through his use of mutes and buckets to vary his instrument's sound and introduce vocal effects. In the decade following Oliver's first recordings, many of his licks and phrases became the stock-in-trade of young jazz trumpeters. Louis Armstrong, Rex Stewart, and Harry James were among those who memorized and performed Oliver's solo choruses from his recording of "Dippermouth Blues," carrying Oliver's innovative trumpet style into the swing era. After trombone lessons as a child, Oliver switched to cornet and was playing in the Melrose Brass Band in 1907. A decade later, Oliver was in trombonist Kid Ory's band when Ory declared him "King" of the New Orleans cornetists—a title Oliver held without dispute. Veteran bassist Bill Johnson invited Oliver to join him in Chicago in 1919, where Oliver began a residence at the Lincoln Gardens that lasted, with time out for a trip to the West Coast, until 1924. Oliver assumed leadership from Johnson, assembling a band with Baby Dodds on drums and Johnny Dodds on clarinet. In 1922, he invited the young Louis Armstrong to join him as second cornetist. This cemented Oliver's place as the central figure in jazz at the time. For the next few years, Oliver led a larger band, the Dixie Syncopators, at the Plantation Cafe, constructing a music that increasingly combined the skills of well-trained "reading" musicians with his more spontaneous, expressive associates from New Orleans, like Johnny Dodds and Kid Ory. A disastrous tour, business mistakes, failing health, and changing tastes all combined to undo Oliver's career. When he moved to New York in 1929, painful dental problems often forced him to cede trumpet solos on his recordings to Louis Metcalf or Red Allen. The later years of Oliver's life were a dismal fall from the celebrity he had known in New Orleans and Chicago.

what to buy: Oliver made his greatest recordings with his Creole Jazz Band in 1923. Though earwitnesses claimed these recordings, made with primitive technology and restricted playing times, did the band little justice, they are unquestionably the first great jazz records. *Louis Armstrong and King Oliver* (Milestone, 1992, prod. Orrin Keepnews) is an excellent single-CD starting point, with 18 selections of the Creole Jazz Band's wondrous work, including "Dippermouth Blues." The two-CD *King Oliver's Creole Jazz Band: 1923–1924* (Retrieval, 1997, prod. various) is the most complete set of Oliver's early work available, including alternate takes and duets with pianist Jelly Roll Morton.

what to buy next: Though Oliver's later recordings have been overshadowed by the sheer impact of the Creole Jazz Band, they have distinctive qualities and often point to the rise of the swing era's sectional play. *King Oliver and His Dixie Syncopators: 1926–28* (Jazz Classics, 1994, prod. various) demonstrates the band's increasing use of arrangement in place of collective improvisation on such tracks as "Deep Henderson." *King Oliver: 1928–30* (Jazz Classics, 1994, prod. various) has the later New York recordings, with surprises ranging from the scintillating piano of James P. Johnson to a rendition of country singer Jimmie Rodgers's "Everybody Does It in Hawaii." The latter features country musician Roy Smeck's steel guitar mingling with Oliver's muted horn in a performance that foreshadows the rise of western swing.

best of the rest:

King Oliver, Vol.2: 1926–31 (Topaz, 1995)

worth searching for: To read about the complete life of this essential figure, find the Walter Allen and Brian Rust book *King Oliver* (Storyville, 1987).

influences:

◀◀ Buddy Bolden, Freddie Keppard, Bunk Johnson

▶▶ Louis Armstrong, Bubber Miley, Muggsy Spanier, Red Allen, Doc Cheatham

see also: *Louis Armstrong*

Stuart Broomer

Oran "Hot Lips" Page

Born January 27, 1908, in Dallas, TX. Died November 5, 1954, in New York, NY.

Oran "Hot Lips" Page was a great swing trumpeter and blues vocalist who worked with the great blues belter Ma Rainey, among others, before joining the legendary Blue Devils from 1928 to 1931. After the Devils broke up, Page played in Bennie Moten's orchestra and appeared on many of Moten's influential recordings in the early 1930s—his trumpet rides out the orchestra's trademark tune, "Moten Swing." After Moten's premature death, Page starred among the featured players in Count Basie's band, but went solo just before Basie left Kansas City. Page led a big band that recorded for Victor, and made a number of other recordings with smaller groups. He was featured in Artie Shaw's Orchestra from 1941 to 1942. After that, he mainly freelanced and frequented jam sessions. A revered jazz figure even after bebop displaced swing, Page played the Paris Jazz Festival in 1949 along with Sidney Bechet, Miles Davis, and Charlie Parker. Many of his later recordings were with small jump bands, and bridged the jazz and R&B genres.

what's available: *The Chronological Hot Lips Page: 1938–1940* (Jazz Chronological Classics, 1991, prod. various) includes small-group recordings Page made for Decca and all of the big-band sides he recorded for Victor's subsidiary, Bluebird. *The Chronological Hot Lips Page: 1940–1944* (Jazz Chronological Classics, 1995) includes small-group sessions of blues vocals and hot swing instrumentals.

worth searching for: *After Hours in Harlem* (Onyx, 1973, reissue prod. Don Schlitten) is an out-of-print vinyl album of Jerry Newman's 1940–1941 wire recordings from the legendary jazz nightclub Minton's, valuable for the appearances of stride pianist Donald Lambert and the great Thelonious Monk. *Basie Beginnings (1929–1932)* (RCA, 1929–32) is a compilation of Bennie Moten big-band recordings, including many of the Moten Band's most famous sides.

influences:

◀◀ Louis Armstrong

⏩ Charlie Parker

Ron Weinstock

The Paladins

Formed 1977, in San Diego, CA.

Dave Gonzales, vocals, guitar, electric bass, percussion; Thomas Yearsley, vocals, acoustic and electric bass, percussion; Brian Fahey, drums.

Hard electric blues, jumping R&B, rockabilly, Tex-Mex, and elemental swing powerfully intersect in the music of the Paladins. Their highly polished musical skills, impassioned vocals, and indefatigable energy all combine to forge a much fuller, more rhythmic sound than any trio has a right to expect. Besides possessing an uncanny ability to find old songs that fit their style, all three members are capable of writing clever songs with a timeless feel and a bluesy, almost punk edge. Initially a high school quartet, they played rockabilly-oriented material years before the official revival, and vigorously helped spread the word once that revival began. The Paladins officially became a trio in 1984, and began contributing to compilation discs on the Government and Rhino labels. Once their first solo disc hit the stores, the band began hitting the road, playing in excess of 200 live dates a year, both in America and abroad. Though they have cut two critically acclaimed LPs for the Chicago-based Alligator label, the Paladins haven't really cracked the big time like their contemporaries (and mentors) Los Lobos and the Fabulous Thunderbirds.

what to buy: There's plenty of rocking jump blues on *Years Since Yesterday* ♪♪♪ (Alligator, 1988, prod. the Paladins, Steve Berlin, Mark Linett), which features such danceable original numbers as "Good Lovin'," "She's Fine," and their masterful remake of Joe Clay's "Right Track." This one's a better introduction to the band and its influences than the debut disc on Wrestler.

what to buy next: A far stronger musical statement, *Let's Buzz* ♪♪♪♪ (Alligator, 1990, prod. the Paladins, Steve Berlin, Mark Linett) boasts the stomping blues of the title track, the rockabilly/Tex-Mex of "Playgirl," the Latin-tempo instrumental "Untamed Melody," and a swinging jump-blues version of Brook Benton's "Kiddio," with New Orleans legend Lee Allen on sax. It's skewed a little more toward Stevie Ray Vaughan–type blues than some swingheads would like, but this is a case where musical excellence transcends genre boundaries.

the rest:

The Paladins ♪♪♪½ (Wrestler, 1989)

worth searching for: Two of the Paladins' better LPs were poorly distributed and, lamentably, are now out of print: *Ticket Home* ♪♪♪½ (Sector 2, 1994, prod.Cesar Rojas, the Paladins) and *Million Mile Club* ♪♪♪ (4AD, 1996, prod. the Paladins, Irvin "Magic" Kramer) are two very satisfying live outings that completely capture their blues-drenched essence.

influences:

⏪ Link Wray, the Fabulous Thunderbirds, Stevie Ray Vaughan, Los Lobos

⏩ The Blasters, X, Hot Rod Lincoln, Cigar Store Indians

Ken Burke

Charlie Parker

Born April 29, 1920, in Kansas City, MO. Died March 12, 1955, in New York, NY.

The man they called "Bird" engineered the rebellion against swing—via the movement he and his aide-de-camp, Dizzy Gillespie, called bop. But like all successful revolutionaries, Charlie Parker came up through swing, learned to idolize its masters (Lester Young, above all of them), and, even at his most iconoclastic, always made sure his breakneck pyrotechnics and his lilting melodies both swung. A decade ago, finding the swing-era Parker required the patience of an archaeologist—only a handful of pre–World War II recordings with Jay McShann's tough Kansas City big band could be found. The CD age changed all that. Now avid listeners can not only find several discs of McShann material, they can revel in seminal sides that show Parker moving from a swingman's world into the new realm of bop. Parker's swing sides are not only important simply as curios, they also show the mainstream foundations of a player who altered all swing bands that followed. Gillespie's pressure-cooker bop band of the late 1940s and Count Basie's re-formed band of the 1950s—to name two aggregations—both were influenced by Parker's vocabulary. And on top of all that, just to listen to Bird is to swing, albeit at 78 rpm.

The bare-bones outline of Parker's life has become achingly familiar—presented more or less accurately in Clint Eastwood's movie, *Bird*. Humiliated as a youth during jam sessions with Count Basie's big band, Parker woodshedded before joining McShann's unit in 1937. A trip to New York brought him into contact with some of the young Turks he would lead later on, but Parker returned to K.C. before moving back to the Apple for good in 1941. There were stints with Earl Hines, Billy Eckstine, and Noble Sissle, but Parker was meant to head his own group. A series of 1945 classics with Gillespie and a changing group of sidemen dropped the bomb. Parker followed with stunning stints on Savoy and Dial, but a worsening heroin habit left him unstrung and confined in a California mental hospital before he emerged stronger in 1947. Between then and the early 1950s, Bird owned the New York scene, joined by an army of fellow musicians. He was recorded repeatedly both by legitimate stu-

Charlie Parker (r) **(Archive Photos)**

dios and by fanatics who turned off their tape players when Parker stopped soloing. But heroin took over and Parker's life slowly unraveled. He died of a heart attack at age 34 in 1955, so ravaged that a coroner mistakenly guessed his age as 64. Bird was never a pied piper for dancers. The beret-topped beats jammed the Royal Roost to listen to Parker play, not to dance. But if you fail to at least snap your fingers to this stuff, Jack, you're dead.

what to buy: Parker shows up for five sides on *Blues from Kansas City* (GRP, 1992, prod. Orrin Keepnews), but the entire disc jumps. Jay McShann's group was gutty and bluesy and would have taken New York by storm if World War II hadn't gotten in the way. *Early Bird* (Stash, 1991, prod. Bernard Brightman) has an entire collection of radio transcriptions of McShann and Parker, and if it's a little wooly, it's even tougher than the official stuff. Hardcore Parker buffs can't live without *The Complete "Birth of the Bebop"* (Stash, 1991, prod. Bernard Brightman), a stunning set of long-unknown recordings of Parker woodshedding his way from life as a swing sideman to jazz trailblazer. He plays in hotel rooms with Diz and Billy Eckstine, noodles over Benny Goodman platters, and one-ups Lester Young on Prez classics.

what to buy next: Parker fanatics will argue until Armageddon over which record label did the most right by Bird—his initial foray on Savoy, the late 1940s Dials, or his 1950s sunset fling with Verve. The most lilting ballads and soaring skywriting are on *The Complete Dial Sessions* (Stash, 1993, prod. Ross Russell). There is nothing treacly about these 79 sides, just stratospheric gyrations and consummate balladry.

best of the rest:

Savoy Recordings (Master Takes) (Savoy, 1988)
Bird: The Complete Charlie Parker on Verve (Verve, 1988)
Jazz at Massey Hall (Original Jazz Classics, 1990)
The Complete Live Performances on Savoy (Savoy, 1998)

influences:

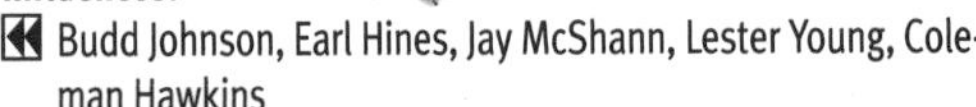

◄◄ Budd Johnson, Earl Hines, Jay McShann, Lester Young, Coleman Hawkins

►► Dizzy Gillespie, Miles Davis, Bud Powell, Max Roach, Sonny Rollins, Sonny Stitt, Dexter Gordon, Jackie McLean, J.J. Johnson

Steve Braun

Carl Perkins

Born April 9, 1932, in Ridgeley, TN. Died January 19, 1998, in Jacksonville, TN.

During rockabilly's very short life as a viable, commercial music, Carl Perkins was its finest singer, songwriter, and guitarist. No one else even came close. As a tunesmith, he brought the status-conscious hunger of the blues to his bopping teen anthems (at which only he and Chuck Berry truly excelled). Vocally, he combined the sorrow and self-deprecating comedy of Hank Williams and Ernest Tubb with the enthusiastic western-swing asides of Bob Wills and the razor-totin' menace of Muddy Waters and Howlin' Wolf. As a guitarist, Perkins adapted John Lee Hooker's electric rhythm to Bill Monroe's beat, and his rapid fire leads yelped with the cathartic release of rock 'n' roll. Born to sharecroppers, Perkins and his brothers were all quite young when they began working in the cotton fields. It was there a gray-haired black man named "Uncle John" Westbrook instructed Carl on the proper technique for picking both cotton and the guitar. Perkins drew his later professional style from his exposure to the cotton-patch gospel-blues of his co-workers and weekly *Grand Ol' Opry* broadcasts. With his brothers Jay and Clayton, on guitar and upright bass, respectively, and W.S. "Fluke" Holland on drums, Perkins played every honky-tonk and bloody bucket in his area. When they heard Elvis Presley's "That's All Right Mama" on the radio, they realized there was indeed a future for their type of music, and they headed straight to Sun Records in Memphis. Paradoxically, label owner Sam Phillips felt Presley had already cornered the market on the new rock 'n' roll beat, and had Perkins relegate his up-tempo songs to the B-sides of unsuccessful hillbilly records. Once Presley had departed for RCA, Perkins (at the suggestion of labelmate Johnny Cash) wrote a song based on an incident he witnessed at a high school hop. Rife with observational humor and hot-scatting rhythm, "Blue Suede Shoes" became the first record to simultaneously top the country, pop, and R&B charts. Perkins's massive hit beat Presley's RCA debut "Heartbreak Hotel" onto the charts, but his days at the top were short. On the way to New York for appearances on the *Perry Como Show*, Perkins and his band were involved in an auto wreck. Injuries from the accident kept Perkins out of commission for months, and contributed to his brother Jay's early demise. When Perkins finally returned to the studio, his momentum as a pop artist was stopped cold. However, such rockabilly classics as "Boppin' the Blues," "Dixie Fried," and "Your True Love" became strong sellers on the country charts and he remained a hot item in the South. When it came time to film the 1957 teen flick *Jamboree*, Perkins was given his choice of two songs to lip-sync—"Glad All Over" or "Great Balls of Fire." He chose the former, and was so disappointed when it sank without a trace that he decided to leave Sun. Unfortunately, Columbia had no idea of how to handle the rock pioneer. They larded his recordings with tinkling pianos, burping saxophones, and syrupy chorus singers. "Pink Pedal Pushers" was a minor country hit and the fine "Pointed Toe Shoes" scraped the bottom of the charts, but that was all. Perkins wouldn't see a significant upturn in his fortunes until 1964, when the Beatles recorded three of his Sun-era songs, "Honey Don't," "Everybody's Trying to Be My Baby," and "Matchbox," for their top-selling albums. Though wildly successful tours resulted in British fans proclaiming him "The King of Rock 'n' Roll," Perkins worked mostly in country music from that point on, cutting many well-reviewed LPs that sold poorly, and touring with Johnny Cash's show. During the late '60s, he had minor hits with "Shine, Shine, Shine," "Country Boy's Dream," and the brilliant Jerry Reed–styled "Restless," but made a greater mark in that genre writing hit songs for Patsy Cline, Johnny Cash, and the Judds among others. Perkins never gave up. He continued to play both rock and country worldwide, recorded for labels big and small, and eventually brought his sons Stan and Greg into his band. The '80s saw the rise of his last country hit, the autobiographical "Birth of Rock 'n' Roll," and his induction to the Rock and Roll Hall of Fame. During the '90s, Perkins survived a bout with cancer, recorded surprisingly fresh sides with some of the industry's biggest name acts, and lived long enough to witness the grassroots revival of the music he helped create.

what to buy: The wealth of material Perkins cut during his few short years at Sun runs far deeper than just "Blue Suede Shoes," as one listen to *Original Sun Greatest Hits* (Rhino, 1986, compilation prod. Bill Inglot) will attest. His classic performances of "Honey Don't," "Everybody's Trying to Be My Baby," "Put Your Cat Clothes On" (with Jerry Lee Lewis on piano), "Boppin' the Blues," and "Gone, Gone, Gone" virtually define the rockabilly movement then and now.

what to buy next: The cream of his later rocking work can be found on *Restless: The Columbia Recordings* (Columbia/Legacy, 1992, compilation prod. Bob Irwin), an engaging set of such high-gloss rockabilly from the late '50s as "Pointed Toe Shoes," "Jive After Five," "Where the Rio De Rosa Flows," and the remarkable title cut. Those seeking validation in star power should check out Perkins's final offering, the 1996 tribute album, *Go Cat Go!* (Dinosaur Entertainment, 1996, executive prod. Jim McCullough), wherein the Rockin' Guitar Man jams with such admirers as Paul McCartney, George Harrison, Johnny Cash, John Fogerty, Ringo Starr, Paul Simon, Tom Petty, and Bono on a strong set of fresh, mostly self-penned tunes.

what to avoid: Watch out for these deceptively titled sets: *Best of Carl Perkins* (Curb, 1993) contains the Sun version of "Blue Suede Shoes" but everything else is from his 1989 Universal LP *Born to Rock*; *The Best of Carl Perkins* (Cleopatra, 1998) contains many '70s tracks first recorded for the tiny Music Mill label; and the import *The Best & The Rest of Carl Perkins* (Jet, 1978/Action Replay, 1997) is a retitled version of his big-selling British LP *Ol' Blue Suede's Back*. Perkins is in fine form vocally on this set of reworked oldies, but his use of guitar FX is irritating.

the rest:

Whole Lotta Shakin' (Columbia, 1958/Sony, 1991)
Country Boy's Dream—The Dollie Masters (CBS, 1968/Bear Family, 1994)
My Kind of Country (Mercury, 1973/Rebound, 1998)
Country Soul (Charvan, 1981/Chicago, 1995)
Honky Tonk Gal: Rare and Unissued Masters (Rounder, 1989)
Born to Rock (MCA/Universal, 1989/Liberty, 1995)
Jive After Five (Rhino, 1991)
Guitar Legends (Prime Cuts, 1995)
The Man and the Legend (Magnum, 1996)
Carl Perkins Live (Silver Eagle, 1997)
Roots of Rock 'n' Roll (Direct Source, 1997)
Turn Around (Culture, 1998)
Blue Suede Shoes: The Very Best of Carl Perkins (Collectables, 1999)

worth searching for: All of Perkins's work for Sun, his first run at Columbia, and his Decca recordings are included on *The Classic Carl Perkins* (Bear Family, 1994, compilation prod. Richard Weize), a five-disc box set from the German record company mixing heartbreaking country with blues-drenched rockabilly. Equally fine is the two-disc, 58-song set *The Definitive Collection* (Charly, 1998), which contains all of Perkins's work for Sun, including alternate takes and early home demos.

influences:

◄◄ Hank Williams, Ernest Tubb, John Lee Hooker, Muddy Waters, Bob Wills, Bill Monroe, Elvis Presley

►► Ricky Nelson, Mac Curtis, Beatles, John Fogerty, Brian Setzer, Kim Lenz

see also: *Jerry Lee Lewis*

Ken Burke

Pinetop Perkins

Born July 13, 1913, in Belzoni, MS.

Boogie-woogie piano master Pinetop Perkins was almost 60 years old when he replaced the legendary bluesman Otis Spann as resident pianist with the Muddy Waters Band. Late starts were not unusual for Perkins, who didn't begin playing piano until he was in his 30s after an injury left him unable to play guitar. In his younger days Perkins was based out of Helena, Arkansas, where he appeared regularly on Robert Nighthawk's blues radio show and Sonny Boy Williamson's *King Biscuit Time* broadcast. An early 1950s stint with guitarist Earl Hooker produced "Pinetop's Boogie Woogie," his first recording. Joining with the Waters band, however, was a decisive turning point in Perkins's career. His style doesn't plumb the pathos-laden depths Spann visited but is brilliant nonetheless. Rich vocals and rolling keyboard work are Perkins's mainstay. A decade with Muddy ended with Pinetop and bandmates splitting to form the Legendary Blues Band, where Perkins presided as an elder blues spokesman. He is considered the premier living blues pianist and has appeared on many blues artists' recordings. Slowed a trifle by age, Perkins remains active on the blues scene.

what to buy: *Eye to Eye* (AudioQuest, 1997, prod. Joe Harley) is a solid back-to-basics blues set with Legendary Blues Band/Muddy Waters alumni Calvin Jones and Willie Smith aboard and featuring guitarist Ronnie Earl. *Portrait of a Delta Bluesman* (Omega, 1993, prod. George Kilby Jr., Bob Ward) offers pure, unadulterated Perkins on a solo outing and excerpts from interviews that give it an autobiographical tone.

what to buy next: *Boogie Woogie King* (Black and Blue, 1976/Evidence, 1992, prod. Jerry Gordon) is a lively disc with great support from Luther Johnson, Jones, and Smith. A host of big names, including Kim Wilson, Matt Murphy, Jimmy Rogers, and Duke Robillard, turn out for *Pinetop's Boogie Woogie* (Antone's, 1992, prod. Clifford Antone), a live and kicking set from the legendary Austin blues club.

what to avoid: Perkins is backed by an Icelandic group, the Blue Ice Band, for *After Hours* (Blind Pig, 1989, prod. Edward Chmelewski), with less than memorable results.

the rest:

On Top (Deluge, 1992)
Live Top (Deluge, 1995)
Born in the Delta (Telarc, 1997)
Down in Mississippi (HighTone, 1998)

influences:

◄◄ Otis Spann, James P. Johnson, Professor Longhair, Sonny Boy Williamson

►► Henry Butler, Ann Rabson

Tali Madden

Oscar Peterson

Born August 15, 1925, in Montreal, Quebec, Canada.

Few major jazz musicians have received as much scathing criticism as Oscar Peterson—which is puzzling, considering he's one of the most prodigious pianists in jazz history. Though his early style was derivative of Nat King Cole, by the early 1950s he had incorporated elements of Teddy Wilson and Earl Hines and played with flawless technique, vast harmonic knowledge, and the overwhelming power of swing. Frequently faulted for a supposed lack of "soul" (a criticism that doesn't bear scrutiny), Peterson has also been attacked for his ostentatious speed and repetitive phrasing.

Peterson gained attention with his tremendous technical skill at a young age, winning an amateur radio contest at 14. He was featured on a weekly radio program in the early 1940s, then developed his touch as an accompanist while working with the Johnny Holms Orchestra in the mid-1940s in Montreal. In the late 1940s, impresario Norman Granz heard Peterson in Canada and presented him at a Carnegie Hall Jazz at the Philharmonic concert in 1949. It was the beginning of one of the most prolific artist/producer relationships in jazz history; Granz made Peterson a cornerstone of each new label he founded. While working as Verve's house pianist in the 1950s, Peterson recorded with a who's who of jazz royalty, including Billie Holiday, Ella Fitzgerald, Lester Young, Ben Webster, Coleman Hawkins, and Louis Armstrong. Granz promoted Peterson's career by featuring him on Jazz at the Philharmonic tours in the early 1950s, but Peterson found his musical home with a piano/bass/guitar trio he created (modeled after Nat King Cole's) in the mid-1950s. Using tight and intricate arrangements, the Oscar Peterson Trio, featuring Herb Ellis's stinging guitar lines and Ray Brown's powerful, blues-drenched bass work, was one of the most popular and commanding groups in jazz. When Ellis left in 1958, drummer Ed Thigpen came on board, creating another stable and popular trio that lasted until 1965. After a few years in the late 1960s and early 1970s recording for the MPS/BASF label, Peterson rejoined forces with Granz on Pablo, where he recorded frequently with such label stalwarts as Joe Pass, Dizzy Gillespie, and Count Basie. He has continued to tour through the 1980s and 1990s, recording for Telarc, and recovered almost completely from a stroke he suffered in 1993. In 1988, lyricist and jazz historian Gene Lees published a fine biography of the pianist, *The Will to Swing*.

what to buy: An excellent two-disc set that documents Peterson with a host of his musical collaborators, *History of an Artist* ♪♪♪♪♪ (Pablo, 1972–74/1993, prod. Norman Granz) recaptures various groupings from Peterson's long career. The level of musicianship is uniformly high, and Peterson is often in astounding form. One of the definitive (and last) recordings by Peterson's trio with Herb Ellis and Ray Brown, *At the Concertgebouw* ♪♪♪♪♪ (Verve, 1957/1994, prod. Norman Granz) was a typically sloppy Granz production (despite the title, the session was recorded at Chicago's Civic Opera House). No matter, after playing together for four years, the trio breathes as one. Highlights include thrilling versions of Clifford Brown's "Joy Spring" and "Daahoud," a relaxed run through "Bluesology," and a medium-tempo take on "I've Got the World on a String," in which Peterson displays his Cole roots. One of Peterson's most enjoyable sessions, *Oscar Peterson Trio + 1* ♪♪♪♪♪ (Emarcy, 1964/1984) features his second great trio, and it's the first time trumpeter Clark Terry recorded his "mumbles" routine. Peterson and Terry are particularly effective together on the delicate but hard-swinging "Squeaky's Blues" and "Brotherhood of Man." Only the second solo session Peterson ever recorded, *Tracks* ♪♪♪♪♪ (MPS, 1971/Verve, 1994, prod. Hans Georg Brunner Schwer) is a tour de force, with 10 pieces in which Peterson gives his imagination full and unfettered freedom. He unveils surprise after surprise, changing tempos and keys and breaking into torrid stride passages. He also waxes sensitive on "A Child Is Born" and "Django."

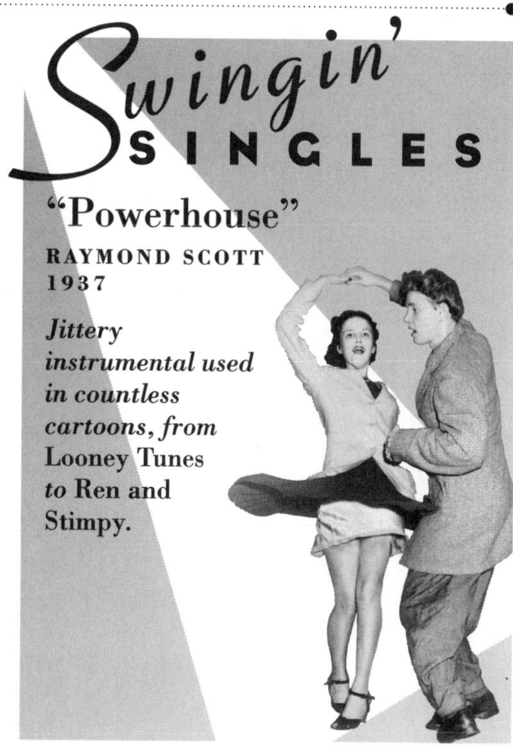
Swingin' SINGLES
"Powerhouse"
RAYMOND SCOTT
1937
Jittery instrumental used in countless cartoons, from Looney Tunes to Ren and Stimpy.

what to buy next: One of five duo sessions Peterson recorded with great trumpeters, *Oscar Peterson & Harry Edison* ♪♪♪♪♪ (Pablo, 1975/Original Jazz Classics, 1992, prod. Norman Granz) is a romp in the park on a sunny day, with the two masters treading lightly through seven standards and two bluesy originals. On paper, pairing Sweets Edison's spare, wryly pungent trumpet style with Peterson's extravagant and effusive piano

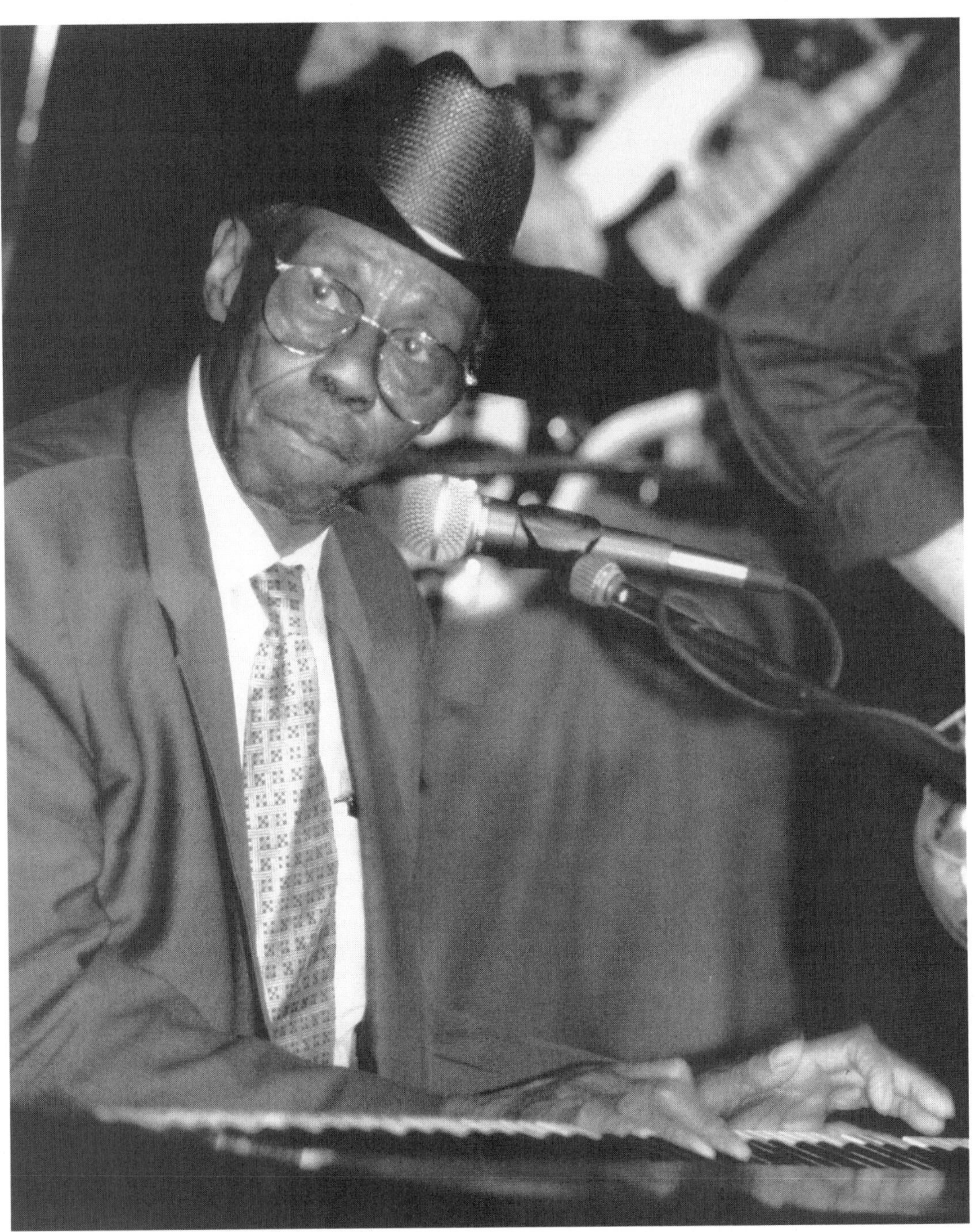

Pinetop Perkins **(© Jack Vartoogian)**

might seem like a nonstarter, but the session is a complete success. A two-disc set that pairs two incomparable masters, *Oscar Peterson et Joe Pass; la Salle Pleyel* (Pablo, 1975/1997, prod. Norman Granz) opens with seven solo tracks by OP, including a trademark chops-busting run through "Sweet Georgia Brown" and a five-tune Ellington medley, followed by five unaccompanied pieces by Pass. Peterson thrived in the trio setting, and *The Trio* (Pablo, 1973/1991, prod. Norman Granz) was one of the most inspired sessions from his prolific Pablo period. Opening with a thrilling version of "Blues Etude," where OP flows through various styles, including stride, boogie woogie, and Cole runs, the set also contains a gorgeous version of Duke Ellington's "Come Sunday." Two masters of swing pair up on *Satch and Josh* (Pablo, 1975/1988, prod. Norman Granz), a session that unites jazz's greatest minimalist, Count Basie, with Peterson, one of the music's most extravagant embellishers.

what to avoid: Though Peterson and Joe Pass were exceptionally consistent musicians, *Porgy & Bess* (Pablo/Original Jazz Classics, 1976, prod. Norman Granz) is a rare dud in their discographies, mostly due to Peterson's unaccountable decision to use a clavichord, a predecessor to the piano. Pass does his best under the circumstances, sticking exclusively to acoustic guitar, but the circumstances quickly move from novelty to boredom.

best of the rest:

The Complete Young Oscar Peterson (Black and Blue, 1945–49/1994)
Plays the Gershwin Songbooks (Verve, 1952–59/1996)
The Oscar Peterson Trio at Zardi's (Pablo, 1955/1994)
Plays Count Basie (Clef, 1956/Verve, 1993)
Oscar Peterson Plays "My Fair Lady" and the Music from "Fiorello!" (Verve, 1958–60/1994)
Plays Porgy and Bess (Verve, 1959/1993)
The Jazz Soul of Oscar Peterson/Affinity (Verve, 1959/1962/1996)
The London House Sessions (Verve, 1962/1996)
Busting Out with the All Star Big Band (Verve, 1962/1996)
We Get Requests (Verve, 1965/1997)
The Good Life (Pablo, 1973/Original Jazz Classics, 1991)
Oscar Peterson & Clark Terry (Pablo, 1975/Original Jazz Classics, 1994)
Oscar Peterson & Dizzy Gillespie (Pablo, 1975/1987)
Oscar Peterson in Russia (Pablo, 1976/1996)
Montreux '77 (Pablo, 1977/Original Jazz Classics, 1989)
Nigerian Marketplace (Pablo, 1982/1988)
Two of the Few (Pablo, 1983/Original Jazz Classics, 1992)
A Tribute to My Friends (Pablo, 1984/Original Jazz Classics, 1996)
Oscar Peterson + Harry Edison + Eddie "Cleanhead" Vinson (Pablo, 1987)
Oscar Peterson Live (Pablo, 1987)
Saturday Night at the Blue Note (Telarc, 1991)
Last Call at the Blue Note (Telarc, 1992)
Encore at the Blue Note (Telarc, 1993)
Side by Side (Telarc, 1994)
The More I See You (Telarc, 1995)
Oscar Peterson Meets Roy Hargrove and Ralph Moore (Telarc, 1996)
Oscar in Paris (Telarc, 1997)
Triple Play (Telarc, 1998)
Ultimate Oscar Peterson (Verve, 1998)

worth searching for: Norman Granz used Peterson frequently as an accompanist, even when his style didn't fit the vocalist, such as Peterson's many sessions with Billie Holiday. But there's no question Peterson was the right man for the job on *How Long Has This Been Going On?* (Pablo, 1978/1987, prod. Norman Granz), Sarah Vaughan's best Pablo recording.

influences:

◀◀ Nat King Cole, Teddy Wilson, Earl Hines

▶▶ Monty Alexander, Ross Tompkins, Benny Green, Phineas Newborn Jr.

Andrew Gilbert

Flip Phillips

Born Joseph Edward Filipelli, February 26, 1915, in Brooklyn, NY.

Flip Phillips was one of the turbulent saxophonists tagged "honkers and shouters"—Arnett Cobb, Illinois Jacquet, Gene Ammons, King Curtis, and others—whose screaming, howling, frantic tempos and improvisations paved the way for R&B musicians. He was one of the earliest swing-era horn players. Phillips began his career on the clarinet, then switched to tenor saxophone in the 1940s before his breakthrough gig in Woody Herman's First Herd, remaining with the big band until it broke up in 1946. Phillips toured annually with the legendary Jazz at the Philharmonic from 1946 to 1957, acquiring a reputation for his venturesome improvisations and for his ability to match his talents against growing saxophone legends Charlie Parker and Lester Young. In 1948, Phillips received accolades in both *Down Beat* and *Metronome* polls for best tenor saxophonist. In the late 1950s, Phillips retired to Pompano Beach, Florida, took occasional gigs, and emerged occasionally to perform with Benny Goodman's band during a 15-year hiatus.

In 1970, Phillips began recording and traveling again, and by 1975 was back into music full time, continuing to record and perform with high energy and peak virtuosity throughout the 1980s. Although Phillips plays ballads, stomps, and standards

Flip Phillips **(Archive Photos)**

with equal ardor, he is the tenor sax player most often remembered for his squawking sound during a frenetic solo on "Perdido," performed during the Jazz at the Philharmonic tours.

what to buy: Phillips and his younger counterpart, Scott Hamilton, came together for *A Sound Investment* (Concord, 1987, prod. Carl E. Jefferson) after years of running into each other at jazz parties. Except for Phillips's smear techniques and a few honks, there's almost no audible difference between the then-seventy-something Phillips and the under-40 Hamilton. The session includes mostly swinging and bluesy Phillips originals, along with the Benny Goodman tune "A Smooth One."

what to buy next: Playing tenor saxophone and bass clarinet, Flip Phillips joins a crew of swing masters from the Concord roster on *Real Swinger* (Concord, 1988, prod. Carl E. Jefferson). On this 11-tune mixture of swing standards and Phillips originals, the reedman is backed by an industrious and masterful swing-jazz crew, including pianist Dick Hyman and young guitarist Howard Alden. Phillips plays tenor sax on the hot racer "Hashimoto's Blues" and Ellington's righteous swinger "Cotton Tail," and finishes the session with a full-bodied solo on the joyous "I Want to Be Happy."

the rest:

A Melody from the Sky (Flying Dutchman, 1944–45/Doctor Jazz, 1993)
The Claw: Live at the Floating Jazz Festival (1986) (Chiaroscuro, 1992)
At the Helm: Live at the 1993 Floating Jazz Festival (Chiaroscuro, 1994)

influences:

Ben Webster

Scott Hamilton

Nancy Ann Lee

Piano Red

Born Willie Perryman, October 19, 1913, in Hampton, GA. Died July 25, 1985, in Decatur, GA.

Willie "Piano Red" Perryman was rewarded for his fine piano skills with a 1961 R&B hit, "Dr. Feelgood." The boogie-woogie house fixture at Atlanta's Magnolia Ballroom for years and the brother of Rufus "Speckled Red" Perryman, Red had been an active southern performer for more than two decades before his hit. (He also scored with 1950's "Red's Boogie.") Blues didn't always pay his bills; he often worked as an upholsterer in the Atlanta area. The blues revival gave him slightly renewed popularity, and he played the Montreux Festival in Switzerland in 1974.

what to buy: The best thing about the solo *Atlanta Bounce* (Arhoolie, 1972/1992, prod. Chris Strachwitz) is Red's rambling and storytelling, which come across much more frequently above the piano than the actual singing of choruses.

the rest:

Blues Blues Blues (Black Lion, 1993)

influences:

Speckled Red, Fats Waller, Art Tatum, Victoria Spivey, Scott Joplin

Ray Charles, Memphis Slim, Dr. John, Professor Longhair

Steve Knopper

Pine Valley Cosmonauts

Formed 1994, in Chicago, IL.

Jon Langford, guitar, vocals; Steve Goulding, drums; Mark Durante, steel guitar; Tom Ray, bass; John Rice, fiddle, guitar, mandolin, tenor banjo; Paul Mertens, clarinet and saxophone; Dave Max Crawford, trumpet and piano; Jane Baxter-Miller, vocals.

Whether playing punk rock, honky-tonk, or reggae, the Mekons have always been too wide-ranging and unruly to be confined within the strictures of a single style or even a single band. One of this legendary British punk collective's more peculiar alter-ego spinoffs is the Pine Valley Cosmonauts, a group specializing in country tribute records. The Cosmonauts' ringleader is head Mekon Jon Langford, who presides over a loose assemblage of fellow travelers from the alternative-country universe, most of whom are affiliated in some way with Bloodshot Records (the Chicago alt-country label that is also home to another of Langford's sidebands, the Waco Brothers). A strange pedigree, to be sure; yet this bunch somehow put together one of the swingin'-est records (western division) of modern times with its second album.

what's available: The Cosmonauts debuted with *Misery Loves Company* (Rough Trade, 1994, prod. Jon Langford, Dave Trumfio), billed as "Jonboy Langford and the Pine Valley Cosmonauts Explore the Dark and Lonely World of Johnny Cash." This was the second Cash tribute Langford oversaw (after 1988's hard-to-find import *'Til Things Are Brighter*), and is quite honestly more ragged than right. But Langford and company took a great leap forward with the followup, *The Pine Valley Cosmonauts Salute the Majesty of Bob Wills* (Bloodshot, 1998, prod. Jon Langford, Mark Durante, John Rice), a fabulous tribute to the late king of western swing. This time out, the Cosmonauts are augmented by guest vocalists including Alejandro Escovedo (whose reading of "San Antonio Rose" is simply heart-stopping), Jimmie Dale Gilmore ("Trouble in Mind" never had it so good), and most of all Robbie Fulks—who sounds like

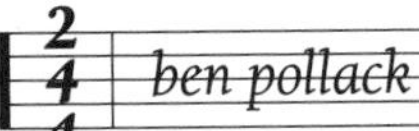

he's having a nervous breakdown as he turns "Across the Alley from the Alamo" into a punk-swing meltdown. Not exactly the stuff of Gap commercials, and therefore brilliant.

influences:

Bob Wills, Asleep at the Wheel

Waco Brothers

David Menconi

Ben Pollack

Born June 22, 1903, in Chicago, IL. Died June 7, 1971, in Palm Springs, CA.

A bandleader who had Benny Goodman, Glenn Miller, Jack Teagarden, Freddie Slack, Bud Freeman, and Harry James working for him had to have been one of the most successful figures in big-band history, right? The fact is, Ben Pollack never made much of a commercial splash. The first of the drumming bandleaders, Pollack had a gift for putting together great musical aggregations, but none for exploiting (or holding on to) their respective talents.

Pollack turned pro in 1924 with the New Orleans Rhythm Kings, a bold Dixieland group that often worked and recorded with the great pianist Jelly Roll Morton. After he took over Harry Bastin's orchestra, the aggressive drummer put together a band whose members would eventually be on the forefront of a musical revolution—big-band swing. The aforementioned future bandleaders, along with some of the best-regarded sidemen of the day, played a scintillating mix of Dixieland, swing, and hot rhythmic jazz, interspersed with the usual array of vocal ballads. However, sales of their recordings on Victor, Variety, and Columbia did not reflect the high esteem in which critics held their work. After a disastrous road trip, Pollack's first great band broke up in 1934, with many defecting to Bob Crosby's organization. He rebounded the following year with an outfit nearly as good (featuring Harry James and Freddie Slack), which appeared on network radio and in the film *New Faces of 1937*. Like others before them, James and Slack went on to greener pastures, though Pollack continued to furnish a pretty solid musical line-up, with only fleeting success. During the early '40s, the cash-strapped Chico Marx toured the world with Pollack's band, with the drummer stepping down to manage the group. Still possessing a fine eye for talent, Pollack hired the very young Mel Tormé to handle vocal chores, but his days as a force in swing music were nearly over by then.

Pollack went on to form his own label, play in several Dixieland combos, and appear as himself in film versions of both *The Glenn Miller Story* and *The Benny Goodman Story*. During the years which followed, various big-band revivals forgot about Pollack's contributions and he grew bitter, eventually committing suicide.

worth searching for: Sadly, there's nothing in print by Pollack's great '20s and '30s bands, though you might find *The 1930s: The Big Bands* (Columbia, 1987, reissue prod. Michael Brooks) hiding in some bins or used shops. *Ben Pollack and His Pick-A-Rib Boys* (Jazzology, 1994, reissue prod. George H. Buck Jr.) is a strong collection of latter-day Dixieland first recorded in 1950. Pollack, along with Dick Cathcart, Moe Schneider, and others, really wails on such standards as "San Antonio Shout," "I Can't Give You Anything but Love," and "Goody Goody." Pollack's early ground-breaking work as a drummer with the New Orleans Rhythm Kings and Jelly Roll Morton are on *New Orleans Rhythm Kings and Jelly Roll Morton* (Milestone, 1992, reissue prod. Orrin Keepnews) and *Introduction: 1922–1935* (Best of Jazz, 1997, prod. various), two fine sets of oldtime Dixieland and ragtime.

influences:

Harry Bastin, King Oliver

Glenn Miller, Benny Goodman, Jack Teagarden, Bob Crosby

see also: *Benny Goodman, Glenn Miller, Harry James*

Ken Burke

Preacher Jack

Born John Lincoln Coughlin, February 12, 1942, in Malden, MA.

Preacher Jack is a colorful fixture in Massachusetts clubs, where he alternates salacious secular music with pedantic, explosive evangelical rants, and convinces the customers he's either a sanctified madman or a compelling entertainer venting rhythm and truth. Jack's musical style is rooted in the traditions of such legendary boogie piano masters as Jimmy Yancey, Albert Ammons, and Meade Lux Lewis. His primary influence is Jerry Lee Lewis: Jack's repertoire includes many of Jerry Lee Lewis's songs, he writes and reinterprets others in JLL's style, and he even inserts his own name into songs like Jerry Lee. But before dismissing him as a mere imitator, consider the following: Preacher Jack is the only piano player of recent vintage to top Lewis as a piano player. His jack-hammer left-hand rhythm is more varied and unfailingly supportive, his right-hand melody is more flexible and evokes greater depth of feeling, and he pounds every bit as hard.

An East Coast legend for many years, Jack counted among his fans blues-rocker George Thorogood and the great rockabilly singer Sleepy LaBeef. Both played behind him on such Rounder LPs as *Rock 'n' Roll Preacher* (1980) and *3,000 Barrooms Later* (1984) before he moved on to George Buck Jr.'s Solo Art label.

Though not a major record-seller, Jack remains a regional cult hero.

what to buy: The best parts of Jack's first two Rounder LPs and seven previously unreleased tracks are on *Return of the Boogie Man* ♫♫♫ (Rounder, 1997, prod. Ken Irwin, compilation prod. Elijah Wald, Jake Guralnick), a stimulating mix of country gospel, Sun Records–era rock 'n' roll, and flat-out boogie-woogie. The Preacher covers his idols Yancey ("Yancey's Bugle Call") and Lewis ("Break-Up," "Lovin' Up a Storm"), and lays down wonderful instrumentals ("Rounder Boogie," "Jessie's Boogie Woogie"). The informative booklet includes a 1959 picture of Jack with his arm around the shoulders of the one and only Jerry Lee Lewis.

what to buy next: The strictly instrumental *Non-Stop Boogie* ♫♫♫♫ (Solo Art, 1995, prod. Richard S. Burwen, John L. Coughlin) is this artist's most potent and pleasing work to date. Opening with a 32-minute medley of "You Are My Sunshine," "Yancey's Bugle Call," "In the Mood," Beethoven's "Moonlight Sonata," and others, Jack proves a master of rhythm, mood, and dramatic nuance. The remaining eight tracks find him paying homage to Albert Ammons and Jimmy Yancey in high style. The sound quality is fat and vibrant throughout and the Preacher's energy doesn't flag for even a second.

worth searching for: The out-of-print *Rock 'n' Roll Preacher* ♫♫♪ (Rounder, 1980, prod. Ken Irwin) and *3,000 Barrooms Later* ♫♫♫ (Rounder, 1984, prod. Ken Irwin) will supply all the missing tracks you need. As many completists know, you can't be truly sanctified until you know all the scriptures by heart.

influences:

◀◀ Jimmy Yancey, Meade Lux Lewis, Albert Ammons, Jerry Lee Lewis

▶▶ Jason D. Williams

Ken Burke

Elvis Presley

Born Elvis Aron Presley, January 8, 1935, in East Tupelo, MS. Died August 16, 1977, in Memphis, TN.

People sometimes forget that Elvis Presley—king of rock 'n' roll, movie star, tragic symbol of garish excess, paragon of moral decay, one of the best-selling pop artists of all time, even a pop-culture Christ figure—actually was talented. Whether or not he invented rock 'n' roll by linking, as myth recalls, white country music and black R&B, he had an innate command of the stage and audience, and he was a terrific singer and interpreter. Born to a poor southern couple, the shy Presley began greasing his hair into a tall pompadour, wearing long sideburns, and choosing his outlandish outfits carefully in pinks, blacks, and whites. Peers thought he was nuts. Eventually, he

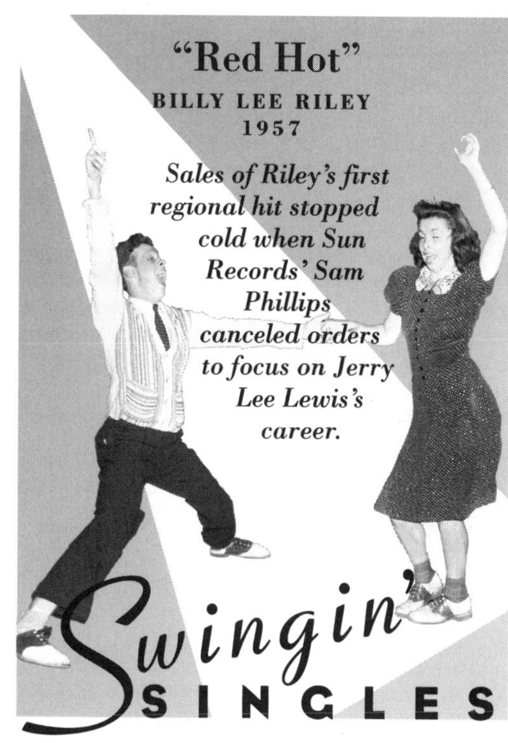

was vindicated: after he hung around Memphis's Sun Records studio for a year, confident entrepreneur and record producer Sam Phillips saw an intangible quality in Presley and set him up for a session. (Phillips, a longtime recorder of black bluesmen and minor R&B stars, from Junior Parker to Rufus Thomas, had long predicted that if he could get a white boy with "the Negro look and the Negro feel," he would make a million dollars. That turned out to be a significant understatement.) With hungry session musicians Scotty Moore on guitar and Bill Black on upright bass, the trio performed take after take until, while fooling around, they came up with reworked versions of Arthur "Big Boy" Crudup's "That's All Right (Mama)" and Bill Monroe's "Blue Moon of Kentucky." An excited Phillips dropped the cuts off to famous Memphis DJ Dewey Phillips, who played "That's All Right (Mama)" countless times in a row, thus creating Presley's first buzz.

"Red Hot"
BILLY LEE RILEY
1957
Sales of Riley's first regional hit stopped cold when Sun Records' Sam Phillips canceled orders to focus on Jerry Lee Lewis's career.
Swingin'
SINGLES

For the subsequent two decades, Presley's career moved so fast he—to say nothing of his friends and family, who were simultaneously excited and suspicious—could barely keep up. "The Colonel," brilliant opportunist and Hank Snow manager Tom Parker, took the young singer under his wing and autocratically began navigating Presley's career trajectory, signing him to RCA Records. As Presley began performing more and more unprecedentedly great concerts, attracting teenage girls by the truckload, his legend started to grow. Then came a rash of tremendous singles: "Hound Dog," "Don't Be Cruel," "Love Me Tender," "All Shook Up," and the classic hits written by the now-legendary songwriting duo of Leiber and Stoller, including "Jailhouse Rock." The King bought a pink Cadillac for his mother, many more Cadillacs for himself and, in 1957, Graceland, a former Memphis church he converted into a mansion. Everything was going perfectly until Presley was inducted into the Army in 1958; shortly after that, a plane carrying Buddy Holly and Ritchie Valens crashed—that was, as Don McLean later lamented, "the day the music died." But despite all this, as well as the advent of Bob Dylan, the Beach Boys, and the Beatles, Presley never went away. He was rock's first careerist, continuing to release hits ("Little Sister," "It's Now or Never," "Can't Help Falling in Love," "Return to Sender," and "Bossa Nova Baby") throughout the '60s. In that decade of hippies, the Vietnam War, and baby boom counter-culture, Presley focused on innocent movies (and soundtracks), starring in total throwaways such as *It Happened at the World's Fair* and *Girl Happy*, and energetic dance flicks such as *Blue Hawaii* and *Clambake*. Presley began creating an insular world for himself and a close circle of friends and relatives in the garishly decorated Graceland. His 1968 television concert was a tremendous comeback, an explosive show with a smash soundtrack. But Presley inevitably drifted toward Las Vegas, gained much weight, and became a parody of himself. Not a total parody, though—some of Presley's late '60s and '70s songs, including "In the Ghetto," "Suspicious Minds," and the underrated "Burning Love," were explosive and funky. Presley had become more famous for his lifestyle, obesity, and white-fringed costumes than he previously had been for his music. Legions of imitators stepped up to create a bizarre and enduring cottage industry in Vegas, Memphis, and elsewhere. Then Presley died in his Graceland bathroom. Though the cause of death has been frequently disputed, the most reliable diagnosis lists drug-related heart failure, advanced arteriosclerosis, and enlargement of the liver. The King left behind his daughter, Lisa Marie, heir to the $100-million Graceland mansion and its 675,000 annual visits from tourists; a manager, Parker, who said upon Presley's death that he would "go right on managing him," which he did until his own death in the mid-'90s; 94 gold singles; 40 gold albums; $180 million in movie grosses; millions more in merchandise sales, and, perhaps most important, the entire pop music industry (rock 'n' roll in particular) as his legacy. Some have said the King is still alive—during the late '80s, shoppers in a Kalamazoo, Michigan, grocery store were among many to report Presley sightings. It's possible that, centuries from now, when the rest of American pop culture has decayed and disappeared, the King's velvet image will remain.

what to buy: RCA's three five-disc box sets were a godsend, because without them it was impossible to navigate the record store binfuls of studio albums and greatest-hits collections for the essential stuff. Start with *Elvis—The King of Rock 'n' Roll: The Complete '50s Masters* (RCA, 1992, compilation prod. Ernst Mikael Jorgensen, Roger Semon) and hear the young truck driver transform from raw talent in the early hits "Blue Moon of Kentucky" and "That's All Right" to accomplished showman in "Jailhouse Rock" and "Love Me Tender." Next stop: *From Nashville to Memphis: The Essential '60s Masters I* (RCA, 1994, compilation prod. Ernst Mikael Jorgensen, Roger Semon) proves that, despite the Beatles and his late '50s stint in the Army, Presley was still a vital performer; "Little Sister," "Suspicious Minds," "In the Ghetto," and "Fever" are among the transcendental tracks. *Walk a Mile in My Shoes: The Essential '70s Masters* (RCA, 1995, compilation prod. Ernst Mikael Jorgensen, Roger Semon) and *Command Performances: The Essential '60s Masters II* (RCA, 1995, compilation prod. Ernst Mikael Jorgensen, Roger Semon) compile the best live tracks and soundtrack songs while eliminating most of the chaff. *The Complete Sun Sessions* (RCA, 1987, prod. Sam Phillips) is mostly revisited on the first box set, but it contains the fascinating sound of Elvis, Moore, Black, and producer Phillips inventing rock 'n' roll in the Sun Records studio; "Milkcow Blues Boogie" finds Elvis stopping a slow blues song, announcing "that don't MOVE me," and proceeding to change it before our ears into something completely different.

what to buy next: The boxes don't necessarily preclude Presley's individual titles. Many are worthwhile, but these are the first to check out: *Loving You* (RCA, 1957, prod. Elvis Presley, Hal Wallis), the first Elvis movie soundtrack; *His Hand in Mine* (RCA, 1960, prod. Elvis Presley), a gospel album that initially confused the record company; *Elvis NBC-TV Special* (RCA, 1968, prod. Steve Binder), the master's triumphant return to television when everybody thought he was washed up; *From Elvis in Memphis* (RCA, 1969, prod. Felton Jarvis, Chips Moman), another solid comeback, this time to where he began his career; *Elvis Country* (RCA, 1971, prod. Felton Jarvis, Steve Sholes), proof that the '70s Elvis wasn't just a fat druggie awaiting death; *Burning Love* (RCA Camden, 1972, prod. various), whose title track still sounds surprisingly fresh and vital; and *The Million Dollar Quartet* (RCA, 1990, prod. Sam Phillips), which features Presley, Jerry Lee Lewis, and Carl Perkins (plus a no-show Johnny Cash), sharing classic '50s rockabilly hits with spontaneity, style, and fun.

what to avoid: Most of Presley's schlock, which became almost as famous as his great stuff, was in either the bad-live-performance or icky-movie soundtrack categories. His bad live albums were most prominent during the '70s, including *As Recorded at Madison Square Garden* (RCA, 1972, prod. Felton Jarvis), *Recorded Live on Stage in Memphis* (RCA, 1974, prod. Felton Jarvis), *Having Fun with Elvis on Stage* (RCA, 1974) (just the King making bad jokes), *Elvis in Concert* (RCA, 1977, prod. Don Wardell), and *Elvis on Stage* (RCA, 1977). Of the soundtracks, stay away from *Fun in Acapulco* (RCA, 1963, prod. Elvis Presley), *Live a Little, Love a Little/Charro!/The Trouble with Girls/Change of Habit* (RCA, 1995, compilation prod. Ernst Mikael Jorgensen, Roger Semon), *Girl Happy/Harum Scarum* (RCA, 1965/1995, prod. Elvis Presley), and *Frankie and Johnny/Paradise, Hawaiian Style* (RCA, 1966/1994, prod. Elvis Presley). Also gloriously bad are *Interviews and Memories Of: The Sun Years* (Sun, 1977, prod. Sam Phillips), *From Elvis Presley Boulevard, Memphis, Tennessee* (RCA, 1976, prod. Chick Crumpacker), both volumes of *Our Memories of Elvis* (RCA, 1979, prod. various), *I Was the One* (RCA, 1983, prod. various), and *The Elvis Presley Interview Record: An Audio Self-Portrait* (RCA, 1984). In the tribute category, avoid *It's Now or Never: The Tribute to Elvis* (Mercury, 1994, prod. various), which does feature Presley fan Dwight Yoakam but unfortunately has loser hacks such as Michael Bolton, Travis Tritt, and Wet Wet Wet as well.

the rest:

Elvis Presley (RCA, 1956)
Elvis (RCA, 1956)
Elvis's Christmas Album (RCA, 1957)
King Creole (RCA, 1958)
Elvis' Golden Records, Vol. 1 (RCA, 1958)
For LP Fans Only (RCA, 1959)
A Date with Elvis (RCA, 1959)
Elvis Is Back! (RCA, 1960)
G.I. Blues (RCA, 1960)
50,000,000 Elvis Fans Can't Be Wrong: Elvis's Golden Records, Vol. 2 (RCA, 1960)
Something for Everybody (RCA, 1961)
Blue Hawaii (RCA, 1961)
Pot Luck (RCA, 1962)
Girls! Girls! Girls! (RCA, 1962)
It Happened at the World's Fair (RCA, 1963)
Elvis' Golden Records, Vol. 3 (RCA, 1963)
Elvis for Everyone (RCA, 1965)
Spinout (RCA, 1966)
Double Trouble (RCA, 1967)
How Great Thou Art (RCA, 1967)
Speedway (RCA, 1968)
Elvis' Golden Records, Vol. 4 (RCA, 1968)
Elvis Sings Hits from His Movies (RCA, 1969)
From Memphis to Vegas/From Vegas to Memphis (RCA, 1969)
Back in Memphis (RCA, 1970)
That's the Way It Is (RCA, 1970)
Almost in Love (RCA, 1970)
On Stage—February 1970 (RCA, 1970)
Elvis in Person at the International Hotel, Las Vegas (RCA, 1970)
World Wide 50 Gold Award Hits, Vol. 1, Nos. 1–4 (RCA, 1970–71)
I Got Lucky (RCA, 1971)
You'll Never Walk Alone (RCA, 1971)
Love Letters from Elvis (RCA, 1971)
C'mon Everybody (RCA, 1971)
Elvis (RCA, 1971)
Elvis Sings the Wonderful World of Christmas (RCA, 1971)
He Touched Me (RCA, 1972)
Elvis Now (RCA, 1972)
Separate Ways (RCA, 1973)
Elvis: Raised on Rock/For Ol' Times Sake (RCA, 1973)
Aloha from Hawaii (RCA, 1973)
A Legendary Performer: Vol. 1 (RCA, 1974)
Let's Be Friends (RCA, 1975)
Promised Land (RCA, 1975)
Pure Gold (RCA, 1975)
A Legendary Performer: Vol. 2 (RCA, 1976)
Welcome to My World (RCA, 1977)
Moody Blue (RCA, 1977)
The Elvis Tapes (Redwood, 1977)
He Walks Beside Me (RCA, 1978)
A Canadian Tribute (RCA, 1978)
Elvis Sings for Children and Grownups Too! (RCA, 1978)
A Legendary Performer: Vol. 3 (RCA, 1978)
Elvis Aron Presley (RCA, 1980)
This Is Elvis (RCA, 1981)
Elvis: The Hillbilly Cat (Music Works, 1982)
Elvis: The First Live Recordings (Music Works, 1982)
Memories of Christmas (RCA, 1982)
A Legendary Performer: Vol. 4 (RCA, 1983)
Elvis—A Golden Celebration (RCA, 1984)
Elvis' Gold Records, Vol. 5 (RCA, 1984)
Reconsider Baby (RCA, 1985)
A Valentine Gift for You (RCA, 1985)
Always on My Mind (RCA, 1985)
Return of the Rocker (RCA, 1986)
The Memphis Record (RCA, 1987)
The Number One Hits (RCA, 1987)
Essential Elvis (RCA, 1988)
Stereo '57 (Essential Elvis, Vol. 2) (RCA, 1988)
Elvis in Nashville (RCA, 1988)
The Alternate Aloha (RCA, 1988)
50 World Wide Gold Award Hits, Vol. 1 (RCA, 1988)
The Top 10 Hits (RCA, 1988)
Known Only to Him: Elvis Gospel, 1957–1971 (RCA, 1989)
The Lost Album (RCA, 1990)
The Great Performances (RCA, 1990)
Elvis Presley Sings Leiber & Stoller (RCA, 1991)
The Essential Elvis, Vol. 3 (RCA, 1991)
Viva Las Vegas/Roustabout (RCA, 1993)
Amazing Grace: His Greatest Sacred Performances (RCA, 1994)

Kissin' Cousins/Clambake/Stay Away, Joe (RCA, 1994)
Flaming Star/Wild in the Country/Follow That Dream (RCA, 1995)
Elvis '56 (RCA, 1996)
Great Country Songs (RCA, 1996)
The Essential Elvis, Vol. 4: 100 Years from Now (RCA, 1996)
An Afternoon in the Garden (RCA, 1997)
Elvis' Greatest Jukebox Hits (RCA, 1997)
Elvis Platinum: A Life in Music (RCA, 1997)
Jailhouse Rock/Love Me Tender (RCA, 1997)
Love Songs (RCA, 1998)
Rhythm 'N' Country: Essential Elvis, Vol. 5 (RCA, 1998)
Tiger Man (RCA, 1998)
Memories: '68 Comeback Special (RCA, 1998)

worth searching for: Great songs about Elvis: "Elvis Is Dead" by Living Colour; "Elvis Is Everywhere" by Mojo Nixon; "My Boy Elvis" by Janis Martin; "Galway to Graceland" by Richard Thompson; "Elvis Ate America" by Passengers (a.k.a. U2, Brian Eno, et al.); and "Johnny Bye Bye" by Bruce Springsteen. Also, the entire soundtrack of *Honeymoon in Vegas* (Epic, 1992, prod. Peter Afterman, Glen Brunman) is worthwhile despite the lifeless carbon-copy Billy Joel versions of "All Shook Up" and "Heartbreak Hotel." Finally, one great disc of Elvis songs: the British import *The Last Temptation of Elvis* (New Musical Express, 1990, executive prod. Roy Carr) has Motörhead's Lemmy doing "Blue Suede Shoes," Bruce Springsteen doing "Viva Las Vegas," the Jesus & Mary Chain demolishing "Guitar Man," and Cath Carroll and legendary weirdo punk-noise producer Steve Albini deconstructing "King Creole."

influences:

◀◀ Bill Monroe, Hank Snow, Arthur "Big Boy" Crudup, Little Richard, Chuck Berry, Lowell Fulson, Big Mama Thornton, Frank Sinatra, Hank Williams Sr., Roy Brown, the Carter Family, Jimmie Rodgers, the Ink Spots, Eddy Arnold

▶▶ Buddy Holly, Carl Perkins, Roy Orbison, the Beatles, Johnny Cash, Bob Dylan, the Beach Boys, Janis Martin, Bruce Springsteen, Billy Joel, Mojo Nixon, Dwight Yoakam, the Band, the Blasters, Elvis Hitler, Elvis Costello, U2, Stray Cats, Living Colour, Public Enemy

Steve Knopper

Louis Prima & Keely Smith

Formed late 1940s.

Louis Prima (born December 7, 1910, in New Orleans, LA; died August 24, 1978, in New Orleans, LA), trumpet, vocals; Keely Smith (born Dorothy Jacqueline Keely Smith, March 9, 1932), vocals.

Borrowing jolly enthusiasm and a horn-heavy jump-blues sound from two other guys named Louis—Jordan and Armstrong—Prima held all-night swing court for years in Las Vegas lounges and showrooms. The trumpeter sang with a slurring boisterousness; led big bands all over the country; played hilariously off his longtime wife and duet partner, Keely Smith; wrote Benny Goodman's enduring swing classic "Sing, Sing, Sing;" sired saxman Sam Butera and his Witnesses; supplied King Louie the Orangutan's voice in the animated 1967 Walt Disney classic *The Jungle Book*; recorded "Jump, Jive, an' Wail," which, thanks to a catchy jitterbugging Gap ad and a hit Brian Setzer Orchestra version, helped launch the late-'90s neo-swing movement; and, long after his death, dominated a movie (1995's *Big Night*) in which he never appeared.

Born just outside New Orleans's famed Storyville district, Prima spent his youth soaking up Dixieland jazz, specifically the horn-rich sounds of Joe "King" Oliver and Armstrong, then dropped out of high school to become a musician. He slowly advanced in the New Orleans nightclub pecking order, finally scoring a major break in 1934, when bandleader Guy Lombardo pushed him to move to New York City. He did, and things moved quickly: clubgoers loved him and his rollicking band, the New Orleans Gang, and he wound up in musicals with established singer Bing Crosby and young talent Martha Raye. In addition to writing his most enduring hit—Goodman's "Sing, Sing, Sing," still a must-play at weddings everywhere—he started recording humorous pop songs like "Robin Hood" and "Civilization." In the late '40s, Prima met 16-year-old Keely Smith, a crooner with a beautiful voice who was willing to play the straightwoman to Prima's rambunctious persona. They married in 1952 and, when big-band nightclub work eroded in New York, negotiated what turned out to be their most important gig, a two-week stint at Las Vegas's Sahara Hotel. They became a mainstay, hooking up with Butera and the Witnesses and amassing enough clout to record for Capitol Records. (The 1958 hit "That Old Black Magic," with Smith singing in her usual smooth, declarative voice and Prima exploding with clipped phrases like "look at the spin I'm in" and "put out the fire!" is one of the most hilarious and exuberant pop songs of all time.)

Prima and Smith recorded successful hits—solo and as a team—and played countless lucrative gigs in Las Vegas, eventually breaking up both the partnership and the marriage in 1961. Prima continued to make hits, including the 1967 Phil Harris duet "I Wanna Be Like You," and perform with Butera in New Orleans. Though Smith and Butera continue to tour and perform, Prima had brain-tumor surgery in 1975 and spent the last three years of his life in a coma. In addition to his general influence on pop music, he was an icon in the Italian-American community—the acclaimed film *Big Night* is about two

Louis Prima **(Archive Photos)**

Italian brothers who emigrate to the U.S. and open a restaurant. They rely on a friend's connection with Louis Prima to save the business, but the anxiously awaited singer never shows up.

what to buy: Prima's recording career peaked in the '50s and '60s, when he recorded several albums for Capitol Records—*Capitol Collector's Series* ♪♪♪♪♪ (Capitol, 1991, prod. Voyle Gilmore, compilation prod. Bob Furmanek), with 26 songs, captures Prima as a dominant and versatile performer. Though the great Smith shows up on just a few tracks, including "That Old Black Magic" and "Embraceable You," Prima careens between blues ("St. Louis Blues"), swing (his "Sing, Sing, Sing"), novelty ("Beep! Beep!"), and romantic ballads ("Lazy River").

what to buy next: *Wonderland by Night* ♪♪♪ (MCA Special Products, 1995, prod. various) recalls Prima's softer, smoother side, including ballads like "By the Light of the Silvery Moon" and "Moonlight in Vermont."

what to avoid: While Rhino Records compilations are almost always the definitive statement on a vintage performer, the Capitol collection immediately outpaced *Zooma Zooma: The Best of Louis Prima* ♪♪♪♪ (Rhino, 1990, prod. various), which overlaps many of the same songs and doesn't give quite as much quality for the price.

best of the rest:
Play Pretty for the People ♪♪ (Savoy, 1990)
Jazz Collectors Edition ♪♪♪ (Laserlight, 1991)
Very Best of Louis Prima ♪♪♪ (Pair, 1997)
Breaking It Up ♪♪♪ (Sony, 1998)
V-Disc Recordings ♪♪♪♪ (Collectors' Choice, 1998)
Let's Fly with Mary Poppins ♪♪♪ (Disney Archives, 1998)

worth searching for: The German eight-disc import *The Capitol Recordings* ♪♪♪♪ (Bear Family, 1994, prod. various) is overkill, but it's the logical next step beyond *Capitol Collector's Series*. Also, the import label Jasmine Records has nicely reissued several classic Prima and Smith albums, including the twisty two-LP combination *Twist with Keely Smith/Doin' the Twist with Louis Prima* ♪♪♪ (Jasmine, 1997, prod. various); Smith's *Cherokeely Swings* ♪♪♪ (Jasmine, 1994) and *Keely Christmas* ♪♪♪ (Jasmine, 1996); and Prima's *His Greatest Hits* ♪♪ (Jasmine, 1994), which is redundant given the superior Rhino and Capitol collections. For original Smith solo LPs and Smith-Prima duet LPs, Jasmine provides pretty much the only stuff available; still, if you're the type who enjoys rooting through used-record bins for original vinyl, *The Wildest!* ♪♪♪♪ (Capitol, 1956, prod. Voyle Gilmore), with "Buona Sera" and "Jump, Jive, an' Wail," makes for an excellent holy grail.

influences:
◀◀ Louis Armstrong, Joe "King" Oliver, Al Jolson, Ethel Merman, Louis Jordan, Bob Wills, Jimmy Witherspoon, Charles Brown, Jelly Roll Morton

▶▶ Benny Goodman, Glenn Miller, Screamin' Jay Hawkins, Squirrel Nut Zippers, Royal Crown Revue

see also: *Sam Butera*

Steve Knopper

Boyd Raeburn

Born October 27, 1913, in Faith, SD. Died August 2, 1966, in Lafayette, LA.

Of all the orchestra leaders from the Golden Age of Big Band, Boyd Raeburn made the most startling transformation. During the early '30s he led a rather undistinguished "sweet" band which recorded for the Grand and Guild record labels. Later that decade, when the swing movement began to heat up, Raeburn tried his hand at that. He made a living in hotels and on radio, but critics tended to scorn his work. In 1944, he assembled one of the best jazz bands in the country, and began to press elements of Bartok, Debussy, and Ravel into the hard bop grooves of his music. The results weren't exactly danceable, but fans of the genre loved the complex arrangements (compliments of Ed Finckel, George Handy, Johnny Mandel, and Johnny Richards) and masterful mix of reeds, horns, and occasional strings.

Though competent on the bass sax, Raeburn was more a visionary than a soloist, and he was held in high esteem by his peers. Some of the finest jazz musicians of the time (such as Dizzy Gillespie and Lucky Thompson), wandered in and out of Raeburn's band. Yet despite the power of that musical aggregation, and the presence of vocalists Ginny Powell, Don Darcy, and David Allen, the orchestra wasn't a consistent commercial force. As a result, Raeburn's band became something of a cause celebre among other musicians. (According to legend, Duke Ellington funneled cash to Raeburn to keep the band going.) But the admiration of other musicians didn't sell more records, and Raeburn's orchestra eventually disbanded in the late '40s. After that, he returned to dance-oriented music—but for a time, he really shook things up.

what to buy: Raeburn's best orchestral line-up and most inventive arrangements are on *Jewells* ♪♪♪♪ (Savoy, 1995, compilation prod. Bob Porter), a 26-song collection featuring such delicious pieces of musical irreverence as "Boyd Meets Stravinsky," "Tonsillectomy," "Hep Boyd's," and his popular version of "Over the Rainbow."

what to buy next: The bandleader's classical influences come across strongly on *Boyd Meets Stravinsky* (Savoy, 1993, prod. Ozzie Cadena), which contains some similar tracks to the above set, plus Raeburn's unique arrangements of "Body and Soul," "Summertime," and "Blue Prelude."

the rest:
The Legendary Jubilee Performances (Hep, 1994)
The Transcription Performances 1946 (Hep, 1994)
Boyd Raeburn and His Orchestra—1944 (Circle, 1995)
Boyd Raeburn and His Orchestra, 1944 & 1945 (Circle, 1995)

worth searching for: The out-of-print *Experiments in Big Band Jazz* (Discovery, 1993, compilation prod. Bob Porter) is a highly regarded cult item among musicians. Guest star Dizzy Gillespie joins Raeburn's crack ensemble on some challenging arrangements of both standards and original material.

influences:
◀◀ Sonny Dunham, Count Basie, Duke Ellington, Stan Kenton
▶▶ Woody Herman, Ike Carpenter, Dizzy Gillespie

Ken Burke

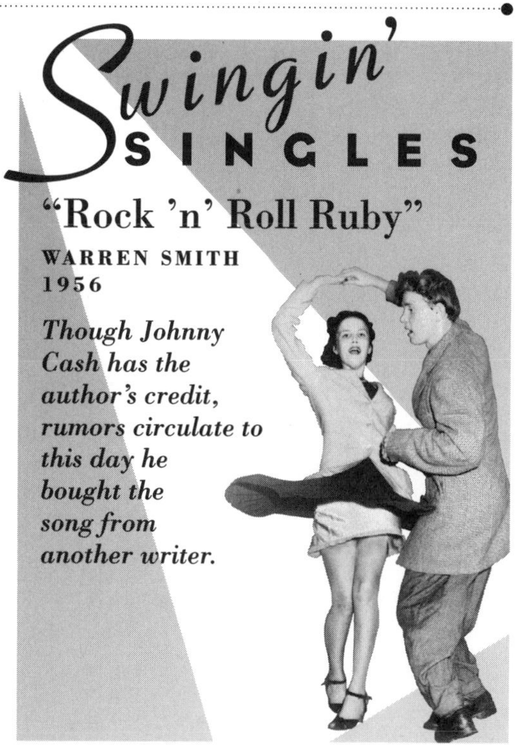

Swingin' SINGLES
"Rock 'n' Roll Ruby"
WARREN SMITH
1956
Though Johnny Cash has the author's credit, rumors circulate to this day he bought the song from another writer.

Johnnie Ray

Born John Alvin Ray, January 10, 1927. Died February 25, 1990, in Los Angeles, CA.

In the years before rock 'n' roll, white pop singer Ray synthesized the post–World War II R&B sounds he heard in nightclubs into the most affecting, highly successful records of his time. He cut his first single, "Whiskey and Gin" (a top-notch supper-club blues), in Detroit and released it on Columbia's "race music" label OKeh, in 1951. After strong regional sales, Ray recorded his two-sided masterpiece "Cry" b/w "The Little White Cloud That Cried"—which became the first time two sides of a single hit both #1 and #2 on the charts. Onstage he was a frantic, nearly hysterical figure who threw himself to his knees, slid across the stage, pounded on his piano, and thrilled his fans with the most beautifully executed dramatic fits in pop-music history. Bobby soxers worshipped him, conventional singers sneered at his hearing aid, and the press had a field day inventing nicknames such as "The Cry Guy," "The Nabob of Sob," and "The Prince of Wails." Ray gave the "Cry" treatment to such hits as "Please, Mr. Sun," and "(Here I Am) Broken Hearted," before turning in a cool and jazzy performance on his sensational hit "Walkin' My Baby Back Home." Then Mitch Miller, Columbia's notoriously schmaltzy and R&B-hating A&R man, took over Ray's song-selection duties. Many of his choices, unfortunately, were Tin Pan Alley dreck such as "Somebody Stole My Gal" and "Hernando's Hideaway." That, combined with bad publicity over an arrest early in his career on an alleged morals charge and a flop film, slowed his chart momentum. Still, his duets with crooners Frankie Laine and Doris Day were especially popular. The bluesiest of the pre-rock pop singers, Ray surprisingly didn't pursue rock audiences; as a result, he became irrelevant to '50s teens. Columbia sought to resurrect his career by recording him as a light-jazz singer, cowboy crooner, and all-around entertainer, but after 1959's "I'll Never Fall in Love Again," the hits stopped coming. A second arrest in 1961—he was loudly accused and quietly acquitted—prompted Columbia to drop Ray from its roster. Subsequent singles and LPs flopped, and Ray's recording career was over, though he continued to perform as a major star in England and Australia. During his last years Elvis Presley publicly acknowledged his stylistic debt to the great Johnnie Ray.

what to buy: The bluesy *High Drama: The Real Johnnie Ray* (Sony, 1997, compilation prod. Al Quaglieri), is a smart compilation of hits mixed with lesser-known sides revealing Ray's love of R&B sounds, which are only slightly hampered by the vanilla wand-waving of Mitch Miller. The brass is blaring, rhythms are jumping and Johnnie Ray is at the peak of his form here. This disc also includes two previously unreleased tracks from his first R&B session in Detroit: "Paths of Paradise" and "She Didn't Say Nothin' at All." Revealing stuff from one of the true originators of rock 'n' roll.

what to buy next: Ray's best-known OKeh and Columbia sides, including a duet with Doris Day, are on *16 Most Requested Songs* (Legacy, 1991, prod. Michael Brooks), wherein his true pop classics, "Cry" and "Little White Cloud That Cried," still shudder with the eternal grief of perpetually lost love.

what to avoid: There's absolutely nothing wrong with *Back to Back: Frankie Laine/Johnnie Ray* (K-Tel, 1989, prod. various), but for the same price you can get much more of the Sultan of Sob on a solo disc. Also, the budget racks still provide sanctuary for *Cry* (ITC, 1997), a cheapie with inferior rerecordings of Ray's best Columbia sides.

the rest:
Best of Johnnie Ray (Columbia Special Products, 1989)
Greatest Hits (K-Tel, 1990)
Here and Now (Columbia Special Products, 1994)
Greatest Songs (Curb Records, 1995)

worth searching for: The German import *Cry* (Bear Family, 1990, prod. Richard Weize) features the largest selection of Ray's OKeh/Columbia sides to date and includes duets with Frankie Laine and Doris Day. Also, Ray is in peak form on *Live at the Paladium* (Bear Family, 1992, reissue prod. Richard Weize), a reissue of his original 1954 LP, recorded live in London, England.

influences:
◀◀ LaVern Baker, Dinah Washington, Al Hibbler, Frankie Laine, Jimmy Scott
▶▶ Four Lads, Elvis Presley, Roy Orbison

Ken Burke

Red & the Red Hots

Formed 1985, in TX.

Red Young, vocals, piano, synthesizer, arranger; Elizabeth Lamers, vocals; Dina Bennett, vocals; Keith Fiddlemont, saxophones; Brian Swartz, trumpet; Kenny Sara, drums; Randy Landas, bass; Chris Maurer, trumpet; Mark Visher, alto sax; Greg Smith, baritone sax.

Red & the Red Hots bring a taste of modern technology to the classic songs of the big-band era. Their leader, Red Young, is not averse to using a digital piano or bolstering the horn section with synthesizers. As a result, whether it plays fast boogie or Latin rhythms, or emotes sentimental pop, his group has a clean sound that recalls keyboard-enhanced '80s pop bands. One of the singing bandleaders, Young doesn't possess much range or expressiveness, but can stay on key and sound like he's having fun. (Which is more than you can say for some bandleaders.) A big component of this group's sound are the vocalists, who in tandem with Young, forge a lush pop sound and wail torchy jazz in their solo spots. Young, a fine pianist, has played with a version of Clyde McCoy's band, worked with famed producer Huey Meaux and a slew of great Texas-based acts, and toured with Tompall Glaser, Sonny and Cher, and Linda Ronstadt and Nelson Riddle. In recent times, he has contributed arrangements to Big Bad Voodoo Daddy, Royal Crown Revue, and many others. With the Red Hots, he plans to record and release a new LP sometime in 1999.

what to buy: The band's best disc, *The Boogie Man* (Red Young Productions, 1998, prod. Red Young), blends hot piano jazz ("Boogie Man") with fine up-tempo originals ("Jumpin' with Red," "Cab to the City"), and a neat Basie tribute ("Jumpin' at the Woodside"). Vocalists Cassie Miller and Dina Bennett ("The Best Thing for You") are standouts, and Young ("Look a There Ain't She Pretty") himself doesn't sound bad.

what to avoid: The inappropriately titled *Red Hot Jazz* (Red Young Productions, 1995, prod. Red Young, Doug Matthews) is a lifeless, sterile set of overlong standards closer to lounge's Muzak side than to swing. The only bright spots are Young's gentle originals ("Song for Travis," "It Happened in the Spring"), and guest Cassie Miller's ("Round Midnight") ethereal vocal. Otherwise, this is pretty somnambulant stuff.

worth searching for: Their debut cassette *Red & the Red Hots* (Red Young Productions, 1987) is still available through the group's Web site and includes jivey renditions of "(Ain't Nobody Here but Us) Chickens," "All Right, OK, You Win," and "Choo-Choo Cha Boogie."

influences:
◀◀ Ray Charles, Manhattan Transfer, the Harlettes, Clyde McCoy, Nelson Riddle

Ken Burke

Don Redman

Born July 29, 1900, in Piedmont, WV. Died November 30, 1964, in New York, NY.

Clarinetist, alto saxophonist, and major jazz arranger Don Redman never achieved the fame of many bandleaders of the '30s, but he did more than any other musician to create the big-band style that defined the swing era. With Fletcher Henderson, McKinney's Cotton Pickers, and his own band, he was the chief ar-

Don Redman **(Archive Photos)**

chitect of swing, integrating popular orchestral dance music and elements of jazz, fusing sections with soloists and intertwining written and improvised parts. He also contributed charts to the big bands of Paul Whiteman, Count Basie, Isham Jones, Jimmy Dorsey, Harry James, and Bing Crosby. He wrote durable songs like "Gee, Baby, Ain't I Good to You," and was an effective vocalist on witty novelty numbers. Redman was a child prodigy who learned to play most of the band instruments. After graduating at age 20 with a degree in music from Storer College in Harper's Ferry, West Virginia, Redman was soon arranging for Billie Paige's Broadway Syncopators. He settled in New York in 1923 and began arranging for Fletcher Henderson's orchestra. In this period he also recorded as accompanist to many of the classic blues singers of the period—Bessie Smith, Ma Rainey, and Alberta Hunter. A major breakthrough occurred when Louis Armstrong joined the Henderson Orchestra; Armstrong's rhythmic fluency provided the impetus for Redman to make his arrangements swing. Redman left Henderson's band in 1927 to lead the Detroit-based McKinney's Cotton Pickers, building another great proto-swing band in the process. He formed his own group in 1931, using many of the same musicians he had recruited for the Cotton Pickers. For most of the '50s, Redman worked as arranger/bandleader for Pearl Bailey.

what to buy: *Doin' What I Please* (Living Era, 1993, prod. Vic Bellerby) has 25 tracks from 1925 to 1938, including "Sugarfoot Stomp," featuring Armstrong with the Henderson Orchestra; takes by McKinney's Cotton Pickers with guest Fats Waller; the 1931 "Chant of the Weed," the complex theme song of Redman's own orchestra; and fine arrangements of "I've Got Rhythm" and Duke Ellington's "Sophisticated Lady." Along the way, there are appearances by the greatest musicians of the era, including Coleman Hawkins and Benny Carter. A comparable alternative choice is *Chant of the Weed* (Pearl, 1996, prod. Tony Watts, Colin Brown), which overlaps much of the key *Doin' What I Please* material.

what to buy next: The Jazz Chronological Classics series covers all of Redman's '30s work under his own name. *Don Redman 1931–33* (Jazz Classics, 1994, prod. various) is the most significant, including terrific instrumental and vocal versions of "Doin' the New Low-down," the latter with Cab Calloway and the Mills Brothers.

best of the rest:

Don Redman and His Orchestra 1933–36 ♪♪♪♪ (Jazz Chronological Classics, 1990)

Don Redman and His Orchestra 1936–39 ♪♪♪½ (Jazz Chronological Classics, 1991)

Don Redman and His Orchestra 1939–40 ♪♪½ (Jazz Chronological Classics, 1992)

worth searching for: Redman's work with Fletcher Henderson is essential to the rise of the big-band era. The Armstrong and Henderson connections are best documented on *Fletcher Henderson 1924–25* ♪♪♪♪ (Jazz Chronological Classics, 1994, prod. various). Additional examples of his arrangements for Armstrong can be heard on *Louis Armstrong Volume IV: Louis Armstrong and Earl Hines* ♪♪♪♪♪ (Columbia, 1989, prod. Richard M. Jones), which includes a piquant "St. James Infirmary." Redman's earliest recordings with Bessie Smith, from 1923, can be heard on her *Complete Recordings Vol. 1* ♪♪♪♪♪ (Columbia/ Legacy, 1991, prod. various), but they're of primarily historical interest. He sounds more confident and idiomatic playing alto saxophone on the 1925 "Golden Rule Blues" on *Complete Recordings, Vol. 3* ♪♪♪♪ (Columbia/Legacy, 1992, prod. various).

influences:

◀◀ James Reese Europe, Eubie Blake, King Oliver, Jelly Roll Morton

▶▶ Duke Ellington, Cab Calloway

see also: *Fletcher Henderson, Louis Armstrong, McKinney's Cotton Pickers*

Stuart Broomer

Eddie Reed Big Band

Formed 1993, in Long Beach, CA.

Eddie Reed, leader, vocals, clarinet; Meghan Ivy, vocals; Barry Cogert, bass; Paul Lines, drums; Quinn Johnson, piano; Kye Palmer, trumpet; Willie Murillo, trumpet; Bob Bennett, trumpet; Dave Ryan, trombone; Rich Berkley, trombone; Dan Barrett, trombone; Danny House, alto saxophone; Albert Alva, alto saxophone; Dave Moody, tenor saxophone; Paul Carman, tenor saxophone; Martin Matthews, baritone saxophone; Al Viola, guitar.

Bandleader-vocalist-clarinetist Eddie Reed leads one of the most polished swing big bands in the business. He comes from a musical family, began playing at an early age in Shady Grove (a country town outside of Dallas), and polished his chops until 1990 in the rockabilly revival (Eddie Reed and the Bluehearts) and in society dance bands before forming his hard-swinging big band.

In addition to trumpeter Kye Palmer, a former member of the Woody Herman Orchestra, the 39-year-old Reed's big band comprises a rotating group of young professional musicians from Southern California, many of them veterans of *The Tonight Show* orchestra and *Arsenio Hall Show* band as well as other groups. These cats are capable of navigating the coveted arrangements Reed procured from legendary bandleaders such as Artie Shaw, charts which accurately capture the spirit of jazz from around 1939. Reed's big band plays regularly at top spots in Southern California, Las Vegas, New York, and other locales.

what to buy: *Hollywood Jump* ♪♪♪♪ (Royal Big Mac Records/ Hep Cat Records, 1997, prod. Anthony Arvizu, Dann Thompson, Eddie Reed) contains 12 authentic-sounding swing and jazz standards that will satisfy nostalgia fans and staunch neo-swing devotees. Classics such as "Boogie Blues" (by Gene Krupa and Ray Biondi) and Duke Ellington's "Cottontail" should satisfy the most particular fans. Vocalist Ivy, who joined the band around age 18 and who has been cited as the "next Doris Day," delivers perfected vocals inspired by the classy swing-era singer, Helen Forrest.

worth searching for: Musicianship prevails on *While the Music Plays On* ♪♪♪½ (self-released/Hep Cat Records, 1999, prod. Dann Thompson, Eddie Reed), and while some tunes date back to the heyday of Harry James, George Gershwin, and Duke Ellington, the session has a more modern, straight-ahead jazz flair to it and focuses attention on Reed's vocals.

influences:

◀◀ Harry James, Artie Shaw, Count Basie, Louis Jordan, Duke Ellington, Frank Sinatra

Nancy Ann Lee

Della Reese

Born Dellareese Taliaferro, July 6, 1932, in Detroit, MI.

Modern audiences know her best from her recurring role on TV's *Touched by an Angel* and for giving Eddie Murphy's character a first-class ass-whuppin' in the movie *Harlem Nights*, yet in the '50s and '60s, Della Reese was a soul chanteuse with a gorgeous face, an eye-catching figure, and a string of hit records. Reese began her professional career at age 14, singing gospel with Mahalia Jackson's troupe for four years before becoming one of the Clara Ward Singers; in 1953, she joined the Erskine Hawkins Orchestra. Her first recordings were raw blends of pop, jazz, and gospel in the Sarah Vaughan and Dinah Washington styles. Her first hit, "And That Reminds Me," reached #12 on the pop charts, but she barely registered with her superior follow-up "Sermonette." Reese signed with RCA in 1959, where her sound became more supper-club chic, and she scored immediately with her biggest pop hit "Don't You Know," a torchy love ballad brimming with gospel intensity. After years of struggling with a direction—her onetime record label, RCA, didn't know whether to sell her records to teenagers or their parents—television has stepped in to bolster Reese's career

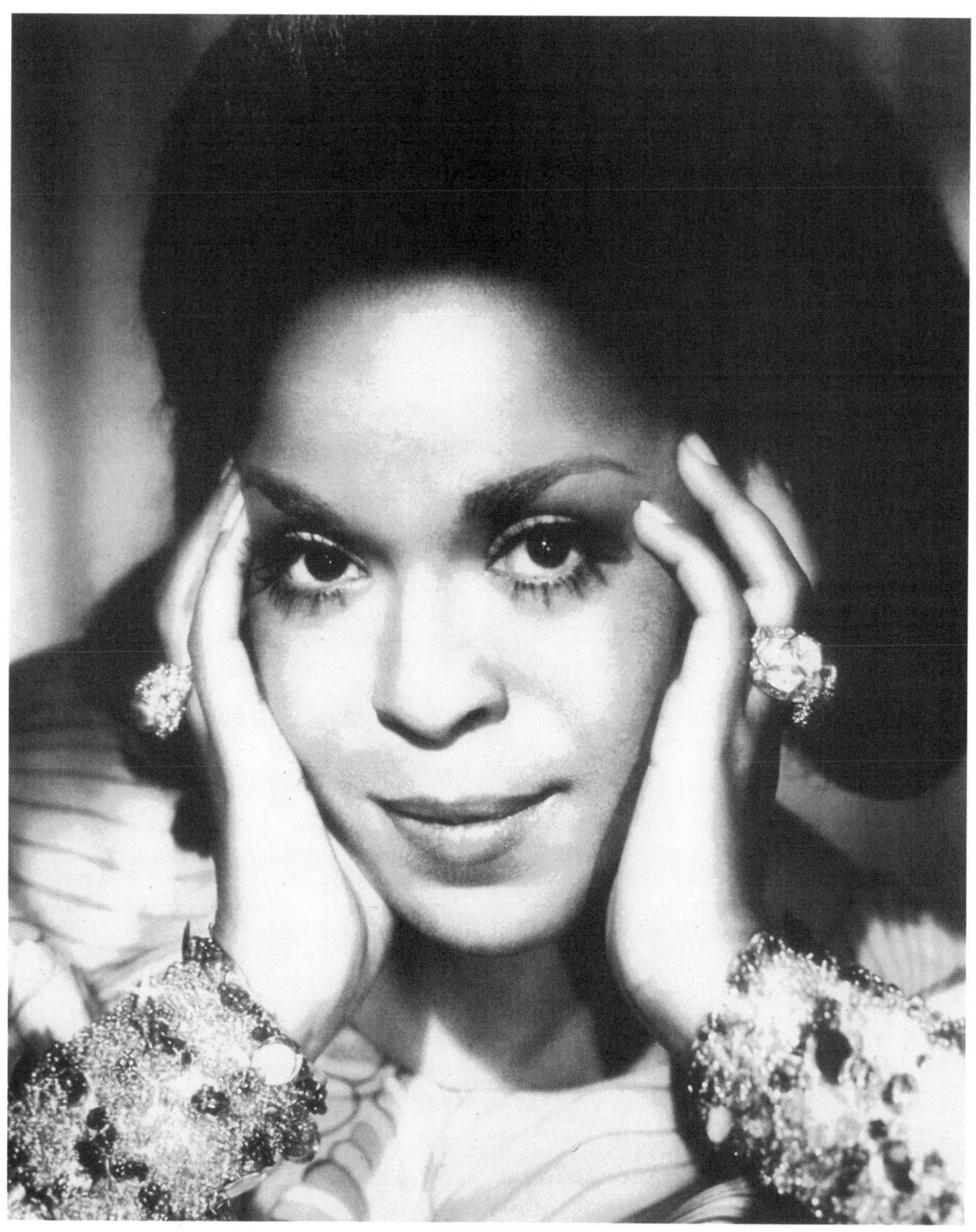

Della Reese **(Archive Photos)**

quite nicely. She has been a guest on practically every major variety program of the last 30 years, hosted her own talk show, and maintained a viable career as a character actress. In 1997, she summed it all up with the title of her autobiography: *Angels Along the Way: My Life with Help from Above*.

what to buy: Reese's run of classy late '50s and early '60s hits, including "Don't You Know," "And Now," and "Someday (You'll Want Me to Want You)," are on *Voice of an Angel* (RCA, 1996, prod. various), which showcases her sophisticated yet personal vocal style.

what to buy next: The best of Reese's '60s studio albums for ABC have been distilled onto *The Della Reese Collection* (Varese Vintage, 1998, compilation prod. Cary E. Mansfield, Marty Wesker), a sparkling mix of uptown soul, blues, and torchy middle-of-the-road music. Reese convincingly taps into the angst of perpetual heartbreak on such numbers as "Drinking Again," "Some of My Best Friends Are the Blues," and the hit "After Loving You" (which Elvis Presley later covered). Equally fine is *The Angel Sings* (Amherst, 1997, compilation prod. Leonard Silver, Chris Beilor), a collection of her '60s sides for the Avco-Embassy label, full of pleasingly gritty soul music, including Reese's last chart hit, "If It Feels Good Do It," and four previously unreleased tracks.

the rest:

(With Duke Ellington) *1962 Live Guard Session & at Basin St. East* (Jazz Band, 1994)
Story of the Blues (Westside, 1998)
The Story of Della Reese/Della Reese Live at Mr. Kelly's (Westside, 1998)

worth searching for: Reese's jazz and gospel roots are joyously displayed on *And That Reminds Me: The Jubilee Years* (Collectors' Choice, 1996/Westside, 1998), a 24-track disc containing everything she recorded for Jubilee, including the title hit.

influences:

◀◀ Clara Ward, Mahalia Jackson, Dinah Washington, Sarah Vaughan

▶▶ Leslie Uggams, Dionne Warwick, Martha Reeves

Ken Burke

Django Reinhardt

Born Jean Baptiste Reinhardt, January 23, 1910, in Belgium. Died May 16, 1953, in Fontainebleau, France.

The name "Django" has been mysterious and powerful in jazz history, and its owner is one of the most unique and individualistic of jazz artists. Reinhardt grew up in a musical Gypsy family, learning to play both violin and guitar proficiently by the time he was 12 years old. In 1928 he was badly injured in a fire, permanently losing the use of the first two fingers on his fret hand. Inventiveness and talent got him around this disability, as he devised his own fingering method and kept playing. In 1934 Django began a lifelong association with violinist Stephane Grappelli, forming the famous Quintet du Hot Club de France and making his first recordings. The Quintet played and recorded throughout Europe in the years leading up to World War II, becoming perhaps the most important group of non-American jazz musicians of the era and creating a distinctive brand of swing using mostly, and often only, stringed instruments. After the war, Django became popular outside Europe, as he toured the U.S. with Duke Ellington and did some recording. But Django would spend most of the rest of his life in France, where he would continue making great swing music, even experimenting some with electric guitar and bebop. After his early death in 1953, Reinhardt's legend was solidified with the hauntingly famous tribute song "Django," and with the documentary film *Django Reinhardt* by director Paul Paviot.

what to buy: The Django Reinhardt discography available domestically is a confusing mess of overlapping reissues and imports. Recorded in 1936–48, *Best of Django Reinhardt* (Blue Note, 1996, prod. Dan Morgenstern) provides an excellent introduction to the music of the great jazz guitarist, with instructive liner notes by producer Dan Morgenstern. Reinhardt is heard on a mix of early jazz standards like "Limehouse Blues," "You Rascal You," and "St. Louis Blues" as well as some of his own originals, including "Nuages," "Blues Claire," and "My Serenade." *Peche à la Mouche* (Verve, 1953/1992, prod. Gerard Leveque) features Reinhardt's last recordings, displaying inventive and distinctive leanings toward bop and electric guitar.

what to buy next: Reinhardt and Grappelli's group arises fully formed on *First Recordings!* (Prestige, 1934/Original Jazz Classics, 1997, prod. Don Schlitten). What is most remarkable is how confident and competent the musicians sound, though they were staking out totally new territory with their all-string band of European musicians. *Djangology 1949* (RCA, 1949/Bluebird, 1990, prod. Orrin Keepnews) consists of a later reunion of Reinhardt and Grappelli in Italy. The two old friends and compatriots constantly challenge each other.

what to avoid: *Gypsy Jazz* (Drive Archive, 1994, prod. Don Grierson) is a rather aimless reissue that randomly includes music from several unrelated sessions from late in Django's career (1947–53). The music is fine, but the same stuff can be acquired better ways.

the rest:

1935–1936 (Original Jazz Classics, 1990)
Djangologie/USA Vols. 1 & 2 (DRG, 1990)
Django Reinhardt and Stephane Grappelli (GNP Crescendo, 1991)

Swing Guitar (Jass, 1991)
Django Reinhardt and Friends (Pearl, 1992)
1934–1935 (Original Jazz Classics, 1992)
1937 (Original Jazz Classics, 1992)
1937: Vol. 2 (Original Jazz Classics, 1992)
1939–1940 (Original Jazz Classics, 1992)
1940 (Original Jazz Classics, 1992)
Compact Jazz: In Brussels (Verve, 1992)
Djangology (Blue Note, 1993)
1937–1938 (Original Jazz Classics, 1993)
1938–1939 (Original Jazz Classics, 1993)
Jazz Masters 38 (Verve, 1994)
The Indispensable Django Reinhardt (RCA, 1994)
Swing de Paris (Iris, 1996)
Nuages (Arcadia, 1997)
Django with His American Friends (DRG, 1998)

worth searching for: A French import, *Paris 1945* (Columbia, 1945, prod. John Hammond) features Reinhardt with an American sextet that includes "Peanuts" Hucko on clarinet and pianist Mel Powell. Highlights include "Homage à Fats Waller" and "Homage à Debussy."

influences:
◄◄ Charlie Christian, Louis Armstrong
►► Les Paul

Dan Keener

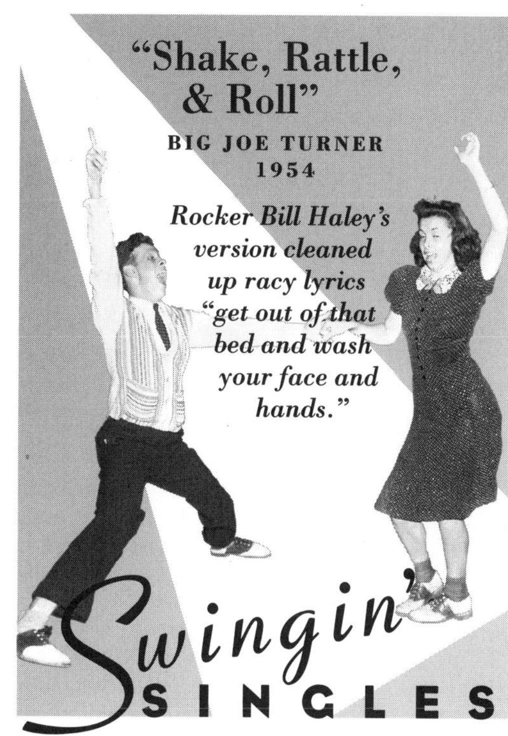

"Shake, Rattle, & Roll"
BIG JOE TURNER
1954
Rocker Bill Haley's version cleaned up racy lyrics "get out of that bed and wash your face and hands."
Swingin' SINGLES

Johnny Reno

Born in AR.

Long before the late-'90s swingers honked onto the scene, saxman Johnny Reno was bar-walking through the '80s with his band, the Sax Maniacs. Reno masterfully fused swing, jump blues, rockabilly, and jazz with impeccable sax and showmanship. The Sax Maniacs also featured the double-barreled, dueling saxophone sound that drives the musical core of many of today's young swing bands. Reno has a talent for finding obscure old tunes and making them sound fresh, while writing new material that neatly fits the old grooves. Much of Reno's Sax Maniac repertoire has found its way into today's swing set lists, from the Mighty Blue Kings' coverage of "Don't Let Go" and "Pink Champagne" to the Brian Setzer Orchestra, which covers Reno's long-time signature tune "Mellow Saxophone." Based in Fort Worth, Texas, the Sax Maniacs were born in 1983 and packed nightclubs throughout the Midwest. Along with Roomful of Blues, Reno's was one of the few touring bands keeping the horn-heavy, jump-blues traditions alive prior to the swing revival. After playing in the late '70s with Stevie Ray Vaughan's Triple Threat Revue, he played sax in Fort Worth's Juke Jumpers, then fronted a stripped-down rock 'n' roll band. Reno spent the early '90s touring as a sideman for rockabilly-pop crooner Chris Isaak, adding hot, driving sax and humor to the thoughtful singer's stage show. His new solo album is due in 1999, on a new EMI-Capitol swing spin-off record label.

what to buy: Reno's latest project is the Lounge Kings, a swing-influenced band focusing on jumping sax-fueled instrumentals and smoky torch songs. On *Swinging & Singing* (Menthol, 1997, prod. Johnny Reno), Reno lays down the vocals in the cool and bittersweet tradition of Chet Baker and Frank Sinatra. For a touch of bebop, beatnik, bachelor-pad cool, Alan Pollard adds groovy bongos on several tracks. The live *For Dancers Only* (Menthol, 1998, prod. Johnny Reno) includes classic swing tunes from Louis Prima and Red Prysock, mixed with unexpected covers like Roger Miller's "King of the Road."

what to buy next: The Johnny Reno Band performs a potent, mixed bag of scorching rockabilly and mainstream pop on *Third Degree* (Wildcat, 1990, prod. Johnny Reno).

worth searching for: Available only on vinyl and cassette, *Full Blown* (Rounder, 1985/1993, prod. Johnny Reno, T-Bone Burnett) includes swingabilly classics recently covered by nouveau swing bands like the Mighty Blue Kings ("Hey There," "Don't Let

Go," and "Hide and Seek.") Reno's vocals on "Thrill Me" and "Feels So Good" are barn-burning screamers. The Sax Maniacs' EP *Born to Blow* (Black Top, 1983, prod. Hammond Scott, Johnny Reno) contains a dynamic version of "Harlem Nocturne."

influences:

◀◀ Illinois Jacquet, Arnett Cobb, King Curtis, Red Prysock, Louis Prima, Sam Butera, Elvis Presley, Frank Sinatra, Chet Baker

▶▶ The Mighty Blue Kings, the Naughty Ones, Royal Crown Revue, Big Bad Voodoo Daddy, the Brian Setzer Orchestra

B.J. Huchtemann

Buddy Rich

Born September 30, 1917, in New York, NY. Died April 2, 1987, in Los Angeles, CA.

One of the most popular drummers in jazz for almost 50 years, Buddy Rich was a muscular, flamboyant player with a powerful sense of swing and enormous talent. Unfortunately, Rich had one of the biggest egos in jazz; a Rich-led band was frequently little more than a vehicle for its leader's rather overstated ensemble style. Still, he cooked. Despite his extreme extroversion (or perhaps because of it), his groups were always exciting; they regularly featured top-notch arrangements and such high-caliber soloists as Ernie Watts, Art Pepper, and Phil Wilson.

Rich was born into show business; he played a part in his parents' vaudeville act when he was little more than a year old. He appeared on Broadway as a drummer and tap dancer at age 4, and toured the U.S. and Australia from the age of six. At 11, Rich led his first band. From 1937 to 1939 he played with the bands of Joe Marsala, Bunny Berigan, Harry James, Artie Shaw, and Benny Carter. In 1939 he joined Tommy Dorsey's band, with whom he would play (interrupted by a war-time stint in the Marines) until 1945. From that point until 1951, he would lead his own groups and tour variously with Charlie Ventura, Les Brown, and Norman Granz's Jazz at the Philharmonic. Rich spent most of his time between 1953 and 1966 with Harry James, aside from periods with Dorsey (1954–55) and his own group (1957–61). From 1966 to 1974, Rich led his own very successful big band. He spent the late 1970s in New York, playing mostly at his own nightclub, Buddy's Place. He took to the road again in the 1980s, leading another big band of mostly young players. In the 1970s and 1980s, Rich developed a reputation as a lovable, egocentric curmudgeon via frequent appearances on Johnny Carson's *The Tonight Show*. According to members of his later groups, that image was only partially earned; Rich's reputed band-bus tirades are the stuff of legend.

what to buy: *Time Being* (RCA Bluebird, 1971/1972, prod. Ed Michel) is a fair representation of his excellent early 1970s band, featuring the underrated tenor saxophonist Pat LaBarbera. The Rich bands of this era were prone to occasional covers of undistinguished rock tunes, but when they kick out the stops and swing—as on this record's particularly aggressive "Straight, No Chaser"—they were among the best in the business.

what to buy next: *Big Swing Face* (Pacific Jazz, 1967/Blue Note, 1996), some of which was recorded live in Hollywood in the late '60s, is the big-band sound as it eased into Las Vegas showrooms. It's upbeat and fun, beginning with a version of the Beatles' "Norwegian Wood" and generally sounding of a piece with Doc Severinsen's enduring *The Tonight Show* theme.

what to avoid: By the early '80s, Rich's swinging arrangements had lost most of their pep, and the six-song *Live at Ronnie Scott's* (DRG, 1994) captures him attempting funky jazz fusion with bland results.

best of the rest:

This One's for Basie (Verve, 1956)
Swingin' New Band (Pacific Jazz, 1966)
Lionel Hampton Presents Buddy Rich (Who's Who, 1977)
Best Band I Ever Had (DCC, 1977/1990)
Best of Buddy Rich (Blue Note, 1997)

worth searching for: Some of Rich's earliest big-band recordings are on obscure and import labels, including *His Legendary '47–'48 Orchestra* (Hep, 1991) and *Legendary 1946–1948* (Hep, 1998).

influences:

◀◀ Harry James, Gene Krupa, Max Roach

▶▶ Keith Moon, Charlie Watts

Chris Kelsey and Steve Knopper

Nelson Riddle

Born June 1, 1921, in Oradell, NJ. Died October 6, 1985, in Los Angeles, CA.

His long and profitable associations as an arranger for performers like Judy Garland, Nat King Cole, Frank Sinatra, Johnny Mathis, Ella Fitzgerald, and others has ensured that Nelson Riddle's name is rarely the first one mentioned in his capsule biographies. Still, his orchestral pop was immensely influential on the big-band and swing genres, and his association with Frank Sinatra helped create '50s cool. Riddle started as a trombonist for Tommy Dorsey and other bandleaders in the mid-'40s and quickly moved on to arranging, working first with Garland, then Cole, and finally with Sinatra on a trio of landmark mid-'50s albums, *In the Wee Small Hours*, *Songs for Young Lovers / Swing Easy*, and *Songs for Swingin' Lovers!* That these are Sinatra's finest albums is due in large part to Riddle's superbly nuanced arrangements and orchestration. His sense of

Buddy Rich **(Archive Photos)**

timing, especially, is faultless, and his control of his orchestra masterful. After the release of these albums Riddle was in high demand as an arranger. As a solo artist, he also recorded several easy-listening and orchestral versions of pop songs, including the Beatles' "I Want to Hold Your Hand," and worked as a television and film composer, creating the theme for *The Untouchables* and *Route 66* and scoring films like *The Pajama Game*. Illness sidelined Riddle in the late '70s, but he returned to arrange a trio of albums for Linda Ronstadt, including the Grammy-winning *What's New* in 1983, as well as a project for opera singer Kiri Te Kanawa.

what to buy: *Songs for Swingin' Lovers!* (Capitol, 1956, prod. Voyle Gilmore) is Frank Sinatra's outright masterpiece, with classics like "You Make Me Feel So Young," "I Thought About You," "It Happened in Monterey," and many more. It's Sinatra's album, of course, but it's Riddle's too—his overall vision as arranger makes this a true collaboration.

what to buy next: *The Best of Nelson Riddle* (Curb, 1997, prod. Don Ovens) is a budget collection of Riddle's best performances as an artist, including "Lisbon Antigua," "Ramblin' Rose," "Walkin' My Baby Back Home," "I Want to Hold Your Hand," and the *Route 66* theme.

worth searching for: Get a sense of Riddle's later work with Linda Ronstadt's *What's New* (Asylum, 1983, prod. Peter Asher), and Kiri Te Kanawa's *Blue Skies* (London, 1985, prod. Don Lewzey).

influences:

◄◄ Gordon Jenkins, Axel Stordahl, George Siravo

►► Billy May, Johnny Mandel, Neal Hefti, Quincy Jones

Ben Greenman

Billy Lee Riley

Born October 5, 1933, in Pocohontas, AK.

Rockabilly legend Billy Lee Riley synthesized the same blend of country, blues, and R&B that characterized the work of his Sun Records labelmates Carl Perkins, Elvis Presley, Warren Smith, Jerry Lee Lewis, and Sonny Burgess. In 1956, Riley and future Sun producer Jack Clement recorded the brooding, Presley-like "Trouble Bound" for Slim Wallace's Fernwood label. When Clement leased the tape to Sun head Sam Phillips, the label hired both him and Riley. Handsome, multi-talented, and a crowd-pleaser on stage, Riley seemed destined for stardom, and with his band, the Little Green Men, he cut two of the wildest rock 'n' roll sides ever: "Flying Saucers Rock 'n' Roll" and "Red Hot." However, neither was more than a regional success and Riley was caught in a classic small-label conundrum: only at Sun could Riley find a sympathetic home for his fire-breathing R&B/country rave-ups, yet Phillips had limited resources. So, at the time Riley was producing his best work, the label was devoting most of its time and cash to Jerry Lee Lewis's booming career. Riley even overheard Phillips cancel pressings of his records so Sun could afford to ship more of Jerry Lee's. So Riley continued to cut hot Little Richard–type rockers and jump blues that didn't sell, and picked up eating money by backing nearly every act that came into the Sun studios through 1960.

Riley's career was dogged by bad luck and missed opportunities. He helped start Rita Records in 1961 but sold his interest in the label just before Harold Dorman hit it big with "Mountain of Love." After moving to Hollywood, Riley found work as the featured harmonica player for Sammy Davis Jr., Dean Martin, and Johnny Rivers, and fronted his own band as well. The Whiskey-A-Go-Go style matched well with Riley's, but no hits were forthcoming. Throughout the '60s Riley recorded under various names (Lightning Leon, Skip Wiley, Darren Lee) for a variety of labels, some of which he partly owned. In 1972, Riley finally hit the charts with "I've Got a Thing about You Baby" on Chips Moman's Entrance label. Moman's lack of promotion doomed the release to mid-chart status and the song, copied note-for-note, became more successful in the hands of Presley. After Presley's death, fresh interest in the original rockers began to build and Riley returned to Memphis to record for Sam Phillips's son, Knox, at Southern Rooster. His rockabilly reworking of "Blue Monday" earned Riley a favorable feature article in *Rolling Stone*, but the disc was poorly distributed and his moment seemed lost. Despite many frustrating years as an underpaid "cult hero," Riley somehow kept pumping. He supplemented his day job in construction with further small label offerings, club dates, and Sun reunion tours. During the '90s, Riley made a stand for the blues, cutting well-received discs for HighTone and Capricorn, while still raving out spirited R&B-flavored rockabilly in concert the world over.

what to buy: All of Riley's best solo tracks at Sun Records reside on *Red Hot: The Very Best of Billy Lee Riley* (Collectables, 1999, prod. Sam Phillips, Jack Clement), a comprehensive, inexpensive collection.

what to buy next: *Blue Collar Blues* (HighTone, 1992, prod. Bruce Bromberg) is a smart, cut-to-the-bone blend of Jimmy Reed–type blues, T. Graham–style country, and updated '50s rockabilly. Some former members of the Little Green Men join on a few songs.

what to avoid: Know what you're getting with *A Tribute to the Legendary Billy Lee Riley* (BSC Records, 1996, prod. various), with songs by various neo-rockabillies and psychobillies—but only one song by the man himself.

the rest:

Rockin' '50s (Icehouse Records, 1995)

Red Hot (Charly, 1997)
Hot Damn! (Capricorn Records, 1997)

worth searching for: The German import *Classic Recordings 1956–1960* (Bear Family, 1994, compilation prod. Richard Weize) is the most satisfying Riley package. The two-disc set includes everything he recorded at Sun during the '50s, plus his first sides at Rita Records and an informative critical essay by Colin Escott. The out-of-print import *Rockin' with Billy Lee Riley* (Charly, 1993, prod. various) includes all of Riley's recordings, false starts, and instrumentals during his days at Sun, plus his later reincarnation as a Creedence Clearwater Revival–style southern soul man at Sun International during the late '60s. Fans who dig his blues style will delight in such gems as "Pilot Town Louisiana," "Sun Goin' down on Frisco," and the tear-jerking "Kay." Also, Riley plays harmonica and guitar and sings duets on Wayne Keeling's *Rockin' & Ballin' the Jack* (Wix, 1997, prod. Tommie Wix) and *Run Fool Run* (Wix, 1998, prod. Tommie Wix), two solid helpings of honky-tonk and rockabilly cut in the legendary Sun studios.

influences:

◀◀ Big Joe Turner, Elvis Presley, Little Richard, Jimmy Reed, Ricky Nelson, Johnny Rivers

▶▶ Robert Gordon, Delbert McClinton, Creedence Clearwater Revival, T. Graham Brown, Wayne Keeling

see also: *Jerry Lee Lewis, Sonny Burgess, Warren Smith*

Ken Burke

Duke Robillard

Born October 4, 1948, in Woonsocket, RI.

There are certainly tons of phenomenal guitarists dotting the history of the blues, but few have ever managed to display a dazzling proficiency in as many diverse styles as Duke Robillard. He founded the jumping Roomful of Blues in 1967 and worked with the seminal outfit until 1979. Along the way he caught the eye of Muddy Waters and jammed onstage with his idol repeatedly for several years. Robillard later signed on with rockabilly singer Robert Gordon's group before founding his own band in 1981. As songwriter, bandleader, and torrid guitarist, Robillard has expanded his exploration of music through forays into rockabilly, jazz, R&B, and rock that build upon his blues roots. Constantly re-inventing himself, Robillard has delved into everything from jazzy horn sections and old-time rock to understated swing and rough, guitar-powered blues standards. In between projects, Robillard also replaced Jimmie Vaughan in the Fabulous Thunderbirds from 1990–92 and recently has produced albums for other top blues acts, including John Hammond and Jay McShann.

what to buy: *Duke Robillard and the Pleasure Kings* (Rounder, 1984, prod. Scott Billington, Duke Robillard), Robillard's debut as bandleader, is filled with tight, polished arrangements from his trio. These stripped-down tunes, mostly originals, connect early electric blues with Robillard's updated vision and edge. *After Hours Swing Session* (Rounder, 1992, prod. Duke Robillard) is an absolute treat, showing off Robillard's crisp journey into swinging jazz, including tunes plucked from Nat King Cole, Billie Holiday, and Tiny Grimes along with a few originals. His band (consisting of several Roomful of Blues pals) provides shimmering lead work on clarinet, sax, and piano while Robillard's guitar rings straight and true. Tribute albums too often pay boring homages to an artist's influences, but *Duke's Blues* (Pointblank, 1996, prod. Duke Robillard) is an exciting blend of Robillard originals and covers that bow to his idols while also giving them a kick in the pants. Robillard's guitar effortlessly darts between scorching assaults and restrained, jazzy fills while his vocals are scuffed or smooth depending on the moment.

what to buy next: *Turn It Around* (Rounder, 1991, prod. Duke Robillard, John Paul Gauthier) is a modern, rock-oriented set that features vocalist Susann Forrest. While Robillard lets his guitar ramble and roar more than on previous albums, Forrest's singing adds a sultry flare that provides a vibrant dimension to Duke's ensemble. *Dangerous Place* (Pointblank, 1997, prod. Duke Robillard) takes Robillard's adventures in swing, including an exceptional horn section, and melds them together with a fuzzed-out, hard-driving guitar. The full-band jams are hard-driving explosions, and the softer stuff displays some towering jazz constructions on saxophone.

the rest:
Too Hot to Handle (Rounder, 1985)
Swing (Rounder, 1987)
Rockin' Blues (Rounder, 1988)
You Got Me (Rounder, 1988)
Temptation (Pointblank, 1994)
Duke Robillard Plays Blues: The Rounder Years (Rounder, 1997)
Duke Robillard Plays Jazz: The Rounder Years (Rounder, 1997)

worth searching for: Robillard and band revisit some of Jay McShann's classic tunes for *Hootie's Jumpin' Blues* (Stony Plain, 1997, prod. Duke Robillard, Holger Peterson).

influences:

◀◀ T-Bone Walker, B.B. King, Lowell Fulson

▶▶ Chris Duarte, Kenny Wayne Shepherd, Royal Crown Revue, Squirrel Nut Zippers

see also: *Roomful of Blues*

Matt Pensinger

Duke Robillard **(© Linda Vartoogian)**

Adrian Rollini

See: California Ramblers

Roomful of Blues

Formed 1968, in RI.

Rich Lataille, alto sax, tenor sax (1970–present); John Rossi, drums (1970–98); Bob Enos, trumpet, (1981–present); Chris Vachon, guitar (1990–present); Mac Odom, vocals (1998–present); John Wolf, tenor and bass trombones (1998–present); Kevin May, baritone sax (1998–present); Greg Silva, bass (1998–present); Steve Kostakes, keyboards (1998–present); Albert Weisman, Hammond B-3, piano (1998); Marty Ballou, bass (1998); Matt McCabe, piano (1993–97); Carl Querfurth, trombone (1978, 1987–97); Ken "Doc" Grace, bass (1992–97); Sugar Ray Norcia, vocals, harmonica (1990–97); Al Copley, piano (1968–84); Larry Peduzzi, bass (1968–early '70s, 1990–93); Chuck Riggs, drums (1968); Fran Christina, drums (1968–70); Greg Piccolo, tenor sax, vocals (1970–94); Preston Hubbard, bass (1970s, 1982–84); Jimmy Wimpfheimer, bass (1979–82); Rory MacLeod, bass (1984–86); Ronnie Earl, guitar (1979–88); Tommy K, guitar (1988–90); Danny Motta, trumpet (1979–81); Porky Cohen, trombone (1979–87); Lou Ann Barton, vocals (1979–80); Curtis Salgado, vocals (1984–86); Ron Levy, piano, organ (1984–88); Jr. Brantley, piano (1988–93), Paul Tomasello, bass (late '80s); Rhandy Simmons, bass (mid-to-late '80s); Duke Robillard, guitar, vocals (1968–79); Mike Warner, drums (1998–present).

Today's swing revival owes a huge debt to Roomful of Blues, which swung when swing wasn't hip. Founded by guitarist Duke Robillard, Roomful of Blues is one of the few bands that preserved and promoted the horn-based, jump-blues sounds of the old '30s and '40s territory bands throughout the '70s and '80s. The band members are not historic archivists; for them it's a love affair and the music is a living, breathing thing.

The Roomful concept gelled in 1971, after Robillard—inspired by old 78 rpm recordings of the classic swing-blues orchestras—added horns to a band he put together for an amateur showcase at the Newport Folk Festival. While rock and disco were the popular musical forms of the early '70s, Roomful perfected its sound gigging for swing dance revivalists at the Westerly, Rhode Island, Knickerbocker Cafe—a '40s-era dance hall that once housed many original jump-blues orchestras. In 1998, after years of lineup changes, it was appropriate that the band's 30th anniversary year (1998) found an almost complete personnel revamping.

what to buy: *Turn It On! Turn It Up!* (Bullseye/Rounder, 1995, prod. Carl Querfurth), with most of the Roomful lineup introduced on 1994's *Dance All Night*, stomps, swaggers, and smokes. "I Left My Baby" is a vibrant, gleaming tribute to Count Basie's original (and that includes vocalist Jimmy Rushing and the swinging Kansas City sound in general). *There Goes the Neighborhood* (Bullseye/Rounder, 1998, prod. Chris Vachon, Phil Greene) introduces the newest generation of Roomfullers—vocalist Mac Odom has a wide range and a big soul/jump-blues sound that's reminiscent of former lead singer Curtis Salgado. The tunes are a mix of originals and covers, including "I Smell Trouble" and Duke Ellington's "Rocks in My Bed," all of which jump hard. The sassy *Dressed Up to Get Messed Up* (Varrick, 1984/Rounder, 1986, prod. Greg Piccolo) includes mostly original tunes, and Piccolo's vocals exude an in-your-face confidence. Listening to Sugar Ray front Roomful on *Dance All Night* (Bullseye/Rounder, 1994, prod. Carl Querfurth), his first CD with the band, it's hard to believe he wasn't part of the lineup from the start. (In fact, he was a long-time fan.) His versatile, emotive vocals and harp are a perfect match for the band's big sound.

what to buy next: The two-in-one CD *Two Classic Albums: Roomful of Blues with Joe Turner/With Eddie "Cleanhead" Vinson* (Muse, 1982/1983/32 Blues, 1997, prod. various) is as good as you'd expect from the brilliant pairing of Roomful of Blues with two of its inspirations. The selection of material isn't quite as engaging as *Turn It On! Turn It Up!*, but on *Under One Roof* (Bullseye/Rounder, 1997, prod. Carl Querfurth), the band is rock-solid. The only in-concert Roomful recording, *Live at Lupo's Heartbreak Hotel* (Varrick/Rounder, 1987, prod. Greg Piccolo, Doug James, Roomful of Blues) documents the contributions of the extraordinary singer-harpist Curtis Salgado. Salgado's appearance on the CD is, unfortunately, limited to three tracks; aside from that "sin of omission," it's a fine CD with Piccolo on lead vocals on two tracks, lots of variety, and two jumping instrumentals. *Hot Little Mama* (Blue Flame, 1981/1985/Varrick/Rounder, 1989, prod. Roomful of Blues), the first Roomful recording with Robillard's "successor," guitarist Ronnie Earl, includes Ellington standards "Caravan" and "Jeep's Blues" and a nod to Lou Ann Barton, "Sugar Coated Love."

the rest:

The First Album (32 Blues, 1996)
Roomful of Christmas (Bullseye/Rounder, 1997)

worth searching for: Out of print is *Let's Have a Party* (Antilles Records, 1979, prod. Joel Dorn). Also, the pre-1998 Roomful horn section, often with drummer Rossi, has been an in-demand unit for other artists' recordings. To name a few examples: Piccolo rejoins the other horn players on five cuts of Luther "Guitar Junior" Johnson and the Magic Rockers' *Doin' the Sugar Too* (Bullseye Blues, 1997); the entire band appears on former Roomful trombone player Porky Cohen's *Rhythm & Bones* (Bullseye Blues, 1996); Roomful horns appear with Mitch Woods & His Rocket 88's *Solid Gold Cadillac* (Blind Pig Records, 1991); and Rossi and the horns have appeared on Pat Benatar's *True Love* (Chrysalis), and Colin James's *Cadillac Baby* (Virgin).

Royal Crown Revue **(© Warner Bros. Records Inc.)**

influences:

⏪ Eddie "Cleanhead" Vinson, Count Basie, T-Bone Walker, Joe Turner, Wynonie Harris, Jimmy Rushing, Joe Williams

⏩ Big Swing, the Vanguard Aces, the Mighty Blue Kings, Indigo Swing, Big Bad Voodoo Daddy, Royal Crown Revue, the Brian Setzer Orchestra.

see also: *Duke Robillard, Sugar Ray Norcia*

B.J. Huchtemann

Royal Crown Revue

Formed 1989, in Los Angeles, CA.

Eddie Nichols, vocals; Mando Dorame, tenor sax; James Achor, guitar; Bill Ungerman, baritone sax; Scott Steen, trumpet; Veikko Lepisto, bass; Daniel Glass, drums.

Swinging ahead of the rest of the swing-music revivalists, Royal Crown Revue helped rescue swing from the past, giving the music a rock-infused shot in the arm in the late '80s. Though they've yet to receive the sort of broad mainstream radio success enjoyed by the likes of the Cherry Poppin' Daddies, Royal Crown singer Eddie Nichols and Co. remain one of the swing revival's most popular bands, in part because of the jump-blues outfit's considerable chops and keen collective sense of style. Of course, an appearance in the Jim Carrey smash *The Mask* didn't hurt: In the pre-*Swingers* film, the then-unsigned septet performed its original song "Hey Pachuco!" as Carrey and Cameron Diaz did their, um, swing. RCR was one of the first modern swing bands to land a major-label recording contract (with Warner Bros. in the spring of 1995). And confirming its coolness quotient, the band—which consistently packs rooms up and down the West Coast, including the Derby in Los Angeles—secured a nine-week stint at the end of 1997 headlining at the Desert Inn, the newly renovated Las Vegas lounge made famous by Louis Prima, Sam Butera, and, of course, Frank Sinatra and the Rat Pack. No slaves to nostalgia, though, Royal Crown Revue—whose members have experienced playing everything from jazz and soul to skiffle, rockabilly, and even punk—give the music a decidedly contemporary spin, playing with the edge and intensity of a rock band. No wonder, then, that RCR landed a gig opening for Kiss, as well as a spot on the punk-oriented Warped Tour.

what to buy: The major-label debut, *Mugzy's Move* 🎵🎵🎵🎵 (Warner Bros., 1996, prod. Ted Templeman), is a mix of brazen originals (the big-band-style "Park's Place," the zippy "Zip Gun Bop," the manic "Hey Pachuco!") and smart covers, including Bobby Darin's somewhat obvious "Beyond the Sea" and Willie Dixon's not-so-obvious "I Love the Life I Live." Veteran rock producer Ted Templeman (Doobie Brothers, Van Halen) does a fine job at capturing, in the studio, the same sort of energy and excitement the band delivers on stage.

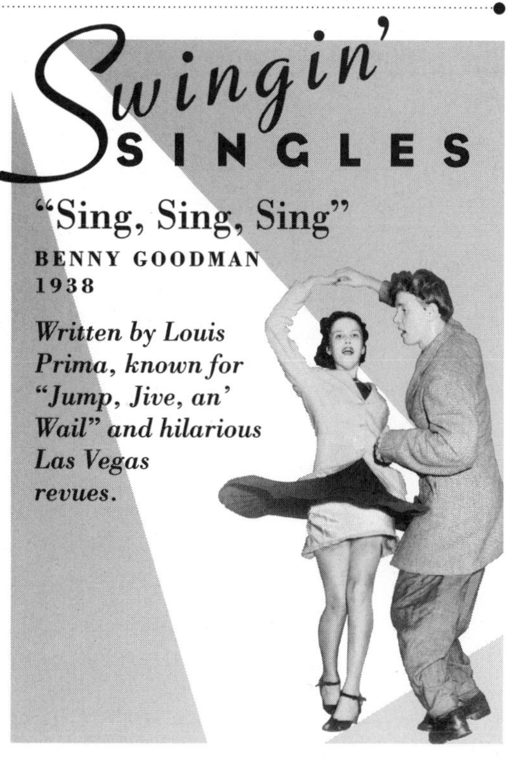
Swingin' SINGLES
"Sing, Sing, Sing"
BENNY GOODMAN
1938
Written by Louis Prima, known for "Jump, Jive, an' Wail" and hilarious Las Vegas revues.

the rest:

Kings of Gangster Bop 🎵🎵🎵 (BYO/Big Daddy, 1991)
Caught in the Act 🎵🎵🎵 (Surfdog, 1997)
The Contender 🎵🎵🎵 (Warner Bros., 1998)

influences:

⏪ Frank Sinatra, Bobby Darin, Bad Religion, Raymond Chandler, David Goodis, Benny Goodman, Louis Jordan

⏩ Big Bad Voodoo Daddy, Indigo Swing, Cherry Poppin' Daddies, *Swingers,* and the rest of the neo-swing movement

Josh Freedom du Lac

Jimmy Rushing

Born August 26, 1903, in Oklahoma City, OK. Died June 8, 1972, in New York, NY.

Jimmy Rushing was not only the singer and primary frontman of Count Basie's orchestra but the glue that held the band together in rough times. (It was big glue: Rushing was known as "Mr. Five by Five" for his intimidating physique.) From 1935 to

Jimmy Rushing **(Archive Photos)**

1950, Rushing sang on Basie swing classics like "Boogie-Woogie," "Evenin'," and even "Did You See Jackie Robinson Hit That Ball." As a teenager, he lived the prototypical bluesman's life, hoboing through the Midwest and singing at occasional parties and churches. He wound up in California and quickly started making connections: Jelly Roll Morton employed him as a singer; Walter Page's Blue Devils, the famous Kansas City band of the late 1920s, made him vocalist; and he toured with Bennie Moten's Kansas City Orchestra. He met Basie in 1936 and frequently sang duets with Billie Holiday. The orchestra disbanded in 1950, and Rushing just couldn't stay retired; he wound up working with Dave Brubeck, Earl Hines, and other sidemen and made small acting appearances in several movies. He and Basie reunited just once—at the 1957 Newport Jazz Festival—but after 1950 neither performer was able to recreate the old orchestra's success.

what to buy: Though the most essential Rushing collection will extensively sample the singer's years with the Count Basie Orchestra, *The Essential Jimmy Rushing* ♪♪♪♪ (Vanguard, 1978/1989, prod. John Hammond) is a fine document of Rushing's mid-1950s solo material. He recreates a number of Basie standards, including "Going to Chicago," often with old Basie friends and sidemen.

what to buy next: With a terrific ensemble, including the great jazz drummer Jo Jones, Rushing's All-Stars make the 1967 recording *Gee, Baby, Ain't I Good to You* ♪♪♪ (Master Jazz, 1968/New World, 1997) into a jumping party that ends far too soon after nine songs (including the Basie classic "One O'Clock Jump").

best of the rest:

Rushing Lullabyes/Little Jimmy ♪♪♪ (Sony, 1959/1997)
(With Champion Jack Dupree) *Mister Five by Five* ♪♪♪ (Columbia, 1980/Topaz, 1996)
Dynamic Duo ♪♪♪ (Collector's Edition, 1996)
Swings the Blues ♪♪ (Louisiana Red Hot, 1997)
Five Feet of Soul ♪♪♪ (Collectables, 1998)

worth searching for: Filled with late material, the out-of-print *The You and Me That Used to Be* ♪♪♪♪ (RCA/Bluebird, 1971/1988) is more slick and pop-oriented and doesn't have quite the same sparkle as the mid-1950s stuff. Still, Rushing's booming voice is nice to hear in many different contexts.

influences:

◀◀ Count Basie, Duke Ellington, Louis Armstrong, Billie Holiday, Bessie Smith

▶▶ Jimmy Witherspoon, Big Joe Turner, Charlie Parker, Louis Jordan, Dinah Washington

Steve Knopper

S

Sax Maniacs

See: Johnny Reno

Raymond Scott

Born Harry Warnow, September 10, 1908, in New York, NY. Died February 8, 1994.

"Dinner Music for a Pack of Hungry Cannibals" was one of the many brilliant song titles devised by Scott, an obsessive tinkerer and perfectionist bandleader who created some of this century's most playful big-band instrumentals. Many listeners already have a thorough knowledge of Scott's music, even if they've never heard of him, because percussion-heavy pieces like "Powerhouse" were the soundtracks for Porky Pig and Bugs Bunny on *Looney Tunes* cartoons. A serious classical music student schooled at Juilliard, Scott joined his brother Mark's CBS orchestra in the early 1930s, then headed his own highly experimental quintet through decade's end. His compositions, such as "Confusion Among a Fleet of Taxicabs upon Meeting with a Fare," were filled with quirky Dixieland horns, playful percussion, and dizzying mood changes. Though he developed a prominent reputation as an arranger, many viewed his songs as novelty music, which explains the songs' later appeal to Warner Bros., which licensed them for *Looney Tunes*.

Scott formed a more traditional big band in the early 1940s, working with Frank Sinatra, Cozy Cole, and Ben Webster, among others, then ran a record label and performed with his wife, singer Dorothy Collins. He was also a prolific inventor, creating one of the first known synthesizers in 1949, and devising contraptions called the electronium and the clavivox. He retired in 1977, but recorded with MIDI computer techniques through 1987, when he suffered his first debilitating stroke.

what to buy: On *Reckless Nights and Turkish Twilights: The Music of Raymond Scott* ♪♪♪♪ (Columbia, 1992, prod. Irwin Chusid), the producer quotes a commentator saying, "Scott's music is very seldom revived nowadays," then responds, "I decided to make that statement untrue." There's novelty appeal here, of course, as the opening song "Powerhouse" evokes any number of Bugs Bunny episodes; but the real surprise is just how inventive, complex, and plain fun Scott's music remains.

what to buy next: Unsurprisingly, Scott's ready-for-the-cartoons style downshifted easily into kids' music, and he put out several volumes of it—*Soothing Sounds for Baby, Vols. I–III* ♪♪♪ (Epic, 1963/Basta, 1997) is certainly as much as you'll need.

what to avoid: Every Scott collection includes "Powerhouse," because it's the most recognizable of his cartoon theme music.

The Columbia set dwarfs past projects such as *The Raymond Scott Project, Powerhouse, Vol. 1* ♪♪ (Stash, 1991).

worth searching for: The hard-to-find *The Uncollected Raymond Scott* ♪♪♪ (Hindsight, 1983) is a live recording from a 1940 Chicago ballroom show; its sequel, *The Uncollected Raymond Scott, Vol. 2* ♪♪♪ (Hindsight, 1985), comes from 1944.

influences:

◀ Benny Goodman, Duke Ellington, Frank Sinatra, Nelson Riddle

▶ Juan Garcia Esquivel, Frank Zappa, They Might Be Giants, Devo

Steve Knopper

The Senders

Formed 1988, in Minneapolis, MN.

Charmin Michelle, vocals; David Brown, guitar and vocals; Bill Black, upright bass; Marty Bryduck, drums; Bruce Pendalty, keyboards; Scott Johnson, tenor sax; Bob Byers, baritone and alto sax; Pete Masters, trombone.

If life was fair, the terrific swing-dancing scene at the heart of the movie *Swingers* would have brought back the big bands the way *Urban Cowboy* once rescued the entire country music industry. But the Squirrel Nut Zippers' popularity notwithstanding, the mid-1990s swing revival's days are probably numbered. Remember, the reason Benny Goodman and his contemporaries eventually died out was because it got too expensive to drag all those people, buses, and equipment around the country. The Senders, whose singer, Charmin Michelle, has a funny Betty Boop–like pitch, have the right spirit. They know how to swing, and they have enough connections to lure guest pianist-legend Charles Brown into the studio to perform energetic covers of B.B. King's "Everything I Do Is Wrong" and Wynonie Harris's "Wasn't That Good." With luck, they, and the Zippers and Royal Crown Revue, will stick around long enough for every American to learn (or re-learn) the jitterbug and the foxtrot.

what to buy: *Jumpin' Uptown* ♪♪♪ (Blue Loon, 1996, prod. Pete Masters) has a lot of great energy, and nice sax and guitar solos—plus Michelle is a fun, charismatic singer—but this is a bar band that hasn't fully captured its live sound in the studio.

what to buy next: The band's debut, *Bar Room Blues* ♪♪♪ (Blue Loon, 1994, prod. Duke Robillard, the Senders), is interesting enough to make listeners pay a cover charge.

influences:

◀ Benny Goodman, Charles Brown, Glenn Miller, Billie Holiday, Doris Day, B.B. King

Steve Knopper

The Brian Setzer Orchestra

Formed 1992, in Los Angeles, CA.

Brian Setzer, guitar, vocals; Michael Acosta, tenor saxophone (1994–1996); Bob Sandman, tenor saxophone (1994–1996); Ray Herrmann, alto saxophone (1994); Steve Fowler, alto saxophone (1994–1996); Don Roberts, baritone saxophone (1994–present); Dan Fornero, trumpet (1994–present); Jon Fumo, trumpet (1994–present); Les Lovitt, trumpet (1994); Ramon Flores, trumpet (1994); Art Valasco, trombone (1994); Dana Hughes, baritone trombone (1994); Bruce Fowler, trombone (1994); Mark Jones, trombone (1994–present); Bernie Dresel, drums (1994–present); Bob Parr, bass (1994–1996); Gary Stockdale, piano (1994); George Shelby, alto saxophone, clarinet (1996); Stan Watkins, trumpet (1996); Sal Cracchiola, trumpet (1996); Charlie Biggs, trumpet (1996); George McMullen, trombone (1996–present); Michael Vlatkovich, trombone (1996–present); Robbie Hioki, bass trombone, tuba (1996–present); Roger Burn, piano, vibes (1996); Tim Misica, saxophone (1998–present); Steve Marsh, saxophone (1998–present); Rick Rossi, saxophone (1998–present); Kevin Norton, trumpet (1998–present); Dennis Farias, trumpet (1998–present); Ernie Nunez, bass (1998–present).

Brian Setzer is a terrific guitarist and a serious student of music history who has had the good fortune of musical fashion following his lead not once, but twice in his serendipitous career. As the leader of the Stray Cats in the '80s, Setzer helped revive '50s-style rockabilly, albeit in a supercharged and somewhat cartoonish fashion. Still, few could deny the pleasures of their MTV-launched hits "Rock This Town" and "Stray Cat Strut." The Cats broke up after the trend ran its course and success went to their heads, but Setzer stayed true to the music, playing '50s guitar hero Eddie Cochran in the Ritchie Valens biopic *La Bamba*, playing in Robert Plant's retro group the Honeydrippers, and recording several solo albums. After sitting in with some neighbors on a big-band jam session, Setzer decided to form his own orchestra, modeling it on the pre–World War II big bands, but not limiting himself to a strictly retro sound. Instead, his 17-piece outfit (count 'em—five saxes, four trumpets, four trombones, drums, bass, piano, and Setzer himself) play a mix of swing, jump blues, sophisticated pop, and rock 'n' roll, including original material. When the swing trend broke wide open in the mid-to-late '90s, Setzer could truthfully claim he'd been on the scene all along.

what to buy: Three albums into his career as a big-band leader, Setzer got the mix of all the various elements almost perfect on *the Dirty Boogie* ♪♪♪♪ (Interscope, 1998, prod. Peter Collins): there are just enough quality cover tunes (including Bobby Darin's "As Long As I'm Singin'," Clint Stacey's country-flavored "This Old House," the Leiber and Stoller chestnut "You're the Boss" (featuring No Doubt's Gwen Stefani), and a sssmokin' version of Louis Prima's "Jump, Jive, an' Wail") alongside some

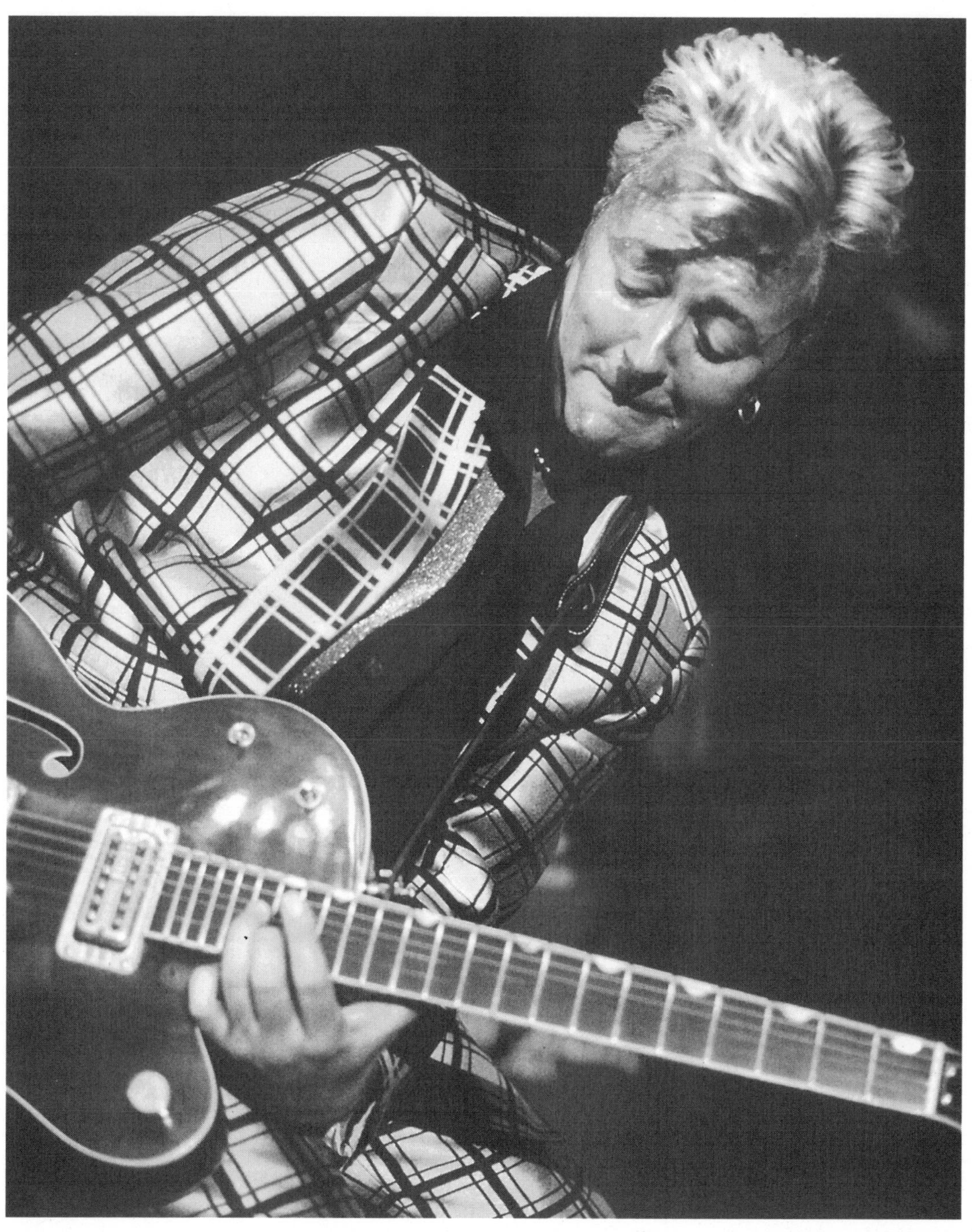

Brian Setzer **(© Ken Settle)**

fine originals (such as "Let's Live It Up," "Hollywood Nocturne," and a new version of "Rock This Town"). The band is in fine form, stepping out when it's required, but leaving Setzer's guitar plenty of room to roam.

what to buy next: On *Guitar Slinger* (Interscope, 1996, prod. Phil Ramone), Setzer realized that even though his band was a kick in the brass, his guitar was still the star of the show. Thus the album title, and a greater emphasis on rock that swings rather than swing that rocks—or something like that. Highlights include a version of the Stray Cats' "Rumble in Brighton," Stevie Ray Vaughan's "The House Is Rockin'," and a couple of collaborations between Setzer and the Clash's Joe Strummer.

the rest:
The Brian Setzer Orchestra (Hollywood, 1994)

worth searching for: To sample Setzer's first rock career, with the hitmaking rockabilly band the Stray Cats, the generous best-of collection *Runaway Boys: A Retrospective '81–'92* (EMI, 1997, prod. various) offers 25 tracks of the group's trademark latter-day rockabilly boogie, from "Rock This Town" and "Stray Cat Strut" to "(She's) Sexy + 17" and many more. It doesn't necessarily swing, but Setzer's recently reissued solo debut, *The Knife Feels Like Justice* (EMI, 1986/Razor & Tie, 1999), is a mature and stylistically varied effort that didn't get a fair hearing the first time around.

influences:
◄◄ Glenn Miller, Louis Prima, Louis Jordan, Bobby Darin, Count Basie, Gene Vincent

►► Cherry Poppin' Daddies, Royal Crown Revue, Big Bad Voodoo Daddy

Daniel Durchholz

Doc Severinsen

Born Carl H. Severinsen, July 7, 1927, in Arlington, OR.

One of the most visible trumpet players of the last 40 years, former *Tonight Show* bandleader Doc Severinsen is a consummate professional who can execute a wide variety of musical genres with equal skill. Whether a leader, guest star, or hired hand, Severinsen has never allowed his legendary sartorial style or immense fame to intrude upon the character of his music. Via Johnny Carson's opening theme music, Severinsen also kept swing music alive before the masses for three decades. Severinsen played trumpet and flugelhorn with bands led by Charlie Barnet, Tommy Dorsey, and Benny Goodman, before joining NBC as a staff musician in 1949. When he wasn't playing on the big network variety shows of the 1950s and early 1960s (the *Steve Allen* show among them), Severinsen recorded solid jazz with the likes of Stan Getz, Tito Puente, Gene Krupa, and Milt Jackson, and softer, more commercial sounds with Dinah Washington and Ray Conniff. When Johnny Carson took over *The Tonight Show* from Jack Paar in 1963, Severinsen was the assistant bandleader behind Skitch Henderson. Carson discovered he had better comedic chemistry with the affable trumpet player than the dour Henderson, and by 1967 made Severinsen the bandleader of his nightly program. Always a colorful dresser, Severinsen began wearing increasingly wilder outfits to accommodate the jokes in Carson's monologues and crystallized his TV persona as the goofy hipster. TV fame led to a series of well-received jazz and pop LPs, as well as being voted the Top Brass Player in more than a dozen *Playboy* music polls. Besides playing standards and appropriate intro music for guests, Severinsen was something of an innovator in that he introduced elements of funk, bebop, and fusion in 20- and 30-second bites to TV audiences. When Carson left *The Tonight Show* in 1992, so did Severinsen, who has since led successful tours with his TV band and been named the principal pops conductor for orchestras in Phoenix, Minnesota, Milwaukee, and Buffalo.

what to buy: *The Very Best of Doc Severinsen* (Amherst, 1997, prod. Jeff Tyzik) works as a solid sampler and introduction to the wildly attired bandleader. However, Severinsen's best recordings with his fabled *Tonight Show* band are on *Once More . . . with Feeling!* (Amherst, 1991, prod. Jeff Tyzik). In addition to the band's fine regular soloists, 14 popular jazz standards, and refreshing, colorful charts (written mostly by top arrangers Bill Holman and Tommy Newsome), this CD features guest appearances by Wynton Marsalis and Tony Bennett on one tune each. It includes classic gems such as "St. Louis Blues," "I Can't Get Started" (featuring Bennett), "Avalon" (with Marsalis), "What Is This Thing Called Love," and "Body and Soul."

what to buy next: Almost as good are *Doc Severinsen & The Tonight Show Orchestra* (Amherst, 1990, prod. Jeff Tyzik) and *Tonight Show Band, Vol. 2* (Amherst, 1990, prod. Jeff Tyzik), where the group alternates between playing big-band standards and fusion workouts in their inimitable, polished style.

what to avoid: There's too much Cincinnati Pops and not enough Severinsen on *Erich Kunzel/Cincinnati Pops* (Telarc, 1991, prod. Robert Woods, Elaine Martone).

best of the rest:
Facets (Amherst, 1988)
Lullabies and Goodnight (Critique, 1992)
Good Medicine (RCA Bluebird, 1992)
Doc Severinsen & Friends (MCA Special Products, 1992)
Merry Christmas from Doc Severinsen & The Tonight Show Orchestra (Amherst, 1992)
Two Sides of Doc Severinsen (The Right Stuff, 1993)

worth searching for: The out-of-print *Tonight Show Band, Vol. 1* (Amherst, 1986, prod. Jeff Tyzik) won a Grammy for Best Jazz Instrumental—Big Band in 1987. Fans of the genre will definitely want *Big Band Hit Parade* (Telarc, 1988, prod. Robert Woods), *Erich Kunzel/Cincinnati Pops Orchestra: Fiesta* (Telarc, 1990, prod. Robert Woods), *Unforgettably Doc* (Telarc, 1992, prod. Robert Woods, Elaine Martone), and *Christmas with the Pops* (Telarc, 1993, prod. Robert Woods). Completists should know that Doc made strong guest appearances on Tony Bennett's *This Is Jazz #33* (Columbia, 1998, prod. various) and Ani DiFranco's *Living In Clip* (Righteous Babe Records, 1997, prod. Ani DiFranco).

influences:

◀◀ Harry James, Ray Anthony

▶▶ Herb Alpert, Chuck Mangione

Ken Burke

Artie Shaw

Born Arthur Jacob Arshawsky, May 23, 1910, in New York, NY.

From his first massive hit, 1938's "Begin the Beguine," to the time he joined the Navy in 1942, clarinetist Artie Shaw led one of the most popular bands of the swing era, employing sterling musicians such as singer Billie Holiday, drummer Buddy Rich, and pianist Johnny Guarnieri. (Unlike other bandleaders, who were content to lead one outfit, Shaw wound up with no less than five during his career.) Cole Porter's formerly obscure "Beguine," which in Shaw's hands became one of the best-selling songs ever, led to a string of orchestra hits, including "Frenesi," "Indian Love Call," "Back Bay Shuffle," and the band's theme, "Nightmare." During the orchestra's peak years, a fan-generated conflict broke out between aficionados of Shaw and the other major clarinet player of the day, Benny Goodman. Neither musician was involved in the hostilities, but fans debated their heroes' merits in conversation and the press.

Mainly self-taught, Artie Shaw played alto saxophone in a dance band in his early teens, and by his mid-teens switched to the clarinet and worked as music director/arranger with Austin Wylie's band in Cleveland, Ohio. With Irving Aaronson's band, Shaw traveled in 1929 to New York where he sat in at late-night jam sessions, including those organized by an early mentor, pianist Willie "The Lion" Smith. When he was 19, Shaw discovered the scores of Igor Stravinsky and Claude Debussy, a factor that would influence much of his future music making. Shaw perfected his playing and became a highly sought-after session musician, especially on alto saxophone and clarinet. He attended Columbia University (to study literature) in the first of his periodic "retirements" from the music business, but re-entered the musical fray in 1934, working with many top-notch swing musicians, including Red Norvo, the Dorsey Brothers, and Bunny Berrigan. Shaw became a bandleader in his own right in 1936, employing several top musicians and a string section before finally earning a hit with "Begin the Beguine." During his Navy years, Shaw was put in charge of an all-star band, which entertained World War II troops fighting in the Pacific. After leaving the Navy, he formed another series of bands before entering his longest "retirement" in the mid-1950s to devote himself to literary pursuits. In addition to his short stories written in the mid-1950s and 1960s, Shaw wrote his autobiography, *The Trouble with Cinderella*, and a trio of short stories, *I Love You, I Hate You, Drop Dead!* He also operated Artixo Productions, a film distribution and production company.

what to buy: Despite the favorable reputation of the Gramercy Five sessions, *The Last Recordings, Vol. 1: Rare & Unreleased* (MusicMasters, 1992, prod. Artie Shaw), a two-CD set of tunes from 1954, could very well contain Shaw's finest music within a small group format. His restless brand of perfectionism has Shaw breaking out of the mold for the last time, since these are among his final recordings. *Begin the Beguine* (RCA/Bluebird, 1938–41/1988, prod. various) is probably the best single volume to start with for a taste of Shaw's major hits. It is filled with 20 of Shaw's most popular chart-toppers, including "Frenesi," "Star Dust," and "Back Bay Shuffle." All the material covered comes from the classic 1938–41 period, when singers Billie Holiday, Helen Forrest, and Tony Pastor were with the band. The band within a band on *The Complete Gramercy Five Sessions* (RCA/Bluebird, 1989, prod. various) allows Shaw, with a select handful of musicians, to step out of the bigger group format and play music that swings harder and more progressively than his larger ensemble. The harpsichord of 1940 gives way to the piano of 1945, but that provides the only minor quibble about which version of the Gramercy Five is better. The recordings on *The Indispensable Artie Shaw: 1944–45* (RCA, 1944–45/1986/1995, reissue prod. Jean-Paul Guiter) date from when Shaw came back to the States after his Navy tour of the South Pacific. His new band featured a large brass/reed section, and the rhythm quartet of piano, guitar, bass, and drums. Although this particular band didn't have quite the commercial success of his earlier outfits, Shaw managed to come up with a jazz classic ("Little Jazz") featuring trumpeter Roy Eldridge.

what to buy next: Shaw stepped out from his career as a session musician to lead his first band in 1936. The import CD *In the Beginning—1936* (Hep, 1994, prod. A. Robertson, J.R.T. Davies) documents that year, when Shaw led his innovative "string quartet" group, which included the usual complement of rhythm and brass/reed instruments in addition to a small string section. It was an experiment that garnered critical acclaim but modest commercial success. There are elements of schmaltz to be found here, but Shaw's clarinet playing is superb, and the performances swing far more than his contemporaries, the Casa Loma Orchestra's Glen Gray or Lawrence Welk (especially on material like "It Ain't Right" and "Copenhagen"). *More Last Recordings: The Final Sessions* (MusicMasters, 1993, prod. Artie Shaw) contains additional tunes from the 1954 small-group sessions that MusicMasters dipped into for their superb *The Last Recordings, Vol. 1: Rare & Unreleased* release. This two-CD set contains some interesting takes on standards long associated with Shaw. His clarinet playing is supple and adventurous on "Frenesi," "Stardust," and "Back Bay Shuffle."

the rest:
Frenesi (RCA, 1992)
Personal Best (RCA, 1992)
Artie Shaw: 1936 (Classics, 1996)
Artie Shaw: Greatest Hits (RCA, 1996)

worth searching for: Shaw's 1937 song "Nightmare," which grew from an extended practice jam during a recording session, appears on *Swing Time! The Fabulous Big Band Era 1925–1955* (Columbia/Legacy, 1993, compilation prod. Aubrey Fell). The three-disc set frames the bandleader with his contemporaries, including Benny Goodman, Duke Ellington, Count Basie, Harry James, and Glenn Miller.

influences:
◀◀ Willie "The Lion" Smith, Claude Debussy, Igor Stravinsky, Jimmy Dorsey, Barney Bigard

▶▶ Bob Wilber, Dick Johnson

Garaud MacTaggart

Dinah Shore

Born Frances Rose Shore, March 1, 1917, in Winchester, TN. Died February 24, 1994, in Beverly Hills, CA.

After naming herself after her own hit song—1939's "Dinah"—this actress and singer achieved massive media stardom in three different decades. First, thanks to timely connections with bandleader Xavier Cugat and singer-TV personality Eddie Cantor, she was a hit singer; in 1941, she earned her own radio show; and for almost 20 years, beginning in the 1950s, she hosted *The Dinah Shore Show*, one of the most popular programs on television. Though Shore's family moved to Nashville when she was six, the pop songs she sang were almost the antithesis of country-western twang. She struggled initially, failing auditions to sing for the Dorsey Brothers and Benny Goodman big bands, then got a job singing at a Long Island, New York, nightclub (which was later canceled). A chance connection with Cugat, then a big-time bandleader, became her first major break, and she used it to sing for radio networks and a well-known chamber music group. By the time Eddie Cantor hired her to sing on his popular radio program, she was ready to sing big, vibrato-filled pop standards like "Baby, It's Cold Outside" and "Buttons and Bows." Her charm was a natural for another medium, television, where she reigned as hostess, mistress of ceremonies, interviewer, and personality through the 1970s.

what to buy: Shore's recorded material comes mostly from the 1940s; the complementary collections *16 Most Requested Songs* (Sony, 1991, prod. various) and *16 Most Requested Songs: Encore* (Sony, 1995, prod. Didier C. Deutsch) show off Shore's clear-voiced, straightforward talent for standards, such as "Willow Weep for Me" and "Mad about the Boy."

what to buy next: "Buttons and Bows," a campy 1940s hit, shows up on several other hits sets, including *Best of Dinah Shore* (Curb, 1991), *Some of the Best* (Laserlight, 1996, prod. Rod McKuen), and *More of the Best* (Laserlight, 1996, prod. Rod McKuen).

what to avoid: *Greatest Hits* (Laserlight, 1994) merely duplicates the other sets on the market.

the rest:
Blues in the Night (Living Era, 1994)
Doin' What Comes Natur'lly (Sony Special Products, 1995)

worth searching for: Shore played comedian-singer-radio-host Eddie Cantor's singing straightwoman for several years, and her material comes across nicely on Cantor's hard-to-find comedy-variety album *The Show That Never Aired* (Original Cast, 1993).

influences:
◀◀ Judy Garland, Billie Holiday, Bing Crosby, Eddie Cantor

▶▶ Jo Stafford, Rosemary Clooney, Rosie O'Donnell

Steve Knopper

Bobby Short

Born September 15, 1926, in Danville, IL.

Bobby Short is a cabaret singer who respects and understands the lyric content of the songs in his vast repertoire. He's in a class by himself: impeccable dresser, stunning smile, and a husky baritone voice frequently tinged with a touch of appealing laryngitis. His piano playing shows influences of the late Nat King Cole and Art Tatum, two of his long-time friends. Short's diction, delivery, personality, and all-around *savoir faire* allow him the ability to connect and communicate with his audiences in ways unlike many other performers.

Short left Danville at age 11, with his family's blessing, to perform in vaudeville as a child singer-pianist in Chicago, 125 miles north of his home. Later he spent a year in New York City, where he got booked at various clubs, including Harlem's famous Apollo Theatre. Early in 1938 Short returned to Danville and remained there for four years while he finished high school. Then he was off to the Capitol Lounge in Chicago. In 1943 he went to Omaha, Nebraska, where he met Nat Cole; then he toured to Milwaukee where he befriended Art Tatum. The next 20 years were spent performing in clubs on both coasts, occasionally in Florida or the Midwest. In 1954 Short acquired the savvy Phil Moore as his manager and sometime music director. Short sold a tape to Atlantic Records, which subsequently landed him a recording contract. Surviving the mid-1960s club doldrums, Short replaced George Feyer at the Café Carlyle in New York City's Carlyle Hotel in 1968; he was recommended for the gig by the Erteguns at Atlantic Records. From 1968 on, Bobby Short has been presenting his stylized versions of lyrics from the Great American Songbook for four to eight months a year at this intimate Madison Avenue spot. As long as Short is performing, the works of composers Cole Porter, Rodgers and Hart, Jerome Kern, Vernon Duke, and George and Ira Gershwin are in good hands.

what to buy: *50 by Bobby Short* 𝅘𝅥𝅮𝅘𝅥𝅮𝅘𝅥𝅮𝅘𝅥𝅮𝅘𝅥𝅮 (Atlantic, 1950s–80/1986, prod. various) offers a look back on Short's recorded output from the 1950s to the 1980s. This two-CD compilation contains 50 tracks of sophistication, swing, and tasteful treatment of both evergreens and obscurities such as "Manhattan," "From This Moment On," and "I've Got Five Dollars." *Late Night at the Café Carlyle* 𝅘𝅥𝅮𝅘𝅥𝅮𝅘𝅥𝅮𝅘𝅥𝅮𝅘𝅥𝅮 (Telarc, 1992, prod. John Snyder) features 17 standards and lesser-known songs recorded by the Bobby Short Trio from June 20–22, 1991, at his comfortable home base. His swinging companions, bassist Beverly Peer and drummer Robert Scott, admirably support the singer-pianist as they ease and swing through chestnuts such as "Night and Day" and "Drop Me off in Harlem." For similar material in an 11-piece band setting, pick up *Celebrating 30 Years at the Café Carlyle* 𝅘𝅥𝅮𝅘𝅥𝅮𝅘𝅥𝅮𝅘𝅥𝅮▽ (Telarc, 1997, prod. John Snyder) reprises 14 of the songs associated with Short during his stay at the Madison Avenue nightclub, all done up in new arrangements.

what to buy next: *Swing That Music* 𝅘𝅥𝅮𝅘𝅥𝅮𝅘𝅥𝅮𝅘𝅥𝅮 (Telarc, 1993, prod. John Snyder) features Short with the Howard Alden–Dan Barrett Quintet. Short plays the role of the hot sophisticate, singing 13 songs arranged by Barrett with the quintet providing a swinging backdrop. The 1936 standard "Gone with the Wind" receives definitive handling and the rarely heard Sam Coslow/Tom Satterfield "Restless" is especially effective. Several of the other tunes are off the beaten path—including "Take Love Easy" and "Killin' Myself"—and are treated kindly by the crew. For a generous taste of Bobby Short's piano playing and a sampling of his thoughts on music, try a delightful hour of *Marian McPartland's Piano Jazz with Guest Bobby Short* 𝅘𝅥𝅮𝅘𝅥𝅮𝅘𝅥𝅮𝅘𝅥𝅮 (Jazz Alliance, 1994, prod. Shari Hutchinson). A November 10, 1986, broadcast for McPartland's National Public Radio *Piano Jazz* series, the recording documents nine musical tracks interspersed with conversation.

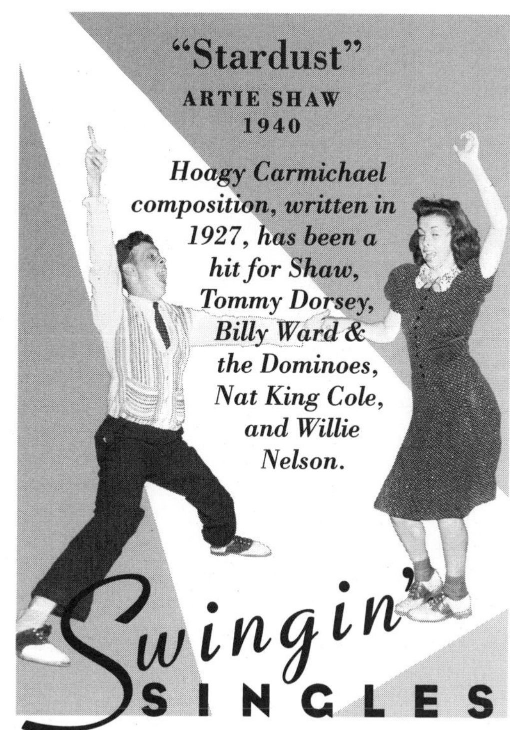
"Stardust"
ARTIE SHAW
1940
Hoagy Carmichael composition, written in 1927, has been a hit for Shaw, Tommy Dorsey, Billy Ward & the Dominoes, Nat King Cole, and Willie Nelson.
Swingin' SINGLES

the rest:
Bobby Short is K-Ra-Zy for Gershwin 𝅘𝅥𝅮𝅘𝅥𝅮𝅘𝅥𝅮𝅘𝅥𝅮▽ (Atlantic, 1959/1990)
The Mad Twenties 𝅘𝅥𝅮𝅘𝅥𝅮𝅘𝅥𝅮𝅘𝅥𝅮 (Atlantic, 1959/1994)
Bobby, Noel & Cole 𝅘𝅥𝅮𝅘𝅥𝅮𝅘𝅥𝅮𝅘𝅥𝅮 (Atlantic, 1971/1972/1989)
Celebrates Rodgers and Hart 𝅘𝅥𝅮𝅘𝅥𝅮𝅘𝅥𝅮𝅘𝅥𝅮▽ (Atlantic, 1975/1994)
Guess Who's in Town 𝅘𝅥𝅮𝅘𝅥𝅮𝅘𝅥𝅮𝅘𝅥𝅮 (Atlantic, 1987)
Songs of New York 𝅘𝅥𝅮𝅘𝅥𝅮𝅘𝅥𝅮𝅘𝅥𝅮 (Telarc, 1995)
How's Your Romance 𝅘𝅥𝅮𝅘𝅥𝅮𝅘𝅥𝅮𝅘𝅥𝅮 (Telarc, 1999)

influences:
◀◀ Mabel Mercer, Hildegarde, Nat King Cole, Art Tatum
▶▶ Ann Hampton Callaway, Nancy LaMott, Harry Connick Jr.

John T. Bitter

Frank Sinatra

Born December 12, 1915, in Hoboken, NJ. Died May 14, 1998, in Los Angeles, CA.

Although Frank Sinatra entered the public consciousness as a laid-back crooner who filled in with slow-dance ballads between the swing era's main course of jumping dance tunes, the mature Sinatra forged a swinging pop sound that is his true legacy. We can hear the sound developing in *Swing and Dance with Frank Sinatra*, a swing collection from his early Columbia Records days, and virtually every album he made for Capitol and Reprise up through the mid '60s was a swingin' affair worth having.

An only child of Italian immigrant parents, the teen-aged Sinatra began singing professionally against their wishes. He stubbornly clung to his ambitions, so his mother caved in and found him a breakthrough gig at the Rustic Cabin in Englewood, New Jersey, in the late '30s. By 1939, he had signed on with Harry James's orchestra, then moved to Tommy Dorsey's big band. Sinatra's voice jumped out of the speakers on "I'll Never Smile Again," the first vocal he recorded with Dorsey. When they played New York's famous Paramount Theater in 1942, Sinatra's effect on the crowd was electric, and the bobby-soxers swooned in their seats. Dorsey was miffed that his singer was getting a better reaction than the band. Sinatra soon left to start a solo career that changed the course of the music business, from big bands to individual star singers.

The young Sinatra sang ballads in a deceptively breathless near-whisper, holding notes with the slightest of quavers, sounding sincere and more vulnerable and sensuous than any mainstream pop singer before him. (Billie Holiday's singing was a major influence.) When his career as a crooner went bust toward the end of the '40s, he methodically reinvented himself as a mature singer (and movie actor). At age 37, he signed with Capitol Records and began to refocus his image as a swinging, rambunctious bon vivant, who sometimes got very low in the wee, small hours of the morning—and developed a confident, huskier sound to match. This was the era of the Rat Pack, the gang of entertainers that included Dean Martin, Sammy Davis Jr., Peter Lawford, and Joey Bishop. Sinatra led the way in swagger, with hat perched at a jaunty angle on his head, a loosened tie, a cigarette, and babes lined up from Las Vegas to Los Angeles. But for all the emphasis on image, there's no imitating Sinatra's talent and command: he picked his phrases carefully and told each song's story as though his way were the only way it could be told.

Despite the swagger of his approach, Sinatra maintained an interesting humility in concert, dutifully crediting the songwriters and arrangers who provided him with crucial springboard material. In the '60s, he continued to swing, but also ventured into folk-influenced contemporary pop and even soft rock. He "retired" in 1971, only to come back in 1973 and continue to release records through 1995. Although his voice was deteriorating (his upper register became raw and his pitch sometimes wavered), his interpretive skills diminished only slightly, and he remained a major concert draw until his 1995 retirement. On the 1993 *Duets* album, in which a collaboration with rock singer Bono slammed against a more conventional one with Bette Midler, the duets reportedly were overdubbed at separate sessions—suggesting that Sinatra needed studio tweaking to make coherent recordings. You can hear technology clamp down the sound as he loses his breath at the end of phrases. Still, these records were big events that extended Sinatra's hit-making punch, if not his swing, into the '90s. The media barrage immediately after his death was unprecedented, except maybe for the death of Princess Diana the previous year. "My Way" filled every airwave for weeks, dozens of tribute magazines hit the stands, sales of greatest-hits collections went through the roof, and newspapers filled entire sections with Sinatra remembrances and essays. A few months after his death, the media obtained his old FBI file, thought to contain juicy details of dalliances with mob figures, but a smoking gun never emerged.

what to buy: *The Capitol Years* (Capitol, 1990, executive prod. Ron McCarrell, Wayne Watkins, prod. Ron Furmanek) is a succinct overview of Sinatra's classic period in three CDs; his best work during this time was in collaboration with Nelson Riddle, whose arrangements on such tunes as "I've Got the World on a String" nailed the optimistic, prime-of-life feeling Sinatra brought to his singing. (Sinatra was also successful working with Gordon Jenkins, whose arrangements had a more stately, reflective feeling, and Billy May, whose arrangements swung more forcefully than Riddle's.) If the price tag for the three-CD set is too high, *Best of "The Capitol Years"* (Capitol, 1992, compilation prod. Wayne Watkins) and *Frank Sinatra: Capitol Collector's Series* (Capitol, 1989, compilation prod. Ron Furmanek) offer excellent single-CD overviews. Capitol released 23 Sinatra albums from 1953 to 1961; 16 of them were cohesive units (ushering in the era of the concept album), all collected in a box called *Concepts* (Capitol, 1992, prod. Voyle Gilmore, David Cavanaugh). You can buy them separately—all 16 are must-buys—but in CD form some questionable bonus tracks have been added. *The Complete Capitol Singles Collection* (Capitol, 1996, compilation prod. Brad Benedict, executive prod. Wayne Watkins) is a four-CD set that lives up to its title with A-sides and B-sides, many of which had not been available on CD before. *The Columbia Years (1943–1952): The Complete Recordings* (Columbia, 1993, compilation prod. Didier C. Deutsch) collects on 12 CDs the Sinatra sides that defined a new role for pop singers. They were revolutionary then and enjoyable now; a four-disc distillation called *The Best of the Columbia Years: 1943–1952* (Columbia, 1995, compilation prod. Didier C. Deutsch) came out later, for the budget-conscious.

what to buy next: *The Song Is You* (RCA, 1993, prod. Paul Williams) is the definitive collection of Sinatra's work with Tommy Dorsey, on five CDs; another version is distilled to one CD: *I'll Be Seeing You* (RCA, 1993, prod. Paul Williams). Then, there's *The Reprise Collection* (Reprise, 1990, compilation prod. Mo Ostin, Joe McEwen, James Isaacs), which isn't as satisfying as the collections of earlier work, but presents a picture of adventurous maturity. The four-CD set is overlong, yet it covers a much longer time period than the Capitol collection—from a 1960 recording of "Let's Fall in Love" to a 1986 recording of "Mack the Knife." In 1991, Reprise released the condensed, single-CD *Sinatra Reprise: The Very Good Years* (Reprise, 1991, compilation prod. Mo Ostin, Joe McEwen, James Isaacs), then went the other way, with *The Complete Reprise Studio Recordings* (Reprise, 1995, compilation prod. Mo Ostin, Joe McEwen, James Isaacs) on 20 discs. Yikes! Definite musts for swing fans are the albums Ol' Blue Eyes recorded with Count Basie—*Sinatra/Basie* (Reprise, 1963/1988) and *Sinatra at the Sands* (Reprise, 1966/1998, prod. Sonny Burke).

what to avoid: *Duets* (Capitol, 1993, prod. Phil Ramone) and *Duets II* (Capitol, 1994, prod. Phil Ramone) may have revived Sinatra's recording career, but they consist of mostly meaningless (and chemistry-less) re-recordings. This is said with infinite sadness. For the first time in his career, Sinatra had to depend on others to carry him. Even the posthumous *Limited Edition Sinatra Duets and Duets II* (Capitol, 1998, prod. Phil Ramone, Steve Johnson) just adds a bonus CD of a radio special about the making of the *Duets* albums. For two-thirds of the over-ambitious *Trilogy* (Reprise, 1980, prod. Sonny Burke), Sinatra summed up where he was in the late '70s. The gorgeous Nelson Riddle arrangement of George Harrison's "Something" and the swaggering "Theme from *New York, New York*" became virtual signature tunes of the early autumn of Sinatra's career. Conceived as a three-LP look at the past, present, and the future, Sinatra could have skipped the future part, which is goofy at best, ponderous at worst. A boiled-down, single album from these sessions could have been dynamite. Also, *All-Time Greatest Hits, Vols.1–4* (RCA, late 1980s) is a poorly done collection of Sinatra's work with Dorsey.

best of the rest:

Songs for Swingin' Lovers! (Capitol, 1956/1997)
A Swingin' Affair! (Capitol, 1957/1991)
Come Fly with Me (Capitol, 1957/1987)
Where Are You? (Capitol, 1957/1991)
(Frank Sinatra Sings for) Only the Lonely (Capitol, 1958/1996)
Come Dance with Me! (Capitol, 1958/1987)
No One Cares (Capitol, 1959/1991)
Nice 'N' Easy (Capitol, 1960/1991)
Sinatra's Swingin' Session!!! (Capitol, 1960/1987)
September of My Years (Reprise, 1965/1988)
Francis Albert Sinatra and Antonio Carlos Jobim (Reprise, 1967/1988)
Francis A. Sinatra & Edward K. Ellington (Reprise, 1968/1988)
V-Discs (Columbia, 1994)
Sinatra and Sextet: Live in Paris (Reprise, 1994)
Swing and Dance with Frank Sinatra (Columbia Legacy, 1996)
Portrait of Sinatra (Columbia, 1997)
Frank Sinatra with the Red Norvo Quartet: Live in Australia 1959 (Blue Note, 1997)
The Popular Frank Sinatra, Sinatra & Dorsey, Vols. 1–3 (RCA, 1998)

worth searching for: There's a wealth of radio, TV, and concert performances available on small labels that aren't often easy to find at your local CD store. The place to start is with such '40s material as *The Unheard Frank Sinatra, Vols. 1–4* (VJC, 1990), and then such '50s material as *Perfectly Frank* (BCD, 1990). The Sinatra-searcher's grail is *From the Vaults*, a 750-copy pressing that's almost impossible to track down.

influences:

◀◀ Billie Holiday, Bing Crosby, Russ Columbo, Louis Armstrong, Nelson Riddle, Duke Ellington, Cole Porter, Al Jolson, Rudy Vallee

▶▶ Tony Bennett, Harry Connick Jr., Vic Damone, Rosemary Clooney, Jo Stafford, Bono, Billy Joel, Bruce Springsteen, Eddie Fisher, Nancy Sinatra, Frank Sinatra Jr.

Salvatore Caputo

Frank Sinatra Jr.

Born 1943.

Best known as a kidnapping victim, the son of Frank Sinatra has been a celebrity all his life. But as a singer, he has been something of a joke, a limited imitator of his father blessed with similar mannerisms, the all-important Sinatra name, and none of his father's talent, voice, or preternatural sense of phrasing. At the end of 1963, when he was only 19, Sinatra Jr. was snatched from a Lake Tahoe motel and held in the San Fernando Valley. The kidnappers demanded a ransom of $240,000 from his father. Lawmen like Robert Kennedy and J. Edgar Hoover, as well as outlaws like Sam Giancana, offered to help. The kidnappers were quickly apprehended, tried, convicted, and sentenced. One of them, Barry Keenan, is now a successful Los Angeles-area businessman. Meanwhile, for the past several years, Frank Jr. has been leader of several touring big bands that play almost exclusively standards, including the ones Frank Sr. made famous. Still, Frank Jr. would not even merit a footnote without his father's legacy. With it, and with his father spreading those coattails wide both in life (Ol' Blue Eyes invited his son to sing with him on the 1991 *Duets* album) and after life (his 1998 death trig-

Noble Sissle (l) and Eubie Blake **(Archive Photos)**

gered renewed interest in the Sinatra name), Frank Jr. is still only a footnote, albeit an interesting one.

what to buy: *As I Remember It* ♪♪♪♪ (Angel, 1996) finds Frank covering Frank, with Sinatra *fils* offering his versions of Sinatra *pere*'s "Night and Day," "I've Got the World on a String," "Three Coins in a Fountain," and "In the Wee Small Hours of the Morning." Not essential by any means, but given the crushing weight of history, not too shabby.

what to buy next: Young Blue Eyes is the centerpiece of Pat Longo's Super Big Band's record *Billy May for President* ♪♪♪ (Townhall Records, 1983, prod. Lincoln Mayorga), a tribute to the venerable jazz arranger and Sinatra collaborator. Here, son takes on a set of mostly originals, and even contributes a song of his own, "Missy."

what to avoid: It seems unfair to point out the lowlights in a recording career as sparse as Sinatra Jr.'s, but his two pallid, neo-conservative guest vocals on Louise Baranger's *Trumpeter's Prayer* ♪♪ (Summit, 1976) demonstrate everything that's wrong with Sinatra.

worth searching for: After cooking up dream projects for vocalists like Iggy Pop and Ozzy Osbourne, Detroit avant-funksters Was (Not Was) assembled an incredibly weird group of musicians for *What Up Dog?* ♪♪♪♪ (Chrysalis, 1988, prod. Don Was, David Was, Paul Staveley O'Duffy). Guitar shredder Stevie Salas is here, along with organ legend Al Kooper, jazz bassist Marcus Miller, horn star Mark Isham—and Frank Sinatra Jr., warbling his way through the Sinatra parody "Wedding Vows in Vegas."

influences:

◄◄ Frank Sinatra

Ben Greenman

Noble Sissle

Born July 10, 1889, in Indianapolis, IN. Died December 17, 1975, in Tampa, FL.

Noble Sissle, along with Eubie Blake, revitalized black musical theater, and helped set the stage for the big swing revolution of the '20s and '30s. During the early 20th century, Sissle scrambled around in vaudeville as a singer, pianist, and songwriter. With Blake he wrote "It's All Your Fault," a hit for the legendary Sophie Tucker, before they joined James Reese Europe's orchestra. Europe's band was the first to break the color barrier in New York nightclubs and showrooms, and its wild, syncopated jazz made it the toast of cafe society. When World War I broke out, Sissle and many other musicians enlisted with Europe and fought in an all-black regiment, the Hellfighters, known for their fierce combat style. Eventually, the Hellfighters were formed into a serviceable military orchestra that entertained its fellow soldiers at home and abroad. They made more than two dozen popular recordings for the Pathe company and were quite renowned for their jazzy renditions of traditional military styles. After being chewed out for making mistakes on the bandstand, a resentful drummer stabbed Europe to death, and Sissle took over leadership of the band until the end of the war. During the early '20s, Sissle reteamed with Blake to write and produce the landmark variety shows *Shufflin' Along* and *Chocolate Dandies*, which launched the careers of Florence Mills and Josephine Baker. These shows featured an all-black cast, capitalized on the public's fascination with jazz and ragtime music, and spawned many hits that have become classics—among them, "I'm Just Wild about Harry," "Love Will Find a Way," and "You Were Meant for Me."

Throughout the '20s, Sissle and Blake also recorded as a team, racking up sizable hits with "Arkansas" and "Down-Hearted Blues." The duo also appeared in many early short musical films ("soundies") before Sissle formed his own orchestra and moved to England. When Sissle returned to America, he started a new swing band, which at one time or another featured such great sidemen as Sidney Bechet, Charlie Parker, and the young singer Lena Horne. Its 1931 hit "Got the Bench, Got the Park" became a standard and was a springboard for several other big-sellers in the Depression era. Sissle's outfit remained popular until he disbanded it in the early '50s to concentrate on music publishing. Though he occasionally reunited with Blake for special appearances, Sissle's main claim to fame during the '60s was as a club owner and the first black DJ at New York's WMGW radio.

what's available: Sissle is one of the featured vocalists on *James Reese Europe's 369th U.S. Infantry "Hellfighters" Band* 𝅘𝅥𝅮𝅘𝅥𝅮𝅘𝅥𝅮𝅘𝅥𝅮 (Memphis Archives, 1996, prod. Richard James Hite), a unique collection of 24 World War I–era military recordings that sound anything but military. The syncopated rhythms and jazzy horns bring timeless life to a series of rags, blues, and popular tunes which prefigured the upcoming swing explosion. Sissle croons the classics "How Ya Gonna Keep 'Em Down on the Farm," "When the Bees Make Honey," and "Jazzola" in grand, old-timey style. The sound quality is excellent when you consider these recordings were remastered from decades-old cylinders and rare Pathe vertical discs.

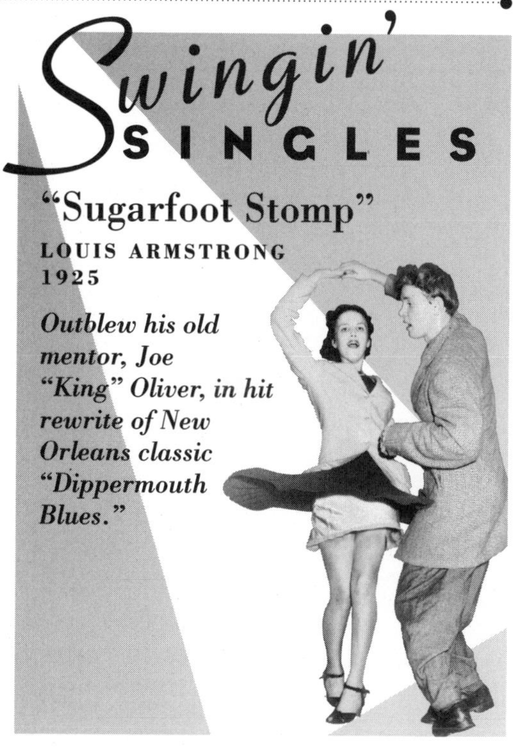
Swingin' SINGLES
"Sugarfoot Stomp"
LOUIS ARMSTRONG
1925
Outblew his old mentor, Joe "King" Oliver, in hit rewrite of New Orleans classic "Dippermouth Blues."

worth searching for: Many prime sides by Sissle's orchestra are on *Noble Sissle & His Sizzling Syncopators (1930–1931)* 𝅘𝅥𝅮𝅘𝅥𝅮𝅘𝅥𝅮 (Fat Cat Jazz, 1986). Also, *Sissle & Blake: Early Rare Recordings* 𝅘𝅥𝅮𝅘𝅥𝅮𝅘𝅥𝅮½ (Stash, 1980) is a collection of classic collaborations by two seminal jazz and swing innovators. Both may be found in shops specializing in out-of-print and collectible releases.

influences:

◀◀ W.C. Handy, James Reese Europe, Eubie Blake, Luckey Roberts

▶▶ Sidney Bechet, Josephine Baker, Pearl Bailey, Lena Horne, Nat King Cole, Charlie Parker

see also: *Eubie Blake*

Ken Burke

Keely Smith

See: Louis Prima & Keely Smith

Stuff Smith

Born Hezekiah Leroy Gordon Smith, August 14, 1909, in Portsmouth, OH. Died September 25, 1967, in Munich, Germany.

Violinist Stuff Smith, who led Fats Waller's band after the pianist died in 1943, was an extraordinary fiddler whose performances lit up Manhattan's thriving jazz scene on 52nd street in the mid-'30s. He developed a hot, swinging style, hoarse-toned and raucous, contrasting vastly with the European-gypsy influences of peers such as Stephane Grappelli. Smith studied early with his father and performed in the family band; by age 15, he was working as a professional musician. Smith lived in Buffalo for several years, then moved to New York in 1936, where, playing amplified violin, he led a quintet at the famed Onyx Club. Impresario Norman Granz recorded several exceptional 1950s Verve sessions with Smith. The violinist toured extensively during the 1960s and settled in Copenhagen in 1965, two years before he died.

what to buy: Guitarist Herb Ellis and the older Smith come together again on the appropriately titled *Together!* (Epic, 1963/Koch Classics, 1995, prod. John Hammond), a reissue of the duo's spunky Hollywood studio session produced by the legendary Columbia talent scout John Hammond. Ellis interacts pleasingly with Stuff and injects some hard-swinging, mellifluous solos, but Stuff's stuff and Bob Enevoldsen's valve trombone solos steal the scene.

what to buy next: On the compilation *Violins No End* (Pablo, 1957/Original Jazz Classics, 1996, prod. Norman Granz), Smith is on three of the seven tracks recorded live in a 1957 concert with Oscar Peterson (piano), Herb Ellis (guitar), Ray Brown (bass), and Jo Jones (drums). Smith often plays chordal harmonies, and swings hot and hard on the seven minutes of "Desert Sands," one of the album's highlights. Smith also delivers a waltz-to-swing version of "How High the Moon" and shows supreme mastery of his instrument on the ballad "Moonlight in Vermont."

influences:

◀◀ A. J. Piron, Joe Venuti, Claude Willliams, Stephane Grappelli, Eddie South

▶▶ Ray Nance, Tom Morley, John Frigo, Vassar Clements, Matt Glaser, Randy Sabien

Nancy Ann Lee

Warren Smith

Born February 2, 1933, in Humphries County, MS. Died January 30, 1980, in Longview, TX.

Though overshadowed by the other great rockabilly artists from Sun Records, Warren Smith was as fine a vocalist as any of them. He could hiccup and wail Elvis Presley–style rock 'n' roll, bring visceral elements of the blues to honky-tonk ballads like Carl Perkins, and emote folk-tinged regret à la Johnny Cash. After his discharge from the air force, Smith began performing at the Cotton Club in Memphis with Clyde Leoppard and His Snearly Ranch Boys. Band member Stan Kessler (who co-wrote "I Forgot to Remember to Forget" for Presley) brought him to Sun head Sam Phillips with the intention of recording the plaintive country ballad "I'd Rather Be Safe Than Sorry." Coincidentally, Johnny Cash was looking for someone to record a song he had written (or bought) titled "Rock 'n' Roll Ruby." Smith tackled both numbers with verve and style, and the resulting record hit #1 in Memphis, becoming the biggest-selling debut disc in Sun history. Smith's living, pulsating waxings, such as "Ubangi Stomp" and "Got Love If You Want It," didn't make a dent outside the mid-South. The good-looking Smith should have been a star, but his fortunes suffered due to the limited resources at Sun, which was concentrating all its efforts on the booming career of Jerry Lee Lewis. Subsequently, Smith gave up on rock 'n' roll and returned to his first love, country music. "I Don't Believe I'll Fall in Love Today" and "Odds and Ends (Bits and Pieces)" became top-10 country smashes at Liberty Records, and Smith was finally living the life of a country star. He appeared on *Louisiana Hayride* and *The Grand Ole Opry*, and toured in major package shows. He recorded several more chart singles until 1965, when a car accident derailed his career. By the late '60s, an addiction to prescription drugs, a jail term, and Smith's own difficult personality had driven him from the music business. He re-emerged during the late '70s, recording for the Swedish Lake Country label and basking in the European rockabilly revival until his death.

what to buy: You'll be surprised at how many great songs and performances are on *Ubangi Stomp: The Very Best of Warren Smith* (Collectables, 1999, prod. Sam Phillips, Jack Clement), a powerful collection of Smith's best country and rockabilly sides for Sun Records, including such gems as "Uranium Rock," "I Like Your Kinda Love," and "Red Cadillac and a Black Moustache."

worth searching for: The out-of-print *Uranium Rock: The Best of Warren Smith* (AVI, 1995, compilation prod. Patti Drosins) is still in some catalogs and store racks. The 31-song import *Classic Recordings 1956–1959* (Bear Family, 1992, reissue prod. Colin Escott), encompasses everything Smith cut for the Sun label, including alternate takes and some of the moodier country numbers not on the Collectables or AVI sets. Smith's run of successful country sides at Liberty are on *Call of the Wild* (Bear Family, 1990, compilation prod. Richard Weize), a 30-song German import that boasts the hits "That's Why I Sing in a Honkytonk," "Odds and Ends," and many others.

influences:

◄◄ Carl Perkins, Johnny Cash, Hank Snow, Elvis Presley

►► Jack Scott, Jerry Jaye, Billy "Crash" Craddock

Ken Burke

Lavay Smith & Her Red Hot Skillet Lickers

Formed 1989, in San Francisco, CA.

Lavay Smith, vocals; Chris Siebert, piano and leader-arranger; Bill Stewart, alto/tenor saxophones; Harvey Robb, tenor/alto saxophones; Noel Jewkes, tenor/baritone saxophones, clarinet; Larry Leight, trombone; Charlie Siebert, guitar; Bing Nathan, string bass; Dan Foltz, drums.

Lavay Smith & Her Red Hot Skillet Lickers is much more than the novelty band the name suggests. The nine-member unit is one of the best swing/jump-blues bands around, established long before the neo-swing movement. Drawing their name from an obscure 1920s–1930s Smithsonian Collection recording by the Skillet Lickers, the modern-day Skillet Lickers evolved out of Bo Grumpus, an old-time jazz/ragtime band in which vocalist Lavay Smith (she doesn't reveal her real name) and pianist-arranger Siebert performed. Among the intergenerational (ages 27 to 74) crew's strengths are Smith's sultry blues-bred vocals and Siebert's solid arrangements of classics by Ella Fitzgerald, Billie Holiday, Bessie Smith, Dinah Washington, and Louis Jordan. The Skillet Lickers play regularly at the San Francisco jazz club Cafe du Nord and other venues, including the festival circuit. By December 1998, their 1996 recording debut on Fat Note Records had sold about 20,000 copies.

what's available: *One Hour Mama* (Fat Note, 1996, prod. Chris Siebert) serves 48 minutes of jump blues, swing, and leader Chris Siebert's swell boogie-woogie piano, with tightly arranged horns and improvised solos adding to the seasoned sound of this nine-musician group. Containing hints of Billie Holiday's bittersweet tones, Ella Fitzgerald's little-girl qualities, and enough blues-whammy to compete with that other Smith (Bessie), Smith's voice sounds like she just stepped out of a 1940s Philco radio. You'll enjoy "Oo Poppa Do" for Smith's vocals, "What's the Matter with You" for Siebert's barrelhouse boogie-woogie piano, Fat Waller's "Squeeze Me" for its seductiveness, and Count Basie's "Goin' to Chicago Blues" for its stately swing.

influences:

◄◄ Louis Armstrong, Bessie Smith, Billie Holiday, Dinah Washington, Duke Ellington, Count Basie, Benny Carter, Johnny Hodges, Fats Waller, Teddy Wilson, Louis Jordan

Nancy Ann Lee

Muggsy Spanier

Born Francis Joseph Spanier, November 9, 1906, in Chicago, IL. Died February 12, 1967, in Sausalito, CA.

Cornetist Muggsy Spanier was a fixture in popular big bands in the '30s and '40s, playing with Ted Lewis, Ben Pollack, and Bob Crosby before running his own successful outfit between 1941 and 1943. The band peaked commercially in 1943, when "Two O'Clock Jump" narrowly missed the Top 20. Spanier, who also helped nurture the Dixieland revival in the late '30s, played late in his career in small jazz groups and with famed bandleader Earl "Fatha" Hines. A vigorous, if predictable, melody-based player who began his professional career in 1921, Spanier became one of Chicago's finest, performing with dance bands there until 1929. Later, he helped develop the Chicago swing style with the school of white musicians, including tenor saxman Bud Freeman and guitarist/banjo player Eddie Condon. Spanier was present on many famous recording sessions by the Chicago Rhythm Kings with Red McKenzie, among others. But when the Depression hit, he and scores of other musicians were looking for work. Spanier soloed with various bands, played overseas, and appeared in two films in 1929 and 1935. While playing a gig in New Orleans at the end of 1936, Spanier became ill (some sources say it was too much alcohol; others claim he had surgery for a serious illness) and was hospitalized at the Touro Infirmary in New Orleans. Upon his recovery, he returned to Chicago, where he opened with his eight-piece Ragtime Band (considered his best band by historians) at the Sherman Hotel's Old Town Room in 1939. The group recorded 16 RCA Bluebird singles, later dubbed "the Great 16" because they virtually defined the Dixieland revival movement and made the band popular in the U.S. and Europe. Although his group performed in Chicago and New York, the demand for big bands was increasing, and the small group disbanded for lack of work after 18 months. Although he wasn't in best of health later in life, Spanier played the Newport Festival in 1964 and a few other gigs.

what to buy: Spanier's only available domestic CD, *The Ragtime Band Sessions* (Bluebird, 1939/BMG, 1995, reissue prod. Orrin Keepnews), contains lovingly restored, rare reissues of "the Great 16," the classic jazz tunes that made his Ragtime Band popular. Sound quality is perfect as Spanier delivers his brawny big-tone solos and melody leads that inspired his sidemen and lifted the swinging band off the ground.

worth searching for: The danceable CDs *Muggshot* (ASV, 1924–42/1993), *Muggsy Spanier 1939–1942* (Jazz Chronological Classics, 1939–42/1994), and *Muggsy Spanier 1944* (Jazz Chronological Classics, 1944/1997) are imports, but they're usually available in jazz-focused music chains such as Borders and Tower.

Muggsy Spanier **(Archive Photos)**

influences:

Joe "King" Oliver, Louis Armstrong

Nancy Ann Lee

Squirrel Nut Zippers

Formed 1993, in Chapel Hill, NC.

Tom Maxwell, guitar, horns, vocals; James Mathus, guitar, piano, vocals; Katherine Whalen, banjo, vocals; Chris Phillips, drums; Ken Mosher, horns, guitar, vocals; Stacy Guess, trumpet (1993–95); Je Widenhouse, trumpet (1996–present); Don Raleigh, bass (1993–96); Stu Cole, bass (1996–present).

The Squirrel Nut Zippers originally came together as a lark—people from a wide variety of alternative rock bands playing prohibition-vintage "hot jazz." Somehow, they wound up as the unwilling breakthrough act for the '90s swing revival, mostly because they dressed the part; they're actually much closer to Dixieland jazz than anybody's definition of "swing." Certainly, the Zippers' shtick is one with a great deal of inherent commercial appeal, although you'd figure it would only get them as far as NPR rather than MTV. Yet MTV was precisely where the Zippers found themselves in 1997 with the Calypso shout-along "Hell." That song was omnipresent enough to earn the quintessentially '90s seal of approval, getting sampled on a rap single (Funkdoobiest's "Papi Chulo"). It also resulted in one of the unlikeliest platinum albums in recent memory, thereby creating a slot on radio playlists for bands with horn sections and vintage wardrobes.

what to buy: *Hot* (Mammoth, 1996, prod. Brian Paulson, Mike Napolitano) is the album that benefitted from the hit status of the aforementioned single "Hell," and it's a wonderful record. Recorded in New Orleans for that Crescent City feel, the album also works in a bit of Memphis and Las Vegas—and swings with a vengeance. The Bessie Smith–styled "Put a Lid on It" stands as Katherine Whalen's finest on-record vocal moment. While not quite as solid as *Hot*, the full-length debut *The Inevitable Squirrel Nut Zippers* (Mammoth, 1995, prod. Brian Paulson) is still tremendous fun. The group's chemistry was evident even then, a balance between Whalen's Betty Boop, James Mathus's loose-limbed soul man, and Tom Maxwell's Fred Schneider (of the B-52's). Actor/director Ben Stiller selected the sly *Inevitable* ballad "Anything but Love" as backing music to play over the opening credits to his 1995 comedy *Flirting With Disaster*, by the way.

what to buy next: Judging from the crankier tone of *Perennial Favorites* (Mammoth, 1998, prod. Mike Napolitano), success has not been entirely agreeable for the Zippers. The video to the album's very pointed lead single, "Suits Are Picking Up the Bill," depicts the band members being offered up as a cannibalistic sacrifice (with Chapel Hill kindred spirit Ben Folds putting in an amusing cameo as the next victim in line). But *Perennial Favorites* still has much to recommend it, especially the light-touch swing ballad "Evening at Lafitte's" and the remarkable voodoo klezmer "Ghost of Stephen Foster." More easygoing is *Sold Out* (Mammoth, 1997, prod. various), a rough but nevertheless charming stopgap live EP. It closes with a handful of unlisted tracks, including the hilarious "Santa Claus Is Smoking Reefer" and some nifty old radio spots for Squirrel Nut Zippers candy, from whence came the group's name.

the rest:

Roasted Right (Merge EP, 1993)
Christmas Caravan (Mammoth, 1998)

worth searching for: Prior to forming the Zippers, Mathus played in the twangy rockabilly band Metal Flake Mother, which left behind the album *Beyond the Java Sea* (Moist, 1991/Hep Cat, 1997, prod. Lou Giordano). Maxwell played drums in the art-rock band What Peggy Wants, whose lone album *Death of a Sailor* (Moist, 1992, prod. Tim Harper) will probably have you scratching your head wondering how he got from there to the Zippers. Drummer Chris Phillips can also be heard on the Two Dollar Pistols' *On Down the Track* (Scrimshaw, 1997, prod. John Plymale), a fabulous album of straight honky-tonk à la Lefty Frizzell. Go figure.

solo outings:

James Mathus:

Jas. Mathus & His Knock-Down Society Play Songs for Rosetta (Mammoth, 1997)

Katherine Whalen:

Katherine Whalen & Her Jazz Squad N/A (Mammoth, 1999)

influences:

B-52's, Red Clay Ramblers, Fats Waller, Louis Prima, Bessie Smith, Billie Holiday, Django Reinhardt

Asylum Street Spankers, Blue Rags

David Menconi

Jo Stafford /Jonathan & Darlene Edwards

Born November 12, 1919, in Coalinga, CA.

Though Jo Stafford's smooth, no-vibrato crooning tone occasionally sounds as serious as Frank Sinatra's "Angel Eyes," she always maintained a terrific underlying sense of humor and camp. In addition to her specialty—solemn romantic ballads, such as 1952's two-million-selling "You Belong to Me"—Stafford sang under aliases, such as Darlene Edwards or Cinderella G. Stump. (Stump's first novelty hit, "Timtayshun," a parody of the earlier standard "Temptation," was so convincing that even diehard Stafford fans didn't recognize—or believe—that their heroine was singing. Edwards, wife of pianist Paul "Jonathan Edwards" Weston, had a blast missing notes and cutting up on record.) After a stint as a teen singer in the Pied Pipers, Stafford hooked up with Tommy Dorsey's big band and developed her straightforward, no-frills singing tone to go with the bandleader's trombone. (Her first recorded solo song, with Dorsey, was "Little Man with a Candy Cigar.") Before long, she became one of the country's most beloved female crooners, singing such hits as "You Belong to Me" and "I'll Be Seeing You," and competing with Dinah Shore as a radio and television star. She got to work with Benny Goodman, Harry James, Lionel Hampton, Buddy Rich, and Duke Ellington, to name just a few swing heroes, before she retired in the 1960s.

what to buy: Stafford was mainly known as a pop singer, especially during World War II, but even at her peak she drew on her roots as a singer fronting big bands. Many of her most swinging albums are out of print; an exception is *The "Big Band" Sound* (Corinthian), which drops her voice seamlessly between a multitude of horns and veteran soloists from the Tommy Dorsey, Glenn Miller, Benny Goodman, and other big-name bands.

what to buy next: A massive three-disc box, *The Portrait Edition* (Sony Special Products, 1994, prod. various) has absolutely everything, but non-obsessives may opt for *16 Most Requested Songs* (Columbia/Legacy, 1995, prod. various), which includes crucial hits like "Jambalaya," "Shrimp Boats," and "If." *Capitol Collector's Series* (Alliance, 1991/1996, prod. Ron Furmanek, Bob Furmanek) focuses more on Stafford's serious stuff, including "I Love You" and "It Could Happen to You," and it's a nice supplement to the more prominent greatest-hits collections.

what to avoid: It's unclear whether Stafford understands the concept of "American folk singer" on *Jo Stafford Sings American Folk Songs* (Corinthian, 1993), in which she uses a full big-band ensemble to augment woodsy heartland classics like "Shenandoah," "Old Joe Clark," and "Cripple Creek." Also, *Greatest Hits* (Curb, 1993), a collection of Stafford's Capitol songs from the '40s, isn't quite as thorough as Corinthian's greatest-hits collection of a year later.

the rest:
G.I. Jo: Jo Stafford Sings Songs of World War II (Corinthian)
Drifting and Dreaming with Jo Stafford (Jazz Classics, 1950/1996)
Jo + Jazz (Corinthian, 1987)
Coming Back Like a Song (Living Era, 1988)
Broadway Revisited (Corinthian, 1991)
Greatest Hits (Corinthian, 1994)
International Hits (Corinthian, 1994)
Music of My Life (Corinthian, 1994)
America's Most Versatile Singing Star (Corinthian, 1994)
Spotlight on . . . Jo Stafford (Alliance, 1996)
They Say It's Wonderful (Sony Special Products, 1996)
The One and Only Jo Stafford (EMI, 1997)
V-Disc Recordings (Collectors' Choice, 1998)

worth searching for: Camp-happy couple Jonathan and Darlene Edwards's sense of fun is infectious, and rare when you're listening to mid-century pop crooners, so *Jonathan and Darlene's Greatest Hits* (Corinthian, prod. various) and *Jonathan and Darlene's Greatest Hits, Vol. 2* (Corinthian, prod. various) are still valuable lighthearted collections.

influences:
◄ Dinah Shore, Frank Sinatra, Judy Garland, Benny Goodman, Tommy Dorsey

► Rosemary Clooney, Patsy Cline, k.d. lang, Sinéad O'Connor, Doris Day

Steve Knopper

Kay Starr

Born Katherine LaVerne Starks, July 21, 1922, in Dougherty, OK.

Had Starr not been a pop crooner who emulated Jo Stafford and Margaret Whiting, she might have made it as a clear-voiced blues belter. Though her songs were mostly pop standards, including Cole Porter's "Allez-Vous-En" and Hoagy Carmichael's "Lazy River," she sang them deep and warm, like a more debutante-ish Patsy Cline or a less salacious Bessie Smith. Born to Native American parents—though not on a reservation, as some 1940s publicists suggested—Katherine Starks began singing as a child to chickens in a family-owned henhouse. A supportive aunt entered her in a radio station's talent contest, which she won, then moved with her parents to Memphis (which may account for the country and blues influences). Inevitably, her singing talent drifted to the right people's ears, and by the late 1930s she was working with bandleaders Joe Venuti, Bob Crosby, Wingy Manone, and even Glenn Miller. After replacing Lena Horne in Charlie Barnet's band, then battling pneumonia for a year, she went solo in 1946 and quickly signed a deal with Capitol Records. Singing older jazz material, Starr started reeling off hits, including 1948's "So Tired" and Pee Wee King's country song, "Bonaparte's Retreat," which led to a collaboration with singer Tennessee Ernie Ford. Unafraid to try any pop-music trend, the versatile-voiced Starr had big country, waltz, rock 'n' roll, jazz, and even polka hits through the 1950s.

what to buy: *Capitol Collector's Series* (Capitol, 1991, compilation prod. Bob Furmanek, Ron Furmanek) generously tours Starr's 1940s material, and you can hear her growing slowly more confident as she shifts from straightforward pop ("You Were Only

Kay Starr **(Archive Photos)**

Fooling (While I Was Falling in Love)") to country ("I'll Never Be Free," with her frequent duet partner Ford) to a superb amalgamation of both (her masterful hit "Wheel of Fortune").

what to buy next: *Greatest Hits* ♪♪♪ (Curb, 1991, prod. various) includes "Wheel of Fortune," of course, and tours material from Starr's hitmaking 1950s years with RCA, so it's more diverse but less thorough than the Capitol set.

what to avoid: *Spotlight on Kay Starr* ♪♪♪ (Capitol/EMI, 1995, prod. various) is a less impressive synthesis of the same Capitol material.

best of the rest:
The Uncollected Kay Starr: In the 1940s ♪♪♪♪ (Hindsight, 1990)
The Uncollected Kay Starr: Vol. 2 ♪♪♪ (Hindsight, 1992)
Back to the Roots ♪♪♪ (Crescendo, 1996)
Them There Eyes ♪♪♪ (Pickwick, 1997)

worth searching for: Starr's early material, which leaned on old, old songs even by 1940s pop standards, are documented on *Back to the Roots* ♪♪♪ (GNP/Crescendo, 1996, prod. various), including "Exactly Like You" and "When a Woman Loves a Man."

influences:
◀ Margaret Whiting, Jo Stafford, Tennessee Ernie Ford, Roy Acuff, Bessie Smith, Judy Garland
▶ Rosemary Clooney, Vic Damone, Jack Jones, Liza Minnelli

Steve Knopper

Dakota Staton

Born Aliyah Rabia, June 3, 1931, in Pittsburgh, PA.

Though she frequently sang jazz and blues material, Dakota Staton's clear, charismatic voice made her a crooner worthy of Rosemary Clooney, Margaret Whiting, or any of the other female vocal stars of the '50s. She's best known for her version of Stan Getz's "Misty" and a superb collaboration with pianist George Shearing in 1958, but she was an excellent pop standards singer—her takes on the Gershwins' "Someone to Watch Over Me" and "I Can't Get Started" are some of the songs' definitive readings. As Staton aged, her voice grew deeper and more commanding and she tended to record more soulful, jazz-oriented albums.

what to buy: Staton's best two original albums, *Dakota Staton at Storyville* ♪♪♪♪ (Capitol, 1962/Collectables, 1994) and *The Late, Late Show* ♪♪♪♪ (Capitol, 1957/Collectables, 1994), have happily made it to CD stores. Staton is still in showtune mode, despite the jazzy piano backing, belting "Broadway" (not to be confused with the more famous "On Broadway") with clarity and command.

best of the rest:
More Than the Most ♪♪♪ (Collectables, 1994)
Spotlight on . . . Dakota Staton ♪♪♪ (Gold Rush, 1996/1997)

worth searching for: Staton's two tracks on *Sweet and Lovely: Capitol's Great Ladies of Song* ♪♪♪♪ (Capitol, 1992, prod. Brad Benedict) place her among some of the most famous crooners of her era, including Betty Hutton, Jo Stafford, Dinah Washington, Dinah Shore, and Judy Garland. She handles the Gershwins' "Someone to Watch Over Me" and "I Can't Get Started" nicely, distinguishing them with a natural swing the other singers lack.

influences:
◀ Billie Holiday, Etta James, Jo Stafford, Nancy Wilson
▶ Rosemary Clooney, Blossom Dearie, Cleo Laine

Steve Knopper

Rex Stewart

Born February 22, 1907, in Philadelphia, PA. Died September 7, 1967, in Los Angeles, CA.

Rex Stewart was one of the great trumpeters of the 1930s, a hard-blowing player who made up for his technical limitations with a huge bag of half-valve effects that allowed him to approximate human speech. His ability to play highly expressive, squeezed, and bent notes with great musical flair made him a key element in Duke Ellington's orchestras of the 1930s and 1940s. Stewart's family moved to Washington, D.C., in 1914 and he got his start playing on riverboats plying the Potomac. His idol was Louis Armstrong, but early on he realized he didn't have the technique to imitate Satchmo, so he began developing his energetic approach. He played with Elmer Snowden in 1925 and replaced Armstrong in the Fletcher Henderson Orchestra in 1926; he soon quit because he felt he wasn't ready for the gig and joined (Fletcher's brother) Horace Henderson's band at Wilberforce College. He rejoined Fletcher's band in 1928 and stayed for five years as a featured soloist in what was still the country's leading jazz orchestra. Stewart joined Ellington in 1934 and stayed through the orchestra's greatest years, leaving in 1945. Ellington quickly incorporated Stewart's unique "talking" style into the band's palette and featured his cornet work in many tunes. He toured extensively with Jazz at the Philharmonic between 1947 and 1951, partly dropped out of jazz in the middle of the decade, then led a Fletcher Henderson reunion band from 1957 to 1958. He was a regular at Eddie Condon's club from 1958 to 1959, and then settled on the West Coast. Working as a disc jockey and as a critic he began writing for *Down Beat*. His profiles have been collected in *Jazz Masters of the '30s*, one of the first and still best books on jazz written by a jazz musician. Named after one of his biggest hits with

Ellington, his wonderful, self-deprecating autobiography, *Boy Meets Horn*, was published posthumously.

what to buy: A two-disc collection of Ellington side projects recorded between 1934 and 1938, *The Duke's Men: Small Groups, Vol. 1* ♪♪♪♪♪ (Columbia/Legacy, 1991, prod. Helen Oakley) features Stewart on about 12 of the 45 tracks, including four excellent tunes (three by Stewart) with Duke at the piano.

what to buy next: Made up of three small-group Ellington sidemen sessions originally recorded for HRS, *Rex Stewart and the Ellingtonians* ♪♪♪♪ (Riverside/Original Jazz Classics, 1990, prod. various) contains a light, Dixieland feel on the 1940 septet session and Stewart's unique, highly expressive trumpet style on the 1946 quartet tracks. *Trumpet Jive!* ♪♪♪♪ (Prestige, 1992, prod. Esmond Edwards) was an album Stewart recorded in 1944–45 with the fine traditional-jazz trumpeter Wingy Manone. Stewart is in fine form, though he's a little too generous in giving his bandmates solo space.

best of the rest:
Rexatious ♪♪♪♪ (Living Era, 1996)
1934–1946 ♪♪♪♪ (Jazz Chronological Classics, 1997)
Late Date ♪♪♪ (Simitar, 1998)
1946–1947 ♪♪♪ (Jazz Chronological Classics, 1999)

influences:
◄◄ Louis Armstrong, Jabbo Smith
►► Charlie Parker, Wynton Marsalis

Andrew Gilbert

Stray Cats

See: The Brian Setzer Orchestra

Billy Strayhorn

Born November 29, 1915, in Dayton, OH. Died May 31, 1967, in New York, NY.

One of jazz's greatest composer/arrangers, Billy Strayhorn played an essential role in the Duke Ellington Orchestra from the time he became a lyricist in 1939 until his death of cancer. Though Strayhorn's contributions were often overlooked during his life, he has gained much wider recognition in the past decade. A sensitive, swinging pianist with great harmonic sophistication and a beautiful touch, Strayhorn could also perfectly imitate Ellington's more percussive approach. His body of tunes, including the Ellington orchestra's theme song "Take the 'A' Train" (which Ellington always introduced by giving Strayhorn credit), is one of the most beautiful and finely crafted *oeuvres* in American music.

"Take the 'A' Train"
DUKE ELLINGTON
1941
Billy Strayhorn wrote eventual showstopper based on Ellington's subway directions to Harlem.
Swingin' SINGLES

Raised in Pittsburgh, Strayhorn began writing songs and musical reviews while still in high school. He was already a preternaturally gifted songwriter before joining the Ellington sphere, composing such stunning art songs as "Lush Life" and "Something to Live For." He began collaborating with Ellington in 1939, at first supplying lyrics but quickly assuming the role of Ellington's cherished collaborator, writing arrangements for the orchestra and such classic instrumentals as "Chelsea Bridge," "Rain Check," and "Johnny Come Lately." After the mid-1940s, Ellington and Strayhorn began sharing credit for many of their collaborations, which led to the widespread misconception that their music was indistinguishable. In truth, when working on their own, Strayhorn and Ellington had profoundly different compositional styles. The depth of their musical pairing is probably unprecedented, with Strayhorn involved in every aspect of the band's creative life, from leading small group sessions with Ben Webster, Cootie Williams, Barney Bigard, and Johnny Hodges, to co-composing and arranging hundreds of tunes and extended works such as *The Deep South Suite*, *Such Sweet Thunder*, and *The Perfume Suite*. Outside of Ellington's bands, Strayhorn recorded only a few of his own sessions, most of which are now available on CD. His death inspired Ellington to record one of the orchestra's last great albums, *And His Mother Called Him Bill*. David Hadju's 1996 biography

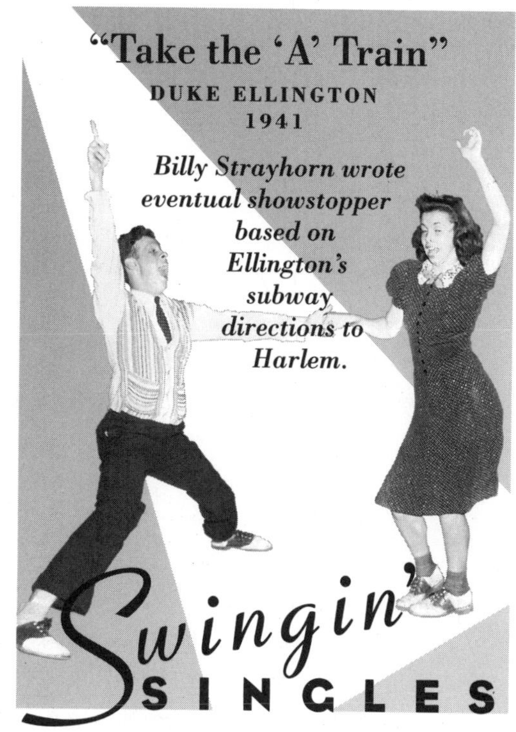

Rex Stewart **(Archive Photos)**

of Strayhorn, *Lush Life*, played an important role in disentangling Strayhorn's accomplishments from Ellington's, shedding light on Strayhorn's genius and his semi-public life as a quietly, though openly, gay man.

what's available: This revelatory set of unreleased material, *Lush Life* (Red Baron, 1964–65/Sony, 1992, prod. Duke Ellington, Mercer Ellington), is absolutely essential for those interested in Strayhorn or Ellington. Willie Ruff's French horn joins an exemplary quintet on five tracks, adding considerable warmth to the arrangements. Strayhorn accompanies the serviceable singer Ozzie Bailey on four tunes, and plays three tunes by himself, among the only solo piano pieces he ever recorded. Perhaps the most memorable track is the album's first, with Strayhorn accompanying his own vocals on "Lush Life." Of the very few albums Strayhorn recorded during his life, *The Peaceful Side* (Capitol, 1961/1996, prod. Alan Douglas), recorded in Paris, was the most intimate and personal. Reworking 10 tunes previously recorded by the Ellington orchestra, Strayhorn pares each tune to its essence. Highlights include the duo versions of "Passion Flower" and "Something to Live For" and the breathtaking string arrangement on "A Flower Is a Lovesome Thing." A completely obscure album when it was released, it was reissued in 1996.

worth searching for: To hear other orchestras performing Strayhorn's wonderful music, seek the following recordings. One of Ellington and Strayhorn's last collaborations, *The Far East Suite—Special Mix* (Bluebird, 1966/RCA, 1995, prod. Brad McCuen) is also one of Duke's best extended works of the 1960s, a highly lyrical nine-piece evocation of their long 1963 State Department–sponsored tour of Asia. The CD reissue adds four alternate takes, including Strayhorn's haunting ballad "Isfahan," featuring Johnny Hodges, and the clever "Bluebird of Dheli." One of the finest Strayhorn tributes ever recorded, Art Farmer's *Something to Live For* (Contemporary, 1987, prod. Helen Keane) is a brilliant quintet session. The album that finally brought tenor saxophonist Joe Henderson the audience and recognition his playing had so long warranted, *Lush Life: The Music of Billy Strayhorn* (Verve, 1992, prod. Richard Seidel, Don Sickler), includes trumpeter Wynton Marsalis. Pianist Marian McPartland used to play Strayhorn's tunes when he came by the Hickory House to catch her trio, and she pays the great composer/arranger a loving tribute with *Plays the Music of Billy Strayhorn* (Concord Jazz, 1987, prod. Carl E. Jefferson), a superior quartet session. *Lush Life: The Billy Strayhorn Songbook* (Verve, 1996, prod. various), an anthology of 15 Strayhorn tunes performed by various jazz artists, came out in conjunction with Hadju's Strayhorn biography. The music ranges from Cecil Taylor's angular rendering of "Johnny Come Lately" to Stan Getz's haunting live version of "Blood Count." Though there are some unaccountable choices made (why include Billy Eckstine singing Ellington's "Satin Doll" or Ella Fitzgerald's blithe version of the wrenching "Something to Live For?"), three tunes alone are worth the CD's price. Strayhorn's string arrangement for Ben Webster's version of "Chelsea Bridge" is a classic, and his piano work on Johnny Hodges's version of "Three and Six," featuring Webster, Ray Nance, Lawrence Brown, and Roy Eldridge, displays a mature style quite distinct from Ellington's. The album ends with a thrilling, star-studded nine-minute Norman Granz jam session on "Take the 'A' Train." Ellington wrote his heart-wrenching tribute to his alter ego (included in the CD liner notes) the day Strayhorn died, and it's as eloquent and moving as the music on *And His Mother Called Him Bill* (Bluebird, 1967/1987, prod. Brad McCuen), recorded three months after Strayhorn's death. The album covers a wide range of Strayhorn's tunes, from his early masterpieces "Daydream" and "Rain Check," to his late works "U.M.M.G." and "Blood Count," which features one of the most emotionally charged solos Johnny Hodges ever recorded, an angry outpouring at Strayhorn's loss.

influences:

◄◄ Duke Ellington

►► Melba Liston, Gil Evans

Andrew Gilbert

Ron Sunshine & Full Swing

Formed 1990, in New York, NY.

Ron Sunshine (born August 24, 1963, in Denver, CO), vocals, harmonica; Craig Dreyer, tenor sax; Dan Hovey, guitar; Paul Tillotson, piano; Andres Villamil, bass; James Wormworth IV, drums.

Full Swing distinguishes itself from many other bands in the New York and West Coast swing scenes by leaning more toward the jazz side of things (though Louis Jordan–style jump-blues tunes figure in its setlists), the high quality of leader Ron Sunshine's original material, and the strong jazz backgrounds of the instrumentalists. Especially noteworthy is drummer James Wormworth IV's truly swinging style, as opposed to the clunky thudding of the ex-rock drummers in other ensembles. (His father, James Wormworth, has stints with Al Haig and Lambert, Hendricks & Ross on his resume.) Sunshine, a music fanatic equally versed in Duke Ellington, Thelonious Monk, Ray Charles, and Parliament-Funkadelic, moved to New York in 1981 and later began playing harmonica. He was a sideman in various groups on the N.Y.C. blues circuit and in 1990 formed a blues/funk band, the Smoking Section, in which he was also

Billy Strayhorn **(Archive Photos)**

the lead vocalist. That summer, he spent some time in Paris, France, playing blues and swing on the streets with, among others, then-young crooner Madeleine Peyroux. After his return to New York that August, the core of the band that became Full Swing was formed to play an outdoor gig in Central Park. At the time, the neo-swing craze was several years off.

what to buy: The initial impression from *Straight Up* ♪♪♪♪ (Daddy-O/Royalty, 1998) is "this guy can sing!" Sunshine has a mellifluous, elegantly soulful vocal style and even displays a talent for ballad singing, not exactly common on the neo-swing scene. The emphasis is on Sunshine's extremely idiomatic yet non-imitative originals. "Enough for You (Mop Mop)" stands out among strong company. The only misstep is the cover of Louis Jordan's "Salt Pork, West Virginia," which gets points for obscurity but just isn't a song that stands up to repeat listening in anyone's version. (That sort of clowning is avoided on the other tracks.)

worth searching for: The mix of high-profile names and grass-roots-level bands on *Hipsters Zoots & Wingtips: The '90s Swingers* ♪♪♪ (Hip-O/Universal, 1998) includes Full Swing on a different version of "Enough for You (Mop Mop)" than the one on *Straight Up*. Also heard are the Brian Setzer Orchestra, Big Bad Voodoo Daddy, Royal Crown Revue, Indigo Swing, Diana Krall, Flying Neutrinos, Big Time Operator, Red & the Red Hots, and six others. On the compilation *Swingin' Christmas* ♪♪♪ (Daddy-O/Royalty, 1998), the Full Swing tracks are "Santa Claus Is Back in Town" and "Blue Christmas." The bands on the other 10 tracks are Flipped Fedoras, Swingtips, Heavenly 7, and Set 'Em Up Joe.

influences:

◀◀ Duke Ellington, Louis Jordan, Nat King Cole, Lost Wandering Blues & Jazz Band

Steve Holtje

Swing, Mr. & Mrs.

See: Mildred Bailey, Red Norvo

Swingerhead

Formed 1997, in Orlando, FL.

Michael "Swingerhead" Andrew, vocals; Quiche Lorraine, guitar; Peter "Spider" Orfanella, acoustic bass; Roger King Jr., drums; Brian Snapp, alto sax, tenor sax, clarinet; Steve Falkner, trumpet; Rick Abbott, trombone.

Swingerhead's sound contains equal parts lounge-lizard attitude and hot big-band rhythms. The brains behind the operation, Michael Andrews sings so close in style and tone to Bobby Darin (replete with the finger-snapper's patented hubris) that one is tempted to call in Oliver Stone to investigate. Though Andrews's songwriting borders on satirical, he never sacrifices the all-important tone of yesteryear. Likewise, his orchestra seems just as comfortable playing vibe-oriented mood music as it does fleet-footed swing, and the musicians include splashes of electric rock guitar and jump blues in their fresh, freewheeling arrangements.

Andrews has been singing swing and lounge long before there was even mention of a revival. He played cruise ships, led the Rainbow Room orchestra in New York City, and even created his own show around a fictitious swing character, *Mickey Swingerhead and the Earth Girls*. Occasionally, the band's approach seems almost too tongue-in-cheek, as if the musicians are carefully plotting an appropriate moment to spring their ironic punchline on the audience. But followers have gleefully been in on the joke since the beginning: Swingerhead has succeeded so well in its home base that the owner of Orlando's Orange Avenue Club totally remodeled his nightery (rechristened Rat Pack's on the Avenue) for the regular turnaway crowds.

what's available: There's retro sass galore on the debut *She Could Be a Spy* ♪♪♪ (Colossal, 1997, prod. Tony Battaglia), which features Michael Andrews's best Bobby Darin–cum–Frank Sinatra vocals and 12 very clever tunes. Whether playing hip would-be movie themes ("She Could Be a Spy"), hot and heavy dance floor anthems ("Pick Up the Phone"), or cozy lounge numbers ("Let's Rendezvous"), Swingerhead effortlessly achieves the lively atmosphere of a late-night Las Vegas showroom.

influences:

◀◀ Bobby Darin, Cab Calloway, Louis Jordan, Juan Garcia Esquivel

Ken Burke

The Swingtips

Formed 1991, in Mesa, AZ.

J. Kregg Barentine, lead vocals, saxophone; Scott Yandell, trumpet; Mark Witt, trombone, harmonica; Gregg Delfiner, percussion; Kyle Nix, upright bass, percussion; Jim Van Wagoner, piano; Paul Lucas, guitar.

One of the leading lights of the Arizona swing revival, the Swingtips bring overtones of bop into their very danceable small-combo sound. Bandleader J. Kregg Barentine, who played clarinet, flute, and sax in the Glenn Miller Orchestra (c. 1993–94), is their creative mastermind in terms of writing, arranging, producing, and marketing. Barentine admired the aggressive feel of Oingo Boingo's horn arrangements, which showed him that, when properly arranged, a smaller lineup of horns can actually swing harder than a full orchestra. Early on,

Barentine shared the bandstand with contemporary lineups of the Duke Ellington, Dorsey Brothers, and Guy Lombardo orchestras. Collaborations with the Arizona Lindy Hop Society and Arizona theater (the Zony Award winning *All Night Strut*) led to high-profile gigs opening for comedians Jay Leno and Bob Newhart. A highly visual act onstage, the band once dressed in old-time baseball uniforms to perform "Let's Play Some Ball!" (dedicated to the memory of Chicago Cubs broadcaster Harry Carey). As a result, the tune has been played at Major League Baseball stadiums all across the country, giving the band an enormous boost with a previously untapped audience.

what's available: The group's debut, *Let's Play Some Ball!* (Ghost Note, 1998, prod. J. Kregg Barentine), mixes fast original bop and boogie ("Too Pooped to Pop," "Checkbook Daddy-O") with band-on-the-run, detective-noir parodies ("Vamanos, Los Gatos") and aggressive remakes of instrumental standards ("Little Brown Jug"). But Barentine's lead vocals are often weak and inconsistent. More satisfying from a cultural reference standpoint, *Santa Swings* (Ghost Note, 1998, prod. J. Kregg Barentine) combines imaginative jazz-oriented remakes of holiday standards ("Parade of the Wooden Soldiers," "Hanukkah Chag Ya'fe") with some amusing original novelties ("Santa Swings," "I've Been a Bad, Bad Christmas Boy"). The band is solid, and Barentine's vocals are a bit warmer and more expressive than on their first disc. However, guest vocalist Angela Barentine steals the show with her moving rendition of "Christmas Time Is Here," the popular song from the animated classic *A Charlie Brown Christmas*.

influences:

Glenn Miller, Louis Prima, Oingo Boingo

Ken Burke

T

Buddy Tate

Born February 22, 1913, in Sherman, TX.

One of the few remaining swing-era players, tenor saxophonist Buddy Tate first made his name as a member of the Count Basie band during the 1930s. His husky, warm, and burnished sound was in the same style as that of the other jazz heavyweights of the time, Ben Webster, Coleman Hawkins, and Herschel Evans. However, Tate's delightful swagger and exuberance, not to mention his distinctive clarinet playing, helped him stand apart from his contemporaries. Throughout the '30s, '40s, and '50s, Tate was an in-demand player and he worked with a variety of popular big bands, including those led by Lucky Millinder, Hot Lips Page, Jimmy Rushing, and Andy Kirk. Over the following few decades, Tate led his own band in a lengthy stay at Harlem's Celebrity Club, in addition to recording a fine series of albums for the Prestige label. During the '70s, the saxophonist kept busy as a touring artist in Europe and through his work with Benny Goodman, Jay McShann, and Paul Quinichette. Tate continues to play and record sporadically, including a recent stint with Lionel Hampton.

what to buy: *Buck and Buddy* (Prestige/Swingville, 1960/Original Jazz Classics, 1992, prod. Esmond Edwards) and *Buck and Buddy Blow the Blues* (Prestige/ Swingville, 1961/Original Jazz Classics, 1995, prod. Esmond Edwards), both quintet dates, catch Tate in the company of swing-era trumpeter Buck Clayton. The material is familiar and the performances, with Tate on his seldom-recorded clarinet, are sublime and inspired.

what to buy next: *Groovin' with Tate* (Prestige/Swingville, 1959/1961/Prestige, 1995, prod. Esmond Edwards) combines on one CD the original albums *Tate's Date* and *Groovin' with Tate*. While the latter is a pleasant quartet outing, the former is an exciting large group date with many of Tate's colleagues from the Celebrity Club.

what to avoid: *Just Jazz* (Uptown, 1984/Reservoir, 1993, prod. Bob Sunenblick) pairs Tate with the legendary trombonist Al Grey, but the results are surprisingly routine.

the rest:

Buddy Tate and His Buddies (Chiaroscuro, 1973/1994)
Swinging Scorpio (Black Lion, 1974/1992)
The Texas Twister (Master Jazz, 1975/New World, 1992)
Jive at Five (Storyville, 1975/1993)
The Ballad Artistry of Buddy Tate (Sackville, 1981)

worth searching for: *Tate-a-Tate* (Prestige/Swingville, 1960/Original Jazz Classics, 1985, prod. Esmond Edwards), available on vinyl only, is an inspiring recording with sidemen Clark Terry and Tommy Flanagan.

influences:

Herschel Evans, Coleman Hawkins, Ben Webster

Ken Peplowski, Tad Shull

Chris Hovan

Jack Teagarden

Born Jack Weldon Leo Teagarden, August 29, 1905, in Vernon, TX. Died January 15, 1964, in New Orleans, LA.

Trombonist-vocalist Jack Teagarden is one of the true giants of jazz. His unique tone and braggadocio style of playing make him identifiable after just one measure of music—even one note can give him away. As a result, many top names of the swing era, from Louis Armstrong to Benny Goodman, sought his talents for their big bands. Born to a musical family, Teagarden was playing trombone by the age of 10. His dad was an amateur trumpet player; his mother played piano, as did his sister, Norma; brother Charlie played trumpet; and brother Clois played drums. By age 15, Teagarden was playing with various bands, and he toured the Southwest and Mexico extensively through the mid-1920s. By then, he had become almost legendary to those who had heard him, and his fame preceded his trip to New York in 1927. His first recordings (with the Roger Wolfe Kahn and Ben Pollack Orchestras) show a trombonist whose skill was almost unmatched by any other jazz trombonist. Teagarden became fast friends with the other titans who were shaping the jazz world of the time, such as Benny Goodman, Coleman Hawkins, Louis Armstrong, Bix Beiderbecke, Fats Waller, and Red Allen. Teagarden's voice was just as good as his trombone playing, making his presence on a record date a most treasured event. Teagarden played with Ben Pollack's band on and off for a good part of the late 1920s and early 1930s. He played briefly with Red Nichols at the Hotel New Yorker and on some excellent recordings for Brunswick during this period. He formed his own band briefly during 1933 and played at the Vienna Gardens, located in the 1933 Chicago World's Fair grounds (and also recorded four titles for Columbia). The Depression caused Teagarden to seek steady income, which he found with Paul Whiteman's Orchestra. Teagarden stayed on for five years and left Pops in 1938 to form his own big band. The business end of the music profession was ultimately too much for Teagarden, and he disbanded his group near the end of World War II. The war years may have been Teagarden's best artistic period. His 1943 and 1944 sessions with the Capitol Jazzmen on Capitol, George Wettling on Keynote, and Louis Armstrong on V-Disc are breathtaking. After the war and his dissolution of his band, he joined Louis Armstrong's All-Stars, playing with Louis until 1951. Upon leaving Armstrong, Teagarden formed his own small group. He toured until his death.

what to buy: Teagarden's Victor recordings are chronicled on the two-CD *The Indispensable Jack Teagarden, 1928–1957* (RCA, 1995, prod. various). They start with his first recorded solo as a sub (for Miff Mole!) with Roger Wolfe Kahn's Orchestra on "She's a Great, Great Girl" and end with the wonderful Bud Freeman's Chicagoans titles. Equally diverse but more focused on his earlier output are two CDs: *I Gotta Right to Sing the Blues* (ASV Living Era, 1992, prod. various) and *The Best of Big T* (Topaz, 1995, prod. various), both of which cover pretty much the same ground. *A Hundred Years from Today* (Conifer, 1994) chronicles the best of Teagarden's bands in the early '30s, while *Jack Teagarden, 1930–1934*

Swingin'
SINGLES
"Whatever Will Be, Will Be (Que Sera Sera)"
DORIS DAY
1956
Day and eccentric funkster Sly Stone redid this on 1972's Fresh; the pair were rumored to be an item.

(Jazz Chronological Classics, 1994, prod. Gilles Petard) is typically complete. Teagarden's first leadership date for the American Record Company produces standard Depression fare, until Teagarden comes and saves the day on "You're Simply Delish." The recording dates get better, especially the 1931 Columbia session with Fats Waller.

what to buy next: *Jack Teagarden, 1934–1939* (Jazz Chronological Classics, 1994); *Jack Teagarden, 1939–1940* (Jazz Chronological Classics, 1994); *Jack Teagarden, 1940–1941* (Jazz Chronological Classics, 1995); and *Jack Teagarden, 1941–1943* (Jazz Chronological Classics, 1996) feature Teagarden's big band. Many instrumental titles are quite good, and Teagarden shines on both vocal and solo outings, but the sweet titles and ballads really slow the band down. His best recordings for Standard Transcriptions are on *Masters of Jazz, Vol. 10—Jack Teagarden, 1941–44* (Storyville, 1941–44/1994). Also worth pursuing are the excellent HRS titles from 1940, which are on *Jack Teagarden–Pee Wee Russell* (Origins of Jazz, 1990).

best of the rest:

Jack Teagarden Live in Chicago, 1960–1961 (Jazzland, 1993)
Club Hangover Broadcasts (Arbors Jazz, 1996)

Jack Teagarden **(Archive Photos)**

worth searching for: For examples of Teagarden's later work, the wonderful limited-edition set *The Complete Capitol Fifties Jack Teagarden Sessions* (Mosaic, 1995, prod. Charlie Lourie, Michael Cuscuna) has outstanding sound and content, superlative vocals and trombone solos by Teagarden, and improvisational as well as arranged venues.

influences:

◀◀ Paul Whiteman, Eddie Condon

▶▶ Kai Winding

Jim Prohaska

Clark Terry

Born December 20, 1920, in St. Louis, MO.

One of Clark Terry's most cherished items, a letter from Louis Armstrong, advises him to "keep playing that trumpet, boy, because you can blow your ass off!" In an amazing career spanning more than 50 years to date, the trumpeter and flugelhornist first made his name in the Count Basie and Charlie Barnet big bands, wound through sessions and live dates with Lester Young, Milt Hinton, Quincy Jones, Ben Webster, Oscar Peterson, Ray Brown, and Gerry Mulligan, and influenced everybody from Miles Davis to whichever future young lion may be listening today. Terry's fascinating yet sometimes difficult career started as a young man of 13 growing up in St. Louis, Missouri. He grew up in a family of 10 children and, at age 9, moved in with his oldest sister and her husband, a tuba player with Dewey Jackson's band, the Musical Ambassadors. As a youngster watching the band practice, Terry met trumpet player Louis Caldwell, who assigned him the duty of watching his horn during breaks. Returning from break one day, Caldwell caught Terry trying to blow his trumpet and told him he was going to grow up to be a trumpet player. After leaving high school to support his family, he played with various local musicians (including classic-blues singer Ida Cox), and entered the navy in 1942. Upon his discharge three years later, he joined Lionel Hampton's band, then returned to St. Louis to work with George Hudson at the Club Plantation. From 1947 to 1948, Terry traveled to California to join Charlie Barnet's big band and became a member of Basie's outfit, where he remained until 1951, when he began an eight-year run with Duke Ellington's band. From late 1959 to 1960, Terry toured Europe with Harold Arlen's *Free and Easy Show*; joined Quincy Jones's orchestra; and became a regular member of the NBC Orchestra and *The Tonight Show* band. Terry continued to record on several recording dates and for a short period in the 1970s led his own band, Clark's Big Bad Band. Today, the recipient of four honorary doctorate degrees and the namesake of two music schools is a staunch supporter of jazz education and continues to devote time to young musicians, teaching improvisational techniques beyond the books and manuals—in addition to his regular performances of blowing, singing, and scat-singing.

what to buy: *Clark Terry* (EmArcy, 1955/Verve, 1997, prod. Bob Shad), part of Verve's Elite Edition series of limited-edition historical recordings, contains bonus tracks from the Leonard Feather-produced LP *Cats vs. Chicks*. With sidemen such as Horace Silver and Oscar Pettiford, Terry's exceptional, smooth trumpet frequently swings at a bop tempo. The gem *The Happy Horns of Clark Terry* (Impulse!, 1964/1994, prod. Bob Thiele), with Ben Webster on tenor sax and Milt Hinton on bass, includes the tender ballad "Do Nothin' 'til You Hear from Me" and many sharp flugelhorn solos. *Portraits* (Chesky Records, 1988, prod. Norman Chesky), dedicated to other legendary trumpeters, includes Terry's original, "Finger Filibuster," which opens with his trademark scatting. The delightfully poignant ballet on "I Can't Get Started" hails Bunny Berigan. *In Orbit* (Riverside, 1958/Original Jazz Classics, 1987, prod. Orrin Keepnews) is possibly the first time a jazz musician uses flugelhorn as the lead horn; combined with the presence of pianist Thelonious Monk, the recording is one of Terry's finest accomplishments.

what to buy next: *Serenade to a Bus Seat* (Riverside, 1957/Original Jazz Classics, 1993, prod. Orrin Keepnews) is a swinging bebop affair, with five Terry originals and two standards. *Duke with a Difference* (Riverside, 1957/Original Jazz Classics, 1990, prod. Orrin Keepnews) is a dedication to Terry's boss at the time, Duke Ellington. Departing from the traditional, disciplined Ellington arrangements, Terry delivers a lighthearted treatment, especially the swinging "Cotton Tail" and the Marian Bruce–sung "In a Sentimental Mood." *Memories of Duke* (Original Jazz Classics, 1980/1990, prod. Norman Granz) includes Terry's muted lead trumpet on pleasing readings of other Ellington gems, such as "Cotton Tail," "Come Sunday," "Passion Flower," and "Echoes of Harlem." *Yes, the Blues* (Original Jazz Classics, 1981/1995, prod. Norman Granz) teams Terry with his old partner, alto saxman Eddie "Cleanhead" Vinson, who achieved fame as a blues player but is just as comfortable playing jazz. Coming together for the first time since 1947 (when Terry was a member of his 16-piece band), they deliver "Diddlin'," with Terry soloing on his mouthpiece, and "Railroad Porter Blues," enhanced by Vinson's vocals and "Harmonica George" Smith.

best of the rest:

Top and Bottom Brass (Riverside, 1959/Original Jazz Classics, 1993)

Live in Chicago—Vol. 1 (Monad Records, 1976/1995)

Live at the Village Gate (Chesky Records, 1990)

The Second Set (Chesky Records, 1990)

worth searching for: With trombonist Bob Brookmeyer, *The Power of Positive Swinging* (Mainstream Records, 1965/1993, prod. Bob Shad) contains relaxed, swinging tunes, including "Battle Hymn of the Republic," with Terry's fluid use of the high register blended with his mute treatments. *The Alternate Blues* (Original Jazz Classics, 1980/1992, prod. Norman Granz) finds Terry fitting in nicely with Dizzy Gillespie and Oscar Peterson, among others. The album is casual and informal, as if these legendary musicians had nothing better to do than an impromptu recording session.

influences:

Louis Armstrong, Roy Eldridge, Bunny Berigan, Louis Caldwell, Doc Cheatham

Miles Davis, Terence Blanchard, Nicholas Payton

Keith Brickhouse

Jean "Toots" Thielemans

Born Jean Baptiste Thielemans, April 29, 1922, in Brussels, Belgium.

Toots Thielemans, who is largely responsible for introducing the chromatic harmonica as a jazz instrument, was present for the roots of swing—although he's considered a bop player today. The onetime Benny Goodman sideman earned his greatest commercial success in 1962, when the catchy waltz "Bluesette" became a worldwide hit and made him an in-demand player. Since then, he has continued playing harmonica and whistling on various studio dates, for film soundtracks such as *Midnight Cowboy*, for TV themes, and on pop and jazz recordings. Inspired after hearing the pop harmonica sounds of Larry Adler in the movies, Thielemans started playing harmonica at age 17, while attending college. But after he contracted a lung infection, he taught himself to play guitar by listening to Django Reinhardt recordings, and he was soon playing in clubs all over Brussels. He took up harmonica again and after World War II performed in American GI clubs in Europe. In 1948 Thielemans emigrated to the U.S.; he became a citizen in 1952 and gained wider notice playing with a variety of top jazz groups, including the Benny Goodman sextet and the George Shearing Quintet. In 1981 Thielemans had a major stroke, but he has mostly recovered and began in the early 1990s to incorporate Brazilian rhythms in his jazz recordings.

what to buy: Despite the curious title, *Man Bites Harmonica* (Riverside/Original Jazz Classics, 1958) is Thielemans's best album as leader. When he takes up the guitar, his fluent, warm sound and sense of swing enhance toe-tapping tunes such as "18th Century Ballroom."

what to buy next: A diverse session of 12 romantic swingers, boppers, ballads, and bossas, *Only Trust Your Heart* (Concord, 1988, prod. Fred Hersch) finds the leader starring solely on harmonica. His trio is tight and light, with drummer Joey Baron creating plenty of splashy and expansive polyrhythms to spur Thielemans's mellow-toned solos. Pianist Fred Hersch's artistry is extremely supportive to the harmonica player and every bit as captivating as he supports Thielemans's mellifluous solos.

what to avoid: *Verve Jazz Masters 59* (Verve, 1996) compiles tracks recorded for Verve between 1953 and 1991 (some with the Quincy Jones Orchestra) that are not honestly representative of Thielemans's best career achievements. Unless you're duly introduced to Thielemans or can't get enough Brazilian jazz, you'll want to wait to acquire *Brasil Project* (Private Music, 1992, prod. Miles Goodman, Oscar Castro-Neves) and *Brasil Project II* (Private Music, 1993, prod. Miles Goodman, Oscar Castro-Neves).

influences:

Larry Adler, John Coltrane, Django Reinhardt, Joe Pass, Antonio Carlos Jobim

Hendrik Meurkens, Kenny Burrell

Nancy Ann Lee

Hank Thompson

Born Henry William Thompson, September 3, 1935, in Waco, TX.

Before he became the King of Honky-Tonk Swing, a seller of more than 60 million albums, and one of the few country singers to have hits in five consecutive decades, Hank Thompson grew up listening to a wide range of country sources, from Jimmie Rodgers to the Grand Ole Opry. His first instrument was the harmonica, and he later was inspired to learn guitar by watching Gene Autry in western movies. Thompson started performing in a Saturday youth program that was broadcast on a Waco radio station. That led to a show called *Hank the Hired Hand*, where Thompson was sponsored by a flour company. After six months of that, Thompson received his high school diploma and enlisted in the navy, attending Princeton University after his discharge. He then returned to Waco and put together a band called the Brazos Valley Boys; they became popular throughout the state, and Thompson signed with Globe Records in 1946.

Thompson's recording caught Tex Ritter's ear, and Ritter introduced Thompson to Capitol Records executives. Thompson signed with Capitol in 1948, beginning an association that lasted until 1966. That first year, Thompson had two songs—"Humpty Dumpty Heart" and "Today"—reach the Top 10. In 1952 he had his first #1 with "Wild Side of Life." The hits continued to pour in: during 1954 Thompson placed five singles in the Top 10. He averaged 240 personal appearances a year throughout much of the 1950s and 1960s, including regular performances at the Texas State Fair, where he often set attendance records. The pace slowed some during the 1970s, although Thompson still toured the United States, Canada, the Far East, and Europe. By the time Thompson signed with Warner Bros. in 1966, he had sold millions of records and had placed almost 50 singles on the charts. For most of his stay at Capitol he was ranked as the top country artist by polls in *Billboard* and *Cashbox*. He signed with ABC/Dot in 1968 and remained there until MCA absorbed the label at the end of the 1970s, at which point his releases appeared on that label. Thompson has had more than 30 Top 10 hits, but he hasn't had a charting single since 1983, although he still continues to record occasionally.

what to buy: *The Best of Hank Thompson 1966–1978* ♪♪♪♪ (Varese Sarabande, 1996, prod. Joe Allison, Larry Butler) contains some of Thompson's strongest stuff and covers his later performances. Eight of the 16 songs were written or co-written by Thompson.

what to buy next: *Vintage Collection Series* ♪♪♪♪ (Capitol, 1996, prod. various) is a 20-song collection that covers the biggest hits of Thompson & His Brazos Valley Boys from 1947 to 1960.

what to avoid: Acquiring more than one of the redundant collections *All-Time Greatest Hits* ♪♪ (Curb, 1990, prod. various), *Greatest Hits Volume 2* ♪♪ (Curb, 1993, prod. various), *Greatest Songs, Volume 1* ♪♪ (Curb, 1995, prod. various), and *Greatest Songs, Volume 2* ♪♪ (Curb, 1995, prod. various) is unnecessary.

the rest:

Live at the Golden Nugget ♪♪♪ (Capitol, 1958/1995)
Wild Side of Life ♪♪ (Richmond, 1985)
Greatest Hits, Volume 1 ♪♪♪ (Step One, 1987)
Greatest Hits, Volume 2 ♪♪♪ (Step One, 1987)
Here's to Country Music ♪♪ (Step One, 1987)
20 Greatest Hits ♪♪♪ (Deluxe, 1987)
The Best of the Best of Hank Thompson ♪♪ (Hollywood, 1990)
Country Music Hall of Fame ♪♪♪ (MCA, 1992)
Hank Thompson and Friends ♪♪♪ (Curb, 1997)

influences:

◀ Bob Wills

▶ Kitty Wells, Asleep at the Wheel

Ronnie McDowell

Claude Thornhill

Born August 10, 1909, in Terre Haute, IN. Died July 1, 1965, in New York, NY.

If there truly was a Birth of the Cool, Claude Thornhill was its father. His band of 1941–48 was one of the most innovative big bands (and a favorite of bebop piano hero Thelonious Monk). In addition to Thornhill's taste for compositions inspired by such European classical composers as Ravel and Debussy, Gil Evans provided the band with groundbreaking charts of bop tunes by Charlie Parker ("Anthropology," "Yardbird Suite"), Miles Davis ("Donna Lee"), and Sir Charles Thompson ("Robbins Nest"). Thornhill and Evans experimented with the very composition of the band, adding several instruments foreign to jazz bands (e.g., french horns, tuba, and flute), as well as having as many as seven reed players, all able to double on clarinet. These developments (with Evans's departure from the band in 1948) led directly to Davis's legendary *Birth of the Cool* sessions. No fewer than seven Thornhill alumni (including Evans and Gerry Mulligan) were involved in the sessions. In the 1930s, after study at the Cincinnati Conservatory and the Curtis Institute, Thornhill worked with several big names in jazz, including Benny Goodman (1934–35), Bud Freeman (1935), and Billie Holiday (1938). Thornhill, through his arranging skills, was largely responsible for Maxine Sullivan's 1938 hit "Loch Lomond" (the pair were once dubbed the Beardless Svengali and the Sepia Trilby). Thornhill crossed paths with Gil Evans in the California band of Skinnay Ennis. After forming his own band in 1940, Thornhill reached back to this association, bringing Evans in as arranger in 1941. Through the 1950s, Thornhill recorded sporadically, doing an album of Mulligan arrangements in 1953 among others.

what to buy: All of the highlights of Thornhill's 1940s band can be found on *Claude Thornhill—Best of the Big Bands* ♪♪♪♪ (CBS, 1990, reissue prod. Michael Brooks). His bebop arrangements are here as well as his biggest hit (and signature tune), "Snowfall." Also included is an Evans arrangement of a segment of the "Nutcracker Suite" not covered in Ellington's treatment.

what to buy next: *Gerry Mulligan Tentet & Quartet* ♪♪♪♪ (GNP/Crescendo, 1996, prod. Gene Norman) features Thornhill's arranging talents.

the rest:

Uncollected ♪♪♪ (Hindsight, 1990)
1948 Transcription Performance ♪♪♪ (Hep, 1994)

worth searching for: The out-of-print LP *Two Sides of Claude Thornhill* ♪♪♪ (Kapp) helps fill in some of the gaping holes in the Thornhill discography.

influences:

◀ Paul Whiteman, Duke Ellington

▶ Miles Davis, Gil Evans Orchestra, Gerry Mulligan

Larry Grogan

Mel Tormé

Born September 13, 1925, in Chicago, IL.

With the exception of Frank Sinatra, Mel Tormé may be the

Claude Thornhill **(Archive Photos)**

most enduring and influential male jazz vocalist of his generation. Graced with an almost absurdly lyrical voice (he hated the nickname critics gave him, "The Velvet Fog"), the cherubic singer is as comfortable scatting with a big band as he is milking ballads with a trio. His pipes have improved with age—his honey-dipped 1940s tenor has lowered to a commanding baritone. More than that, Tormé has been blessed by the fact that his voice is instantly recognizable; there's simply no one who sounds like him. Tormé has been in show business since he was four, when he began singing professionally on Chicago's South Shore. After getting some radio airplay with a local band in the 1930s, he joined Chico Marx's band as a boy singer and eventually formed his own vocal group, the Mel-Tones, with singers like Les Baxter and Henry Mancini's future wife, Ginny O'Connor. The Mel-Tones had plenty of hits, such as the swinging "Truckin'," and recorded other songs with Artie Shaw's band. They also laid the groundwork for other jazz vocal groups like the Manhattan Transfer. Tormé came out of a generation of singers in the 1940s who could do it all—Sammy Davis Jr. and Mickey Rooney, for instance. Like those entertainers, Tormé could sing, dance, act, and tell a joke. It wasn't long before he embarked on what became a respectable movie career, debuting in 1943's *Higher and Higher* for R.K.O. Pictures. Unlike Sinatra, Tormé's talent runs beyond vocals: he played drums for Count Basie's band on occasion, he arranges, and he even accompanies many of his own charts. Since the 1980s, he has written novels (his best one is a book called *Wynner*), biographies of Judy Garland and Buddy Rich, and an autobiography titled *It Wasn't All Velvet*. Every Christmas, the nation swoons to his most famous composition, "The Christmas Song," which he co-wrote on an extremely hot day in 1940 while trying to think of something cool. By the time Nat King Cole recorded it in 1947, the song was set in the exclusive club of successful 20th-century Christmas carols. Maligned by some as a cheesy lounge singer, Tormé has probably been underrated for his entire career. But in the 1980s and 1990s, he experienced a professional rebirth—building a string of accomplished albums (including some terrific live recordings), becoming a spokesman for Mountain Dew, and doing a series of guest spots on NBC's sitcom *Night Court*. The reason for the latter: the show's star, Harry Anderson, idolized him. *Night Court* turned Tormé into something of a curiosity—the legendary jazz singer reborn as retro pitch-man. But that renaissance was cut short in 1996 when he was hit with a massive stroke. Tormé hasn't resumed touring, but is reportedly enjoying his enormous video collection and model railroad setup.

what to buy: *Swingin' on the Moon* ♪♪♪♪ (Verve, 1960/1998, prod. Russell Garcia) is a '60s novelty album in which every song includes the word "moon": "Oh, You Crazy Moon," "Moonlight in Vermont," and "How High the Moon," to name a few. Despite the shtick, it shows off Tormé's unparalleled ability to coalesce with a big band. *Fujitsu-Concord Jazz Festival in Japan* ♪♪♪♪♪ (Concord, 1990, prod. Carl E. Jefferson, George Otaki), one of Tormé's finest performances, shows off a charm so infectious even an audience full of non-English speakers gets into the mood. Frank Wess, one of Count Basie's favorite sax players, brings his own orchestra to back up the singer. Tormé even shows off his drumming skills on Basie's "Swingin' the Blues." There are also terrific renditions of "Wave" and "Tokyo State of Mind"—a takeoff on Billy Joel's "New York State of Mind." The live album *A Vintage Year* ♪♪♪♪ (Concord, 1988, prod. Carl E. Jefferson) puts Tormé in the middle of a Paul Masson vineyard with George Shearing on piano, and the results are fabulous. Shearing and Tormé share a terrific wit, as seen on a hilarious medley of "New York" songs. Shearing's impressionistic style works well with Tormé's laid-back sound.

what to buy next: *Night at the Concord Pavilion* ♪♪♪♪ (Concord, 1990) is a charming, live performance with some of Tormé's best swing tunes: "Sing, Sing, Sing" and "Sent for You Yesterday (But Here You Come Today)." It features the Frank Wess–Harry Edison Orchestra—two heavy-hitters from Count Basie's big-band era. For *That's All* ♪♪♪♪ (Columbia, 1997, prod. Robert Mersey), the liner notes simply say, "A lush, romantic album." That's a fair enough assessment. Some of the tracks border on mushiness, but Tormé's voice is in its prime, and tracks like "Ho-Ba-La-La" and "Haven't We Met?" will be with you long after the CD player has been turned off. *A Tribute to Bing Crosby* ♪♪♪♪ (Concord, 1994, prod. Carl E. Jefferson), a quiet and tasteful album, celebrates one of the few who came close to out-crooning Tormé. An orchestra of violins sometimes gets in the way of Tormé's interpretations, but others will make you want to dance on a moonlit balcony.

what to avoid: Tormé and Marty Paich had a strong partnership prior to *Reunion: Mel Tormé and the Marty Paich Dek-tette* ♪♪♪ (Concord, 1988, prod. Mel Tormé, Marty Paich), but the sparks never materialize. The album also falls victim to one of Tormé's few shortcomings: an inexplicable affinity for song medleys in which each song gets little more than three seconds of airtime.

best of the rest:

Mel Tormé Swings Shubert Alley ♪♪♪♪ (Verve, 1960/1989)
Encore at Marty's ♪♪♪♪ (DCC Jazz, 1982)
Mel Tormé with Rob McConnell and the Boss Brass ♪♪♪♪ (Concord, 1986)
Mel & George "Do" World War II ♪♪♪ (Concord, 1991)
Sing, Sing, Sing ♪♪♪♪ (Concord, 1993)
Velvet and Brass ♪♪♪♪ (Concord, 1995)
A&E: An Evening with Mel Tormé ♪♪♪♪ (Concord, 1996)
The Mel Tormé Collection: 1942–1985 ♪♪♪♪ (Rhino, 1996)

Frankie Trumbauer **(Archive Photos)**

worth searching for: *Smooth as Velvet* ♫♫♫ (Laserlight, 1991) is a nice reissue of some of Tormé's earlier, smooth ballads—including a great rendition of "Prelude to a Kiss." Tormé's voice here is so smooth, it almost cries out for a shriek. But it's still a terrific moodsetter.

influences:

◀ Mickey Rooney, Bing Crosby, Sammy Davis Jr., Nat King Cole

▶ Harry Connick Jr., Mandy Patinkin, Johnny Hartman

Carl Quintanilla

Frankie Trumbauer

Born May 30, 1901, in Carbondale, IL. Died June 11, 1956, in Kansas City, MO.

Master of the C-melody saxophone, Frankie Trumbauer was revered by his fellow musicians, but not a particularly successful big-band leader. Although largely forgotten, his work on the alto sax brought a much-appreciated sense of jazz fluidity to countless sessions for a series of big-name orchestras during the mid-'20s through the late '40s. Trumbauer gigged with several small Midwestern outfits before he latched on with the Detroit-based Jean Goldkette's Orchestra in 1924. He met famed cornetist Bix Beiderbecke, who nicknamed him "Tram," and the two became fast friends, bringing an element of hot jazz to a band that already contained the Dorsey Brothers, Eddie Lang, Joe Venuti, and a young Artie Shaw. Goldkette was a piano player and, while onstage, could not lead the band in the traditional manner. As a result, he had Joe Venuti, Russ Morgan, and Trumbauer take turns as musical director. (Through the years, Goldkette's orchestra featured an astonishing number of future bandleaders.) The experience gave Trumbauer the itch to start his own outfit, and he took many of his boss's best musicians with him when the Goldkette group broke up in 1927. The Frankie Trumbauer Orchestra's best work featured strong interplay between Trumbauer and Beiderbecke on a series of fine recordings for the OKeh label, some done in a subgroup with Lang called Tram, Bix, and Eddie. Today, the group is considered one of the best jazz aggregations ever, but at the time it was a financial disaster. Eventually, it disbanded and Beiderbecke and Trumbauer went to work for the King of Jazz, Paul

Whiteman. During his 10-year association with Whiteman, the sax man continued to lead studio groups and cut commercial sessions with such big-name vocalists as Mildred Bailey and Bing Crosby. He left Whiteman in 1936 to lead the popular subgroup the Three T's (Jack and Charlie Teagarden) as a solo act. Teagarden, of course, went on to bigger fame, while Trumbauer continued to push the jazz envelope in well-respected, gonowhere bands well into the WW II years. The bop era of jazz rendered his style irrelevant during the early '50s, and although he continued to take session work, the Tram's last days were spent as a flight instructor.

what to buy: Trumbauer's finest early work as a bandleader, session man, and guest star have been compiled on *Vol. 1—Tram, 1923–29* (The Old Masters, 1997, prod. various) and *Vol. 2—Tram 2, 1929–30* (The Old Masters, 1997, prod. various). His collaborations with Beiderbecke won't be found here, but some great stuff recorded with the likes of Red Nichols, Paul Whiteman, Joe Venuti, Bee Palmer, Mildred Bailey, and Bing Crosby are included, as well as many other fine sides originally cut for the old OKeh label.

what to buy next: Drawn from several sessions in the early '30s, *Vol. 3—Tram 3, 1931–34* (The Old Masters, 1997, prod. various) is heavy on vocals by Bing Crosby, Johnny Mercer, Jack Teagarden, and assorted groups, but Trumbauer's grooving solos will be of primary interest to swing fans.

worth searching for: Trumbauer supports his frequent partner Bix Beiderbecke on the cornetist's *Vol. 1—Singin' the Blues* (Columbia, 1990, prod. Michael Brooks), a brilliant 20-song collection of late '20s jazz with stellar versions of "Riverboat Shuffle," "Way Down Yonder in New Orleans," and the alto-sax legend's masterpiece, "Trumbology."

influences:

◀◀ Bix Beiderbecke, Jean Goldkette, Paul Whiteman

▶▶ Lester Young, Jack Teagarden

see also: *Bix Beiderbecke, Paul Whiteman*

Ken Burke

Tommy Tucker

Born Gerald Duppler, May 18, 1908, in Souris, ND.

Not to be confused with the R&B artist who recorded the '60s classic "High Heel Sneakers," this Tommy Tucker led a successful "sweet" band during the 1930s and '40s. His specialty was the soft, romantic sounds of slow ballads, muted horns, and sentimental vocal groups. The baton-waving Tucker didn't play an instrument on stage, but he wrote many of his orchestra's hits, such as "The Man Who Comes Around," "How Come Baby," "All Things Come to Those Who Wait," and "The Man Don't Come to Our House Anymore." Like many others of this type, Tucker's band was based in the Midwest and East Coast, where remote radio broadcasts from plush hotels spread his fame nationwide. Particular favorites were his vocalists: handsome baritone Don Brown, the dramatic Amy Arnell, novelty singer Kerwin Somerville, and the chirping Voices Three, who sang the band's theme "I Love You (Oh How I Love You)." Their popular recordings led to regular spots on such network radio programs as *The Lucky Strike Show with Walter Winchell* and *The George Jessel Show.* Tucker's outfit peaked in 1941 with its smash "I Don't Want to Set the World on Fire" (which beat out a competing version from Harlan Leonard's band). A few years later, when his band's popularity began to ebb, Tucker changed musical direction. He brought in arrangers Claude Hopkins and Van Alexander to help him fashion some fuller sounding, hotter swinging sides and, for a brief period, competed with the big boys of swing. Unfortunately, the transformation didn't last. Longtime fans preferred the band's old style, and hardcore swing cats wouldn't be caught dead with one of their discs, no matter what it sounded like. (This type of snobbishness still exists today, folks.) Subsequently, Tucker and his crew returned to their "sweet" style until they disbanded in the mid-1950s.

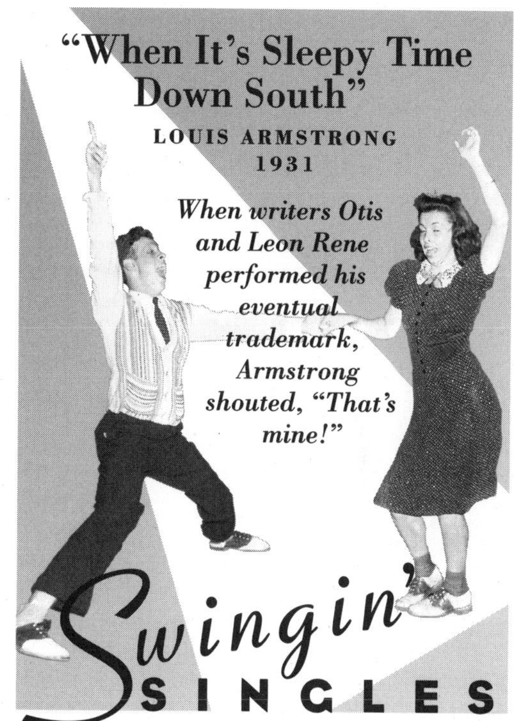

what's available: None of Tucker's big hits are even remotely in print at this time. However, those curious about Tucker's sound are advised to check into *Tommy Tucker and His Orchestra, 1941–47* (Circle, 1995, compilation prod. George Buck Jr.) and *Tommy Tucker and His Orchestra, More 1941–47* (Circle, 1993, compilation prod. George Buck Jr.), two generous collections of radio broadcasts and sessions featuring vocalists Amy Arnell, Kerwin Somerville, Don Brown, and various line-ups of Voices Three. These performances were recorded (in part) during a time Tucker was attempting a fuller big-band sound, but the numbers are closer to his earlier "sweet" sound.

influences:

◀◀ Isham Jones, Hal McIntyre

▶▶ Claude Hopkins

Ken Burke

Big Joe Turner

Born May 18, 1911, in Kansas City, MO. Died November 24, 1985, in Inglewood, CA.

Next time you're trying to hash out who was the first-ever rock 'n' roll singer, consider the following: blues shouter Big Joe Turner (along with pianist Pete Johnson) helped stir up the boogie-woogie craze of the '30s, belted some of the nastiest jump blues of the '40s, and was one of the driving forces in the ascendancy of '50s R&B. His booming vocals and illuminated carnal appetites run rampant in a sea of leering saxophones, salacious piano breaks, and the low-down big beat of after-hours clubs. Turner was a bartender in Prohibition-era Kansas City when he first began shouting the blues. His work with pianist Pete Johnson in the 1930s and 1940s—such as his first records, "Roll 'Em Pete" and "Cherry Red"—helped popularize boogie-woogie and laid the groundwork for the R&B revolution of the 1950s. Through the 1940s he recorded swing, jazz, and raw blues with some of the hottest players of that period (including Johnson, Meade Lux Lewis, and Freddie Slack). Many of Turner's sides were strong regional sellers, but his first national R&B hit was 1947's "My Gal's a Jockey," one of the most lascivious records of that era. In 1951 he signed with Atlantic, where producers sweetened his hard-swinging sound with female chorus-singers and let him loose on teenage America. "Chains of Love," "Sweet Sixteen," "Honey Hush," "TV Mama," and "Don't You Cry" were major R&B hits, but biggest of all was 1954's "Shake, Rattle & Roll," which leered almost as much as it rocked. Bill Haley and Elvis Presley would cut later versions, but they couldn't match the stomp and sass of Big Joe's original. At his commercial peak, Turner appeared in two motion pictures, *Rhythm and Blues Revue* (1955) and *Shake, Rattle and Rock* (1956). When rock 'n' roll became the province of white teenagers, Turner's days as a hitmaker came to an end, although he made many superb recordings for Atlantic until 1959. In the '70s, although he recorded many well-regarded jazz LPs with Dizzy Gillespie, Milt Jackson, Roy Eldridge, and Eddie "Cleanhead" Vinson, Turner never really stopped rocking. Even when old age, obesity, and diabetes forced him to sit while singing, he would pound out the beat with his cane and sing with impressive power until he died.

what to buy: If you're just looking for Big Joe's most popular R&B jumpers from the 1950s in crisp digital sound, you're sure to dig *The Very Best of Big Joe Turner* (Rhino, 1998, compilation prod. Billy Vera), with such cool jive as "Shake, Rattle & Roll," "Flip Flop and Fly," "Corrine, Corrina," and the infamous "TV Mama." If you really want to indulge yourself, *Big, Bad and Blue: The Big Joe Turner Anthology* (Rhino, 1994, prod. James Austin), a 61-song, three-disc set, comprises Turner's best sides for several labels from the 1930s through the 1950s.

what to buy next: To hear Turner onstage in his rocking prime, *Big Joe Rides Again* (Rhino, 1987, prod. Nesuhi Ertegun) contains 10 songs from his 1959 Carnegie Hall appearance. *The Boss of the Blues* (Rhino, 1981, prod. Nesuhi Ertegun) is a 10-track reproduction of Turner's 1956 Atlantic LP that still cooks today. *Tell Me Pretty Baby* (Arhoolie, 1992, prod. Jack Lauderdale) features many of Turner's great sides with Pete Johnson and his orchestra from the 1940s. Despite an ugly cover, *Shake, Rattle & Roll* (Tomato, 1994, prod. various) is a really good budget compilation with many strong Atlantic sides and great notes by Pete Welding. *Blues Train* (Muse, 1995, prod. Doc Pomus, Bob Porter), a reissue of Turner's 1983 LP with Roomful of Blues, shows he still had it late in life.

what to avoid: Turner re-recorded his big hits several times, some of which pop up on *The Best of Joe Turner* (Pablo, 1987, prod. Norman Granz), which is mostly material from the 1970s, not his all-time classics. And beware *Stormy Monday* (Pablo, 1991, prod. Norman Granz), a reissue of one of Turner's lesser LPs from 1976.

the rest:

Nobody in My Corner (Pablo, 1975/Original Jazz Classics, 1992)
Rhythm & Blues Years (Rhino, 1986)
Greatest Hits (Rhino, 1987)
The Midnight Special (Pablo, 1987)
(With T-Bone Walker) *Bosses of the Blues* (RCA Bluebird, 1989)
Flip Flop and Fly (Pablo, 1989)
I've Been to Kansas City, Vol. 1 (MCA Special Products, 1990)
Singing the Blues (Mobile Fidelity, 1990)
The Trumpet Kings Meet Joe Turner (Original Jazz Classics, 1990)
Everyday I Have the Blues (Original Jazz Classics, 1991)
Kansas City Here I Come (Original Jazz Classics, 1992)

Let's Boogie: The Freedom Story, 1959–64 (Collectables, 1992)
Texas Style (Evidence, 1992)
Every Day in the Week (Decca Jazz, 1993)
I Don't Dig It (Mr R&B, 1994)
Life Ain't Easy (Original Jazz Classics, 1994)
Have No Fear, Big Joe Turner Is Here (Savoy, 1995)
In the Evening (Original Jazz Classics, 1995)
Things That I Used to Do (Original Jazz Classics, 1995)
Patcha, Patcha All Night Long (Original Jazz Classics, 1996)
Shouting the Blues (Eclipse, 1996)
Corrine, Corrina (Magnum, 1997)
1938–1940 (Masters of Jazz, 1998)
Joe Turner's Blues (Topaz Jazz, 1998)

worth searching for: Be on the lookout for the out-of-print *Jumpin' with Joe: The Complete Aladdin & Imperial Recordings* (EMI, 1993), which has a couple of hot duets with Turner rival Wynonie Harris and jumping solo tracks as well. Also, if you dig the great boogie and jazz pianists, Pete Johnson, Freddie Slack, Willie "The Lion" Smith, and Art Tatum back up Turner with gusto on *The Complete 1940–44* (Official, 1991), which has 25 tracks from his heart-pumping days at Decca.

influences:
◀◀ Pete Johnson, Jimmy Rushing

▶▶ Wynonie Harris, Roy Brown, Bill Haley, B.B. King, Elvis Presley

Ken Burke

Rudy Vallee

Born Hubert Prior Vallee, July 28, 1901, in Island Pond, VT. Died July 3, 1986, in Hollywood, CA.

"I've never had much of a voice," Rudy Vallee, one of the first crooners and in many ways the prototypical big-band singer, once said. He didn't sing; he crooned. He didn't emote; he said, "Heigh-ho, everybody!" and used his personality, good looks, and charisma to endear himself to huge audiences. He even used a megaphone—which became his famous concert prop—so people could hear his soft, gentle voice. It all worked; he was a major singing star in the 1920s and 1930s until the more-talented Bing Crosby took over the mass market. Nicknamed "The Vagabond Lover" after an early song and a 1929 film, Vallee was a self-taught saxophonist who served in the U.S. Coast Guard and later enrolled at Yale University. His talented first band, the Yale Collegians, was quickly booked to a long run at the Heigh-Ho Club in New York City; by coincidence, WABC Radio chose the club as a site for broadcasts, which was Vallee's first step to the big time. Vallee proved a major radio talent, with the ability to charm countless female listeners who had never even seen his face. But Crosby usurped his popularity, and, beginning in the early 1940s, Vallee's still-young career was relegated to a series of character roles in bad movies. He eventually hit the nostalgia circuit, did cameos on TV's *Batman*, and maintained a decent nightclub career until his death.

what to buy: *Heigh-Ho Everybody, This Is Rudy Vallee* (Living Era, 1992/Pearl Flapper, 1995), a collection of Vallee's 1928 to 1930 radio broadcasts with the Connecticut Yankees and Yale Collegians, leans heavily on college rah-rah crooning, such as "Betty Co-Ed" and "Let's Do It."

what to buy next: Moving on into the 1930s, *Rudy Vallee, Sing for Your Supper* (Conifer) includes "The Whiffenpoof Song," "This Can't Be Love," and 16 other tracks.

the rest:
As Time Goes By (Varese Sarabande, 1998)

worth searching for: *How to Succeed in Business without Really Trying* (RCA, 1962) documents Vallee's successful comeback stint in the 1961 Broadway musical, and it includes several excellent Vallee croons.

influences:
◀◀ Al Jolson

▶▶ Bing Crosby, Fabian, Elvis Presley, Frank Sinatra, Tony Bennett, Vic Damone

Steve Knopper

Vanguard Jazz Orchestra

See: Mel Lewis

Sarah Vaughan

Born March 27, 1924, in Newark, NJ. Died April 3, 1990, in Los Angeles, CA.

Sarah Vaughan earned the nickname "Sassy" for her feistiness, but as a vocal performer she was nothing short of divine. Ella Fitzgerald once called Vaughan—who launched her prolific career as a big-band vocalist during the heart of the swing era—"the greatest singing talent in the world today." And Frank Sinatra thought Vaughan was one of the finest vocalists in the history of pop music. She was considered bop's greatest diva, the queen of jazz vocals, who wielded her voice like a brass horn. Vaughan could improvise, quickly change a song's mood, and embellish it with rhythms and melodies that made any music to which she contributed unique and inspired.

Rudy Vallee **(Archive Photos)**

The daughter of a carpenter father and laundress mother, Vaughan began her singing career in a church choir and by age 12 was the church's organist. In 1942, she won a Harlem talent contest and launched her professional singing career. After working with Earl Hines and Billy Eckstine, Vaughan went solo in 1945. She continued to collaborate with Eckstine, though one of her breakthrough songs was the jazz tune "Lover Man," which she recorded with Dizzy Gillespie and Charlie Parker in 1945. Though Vaughan's roots were in jazz, she recorded many early-career albums simply backed by an orchestra. When she hopped to Mercury in 1954, Vaughan began working in jazz again and collaborated with some of the greats of her time, including Count Basie, Clifford Brown, and Cannonball Adderley. She made some of her best music during this period, especially her big hit "Broken-Hearted Melody." By the 1950s, Vaughan was an international star, touring the world and drawing huge crowds for her concerts in the United States. She continued this success through the 1960s, but eventually took a five-year break from recording. She returned in 1971, and while many of her 1970s ventures were disappointing, her Duke Ellington songbook project with Count Basie and Oscar Peterson was a career standout. Vaughan's health declined during the 1980s, forcing her to cut back on her performances. In 1989, she won a Grammy for her lifetime achievement in music. That same year, she was diagnosed with cancer, and she died in 1990. Vaughan's albums have since been reissued by the dozens, though many of her fans are still not satisfied and wait for more of her work to be reissued and collected.

what to buy: Though you can get *In the Land of Hi-Fi* (Verve, 1955/Emarcy, 1987) if you buy the massive (and pricey) *The Complete Sarah Vaughan on Mercury, Vol. 1*, the individual album is a good place to start. One of Vaughan's best efforts, this album offers up some solid jazz with an Ernie Wilkins orchestra that features a young Cannonball Adderley. *Sarah Sings Soulfully* (EMD/Capitol, 1963/1993) was Vaughan's final Roulette session before she returned to Mercury, and features some of the best vocals of her career on "A Taste of Honey," "What Kind of Fool Am I," "'Round Midnight," and "Moanin'." *1960s, Vol. 4* (PGD/Verve, 1963, prod. various) and *The Divine Sarah Vaughan: The Columbia Years, 1949–1953* (Deuce/Sony, 1988, prod. various) feature a wider selection of some of Vaughan's best work.

what to buy next: If you get *1960s, Vol. 4*, you'll have a lot of the material on *Sassy Swings the Tivoli* (Verve, 1963/1987, prod. Quincy Jones), but this individual release shows how Vaughan does the songs live, with great accompaniment on "I Cried for You," "Misty," and "Tenderly." Likewise, if you're looking for hip Sassy that busts loose and hits the stratosphere in that best-of-career way, then *Sarah Vaughan with Clifford Brown* (Verve, 1954/Emarcy, 1990) is a choice pick. Vaughan didn't record as much with Brown as she should have, but the light that burns half as long burns twice as bright, and this one's blinding. *Crazy and Mixed Up* (Fantasy, 1982/Pablo, 1987, prod. Sarah Vaughan) is Vaughan in total control and at her best. This is not a reissue; in 1982, she had been singing and recording for almost 50 years.

what to avoid: Vaughan actually has some weak collections, including *Rodgers & Hart Songbook* (Verve, 1954/Emarcy, 1991) and the unfortunate *Send in the Clowns* (Sony, 1981, prod. Norman Granz). The songbook does not feature Vaughan at her best; Rodgers & Hart is not the kind of music that made her famous. And "Send in the Clowns" is considered cruel and unusual torture in some countries.

best of the rest:
It's You or No One (Pair, 1946/1992)
Duke Ellington Songbook #1 (Fantasy, 1953/Pablo, 1987)
Swingin' Easy (Verve, 1954/Emarcy, 1992)
The George Gershwin Songbook, Vol. 1 (Verve, 1955/Emarcy, 1990)
At Mister Kelly's (Verve, 1957/Emarcy, 1991)
(With Quincy Jones) *Misty* (Verve, 1958/1964/Mercury, 1990)
The George Gershwin Songbook, Vol. 2 (Verve, 1958/Emarcy, 1990)
Sarah Vaughan's Golden Hits (Verve, 1958/Mercury, 1990)
After Hours (Capitol, 1961/Blue Note, 1997)
Sassy Swings Again (Verve, 1967/1989)
Jazz Fest Masters (WEA, 1969/Scotti Bros., 1992)
I Love Brazil! (Fantasy, 1977/Pablo, 1994)
Copacabana (Fantasy, 1979/Pablo, 1988)
Duke Ellington Songbook #2 (Fantasy, 1979/Pablo, 1987)
Gershwin Live! (Sony, 1982)
Mystery of Man (Kokopelli, 1984)
The Complete Sarah Vaughan on Mercury, Vol. 1 (Mercury, 1986)
The Complete Sarah Vaughan on Mercury, Vol. 2 (Mercury, 1986)
The Complete Sarah Vaughan on Mercury, Vol. 3 (Mercury, 1986)
The Complete Sarah Vaughan on Mercury, Vol. 4 (Mercury, 1986)
Compact Jazz (Verve, 1987/Emarcy, 1990)
Songs of the Beatles (WEA/Atlantic, 1990)
The Roulette Years (Roulette, 1991)
The Essential Sarah Vaughan: The Great Songs (PGD/PolyGram, 1992)
Jazz 'Round Midnight (PGD/Verve, 1992)
Sassy Sings & Swings (Capitol, 1992)
16 Most Requested Songs (Sony, 1993)
Benny Carter Sessions (EMD, 1994)
Essence of Sarah Vaughan (Sony, 1994)
Verve Jazz Masters: Vol. 18 (Verve, 1994)
Verve Jazz Masters: Vol. 42 (Verve, 1995)
Memories (Black Label)
Sings Broadway (PGD/Verve, 1995)

Sarah Vaughan **(Archive Photos)**

Sings Great American Songs, Vol. 2: '56–'57 (Verve)
This Is Jazz #20 (Sony, 1996)
You're Mine You (Member's Edition, 1997)
Ultimate Sarah Vaughan (Verve, 1997)
(With Lester Young) *The Town Hall Concert* (Pacific Jazz, 1997)
Jazz Profile (Blue Note, 1998)

worth searching for: When Fantasy reissued *How Long Has This Been Going On* (Fantasy, 1978/Pablo, 1987), Vaughan fans wept with delight. This disc collects 10 best-of selections that will disappoint neither the newcomer nor the veteran Vaughan lover. Likewise, if you need a good Vaughan fix, *No Count Sarah* (PGD/Verve, 1958) offers her collaboration with the Count Basie Orchestra, which is ultimate Vaughanism.

influences:

◀◀ Billie Holiday, Bessie Smith, Ella Fitzgerald

▶▶ Carmen McRae, Shirley Horn, Lena Horne, Maxine Sullivan, Diana Ross, Whitney Houston

Chris Tower

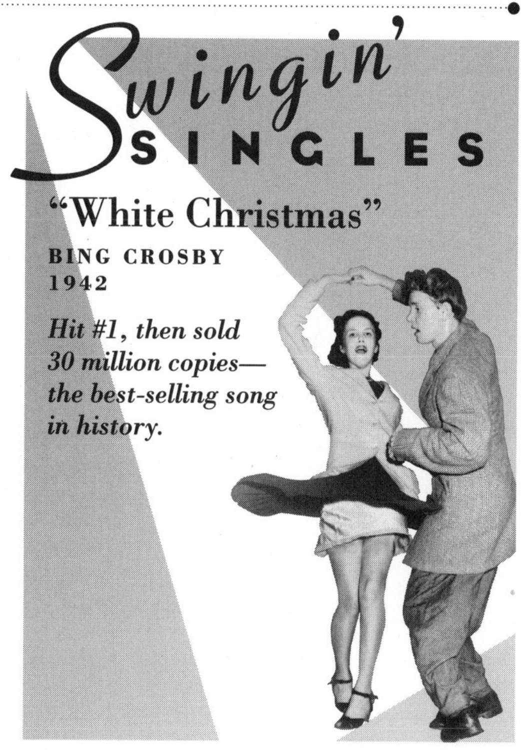

Swingin'
SINGLES
"White Christmas"
BING CROSBY
1942
Hit #1, then sold 30 million copies— the best-selling song in history.

Joe Venuti

Born Giuseppi Venuti, September 6, 1903, in Philadelphia, PA. Died August 14, 1978, in Seattle, WA.

The undisputed father of jazz violin, Joe Venuti created some of the most inventive and energetic solos of the swing era with his searing tone and flawless bow technique. Venuti and his partner, guitarist Eddie Lang, played with Bert Estlow's and Red Nichols's respective bands before they hit the big time with Jean Goldkette's orchestra in 1924. Like many of Goldkette's discoveries, including the Dorsey Brothers, Venuti and Lang were lured away five years later by self-proclaimed "King of Jazz" Paul Whiteman. Whether working solo or in their own combo, the Blue Four, Venuti and Lang were tremendously popular session musicians who cut sides with just about every major swing band of their era. After Lang's death in 1933 (during a botched tonsillectomy), Venuti made several attempts at leading his own bands well into the 1940s; none were successful. A popular featured performer on Bing Crosby's radio show, Venuti also made appearances in such films as *Garden of the Moon, Sing, Helen, Sing,* and *Syncopation.* Though he never really stopped working, the ravages of alcoholism put Venuti's career in a tailspin by the early 1960s. Acclaimed appearances at the Newport Jazz Festival and England's Jazz Expo rekindled public interest and led to a series of well-received recordings with Earl Hines, George Barnes, Zoot Sims, and many others. He continued taking gigs and recording even while fighting cancer during the 1970s.

what to buy: You can sample Venuti's groundbreaking early period with Eddie Lang on *Stringin' the Blues* (Topaz Jazz, 1995, prod. various), which features guest appearances by the Dorsey Brothers, King Oliver, and Bing Crosby from the late '20s and early '30s. *Fiddlesticks* (Happy Days, 1994, prod. various) combines recordings with Venuti and Lang's group, the Blue Four, with exciting sessions with Charlie and Jack Teagarden from the early to late '30s. Or you could opt for *Violin Jazz 1927–34* (Yazoo, 1991, prod. various), a nice sampler of both periods.

what to buy next: A particularly delightful later outing, *Joe Venuti and Zoot Sims* (Chiaroscuro, 1994, prod. Hank O'Neal) features Venuti and sax legend Sims on some solid small-group swing. Smartly reworked standards such as "I Got Rhythm," "I'll See You in My Dreams," and "I Surrender Dear" showcase the soloists at their best. There's plenty of mood and vigor in *'S Wonderful: 4 Giants of Swing* (Flying Fish, 1976/1992, prod. Robert Hoban, Bruce Kaplan), which includes violin-led takes on "Take the 'A' Train," "Lime House Blues," and "Rhapsody in Blue/I Got Rhythm."

the rest:

(With George Barnes) *Gems* (Concord, 1975/1994)

(With Dave McKenna) *Alone at the Palace* ♪♪♪½ (Chiaroscuro, 1977/1992)
(With Stephane Grappelli) *Best of the Jazz Violins* ♪♪♪ (Lester Recording Catalog, 1989)
Sliding By ♪♪♪ (Gazell, 1991)
Pretty Trix ♪♪♪ (IAJRC, 1992)
Joe Venuti in Chicago, 1978 ♪♪½ (Flying Fish, 1993)
Essential Joe Venuti ♪♪♪ (Vanguard Classics, 1995)
15 Jazz Classics ♪♪♪½ (Omega, 1995)

worth searching for: Venuti's work with Eddie Lang never sounded better than on *Great Original Performances, 1926–33* ♪♪♪♪ (Mobile Fidelity, 1992), a now out-of-print digitally remastered compilation of superior quality. Venuti backs Louis Armstrong and Bing Crosby on *Havin' More Fun* ♪♪♪ (Jazz Unlimited, 1997) and jams with Gene Krupa, Eddie Condon, and Benny Goodman on Bud Freeman's *Swingin' with "The Eel"* ♪♪♪ (Living Era, 1998).

influences:
◀◀ Paul Whiteman, Eddie Lang
▶▶ Stephane Grappelli, Django Reinhardt, Stuff Smith

Ken Burke

Gene Vincent

Born Eugene Vincent Craddock, February 11, 1935, in Norfolk, VA. Died October 12, 1971, in Los Angeles, CA.

It's surprising how many knowledgeable people believe Gene Vincent was a mere Elvis Presley soundalike. Indeed, upon hearing Vincent's 1956 rockabilly smash "Be-Bop-a-Lula," Presley's own mother couldn't tell the difference and fired off a congratulatory telegram to her son. Yet not even the King himself could conjure the erotic, edgy feel of Vincent's best Capitol sides. With his band, the Blue Caps, Vincent brought elements of quavering, jazzy bop into rockabilly. Possessing extraordinary vocal control, he combined terse phrasing and gliding pitch to create a palpable aura of tension and danger. As a result, when the Blue Caps cut loose on an instrumental break (with accompanying shouts and screams), they sounded like a motorcycle gang commandeering a roadhouse on a Saturday night. "Be-Bop-a-Lula" became one of the few records to simultaneously scale the upper regions of the pop, country, and R&B charts, despite a B-side ("Woman Love") that caused a Virginia court to fine Vincent $10,000 for lewd behavior. (Did he sing "huggin'" or "fuggin'"? The debate rages on.) "Race with the Devil," "Blue Jean Bop," "Lotta Lovin'" and "Dance to the Bop" made less of an impact on the charts, but they too were masterful examples of tough, yet commercial, rockabilly. However, Vincent's recording career wasn't all switchblades and hot bop. Like Presley, he was also a frustrated R&B group singer, and sang with purity and skill on his share of group ballads, such as "Wear My Ring" and "Important Words."

At his peak, Vincent appeared in such films as *The Girl Can't Help It!* and *Hot Rod Gang,* and became the first rock singer to be awarded a star on the Hollywood Walk of Fame. When the hits and lucrative bookings dried up in America, he moved to England where legendary TV producer Jack Good dressed him in black leather and encouraged him to openly display the brace on his right leg. That game leg (previously injured in a motorcycle mishap) was further mangled in the same auto accident that killed fellow rocker Eddie Cochran, and it caused Vincent unrelenting pain during the remainder of his lifetime. An icon of greasy, primal rockabilly, Vincent paradoxically cut mostly pop sides in England, where he scored his final chart records ("Wild Cat," "Temptation Baby," "Spaceship to Mars") and appeared in a few teen flicks. The emergence of the Beatles, poor health, and a wide array of soul-wracking personal problems forced Vincent to return to the U.S. for an ill-fated comeback. He cut some well-reviewed, low-selling country and modern rock LPs during the late '60s, but nothing could revive his failing health or career. Though his talent remained intact up until the end, he died broke and nearly forgotten. Since his death, dozens of neo-rockabilly acts have helped revive interest in Vincent's music and, in 1998, diligent fans (both old and new) helped get Vincent inducted into the Rock and Roll Hall of Fame. Reissues of his early work have finally become available, and a major biography on Vincent's life and music, written by *Original Cool* magazine publisher Sue Van Hecke, is due out in 1999.

what to buy: Both *Capitol Collector's Series* ♪♪♪♪½ (Capitol, 1990, compilation prod. Ron Furmanek) and *The Screaming End: The Best of Gene Vincent & His Blue Caps* ♪♪♪♪½ (Razor & Tie, 1997, compilation prod. Matt Goldman, Dave "Daddy Cool" Booth) are remarkably potent introductions to this bedrock vital artist. While the track listings are somewhat similar, the Razor & Tie set is the better package for liner notes and flat-out rock, and the Capitol disc contains a few choice ballads that demonstrate Vincent's artistic range.

what to buy next: All of Vincent's original Capitol LPs have been reissued on such strong two-for-one compilations as *Bluejean Bop!/Gene Vincent & His Blue Caps* ♪♪♪♪ (Capitol, 1956/1957/Collectables, 1998, prod. Ken Nelson), *Gene Vincent Rocks & The Blue Caps Roll/A Gene Vincent Record Date* ♪♪♪ (Capitol, 1958/Collectables, 1998, prod. Ken Nelson), and *Sounds Like Gene Vincent/Crazy Times* ♪♪♪½ (Capitol, 1959/1960/Collectables, 1998, prod. Ken Nelson), and they have been further fleshed out with bonus tracks. Vincent's great sidemen, particularly guitarists Cliff Gallup and Johnny Meeks, are expertly showcased on these great sides from the '50s.

what to avoid: The budget racks are glutted with releases featuring Vincent's final recordings, such as *Be-Bop-a-Lula* (Prime Cuts, 1997), *Be-Bop-a-Lula* (Columbia River, 1998), and *Roots of Rock 'n' Roll* (Direct Source, 1997). These discs feature a late '60s remake of "Be-Bop-a-Lula," as well as "The Story of the Rockers," "Pickin' Poppies," and a sickly version of "Hi Lilli Hi Lo." If you absolutely must own these sides, track down *The Masters* (Eagle, 1998), a two-disc, 36-song set that contains all of the above plus Vincent's Challenge LP in its entirety, the British hit "Temptation Baby," his last tracks for Ron Weiser's Rollin' Rock label, some solid cuts with the Wild Angels, and previously released (in the U.S.) demos. This compilation usurps most of the quality material on Magnum's *Rebel Heart* series as well, and will more than satisfy completists.

the rest:

Shakin' up a Storm (EMI, 1964/1998)
Ain't That Too Much (Challenge, 1967/Sundazed, 1993)
I'm Back & I'm Proud (Dandelion, 1970/See for Miles, 1995)
Gene Vincent's Legendary Blue Caps (Magnum, 1993)
Greatest Hits (Curb, 1993)
The Gene Vincent Tapes (Jerden, 1995)
The EP Collection (See for Miles, 1996)
Rebel Heart, Vol. 2 (Magnum, 1996)
Rebel Heart, Vol. 3 (Magnum, 1996)
Rebel Heart, Vol. 4 (Magnum, 1996)
Rebel Heart, Vol. 5 (Magnum, 1998)

worth searching for: Some import services may still carry *The Gene Vincent Box Set* (EMI, 1990, reissue prod. Roger Nunn, Steve Aynsly), a six-disc, 151-song set that includes everything he recorded for Capitol and England's Columbia label from the '50s through the early '60s. Also, longtime fans will definitely want to own *The Lost Dallas Sessions, '57–'58* (Dragon Street, 1998, compilation prod. David Dennard), which contains previously unreleased demos, alternate takes, and a driving live appearance on the *Big D Jamboree* radio show we have all waited too long to hear.

influences:

◄ The Delmore Brothers, Elvis Presley, Red Foley, Ivory Joe Hunter

► The Beatles, Stray Cats, Ronnie Dawson, Johnny Carroll, Jeff Beck, just about every rockabilly act working today

Ken Burke

Eddie "Cleanhead" Vinson

Born December 19, 1917, in Houston, TX. Died July 2, 1988, in Los Angeles, CA.

Eddie "Cleanhead" Vinson's voice cracked as badly as that of a 12-year-old boy with his first chin hairs, but adoring female fans had no complaints about the man's macho swagger. Though Vinson was a horn man first and an R&B crooner later, it was his earthy, ribald singing that sold records. Called "Cleanhead" after he became bald as a result of an accident with a lye hair straightener, Vinson took off in the late 1930s with Milt Larkin's territory swing band, blowing sax with fellow Texans Illinois Jacquet and Arnett Cobb. He detoured to play behind bluesman Big Bill Broonzy for a year, then found a home as saxophonist and vocalist with Cootie Williams, who had only recently left Duke Ellington's streamlined unit to build his own booting swing band. Vinson struck gold almost immediately with his monster blues squeal "Cherry Red Blues," which he would record repeatedly over his 50-year-career. Going it alone, Vinson churned out three dozen tough R&B sides for Mercury and a lesser number of swinging recordings for King. Vinson loved to prove his mettle with the top sax aces of his day, blowing with every jazzman from the growling Ben Webster to Cannonball Adderley. (Vinson's 1950s band even included a young John Coltrane.) Vinson joined fellow blues shouter Joe Turner, churning out sessions for the Pablo label in the 1960s and 1970s, then toured regularly with tough mama Etta James until his death.

what to buy: *Battle of the Blues, Vol. 3* (King, 1988, prod. Syd Nathan), a reproduction of the 1950s-vintage King album, splits 16 cuts evenly between Vinson and fellow lungsman Jimmy Witherspoon, another product of southwestern swing bands. Vinson sails on "Person to Person" and "Ashes on My Pillow." Witherspoon's Kansas City shouting is a fine complement to Cleanhead's Texas twisters.

what to buy next: There are only five Vinson tracks on *Cootie Williams and His Orchestra, 1941–1944* (Classics, 1995), but one of them is his seminal version of "Cherry Red." The rest are up-tempo big-band instrumentals verging on R&B, with some of bop pianist Bud Powell's earliest performances.

the rest:

Kidney Stew Is Fine (Delmark, 1969)
I Want a Little Girl (Pablo, 1981)
Blues in the Night, Vol. 1: The Early Show (Fantasy, 1992)
The Late Show (Fantasy, 1992)
Back in Town (Bethlehem, 1996)
Cherry Red (One Way, 1996)

worth searching for: *Blues, Boogie and Bop: The 1940s Mercury Sessions* (Verve, 1995, prod. Richard Seidel, Kazu Yanagida), a prohibitively expensive, limited-edition, seven-CD box set, contains nearly three dozen Vinson sides from the late 1940s. They're all blaring R&B with hardboiled titles like "Juicehead Baby," "Luxury Tax Blues," and "Shavetail." Included in this expansive collection are swing-and-blues oriented sets by such luminaries as Helen Humes, Jay McShann, Rex Stewart, Cootie Williams, and Buddy Rich.

influences:

◀◀ Louis Jordan

▶▶ Nappy Brown, Big Joe Williams

Steve Braun

T-Bone Walker

Born Aaron Thibeaux Walker, May 28, 1910, in Linden, TX. Died March 16, 1975, in Los Angeles, CA.

The undisputed cornerstone of the modern electric blues guitar movement, T-Bone Walker single-handedly revolutionized the blues—and did so with a horn-heavy band that influenced such jump-blues notables as Clarence "Gatemouth" Brown and, much later, the Brian Setzer Orchestra. With elegant fluidity and a unique gritty sophistication, the onetime Cab Calloway orchestra member triumphed throughout the 1940s and 1950s as the pathfinder of the modern electric guitar movement—he was the original link between the rural blues of singers like Blind Lemon Jefferson and the contemporary blues of the electric combos he pioneered. His fascination with electrified guitar led him to experiment with amplification, an interest that had to do with his crossing paths earlier with another electrified guitar proponent, Charlie Christian. The first to record electric blues, Walker was a commanding guitarist, excellent vocalist, and author of numerous classics. Smitten by wanderlust and a love of the entertainment world while still in grade school, Walker ran off with a medicine show. His insatiable thirst for learning instrumental and performing skills led him to a week's membership in the Cab Calloway Band. After he took a solo in Houston, playing banjo and doing splits and dance moves, Walker was a hit, and by the early 1930s had logged numerous miles on the road and was already beginning to fall victim to health and drinking problems. Walker found a new audience in the European tour circuit during the 1960s, when a new generation discovered the magic of his anthem, "Stormy Monday," through its considerable exposure by the Allman Brothers Band. Despite declining health and a car accident, Walker mounted a domestic comeback of sorts in the early 1970s. Health and financial setbacks got the best of him, and he never fully recovered after being sidelined by a stroke in 1974.

what to buy: The vast and rich Walker discography is complete enough to satisfy the most avid collector or casual listener. Must-haves include *The Complete Capitol/Black and White Recordings* (Capitol, 1995, prod. Pete Welding), 75 tracks on three CDs that chronicle the 1940s phase, with extensive notes and many alternate takes. Another collector's dream set is the specially priced, two-disc *The Complete Imperial Recordings* (EMI America, 1991), which covers his prolific early 1950s stint with Imperial. Among the 52 selections is the stellar instrumental "Strollin' with Bones." For those who are not ready to invest as heavily, try the single-disc *T-Bone Blues* (Atlantic Jazz, 1989, prod. Bob Porter), a solid collection of some better-known Walker compositions, including the classic "Stormy Monday." Originally recorded in the late 1960s for the Black and Blue label, *I Want a Little Girl* (Delmark, 1973, prod. Robert Koester) is another winner. Backed by a polished and empathetic band, T-Bone radiates all that he is legendary for—from up-tempo jazz/blues grooves to smoldering slow blues.

what to buy next: Originally recorded in France in 1969, *Good Feelin'* (Verve, 1993) is rather uneven instrumentally, with the French backup band not quite meshing as well as others have with T-Bone. Oddly, this effort won Walker a Grammy, belatedly, toward the end of his life.

what to avoid: Unless you just want another version of "Stormy Monday," steer clear of *Rare T-Bone Walker* (Offbeat, 1996).

best of the rest:

Inventor of the Electric Blues Guitar (Blues Collection, 1991)
T-Bone Shuffle: Charly Masterworks, Vol. 14 (Charly, 1992)
Rare and Well Done (Magnum America, 1996)
Legendary T-Bone Walker (Brunswick, 1996)
Stormy Monday (Laserlight, 1996)
(With Eddie Vinson) *Blues Collective* (Laserlight, 1997)

worth searching for: *The Complete Recordings of T-Bone Walker, 1940–52* (Mosaic, 1990) is a compelling six-disc collection that demonstrates Walker's remarkable impact.

influences:

◀◀ Blind Lemon Jefferson, Charlie Christian

▶▶ Freddie King, B.B. King, Albert Collins, Clarence "Gatemouth" Brown, the Brian Setzer Orchestra, Stevie Ray Vaughan

Tali Madden

Fats Waller

Born Thomas Wright Waller, May 21, 1904, in New York, NY. Died December 15, 1943, in Kansas City, MO.

Fats Waller—one of the great showmen of jazz, a terrific organist, an underrated soloist, an architect of swing, and an important figure who worked with Bessie Smith, Sidney Bechet, and Fletcher Henderson—first became famous in the 1920s with enduring hits such as "Honeysuckle Rose" and "Ain't Misbehavin'." Waller, whose father was a street-corner preacher with his own trucking business, began his career playing organ during his father's services. His first paying job came when he was 15 years old, as house organist at the Lincoln Theatre. In the early 1920s he became a protégé of the great Harlem stride pianist James P. Johnson, and through him he cut player piano rolls and lined up his first recording date. He also started accompanying a number of classic blues singers (including Bessie Smith and Alberta Hunter) and writing songs. By the end of the '20s, Waller was becoming a force in New York City jazz. He did regular radio broadcasts and had already recorded with stars like Fletcher Henderson, Clarence Williams, and Sidney Bechet, and his songs were garnering both commercial and critical acclaim. With Andy Razaf, grandson of the former Madagascarian consul to the United States, he created such classics as "Honeysuckle Rose," "Ain't Misbehavin'," and "My Fate Is in Your Hands." With his recording career also in full swing, Waller made substantial contributions to dates led by big-band notables Ted Lewis and Jack Teagarden. By the mid-1930s, Waller had created the sextet Fats Waller and His Rhythm, one of the finest small-jazz groups of the time. Though he recorded a lot of material mandated by his record company—much of it trite, hackneyed themes—Waller still imbued it with wit and humor. (Gems included "Christopher Columbus," "Until the Real Thing Comes Along," and "Cabin in the Sky.") He also appeared in a variety of short films (including *Stormy Weather,* with Lena Horne) and radio shows, toured Europe, and played the organ in Paris's Notre Dame Cathedral. On a return train trip from Hollywood to New York City, after working a solo piano gig at the Zanzibar Room, he died of pneumonia.

what to buy: *Turn on the Heat: Piano Solos* ♪♪♪♪♪ (RCA/Bluebird, 1991, prod. various), which includes multiple takes from 1929 RCA sessions, is a must-have for anyone with more than a passing interest in great piano playing. It includes more than half the recording dates from 1927 through 1934, the period when Waller's reputation as a pianist was beginning to pick up steam nationally. Classics like "Handful of Keys," "Ain't Misbehavin'," and "Smashing Thirds" are the highlights, but it is also instructive to hear the differences in two run-throughs of "Carolina Shout," the showpiece written by his mentor, James P. Johnson. *Greatest Hits* ♪♪♪♪♪ (RCA Victor, 1996, prod. various) has been around in various forms since the dawn of the LP era, but CD remastering has improved it tremendously. *Breakin' the Ice: The Early Years, Part 1 (1934–1935)* ♪♪♪♪♪ (RCA/Bluebird, 1995, prod. various) and *I'm Gonna Sit Right Down: The Early Years, Part 2 (1935–1936)* ♪♪♪♪♪ (RCA/Bluebird, 1995, prod. various) have better overall sound than the corresponding releases for Jazz Chronological Classics. Songs like "A Porter's Love Song to a Chambermaid" and "Honeysuckle Rose" were deserved hits, but the solos on "Then I'll Be Tired of You" and the bouncy instrumental "Serenade for a Wealthy Widow" are underrecognized classics. "I Got Rhythm," "Dinah," and the title song from the second album are higlights of *Part 2.*

what to buy next: The standard Fats Waller hits like "Ain't Misbehavin'" and "Honeysuckle Rose" aren't on *Fats and His Buddies* ♪♪♪♪ (RCA/Bluebird, 1992, reissue prod. Orrin Keepnews), but it's still the perfect single-disc complement for a greatest hits set. On material from 1927 through 1929, Waller plays in three different group configurations and reveals his skills at the pipe organ. The Louisiana Sugar Babes' material with James P. Johnson on piano and Waller on organ is particularly delightful, though it doesn't quite capture the two men's greatness. *Fats Waller and His Rhythm: The Middle Years, Part I* ♪♪♪♪ (RCA/Bluebird, 1992, prod. various) and *A Good Man Is Hard to Find: The Middle Years, Part II* ♪♪♪♪ (RCA/Bluebird, 1995, prod. various) represent 1936 to 1940, during which time Waller reveled in vocal shtick. He still played prodigious piano, but seemed to realize that pop tastes preferred bouncy melodies, clever-sounding lyrics, and outrageous mugging rather than straightforward instrumental genius. But these performances aren't trite, especially when compared to much of the stuff his contemporaries were unleashing in faux Waller style. Especially affecting are his takes on "Yacht Club Swing," "Hold Tight," and the alternate "I'll Dance at Your Wedding," where maudlin sentimentality, fortunately, loses to the pianist's formidable wit and skill. *The Jugglin' Jive of Fats Waller and His Orchestra* ♪♪♪♪ (Sandy Hook, 1985), a document of 1938 radio broadcasts from New York City, reveals Waller's live performance genius. The disc is filled with shameless mugging, double-entendre asides, and plenty of classic Waller cuts, including "Honeysuckle Rose," "Ain't Misbehavin'," and little gems like "Pent up in a Penthouse" and "Hallelujah."

what to avoid: There are a couple Waller titles on the market that unwary buyers could pick up in a careless moment and regret later. *Low Down Papa* ♪♪♪ (Biograph, 1990, prod. Arnold S. Caplin) is actually quite interesting, taking player piano rolls that Waller "cut" for the QRS and Play-A-Roll companies, putting them on a modern player piano, and then recording the result in digital sound. *Fats at the Organ* **woof!** (ASV, 1992) is another matter, however, because it takes piano rolls and transcribes them for organ. While Waller did play the organ, the approach he used was different than the one he used for piano, making these mechanical transcriptions more than one step away from the real thing.

best of the rest:

Last Years: Fats Waller and His Rhythm, 1940–1943 ♪♪♪♪ (RCA, 1989)
1936 ♪♪♪♪ (Jazz Chronological Classics, 1995)
1936–1937 ♪♪♪♪ (Jazz Chronological Classics, 1995)
1937 ♪♪♪♪ (Jazz Chronological Classics, 1995)
1929–1934 ♪♪♪♪ (Jazz Chronological Classics, 1996)

Fats Waller **(Archive Photos)**

1934–1935 ℐℐℐℐ (Jazz Chronological Classics, 1996)
1935 ℐℐℐℐ (Jazz Chronological Classics, 1996)
1935, Vol. 2 ℐℐℐℐ (Jazz Chronological Classics, 1996)
1935–1936 ℐℐℐℐ (Jazz Chronological Classics, 1996)
1937, Vol. 2 ℐℐℐℐ (Jazz Chronological Classics, 1996)
1937–1938 ℐℐℐℐ (Jazz Chronological Classics, 1996)
1939 ℐℐℐℐ (Jazz Chronological Classics, 1998)

worth searching for: Maurice Waller wrote a biography of his famous father, *Fats Waller* (Macmillan/Schirmer Books, 1977), with Anthony Calabrese. The book reads well, even if it is a tad starchy. The senior Waller was also one of the first major jazz artists ever bootlegged: organ solos from the RCA vaults emerged when some enterprising soul compiled them and released two 10-inch vinyl albums on the Jolly Roger label. These recordings pre-date all those European concert recordings that keep showing up on the market.

influences:

◀ Luckey Roberts, James P. Johnson, Willie "The Lion" Smith

▶ Art Tatum, Teddy Wilson, Count Basie, Squirrel Nut Zippers

Garaud MacTaggart

Wally's Swing World

Formed 1992, in Santa Cruz, CA.

Wally Trindade, vocals, guitar; Bill Bosch, upright bass; Eliot Kalman, piano; Andy Weis, drums; Curtis Nash, trumpet; Brad Hecht, tenor sax; Paul Tarantino, alto sax.

Critics have called singer Wally Trindade a "Sinatra soundalike," but as a low-key version of "Mack the Knife" proves, his high pitch gives him more in common with Bobby Darin. Still, because the neo-swing movement is dominated by fast, hot bands and flat lead singers, it's refreshing to hear a group built around a voice. Wally's Swing World has been performing live since 1992, including an opening date for honorary swinger Chris Isaak and a regular gig at San Francisco's Top of the Mark, but its repertoire is still mostly covers—from Elvis Presley's "Heartbreak Hotel" to Count Basie's "Shiny Stockings." Trindade's men are destined to stick to the wedding circuit for as many years as they can stand it.

what's available: The band's self-released debut, *Full Swing Ahead* ℐℐℐ (1996, prod. Daniel Thomas, Wally Trindade), leans heavily on vocal standards, as if singer Trindade is positioning himself to be the next Jack Jones or Andy Williams. He croons nicely on "All of Me" and "Saturday Night Is the Loneliest Night," even if he doesn't have quite enough humor or personality for the "you give me a boot" line in "I Get a Kick out of You." It's strong vocal swing music overall, docked slightly for muffled homemade production.

"Whole Lotta Shakin' Goin' On"
JERRY LEE LEWIS
1957
Blues belter Big Maybelle scored a modest R&B hit with this before the Killer made it a rockabilly classic.
Swingin' SINGLES

influences:

◀ Bobby Darin, Frank Sinatra, Nat King Cole, Count Basie, Benny Goodman, Glenn Miller

Steve Knopper

Helen Ward

Born September 19, 1916, in New York, NY. Died April 21, 1998, in Arlington, VA.

One of the finest big-band singers ever, Helen Ward worked with many of the best musical aggregations of the 1930s and '40s. Exuberant but technically skilled, everything Ward cut showcases a sophisticated edge and sultry rhythmic command, which belied her tender years. Ward turned pro at age 16, when she and songwriter Burton Lane formed a piano-vocal duo. Stints with Enrique Madriguera's Latin Band as well as "sweet" bands led by Nye Mayhew, Eddie Duchin, David Rubinoff, and Will Osborne led to her own radio show on WOR. Ward joined Benny Goodman in 1934, just as swing was heating up, and gave voice to such hits as "Goody Goody," "You Turned the Tables on Me," "It's Been So Long," and "These Foolish Things." Though she was on a major commercial roll, Ward chose to semi-retire from show business in 1934 so she could start a family. Always in demand, she made guest appearances on recordings led by Teddy Wilson, Gene Krupa, Hal McIntyre, Red Norvo, Bob Crosby, and Harry James, among others. Though she didn't tour, Ward sang in motion picture "soundies" and made sporadic radio appearances through the 1940s. For a time, Ward worked in radio production, but by the early '50s she returned to the road, singing with Benny Goodman and recording with Wild Bill Davison and Peanuts Hucko. She retired not long after that, appearing on record for the last time in 1979.

what's available: To hear Ward singing "Goody Goody" and "There's a Small Hotel" with Benny Goodman's band, check out *Benny & the Singers* (Memoir Classics, 1997, prod. various), a 24-song set with vocal turns by the likes of Ella Fitzgerald, Helen Forrest, Peggy Lee, Fred Astaire, Johnny Mercer, and Jimmy Rushing. If it's just Ward you want, search the import bins and online services for the 25-song *The Queen of Big Band Swing* (ASV/Living Era, 1998, prod. various), which compiles all of her most famous numbers as recorded with Gene Krupa, Teddy Wilson, Bob Crosby, Harry James, and, of course, Benny Goodman.

worth searching for: You can hear Ward singing live on albums featuring some of the great bandleaders and their bands. She appears on Harry James's *Jump Sauce (1943–44)* (Viper's Nest, 1990) and Red Norvo's *1943–1944: Legendary V-Disc Masters* (Vintage Jazz Classics, 1990)—both solid transcription recordings from the days of World War II.

influences:

◀◀ Mildred Bailey, Ella Fitzgerald, Lee Wiley

▶▶ Martha Tilton, Louise Tobin, Edythe Wright, Ella Mae Morse

Ken Burke

Dinah Washington

Born Ruth Lee Jones, August 29, 1924, in Tuscaloosa, AL. Died December 14, 1963, in Detroit, MI.

Unquestionably, Dinah Washington is one of the greatest, most versatile voices in the entire canon of American song. A consummate master of jazz, blues, R&B, swing, and pop, Washington spent most of her career imprisoned in the ghetto divadom constructed for the likes of Ella Fitzgerald, Billie Holiday, and Sarah Vaughan, and she didn't escape until 1959's "What a Diff'rence a Day Makes." Washington's ascent to that point was long and arduous, yet fruitful. She started as a piano prodigy in her mother's church at the age of 10. In 1939, a 15-year-old Ruth won an amateur contest at Chicago's famous Regal Theater, singing "I Can't Face the Music." From that point on, the sinful call of the secular world was ringing in her ears. The gospel circuit beckoned, but by the early 1940s, Dinah Washington (as she was now called) quit that and plunged into the jazz underworld. After a brief stint with trumpeter Henry "Red" Allen, Washington hooked up with Lionel Hampton's big band. Her work with him earned her a contract with Keynote Records, and her first single, 1943's "Evil Gal Blues," heralded the promise of a new voice to jukeboxes throughout African America. By the 1950s, Washington became a quiet people's favorite, triumphing with excellent and pedestrian material alike. More prolific than most (she would cut almost 500 sides for the Emarcy, Keynote, Mercury, and Wing labels between 1943 and 1961), when she finally hit her stride she was unbeatable. Her crossover successes ("Unforgettable," "This Bitter Earth"), plus 1960 duets with Brook Benton on "A Rockin' Good Way (To Mess Around and Fall in Love)" and "Baby (You've Got What It Takes)," made her the toast of pop and the darling of *Jet* magazine. Washington would leave Mercury in 1961 for a more lucrative deal with Roulette Records, but she never had the same impact again. She died from an accidental overdose of diet pills in 1963. Since her prominence as the musical leitmotif of Clint Eastwood's film *The Bridges of Madison County,* Washington's legacy has undergone a renaissance. For an artist of her caliber, it's long overdue.

what to buy: *First Issue: The Dinah Washington Story* (Verve, 1993, prod. various) is the definitive collection. Buy it. Her classic *What a Diff'rence a Day Makes* (Mercury, 1959/1987) is also available in a nicely polished Mobile Fidelity audiophile issue released in 1997.

what to buy next: *Mellow Mama* (Delmark, 1945/1993, prod. Robert Koester, Steve Wagner) and *Dinah Jams* (PSM, 1954/Verve, 1997) are tremendous early works that set the tone for her future magic. *The Bessie Smith Songbook* (Emarcy, 1957/1986) is one of the finest interpretive efforts of our time. *The Best of Dinah Washington: The Roulette Years* (Roulette, 1993) is a fine chronicling of her later work.

what to avoid: *Golden Classics* (Collectables, 1990) is a hodgepodge affair that doesn't serve Washington's memory well, though she sounds fine throughout.

best of the rest:

For Those in Love (Emarcy, 1955/1992)
In the Land of Hi-Fi (Emarcy, 1956/1987)
Dinah (Emarcy, 1956/1991)
The Fats Waller Songbook (Emarcy, 1957/1987)
Unforgettable (Mercury, 1959/1991)
(With Brook Benton) *The Two of Us* (Verve, 1960/1995)
Compact Jazz (Verve, 1987)
Compact Jazz: Dinah Washington Sings the Blues (Verve, 1987/1990)

Benny Waters (**© Jack Vartoogian**)

The Complete Dinah Washington on Mercury, Vol. 1–7 (Mercury, 1989)
In Love (Roulette, 1991)
The Essential Dinah Washington: The Great Songs (Verve, 1992)
Jazz 'Round Midnight (Verve, 1993)
Verve Jazz Masters #19 (Verve, 1994)
Sings Standards (Verve, 1994)
Blue Gardenia: Songs of Love (Emarcy, 1995)
Jazz Profile (Blue Note, 1997)
Back to the Blues (Blue Note, 1997)
Live at Birdland '62 (Baldwin, 1997)

worth searching for: The 1992 video *The Swingin' Years: Vintage Jazz Classics* features performances by Washington, Stan Kenton, Louis Jordan, and others on a 1960 telecast hosted by Ronald Reagan.

influences:

◄◄ Maxine Sullivan, Sarah Vaughan, Mildred Bailey

►► Patti LaBelle, Patti Austin, Aretha Franklin, Erykah Badu

Tom Terrell and Gary Graff

Benny Waters

Born January 23, 1902, in Brighton, MD. Died August 11, 1998, in Columbia, MD.

Saxophonist Benny Waters lived through all the major jazz eras and the entire history of jazz recording, but pretty much stuck with swing. He played jazz as it was being invented, and continued playing until he died. Waters came from a big, musical family and began musical studies on piano and learned clarinet from his brother. His mother died when he was a youngster and he went to live with his aunt and uncle in Haverford, Pennsylvania. There, he began his professional career in 1918, playing hot syncopated music in a pre-jazz dance band where he also learned to play saxophones. Around age 18, Waters entered the Boston Conservatory of Music where he studied piano and theory. Waters was soon playing all the saxophones and his gigging (often out-of-town) was overshadowing his studies. In 1924, Waters went to New York to play a show at Harlem's Lafayette Theatre, and heard trumpeter Louis Armstrong with bandleader Fletcher Henderson's orchestra. Inspired, Waters left Boston and school, and, based in

Philadelphia, earned full-time work as a dance-band musician in many famed bands of the day.

Waters led his own band for four years in the 1940s and joined drummer Roy Milton's R&B band before hooking up with Jimmy Archey's Dixieland band for a month-long European tour. Waters easily found work in Europe, decided to become an expatriate, quit drinking, and eventually settled in Paris, where he worked steadily (with many American jazz expatriates) from 1952 to 1992. In 1979, Waters began his annual trips to the U.S. He recorded his first album as a leader, *From Paradise (Small's) to Shangri-la*, in 1987. Waters later returned to the United States for cataract surgery, which failed and left him blind. Undeterred, Waters resumed his career in New York City, practicing every day and receiving rave reviews for his performances on alto and tenor saxophones, clarinet, and baritone vocals. He died in 1998 at the age of 96.

what to buy: At age 95, Waters climbed on the bandstand at Manhattan's historically named new Birdland to record the swinging *Benny Waters Birdland Birthday: Live at 95* ♪♪♪♪♪ (Enja, 1997, prod. Russ Dantzler). Kicking off with "Exactly Like Me," Waters maintains the danceable pace and hits the final upper register notes with crisp precision. His original, "Blues Amore," slows the pace for his drawling alto saxophone renderings ranging from full-bodied blowing to soft subtleness injected with raspy, seductive notes. To the amusement of the audience (and to armchair fans), Waters sings and scats on the delightful jump-swing version of "Everybody Loves My Baby."

what to buy next: *Statesmen of Jazz* ♪♪♪♪ (American Federation of Jazz Societies, 1995, prod. Arbors Records) spotlights Waters in a performance with his contemporaries (ranging in age from middle 60s to early 90s). This is no jam, but an intelligent session offering some of the hottest soloing and best ensemble work on record.

worth searching for: Waters was 85 years old when *From Paradise (Small's) to Shangri-la* ♪♪♪♪♪ (Muse, 1989, prod. Phil Schaap) was recorded. Hearing his flawless, robust-toned saxophone playing, his smooth clarinet renderings, and his fine baritone voice, you'd never guess his age. Backed by piano, bass, and drums, Waters delivers nine tunes with sparkling vitality, often switching within one tune to play both alto and tenor, and putting his horns down momentarily to deliver, with crisp perfection, vocal versions of the novelty tunes "Hit That Jive Jack" and "Romance without Finance."

influences:

◀◀ Coleman Hawkins

▶▶ Stanley Turrentine, Hank Crawford, Houston Person

Nancy Ann Lee

Ethel Waters

Born October 31, 1896, in Chester, PA. Died September 1, 1977, in Chatsworth, CA.

Actress-singer Ethel Waters's long and diverse career included many firsts. She was the first genuine jazz singer to record and she eventually worked her way onto the Broadway stage and into many Hollywood films, defying racism and paving the path for other African-American entertainers. She was an adept jazz vocalist with precise, clear diction and a sterling sense of swing, yet also could deliver Bessie Smith–like blues and sing compelling spirituals. Raised near Philadelphia, Waters began her career there before moving to New York City in 1919. During the 1920s, she made her debut two-sided record ("Down Home Blues"/"Oh Daddy") for the first black-owned recording label, Black Swan, and toured with the Black Swan Troubadours, headed by the house accompanist, pianist Fletcher Henderson. She worked the best theaters, nightclubs, and revues, toured the vaudeville and Theater Owners Booking Association circuits, and was the first black singer to broadcast in the deep South. Waters was also the first black singer to work with a white band, singing with Benny Goodman and the Dorsey Brothers in 1929. She appeared at the Cotton Club in 1933, where she first became associated with the song "Stormy Weather." Following that stint she landed vital roles in musicals and played Carnegie Hall in 1938. As a dramatic actress, Waters appeared in Hollywood films, including *Cabin in the Sky*, the 1943 movie in which she sang the classic "Happiness Is Just a Thing Called Joe." Her best-selling 1951 autobiography, *His Eye Is on the Sparrow*, reveals her determination to succeed over all obstacles. Waters performed throughout the classic blues and jazz eras and the beginnings of traditional pop. From the 1960s until her death her performances were restricted mostly to singing spirituals with evangelist Billy Graham.

what to buy: *1931–1934* ♪♪♪♪ (Jazz Chronological Classics, 1997, prod. Gilles Petard) contains 23 tracks, two of which—"I Can't Give You Anything but Love" and "Porgy"—feature Waters singing with the Duke Ellington Orchestra. This volume also includes the original version of "Stormy Weather," jazz gems such as "Don't Blame Me" and "Harlem on My Mind," and other favorites that were popular well into successive decades.

what to buy next: Of the earlier Jazz Chronological Classics volumes, the best are *1925–1926* ♪♪♪♪ (Jazz Chronological Classics, 1997, prod. Gilles Petard), which features Smith singing 23 playful blues and jazz classics, some with backing from Fletcher Henderson on piano; and *1926–1929* ♪♪♪♪ (Jazz Chronological Classics, 1994, prod. Gilles Petard), which finds James P. Johnson in the piano chair. Other volumes include sides with Jack Teagarden, Fletcher Henderson, Benny Goodman, and the Dorsey brothers, and versions of "Dinah" and "Stormy Weather."

influences:

◀◀ Bessie Smith, Ma Rainey, Victoria Spivey

▶▶ Billie Holiday, Mildred Bailey, Aretha Franklin, Dinah Washington, Mahalia Jackson

Nancy Ann Lee

Chick Webb

Born William Webb, February 10, 1909, in Baltimore, MD. Died June 16, 1939, in Baltimore, MD.

Drummer-bandleader Chick Webb had a short-lived career, but his influential dance band specializing in the foxtrot and boogie-woogie–influenced swing inspired countless jazz drummers, including luminaries such as Gene Krupa. A childhood accident left Webb with a deformed spine and small stature, but that didn't hinder propulsive playing in his preteen years. By 1924, Webb was in New York City freelancing, and soon formed his own band. Although Webb never learned to read music, he played drums from a platform in the middle of his band and was able to cue musicians with his dazzling drumming and rhythmic skills. His band worked Harlem clubs and recorded one session for Brunswick in 1931, but continued to struggle for wider notice until he hired 17-year-old jazz singer Ella Fitzgerald on the advice of saxophonist Benny Carter. Webb began to regularly feature Fitzgerald on recordings and the band enjoyed its broadest popularity from June 1935 until February 1939. Fitzgerald's name eventually became bigger than the Webb orchestra, and they achieved popularity with frequent engagements broadcast from the Savoy Ballroom and a lengthy series of recordings for Decca. Although Webb's failing health was in steady decline, he managed to record eight studio sides for Decca on April 21, 1939, and continued live radio broadcasts through May, 4, 1939, before he died of spinal tuberculosis. Following his death, Ella Fitzgerald led the band for two years until July 1941.

what to buy: *An Introduction to Chick Webb, 1929–1939* (Best of Jazz, 1994, reissue prod. Gilles Petard) almost equally splits the 22 tunes between sides recorded with and without Fitzgerald. Webb's drumming drives orchestras led by jazz bandleaders Louis Armstrong and Mezz Mezzrow, as well as his own orchestras. In addition to Webb's first recorded single ("Dog Bottom"), this collection contains a rare track ("My Honey's Loving Arms") that features Webb propelling the Gotham Stompers, a small combo of Duke Ellington soloists. There really isn't a dull cut on this album, but you'll probably best enjoy the 1937 selections that feature Webb engineering his orchestra though fast-paced swing numbers like "Sweet Sue, Just You" and "Harlem Congo." The bonus is Ella Fitzgerald singing her popular late-1930s classics "A-Tisket, A-Tasket" and "Undecided," as well as others.

what to avoid: *Standing Tall* (Almac Records/Drive Archive, 1996) isn't a definitive, career-spanning album by Chick Webb and his orchestra. Only three of the 12 tinny-sounding tunes—"Blue Room," "One O'Clock Jump," and "Breakin' 'Em Down"—offer danceable beats.

best of the rest:

Spinnin' the Web (Decca, 1929–39/1994)
Chick Webb, 1929–1936 (Jazz Chronological Classics, 1994)
Chick Webb, 1935–1938 (Jazz Chronological Classics, 1994)

worth searching for: The two-CD *Ella Fitzgerald: The Early Years, Part 2* (Decca Jazz, 1993, prod. various) contains 42 tunes featuring Fitzgerald. The superior disc one has 1939 sessions near the end of Ella's stint with the Chick Webb Orchestra, only months before Webb's death in June. After his death, the orchestra stayed intact, but when numerous original members departed, the band lost its spirit.

influences:

◀◀ Baby Dodds, Zutty Singleton, George Wettling

▶▶ Sid Catlett, Bill Beason, Jesse Price, Gene Krupa

see also: *Ella Fitzgerald*

Nancy Ann Lee

Ben Webster

Born March 27, 1909, in Kansas City, MO. Died September 20, 1973, in Amsterdam, Holland.

Known as "The Brute" for his barely sheathed violent temper, tenor sax giant Ben Webster could never hide his romantic core. A master of gruff blues and pulsing swing when he played as a sideman for Fletcher Henderson, Benny Moten, and, most persuasively, Duke Ellington's legendary 1940–1942 cabal, Webster developed a gorgeous, breathy sax tone that he honed as a studio nomad in the 1950s. He put out a series of classic ballad and gentle swing records, sometimes recording with swing giants like Art Tatum, Illinois Jacquet, and even Gerry Mulligan. Starting out playing in territory bands in the 1920s, Webster broke onto the scene with the Young family band (as in Lester Young), then hobnobbed through outfits headed by Blanche Calloway (Cab's sister), Benny Moten, Andy Kirk, Benny Carter, Cab Calloway, and Teddy Wilson before two stints with Ellington: one in the mid-1930s, another, more famously, in the '40s. The collapse of the big bands left Webster on his own. First he cocooned in Jazz at the Philharmonic tours, but he found a new home in recording studios, laboring mostly

Chick Webb **(Archive Photos)**

for Norman Granz. Moonlighting on R&B records for everyone from the Ravens to Johnny Otis, Webster finally had his fill of the hard life of an American jazzman. He relocated to Europe and found new life playing in jazz clubs from Amsterdam to Copenhagen. He died there, a tough soul but a happy man.

what to buy: Nothing swings more assuredly than *The Soul of Ben Webster* ♫♫♫♫♫ (Verve, 1995, prod. Norman Granz), a collection of three early 1950s sessions, two featuring Webster and one with Webster backing up Ellington loyalist and alto sax ace Johnny Hodges. Every tune on this two-CD set works, from the inward strains of Duke's "Chelsea Bridge" to the rocking "Gee, Baby, Ain't I Good to You?" For an expansive look at Webster's work inside a big band, the genuine article is *Duke Ellington: The Blanton-Webster Band* ♫♫♫♫♫ (RCA, 1986, prod. Steve Backer), a three-CD treatment of the Duke's early 1940s glory years. Webster's role in the band was so instrumental—he waxes poetic on "Blue Goose" and rumpuses on "Cotton Tail"—that his name has become synonymous with the band's success.

what to buy next: Webster tools through a whole series of swing sessions recorded live in Copenhagen in 1965. While all are superb, the one to get is *Gone with the Wind* ♫♫♫♫♫ (Black Lion, 1989, prod. Alan Bates), which finds the Brute cruising on Juan Tizol's "Perdido," then lilting on the title track and the Arlen-Harburg chestnut "Indiana."

best of the rest:
Ben Webster and Associates ♫♫♫♫♫ (Verve, 1988)
Ben Webster at the Renaissance ♫♫♫♫ (Original Jazz Classics, 1989)
Soulville ♫♫♫♫ (Verve, 1989)
Ben Webster with Strings ♫♫♫ (Discovery, 1989)
Music for Loving ♫♫♫♫♫ (Verve, 1995)
Ben Webster Meets Oscar Peterson ♫♫♫♫♫ (Verve, 1997)
Gerry Mulligan Meets Ben Webster ♫♫♫♫ (Verve, 1997)

worth searching for: Webster fanatics would pay a small fortune to lay their hands on *Ben Webster on Emarcy: The Master Takes* ♫♫♫♫ (Emarcy, 1992), a long-out-of-print Japanese import disc that sometimes pops up in American bins. What's inside is a raucous collection of early 1950s Webster swing and R&B cuts, ranging from sideman sessions with Dinah Washington and the Ravens to big-band stylings with Jay McShann and Johnny Richards.

influences:
◀◀ Coleman Hawkins, Budd Johnson, Duke Ellington, Fletcher Henderson
▶▶ Sonny Rollins, Charlie Rouse, Archie Shepp

Steve Braun

Ted Weems

Born Wilfred Theodore Weymes, September 26, 1901, in Pitcairn, PA. Died May 6, 1963, in Tulsa, OK.

Ted Weems is best remembered as the bandleader who, in 1936, gave crooner Perry Como his first crack at national audiences. But Weems and company had been big stars long before they hired the ex-barber away from Freddy Carlone's band. Their intimate, unpretentious style had been going over big in the Midwest since 1923, and garnered even greater popularity through appearances on such radio programs as *The Fibber McGee and Molly Show* and *Hildegarde's "Beat the Band" Show.* Together they made a series of popular, though not spectacular, records for the various record labels. Weems didn't even try to compete with huge big-band hitmakers such as Benny Goodman and Artie Shaw—his 11-piece outfit kept the solos short and didn't feature many instrumentals. Instead, Weems preferred to showcase his wealth of fine vocalists, such as Mary Lee, Marvell Maxwell (later actress Marylin Maxwell), Dusty Rhodes, and novelty singer Red Ingle. Weems also helped develop Como's style, encouraging the young singer to drop vocal trickery and affectations in favor of an honest, from-the-heart approach. An unusual addition to Weems's sound was a whistler, Elmo Tanner, an important ingredient in the band's fluke hit "Heartaches." First recorded in 1933, the tune stiffed. When it was included as the B-side of "Mickey" (sung by Bob Edwards), disc jockeys began to flip the record over. As a result, "Heartaches" became one of the biggest hits of 1947, and Weems's career was temporarily revived just as the big-band era began to die out.

what to buy: The cream of the bandleader's late '20s work with vocalists Dusty Rhodes, Country Washburn, and Parker Gibbs can be found on *Marvelous: Ted Weems & His Orchestra, 1926–1929* ♫♫♫ (Memphis Archives, 1996, compilation prod. Eddie Dattel, Kevin Daly), which features Weems's hit "Piccolo Pete" and such favorites as "You're the Cream in My Coffee" and "What a Day!"

what to buy next: You'll really get the idea of what a Weems concert was all about with *1940–41 Broadcast Recordings* ♫♫♫ (Jazz Hour, 1993, reissue prod. Edward Burke). The young Perry Como makes his mark as one of the regular vocalists, and whistler supreme Lucas Tanner takes masterful turns on "Canadian Capers" and the biggest Weems band hit, "Heartaches."

the rest:
Ted Weems & His Orchestra ♫♫ (Demand Performance, 1996)

worth searching for: Previously available only on cassette, *Marvellous!* ♫♫♫ (Living Era, 1992) features a nice grab bag of Weems tracks from 1926 to 1934, including "Egyptian Ella," "Washing Dishes with My Sweetie," and "Chick, Chick, Chicken."

influences:

◀◀ Paul Whiteman, Jean Goldkette

▶▶ Sammy Watkins, Red Ingles, Perry Como

Ken Burke

Lawrence Welk

Born March 11, 1903, in Strasburg, ND. Died May 17, 1992, in Santa Monica, CA.

Born in a sod farmhouse, Welk rose from his humble Great Plains beginnings to become one of the world's best-known entertainers, especially after July 2, 1955, when *The Lawrence Welk Show* was first telecast as a summer replacement program on the ABC television network. Critics panned it as mechanical and out of date, and his distinctive "uh one and uh two" countdowns and "wunnaful, wunnaful" critiques alienated an entire population of nascent rock 'n' rollers, but Welk's trademark "champagne music" and perspicuous performance style has endured long after his death.

Welk recreated the music of his times—mostly big-band, country swing, and polka—by emphasizing songs and melodies over solos and improvisation. Welk ran his operation like a big family, and his musicians, whom he chose as much for their Christian morality as the heftiness of their chops, performed without hyperbole behind their stiff yet charismatic chief. His generous revue style, from which he never wavered, allowed nearly everyone, and certainly the cream of the crop—"da lovely Lennon Sisters" singing group, piano-pounding Jo Ann Castle, the mustachioed violinist Aladdin, booming bass man Larry Hooper—to take center stage at one time or another. Though he didn't consider himself anything more than an average musician, Welk was a keen businessman and a perfectionist, a rigorous taskmaster who demanded the same from his musicians. (He fired the popular Champagne Lady, Alice Lon, in 1959 for showing too much skin after she sat on a desk and crossed her legs on camera, a hugely unpopular move for the fan-conscious Welk at the time.)

It was a long road for the German-Russian boy from North Dakota who left home at age 21 to fulfill a childhood dream of being a musician. After frustration as a soloist, the accordionist soon formed his own band and endlessly roamed prairie dance halls and ballrooms. By 1938 Welk had a 13-piece orchestra, but it took more than another decade of perseverance before a local television crew broadcast one of his Los Angeles–area dances in 1951. The ensuing four-year local stint eventually ended 28 years of hard touring when ABC gave Welk and Company an open Saturday night invitation to reach a place their travels never took them—into practically every American home, most of them filled with a nostalgic, post–World War II generation of adults aware that rock and R&B were attracting their children. At 52 years of age, Welk was the ultimate late bloomer and a symbol of adult, Wonder-Bread America. When ABC canceled his program in 1971, on the grounds that it was too old-fashioned and out of touch, Welk signed a syndication deal that made him richer and even more popular and practically guaranteed his immortality. He also built an enviable real estate, publishing, and recording empire. Today, more than 17 years after the last program was taped and several years after Welk's death, *The Lawrence Welk Show* is still one of PBS's top-rated and requested programs; on Saturday nights the bubble machine is still bubbling and champagne music flows into America's living rooms. Videos have proliferated, "new" records continue to be released under his name, and Welk Entertainment operates the Welk Resort Center & Champagne Theatre in Branson, Missouri. All are dedicated to keeping the Welk legacy alive and well for generations to come.

what to buy: Very little of Welk's original work has made the transition to CD, which makes the best buy the budget-priced *Musical Anthology* ♪♪♪½ (Ranwood, 1992), a three-disc mix of full-tilt champagne music in all its guises: big-band classics ("Begin the Beguine"), novelties ("Winchester Cathedral"), Americana ("Scarlet Ribbons," "Old Man River"), country ("San Antonio Rose"), religious/inspirational ("How Great Thou Art," "Climb Every Mountain"), covers ("Raindrops Keep Falling on My Head," "Tie a Yellow Ribbon 'round the Old Oak Tree"), actual Welk charters ("Calcutta," "Baby Elephant Walk"), and numerous other polkas and waltzes. It even opens with the familiar bubble-popping "Champagne Time" opening segment from the show.

what to buy next: Many Welk titles are available only on cassette tape, a reflection of the strength of his elderly audience. Of the many recent releases on his own label, *22 All-Time Big Band Favorites* ♪♪♪ (Ranwood, 1989) includes "Woodchopper's Ball," "Take the 'A' Train," and "String of Pearls," although *16 Most Requested Songs* ♪♪♪ (Sony, 1989) and *22 All-Time Favorite Waltzes* ♪♪♪ (Ranwood, 1988) are equally proficient in more specific categories.

what to avoid: Even given his eclecticism—Welk once had "One Toke Over the Line" performed on his TV show under the guise of a "rock hymn"—nobody really needs to hear *22 Country Music Hits* **woof!** (Ranwood, 1994), do they?

best of the rest:

22 Great Waltzes ♪♪ (Ranwood, 1987)
Best of Lawrence Welk ♪♪½ (MCA, 1987)
22 Great Songs for Dancing ♪♪½ (Ranwood, 1988)
Blowing Bubbles ♪♪ (Ranwood, 1988)
Champagne and Romance ♪♪ (Hamilton, 1992)
22 Great Songs for Easy Listening ♪♪½ (Ranwood, 1993)

The Champagne Music of Lawrence Welk ♪♪♪ (MCA Special Products, 1993)
American Favorites ♪♪ (Ranwood, 1996)
Hallelujah ♪♪ (Ranwood, 1997)

worth searching for: The North Dakota State University Welk Archive includes 352 albums in its collection, and Welk's best recordings can only be found on his early Coral and Dot sides. Although highly collectible, the good stuff is hard to find. Two vinyl-only platters to begin with are *Calcutta* ♪♪♪♪ (Dot, 1961), which includes the harpsichord-drenched title track (and Welk's only #1 hit), and *Baby Elephant Walk* ♪♪♪ (Dot, 1962).

influences:

◀◀ Benny Goodman, Glenn Miller, Tommy Dorsey, Jimmy Dorsey, Guy Lombardo, Paul Whiteman, Artie Shaw, Woody Herman, Red Nichols & His Five Pennies, Cab Calloway, Louis Armstrong

▶▶ Myron Floren, Pete Fountain, Jo Ann Castle, the Lennon Sisters, Lynn Anderson, k.d. lang

see also: *Myron Floren*

Leland Rucker

Pete Wernick

See: Hot Rize

Paul Weston

Born March 12, 1912, in Springfield, MA. Died September 20, 1996, in Santa Monica, CA.

Swingin' SINGLES
"Woodchopper's Ball"
WOODY HERMAN
1939
"I've been sick of it for 20 years," Herman once said of his most requested standard, originally a blues riff.

Ever wonder how certain elements of the '40s big-band swing sound morphed into the lush, overproduced strings of Ray Conniff and Mantovani? Blame this man. He came from the big bands, working with Tommy Dorsey and Rudy Vallee, among others, then put out 1945's easy-listening blueprint *Music for Dreaming*. A wicked sense of humor separated Weston, a composer, arranger, and conductor, from stodgy counterparts like Conniff and Mantovani, but for every *Laugh-In* television episode he oversaw, Weston also wrote a solemn standard like "Autumn in Rome" or "Day by Day." After graduating from Dartmouth University in 1933, Weston was attending graduate school when singer Rudy Vallee heard his previously sold arrangements and hired him to work on the radio show "Fleischman Hour." The connection led to work with Bing Crosby, Fred Astaire, Tommy Dorsey, and Weston's eventual wife, Jo Stafford. He nailed lucrative management gigs at both Capitol and Columbia Records, then slowly started shifting from swing to "mood music." In addition to his moody solo work, Weston spent his later career arranging for Sarah Vaughan, Dinah Shore, Doris Day, and many others; working on *Laugh-In*; directing music for *The Bob Newhart Show* and *Disney on Parade*;

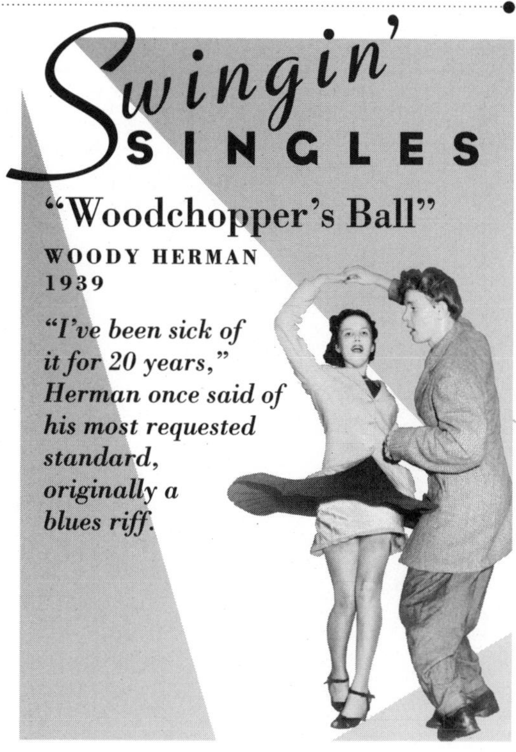

and recording tongue-in-cheek lounge albums with his wife, Stafford, under the pseudonym Jonathan and Darlene Edwards.

what to buy: Weston's first "mood-music" album, *Music for Dreaming* ♪♪♪ (Capitol, 1945/1992), which is packaged on CD with *Music for Memories*, was the exact point where big-band swing music gave way to heavily orchestrated "beautiful music" ballads. With gentle, unobtrusive instrumentals like "I'm in the Mood for Love" and "I Only Have Eyes for You," it was a precursor—although Weston later criticized elevator-music purveyors for stamping out the swing-jazz elements entirely—for Ray Conniff, Percy Faith, and Mantovani.

best of the rest:

Crescent City: Music of New Orleans ♪♪♪♪ (1957/Corinthian, 1994)
Columbia Album of Jerome Kern ♪♪♪ (Sony Special Products, 1991)
Easy Jazz ♪♪ (Corinthian, 1992)
The Original Music for Easy Listening ♪♪ (Corinthian, 1994)

worth searching for: Weston's deliberate missed notes and campy conversation make *Jonathan and Darlene's Greatest Hits* ♪♪♪ (Corinthian, prod. various) and *Jonathan and Darlene's Greatest Hits, Vol. 2* ♪♪♪ (Corinthian, prod. various) valuable lighthearted collections.

Paul Whiteman **(Archive Photos)**

influences:

⏪ Rudy Vallee, Benny Goodman, Glenn Miller, Bing Crosby, Al Jolson

⏩ Jackie Gleason, Ray Conniff, Percy Faith, Mantovani

see also: *Jo Stafford*

Steve Knopper

Paul Whiteman

Born March 28, 1880, in Denver, CO. Died December 26, 1967, in Doylestown, PA.

Pre-swing bandleader Paul Whiteman, who presided over a massive number of pop hits from the '20s to the '40s, was important in the history of jazz, but it was more for the band members he hired than for the music he played. Though he toured as "The King of Jazz," Whiteman blended symphonic and pop music with just a hint of jazz to give it flavor and bring "respectability" to jazz among the upper crust. To be fair, Whiteman hired the best possible musicians (many of them excellent jazz practitioners) and paid them better than anyone else in the business. The roll call of major figures that passed through his band is impressive, including Bix Beiderbecke, Jimmy and Tommy Dorsey, Joe Venuti, Jack Teagarden, Bunny Berigan, and Eddie Lang—plus singers Bing Crosby, Mildred Bailey, and Johnny Mercer. Whiteman first came to public notice in the early 1920s, when he and his band recorded a song called "Whispering" that sold phenomenally well for its time. He commissioned George Gershwin to write "Rhapsody in Blue" and premiered the piece (with the composer playing the piano) in 1924's famous "An Experiment in Modern Music" concert in New York's Aeolian Hall. The success of this concert led Whiteman to feature symphonic arrangements of other American composers, including Victor Herbert, William Grant Still, and Duke Ellington. In the early 1930s, Whiteman starred in an Academy Award–winning (for "Best Interior Decoration") film called *The King of Jazz*. Busby Berkeley engaged in his usual flamboyant scene-shifting for this picture, and Bing Crosby made his first celluloid appearance as part of Whiteman's male vocal group, the Rhythm Boys. By the end of the decade Whiteman and his orchestra found it harder to get jobs as the big-band era started to swing to its demise. During the '40s he appeared in a few more movies (including 1947's *The Fabulous Dorseys*), but a larger portion of his time was spent as a musical director for ABC and hosting his own television show. He had by then given up his band, although he still made guest appearances fronting other orchestras.

what to buy: *Paul Whiteman and His Orchestra* ♪♪♪♪ (Pearl, 1990, prod. various) covers the period from 1921 to 1934 and has most of the big Whiteman hits, including "Whispering" and its hit-parade follow-up, "Japanese Sandman." Standards like "Nola," "Deep Purple," and "Liebestraum" fill up the set, but interesting jazz moments peek through in the band's versions of "St. Louis Blues" and "Wabash Blues."

what to buy next: While *The King of Jazz* ♪♪♪½ (ASV/Living Era, 1996, prod. various) covers roughly the same time period, there is more of an emphasis on jazz inflection here. As in the other set, Bix Beiderbecke, Jack Teagarden, and Joe Venuti are present, as are singers Bing Crosby and Mildred Bailey, but it also offers Whiteman's early recording of "Rhapsody in Blue" for Gershwin fans.

worth searching for: The out-of-print *The Complete Capitol Recordings of Paul Whiteman and His Orchestra* ♪♪♪½ (Capitol, 1995) is still worth hunting up for anyone interested in the back end of Whiteman's career. Johnny Mercer, a former singer with Whiteman's band, was one of the three cofounders of Capitol, and he coaxed his old boss into recording for the label during the '40s. The resultant material wasn't as popular with the audiences of the time, wrapped up as they were in swing and bebop bands of the day, but Whiteman managed to wax a few charmers anyhow. Included is Billie Holiday vocalizing on "Traveling Light" under the alias of "Lady Day."

influences:

◀◀ Al Jolson, Jean Goldkette

▶▶ Benny Goodman, Glenn Miller, Lawrence Welk

Garaud MacTaggart

Margaret Whiting

Born July 22, 1924, in Detroit, MI.

After Perry Como and Frank Sinatra shifted pop music's focus from the big dance band to the charismatic singer, the well-connected and well-voiced Margaret Whiting stepped in to become one of World War II–era America's most beloved female singers. She crooned the definitive versions of "Moonlight in Vermont" (which sold more than two million copies) and "It Might As Well Be Spring," scored 13 gold records, and, while she doesn't quite have the name recognition of her pop-singer forebears, her nightclub gigs continue to draw huge crowds all over the country. Thanks to her father, songwriter Richard Whiting, Margaret was born with an impeccable musical pedigree and, more important, great connections. Johnny Mercer became an important mentor when her father died, setting her up with a microphone for the first time (on an NBC tribute to her father), collaborating on a duet, and feeding her terrific material. Whiting was a smart, confident teen singer, and talent took her the rest of the way. After the war, like her contemporary Jo Stafford, she affected a smooth, clear style, which fit perfectly with the big easy-listening arrangements developing from mood-music pioneers Paul Weston and Percy Faith. But her sidestep into television didn't have much impact—she and her singing sister Barbara starred briefly in a forgotten *I Love Lucy* summer replacement called *Those Whiting Girls*—and her career quickly lost momentum to rock 'n' roll. In one of the most interesting examples of strange pop-music bedfellows this side of Michael Jackson and Lisa Marie Presley, the high-society Whiting married a 20-years-younger adult-film star, Jack Wrangler, in the early 1980s. She continues to sing at countless charity benefits.

what's available: Both *Spotlight on Margaret Whiting* ♪♪♪ (Gold Rush, 1995/1997) and *Then and Now* ♪♪♪ (DRG, 1990, prod. various) are far from definitive—the ultimate Whiting collection has yet to be compiled on CD—but the latter contains her signature first hit "Moonlight in Vermont," plus excellent versions of "That Old Black Magic," "What Is a Man," and "My Best Friend," and guest help from jazzman Gerry Mulligan. *Come a Little Closer* ♪♪½ (Audiophile, 1994) and *Too Marvelous for Words* ♪♪½ (Audiophile, 1995) focus on more recent material.

influences:

◀◀ Art Tatum, Frank Sinatra, Perry Como, Jo Stafford, Johnny Mercer, Al Jolson, Judy Garland

▶▶ Rosemary Clooney, Ann Hampton Callaway, Nancy LaMott

Steve Knopper

Bob Wilber

Born Robert Sage Wilber, March 15, 1928, in New York, NY.

Bob Wilber is a pre-bop reeds player and composer-arranger who studied with the influential jazz clarinetist Sidney Bechet in the 1940s. Though he struggled to separate his style from that of his idol, Wilber was significantly influenced by Bechet, and later formed his Bechet Legacy band (1981–83) to bring attention to the late composer-performer. Wilber began his career in classic jazz as a teenager and, following World War II, fostered the revival of traditional jazz on the East Coast as leader of the Wildcats and other notable groups. After army service (1952–54), Wilber became a member of the Six, then worked with several bands, including Benny Goodman's orchestra and the Soprano Summit, which he co-led from 1974 to 1978. Dedicated to the preservation of the jazz tradition, Wilber served as director of the Smithsonian Jazz Repertory Ensemble; formed his own record company; became director of jazz studies at Wilkes College; wrote the Grammy-winning score for the 1984 film *The Cotton Club*; and, in 1987, published his autobiography, *Music Was Not Enough* (Macmillan). He has led tribute concerts at the world's most prestigious halls and been honored many times for his contributions. Wilber continues to perform on clarinet and saxophones in the swing and Dixieland styles, and to record, compose, arrange, lecture, and write articles.

what to buy: Initially recorded in 1982 on his Bodeswell label, *Ode to Bechet* (Bodeswell, 1982/Jazzology, 1996, prod. Joanne Horton) features Bob Wilber and the Bechet Legacy band. This session remains one of Wilber's hottest, most upbeat swing recordings. Hardy swing and stomp tempos on gems such as Duke Ellington's "The Mooche" and Bechet classics such as "Blues in the Air" and "Quincy Street Stomp" make this CD a delight for both dancers and armchair fans. Recorded 15 years later, *Reunion at Arbors* (Arbors, 1998, prod. Bob Wilber, Kenny Davern) doesn't quite nurture the steady sting and swing of *Ode to Bechet*, but nicely captures swing stalwarts Wilber and Kenny Davern, collaborators since 1974, merging their special chemistries on a set of nine studio-recorded classics. Sterling versions of warhorses "Sentimental Journey," "The Sheik of Araby," and other hot-to-medium swing marvels and ballads make this an attractive album.

what to buy next: Although he has been leading big bands for years, Wilber had never recorded with a big band until *Bufadora Blow-Up* (Arbors, 1997, prod. Bob Wilber), a live performance at the 1996 March of Jazz. Among the 16 tunes are swing classics like "It's Been So Long," "Goodnight My Love," and "I'm Checking Out, Goom Bye" (featuring vocals by Wilber's wife, Joanne "Pug" Horton).

what to avoid: Musicianship is usually solid on any Bob Wilber recording, but some of his late-career albums lack the fiery passion of his earlier, best-swinging dates. *Nostalgia* (Arbors, 1996, prod. Rachel Domber, Mat Domber) is a dreamier, more relaxed studio session of mostly ballads and medium-swing tunes. This CD is a pleasant listen if you want to settle back into an easy chair, but is not particularly recommended for swing-dance fans.

best of the rest:

(With Soprano Summit) *In Concert* (Concord, 1976/1992)
On the Road (Bodeswell, 1982/Jazzology, 1992)
Summit Reunion (Chiaroscuro, 1990)
Live at Concord '77 (Concord, 1991)
Soprano Summit (Chiaroscuro, 1994)
Horns A-Plenty (Arbors, 1994)
Bean: Bob Wilber's Tribute to Coleman Hawkins (Arbors, 1995)

worth searching for: The video version of *Bufadora Blow-Up* features the musicians playing all the tunes from the CD, plus interesting interviews with Wilber and his wife, singer Joanne "Pug" Horton.

influences:

◀◀ Sidney Bechet, Benny Goodman, Artie Shaw, Coleman Hawkins, Johnny Hodges, Charlie Parker, Benny Carter, Dick Wellstood, Buddy DeFranco

▶▶ Ken Peplowski, Scott Hamilton, Chuck Hedges

Nancy Ann Lee

Claude Williams

Born February 22, 1908, in Muskogee, OK.

Kansas City, Missouri, was a hotbed of swing by the time Claude Williams moved there in 1928. And since Williams played most string instruments he easily found work. From his earliest performing days, his favored instrument has always been violin and he has produced horn-like jazz improvisations inspired by saxophonists Charlie Parker and Lester Young. Williams first recorded playing guitar and violin with the Twelve Clouds of Joy (a legendary band led first by Terrence Holder, then Andy Kirk) for the Brunswick label in 1928. In New York City, the band made its debut at the best ballrooms (Roseland and Harlem's Savoy). Upon returning to Kansas City, the band became part of the thriving scene where musicians at 50 clubs near 18th and Vine battled it out in jams and cutting contests. After working awhile in Kansas City, Williams headed for Chicago and played guitar with the band of Eddie Cole (Nat King Cole's brother). Williams gained brief national fame when bandleader Count Basie hired him in a prominent role playing rhythm guitar, but he was eventually replaced by the now-acclaimed Freddie Green. Beginning in the '50s, Williams led his own groups, freelanced around Kansas City, toured Europe, and worked with bluesy pianist Jay McShann into the 1980s. His last album of guitar work was 1980's *Fiddler's Dream*. Since then, he has focused exclusively on violin, recording a couple of albums during the 1980s and 1990s.

what to buy: *Live at J's, Vol. 1* (Arhoolie, 1993, prod. Russ Dantzler, Chris Strachwitz) is an enthusiastic performance that features the then 81-year-old fiddler mixing it up on 12 tunes recorded during two spring 1989 performances at "J's," a New York City venue. Williams's fiddle sings and swings on classics such as "(Going to) Kansas City," "After You've Gone," and "Cherokee." He also delivers a delightful, lightning-quick hoedown on "The Fiddler." The sequel, *Live at J's, Vol. 2* (Arhoolie, 1993, prod. Russ Dantzler, Chris Strachwitz), is also a lively, swinging affair—with Williams adding his spirited fiddling to the 11-tune mixture of familiar ballads and bouncers. Williams's fluency, polished technique, and blissfully swinging personalized style (somewhere between the warm romanticism

Claude Williams (© Jack Vartoogian)

of Stephane Grappelli and bluesy verve of Stuff Smith) will make you wonder why he hasn't produced more recordings as leader.

what to buy next: *King of Kansas City* ♪♪♪♪ (Progressive, 1997, prod. Claude Williams, Russ Dantzler) hits hearty grooves right from the start, bolstered by a sideteam that includes the Claude Williams Swing String Trio. Williams performs 13 standards, singing on "St. Louis Blues" and "Gee Baby, Ain't I Good to You?" The diverse session doesn't contain much Kansas City swing, but Williams gets some especially hot fiddle licks in on Arnett Cobb's jump tune "Smooth Sailing." Fans of hot swing tempos might want to pick up *Swing Time in New York* ♪♪♪½ (Progressive, 1995, prod. Russ Dantzler) after they're duly acquainted with and enamored of Williams's violin artistry. Recommended mainly for jazz fans and completists, this disc features a few medium- to fast-paced danceable swing classics ("Limehouse Blues," "I've Got the World on a String," "Just You, Just Me," and "Lester Leaps In"). Eighty-six years old at the time of this recording, Williams is still in peak form, swinging, fiddling, singing (yes!), and romancing his way through a set of 14 classics (11 done in one take each).

worth searching for: Williams is at comfortable ease with his contemporaries (ranging in age from middle sixties to early nineties) on *Statesmen of Jazz* ♪♪♪♪½ (American Federation of Jazz Societies, 1995, prod. Arbors Records). The 10 classics (some from band members) serve up some of the hottest soloing and best ensemble work in recorded jazz history.

influences:

◀◀ Charlie Parker, Lester Young, A.J. Piron, Joe Venuti, Eddie South, Stephane Grappelli, Stuff Smith

▶▶ Ray Nance, John Frigo, Vassar Clements, Matt Glaser, Randy Sabien, Tom Morley

Nancy Ann Lee

Cootie Williams

Born Charles Melvin Williams, June 24, 1910, in Mobile, AL. Died September 14, 1985, in New York, NY.

Cootie Williams was the brass linchpin of Duke Ellington's suave 1930s orchestra. He was renowned for his adept use of the plunger mute, which allowed his horn to moan, growl, squeal, and produce other kinds of almost-human effects. Williams abandoned Ellington's band in 1940, at the height of his own fame and during the unit's most celebrated era, a move many jazz critics question in hindsight, but on which Williams never looked back. Defecting to Benny Goodman's swing group briefly, Williams became a bandleader himself, fashioning a crackerjack ensemble that quickly churned out a passel of powerful hits and gave the world such artists as vocalists Eddie "Cleanhead" Vinson and Pearl Bailey, and bop titans Bud Powell, Eddie "Lockjaw" Davis, and, for a brief spell, Charlie Parker. Enlisting as a teenage musician in southern pit orchestras, Williams paraded through the Chick Webb and Fletcher Henderson bands before taking over the critical trumpet spot vacated in 1929 by Bubber Miley. Over the next 11 years, Ellington featured Williams prominently in some of his most experimental pieces, including "Echoes of Harlem (Concerto for Cootie)," "Black and Tan Fantasy," and "Reminiscing in Tempo." Williams also led small groups of Ellington stalwarts and his occasional moonlighting with Lionel Hampton, Teddy Wilson, and Billie Holiday whetted his appetite for work beyond Ellington's sphere of influence. After his sojourn with Goodman, Williams moved his big band in the direction of hard-driving swing with an R&B feel. Vinson's "Cherry Red Blues" and "Gator," which featured the hard-edged tenor of Willis "Gatortail" Jackson, were just two examples. As big bands died like dinosaurs during the rock and roll age, Williams finally drifted back into Ellington's orbit, rejoining the Duke in 1962 and staying put even after Duke himself exited in 1974. Williams finally took a well-deserved retirement before his death in 1985.

what to buy: The entire Ellington catalog is studded with shimmering examples of Williams's horn work, but the most adventurous are Columbia's two volumes that collect classics of Ellington's small groups. *The Duke's Men: Small Groups, Vol. 1* (Columbia/Legacy, 1991, prod. Michael Brooks) ranges from 1934 to 1938 and includes blueprint versions of later Ellington big-band perennials like "Caravan" and "Stompy Jones." *The Duke's Men: Small Groups, Vol. 2* (Columbia/Legacy, 1993, prod. Michael Brooks) is littered with an even lusher and more danceable selection that includes "Jeep's Blues," "Prelude to a Kiss," and "Dooji Wooji."

what to buy next: For full-bore big-band Ellington, enthusiasts can quibble over years, but the most sublime for Williams himself was 1938, which is covered by a two-disc set, *Braggin' in Brass: The Immortal 1938 Year* (Columbia, 1989, prod. Bob Thiele). While not quite as immortal as Ellington's pivotal band from 1940 to 1942, this edition can still lay claim to "I Let a Song Go out of My Heart," "Braggin' in Brass," and "Boy Meets Horn."

best of the rest:
The Big Challenge (Fresh Sound, 1989)

worth searching for: Williams's peppy war-era swing, absent for years, now fills two import volumes. *Cootie Williams and His Orchestra: 1941–1944* (Classics, 1995) collects OKeh and Hits sides, among them "Cherry Red" and Bud Powell's early bop-influenced workout on "Round Midnight." *Cootie Williams and His Orchestra: 1945–1946* (Classics, 1998) wraps up most of the trumpeter's pumping Mercury recordings.

influences:
◀◀ Louis Armstrong, Bubber Miley, Red Allen
▶▶ Roy Eldridge, Miles Davis, Wynton Marsalis

Steve Braun

Joe Williams

Born Joseph Goreed Williams, December 12, 1918, in Cordele, GA. Died March 29, 1999, in Las Vegas, NV.

Joe Williams was the last of the great big-band singers, a powerful baritone with the rare ability to offer definitive versions of blues, standards, and ballads. A warm performer with a confidently swinging style, Williams brought an urbane sophistication to a role pioneered in the Count Basie band by Jimmy Rushing. Raised in Chicago, Williams began singing in nightclubs while still a teenager. He worked with Jimmy Noone in the late 1930s and performed with Coleman Hawkins and Lionel Hampton in the early '40s. A tour with Andy Kirk and his Clouds of Joy during 1946 and 1947 led to Williams's first recording, but he continued to struggle. In the late '40s he had brief stints with the Albert Ammons/Pete Johnson band and the Red Saunders band back in Chicago. In 1950 he worked with trumpeter Hot Lips Page and the septet Count Basie founded after breaking up his big band. Williams scored a minor hit with King Kolax in 1951 with "Everyday I Have the Blues," which would become one of his signature songs, but he scuffled for another few years before hooking up with Basie again in 1954. During his seven-year tenure with the revitalized Basie band, Williams became an international star and was one of the key elements behind Basie's resurgence. Williams worked with trumpeter Harry "Sweets" Edison's small group from 1961 to 1962 and toured with his own rhythm section after that. Over the years Williams occasionally reunited with Basie and also recorded memorable sessions with the Thad Jones/Mel Lewis Orchestra, the Capp/Pierce Juggernaut, Cannonball Adderley, and George Shearing. He continued to perform and record with the energy and chops of a man half his age well into the 1990s.

what to buy: The first and still definitive Williams/Basie album, *Count Basie Swings, Joe Williams Sings* (Verve, 1955/1993, prod. Norman Granz), is a powerhouse session with tight, driving arrangements. Many of the tunes, including "Every Day I Have the Blues," "The Comeback," "In the Evening," and "Alright, Okay, You Win," were in Williams's repertoire right up until the end. A classic session pairing two jazz institutions at the peak of their powers, *Joe Williams and the Thad Jones/Mel Lewis Orchestra* ♪♪♪♪♪ (Blue Note, 1966/1994, prod. Alfred Lion) features Jones's complex but streamlined arrangements. Williams responds with tour de force versions of "Smack Dab in the Middle" and "It Don't Mean a Thing . . .," where he scats up a storm. Also memorable is his hilarious version of "Evil Man Blues." Recorded live at Hollywood's Vine Street Bar and Grill, *Ballad and Blues Master* ♪♪♪♪♪ (Verve, 1992, prod. Eulis Cathey) captures the great singer in a relaxed, swinging mood. With his longtime accompanist, pianist Norman Simmons, leading a crack rhythm section featuring the soulful guitarist Henry Johnson, Williams displays his remarkable versatility, crooning ballads such as "Everyday (I'll Fall in Love)" and "A Hundred Years from Today," then tearing into the raunchy blues of "Who She Do" and a three-song medley that ends the album.

what to buy next: Taken from the same performances from which *Ballad and Blues Master* was drawn, *Every Night: Live at Vine St.* ♪♪♪♪♪ (Verve, 1987, prod. Miriam Cutler, David Kreisberg, Ron Berinstein) features Williams at his best with his excellent working rhythm section. Highlights include his much-copied arrangement linking "Every Day I Have the Blues" with Miles Davis's "All Blues," a raucous version of "Roll 'em Pete," and a beautifully rendered "Too Marvelous for Words." A diverse selection of material makes *In Good Company* ♪♪♪♪ (Verve, 1989, prod. Miriam Cutler, Ron Berinstein) one of Williams's more representative albums.

best of the rest:

Every Day: Best of the Verve Years ♪♪♪♪♪ (Verve, 1954–89/1993)
At Newport '63/Jump for Joy ♪♪♪♪♪ (Collectables, 1963/BMG, 1997)
Joe Williams Live ♪♪♪♪ (Fantasy, 1974/Original Jazz Classics, 1990)
Prez Conference: Prez and Joe ♪♪♪♪♪ (GNP, 1979/Crescendo, 1986)
Live at Orchestra Hall, Detroit ♪♪♪♪ (Telarc, 1993)
Here's to Life ♪♪♪ (Telarc, 1994)
Feel the Spirit ♪♪♪♪ (Telarc, 1995)

worth searching for: For his second album with Basie, Williams wanted to show he wasn't just a bluesman. On *The Greatest!! Count Basie Plays, Joe Williams Sings Standards* ♪♪♪♪♪ (Verve, 1957/1990, prod. Buddy Bregman), he proves himself to be a top-shelf jazz singer capable of transforming pop tunes and ballads into swinging vehicles. There's hardly a weak track among the 12 tunes, but standouts include Duke Ellington's "I'm Beginning to See the Light," the Gershwins' "Our Love Is Here to Stay" and "'S Wonderful," and the Johnny Mercer/Harold Arlen gem "Come Rain or Come Shine."

influences:

◀◀ Jimmy Rushing, Billy Eckstine

▶▶ Kevin Mahogany

Andrew Gilbert

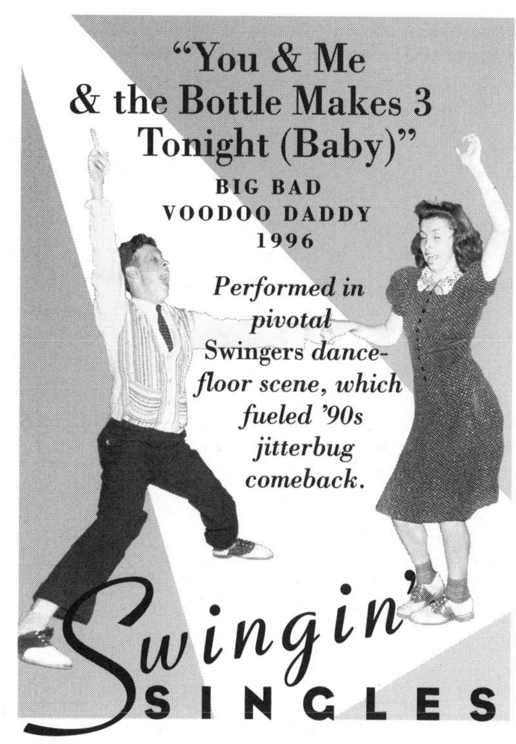

"You & Me & the Bottle Makes 3 Tonight (Baby)"
BIG BAD VOODOO DADDY
1996
Performed in pivotal Swingers dance-floor scene, which fueled '90s jitterbug comeback.
Swingin' SINGLES

Mary Lou Williams

Born Mary Scruggs, May 8, 1910, in Atlanta, GA. Died May 28, 1981, in Durham, NC.

Pianist Mary Lou Williams was a highly regarded instrumentalist and gifted composer who contributed to the success of many notable jazz orchestras during the swing era. More importantly, she is the only major jazz artist who lived and adapted her playing style throughout the development of all of the jazz eras: spirituals, ragtime, the blues, Kansas City swing, boogie-woogie, bop or modern, and avant-garde. Williams grew up in Pittsburgh and performed from age 6 to 16 at parties and in vaudeville, using the name Mary Lou Burley (her stepfather's surname). In 1925, she joined a group led by baritone saxophonist John Williams, whom she married in 1927, and afterwards performed as Mary Lou Williams. She arranged for Andy Kirk's bands, including the Kansas City–based Twelve Clouds of Joy, who owed much of their fame to Williams's distinctive arrangements and original compositions. She also wrote and arranged for other popular big bands of the day, including those of Benny Goodman, Earl Hines, and Tommy Dorsey. In 1942, the Williams couple divorced, and Mary Lou left Kirk's band to return to Pittsburgh where she formed her own band that included the up-and-coming young drummer Art Blakey. Williams married trumpeter Harold "Shorty" Baker, and in 1943 they moved to New York, where she was eventually drawn into the bop scene. After working in Duke Ellington's band, she escaped to Europe, performing with trios and quartets in England and France for two years. Williams returned to New York in 1944 and, disillusioned about the business, retired from music, converted to Catholicism, and established a charitable foundation for musicians with alcohol and drug addiction problems. Coaxed back into the music business by fellow musicians and her spiritual advisors, she began playing publicly again in 1957, joining Dizzy Gillespie at the Newport Jazz Festival, taking jobs in New York's premier jazz clubs, and running her own record label. During the '70s, with Father Peter O'Brien as her personal manager, Williams actively performed and recorded, including a famed late-career duet gig with bassist Brian Torff documented on *Live at the Cookery*, a recording that takes listeners through the development of jazz from spirituals and blues to stride, swing, and bop. Williams also began devoting her time to educational activities, and in 1977 joined the faculty of Duke University, where she taught the history of jazz, wrote arrangements, and gave private instruction until she was incapacitated in 1980. She died of cancer in 1981.

what to buy: Of her domestic recordings in print, *Piano Jazz: McPartland/Williams* ♫♫♫♫ (The Jazz Alliance, 1978/1995, prod. Dick Phipps) finds Williams demonstrating her versatile piano style, discussing her role in jazz history, and talking about influences from Fats Waller to Cecil Taylor. Backed by bassist Ronnie Boykins, Williams plays illuminating works that display her flexibility and command of the keyboard (especially her swinging improvisations on the Duke Ellington classic "The Jeep Is Jumpin'").

what to avoid: Often billed as Williams's "solo recital," *Embraced* ♫♫♪ (Pablo, 1978/OJC, 1995, prod. Mary Lou Williams, Cecil Taylor) pairs Williams with the eccentric avant-garde pianist Cecil Taylor. The performance is a struggle for Williams, even though she was among the vanguard players of the 1960s avant-garde movement. Although Williams manages to play with strength and voracity, Taylor rudely dominates the session. Williams injects some Kansas City swing ("K.C. 12th Street") and delivers a "Good Ole Boogie," but this controversial 10-track album has been slammed by many jazz critics and holds best appeal for Williams devotees and jazz fans able to tolerate the audacious Taylor.

influences:

◀◀ Fats Waller, Earl Hines, Count Basie

▶▶ Marian McPartland, Bud Powell, Thelonious Monk, Tadd Dameron, JoAnne Brackeen, Geri Allen, Hilton Ruiz

Nancy Ann Lee

Tex Williams

Born Sollie Paul Williams, August 23, 1917, near Ramsey, IL. Died October 11, 1985.

A singer from Illinois nicknamed for the Lone Star State, Tex Williams first came to the attention of western-swing fans by singing on fiddler Spade Cooley's Columbia Records hits "Shame on You" and "Detour." When Cooley fired him in 1946, Williams took a good chunk of Cooley's band with him and formed the Western Caravan, one of the more musically inventive swing bands. He had his first big hit under his own name with "Smoke! Smoke! Smoke! (That Cigarette)," a talking-blues novelty written by Merle Travis (Williams shared a writing credit for altering one line). The song was a country and pop smash, making Williams's Western Caravan one of the few western bands to be popular on both sides of the Mississippi. Williams's reliance on the talking-blues gimmick (later singles included "That's What I like about the West" and "Never Trust a Woman") denied him the critical credibility and commercial longevity that other bands had. His heyday was from 1946 to 1949 for Capitol Records; subsequent recordings for RCA and Decca were never as popular. The Western Caravan broke up in 1957, and Williams recorded solo into the 1970s. Ironically (considering the title of his biggest hit), Williams died of lung cancer in 1985 (and he smoked).

what's available: Williams's minor impact beyond a handful of well-known singles means his recordings become available only sporadically in the States, although his crooning baritone is featured prominently on Spade Cooley's *Spadella! The Essential Spade Cooley* ♫♫♫ (Columbia, 1994, prod. various). A particularly impressive example of the breadth of the Western Caravan's musical abilities is contained on the compilation *Hillbilly Fever! Vol. 1: Legends of Western Swing* ♫♫♫♫♪ (Rhino, 1995, prod. various). On this album the band plays a western-swing arrangement of Stan Kenton's "Artistry in Rhythm" that prominently features pedal steel, accordion, flute, and harp.

worth searching for: The out-of-print *Vintage Collections Series* ♫♫♫♫ (Capitol, 1996, compilation prod. Rich Kienzle, John Johnson) captures the essence of Williams's band with his 1940s talking-blues hits, instrumental radio transcriptions, and a healthy helping of previously unissued recordings. Despite his fondness for spoken numbers, Williams is a smooth singer, and the band, which might feature accordion, triple fiddles, vibes, and/or trumpets, is top-notch. "Wild Card," which features guest guitarist Jimmy Bryant, was co-written by actor Buddy Ebsen. This isn't all the good stuff Williams recorded, but it is his most successful.

influences:

◀◀ Jimmy Wakely, Bob Wills

▶▶ Asleep at the Wheel, Dave & Deke Combo

see also: *Spade Cooley*

Brian Mansfield

Bob Wills

Born James Robert Wills, March 6, 1905, near Kosse, TX. Died May 13, 1975, in Fort Worth, TX.

Inducted into the Country Music Hall of Fame in 1968 for, among other accomplishments, effectively inventing western swing, Bob Wills never cared much for the fiddle as a youth—that is, until he stood before an anxious crowd. His father was late for the gig, and somebody had to play. So "Jim Rob" did what he could: repeated the same six songs until his dad showed up. The audience responded to the 10-year-old, and an entertainer was born. In 1931 Wills helped found the Light Crust Doughboys, named after the sponsor of the group's radio show. When band member Milton Brown couldn't take Wills's bawdy demeanor, he was replaced by Tommy Duncan. Both Wills and Duncan left the Doughboys in 1933 and created the first of many incarnations of the Texas Playboys. Wills blended electric steel with standard guitar for a thrilling new sound, while Duncan supported his reputation as perhaps the greatest of the Playboys' vocalists. Oklahoma farmers and Texas ranch-hands packed dancehalls throughout the region to see the Playboys, and at the end of the Depression Wills was among the most famous musicians alive. The band had broadened to 18 members under the supervision of guitarist Eldon Shamblin. A revamped vocal version of "New San Antonio Rose," the group's signature tune, swept the country.

World War II threatened to end all their careers, however. Duncan enlisted in the army shortly after Pearl Harbor, and other members followed right behind him. Wills temporarily disbanded the Playboys and joined the army himself in late 1943. Taking orders was never his strong suit, though, and he and Duncan were soon discharged. The two reunited and formed a smaller, tighter version of the Playboys. In 1943 Wills also married for the sixth time, to Betty Anderson; that union would last until his death. Though Wills outsold his pop-oriented swing contemporaries Tommy Dorsey and Benny Goodman for the next decade, the advent of television decimated the dancehall crowds. Poor health, due to his fondness for cigars and drink, kept Wills out of the spotlight as well (he would lead his last sessions from a wheelchair, after suffering a stroke during 1970). Country radio didn't play Wills much, either, but he never considered himself a country artist. Instead, he was "The King of Western Swing." To Wills, they were two separate styles of music. Merle Haggard had the opportunity to play fiddle on Wills's final project, and the singer championed the innovator with the 1982 album *Tribute to the Best Damn Fiddle Player in the World (Or My Salute to Bob Wills)*. Asleep at the Wheel paid similar tribute in 1994 with *Tribute to the Music of Bob Wills & the Texas Playboys*.

what to buy: Assembled with Rhino's usual flair and passion, the two-disc *Anthology: 1935–1973* 55555 (Rhino, 1991, compilation prod. James Austin, Bob Fisher) spans nearly 40 years of Wills's recordings, from his early days on the Vocalion label to his final sessions in December 1973, just a year and a half before his death. The compilation includes most of the Playboys' biggest hits, but it tends (probably rightly) to concentrate on the years when Tommy Duncan was the group's vocalist.

what to buy next: *Encore* 5555 (Capitol, 1994, compilation prod. John Johnson) surveys Wills's career another way. This three-disc box set compiles studio recordings made for Liberty Records between 1960 and 1963; seven cuts from 1963 to 1964 Ft. Worth, Texas, radio shows; and Wills's final recordings, made in December 1973. (Wills had a stroke the night of the first session and remained in a coma for 15 months until his death; Haggard plays fiddle on the final four tracks, recorded the next day.) It's a fascinating look at the last days of a legend. *Columbia Historic Edition* 5555 (Columbia, 1982) is an excellent one-disc collection of hits from the Playboys' commercial heyday.

what to avoid: Bob Wills and the McKinney Sisters' *Tiffany Transcriptions* 5 (Rhino, 1991) is a largely pop-oriented outing with yodeling sisters Dean and Evelyn McKinney.

best of the rest:

The Tiffany Transcriptions, Volume 1 5555 (Rhino, 1982)
The Tiffany Transcriptions, Volume 2 5555 (Rhino, 1984)
The Tiffany Transcriptions, Volume 3 5555 (Rhino, 1984)
The Tiffany Transcriptions, Volume 4 5555 (Rhino, 1985)
The Tiffany Transcriptions, Volume 5 5555 (Rhino, 1986)
The Tiffany Transcriptions, Volume 6 5555 (Rhino, 1987)
The Tiffany Transcriptions, Volume 7 5555 (Rhino, 1987)
Fiddle 5555 (Country Music Foundation, 1987)
The Golden Era 5555 (Columbia, 1987)
King of Western Swing/Wills & His Playboys 555 (MCA, 1987)
The Tiffany Transcriptions, Volume 8 5555 (Rhino, 1988)
The Tiffany Transcriptions, Volume 9 5555 (Rhino, 1990)
Greatest Hits 555 (Curb, 1990)
The Essential Bob Wills & His Texas Playboys (1935–1947) 555 (Columbia/Legacy, 1992)
Country Music Hall of Fame 555 (MCA, 1992)
For the Last Time 555 (Capitol, 1994)
Special 555 (Sony Music Special Products, 1995)
American Legends: Vol. 13 555 (Laserlight, 1996)
The Hits 555 (Mercury, 1997)

worth searching for: In the United States, only a misleadingly named *21 Golden Hits* ♪♪♪ (Hollywood, 1992) collects Wills's 1960s recordings for the Dallas, Texas–based Longhorn label. *The Longhorn Recordings* ♪♪♪♪ (Bear Family, 1993), a 23-track German import, does a better and more complete job.

influences:

◄◄ Milton Brown, Adolph Hofner

►► Spade Cooley, Willie Nelson, Merle Haggard, Asleep at the Wheel, George Strait

Craig Shelburne and Brian Mansfield

Michelle Willson

Born in Boston, MA.

An excellent R&B singer who belts with the right jump-blues spirit and slows down just as easily into a seductive ballad, Willson switched as a teenager from actress in musicals to singer with a strange affinity for naming her bands after nonexistent characters (Alex Clayton and Mimi Jones, for instance). After she organized a tribute to her favorite singers—such as Dinah Washington and Ruth Brown—she wound up in a band (Evil Gal) and won several local and national awards.

what to buy: Though Willson tries a little too hard to jam disparate styles together on *Tryin' to Make a Little Love* ♪♪♪♪ (Bullseye Blues/Rounder, 1999, prod. Scott Billington), it's a sexy, jumping record with songs by rock singer Joan Osborne and R&B hero Johnny Otis. The neo-swing movement desperately needs a voice, and the endearingly scratchy Willson is perfect for the job—she can make a ballad swoon and a rocker kick.

what to buy next: Willson's thing is jump and swing blues, and she belts energetically and playfully throughout both *Evil Gal Blues* ♪♪♪ (Bullseye Blues/Rounder, 1994, prod. Ron Levy) and *So Emotional* ♪♪♪ (Bullseye Blues/Rounder, 1996, prod. Ron Levy).

influences:

◄◄ Dinah Washington, Ruth Brown, Bessie Smith, Etta James, Big Maybelle, Aretha Franklin, Marcia Ball

Steve Knopper

Teddy Wilson

Born Theodore Shaw Wilson, November 24, 1912, in Austin, TX. Died July 31, 1986, in New Britain, CT.

The first black member of a prominent white jazz group, Teddy Wilson participated in some of swing king Benny Goodman's finest small-group recordings, then drew from that experience to lead his own star-studded ensemble. (Swing heroes Ben Webster, Doc Cheatham, J.C. Heard, Cozy Cole, Chu Berry, and Al Casey, not to mention lead singers Billie Holiday and Ella Fitzgerald, were among the Wilson group's members.) Though Wilson's orchestra never achieved the commercial power of, say, Goodman or Glenn Miller, 1937's "You Can't Stop Me from Dreaming" and "Carelessly" each hit #1, and the group scored several hits during the mid-'30s. Wilson grew up in Tuskegee, Alabama, where his parents worked for the university. After a brief spell at Talladega College, he moved to Chicago, eventually finding work with Jimmie Noone, Speed Webb, and Louis Armstrong, among others. Wilson also started touring the after-hours clubs in the company of one of his idols, Art Tatum, playing piano duets and making a name for himself. One night in 1933, while subbing on a gig for Earl Hines, Wilson was heard by record producer John Hammond, who convinced Benny Carter that the young pianist would be the perfect fit for his band. With this endorsement, Wilson moved to New York City. Playing with Carter and various other musicians (including recording sessions under his own name with high caliber players like Billie Holiday, Ben Webster, and Johnny Hodges) further honed Wilson's skills. This attracted the attention of Benny Goodman, then at the height of his powers as a bandleader. In 1940, after his stint with Goodman's orchestra and fronting his own ensemble, Wilson toured and recorded with small groups and as a solo artist. He also worked staff jobs in various New York radio and television studios in addition to teaching at the Juilliard School and joining Goodman for occasional reunion tours.

what to buy: *1937* ♪♪♪♪♪ (Classics, 1991, prod. various) may be the best available set to display what Teddy Wilson's wonderful 1930s-era bands sounded like. Certainly the recording lineups are impressive, with Billie Holiday, Duke Ellington band members Harry Carney and Johnny Hodges, and Count Basie stars Lester Young, Walter Page, and Freddie Green. Classic jazz interpretations of "Mean to Me" and "I'll Get By" are only two of the tunes to emerge from these sessions. *With Billie in Mind* ♪♪♪♪♪ (Chiaroscuro, 1972/1995, prod. Hank O'Neal) features solo piano renditions of tunes associated with the great Billie Holiday—a fine tribute to Wilson's former band singer. Especially effective are versions of "What a Little Moonlight Can Do," "Body and Soul," and "Miss Brown to You," but Wilson makes all the songs swing with grace and a wistful, emotional undercurrent.

what to buy next: More fine performances with Billie Holiday and appearances by stars like Benny Goodman, Ben Webster, and Johnny Hodges make *1934–35* ♪♪♪♪ (Classics, 1990, prod. various) another highlight in Classics' journey through Wilson's bands of the 1930s and '40s. It is also interesting to compare the Holiday versions of "What a Little Moonlight Can Do" and "Miss Brown to You" with the solo renditions on Wilson's tribute album (mentioned above). There is also a fine version of

Teddy Wilson **(Archive Photos)**

"Rosetta" that does justice to one of Wilson's pianistic idols, Earl Hines.

best of the rest:

(With Lester Young) *Pres and Teddy* ♪♪♪♪ (Verve, 1956/1987)
Runnin' Wild ♪♪♪½ (Black Lion, 1974/1993)
1935–36 ♪♪♪½ (Jazz Chronological Classics, 1991)
1936–37 ♪♪♪½ (Jazz Chronological Classics, 1991)
1938 ♪♪♪½ (Jazz Chronological Classics, 1991)
1939 ♪♪♪½ (Jazz Chronological Classics, 1991)
How High the Moon ♪♪♪½ (Tradition, 1997)

worth searching for: The double-album set *Concert in Argentina* ♪♪♪♪ (Halcyon, 1975, prod. Alejandro Szterenfeld) is the result of a 1974 concert in Buenos Aires, Argentina, featuring Marian McPartland, Ellis Larkins, Earl Hines, and Wilson. Wilson uses his side for standards by Gershwin and Waller, and well-articulated versions of "Body and Soul," "Flying Home," and Earl Hines's "Rosetta." While the Wilson sides alone are fine, when combined with performances by three other outstanding pianists, the whole set is spectacular. Though out of print, *Cole Porter Standards* ♪♪♪♪ (Black Lion, 1978, prod. Alan Bates), a solo piano release, features beautiful interpretations of 20th-century masterpieces and a classy improvisation ("Too Darn Blue"). The swing is palpable on tunes like "Just One of Those Things" and "I Get a Kick out of You," but it also infuses ballad material such as "Why Shouldn't I" and "Easy to Love."

influences:

◀◀ Earl Hines, Art Tatum, Willie "The Lion" Smith

▶▶ Marcus Roberts, Marian McPartland

Garaud MacTaggart

Jimmy Witherspoon

Born August 8, 1923, in Gurdon, AR. Died September 18, 1997, in Los Angeles, CA.

Instead of following the exodus of southern bluesmen to Chicago, Jimmy "Spoon" Witherspoon turned in the opposite direction, both geographically and musically: Los Angeles. So instead of discovering the raw, dirty, electric blues that later influenced so many British rock 'n' rollers, Witherspoon downshifted into a slick, jazzy, cocktail style that recalled Duke Ellington and Count Basie as much as it did Muddy Waters and Charley Patton. Witherspoon started out singing in his church but didn't get his first real professional opportunity until guitarist T-Bone Walker asked Witherspoon, who had been washing dishes at a drugstore, to sing with him during a Little Harlem nightclub show in Watts. After that, Spoon became a cook in the Merchant Marine and earned opportunities to sing on Armed Forces Radio; in 1945, after his discharge, he hooked up with bandleader Jay McShann, and the two recorded the classic "Confessin' the Blues" and spent four years together. When Spoon left the band he was primed for a solo career, which began lucratively with the hits "Ain't Nobody's Business, Parts 1 & 2" and, later, "No Rollin' Blues" and "Wind Is Blowing." After several more hits, rock 'n' roll destroyed his R&B career, but the irrepressible Witherspoon re-emerged as a jazz singer, playing festivals, touring the world, appearing on the Steve Allen and Johnny Carson shows, recording for many influential labels, and even notching the minor 1975 hit "Love Is a Five Letter Word." (He also hooked up with jazzmen Roy Eldridge, Coleman Hawkins, and Earl Hines.) When throat cancer threatened to kill his career in the early 1980s, Witherspoon overcame it with radiation treatments and returned to singing. He performed regularly until dying of natural causes in 1997.

what to buy: Witherspoon had an amazingly consistent, prolific career, so it's tough to pick a starting point: *Blowin' in from Kansas City* ♪♪♪♪♪ (Flair/Virgin, 1991, prod. various) is not only an essential historic document of the singer's jazzy jump blues, but it swings wonderfully, with a horn section and the presence of arrangers Jay McShann and Tiny Webb; *'Spoon and Groove* ♪♪♪♪ (Tradition/Rykodisc, 1996, prod. various) tours Witherspoon's 1960s material with organist Richard Arnold "Groove" Holmes; and *Call My Baby* ♪♪♪♪ (Night Train, 1991, prod. Dan Nooger) reissues Spoon's 1940s classics for Supreme and Swing Time, including both versions of "Ain't Nobody's Business" and "Hey Mr. Landlord."

what to buy next: *Evenin' Blues* ♪♪♪½ (Original Blues Classics, 1963/Fantasy, 1993) operates in that gray zone between rock 'n' roll (a version of "Good Rockin' Tonight"), jazz ("Kansas City"), and pure blues ("How Long Blues"). The compilation *Ain't Nobody's Business* ♪♪♪½ (Polydor, 1967/Drive, 1994) is somewhat mysterious because the liner notes don't refer specifically to the performances on this disc; they're from 1948, 1949, and 1950, and these versions of "Ain't Nobody's Business" and "New Orleans Woman" are among the best Witherspoon recorded.

what to avoid: Even Spoon made missteps, including *Midnight Lady Called the Blues* ♪♪ (Muse, 1986, prod. Doc Pomus, Mac Rebennack), on which he sings bland, uninspired versions of songs written by Pomus and Dr. John. (Note ridiculous cover photo of babe in blue sequins.)

the rest:

Jimmy Witherspoon and Jay McShann ♪♪♪½ (DA, 1949/Black Lion, 1992)
Singin' the Blues ♪♪♪ (Blue Note, 1958/1998)
Baby Baby Baby ♪♪½ (Original Blues Classics, 1963/Fantasy, 1990)
Blues around the Clock ♪♪♪ (Original Blues Classics, 1963/Fantasy, 1995)

Some of My Best Friends Are the Blues ♪♪♪ (Original Blues Classics, 1964/Fantasy, 1995)
Blues for Easy Livers ♪♪♪ (Original Blues Classics, 1966/Fantasy, 1996)
The Spoon Concerts ♪♪♪ (Fantasy, 1972/1989)
Spoonful ♪♪♪ (Avenue Jazz, 1975/Rhino, 1994)
Love Is a Five Letter Word ♪♪♪ (1976/Rhino, 1998)
Rockin' L.A. ♪♪ (Fantasy, 1989)
Spoon So Easy: The Chess Years ♪♪♪♪ (Chess/MCA, 1990)
Spoon's Life ♪♪♪ (Evidence, 1994)
Spoon's Blues ♪♪♪ (Stony Plain, 1995)
(With Robben Ford) *Live at the Mint* ♪♪♪ (On the Spot/Private, 1996)
Jimmy Witherspoon with the Junior Mance Trio ♪♪♪ (Stony Plain, 1997)
Jazz Me Blues ♪♪♪ (Fantasy, 1998)

worth searching for: *Jimmy Witherspoon Sings the Blues* ♪♪♪♪ (Aim, 1993, prod. Peter Noble) comes from 1980 studio sessions with a Melbourne, Australia, band. Witherspoon is in powerful, happy voice on relaxed versions of "C.C. Rider," "Kansas City," and "Roll 'Em Pete," a song by his hero, Joe Turner.

influences:

◄◄ Louis Jordan, T-Bone Walker, Muddy Waters, Big Joe Turner, Charles Brown

►► Robben Ford, B.B. King, Roy Eldridge, Chris Daniels & the Kings

Steve Knopper

The Wolverines

See: Bix Beiderbecke

Mitch Woods & His Rocket 88's

Formed 1980, in San Francisco, CA.

Mitch Woods (born 1951, in New York, NY), piano, organ, vocals. Other members have included: John Firmin, saxophones, background vocals; Rob Sudduth, saxophones, background vocals; Michael Peloquin, saxophones, background vocals; Jonny Viau, saxophones, background vocals; Curtis Lindberg, trombone, background vocals; Rich Welter, guitar; Danny Caron, guitar; Kenny Ray, guitar; Derek Irving, guitar; Dave Schallock, bass; Steve Wolf, bass; Lance Dickerson, drums; Ben Holmes, drums; Mike Rosas, drums.

Acclaimed by music critics as a young master of boogie-woogie piano, singer Mitch Woods was drawing swing dancers to his gigs long before the recent revival. Before he moved from New York—where he became a bandleader in his teens—to San Francisco in the early 1970s, Woods had developed a keyboard technique much like early boogie-woogie stylists Meade Lux Lewis and Albert Ammons, with influences of blues players such as Otis Spann and Champion Jack Dupree. In San Francisco, he formed Mitch Woods & His Red Hot Mama, a duo with a girlfriend who belted out Bessie Smith–style blues. They relocated to Hawaii, but after they broke up Woods was forced to play *and* sing. Competition was stiff among singers and Woods returned to the Bay Area, where he joined with members of the disbanded David Bromberg unit to form the first version of the Rocket 88's. Originally an 11-piece band, the group these days consists of five core musicians drawn from a pool of familiar players and features Woods singing and playing his energetic piano, often with guest soloists. To create the personal style that he calls "rock-a-boogie," Woods borrows from the jump blues of Louis Jordan, New Orleans second-line polyrhythms, Chicago blues, Kansas City boogie-woogie, and West Coast jump blues. Although early albums contain covers of 1940s to late 1950s tunes performed by jump-blues forebears Louis Jordan, Roy Milton, Joe Liggins, and others, Woods also mines his roots styles to write original material for the band.

what to buy: *Mr. Boogie's Back in Town* ♪♪♪♪ (Blind Pig Records, 1988, prod. Mitch Woods) finds Mitch Woods & His Rocket 88's in top form on 11 tunes that dig into boogie-woogie, jump blues, R&B, and tinges of rock 'n' roll. Arrangements by Woods and bandmates enhance classics, such as Roy Milton's "What Can I Do?" and Louis Jordan's "I Want You to Be My Baby," as well as three originals by Woods.

what to buy next: Woods's earliest Rocket 88's recording, *Steady Date* ♪♪♪♪ (Blind Pig, 1984, prod. Mitch Woods), shows off his New Orleans–influenced piano chops (and lyrics) with the infectious tune "Mojo Mambo." Swing dancers will find satisfaction in the livelier numbers—"Juke Box Drive," "Rocket 88," "Nite Life Boogie," and "Boogie-Woogie Bar-B-Que."

what to avoid: *Keeper of the Flame* ♪♪♪ (Viceroy, 1997, prod. Mitch Woods) does not feature the Rocket 88's, but finds Woods performing with blues heavies John Lee Hooker and Earl King (vocals, guitar), James Cotton (harmonica), and others. The Rocket 88's join Woods on the more raucous *Solid Gold Cadillac* ♪♪♪ (Blind Pig Records, 1991, prod. Mitch Woods), but this album also features a slew of blues stars, including Charlie Musselwhite, the Roomful of Blues horns, and Ronnie Earl, making this a better choice for blues fans than swing fans.

the rest:
Shakin' the Shack ♪♪♪♪ (Blind Pig, 1993)

worth searching for: Mitch Woods & His Rocket 88's appear on two entertaining neo-swing compilation CDs: the 15-track *Swing This, Baby! Vol. 2* ♪♪♪ (Beyond, 1999, prod. various) and the 20-track *Swing Sucks* ♪♪♪ (Liberation, 1999, prod. various). At last word, Woods was also shopping around his newest Rocket 88's recording, a big-band venture that takes full advantage of the swing dance craze.

influences:

◀◀ Meade Lux Lewis, Albert Ammons, Professor Longhair, Roy Milton, Louis Jordan, Louis Prima, Jimmy Liggins, Otis Spann, Champion Jack Dupree

Nancy Ann Lee

Jimmy Yancey

Born February 10, 1898, in Chicago, IL. Died September 18, 1951, in Chicago, IL.

Jimmy Yancey was the father of boogie-woogie piano. A self-taught musician, he transformed elements of ragtime and blues into the driving, danceable boogie that became the backbone of both jump blues and rock 'n' roll. Yancey, a vaudeville tap-dancer as a child, had his fill of show-biz by the time he hit his early 20s. After settling down, he learned the elements of ragtime and blues from his older brother, Alonzo, picking up wrinkles from local players to mesh into his early boogie style. Eschewing a professional career, Yancey relegated his playing to house rent parties, club jams, and open house gatherings for other pianists. Among the many players he influenced at these get-togethers were Albert Ammons and Meade Lux Lewis. When the latter recorded the torrid tribute "Yancey Special," it piqued the interest of his producer, who tracked down Yancey and persuaded him to make his belated recording debut in 1939. The boogie-woogie craze had run its course by the time Yancey's first recordings were released, but he was held in high esteem by genre enthusiasts, and he played club dates and concerts at his leisure. During his later years, he also recorded with his wife, Estelle Harris (a.k.a. Mama Yancey), a first-rate blues singer. Possessing a lighter touch than any of his followers, Yancey brought a unique tango rhythm to many of his left-hand bass runs, which he could vary endlessly. He was also an especially affecting blues player, establishing mood and pathos with minimal stabs from his melodic right hand. Music was never anything more than a part-time job to Jimmy Yancey. From 1925 until the year before his death, he worked as a groundskeeper for the Chicago White Sox.

what to buy: Selected cuts from Yancey's recording debut are on *In the Beginning* (Solo Art, 1989, prod. Dan Qualey), which contains 12 tracks of rolling boogie, blues, and subtle jump, including "Steady Rock Blues," "Yancey's Getaway," "La Salle Street Breakdown," and "Big Bear Train."

what to buy next: Yancey's last studio sessions are lovingly enshrined on *Chicago Piano, Vol. 1* (Atlantic, 1951/1992, prod. Ahmet Ertegun), a 14-track collection of fast boogie and thoughtful blues. Mama Yancey vents her considerable vocal chops on five tracks. You'd never guess the pianist was only weeks away from dying.

the rest:

1939, Vol. 1 (Masters of Jazz, 1995)

worth searching for: The Austrian imports *Complete Recorded Works, Vol. 1 (1939–1940)* (Document, 1991, compilation prod. Johnny Parth), *Complete Recorded Works, Vol. 2 (1940–1943)* (Document, 1997, compilation prod. Johnny Parth), and *Complete Recorded Works, Vol. 3 (1943–1950)* (Document, 1997, compilation prod. Johnny Parth) are worth seeking out. The latter contains the only known recordings by Yancey's older brother, Alonzo, a crack ragtime player. Also, completists will need *Recorded at Yancey's Apartment* (Document, 1998, compilation prod. Johnny Parth).

influences:

◀◀ Alonzo Yancey, Cow Cow Davenport, Bessie Smith

▶▶ Albert Ammons, Meade Lux Lewis, Pete Johnson

Ken Burke

Lester Young

Born August 27, 1909, in Woodville, MS. Died March 15, 1959, in New York, NY.

"Pres"—short for "President," the nickname Billie Holiday gave him—was an original hipster and part of the foundation of modern tenor saxophone jazz improvisation. With a high yet warm tone and an engaging improvisational style, Young was one of the two pillars of tenor jazz during his day and a seminal influence on the development of bebop. Jazz enthusiasts of the late 1930s were either in the Pres camp (he was a laid-back, rhythmic improviser who seldom strayed far from the melody) or in the Coleman Hawkins camp (an aggressive, complex improviser). After early years that included playing hot music in a family band and a few other stops, Young became a major attraction with Count Basie during the 1930s. His subsequent career included classic work on stints with others (he was Holiday's favorite accompanist) and an uneven but substantive solo career. His was the style that formed the bridge between swing and bebop, and even helped inspire the post-bop cool school. His idiosyncratic speech mannerisms in large part became the basis for hip language and he provided nicknames for many, such as Billie "Lady Day" Holiday and Harry "Sweets" Edison. Without the Pres influence, jazz tenor would sound very different.

Lester Young **(Archive Photos)**

what to buy: *The Complete Aladdin Recordings* (Blue Note, 1945/1995), a two-CD set, collects Young's total Aladdin output, including a 1942 session with Nat King Cole and a 1945 version of "Body and Soul." Young's solos on Count Basie's "One O'Clock Jump" and a honking, R&B-style cut, "Sax-O-Be-Bop," are tremendous.

what to buy next: Young shone brightest when great musicians pushed him and *Lester Young with the Oscar Peterson Trio* (Verve, 1959/1997, prod. Norman Granz) provides some post-Basie punch, including a couple of great takes of "I Can't Get Started."

best of the rest:

(With Harry "Sweets" Edison) *Pres and Sweets* (Verve, 1955/1991)
(With Teddy Wilson) *Pres and Teddy* (Verve, 1956/1987)
The Jazz Giants (PolyGram, 1956/1987)
Master Takes (Savoy/Arista, 1980)
The Complete Lester Young (Mercury, 1987)
Lester Young and the Piano Giants (Verve, 1988)
Jazz Masters 30 (Verve/PolyGram, 1994)
Lester Leaps In (Living Era, 1995)
The "Kansas City" Sessions (GRP, 1997)
Ultimate Lester Young (Verve, 1998)

worth searching for: Some of Young's best solos were driven by the Basie band and *Lester Young Memorial Album* (Fontana, 1936–40) captures those early golden years. The classic "Lester Leaps In" alone is well worth the price. *Prized Pres* (Official, 1936–57) compiles some of his best work in a number of different settings, including some backbone-shivering collaborations with Holiday. Both collections are out of print.

influences:

◀◀ Frankie Trumbauer, Jimmy Dorsey, Louis Armstrong, Count Basie

▶▶ Charlie Parker, Dexter Gordon, Gerry Mulligan

Lawrence Gabriel

Snooky Young

Born Eugene Edward Young, February 3, 1919, in Dayton, OH.

"Snooky" Young, whom Buck Clayton and Count Basie called "the most dependable trumpet player in the business," is one of the best lead trumpet players to have come through the Basie organization. Young began performing at an early age with his family's band, the Black and White Revue, traveling on the vaudeville circuit during the late 1930s. A true disciple of the late Louis Armstrong, Young first saw Armstrong while standing outside the Palace Ballroom in Dayton, and though Young was too young to enter the Ballroom, Armstrong made an indelible impression (as he did with many young trumpeters of the era) and became Young's lifelong idol. Young went on to join the Jimmie Lunceford Orchestra in 1939 at age 19, and stayed with the band for three years. During the course of his illustrious career, Young has performed with renowned big bands led by Chic Carter, Les Hite, Benny Carter, Gerald Wilson, Lionel Hampton, Lester Young, and Charles Mingus. Young was an original member of the Thad Jones–Mel Lewis Band, and a member of the NBC Orchestra under the direction of Doc Severinsen on Johnny Carson's *Tonight Show.* In addition to his session work, Young is also credited with several film soundtracks, including *Blues in the Night,* but is mainly remembered for his various stints as section leader while a member of the Count Basie Band.

what's available: Recognized as an outstanding musician and an excellent soloist, Young is a powerhouse in any trumpet section. His only in-print CD as leader is *Snooky and Marshal's Album* (Concord Jazz, 1978/1989, prod. Carl E. Jefferson), with saxophonist Marshal Royal. The album includes a fine version of "Cherry," with a beautiful exchange between the two soloists, and the true blues number "Mean Dog Blues." The medley "You've Changed/I'm Confessin'/Come Sunday" melds melodic interpretations of Louis Armstrong's tune "Confessin'" with a heartfelt version of Duke Ellington's classic from *Black, Brown, and Beige Suite.*

influences:

◀◀ Louis Armstrong, Roy Eldridge, Harry "Sweets" Edison

▶▶ Dizzy Gillespie, Miles Davis

Keith Brickhouse

musicHound SWING!

Resources and Other Information

Compilation Albums

Books, Magazines, and Newsletters

Web Sites

Record Labels

Radio Stations

If you're looking for swing and related styles of music by a variety of performers, these compilation albums would be a good place to start.

Boogie-Woogie

Atlantic Blues: Piano (Atlantic, 1986)

Blues 88's: Boogie Woogie Piano Instrumentals (Easydisc, 1998)

Boogie Woogie & Barrelhouse Piano, Vol. 1 (1928–1932) (Document, 1992)

Boogie Woogie & Barrelhouse Piano, Vol. 2 (1928–1930) (Document, 1992)

Boogie Woogie Blues (Biograph, 1991)

The Boogie Woogie Boys—The Complete Library of Congress Recordings in Chronological Order, 1938–1941 (Document, 1995)

Boogie Woogie Riot (Arhoolie, 1985/1995)

Boogie Woogie Special (Pearl, 1995)

Jazz Orchestras

Beethoven Wrote It . . . But It Swings! (Sony, 1996)

Masters of Jazz: Big Bands of the '30s and '40s (BMG, 1996)

Swingin' Talkin' Verve (PolyGram, 1998)

Swing's the Thing (Simitar, 1998)

Jump Blues

Big Band Blues (Collectables, 1991)

Blues Masters, Vol. 5: Jump Blues Classics (Rhino, 1992)

Blues Masters, Vol. 14: More Jump Blues (Rhino, 1993)

Juke Joint Jump (Legacy, 1996)

Jump Blue: Rockin' the Jooks (Blue Note, 1999)

Jump with a Shuffle (Indigo, 1998)

Jumpin' & Jivin' (Specialty, 1997)

Jumpin' Like Mad: Cool Cats & Hip Chicks (Capitol Blues, 1997)

Shouting the Blues (Specialty, 1992)

Specialty Legends of Jump Blues, Vol. 1 (Specialty, 1994)

Swing Is the Thing (Rounder, 1999)

Neo-Swing

Arizona Swings (Hepcat, 1998)

Big Band Crazy: The Swinging Party Album (Starbound, 1997)

The HiBall Lounge Sessions, Vol. 1 (HiBall, 1998)

Hipsters, Zoots & Wingtips, Vol. 1: The '90s Swingers (Hip-O/MCA, 1998)

House of Blues Swings! (House of Blues, 1999)

Jump Up & Boogie: The New Swing (Elektra, 1998)

New York City Swing (Flattop, 1998)

Next Generation Swing (Beast, 1998)

Swing Hit Mix (Wax Works, 1998)

Swing This, Baby! (Beyond, 1998)

Ultra Swing Nouveau (DM, 1998)

Old-School Jive

Jump 'n' Jive (Aladdin, 1999)

Hipsters, Zoots & Wingtips, Vol. 2: Original Swingers (Hip-O/MCA, 1999)

Swing, Baby, Swing! House Rockin' Swing and Jump Jive Boogie (Music Club, 1998)

Rockabilly

Be Bop Boogie (Collectables, 1991)

Best of Sun Rockabilly, Vol. 1 (Charly, 1991)

Best of Sun Rockabilly, Vol. 2 (Charly, 1992)

Cat Music (HighTone, 1998)

Essential Sun Rockabilly (Charly, 1995)

Essential Sun Rockabilly, Vol. 2 (Charly, 1995)

Essential Sun Rockabilly, Vol. 3 (Charly, 1997)

Essential Sun Rockabilly, Vol. 5 (Charly, 1998)

Get Hot or Go Home: Vintage RCA Rockabilly, '56–'59 (CMF, 1990)

Long Gone Daddy (Collectables, 1991)

Memphis Rocks: Rockabilly in Memphis, 1954–1968 (Smithsonian/Folkways, 1992)

Rock This Town: Rockabilly Hits, Vol. 1 (Rhino, 1991)

Rock This Town: Rockabilly Hits, Vol. 2 (Rhino, 1991)

Rockabilly (Life, Times & Music, 1996)

Rockabilly Essentials (Hip-O, 1998)

Rockabilly Hall of Fame, Vol. 1 (Hepcat, 1998)

Rockabilly Hall of Fame, Vol. 2 (Hepcat, 1998)

Rockabilly Riot (K-Tel, 1995)

Rockabilly Stars, Vol. 1 (Epic, 1981/Collectors, 1993)

Rockabilly Stars, Vol. 2 (Epic, 1981/Collectors, 1993)

Rockabilly Stars, Vol. 3 (Epic, 1982/Collectors, 1996)

Rollin' Rock Got the Sock, Vol. 1 (HighTone, 1997)

Rollin' Rock Got The Sock, Vol. 2 (HighTone, 1997)

The Sun Records Collection (RCA/Rhino, 1994)

Sun Rockabilly—Classic Recordings (Rounder, 1995)

Sun Singles, Vol. 1 (Bear Family, 1994)

Sun Singles, Vol. 2 (Bear Family, 1995)

Sun Singles, Vol. 3 (Bear Family, 1996)

Sun Singles, Vol. 4 (Bear Family, 1997)

Sun Singles, Vol. 5 (Bear Family, 1998)

The Sun Story (Rhino, 1987)

Very Best of Sun Rockabilly (Charly, 1997)

Swing Era

An Anthology of Big-Band Swing (1930–1955) (Decca/GRP, 1993)

Best of the Big Bands (Hindsight, 1979)

Best of the Big Bands: The '40s (Ranwood, 1996)

Best of the Big Bands: Male Singers (Ranwood, 1996)

Big Band Greatest Hits (BMG, 1996)

Big Band Instrumentals (Columbia/Legacy, 1992)

Big Band More Greatest Hits (BMG, 1998)

College Rhythm (Memphis Archives, 1996)

The Essential Big Bands (PolyGram, 1992)

The Fabulous Big Band Collection (RCA Victor, 1998)

The Fabulous Swing Collection (RCA Victor, 1998)

The Legendary Big Band Singers (GRP/MCA, 1994)

Lovers' Swing (BMG, 1999)

Masters of the Big Bands: The Vocalists (BMG, 1992)

Oscillatin' Rhythm (Blue Note/Capitol Jazz, 1997)

Roots of Swing (Madacy, 1998)

16 Most Requested Songs of the '40s, Vol. 2 (Columbia, 1989)

Swing Is Alive (MCA Special Products, 1998)

Swing! More Greatest Hits (BMG, 1998)

Swing: The Best of the Big Bands (MCA, 1988)

Swing Time! (1925–1955) (Columbia/Legacy, 1993)

Swingin' at Capitol (Capitol, 1999)

Swingin' the Classics (Viper's Nest, 1996)

Swingin' Uptown (BMG, 1998)

The Swingingest Sounds Ever Heard (Hip-O/MCA, 1997)

Swingsation Sampler (GRP, 1998)

21 Swing Band All-Time Hits (Living Era, 1994)

Ultra-Lounge, Vol. 5: Wild, Cool & Swingin' (Capitol, 1996)

Wicked Swing (RCA Victor, 1998)

Swing-Era Experimentalists

Saturday Night Swing Club (Memphis Archives, 1994)

Can't get enough information about swing music? Here are some books, magazines, and newsletters you can check out for further information. Happy reading!

Books

BIOGRAPHIES

Bass Line: The Stories and Photographs of Milt Hinton
Milt Hinton and David G. Berger (Temple University Press, 1991)

Benny Goodman and the Swing Era
James Lincoln Collier (Oxford University Press, 1989)

Benny Goodman: Listen to His Legacy (Studies in Jazz, No. 6)
D. Russell Connor (Scarecrow Press, 1988)

Benny Goodman: Wrappin' It Up (Studies in Jazz, No. 23)
D. Russell Connor (Scarecrow Press, 1996)

Beyond Category: The Life and Genius of Duke Ellington
John Edward Hasse (Da Capo Press, 1995)

Billie Holiday
Stuart Nicholson (Northeastern University Press, 1995)

Billie's Blues: The Billie Holiday Story, 1933–1959
John Chilton and Buck Clayton (Da Capo Press, 1989)

Bird: The Legend of Charlie Parker
Robert George Reisner (Da Capo Press, 1988)

Bird Lives! The High Life & Hard Times of Charlie (Yardbird) Parker
Ross Russell (Da Capo Press, 1996)

Bird's Diary: The Life of Charlie Parker, 1945–1955
Ken Vail (Harvill Press, 1996)

Bix: Man and Legend
Richard M. Sudhalterr and Philip R. Evans (Arlington House Publishers, 1974)

Blue Flame: Woody Herman's Life in Music
Robert C. Kriebel (Purdue University Press, 1995)

Celebrating the Duke: And Louis, Bessie, Billie, Bird, Carmen, Miles, Dizzy, and Other Heroes
Ralph J. Gleason (Da Capo Press, 1995)

Charlie Christian
Peter Broadbent (Hal Leonard Publishing Corp., 1997)

Charlie Parker (Black Americans of Achievement)
Ron Frankl (Chelsea House, 1992)

Charlie Parker: His Music and Life (Michigan American Music Series)
Carl Woideck (University of Michigan Press, 1996)

Count Basie: Bandleader and Musician
Bud Kliment (Holloway, 1994)

Crazy Fingers: Claude Hopkins' Life in Jazz
Claude Hopkins and Warren W. Vache (Smithsonian Institute Press, 1992)

Dizzy Gillespie (Black Americans of Achievement)
Tony Gentry (Chelsea House, 1994)

Django Reinhardt
Charles Delaunay (Da Capo Press, 1988)

Duke Ellington (Black Americans of Achievement)
Ron Frankl (Chelsea House, 1988)

Duke Ellington (Impact Biography)
Eva Stwertka and Eve Stwertka (Franklin Watts Inc., 1994)

Duke Ellington: Jazz Composer
Ken Rattenbury (Yale University Press, 1993)

The Duke Ellington Reader
Mark Tucker (Oxford, 1995)

Duke Ellington: The Piano Prince and His Orchestra
Andrea Davis Pinkney (Disney Press, 1998)

Ella Fitzgerald: A Biography of the First Lady of Jazz
Stuart Nicholson (Scribner, 1994)

Ellington: The Early Years (Music in American Life Series)
Mark Tucker (University of Illinois Press, 1991)

Fats Waller
Maurice Waller (Macmillan General Reference, 1997)

First Lady of Song: Ella Fitzgerald for the Record
Geoffrey Mark Fidelman (Birch Lane Press, 1994)

Glenn Miller and His Orchestra
George Thomas Simon (Da Capo Press, 1988)

Good Morning Blues: The Autobiography of Count Basie
Albert Murray (Da Capo Press, 1995)

Hamp: An Autobiography
Lionel Hampton, with James Haskins (Amistad, 1993)

If I Only Had a Horn: Young Louis Armstrong
Roxanne Orgill (Houghton Mifflin, 1997)

It's About Time: The Dave Brubeck Story
Fred Hall (University of Arkansas Press, 1996)

Jack Teagarden: The Story of a Jazz Maverick
Jay D. Smith (Da Capo Press, 1988)

Just a Gigolo: The Life and Times of Louis Prima
Gary Boulard (University of Southwestern Louisiana Press, 1989)

The King of Western Swing: Bob Wills Remembered
Rosetta Wills (Watson-Guptill Publishing, 1998)

Lady Sings the Blues
Billie Holiday, with William Dufty (Penguin, 1995)

Leader of the Band: The Life of Woody Herman
Gene Lees and Graham Lees (Oxford University Press, 1995)

Louis Armstrong: A Cultural Legacy
Marc H. Miller (University of Washington Press, 1994)

Louis Armstrong: An Extravagant Life
Laurence Bergreen (Broadway Books, 1997)

Louis Armstrong Odyssey: From Jane Alley to America's Jazz Ambassador
Dempsey J. Travis (Urban Research Press, 1997)

Lush Life: A Biography of Billy Strayhorn
David Hajdu (Farrar, Straus & Giroux, 1996)

Music Is My Mistress
Duke Ellington (Da Capo Press, 1988)

Pres: The Story of Lester Young
Luc Delannoy (University of Arkansas Press, 1993)

Quincy Jones (I Have a Dream)
Stuart A. Kallen (Abdo & Daughters, 1996)

Sassy: The Life of Sarah Vaughan
Leslie Gourse (Da Capo Press, 1994)

Satchmo
Gary Giddins (Da Capo Press, 1998)

Satchmo: My Life in New Orleans
Louis Armstrong (Da Capo Press, 1988)

Sidney Bechet: The Wizard of Jazz
John Chilton (Da Capo Press, 1996)

Sinatra: The Artist and the Man
John Lahr (Random House, 1998)

Sinatra! The Song Is You: A Singer's Art
Will Friedwald (Da Capo Press, 1997)

Swing, Swing, Swing: The Life & Times of Benny Goodman
Ross Firestone (W.W. Norton & Company, 1994)

Those Swinging Years: The Autobiography of Charlie Barnet
Charlie Barnet and Stanley Dance (Da Capo Press, 1992)

Tommy and Jimmy: The Dorsey Years
Herb Sanford (Da Capo Press, 1980)

Tommy Dorsey: On the Side
Robert L. Stockdale (Da Capo Press, 1995)

The Way You Wear Your Hat: Frank Sinatra and the Lost Art of Livin'
Bill Zehme (HarperCollins, 1997)

What My Heart Has Seen
Tony Bennett (Rizzoli, 1996)

Wishing on the Moon: The Life and Times of Billie Holiday
Donald Clarke (Penguin USA, 1995)

The Woodchopper's Ball: The Autobiography of Woody Herman
Woody Herman and Stuart Troup (Limelight Editions, 1994)

Woody Herman: Chronicles of the Herds
William D. Clancy and Audree Coke Kenton (MacMillan, 1995)

The World of Count Basie
Stanley Dance (Da Capo Press, 1985)

The World of Duke Ellington
Stanley Dance (Da Capo Press, 1981)

GENERAL INTEREST

Benny Goodman and the Swing Era
James Lincoln Collier (Oxford University Press, 1991)

The Best Damn Trumpet Player: Memories of the Big Band Era and Beyond
Richard Grudens and Frankie Laine (Celebrity Profiles Inc., 1996)

The Big Band Almanac
Leo Walker (Da Capo Press, 1989)

The Big Bands
George Thomas Simon (Schirmer Books, 1981)

The Big Bands Go to War
Chris Way (Trafalgar Square, 1992)

The Big Book of Swing
(Hal Leonard Publishing Corp., 1998)

A Century of Jazz: From Blues to Bop, Swing to Hiphop—A Hundred Years of Music, Musicians, Singers and Styles
Roy Carr (Da Capo Press, 1997)

Dialogues in Swing
(Pathfinder Publishing, 1989)

Drummin' Men: The Heartbeat of Jazz—The Swing Years
Burt Korall (Schirmer Books, 1990)

From Jazz to Swing: African-American Jazz Musicians and their Music, 1890–1935 (Jazz History, Culture, and Criticism Series)
Thomas J. Hennessey (Wayne State University Press, 1994)

From Satchmo to Miles
Leonard Feather (Da Capo Press, 1988)

Jazz Masters of the Thirties (MacMillan Jazz Masters Series)
Rex William Stewart (Da Capo Press, 1988)

The Jazz of the Southwest: An Oral History of Western Swing
Jean Ann Boyd (University of Texas Press, 1998)

Jitterbug Swing: Beginners Handbook—Ballroom to Barroom
John Kersten (Stumble Bum Press, 1990)

Joel Whitburn's Pop Memories: The History of American Music, 1890–1954
Joel Whitburn (Record Research, 1986)

The Joy of Jazz: Swing Era, 1935–1947
Tom Scanlan (Fulcrum Publishing, 1996)

Lone Star Swing: On the Trail of Bob Wills and His Texas Playboys
Duncan McLean (W.W. Norton & Company, 1998)

Milton Brown and the Founding of Western Swing
Cary Ginell, with Roy Lee Brown (University of Illinois Press, 1994)

More Dialogues in Swing: Intimate Conversations with the Stars of the Big Band Era
Fred Hall and Eugene D. Wheeler, ed. (Pathfinder Publishing, 1992)

The Song Stars: The Ladies Who Sang with the Bands and Beyond
Richard Grudens (Celebrity Profiles Inc., 1997)

Swing!
(Hal Leonard Publishing Corp., 1995)

Swing Changes: Big-Band Jazz in New Deal America
David W. Stowe (Harvard University Press, 1996)

Swing Era New York: The Jazz Photographs of Charles Peterson
W. Royal Stokes (Temple University Press, 1996)

Swing Kings
Julie Koerner (Michael Friedman/Fairfax Publishing, 1997)

Swing Out: Great Negro Dance Bands
Gene Fernett (Da Capo Press, 1993)

Swing That Music
Louis Armstrong (Da Capo Press, 1993)

Swing! The New Retro Renaissance
V. Vale (V/Search, 1998)

Swing to Bop: An Oral History of the Transition in Jazz in the 1940s
Ira Gitler (Oxford University Press, 1987)

Swingin' the Dream: Big Band Jazz and the Rebirth of American Culture
Lewis A. Erenberg (University of Chicago Press, 1998)

200 of the Best Songs from the Swing Era (Jazz Bible Fake Book Series)
Rob Duboff, ed. (Hal Leonard Publishing Corp., 1997)

Western Swing (Life, Times & Music Series)
Andrew G. Hager (Michael Friedman/Fairfax Publishing, 1997)

The Wonderful Era of the Great Dance Bands
Leo Walker (Da Capo Press, 1990)

DANCE HOW-TO

Betty White Learn to Dance Set: Lindy, Swing
(Conversa-Phone, 1998)

Jitterbug Swing: Beginners' Handbook—Ballroom to Barroom
John Kersten (Stumble Bum, 1990)

Let's Dance! Learn to Swing, Jitterbug, Rumba, Tango, Line Dance, Lambada, Cha-Cha, Waltz, Two-Step, Foxtrot and Salsa with Style, Grace and Ease
Paul Bottomer (Black Dog and Leventhal, 1998)

Shall We Dance? Eight Classic Ballroom Dances in Eight Quick Lessons
Manine Rosa Golden (Hyperion, 1997)

Magazines and Newsletters

Billboard
1515 Broadway
New York, NY 10036
(212) 764-7300

Cadence
Cadence Building
Redwood, NY 13679

CMJ New Music Monthly
11 Middleneck Rd., Ste. 400
Great Neck, NY 11021
(516) 466-6000

Coda
PO Box 1002
Station "O"
Toronto, Ontario M4A 2N4
Canada
(250) 335-2911

Down Beat
102 N. Haven Rd.
Elmhurst, IL 60126
(800) 535-7496

ICE
PO Box 3043
Santa Monica, CA 90408
(800) 647-4ICE

Jazz Now
PO Box 19266
Oakland, CA 94519-0266
(800) 840-0465

The Jazz Report
14 London St.
Toronto, Ontario M6G 1M9
Canada

Jazziz
3620 NW 43 St.
Gainesville, FL 32606
(352) 375-3705

JazzTimes
8737 Colesville Rd., 5th Fl.
Silver Spring, MD 20910
(301) 588-4114

Mississippi Rag
PO Box 19068
Minneapolis, MN 55419
(619) 861-2446

Musician
1515 Broadway
New York, NY 10036
(212) 536-5208

Rolling Stone
1290 Avenue of the Americas, 2nd Fl.
New York, NY 10104
(212) 484-1616

Strictly Jazz
PO Box 492008
College Park, GA
(404) 768-4450

Swing Time
30 Baker, Ste. B
San Francisco, CA 94117
(415) 255-8306

Swing and big-band music are everywhere, even out in cyberspace. Point your Web browser to these pages for more information on your favorite artists or the music in general.

Artists

Howard Alden
www.riverwalk.org/alden.htm

Red Allen
www.technoir.net/jazz/red.html

Joey Altruda/Jump with Joey
www.willrecords.com/joeyaltruda/index.htm
www.princeton.edu./~tompilla/jwj.html

Andrews Sisters
holly.colostate.edu/~carleen/andrews/
www.cmgww.com/music/andrews/andrews.html

Louis Armstrong
www.foppejohnson.com/armstrong/
www.satchmo.net/

Asleep at the Wheel
www.bigjam.com/thewheel/htm/history.htm

Fred Astaire
members.aol.com/AstaireFan/

Pearl Bailey
www.gateway-va.com/pages/bhistory/bailey.htm

Count Basie
www.soros.org.mk/mk/skopje/jazz/en/count.htm

Les Baxter
home.earthlink.net/~spaceagepop/baxter.htm

Bix Beiderbecke
www.riverwalk.org/bix.htm
www.qconline.com/bix/

Bellevue Cadillac
www.bellevuecadillac.com/

Tony Bennett
www.tonybennett.net/

Elmer Bernstein
home.earthlink.net/~spaceagepop/bernstei.htm

Big Bad Voodoo Daddy
www.coolsvillerecords.com/bbvd/index.htm

Big Six
www.big.six.org/

Big Time Operator
members.aol.com/BigTimeOp/index.html
www.bigtimeoperator.com/

The Blasters
bullwinkle.as.utexas.edu/scot/blasters.html

Blue Plate Special
www.zapt.com/blueplate/

Clarence "Gatemouth" Brown
www.rounder.com/rounder/catalog/byartist/b/brown_clarence_gatemouth_/

Junior Brown
www.juniorbrown.com/

Dave Brubeck
www.schirmer.com/composers/brubeck_bio.html

Sonny Burgess
www.deltaboogie.com/deltamusicians/burgess.htm

Hoagy Carmichael
www.hoagy.com/

Benny Carter
www.lpb.com/benny/

Chazz Cats
www.chazzcats.com/

Doc Cheatham
www.npr.org/programs/jazzprofiles/cheatham.html

Cherry Poppin' Daddies
www.daddies.com/index.html
www.geocities.com/SunsetStrip/Pit/4564/daddies.html

Charlie Christian
personal.nbnet.nb.ca/hansen/Charlie/

Cigar Store Indians
www.cigarstoreindians.com/

Rosemary Clooney
www.clooney.com/

Eddie Cochran
www.oliveweb.clara.net/r-ccoche.htm

Nat King Cole
www.tip.net.au/~bnoble/natkcole/nat_cole.htm

Commander Cody & His Lost Planet Airmen
www.globerecords.com/Cody.html
www.awpi.com/CommanderCody/

Harry Connick Jr.
www.hconnickjr.com/
www.connick.com/connick.html
weber.u.washington.edu/~no1husky/harry/connick.html

Bing Crosby
www.kcmetro.cc.mo.us/pennvalley/biology/lewis/crosby/bing.htm
www.geocities.com/BourbonStreet/3754/bing.html
www.tir.com/~rtw/bing.htm

Bob Crosby
members.aol.com/famemgt/fame/crosby.htm

Sammy Davis Jr.
www.geocities.com/CollegePark/8182/samtro.htm
www.interlog.com/~wad/sambio.html
www.sammydavis-jr.com/

Ronnie Dawson
www.mountainx.com/ae/1998-1/dawson.html

Doris Day
www.netlink.co.uk/users/funkin/dorisday/dorisday.html
www.ozemail.com.au/~bywaters/index.html
laurie.dreamhost.com/doris.html

The Delmore Brothers
www.alamhof.org/delmores.htm

Jimmy Dorsey
www.technoir.net/jazz/jimmy.html

Tommy Dorsey
www.teleport.com/~rfrederi/wtommy01.htm
spaceformusic.com/tommydorsey.html

Billy Eckstine
www.servtech.com/~pnm/stardust/billy.htm

8½ Souvenirs
www.haz.com/souvenirs/

Duke Ellington
duke.fuse.net/
www.dnsmith.com/ellington/
www.ilinks.net/~holmesr/duke.htm

Bill Elliott Swing Orchestra
studio8h.com/swingorch/

Dutch Falconi Orchestra
www.mother.com/~foy323/falconi.html
www.dutchfalconi.com/

Ella Fitzgerald
jazzcentralstation.com/jcs/station/musicexp/artists/ella/index.html
www.public.iastate.edu/~vwindsor/Ella.html
www.seas.columbia.edu/~tts6/ella.html

Rosie Flores
lonestar.texas.net/~dqkidd/

Flying Neutrinos
www.flyingneutrinos.com/

Frantic Flattops
our.tentativetimes.net/rrw98/flattops.html

Ray Gelato & His Giants of Jive
www.raygelato.com/

Banu Gibson
www.riverwalk.org/banu.htm

Dizzy Gillespie
www.duke.edu/~jlb18/
Lumberjack.humboldt.edu/bird/index.html
www.geocities.com/BourbonStreet/8446/

Benny Goodman
www.flash.net/~rdreagan/index.shtml
qlink.queensu.ca/~3pje2/bg.html

Robert Gordon
www.athenet.net/~genevinc/RobertGordon.html

Stephane Grappelli
www.digitalrain.net/bowed/grapelli.htm

Buddy Greco
www.buddy-greco.com/index.htm

Merle Haggard
www.TheHag.com/

Bill Haley
www.rockabilly.nl/artists/bhaley.htm

Lionel Hampton
www.duboislc.com/JazzHallFame/html/LionelHampton.html

Hipster Daddy-O & the Hand Grenades
www.hipsterdaddyo.com/

Hot Rize
www.banjo.com/Profiles/HotRize.html

Hot Rod Lincoln
v-music.com/artists/hot.rod.lincoln/

Betty Hutton
web.starlinx.com/fwsiegle/bh/index.htm-ssi

Dick Hyman
easyweb.easynet.co.uk/~rcb/light/

Indigo Swing
www.slip.net/~indigos/

Joe Jackson
www.joejackson.com/

Wanda Jackson
www.netreach.net/~mcreep/mw/jackson.html

Jive Aces
jiveaces.scientology.org/

Al Jolson
www.jolson.org/
www.btinternet.com/~jolson/main.htm

Quincy Jones
www.wbr.com/quincyjones/

Spike Jones
www.geocities.com/SunsetStrip/4020/spike.html

Gene Krupa
www.geocities.com/BourbonStreet/Delta/3898/
www.concentric.net/~thompjr/gene_krupa/index.shtml

Peggy Lee
www.geocities.com/Broadway/Stage/2481/home.html

Lee Press-On & the Nails
www.swingordie.com/

Kim Lenz
www.kimlenz.com/

Jerry Lee Lewis
www.ciagri.usp.br/~gmsenato/jerry2.html
www.student.tdb.uu.se/~m93aum/jerry.html
www.generation.net/~elbonne/fcjllewis/ejerry.htm

Guy Lombardo
members.aol.com/famemgt/fame/lombardo.htm

Steve Lucky & the Rhumba Bums
www.luckylounge.com/

The Manhattan Transfer
www.west.net/~jrpprod/tmt/tmt.html
www.singers.com/manhattantransfer.html

Dean Martin
www.deanmartinfancenter.com/index.html

Carmen McRae
www.ddg.com/LIS/InfoDesignF96/Ismael/jazz/1950/McRae.html

Bette Midler
www.geocities.com/Hollywood/Picture/2757/
www.nwrain.net/~jstewart/bette.htm
www.geocities.com/Hollywood/4863/

Glenn Miller
www.heartland.net/local/pages/glenn-miller/member.htm

Matt Monro
www.clark.net/pub/eisinger/monro.htm

Bill Monroe
www.banjo.com/BG/Profiles/BillMonroe.html

Moon Mullican
www.webspawner.com/users/MoonMullican/

The New Morty Show
www.newmortyshow.com/

The Paladins
www.rockabilly.com/paladin.html

Charlie Parker
www.cmgww.com/music/parker/parker.html
www.wam.umd.edu/~losinp/music/bird.html

Pinetop Perkins
www.mint.net/deluge/bio/pinetop.html

Oscar Peterson
www.duke.edu/~jhs7/jazz/index.html

Elvis Presley
www.elvis-presley.com
users.aol.com/petedixon/elvis/index.html
sunsite.unc.edu/elvis/elvishom.html
www.pathfinder.com/people/sp/elvis
wsrv.clas.virginia.edu/~acs5d/elvis.html

Louis Prima
home.earthlink.net/~spaceagepop/prima.htm

Django Reinhardt
ourworld.compuserve.com/homepages/SRoyall/homepage.htm

Buddy Rich
members.aol.com/Azhosers/hosers-c.html

Billy Lee Riley
www.athenet.net/~genevinc/BLR.html

Duke Robillard
www.rosebudus.com/robillard/bio.html

Adrian Rollini
www.redhotjazz.com/Rollini.html

Royal Crown Revue
www.rcr.com/

Jimmy Rushing
www.blueflamecafe.com/

Raymond Scott
RaymondScott.com/

Brian Setzer Orchestra/Stray Cats
www.geocities.com/SunsetStrip/Arena/1198/brian_setzer/briansetzertribute.html
www.listen.to/briansetzer
www.jps.net/mrjazz/

Doc Severinsen
www.trb.ayuda.com/~dnote/doc.html

Artie Shaw
www.artieshaw.com/

Frank Sinatra
www.blue-eyes.com/
www.sinatralist.com
www.sinatraclub.com/
www.Sinatrafamily.com
members.aol.com/BrianC101/Sinatra.htm

Lavay Smith & Her Red Hot Skillet Lickers
www.lavaysmith.com/

Squirrel Nut Zippers
www.mammoth.com/mammoth/bands/snz/
www.squirrelnutzippers.com/

Billy Strayhorn
www.billystrayhorn.com/

Ron Sunshine & Full Swing
www.goldenbug.com/

Swingerhead
www.swingerhead.com/

Jack Teagarden
www.geocities.com/BourbonStreet/2508/

Jean "Toots" Thielemans
houbi.simplenet.com/belpop/groups/toots.htm

Hank Thompson
www.infocs.com/hank/

Merle Travis
www.comsource.net/~darrelw/

Billy Vaughn
home.earthlink.net/~spaceagepop/vaughn.htm

Sarah Vaughan
members.xoom.com/sarahvaughan/

Gene Vincent
www.athenet.net/~genevinc/index20.html

T-Bone Walker
www.io.com/~tbone1/blues/bios/tbone.html

Ethel Waters
library.advanced.org/10320/Waters.htm

Lawrence Welk
welk.buffnet.net/
www.zeldman.com/welk.html

Jimmy Yancey
homepages.munich.netsurf.de/Andreas.Busch/boogie/bframe2.html

Lester Young
www.duke.edu/~crt/jazz/lester_young.html

Other Swing, Dance, and Music-Related Sites

Amazon.com
www.amazon.com/music

Any Swing Goes
www.anyswinggoes.com/

Arthur Murray International
www.arthurmurray.com/

Ballroom Dance Club
dancetv.com/

Billboard Magazine
www.billboard.com/

BlackCat Rockabilly Homepage
www.mara.nl/

The Blue Flame Cafe
www.blueflamecafe.com/

BMG Music Service
www.bmgmusicservice.com/
www.borders.com/music

Borders.com
www.borders.com/music

CD Universe
www.cduniverse.com/

CDnow
www.cdnow.com/

Collectors' Choice Music
www.ccmusic.com

Columbia House Music Club
www.columbiahouse.com/

Dance! Dance! Dance!
www.dancedancedance.com

eSwing
www.eSwing.com/

ICE Magazine
www.icemagazine.com/

Jump Site
NCLS.com/graphicsrich/index.html

The Lindy Hop and Swing Bands Page
www.geocities.com/BourbonStreet/Bayou/2150/

Music Boulevard
www.musicblvd.com/

Music Newswire
www.musicnewswire.com/

neoSwing
www.neoswing.com/

Past Perfect: The Sounds of the '20s, '30s and '40s Digitally Re-mastered
www.pastperfect.com/first.html

Pennsylvania 65000
www.pennsylvania65000.com/

Raper's Dance Corner
www.dancecorner.com/dance/

Rock and Roll Hall of Fame
www.rockhall.com/

Rockabilly Hall of Fame
www.rockabillyhall.com/

SavoyStyle
www.savoystyle.com/

Swing It!
swingit.apollonet.net/

Total Swing Online
www.totalswing.com/

Tunes.com
www.tunes.com/

U.S. Swing Dance Server
simon.cs.cornell.edu/Info/People/aswin/SwingDancing/swing_dancing.html

Wall of Sound
www.wallofsound.com

Zootsuitstore.com
www.zootsuitstore.com

The following record labels are just some of the labels that have swing, jump blues, and rockabilly catalogs. You may want to contact them if you have questions regarding specific releases.

Arista Records
6 W. 57th St.
New York, NY 10019
(212) 489-7400
Fax: (212) 830-2238

Atlantic Recording Corp.
1290 Avenue of the Americas
New York, NY 10104
(212) 707-2000
Fax: (212) 405-5507

Bear Family Records
PO Box 1154
27727 Hambergen, Germany
(49) 04794-93000
Fax: (49) 04794-930020

Bellmark Records/Life Records
7060 Hollywood Blvd., 10th Fl.
Hollywood, CA 90028
(213) 464-8492
Fax: (213) 464-0785

Biograph Records
35 Medford St., Ste. 203
Somerville, MA 02143
(617) 426-7500
Fax: (617) 426-5222

Blue Note Records
1290 Avenue of the Americas, 35th Fl.
New York, NY 10104
(212) 492-5300
Fax: (212) 492-5458

Capricorn Records
1100 Spring St. NW, Ste. 103.
Atlanta, GA 30309-2823
(404) 873-3918
Fax: (404) 873-1807

Chiaroscuro Records
830 Broadway
New York, NY 10003
(212) 473-0479

Collectables Records
2320 Haverford Rd.
Ardmore, PA 19003
(800) 446-8426
(610) 649-7650
Fax: (610) 649-0315

Collectors' Choice Music
PO Box 838
Itasca, IL 60143-0838
(800) 923-1122

Columbia Records
550 Madison Ave.
New York, NY 10022-3211
(212) 833-8000
Fax: (212) 833-7731

Concord Records
2450-A Stanwell Dr.
Concord, CA 94520
(510) 682-6770
Fax: (510) 682-3508

Corinthian Records
PO Box 6296
Beverly Hills, CA 90212
Fax: (310) 455-2649

The Curb Group
47 Music Sq. E.
Nashville, TN 37203
(615) 321-5080
Fax: (615) 255-2855

Decca Records
60 Music Sq. E.
Nashville, TN 37203
(615) 244-8944
Fax: (615) 880-7475

Delmark Records
4121 N. Rockwell
Chicago, IL 60618
(773) 539-5001
Fax: (773) 539-5004

EastWest Records
75 Rockefeller Plz.
New York, NY 10019
(212) 275-2500
Fax: (212) 974-9314

Elektra Entertainment Group
75 Rockefeller Plz.
New York, NY 10019-6907
(212) 275-4000
Fax: (212) 974-9314

EMI-Capitol Records
1750 N. Vine St.
Hollywood, CA 90028
(213) 462-6252
Fax: (213) 467-6550

Epic Records
550 Madison Ave.
New York, NY 10022-3211
(212) 833-8000
Fax: (212) 833-5134

Evidence Music
1100 E. Hector St., Ste. 392
Conshohocken, PA 19428
(610) 832-0844
Fax: (610) 832-0807

Fantasy Records
2600 Tenth St.
Berkeley, CA 94710
(510) 549-2500
Fax: (510) 486-2015

GNP Crescendo Records
8480-A Sunset Blvd.
West Hollywood, CA 90069
(213) 656-2614
Fax: (213) 656-0693

GRP Recording Co.
555 W. 57th St., 10th Fl.
New York, NY 10019
(212) 424-1000
Fax: (212) 424-1007

Hep Cat Records
PO Box 1108
Orange, CA 92856
(800) 404-4117
Fax: (714) 532-1474

Hollywood Records
500 S. Buena Vista St.
Burbank, CA 91521
(818) 560-5670
Fax: (818) 841-5140

Ichiban Records
PO Box 724677
Atlanta, GA 31139-1677
(770) 419-1414
Fax: (770) 419-1230

Impulse!
555 W. 57th St., 10th Fl.
New York, NY 10019
(212) 424-1000
Fax: (212) 424-1007

Interscope/Geffen/A&M Records
10900 Wilshire Blvd., Ste. 1230
Los Angeles, CA 90024
(310) 209-7600
Fax: (310) 208-7343

Koch International
2 Tri Harbor Ct.
Port Washington, NY 11050-4617
(516) 484-1000
Fax: (516) 484-4746

Laserlight Digital
Delta Music Company
1663 Sawtelle Blvd.
Los Angeles, CA 90025
(310) 268-1205
Fax: (310) 268-1279

London Records
825 Eighth Ave., 23rd Fl.
New York, NY 10019
(212) 333-8000
Fax: (212) 333-8030

MCA Records
70 Universal City Plz.
Universal City, CA 91608
(818) 777-4000
Fax: (818) 733-1407

Metropolitan Recording Corp.
900 Passaic Ave.
East Newark, NJ 07029
(201) 483-8080
Fax: (201) 483-0031

N-Coded Music
55 Broad St., 18th Fl.
New York, NY 10004
(212) 378-6100
Fax: (212) 742-1775

Polydor Records
1416 N. La Brea Ave.
Hollywood, CA 90028
(213) 856-6600
Fax: (213) 856-6610

Private Music
8750 Wilshire Blvd.
Beverly Hills, CA 90211
(310) 358-4500
Fax: (310) 358-4520

Qwest Records
3800 Barham Blvd., Ste. 503
Los Angeles, CA 90068
(213) 874-7770
Fax: (213) 874-5049

Ranwood Records
Welk Music Group
1299 Ocean Avenue
Santa Monica, CA 90401
(310) 451-5727

Razor & Tie Records
214 Sullivan St., #4A
New York, NY 10012
(212) 473-9173
Fax: (212) 473-9174

RCA Records
1540 Broadway
New York, NY 10036
(212) 930-4000
Fax: (212) 930-4468

Reader's Digest Music
261 Madison Ave.
New York, NY 10016
(212) 907-6968
Fax: (212) 986-2507

Relativity Records
79 Fifth Ave., 16th Fl.
New York, NY 10003
(212) 337-5300

Reprise Records
3300 Warner Blvd.
Burbank, CA 91505-4694
(818) 846-9090
(818) 953-3223
Fax: (818) 953-3211

Restless Records
1616 Vista Del Mar Ave.
Hollywood, CA 90028
(213) 957-4357
(800) 573-7853
Fax: (213) 957-4355

Rhino Records
10635 Santa Monica Blvd.
Los Angeles, CA 90025-4900
(310) 474-4778
Fax: (310) 441-6575

The Right Stuff
1750 N. Vine St.
Hollywood, CA 90028
(213) 960-4634
Fax: (213) 960-4666

Rounder Records
One Camp St.
Cambridge, MA 02140
(617) 354-0700
Fax: (617) 491-1970

Rykodisc
27 Congress St.
Salem, MA 01970
(508) 744-7678
Fax: (508) 741-4506

Scamp/Caroline Records
104 West 29th St.
New York, NY 10001
(212) 886-7500

Sire Records
75 Rockefeller Plz., 17th Fl.
New York, NY 10019
(212) 275-2500
Fax: (212) 275-3562

Smithsonian Folkways Recordings
955 L'Enfant Plaza, Ste. 2600, MRC 914
Washington, DC 20560
(202) 287-3251
Fax: (202) 287-3699

Sony 550 Music
550 Madison Ave.
New York, NY 10022
(212) 833-8000
Fax: (212) 833-7120

Tag Recordings
14 E. 60th St., 8th Fl.
New York, NY 10022
(212) 508-5450
Fax: (212) 593-7663

Telarc International
23307 Commerce Park Rd.
Cleveland, OH 44122
(216) 464-2313
Fax: (216) 464-4108

32 Records
250 W. 57th St.
New York, NY 10107
(800) 771-9553
(212) 265-0740

TVT Records
23 E. Fourth St., 3rd Fl.
New York, NY 10003
(212) 979-6410
Fax: (212) 979-6489

Universal Records
1755 Broadway, 7th Fl.
New York, NY 10019
(212) 373-0600
Fax: (212) 247-3954

Varese Sarabande Records
11846 Ventura Blvd., Ste. 130
Studio City, CA 91604
(818) 753-4143

Verve Records
825 Eighth Ave., 26th Fl.
New York, NY 10019
(212) 333-8000
Fax: (212) 333-8194

Virgin Records
338 N. Foothill Rd.
Beverly Hills, CA 90210
(310) 278-1181
Fax: (310) 278-6231

Warner Bros. Records
3300 Warner Blvd.
Burbank, CA 91510
(818) 846-9090
(818) 953-3223
Fax: (818) 846-8474

The Work Group
2100 Colorado Ave.
Santa Monica, CA 90404
(310) 449-2666
Fax: (310) 449-2095

The following are some of the U.S. radio stations that feature a swing, big band, or nostalgia format. Please be advised that radio station formats often change like the weather. Your best bet would be to check the local radio listings in the cities below. (Radio listings courtesy of BIA Research Inc.'s. MediaAccess Pro)

Alabama

Alexander City
WRFS (1050 AM)

Auburn
WAUD (1230 AM)

Birmingham
WODL (106.9 FM)

Glencoe
WGMZ (93.1 FM)

Mobile
WABF (1220 AM)

Montgomery
WNZZ (950 AM)

York
WYLS (670 AM)

Alaska

Anchorage
KHAR (590 AM)

Homer
KGTL (620 AM)

Arizona

Bullhead City
KBAS (1490 AM)

Cottonwood
KYBC (1600 AM)

Lake Havasu City
KBBC (980 AM)

Phoenix
KMYL (105.3 FM/1190 AM)
KOY (550 AM)

Tucson
KCEE (940 AM)
KGVY (1080 AM)
KSAZ (580 AM)
KTUC (1400 AM)

Arkansas

Beebe
KPIK (101.5 FM)

Benton
KEWI (690 AM)

Corning
KBKG (93.5 FM)
KCCB (1260 AM)

Fairfield Bay
KFFB (106.1 FM)

Ft. Smith
KFPW (1230 AM)

Hot Springs
KXOW (1420 AM)

Nashville
KBHC (1260 AM)

California

Bakersfield
KBID (1350 AM)
KCOO (104.3 FM)
KQAB (1140 AM)
KVLI (104.5 FM)

Barstow
KIQQ (1310 AM)

Chico
KJAZ (1340 AM)

Crescent City
KFVR (1310 AM)

Eureka
KWSW (790 AM)

Fresno
KJWL (99.3 FM)

Los Angeles
KLAC (570 AM)

Modesto
KVIN (1390 AM)

Monterey-Salinas-Santa Cruz
KIDD (630 AM)

Mt. Shasta
KMJC (107.9 FM)

Palm Springs
KCMJ (1140 AM)

Quincy
KPCO (1370 AM)

Red Bluff
KBLF (1490 AM)

Redding
KLXR (1230 AM)

Sacramento
KCTC (1320 AM)

San Diego
KPOP (1360 AM)
KSPA (1450 AM)

San Francisco
KABL (960 AM)

San Luis Obispo
KKJL (1400 AM)

Santa Barbara
KZBN (1290 AM)

Twentynine Palms
KQYN (1250 AM)

Colorado

Burlington
KNAB (1140 AM)

Colorado Springs
KCMN (1530 AM)
KTWK (740 AM)

Ft. Collins-Greeley
KEZZ (1470 AM)
KIIX (600 AM)

Montrose
KUBC (580 AM)

Connecticut

Hartford-New Britain-Middletown
WDRC (1360 AM)
WSNG (610 AM)

New Haven
WQUN (1220 AM)

New London
WWJY (1510 AM)

Delaware

Wilmington
WJBR (1290 AM)

Florida

Daytona Beach
WROD (1340 AM)
WSBB (1230 AM)

Ft. Myers-Naples-Marco Island
WJST (106.3 FM)
WKII (1070 AM)
WODX (1480 AM)

Ft. Pierce-Stuart-Vero Beach
WAXE (1370 AM)
WOSN (97.1 FM)
WTTB (1490 AM)

Ft. Walton Beach
WFAV (1400 AM)
WFSH (1340 AM)

Gainesville-Ocala
WAVQ (104.3 FM)
WRZN (720 AM)

Jacksonville
WKLN (1170 AM)

Lakeland-Winter Haven
WONN (1230 AM)

Melbourne-Titusville-Cocoa
WMMV (1350 AM)

Orlando
WHOO (990 AM)

Panama City
WDIZ (590 AM)
WEBZ (93.5 FM)

Sebring
WITS (1340 AM)

Tampa-St. Petersburg-Clearwater
WLVU (1470 AM)
WZHR (1400 AM)

West Palm Beach-Boca Raton
WDBF (1420 AM)
WJNA (1230 AM)

Georgia

Augusta
WAJY (102.7 FM)

Brunswick
WMOG (1490 AM)

Clayton
WGHC (1370 AM)

Douglas
WOKA (1310 AM)

Eatonton
WKVQ (1520 AM)

Macon
WPGA (980 AM)

Manchester
WFDR (1370 AM)

Savannah
WLOW (107.9 FM)

Hawaii

Honolulu
KUMU (1500 AM)

Idaho

Boise
KGEM (1140 AM)

Moscow
KRPL (1400 AM)

Illinois

Chicago
WAIT (850 AM)
WAKE (1500 AM)
WCSJ (1550 AM)
WLIP (1050 AM)

Danville
WITY (980 AM)

Freeport
WFRL (1570 AM)

Watseka
WGFA (1000 AM)

Indiana

Anderson
WGNR (1470 AM)

Indianapolis
WMYS (1430 AM)

La Porte
WLOI (1540 AM)

Lafayette
WILO (1570 AM)

South Bend
WTRC (1340 AM)

Terre Haute
WAXI (104.9 FM)
WQTY (93.3 FM)

Iowa

Cedar Rapids
KMRY (1450 AM)

Clinton
KLNT (1390 AM)

Decorah
KDEC (1240 AM)

Des Moines
KRNT (1350 AM)

Ft. Dodge
KVFD (1400 AM)

Sioux City
KLEM (1410 AM)

Waterloo-Cedar Falls
KXEL (1450 AM)

Kansas

Abilene
KABI (1560 AM)

Arkansas City
KSOK (1280 AM)

Salina
KINA (910 AM)

Topeka
KTOP (1490 AM)

Kentucky

Frankfort
WKED (1130 AM)

Louisville
WAVG (1450 AM)
WCND (940 AM)

Owensboro
WVJS (1420 AM)

Paducah
WPAD (1560 AM)

Somerset
WTLO (1480 AM)

Louisiana

Houma
KJIN (1490 AM)

Lafayette
KNIR (1360 AM)
KSIG (1450 AM)

New Orleans
WBYU (1450 AM)

Shreveport
KASO (1240 AM)

Vidalia
KVLA (1400 AM)

Maine

Augusta-Waterville
WFAU (1280 AM)

Bangor
WABI (910 AM)
WDEA (1370 AM)

Lewiston-Auburn
WZOU (1470 AM)

Portland
WLAM (106.7 FM/870 AM)

Rumford
WLLB (790 AM)

Maryland

Baltimore
WWLG (1360 AM)

Cumberland
WTBO (1450 AM)

Easton
WCEI (1460 AM)

Oakland
WMSG (1050 AM)

Salisbury-Ocean City
WJWL (900 AM)

Massachusetts

Boston
WLLH (1400 AM)
WXKS (1430 AM)

Southbridge
WESO (970 AM)

Springfield
WARE (1250 AM)
WMAS (1450 AM)

Michigan

Battle Creek
WRCC (1400 AM)

Cadillac
WKJF (1370 AM)

Cassopolis
WGTO (910 AM)

Detroit
CKWW (580 AM)

Grand Rapids
WMJH (810 AM)

Greenville
WPLB (1380 AM)

Houghton
WCCY (1400 AM)

Houghton Lake
WHGR (1290 AM)

Kalamazoo
WAKV (980 AM)

Manistee
WMTE (1340 AM)

Munising
WQXO (1400 AM)

Northwest Michigan
WCBY (1240 AM)
WCCW (1310 AM)

Rogers City
WVXA (106.7 FM)

Saginaw-Bay City-Midland
WMPX (1490 AM)
WMRX (97.7 FM)

Minnesota

Aitkin
KKIN (930 AM)

Duluth-Superior, WI
KZIO (104.3 FM)

Mankato
KYSM (1230 AM)

Minneapolis-St. Paul
KLBB (1400 AM)
WLOL (1470 AM)

Park Rapids
KDKK (97.5 FM)

St. Cloud
KXSS (1390 AM)

Virginia
WHLB (1400 AM)

Mississippi

Biloxi-Gulfport-Pascagoula
WXBD (1490 AM)

Jackson
WVIV (93.9 FM)

Laurel-Hattiesburg
WQIS (890 AM)

Missouri

Branson
KOMC (1220 AM)

Cape Girardeau
KAPE (1550 AM)

Joplin
KWAS (1230 AM)

Kansas City
KPHN (1190 AM)

Kimberling City
KOMC (100.1 FM)

Lebanon
KLWT (1230 AM)

Malta Bend
KRLI (97.5 FM)

St. Joseph
KSFT (1550 AM)

St. Louis
WEW (770 AM)

Springfield
KGMY (1400 AM)

Montana

Bozeman
KOBB (1230 AM)

Great Falls
KXGF (1400 AM)

Helena
KMTX (950 AM)

Nebraska

Kearney
KKPR (1460 AM)

Ogallala
KOGA (930 AM)

Nevada

Las Vegas
KJUL (104.3 FM)

New Hampshire

Berlin
WMOU (1230 AM)

Manchester
WFEA (1370 AM)

Portsmouth-Dover-Rochester
WGIN (930 AM)
WGIP (1540 AM)

New Jersey

Atlantic City-Cape May
WCMC (1230 AM)
WRDR (104.9 FM)

Monmouth-Ocean
WADB (1310 AM)
WHTG (1410 AM)

Morristown
WMTR (1250 AM)

Sussex
WNNJ (1360 AM)

New Mexico

Albuquerque
KIVA (1310 AM)

Bayard
KNFT (950 AM)

Portales
KSEL (1450 AM)

Roswell
KCRX (1430 AM)

Ruidoso
KBUY (1360 AM)

Santa Fe
KTRC (1400 AM)

New York

Albany-Schenectady-Troy
WIZR (930 AM)
WKAJ (900 AM)

Binghamton
WKOP (1360 AM)

Buffalo-Niagara Falls
WECK (1230 AM)

Catskill
WCKL (560 AM)

Elmira-Corning
WCBA (1350 AM)
WEHH (1590 AM)

Hudson Falls
WENU (101.7 FM)

Liberty
WVOS (1240 AM)

Nassau-Suffolk
WLIM (1580 AM)
WLUX (540 AM)

New York
WLIR (1300 AM)
WLNA (1420 AM)
WQEW (1560 AM)
WRTN (93.5 FM)
WVNJ (1160 AM)

Newburgh-Middletown
WDLC (1490 AM)
WGNY (1620 AM)

Poughkeepsie
WEOK (1390 AM)
WWLE (1170 AM)

Rochester
WDNY (1400 AM)
WEZO (950 AM)

Syracuse
WFBL (1050 AM)
WTLA (1200 AM)

Utica-Rome
WADR (1480 AM)
WRNY (1350 AM)
WTLB (1310 AM)
WUTQ (1550 AM)

North Carolina

Charlotte-Gastonia-Rock Hill
WNMX (106.1 FM)

Elizabeth City
WCNC (1240 AM)

Fayetteville
WAZZ (1490 AM)

Greensboro-Winston Salem-High Point
WIST (98.3 FM)

Greenville-New Bern-Jacksonville
WLNR (1230 AM)
WMBL (740 AM)
WNOS (1450 AM)
WZXS (103.9 FM)

Ohio

Bryan
WQCT (1520 AM)

Cambridge
WILE (97.7 FM/1270 AM)

Canton
WDPN (1310 AM)

Cleveland
WRMR (850 AM)

Columbus
WLOH (1320 AM)
WMNI (920 AM)

Dayton
WONE (980 AM)
WPFB (910 AM)
WPTW (1570 AM)

Galion
WGLN (102.3 FM)

Norwalk
WVAC (1510 AM)

Toledo
WCWA (1230 AM)

Van Wert
WERT (1220 AM)

Youngstown-Warren
WNIO (1540 AM)

Oklahoma

Frederick
KTAT (1570 AM)
KYBE (95.9 FM)

Pawhuska
KOMH (1500 AM)

Stillwater
KSPI (780 AM)

Tulsa
KGTO (1050 AM)

Oregon

Bend
KXUX (940 AM)

Corvallis
KEJO (1240 AM)

Eugene-Springfield
KKXO (1450 AM)

Lebanon
KSHO (920 AM)

Lincoln City
KBCH (1400 AM)

Medford-Ashland
KMED (1440 AM)

Seaside
KSWB (840 AM)

Pennsylvania

Allentown-Bethlehem
WEST (1400 AM)
WKAP (1470 AM)
WLSH (1410 AM)

Altoona
WKMC (1370 AM)

Erie
WRIE (1260 AM)

Franklin
WFRA (1450 AM)

Harrisburg-Lebanon-Carlisle
WHYL (960 AM)
WKBO (1230 AM)

Johnstown
WYSN (1330 AM)

Lancaster
WLAN (1390 AM)

Mt. Carmel
WMIM (1590 AM)

Philadelphia
WPEN (950 AM)
WWJZ (640 AM)

Pittsburgh
WJAS (1320 AM)

Reading
WRAW (1340 AM)

Smethport
WQRM (106.3 FM)

Williamsport
WMYL (95.5 FM)

Wilkes Barre-Scranton
WAAT (750 AM)
WAZL (1490 AM)
WEJL (630 AM)
WJMW (550 AM)

South Carolina

Camden
WCAM (1590 AM)

Columbia
WBLR (1430 AM)
WSCQ (100.1 FM)

Florence
WHYM (1260 AM)
WOLS (1230 AM)

Greenville-Spartanburg
WDAB (1580 AM)

Myrtle Beach
WJXY (1050 AM)

South Dakota

Brookings
KBRK (1430 AM)

Mobridge
KOLY (1300 AM)

Rapid City
KTOQ (1340 AM)

Tennessee

Chattanooga
WBAC (1340 AM)
WDOD (1310 AM)

Johnson City-Kingsport-Bristol
WKPT (1400 AM)
WKTP (1590 AM)
WOPI (1490 AM)

Knoxville
WLOD (1140 AM)

Nashville
WAMB (98.7 FM/1160 AM)

Waverly
WPHC (1060 AM)

Texas

Abilene
KMPC (1560 AM)

Amarillo
KIXZ (940 AM)

Beeville
KYTX (97.9 FM)

Bryan-College Station
KTAM (1240 AM)

Burnet
KHLB (1340 AM)

Dallas-Ft. Worth
KDMM (1150 AM)
KPYK (1570 AM)
KXEB (910 AM)

Houston-Galveston
KQUE (1230 AM)

Kerrville
KERV (1230 AM)

Lubbock
KRFE (580 AM)

Madisonville
KMVL (1270 AM)

San Antonio
KLUP (930 AM)

Sherman
KJIM (1500 AM)

Stephenville
KSTV (1510 AM)

Victoria
KNAL (1410 AM)

Utah

Delta
KZEZ (95.7 FM)

Logan
KLGN (1390 AM)

St. George
KEOT (99.7 FM)

Salt Lake City
KDYL (1280 AM)
KKDS (1060 AM)
KLO (1430 AM)
KMGR (92.1 FM)

Vermont

Burlington
WDEV (96.1 FM)

St. Johnsbury
WSTJ (1340 AM)

Springfield
WCFR (1480 AM)

Virginia

Blacksburg-Christiansburg-Radford-Pulaski
WRAD (1460 AM)

Culpeper
WCVA (1490 AM)

Fredericksburg
WFVA (1230 AM)

Norfolk-Virginia Beach-Newport News
WBYM (1490 AM)
WMBG (740 AM)

Richmond
WTVR (1380 AM)

Roanoke-Lynchburg
WLQE (106.9 FM)
WLVA (590 AM)
WVLR (880 AM)

Tappahannock
WRAR (1000 AM)

White Stone
WNDJ (104.9 FM)

Winchester
WAZR (93.7 FM)

Washington

Goldendale
KLCK (1400 AM)

Richland-Kennewick-Pasco
KALE (960 AM)

Spokane
KAZZ (107.1 FM)
KKPL (630 AM)

Yakima
KREW (1210 AM)

West Virginia

Charles Town
WMRE (1550 AM)

Charleston
WCAW (680 AM)

Keyser
WKLP (1390 AM)

Parkersburg
WADC (1050 AM)

Weirton
WEIR (1430 AM)

Wheeling
WBBD (1400 AM)

Wisconsin

Algoma
WBDK (96.7 FM)

Appleton-Oshkosh
WNAM (1280 AM)
WRJQ (1570 AM)

Ashland
WATW (1400 AM)

Clintonville
WFCL (1380 AM)

Eagle River
WERL (950 AM)

Eau Claire
WEIO (1050 AM)

Madison
WNWC (1190 AM)
WTSO (1070 AM)

Milwaukee-Racine
WOKY (920 AM)

Neillsville
WCCN (1370 AM)

Sheboygan
WCNZ (950 AM)

Tomah
WTMB (1460 AM)

Waupun
WMRH (1170 AM)

Wausau-Stevens Point
WRIG (1390 AM)

musicHound SWING!

Indexes

Five-Bone Album Index

Band Member Index

Producer Index

Roots Index

Category Index

Series Index

The following albums achieved the highest rating possible— —from our discriminating MusicHound Swing *writers. You can't miss with any of these recordings. (Note: Albums are listed under the name of the entry (or entries) in which they appear and are not necessarily albums by that individual artist or group. The album could be a compilation album, a film soundtrack, an album on which the artist or group appears as a guest, etc. Consult the artist or group's entry for specific information.)*

Howard Alden
Your Story—The Music of Bill Evans (Concord Jazz, 1994)

Henry "Red" Allen
World on a String (RCA/Bluebird, 1957/1991)

Harold Arlen
The Capitol Years (Capitol, 1990)

Louis Armstrong
The Complete Studio Recordings of Louis Armstrong and the All Stars (Mosaic, 1993)
Ella Fitzgerald and Louis Armstrong (Verve, 1957)
Hot Fives and Hot Sevens—Vol. 2 (CBS, 1926/Columbia, 1988)
Louis Armstrong and Earl Hines (CBS, 1927/Columbia Jazz Masterpieces, 1989)
Portrait of the Artist As a Young Man, 1923–1934 (Columbia/Legacy, 1994)

Fred Astaire
The Astaire Story (Verve, 1988)

Charlie Barnet
Complete Charlie Barnet, Vols. 1–6 (Bluebird, 1942)

Dave Bartholomew
Crescent City Soul: The Sound of New Orleans (1947–1974) (EMI, 1996)
The Genius of Dave Bartholomew (EMI, 1992)

Count Basie
April in Paris (Verve, 1956)
Basie (Roulette, 1957/1994)
Basie in London (Verve, 1957/1988)
Basie, Lambert, Hendricks, Ross (Europa/Giganti Jazz)
Beaver Junction (VJC, 1991)
The Complete Decca Recordings (GRP–Decca Jazz, 1992)
The Complete Roulette Live Recordings of Count Basie & His Orchestra (Roulette/Mosaic, 1991)
The Complete Roulette Studio Recordings of Count Basie & His Orchestra (Roulette/Mosaic, 1993)
The Count at the Chatterbox (Jazz Archive, 1974)
Count Basie & the Kansas City Seven (Impulse!, 1962/1996)
Count Basie at Newport (Verve, 1957/1989)
Count Basie Swings, Joe Williams Sings (Verve, 1955/1993)
Sing Along with Basie (Roulette, 1959/1991)

Sidney Bechet
Best of Sidney Bechet on Blue Note (Blue Note, 1953)
Really the Blues (Living Era, 1993)
Volume 2: 1923–1932 (Masters of Jazz, 1992)

Bix Beiderbecke
Bix Beiderbecke and the Wolverines (Timeless, 1993)
Bix Beiderbecke 1924–1930 (Jazz Classics in Digital Stereo, 1995)
Bix Beiderbecke, Vol. 1: Singin' the Blues (1927) (Columbia, 1990)
Bix Beiderbecke, Vol. 2: At the Jazz Band Ball (1927–28) (Columbia, 1991)
The Complete New Orleans Rhythm Kings, Vol. 2 (1923)/The Complete Wolverines (1924) (King Jazz, 1923–24/1992)
Masters of Jazz Series: The Complete Bix Beiderbecke (Media 7, 1997)

Tony Bennett
Forty Years: The Artistry of Tony Bennett (Columbia, 1991)
Tony's Greatest Hits, Vol. III (Columbia, 1965)

Bunny Berigan
Bunny Berigan and His Boys: 1935–36 (Jazz Chronological Classics, 1993)
Mound City Blues Blowers (Timeless, 1994)
Portrait of Bunny Berigan (ASV Living Era, 1992)
Swingin' High (Topaz, 1993)

Eubie Blake
The Greatest Ragtime of the Century (Biograph, 1987)

Ruby Braff
Ruby Braff and His New England Songhounds, Vol. 1 (Concord, 1991)
Ruby Braff and His New England Songhounds, Vol. 2 (Concord, 1992)

Jackie Brenston
Sun Records: The Blues Years 1950–58 (Charly, 1996)

Clarence "Gatemouth" Brown
The Original Peacock Recordings (Rounder, 1990)

Roy Brown
Good Rocking Tonight: The Best of Roy Brown (Rhino, 1994)

Ruth Brown
Miss Rhythm: Greatest Hits and More (Atlantic, 1989)
Rockin' in Rhythm: The Best of Ruth Brown (Rhino, 1996)

Dave Brubeck
The Dave Brubeck Quartet featuring Paul Desmond (Fantasy, 1986)
Time Further Out (Columbia/Legacy, 1961/1996)
Time Out (Columbia/Legacy, 1959/1997)
Time Signatures: A Career Retrospective (Columbia/Legacy, 1992)

Milt Buckner
Hamp (MCA, 1996)

Cab Calloway
Are You Hep to the Jive? (Columbia/Legacy, 1994)

Hoagy Carmichael
The Classic Hoagy Carmichael (Smithsonian, 1994)

Benny Carter
Benny Carter: The Complete Recordings, 1930–40, Volume I (Various, 1930–40/Charly/Affinity, 1991)
Benny Carter: The King (Pablo, 1976/Original Jazz Classics, 1996)
Live and Well in Japan (Pablo, 1978/Original Jazz Classics, 1992)

Doc Cheatham
The 87 Years of Doc Cheatham (Columbia, 1993)

Arnett Cobb
Arnett Blows for 1300 (Apollo, 1947/Delmark, 1994)
Blow, Arnett, Blow (Prestige, 1959/Original Jazz Classics, 1993)
Blue and Sentimental (Prestige, 1960/Original Jazz Classics, 1993)

Nat King Cole
Anatomy of a Jam Session (Black Lion, 1945)
The Complete after Midnight Sessions (Capitol/EMI, 1996)
The Complete Capitol Recordings of the Nat King Cole Trio (Capitol/EMI, 1991)
The Greatest Hits (Capitol/EMI, 1994)
Jazz Encounters (Blue Note, 1992)
Lush Life (Capitol/EMI, 1993)
Nat King Cole (Capitol/EMI, 1992)
The Very Thought of You (Capitol/EMI, 1991)

Chris Connor
Sings the George Gershwin Almanac of Song (Atlantic, 1956–61/1989)

Bing Crosby
Bing Crosby: His Legendary Years, 1931–57 (MCA, 1993)
Bing's Gold Records (Decca, 1997)
Greatest Hits (MCA, 1995)

Bob Crosby
Swing Time! The Fabulous Big Band Era, 1925–55 (Columbia/Legacy, 1993)

Eddie "Lockjaw" Davis
Live at Minton's (Prestige, 1961/1998)

The Delmore Brothers
Brown's Ferry Blues (County, 1995)
Freight Train Boogie (Ace, 1993)
Sand Mountain Blues (County, 1986)
When They Let the Hammer Down (Bear Family, 1984)

Harry "Sweets" Edison
Edison's Lights (Pablo, 1976/Original Jazz Classics, 1994)
The Inventive Mr. Edison (Pacific Jazz, 1953)
Just Friends (Pablo, 1983)
Oscar Peterson and Harry Edison (Pablo, 1975/Original Jazz Classics, 1992)
The Soul of Ben Webster (Verve, 1958/1995)

Roy Eldridge
Little Jazz (Columbia, 1989)
Montreux '77 (Pablo, 1978/Original Jazz Classics, 1989)
Roy and Diz (Verve, 1955/1994)

Duke Ellington
All Star Road Band Vol. II (Signature, 1957/CBS Special Products, 1990)
Anatomy of a Murder (Anadisq, 1959/Rykodisc, 1987)
The Best of Duke Ellington (Blue Note, 1995)
Black, Brown, and Beige—Mastersound Series (Columbia, 1994)
Blues in Orbit—1960 (Columbia, 1988)
The Cornell University Concert—December 1948 (MusicMasters, 1995)
Duke Ellington & His Orchestra Live at Newport—1958 (Columbia/Legacy, 1994)
Duke Ellington: Greatest Hits (RCA, 1996)
Duke Ellington Meets Coleman Hawkins (MCA, 1986)
Duke Ellington, 1924–30 (Classics 6, 1995)
Duke Ellington: The Blanton-Webster Band, 1939–1942 (Bluebird, 1986)
Duke Ellington, Vol. II: Swing 1930–38 (ABC Music, 1994)
Duke Ellington's My People (Red Baron, 1992)
Duke's Big Four (Pablo, 1973/1988)
Ellington at Basin Street East: The Complete Concert of 14 January 1964 (Music & Arts, 1996)
Ellington at Newport (Columbia, 1956/1987)
Ellington Indigos: Sept.–Oct. 1957 (Columbia, 1989)
Ellingtonia (Fat Boy, 1996)
The Great London Concerts—1964 (MusicMasters, 1993)
The Great Paris Concert (Atlantic, 1963/1989)
In a Mellotone—1940–44 (RCA, 1995)
Live at the Blue Note (Roulette Jazz, 1994)
Lullaby of Birdland (Intermedia)
Money Jungle—1962 (Blue Note, 1986)
Mood Indigo (EPM Musique, 1994)
New Orleans Suite–1970 (Atlantic)
Original Hits, Vol. I: 1927–31 (King Jazz, 1993)
Original Hits, Vol. II: 1931–38 (King Jazz, 1993)
The Pianist: 1966, 1970 (Fantasy, 1992)
The Piano Album (Capitol, 1989)
The Private Collection, Vol. V: "The Suites" 1968 (Saja, 1989)
Satin Doll, 1958–59 (Jazz Time, 1995)
70th Birthday Concert—Nov. 1969 (Blue Note, 1995)
Side by Side (Verve, 1986)
Sophisticated Lady: Masters of the Big Bands (Bluebird, 1992)
Uptown Downbeat with His Orchestra: Cotton Club, Jungle Band 1927–40 (Empire/Avid, 1995)
Uptown—Early 1950s (Columbia, 1987)
Vol. IV: The Mooche, 1928 (EPM Musique, 1996)
Vol. IX: Mood Indigo, 1930 (EPM Musique, 1996)

Ella Fitzgerald
The Best Is Yet to Come (Pablo, 1996)
The Best of Ella Fitzgerald & Louis Armstrong on Verve (Verve, 1997)
The Cole Porter Songbook (Verve, 1956/DCC, 1995)
The Complete Duke Ellington Songbook (Verve, 1956)
The Complete Ella Fitzgerald & Louis Armstrong on Verve (Verve, 1997)
The Complete Ella Fitzgerald Song Books (Verve, 1993)

Ella Fitzgerald & Duke Ellington: The Stockholm Concert, Feb. 7, 1966 (Pablo, 1989)
Ella Fitzgerald/Count Basie/Joe Pass: Digital III at Montreux (Pablo, 1988)
Ella: The Legendary Decca Recordings (Decca Jazz, 1995)
First Lady of Song (Verve, 1993)
Love Songs: Best of the Verve Songbooks (Verve, 1996)
Mack the Knife: The Complete Ella in Berlin Concert (Verve, 1993)
75th Birthday Celebration (Decca, 1993)
Sings the Rodgers & Hart Songbook (Verve, 1997)
These Are the Blues (Verve, 1986)

Cecil Gant
Mean Old World: The Blues from 1940–94 (Smithsonian, 1996)

Erroll Garner
Concert by the Sea (Columbia, 1970/1987)

Dizzy Gillespie
Birks Works: The Verve Big-Band Sessions (Verve, 1995)
Dizzy Gillespie 1945 (Classics, 1996)
Dizzy Gillespie—The Complete RCA Recordings (RCA Bluebird, 1995)
Dizzy's Diamonds (Verve, 1993)
Duets (Verve, 1997)
Most Important Recordings of Dizzy Gillespie (Official, 1989)
Shaw Nuff (Discovery, 1988)

Benny Goodman
Air Play (Signature, 1989)
Benny Goodman Carnegie Hall Jazz Concert (Columbia, 1987)
Benny Goodman: Complete Capitol Small Group Recordings (Mosaic, 1993)
Jam (Swing House, 1983)
On the Air, 1937–1938 (Columbia, 1993)
Session (Swing House, 1981)
Treasure Chest Series (MGM, 1959)

Stephane Grappelli
Stephane Grappelli Live (Justin Time, 1998)

Wardell Gray
The Chase! (Dial, 1947/Stash, 1995)
Wardell Gray Memorial Album, Vol. II (Prestige, 1950/1952/OJC, 1992)

Merle Haggard
Down Every Road (Capitol, 1995)
The Lonesome Fugitive: The Merle Haggard Anthology (1963–77) (Razor & Tie, 1995)
A Tribute to the Best Damn Fiddle Player in the World (or, My Salute to Bob Wills) (Capitol, 1970/Koch, 1995)
Untamed Hawk (Bear Family, 1995)

Lionel Hampton
After You've Gone: The Original Benny Goodman Trio and Quartet Sessions, Vol. I (Bluebird, 1935–37/1987)
Hamp and Getz (Verve, 1955)
Midnight Sun (Decca, 1946–47/1993)

Sir Roland Hanna
Perugia (Freedom, 1975)

Wynonie Harris
Bloodshot Eyes—The Best of Wynonie Harris (Rhino, 1994)

Coleman Hawkins
At the Opera House (Verve, 1994)
Coleman Hawkins Encounters Ben Webster (Verve, 1997)
The Genius of Coleman Hawkins (Verve, 1997)
Hollywood Stampede (Capitol, 1989)
The Indispensable Coleman Hawkins (1927–56) (BMG, 1992)

Fletcher Henderson
Fletcher Henderson: 1924, Vol. III (Jazz Chronological Classics)
Fletcher Henderson: 1924–25 (Jazz Chronological Classics)
Fletcher Henderson: 1932–34 (Jazz Chronological Classics)
A Study in Frustration (Columbia, 1994)

Woody Herman
The First Herd (Le Jazz, 1996)
The 1940s—The Small Groups: New Directions (Columbia, 1988)
The Thundering Herds, 1945–47 (Columbia, 1988)
Woody Herman: The V-Disc Years, Vols. I & II, 1944–46 (Hep, 1994)

Earl "Fatha" Hines
Earl Hines Plays Duke Ellington (New World, 1988)
Earl Hines Plays Duke Ellington, Vol. II (New World, 1997)
Tour de Force (Black Lion, 1973/1990)
Tour de Force Encore (Black Lion, 1973)

Milt Hinton
Piano Jazz with Guest Milt Hinton (Concord/Jazz Alliance, 1995)

Johnny Hodges
Caravan (Prestige, 1992)
Complete Johnny Hodges Sessions: 1951–55 (Mosaic, 1989)
The Duke's Men: Small Groups, Vol. 1 (Columbia/Legacy, 1991)
The Duke's Men: Small Groups, Vol. 2 (Columbia/Legacy, 1993)
Everybody Knows Johnny Hodges (Impulse!, 1964)
Hodge Podge (Legacy/Epic, 1995)
Johnny Hodges at Sportpalast, Berlin (Pablo, 1993)
Passion Flower: 1940–46 (Bluebird, 1995)
A Smooth One (Verve, 1979)
Triple Play (Bluebird, 1967/RCA Victor, 1996)

Billie Holiday
The Complete Decca Recordings (GRP, 1991)

Claude Hopkins
1932–34 (Jazz Chronological Classics, 1994)

Illinois Jacquet
The Blues: That's Me! (Prestige, 1969/Original Jazz Classics, 1991)
The Soul Explosion (Prestige, 1969/Original Jazz Classics, 1991)

Buddy Johnson
Buddy and Ella Johnson 1953–1964 (Bear Family, 1992)
Walk 'Em: The Decca Sessions (Decca, 1941–52/Ace, 1996)

Pete Johnson
Boss of the Blues (Atlantic, 1956/1981)

Al Jolson
The Best of Al Jolson (MCA, 1962)
The Best of the Decca Years (MCA, 1992)

Thad Jones
The Complete Blue Note/UA/Roulette Recordings of Thad Jones (Mosaic, 1956–59)
The Complete Solid State Recordings of the Thad Jones/Mel Lewis Orchestra (Mosaic, 1970/1994)

Louis Jordan
The Best of Louis Jordan (MCA, 1975)

Andy Kirk
Andy Kirk, 1929–31 (Jazz Chronological Classics, 1994)
An Anthology of Big Band Swing 1930–1955 (Decca/GRP, 1993)

Rahsaan Roland Kirk
Rahsaan—The Complete Mercury Recordings (Mercury, 1961–65/PolyGram, 1990)

Sonny Lester
Ann Corio Presents: How to Strip for Your Husband/Music to Make Marriage Merrier (Roulette, 1962)

Jerry Lee Lewis
Live at the Star Club, Hamburg (Rhino, 1992)
Original Sun Greatest Hits (Rhino, 1984)
Sings the Rock 'n' Roll Classics (Eagle, 1998)

Mel Lewis
Definitive Thad Jones, Volume 1 (MusicMasters, 1989)
Live at the Village Vanguard (DCC, 1980/1991)
Lost Art (MusicMasters, 1990)
Mel Lewis (VSOP, 1957/1995)

Joe Liggins
Joe Liggins and the Honeydrippers (Specialty, 1990)

Henry Mancini
The Music from "Peter Gunn" (RCA Victor, 1958)

Dean Martin
Dean Martin: Capitol Collector's Series (Capitol, 1989)
Greatest Hits: King of Cool (Capitol, 1998)

Billy May
Come Fly with Me (Capitol, 1957)

McKinney's Cotton Pickers
McKinney's Cotton Pickers: 1928–1929 (Jazz Chronological Classics, 1994)
McKinney's Cotton Pickers: 1929–1930 (Jazz Chronological Classics, 1994)

Carmen McRae
The Great American Songbook (Atlantic, 1992)

Jay McShann
The Early Bird Charlie Parker (MCA, 1982)

Amos Milburn
The Best of Amos Milburn—Down the Road Apiece (Alliance, 1997)

Glenn Miller
Glenn Miller: A Memorial (Bluebird, 1992)
Glenn Miller: The Lost Recordings (RCA, 1995)
The Spirit Is Willing (1939–42) (Bluebird, 1995)
Swing Time! The Fabulous Big Band Era 1925–1955 (Columbia/Legacy, 1993)

Roy Milton
Grandfather of R&B (Mr. R&B, 1994)
Roy Milton & His Solid Senders (Specialty, 1990)

Ella Mae Morse
Jumpin' Like Mad: Cool Cats & Hip Chicks (Capitol Blues, 1996)
The Very Best of Ella Mae Morse (Collectables, 1998)

Jelly Roll Morton
Anamule Dance: The Library of Congress Recordings, Volume 2 (Rounder, 1993)
The Jelly Roll Morton Centennial: His Complete Victor Recordings (RCA, 1926/1990)
Jelly Roll Morton, Volume 1 (JSP, 1990)
Kansas City Stomp: The Library of Congress Recordings, Volume 1 (Rounder, 1993)
The Pearls: The Library of Congress Recordings, Volume 3 (Rounder, 1993)
Winin' Boy Blues: The Library of Congress Recordings, Volume 4 (Rounder, 1993)

Bennie Moten
Basie Beginnings (1929–1932) (RCA, 1929–32)

Sugar Ray Norcia
Sweet & Swingin' (Bullseye Blues and Jazz, 1998)

Joe "King" Oliver
King Oliver's Creole Jazz Band: 1923–1924 (Retrieval, 1997)
Louis Armstrong and King Oliver (Milestone, 1992)

Oran "Hot Lips" Page
Basie Beginnings (1929–1932) (RCA, 1929–1932)

Charlie Parker
Bird: The Complete Charlie Parker on Verve (Verve, 1988)
Blues from Kansas City (GRP, 1992)
The Complete "Birth of the Bebop" (Stash, 1991)
The Complete Dial Sessions (Stash, 1993)
Early Bird (Stash, 1991)
Jazz at Massey Hall (Original Jazz Classics, 1990)
Savoy Recordings (Master Takes) (Savoy, 1988)

Oscar Peterson
At the Concertgebouw (Verve, 1957/1994)
History of an Artist (Pablo, 1972–74/1993)
How Long Has This Been Going On? (Pablo, 1978/1987)
Oscar Peterson & Clark Terry (Pablo, 1975/Original Jazz Classics, 1994)
Oscar Peterson & Harry Edison (Pablo, 1975/Original Jazz Classics, 1992)
Oscar Peterson et Joe Pass; la Salle Pleyel (Pablo, 1975/1997)
The Oscar Peterson Trio at Zardi's (Pablo, 1955/1994)
Oscar Peterson Trio + 1 (Emarcy, 1964/1984)
Plays Count Basie (Clef, 1956/Verve, 1993)
Plays the Gershwin Songbooks (Verve, 1952–59/1996)
Tracks (MPS, 1971/Verve, 1994)
The Trio (Pablo, 1973/1991)

Flip Phillips
A Sound Investment (Concord, 1987)

Elvis Presley
The Complete Sun Sessions (RCA, 1987)
Elvis—The King of Rock 'n' Roll: The Complete '50s Masters (RCA, 1992)
Elvis' Golden Records, Vol. 1 (RCA, 1958)
Elvis' Golden Records, Vol. 3 (RCA, 1963)
50,000,000 Elvis Fans Can't Be Wrong: Elvis' Golden Records, Vol. 2 (RCA, 1960)
From Nashville to Memphis: The Essential '60s Masters I (RCA, 1994)
The Million Dollar Quartet (RCA, 1990)

Louis Prima & Keely Smith
Capitol Collector's Series (Capitol, 1991)

Don Redman
Complete Recordings, Vol. 1 (Columbia/Legacy, 1991)
Louis Armstrong, Volume IV: Louis Armstrong and Earl Hines (Columbia, 1989)

Django Reinhardt
Best of Django Reinhardt (Blue Note, 1996)
Peche à la Mouche (Verve, 1953/1992)

Nelson Riddle
Songs for Swingin' Lovers! (Capitol, 1956)

Roomful of Blues
Turn It On! Turn It Up! (Bullseye/Rounder, 1995)

Artie Shaw
The Last Recordings, Vol. 1: Rare & Unreleased (MusicMasters, 1992)
Swing Time! The Fabulous Big Band Era, 1925–1955 (Columbia/Legacy, 1993)

Bobby Short
50 by Bobby Short (Atlantic, 1950s–80/1986)
Late Night at the Café Carlyle (Telarc, 1992)

Frank Sinatra
Best of "The Capitol Years" (Capitol, 1992)
The Best of the Columbia Years: 1943–1952 (Columbia, 1995)
The Capitol Years (Capitol, 1990)
The Columbia Years (1943–1952): The Complete Recordings (Columbia, 1993)
The Complete Capitol Singles Collection (Capitol, 1996)
Concepts (Capitol, 1992)
Frank Sinatra: Capitol Collector's Series (Capitol, 1989)

Stuff Smith
Together! (Epic, 1963/Koch Classics, 1995)

Muggsy Spanier
The Ragtime Band Sessions (Bluebird, 1939/BMG, 1995)

Can't remember what band a certain musician is in? Wondering if a person has been in more than one band? The Band Member Index will guide you to the appropriate entry (or entries).

The Producer Index lists the albums in MusicHound Swing *that have a producer noted for them. Under each producer's name is the name of the artist or group in whose entry the album can be found, followed by the album title. If an album is produced by more than one individual or group, the album name will be listed separately under the names of each of the producers. (Note: The entry in which the album can be found is not necessarily that of the artist or group whose album it is. The album could be a compilation album, a film soundtrack, an album on which the artist or group appears as a guest, etc. Consult the artist or group's entry for specific information.)*

Which artists or groups have had the most influence on the acts included in MusicHound Swing? *The Roots Index will help you find out. Under each artist or group's name—not necessarily a swing act—are listed the acts found in* MusicHound Swing *that were influenced by that artist or group. By the way, Louis Armstrong is the influence champ: he appears in the ◀◀ section of a whopping 44 artists or groups.*

The Category Index represents an array of categories put together to suggest some of the many groupings under which swing and big band music and acts can be classified. The Hound welcomes your additions to the existing categories in this index and also invites you to send in your own funny, sarcastic, prolific, poignant, or exciting ideas for brand new categories.

Bobby Short
Frank Sinatra
Jo Stafford
Kay Starr
Dakota Staton
Mel Tormé
Rudy Vallee
Helen Ward
Margaret Whiting
Joe Williams

Divas
Pearl Bailey
Rosemary Clooney
Doris Day
Ella Fitzgerald
Billie Holiday
Candye Kane
Peggy Lee
Carmen McRae
Bette Midler
Anita O'Day
Della Reese
Sarah Vaughan
Dinah Washington
Ethel Waters

Jive Talkin'
Cab Calloway
Slim Gaillard
Harry "The Hipster" Gibson
Phil Harris
Al Hirt
Spike Jones
Preacher Jack
Louis Prima
Fats Waller

Jumping the Blues (Good Old Days)
Tiny Bradshaw
Jackie Brenston & His Delta Cats
Clarence "Gatemouth" Brown
Roy Brown
Ruth Brown
Milt Buckner
Arnett Cobb
Eddie "Lockjaw" Davis
Esquirita
Cecil Gant
Bill Haley
Wynonie Harris
Milt Hinton
Bullmoose Jackson & His Buffalo Bearcats
Pete Johnson
Little Johnny Jones
Louis Jordan
Jimmy Liggins
Joe Liggins
Floyd McDaniel
Big Jay McNeely
Amos Milburn
Roy Milton
Joe Newman
Pinetop Perkins
Piano Red
Louis Prima
Jimmy Rushing
Big Joe Turner
Eddie "Cleanhead" Vinson
T-Bone Walker
Charles "Cootie" Williams
Jimmy Witherspoon

Jumping the Blues (Today)
Big Joe & the Dynaflows
Clarence "Gatemouth" Brown
The Hucklebucks
Love Dogs
Paladins
Duke Robillard
Roomful of Blues
Sugar Ray Norcia

Kids
Junior Brown
Collins Kids
Harry Connick Jr.
Sammy Davis Jr.
Mercer Ellington
Frank Sinatra Jr.

A Little Bit Loungey
Beau Hunks
Buddy Greco
Dick Hyman
Gordon Jenkins
Sonny Lester
Nelson Riddle
Raymond Scott
Bobby Short
Lawrence Welk
Paul Weston

Ring-A-Ding-Ding
Sammy Davis Jr.
Dean Martin
Frank Sinatra

Rockabilly Cats
The Blasters
Lord Buckley
Sonny Burgess
Johnny Burnette
Ray Campi
Eddie Cochran
Collins Kids
Ray Condo
Ronnie Dawson
Charlie Feathers
Rosie Flores
Robert Gordon
Hot Rod Lincoln
Wanda Jackson
Johnny Legend
Kim Lenz
Jerry Lee Lewis
Moon Mullican
Carl Perkins
Elvis Presley
Boyd Raeburn
Billy Lee Riley
Warren Smith
Tommy Tucker
Gene Vincent

Snappy Songwriters
Harold Arlen
Hoagy Carmichael
Erroll Garner
Louis Jordan
Henry Mancini
Jelly Roll Morton
Louis Prima
Don Redman
Billy Strayhorn

Straight Outta New Orleans
Louis Armstrong
Dave Bartholomew
Sidney Bechet
Pete Fountain
Jelly Roll Morton
Joe "King" Oliver
Red Allen

Straight Into Vegas
Sam Butera
Buddy Greco
New Morty Show
Louis Prima
Frank Sinatra

Strings the Things
Charlie Christian
Stephane Grappelli
Django Reinhardt
Stuff Smith
Claude "Fiddler" Williams

Sweet, Not Petite
Tex Beneke
Xavier Cugat
Harry "Sweets" Edison
Les Elgart
Glen Gray & the Casa Loma Orchestra
Horace Heidt
Kay Kyser
Lester Lanin
Guy Lombardo
Ozzie Nelson
Paul Whiteman

Western Style
Asleep at the Wheel
Big Sandy & His Fly-Rite Boys
Junior Brown
Commander Cody & His Lost Planet Airmen
Spade Cooley
Delmore Brothers
Merle Haggard
Hot Club of Cowtown
Hot Rize
Sid King
Sleepy LaBeef
Maddox Brothers & Rose
Emmett Miller
Pine Valley Cosmonauts
Hank Thompson
Tex Williams
Bob Wills

Where's Mommy?
Big Bad Voodoo Daddy
Cherry Poppin' Daddies

Young, Jazzy, and Swinging
Howard Alden
Dan Barrett
Harry Connick Jr.
Joe Jackson
Diana Krall
The Manhattan Transfer
Ron Sunshine & Full Swing

Zoot Suits, '90s Style
Alien Fashion Show
Atomic Fireballs
Beau Hunks
Bellevue Cadillacs
Big Bad Voodoo Daddy
Big Dave & the Ultrasonics
Blue Plate Special
Blues Jumpers
Cherry Poppin' Daddies
Crescent City Maulers
Chris Daniels & the Kings
8 1/2 Souvenirs
Bill Elliott Swing Orchestra
Flattop Tom & His Jumpcats
Flying Neutrinos
Frantic Flattops
George Gee & His Make-Believe
The Ray Gelato Giants
Hipster Daddy-O & the Hand Grenades
Indigo Swing
Jellyroll
Jet Set 6

This index is a guide to all of the artists and groups included in the MusicHound series of books (MusicHound Rock, MusicHound Country, MusicHound Blues, MusicHound R&B, MusicHound Lounge, MusicHound Folk, MusicHound Jazz, *and* MusicHound Swing). *Following the artist or group's name you'll find the book (or books) they appear in.*

SERIES INDEX

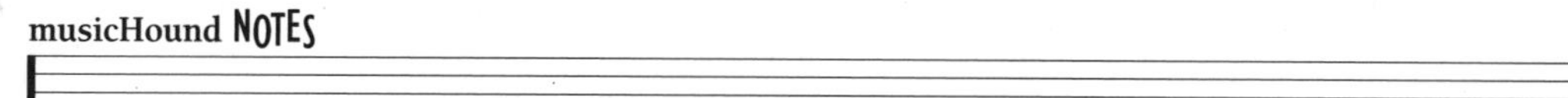
musicHound NOTES

DO YOU HAVE ALL THE ESSENTIALS?

These vital guides tell you what to buy – and why

"This is a great buying guide to smooth and swingin' music."

— Dance USA Magazine

MUSICHOUND® LOUNGE

The Essential Album Guide to Martini Music and Easy Listening

As long as there are dimly lit hideaways, smokey bars, hushed conversations and dinner for two, there will always be lounge music. The resurgence of the smooth and easy stylings of singers like Tony Bennett, Frank Sinatra and Julie London combined with the popularity of chic cigar and martini bars has brought about the need for the first comprehensive buyer's guide to this familiar yet elusive form of music. *MusicHound Lounge* reviews the work of nearly 500 performers – from Harry Belafonte to the Squirrel Nut Zippers – offering recommendations on what to buy and what to avoid, as well as backgrounds on performers. A free CD from Capitol's Ultra-Lounge series of music is included, as well as a guide to Web sites, radio stations, publications and other resources.

Steve Knopper • 1998 • paperback with music CD
600 pages • ISBN 1-57859-048-5

"The best of any jazz guide that I've ever seen."

— Nat Hentoff, columnist
The New York Times,
The Washington Post

MUSICHOUND® JAZZ

The Essential Album Guide

Jazz speaks a language all its own. Whether fusion, avant-garde, bebop, big band, straight-ahead or Dixieland, the music is the message. Now there's a guide that interprets the best of jazz for everyone. *MusicHound Jazz* reviews the work of nearly 1,300 prominent performers, then offers recommendations on what to buy and what to avoid. Compelling essays provide personal information and discuss artists' influences, musical development, trademark sound and more. A free CD sampler from Blue Note is included as well as a guide to jazz resources (Web sites, radio stations, publications, etc.).

Steve Holtje and Nancy Ann Lee • 1998 • paperback with music CD
1,500 pages • ISBN 1-57859-031-0

Available at fine bookstores everywhere, or in the U.S. call 1-800-776-6265

Free Music from Rounder Records

1. Ay La Bas

Michelle Willson
(copyright control)
From *Tryin' to Make a Little Love* (BEYE 9610)

Michelle's voice has been compared to that of Dinah Washington, Ruth Brown, and Big Maybelle. "Ay La Bas" is a gem of a tune—Michelle first heard the hard-to-find Dolly Cooper track and fell in love with it while on a European tour.

2. House of the Blues

Jimmy "T99" Nelson
(Jimmy Nelson/T99 Music, BMI)
From *House of the Blues* (BEYE 9593)

One of the last of the great blues shouters, 79-year-old Jimmy Nelson is a stand up, big-voiced singer with a recording career spanning 50 years. A Big Joe Turner protégé, Jimmy first gained fame in 1951 with "T-99 Blues" (referring to the old Texas Highway 99 heading out of Ft. Worth).

3. Twist Top

Duke Robillard
(Duke Robillard/Blue Duchess Music, BMI)
From *After Hours Swing Session* (ROUN 3114)

Duke Robillard is one of the few contemporary masters of the classic swing-jazz guitar style pioneered by such giants of the genre as Tiny Grimes, Charlie Christian, and Freddie Green.

4. If It's News to You

The Johnny Nocturne Band
(copyright control)
From *Shake 'Em Up* (BEYE 9553)

Hard-blowing tenor saxist John Firman leads a West Coast band that swings as hard as Count Basie's Kansas City Seven, jumps as much as Louis Jordan's Tympany Five, and bops like Lionel Hapmton's great bands of the 1940s.

5. You Knock Me Out

Sax Gordon
(Gordon Beadle/Bonky Music—Happy Valley Music, BMI)
From *You Knock Me Out* (BEYE 9604)

Stints with Roomful of Blues and Duke Robillard have cemented tenor man Sax Gordon's association with the swingin' blues. His music is the spirit of hip and cool—from Jackie Gleason to Bill Doggett and Gene Ammons, Gordon wraps it all together in style!

6. Rockin' at the Doghouse

The Love Dogs
(Scheer/Cooltonic Music, BMI)
From *Heavy Petting* (TCOO 1168)

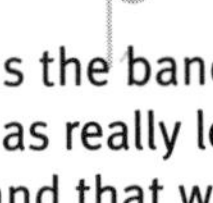

Lead singer Ed Scheer explains the band's curious name: "I think of dogs as really lovable animals. I think of the band that way. It's like this big dog that runs up to you and just smothers you." The Love Dogs' tribal love vibe is impossible to resist!

7. '59 Tweedle Dee

Rosie Flores
(Rosie Flores/Pink Suede Music, ASCAP) From *Dance Hall Dreams* (ROUN 3150)

The tracks on *Dance Hall Dreams* were recorded live during two nights at Cibolo Creek, a turn-of-the-century Texas dance hall in Rosie's hometown of San Antonio, giving this record its spontaneous feel and vibrant energy.